WORD BIBLICAL COMMENTARY

WORD BIBLICAL COMMENTARY

VOLUME 44

Colossians, Philemon

PETER T. O'BRIEN

WORD PUBLISHING

Word (UK) Ltd
Milton Keynes, England

WORD BOOKS AUSTRALIA
Heathmont, Victoria, Australia
SUNDAY SCHOOL CENTRE WHOLESALE
Salt River, South Africa
ALBY COMMERCIAL ENTERPRISES PTE LTD
Scotts Road, Singapore
CHRISTIAN MARKETING LTD
Auckland, New Zealand
CROSS (HK) CO
Hong Kong
EUNSUNG CORP
Seoul, Korea
PRAISE INC
Quezon City, Philippines

THE COMMUNICATORS COMMENTARY SERIES
Volume 1 (NT) Matthew

First British edition 1987.

ISBN 0–85009–415–1 (Australia 1–86258–004–9)

Printed and bound in Great Britain by
Robert Hartnoll (1985) Ltd., Bodmin, Cornwall

To
my wife, Mary
and our children
David, Stephen,
Libby and Sarah

Contents

Author's Preface

It was toward the end of 1977 that I first received an invitation from the Editors of the *Word Biblical Commentary* to write a volume on Colossians and Philemon in their newly projected series and I am grateful to them for taking the risk with one who had not written a commentary before. Over the last four years I have pondered the issues raised by these two Pauline letters, and have been amazed how again and again God has spoken through these parts of his word to contemporary pastoral and theological issues.

I am especially grateful to Professor Ralph Martin through whom the initial invitation came to contribute a volume in this series, for his unfailing help and encouragement over the past four years, and the stimulation I have received from his own writings on these two NT letters. The climax was a personal visit he made to Moore College in June–August, 1981.

Anyone who attempts to write a commentary in the area of the Pauline letters quickly realizes how indebted he is to those who have trodden the path before. Bishop Eduard Lohse's magisterial volume in the Hermeneia series has been constantly at my side while the many writings of Professor Eduard Schweizer, including his commentary in the EKKNT series, have been a source of stimulation and help. Even when I have parted company with these two writers on a particular point of interpretation I have been grateful for the clarity and freshness with which they have presented the issues. There are many other writers to whom I am indebted as the reader will quickly discover.

It would not have been possible to complete this volume within the deadlines set by the Editors without a period of uninterrupted study and I am thankful to the Moore College Committee, especially its Chairman, Sir Marcus Loane, Archbishop of Sydney, and Canon Broughton Knox, Principal of the College, for granting a period of six months' study leave in 1978–79 which I was able to spend in Cambridge, England at Tyndale House. I am grateful to the staffs of the University of Cambridge and Tyndale Libraries for their assistance and for the stimulation received from fellow-researchers while working at Tyndale House.

Messrs. E. J. Brill of Leiden have kindly permitted me to quote from my volume, *Introductory Thanksgivings in the Letters of Paul*, NovTSup 49, published in 1977.

My thanks are due to Miss Jeanette Logan, Miss Wendy Dahl, Mrs. Jenny Gardner and Mrs. Joan Skillicorn for their patience in typing and retyping a lengthy manuscript.

My wife Mary, and our children David, Stephen, Libby and Sarah, to whom this book is dedicated, must have felt at times that they ate, drank and slept the issues of Colossians and Philemon. They have helped me in so many ways to a deeper understanding of this part of God's word not least in the household code of Colossians 3.

Sydney, Australia
January, 1982

PETER T. O'BRIEN

Editorial Preface

The launching of the *Word Biblical Commentary* brings to fulfillment an enterprise of several years' planning. The publishers and the members of the editorial board met in 1977 to explore the possibility of a new commentary on the books of the Bible that would incorporate several distinctive features. Prospective readers of these volumes are entitled to know what such features were intended to be; whether the aims of the commentary have been fully achieved time alone will tell.

First, we have tried to cast a wide net to include as contributors a number of scholars from around the world who not only share our aims, but are in the main engaged in the ministry of teaching in university, college and seminary. They represent a rich diversity of denominational allegiance. The broad stance of our contributors can rightly be called evangelical, and this term is to be understood in its positive, historic sense of a commitment to scripture as divine revelation, and to the truth and power of the Christian gospel.

Then, the commentaries in our series are all commissioned and written for the purpose of inclusion in the *Word Biblical Commentary.* Unlike several of our distinguished counterparts in the field of commentary writing, there are no translated works, originally written in a non-English language. Also, each commentator was asked to prepare his own rendering of the original biblical text and to use those languages as the basis of his own comments and exegesis. What may be claimed as distinctive with this series is that it is based on the biblical languages, yet it seeks to make the technical and scholarly approach to a theological understanding of scripture understandable by—and useful to—the fledgling student, the working minister as well as to colleagues in the guild of professional scholars and teachers.

Finally, a word must be said about the format of the series. The layout in clearly defined sections has been consciously devised to assist readers at different levels. Those wishing to learn about the textual witnesses on which the translation is offered are invited to consult the section headed "Notes." If the readers' concern is with the state of modern scholarship on any given portion of scripture, then they should turn to the sections on "Bibliography" and "Form/Structure/Setting." For a clear exposition of the passage's meaning and its relevance to the ongoing biblical revelation, the concluding "Explanation" is designed expressly to meet that need. There is therefore something for everyone who may pick up and use these volumes.

If these aims come anywhere near realization, the intention of the editors will have been met, and the labor of our team of contributors rewarded.

General Editors: *David A. Hubbard*
Glenn W. Barker
Old Testament: *John D. W. Watts*
New Testament: *Ralph P. Martin*

Abbreviations

A. General Abbreviations

A	Codex Alexandrinus
Akkad.	Akkadian
a	Codex Sinaiticus
Ap. Lit.	Apocalyptic Literature
Apoc.	Apocrypha
Aq.	Aquila's Greek Translation of the Old Testament
Arab.	Arabic
Aram.	Aramaic
B	Codex Vaticanus
C	Codex Ephraemi Syri
c.	*circa,* about
cf.	*confer,* compare
ch., chs.	chapter, chapters
cod., codd.	codex, codices
contra	in contrast to
D	Codex Bezae
DSS	Dead Sea Scrolls (see **F.**)
ed., edd.	edited, edition, editor; editions
e.g.	*exempli gratia,* for example
Egyp.	Egyptian
et al.	*et alii,* and others
EV	English Versions of the Bible
f., ff.	following (verse or verses, pages, etc.)
fem.	feminine
ft.	foot, feet
gen.	genitive
Gr.	Greek
Heb.	Hebrew
Hitt.	Hittite
ibid.	*ibidem,* in the same place
id.	*idem,* the same
i.e.	*id est,* that is
impf.	imperfect
infra.	below
in loc.	*in loco,* in the place cited
Lat.	Latin
LL.	Late Latin
LXX	Septuagint
M	Mishna
masc.	masculine
mg.	margin
MS(S)	Manuscript(s)
MT	Masoretic text
n.	note
n.d.	no date
Nestle	Nestle (ed.) *Novum Testamentum Graece*
no.	number
NS	New Series
NT	New Testament
obs.	obsolete
OL	Old Latin
OS	Old Syriac
OT	Old Testament
p., pp.	page, pages
par.	paragraph
Pers.	Persian
Pesh.	Peshitta
Phoen.	Phoenician
pl.	plural
Pseudep.	Pseudepigrapha
Q	Quelle ("Sayings" source in the Gospels)
qt.	quoted by
q.v.	*quod vide,* which see
rev.	revised, reviser, revision
Rom.	Roman
RVm	Revised Version margin
Samar.	Samaritan recension
Sem.	Semitic
sing.	singular
Sumer.	Sumerian
s.v.	*sub verbo,* under the word
Syr.	Syriac
Symm.	Symmachus
Targ.	Targum
Theod.	Theodotion
TR	Textus Receptus
tr.	translation, translator, translated
UBS	The United Bible Societies' Greek Text
Ugar.	Ugaritic
u.s.	*ut supra,* as above
viz.	*videlicet,* namely
vol.	volume
v., vv.	verse, verses
vs.	versus
Vul.	Vulgate
WH	Westcott and Hort, *The New Testament in Greek*

B. Abbreviations for Modern Translations and Paraphrases

AmT	Smith and Goodspeed, *The Complete Bible, An American Translation*
ASV	American Standard Version, American Revised Version (1901)
Beck	Beck, *The New Testament in the Language of Today*
BV	Berkeley Version (The Modern Language Bible)
JB	The Jerusalem Bible
JPS	*Jewish Publication Society Version of the Old Testament*
KJV	King James Version
Knox	R. A. Knox, *The Holy Bible: A Translation from the Latin Vulgate in the Light of the Hebrew and Greek Original*
LB	The Living Bible
Mof	J. Moffatt, *A New Translation of the Bible*
NAB	The New American Bible
NASB	New American Standard Bible
NEB	The New English Bible
NIV	The New International Version
Ph	J. B. Phillips, *The New Testament in Modern English*
RSV	Revised Standard Version
RV	Revised Version—1881–1885
TEV	Today's English Version
Wey	R. F. Weymouth, *The New Testament in Modern Speech*
Wms	C. B. Williams, *The New Testament: A Translation in the Language of the People*

C. Abbreviations of Commonly Used Periodicals, Reference Works, and Serials

AAS	*Acta apostolicae sedis*
AASOR	Annual of the American Schools of Oriental Research
AB	Anchor Bible
AbrN	*Abr-Nahrain*
AcOr	*Acta orientalia*
ACW	Ancient Christian Writers
ADAJ	Annual of the Department of Antiquities of Jordan
AER	*American Ecclesiastical Review*
AfO	*Archiv für Orientforschung*
AGJU	Arbeiten zur Geschichte des antiken Judentums und des Urchristentums
AH	F. Rosenthal, *An Aramaic Handbook*
AHR	*American Historical Review*
AHW	W. von Soden, *Akkadisches Handwörterbuch*
AION	*Annali dell'istituto orientali di Napoli*
AJA	*American Journal of Archaeology*
AJAS	*American Journal of Arabic Studies*
AJBA	*Australian Journal of Biblical Archaeology*
AJSL	*American Journal of Semitic Languages and Literature*
AJT	*American Journal of Theology*
ALBO	Analecta lovaniensia biblica et orientalia
ALGHJ	Arbeiten zur Literatur und Geschichte des hellenistischen Judentums
ALUOS	Annual of Leeds University Oriental Society
AnBib	Analecta biblica
AnBoll	Analecta Bollandiana
ANEP	J. B. Pritchard (ed.), *Ancient Near East in Pictures*
ANESTP	J. B. Pritchard (ed.), *Ancient Near East Supplementary Texts and Pictures*
ANET	J. B. Pritchard (ed.), *Ancient Near Eastern Texts*
ANF	The Ante-Nicene Fathers
Ang	*Angelicum*
AnOr	Analecta orientalia
ANQ	*Andover Newton Quarterly*
Anton	*Antonianum*
AOAT	Alter Orient und Altes Testament
AOS	American Oriental Series
AP	J. Marouzeau (ed.), *L'année philologique*

APOT	R. H. Charles (ed.), *Apocrypha and Pseudepigrapha of the Old Testament*
ARG	*Archiv für Reformationsgeschichte*
ARM	Archives royales de Mari
ArOr	*Archiv orientální*
ARW	*Archiv für Religionswissenschaft*
ASNU	Acta seminarii neotestamentici upsaliensis
ASS	*Acta sanctae sedis*
AsSeign	*Assemblées du Seigneur*
ASSR	*Archives des sciences sociales des religions*
ASTI	*Annual of the Swedish Theological Institute*
ATAbh	Alttestamentliche Abhandlungen
ATANT	Abhandlungen zur Theologie des Alten und Neuen Testaments (AThANT)
ATD	Das Alte Testament Deutsch
ATR	*Anglican Theological Review*
AusBR	*Australian Biblical Review*
AUSS	*Andrews University Seminary Studies*
BA	*Biblical Archaeologist*
BAC	Biblioteca de autores cristianos
BAG	W. Bauer, W. F. Arndt, and F. W. Gingrich, *Greek-English Lexicon of the NT*
BAR	*Biblical Archaeologist Reader*
BASOR	*Bulletin of the American Schools of Oriental Research*
BASP	*Bulletin of the American Society of Papyrologists*
BBB	Bonner biblische Beiträge
BCSR	*Bulletin of the Council on the Study of Religion*
BDB	F. Brown, S. R. Driver, and C. A. Briggs, *Hebrew and English Lexicon of the Old Testament*
BDF	F. Blass, A. Debrunner, and R. W. Funk, *A Greek Grammar of the NT*
BeO	*Bibbia e oriente*

BETL	Bibliotheca ephemeridum theologicarum lovaniensium
BEvT	Beiträge zur evangelischen Theologie (BEvTh)
BFCT	Beiträge zur Förderung christlicher Theologie (BFCTh)
BGBE	Beiträge zur Geschichte der biblischen Exegese
BHH	B. Reicke and L. Rost (eds.), *Biblisch-Historisches Handwörterbuch*
BHK	R. Kittel, *Biblia hebraica*
BHS	*Biblia hebraica stuttgartensia*
BHT	Beiträge zur historischen Theologie (BHTh)
Bib	*Biblica*
BibB	Biblische Beiträge
BibLeb	*Bibel und Leben*
BibOr	Biblica et orientalia
BibS(F)	Biblische Studien (Freiburg, 1895–) (BSt)
BibS(N)	Biblische Studien (Neukirchen, 1951–) (BibSt)
BIES	*Bulletin of the Israel Exploration Society (= Yediot)*
BIFAO	*Bulletin de l'institut français d'archéologie orientale*
BJRL	*Bulletin of the John Rylands University Library of Manchester*
BK	*Bibel und Kirche*
BKAT	Biblischer Kommentar: Altes Testament
BL	*Book List*
BLE	*Bulletin de littérature ecclésiastique*
BLit	*Bibel und Liturgie*
BO	*Bibliotheca orientalis*
BR	*Biblical Research*
BSac	*Bibliotheca Sacra*
BSO(A)S	*Bulletin of the School of Oriental (and African) Studies*
BT	*The Bible Translator*
BTB	*Biblical Theology Bulletin*
BTS	*Bible et terre sainte*
BU	Biblische Untersuchungen
BVC	*Bible et vie chrétienne*
BWANT	Beiträge zur Wissenschaft vom Alten und Neuen Testament
BZ	*Biblische Zeitschrift*

BZAW Beihefte zur *ZAW*
BZNW Beihefte zur *ZNW*
BZRGG Beihefte zur *ZRGG*

CAD *The Assyrian Dictionary of the Oriental Institute of the University of Chicago*
CAH *Cambridge Ancient History*
CAT Commentaire de l'Ancien Testament
CB *Cultura bíblica*
CBQ *Catholic Biblical Quarterly*
CBQMS Catholic Biblical Quarterly—Monograph Series
CCath Corpus Catholicorum
CChr Corpus Christianorum
CH *Church History*
CHR *Catholic Historical Review*
CIG *Corpus inscriptionum graecarum*
CII *Corpus inscriptionum iudaicarum*
CIL *Corpus inscriptionum latinarum*
CIS *Corpus inscriptionum semiticarum*
CJT *Canadian Journal of Theology*
CNT Commentaire du Nouveau Testament
ConB Coniectanea biblica
ConNT *Coniectanea neotestamentica*
CQ *Church Quarterly*
CQR *Church Quarterly Review*
CRAIBL *Comptes rendus de l'Académie des inscriptions et belles-lettres*
CSCO Corpus scriptorum christianorum orientalium
CSEL Corpus scriptorum ecclesiasticorum latinorum
CTA A. Herdner, *Corpus des tablettes en cunéiformes alphabétiques*
CTM *Concordia Theological Monthly* (or *CTM*)
CurTM *Currents in Theology and Mission*

DACL *Dictionnaire d'archéologie chrétienne et de liturgie*
DBSup *Dictionnaire de la Bible, Supplément*
DISO C.-F. Jean and J. Hoftijzer, *Dictionnaire des inscriptions sémitiques de l'ouest*
DJD Discoveries in the Judean Desert
DOTT D. W. Thomas (ed.), *Documents from Old Testament Times*
DS Denzinger-Schönmetzer, *Enchiridion symbolorum*
DTC *Dictionnaire de théologie catholique (DTHC)*
DTT *Dansk teologisk tidsskrift*
DunRev Dunwoodie Review

EBib Etudes bibliques (EtBib)
EDB L. F. Hartman (ed.), *Encyclopedic Dictionary of the Bible*
EHAT Exegetisches Handbuch zum Alten Testament
EKKNT Evangelisch-katholischer Kommentar zum Neuen Testament
EKL *Evangelisches Kirchenlexikon*
EncJud *Encyclopaedia judaica* (1971)
EnchBib *Enchiridion biblicum*
ErJb *Eranos Jahrbuch*
EstBib *Estudios bíblicos*
ETL *Ephemerides theologicae lovanienses (EThL)*
ETR *Etudes théologiques et religieuses (EThR)*
EvK *Evangelische Kommentare*
EvQ *The Evangelical Quarterly*
EvT *Evangelische Theologie (EvTh)*
ExpTim *The Expository Times*

FBBS Facet Books, Biblical Series
FC Fathers of the Church
FRLANT Forschungen zur Religion und Literatur des Alten und Neuen Testaments
FTS Frankfurter Theologischen Studien

GCS Griechische christliche Schriftsteller
GAG W. von Soden, *Grundriss der akkadischen Grammatik*

GKB	Gesenius-Kautzsch-Bergsträsser, *Hebräische Grammatik*
GKC	*Gesenius' Hebrew Grammar*, ed. E. Kautzsch, tr. A. E. Cowley
GNT	Grundrisse zum Neuen Testament
GOTR	*Greek Orthodox Theological Review*
GRBS	*Greek, Roman, and Byzantine Studies*
Greg	*Gregorianum*
GuL	*Geist und Leben*
HALAT	W. Baumgartner et al., *Hebräisches und aramäisches Lexikon zum Alten Testament*
HAT	Handbuch zum Alten Testament
HDR	Harvard Dissertations in Religion
HeyJ	*Heythrop Journal*
HibJ	*Hibbert Journal*
HKAT	Handkommentar zum Alten Testament
HKNT	Handkommentar zum Neuen Testament
HNT	Handbuch zum Neuen Testament
HNTC	Harper's NT Commentaries
HR	*History of Religions*
HSM	Harvard Semitic Monographs
HTKNT	Herders theologischer Kommentar zum Neuen Testament (HThKNT)
HTR	*Harvard Theological Review*
HTS	Harvard Theological Studies
HUCA	*Hebrew Union College Annual*
IB	*Interpreter's Bible*
ICC	International Critical Commentary
IDB	G. A. Buttrick (ed.), *Interpreter's Dictionary of the Bible*
IDBSup	Supplementary volume to *IDB*
IEJ	*Israel Exploration Journal*
Int	*Interpretation*
ITQ	*Irish Theological Quarterly*
JA	*Journal asiatique*
JAAR	*Journal of the American Academy of Religion*
JAC	Jahrbuch für Antike und Christentum
JANESCU	*Journal of the Ancient Near Eastern Society of Columbia University*
JAOS	*Journal of the American Oriental Society*
JAS	*Journal of Asian Studies*
JB	A. Jones (ed.), *Jerusalem Bible*
JBC	R. E. Brown et al. (eds.), *The Jerome Biblical Commentary*
JBL	*Journal of Biblical Literature*
JBR	*Journal of Bible and Religion*
JCS	*Journal of Cuneiform Studies*
JDS	Judean Desert Studies
JEA	*Journal of Egyptian Archaeology*
JEH	*Journal of Ecclesiastical History*
JEOL	*Jaarbericht . . . ex oriente lux*
JES	*Journal of Ecumenical Studies*
JHS	*Journal of Hellenic Studies*
JIBS	*Journal of Indian and Buddhist Studies*
JIPh	*Journal of Indian Philosophy*
JJS	*Journal of Jewish Studies*
JMES	*Journal of Middle Eastern Studies*
JMS	*Journal of Mithraic Studies*
JNES	*Journal of Near Eastern Studies*
JPOS	*Journal of the Palestine Oriental Society*
JPSV	*Jewish Publication Society Version*
JQR	*Jewish Quarterly Review*
JQRMS	Jewish Quarterly Review Monograph Series
JR	*Journal of Religion*
JRAS	*Journal of the Royal Asiatic Society*
JRE	*Journal of Religious Ethics*

JRelS *Journal of Religious Studies*
JRH *Journal of Religious History*
JRS *Journal of Roman Studies*
JRT *Journal of Religious Thought*
JSJ *Journal for the Study of Judaism in the Persian, Hellenistic and Roman Period*
JSS *Journal of Semitic Studies*
JSSR *Journal for the Scientific Study of Religion*
JTC *Journal for Theology and the Church*
JTS *Journal of Theological Studies*
Judaica *Judaica: Beiträge zum Verständnis . . .*

KAI H. Donner and W. Röllig, *Kanaanäische und aramäische Inschriften*
KAT E. Sellin (ed.), Kommentar zum A.T.
KB L. Koehler and W. Baumgartner, *Lexicon in Veteris Testamenti libros*
KD *Kerygma und Dogma*
KJV *King James Version*
KIT Kleine Texte

LCC Library of Christian Classics
LCL Loeb Classical Library
LD Lectio divina
Leš *Lešonénu*
LLAVT E. Vogt, *Lexicon linguae aramaicae Veteris Testamenti*
LPGL G. W. H. Lampe, *Patristic Greek Lexicon*
LQ *Lutheran Quarterly*
LR *Lutherische Rundschau*
LSJ Liddell-Scott-Jones, *Greek-English Lexicon*
LTK *Lexikon für Theologie und Kirche (LThK)*
LUÅ Lunds universitets årsskrift
LW *Lutheran World*

McCQ *McCormick Quarterly*
MDOG Mitteilungen der deutschen Orient-Gesellschaft
MeyerK H. A. W. Meyer, Kritischexegetischer Kommentar über das Neue Testament
MGWJ *Monatsschrift für Geschichte und Wissenschaft des Judentums*
MM J. H. Moulton and G. Milligan, *The Vocabulary of the Greek Testament*
MNTC Moffatt NT Commentary
MPAIBL *Mémoires présentés à l'Académie des inscriptions et belles-lettres*
MScRel *Mélanges de science religieuse*
MTZ *Münchener theologische Zeitschrift (MThZ)*
MUSJ *Mélanges de l'université Saint-Joseph*
MVAG Mitteilungen der vorder-asiatisch-ägyptischen Gesellschaft

NAB *New American Bible*
NCB New Century Bible
NCCHS R. C. Fuller et al. (eds.), *New Catholic Commentary on Holy Scripture*
NCE M. R. P. McGuire et al. (eds.), *New Catholic Encyclopedia*
NEB *New English Bible*
NedTTs *Nederlands theologisch tijdschrift* (NedThTs)
Neot *Neotestamentica*
NFT New Frontiers in Theology
NHS Nag Hammadi Studies
NICNT New International Commentary on the New Testament
NIDNTT C. Brown (ed.), *The New International Dictionary of New Testament Theology*
NKZ *Neue kirchliche Zeitschrift*
NorTT *Norsk Teologisk Tidsskrift (NTT)*
NovT *Novum Testamentum*
NovTSup Novum Testamentum, Supplements
NRT *La nouvelle revue théologique (NRTh)*
NPNF Nicene and Post-Nicene Fathers
NTA *New Testament Abstracts*
NTAbh Neutestamentliche Abhandlungen
NTD Das Neue Testament Deutsch

NTF Neutestamentliche Forschungen
NTS *New Testament Studies*
NTTS New Testament Tools and Studies
Numen *Numen: International Review for the History of Religions*

OIP Oriental Institute Publications
OLP Orientalia lovaniensia periodica
OLZ *Orientalische Literaturzeitung*
Or *Orientalia* (Rome)
OrAnt *Oriens antiquus*
OrChr *Oriens christianus*
OrSyr *L'orient syrien*
OTM Oxford Theological Monographs
OTS *Oudtestamentische Studiën*

PAAJR *Proceedings of the American Academy of Jewish Research*
PCB M. Black and H. H. Rowley (eds.), *Peake's Commentary on the Bible*
PEFQS *Palestine Exploration Fund, Quarterly Statement*
PEQ *Palestine Exploration Quarterly*
PG J. Migne, *Patrologia graeca*
PGM K. Preisendanz (ed.), *Papyri graecae magicae*
PhEW *Philosophy East and West*
PhRev *Philosophical Review*
PJ *Palästina-Jahrbuch*
PL J. Migne, *Patrologia latina*
PO Patrologia orientalis
PRU *Le Palais royal d'Ugarit*
PSTJ *Perkins (School of Theology) Journal*
PVTG Pseudepigrapha Veteris Testamenti graece
PW Pauly-Wissowa, *Real-Encyclopädie der klassischen Altertumswissenschaft*
PWSup Supplement to PW

QDAP *Quarterly of the Department of Antiquities in Palestine*

RA *Revue d'assyriologie et d'archéologie orientale*
RAC *Reallexikon für Antike und Christentum*
RArch *Revue archéologique*
RB *Revue biblique*
RBén *Revue bénédictine*
RCB *Revista de cultura biblica*
RE *Realencyklopädie für protestantische Theologie und Kirche*
RechBib Recherches bibliques
REg *Revue d'égyptologie*
REJ *Revue des études juives*
RelArts Religion and the Arts
RelS *Religious Studies*
RelSoc *Religion and Society*
RelSRev *Religious Studies Review*
RES *Répertoire d'épigraphie sémitique*
RevExp *Review and Expositor*
RevistB *Revista biblica*
RevQ *Revue de Qumran*
RevScRel *Revue des sciences religieuses*
RevSém *Revue sémitique*
RevThom *Revue thomiste*
RGG *Religion in Geschichte und Gegenwart*
RHE *Revue d'histoire ecclésiastique*
RHPR *Revue d'histoire et de philosophie religieuses (RHPhR)*
RHR Revue de l'histoire des religions
RivB *Rivista biblica*
RNT Regensburger Neues Testament
RQ *Römische Quartalschrift für christliche Altertumskunde und Kirchengeschichte*
RR *Review of Religion*
RSO *Rivista degli studi orientali*
RSPT *Revue des sciences philosophiques et théologiques (RSPhTh)*
RSR *Recherches de science religieuse (RechSR)*
RSV *Revised Standard Version*
RTL *Revue théologique de Louvain (RThL)*
RTP *Revue de théologie et de philosophie (RThPh)*

RTR	*The Reformed Theological Review*
RUO	*Revue de l'université d'Ottawa*
RV	*Revised Version*
SANT	Studien zum Alten und Neuen Testament
SAQ	Sammlung ausgewählter kirchen- und dogmengeschichtlicher Quellenschriften
SB	Sources bibliques
SBFLA	*Studii biblici franciscani liber annuus*
SBJ	*La sainte bible de Jérusalem*
SBLASP	Society of Biblical Literature Abstracts and Seminar Papers
SBLDS	SBL Dissertation Series
SBLMasS	SBL Masoretic Studies
SBLMS	SBL Monograph Series
SBLSBS	SBL Sources for Biblical Study
SBLSCS	SBL Septuagint and Cognate Studies
SBLTT	SBL Texts and Translations
SBM	Stuttgarter biblische Monographien
SBS	Stuttgarter Bibelstudien
SBT	Studies in Biblical Theology
SC	Sources chrétiennes
SCR	*Studies in Comparative Religion*
ScEs	*Science et esprit*
Scr	*Scripture*
ScrB	*Scripture Bulletin*
SD	Studies and Documents
SE	Studia Evangelica I, II, III (=TU 73[1959], 87 [1964], 88 [1964], etc.) *(StEv)*
SEÅ	*Svensk exegetisk årsbok*
Sef	*Sefarad*
Sem	*Semitica*
SHAW	Sitzungsberichte heidelbergen Akademie der Wissenschaften
SHT	Studies in Historical Theology
SHVL	Skrifter Utgivna Av Kungl. Humanistika Vetenskapssamfundet i Lund.
SJLA	Studies in Judaism in Late Antiquity
SJT	*Scottish Journal of Theology*
SMSR	*Studi e materiali di storia delle religioni*
SNT	Studien zum Neuen Testament (StNT)
SNTSMS	Society for New Testament Studies Monograph Series
SO	Symbolae osloenses
SOTSMS	Society for Old Testament Study Monograph Series
SPap	*Studia papyrologica*
SPAW	Sitzungsberichte der preussischen Akademie der Wissenschaften
SPB	Studia postbiblica
SR	*Studies in Religion/Sciences religieuses*
SSS	Semitic Study Series
ST	*Studia theologica (StTh)*
STÅ	*Svensk teologisk årsskrift*
StBibT	*Studia Biblical et Theologica*
STDJ	Studies on the Texts of the Desert of Judah
STK	*Svensk teologisk kvartalskrift*
Str-B	[H. Strack and] P. Billerbeck, *Kommentar zum Neuen Testament*
StudNeot	Studia neotestamentica, Studia
StudOr	Studia orientalia
SUNT	Studien zur Umwelt des Neuen Testaments
SVTP	Studia in Veteris Testamenti pseudepigrapha
SWJT	*Southwestern Journal of Theology*
SymBU	Symbolae biblicae upsalienses (SyBU)
TAPA	*Transactions of the American Philological Association*
TB	*Tyndale Bulletin*
TBl	*Theologische Blätter (ThBl)*
TBü	Theologische Bücherei (ThBü)
TBT	*The Bible Today*
TD	*Theology Digest*
TDNT	G. Kittel and G. Friedrich (eds.), *Theological Dictionary of the New Testament*
TextsS	Texts and Studies
TF	*Theologische Forschung (ThF)*

TGI *Theologie und Glaube (ThGI)*
ThA *Theologische Arbeiten*
ThBer *Theologische Berichte*
THKNT Theologischer Handkommentar zum Neuen Testament (ThHKNT)
TLZ *Theologische Literaturzeitung (ThLZ)*
TNTC Tyndale New Testament Commentary
TP *Theologie und Philosophie (ThPh)*
TPQ *Theologisch-Praktische Quartalschrift*
TQ *Theologische Quartalschrift (ThQ)*
TRev *Theologische Revue*
TRu *Theologische Rundschau (ThR)*
TS *Theological Studies*
TSK *Theologische Studien und Kritiken (ThStK)*
TT *Teologisk Tidsskrift*
TToday *Theology Today*
TTKi *Tidsskrift for Teologi og Kirke*
TTS Trierer Theologische Studien
TTZ *Trierer theologische Zeitschrift (TThZ)*
TU Texte und Untersuchungen
TWAT G. J. Botterweck and H. Ringgren (eds.), *Theologisches Wörterbuch zum Alten Testament (ThWAT)*
TWNT G. Kittel and G. Friedrich (eds.), *Theologisches Wörterbuch zum Neuen Testament (ThWNT)*
TZ *Theologische Zeitschrift (ThZ)*

UBSGNT United Bible Societies *Greek New Testament*
UF *Ugaritische Forschungen*
UNT Untersuchungen zum Neuen Testament
US *Una Sancta*
USQR *Union Seminary Quarterly Review*
UT C. H. Gordon, *Ugaritic Textbook*
UUÅ Uppsala universitetsårsskrift

VC *Vigiliae christianae*
VCaro *Verbum caro*
VD *Verbum domini*
VF *Verkündigung und Forschung*
VKGNT K. Aland (ed.), *Vollständige Konkordanz zum griechischen Neuen Testament*
VS Verbum salutis
VSpir *Vie spirituelle*
VT *Vetus Testamentum*
VTSup Vetus Testamentum, Supplements

WA M. Luther, Kritische Gesamtausgabe (= "Weimar" edition)
WC Westminster Commentary
WDB *Westminister Dictionary of the Bible*
WHAB *Westminster Historical Atlas of the Bible*
WMANT Wissenschaftliche Monographien zum Alten und Neuen Testament
WO *Die Welt des Orients*
WTJ *Westminster Theological Journal*
WUNT Wissenschaftliche Untersuchungen zum Neuen Testament
WZKM *Wiener Zeitschrift für die Kunde des Morgenlandes*
WZKSO *Wiener Zeitschrift für die Kunde Süd- und Ostasiens*

ZA *Zeitschrift für Assyriologie*
ZAW *Zeitschrift für die alttestamentliche Wissenschaft*
ZDMG *Zeitschrift der deutschen morgenländischen Gesellschaft*
ZDPV *Zeitschrift des deutschen Palästina-Vereins*
ZEE *Zeitschrift für evangelische Ethik*
ZHT *Zeitschrift für historische Theologie (ZHTh)*
ZKG *Zeitschrift für Kirchengeschichte*
ZKT *Zeitschrift für katholische Theologie (ZKTh)*

ZMR	*Zeitschrift für Missionskunde und Religions-wissenschaft*	*ZST*	*Zeitschrift für systematische Theologie (ZSTh)*
ZNW	*Zeitschrift für die neutestamentliche Wissenschaft*	*ZTK*	*Zeitshcrift für Theologie und Kirche (ZThK)*
ZRGG	*Zeitschrift für Religions- und Geistesgeschichte*	*ZWT*	*Zeitschrift für wissenschaftliche Theologie (ZWTh)*

D. Abbreviations for Books of the Bible, the Apocrypha, and the Pseudepigrapha

OLD TESTAMENT

Gen	2 Chron	Dan
Exod	Ezra	Hos
Lev	Neh	Joel
Num	Esth	Amos
Deut	Job	Obad
Josh	Ps(Pss)	Jonah
Judg	Prov	Mic
Ruth	Eccl	Nah
1 Sam	S of Sol	Hab
2 Sam	Isa	Zeph
1 Kings	Jer	Hag
2 Kings	Lam	Zech
1 Chron	Ezek	Mal

NEW TESTAMENT

Matt	1 Tim
Mark	2 Tim
Luke	Titus
John	Philem
Acts	Heb
Rom	James
1 Cor	1 Peter
2 Cor	2 Peter
Gal	1 John
Eph	2 John
Phil	3 John
Col	Jude
1 Thess	Rev
2 Thess	

APOCRYPHA

1 Esd	1 Esdras	Ep Jer	Epistle of Jeremy
2 Esd	2 Esdras	S Th Ch	Song of the Three Children (or Young Men)
Tobit	Tobit	Sus	Susanna
Jud	Judith	Bel	Bel and the Dragon
Add Esth	Additions to Esther	Pr Man	Prayer of Manasseh
Wisd Sol	Wisdom of Solomon	1 Macc	1 Maccabees
Ecclus	Ecclesiasticus (Wisdom of Jesus the Son of Sirach)	2 Macc	2 Maccabees
Baruch	Baruch		

E. Abbreviations of the Names of Pseudepigraphical and Early Patristic Books

Adam and Eve	Books of Adam and Eve	*Sib. Or.*	Sibylline Oracles
2–3 Apoc. Bar.	Syriac, Greek Apocalypse of Baruch	*T. 12 Patr.*	Testaments of the Twelve Patriarchs
Apoc. Abr.	Apocalypse of Abraham	*T. Levi*	Testament of Levi
Apoc. Mos.	Apocalypse of Moses	*T. Benj.*	Testament of Benjamin, etc.
As. Mos.	Assumption of Moses		
Bib. Ant.	Ps.-Philo, Biblical Antiquities	*Acts Pil.*	Acts of Pilate
		Apoc. Pet.	Apocalypse of Peter
1–2–3 Enoch	Ethiopic, Slavonic, Hebrew Enoch	*Gos. Eb.*	Gospel of the Ebionites
		Gos. Eg.	Gospel of the Egyptians
Ep. Arist.	Epistle of Aristeas	*Gos. Heb.*	Gospel of the Hebrews
Jub.	Jubilees	*Gos. Naass.*	Gospel of the Naassenes
Mart. Isa.	Martyrdom of Isaiah	*Gos. Pet.*	Gospel of Peter
Odes Sol.	Odes of Solomon	*Gos. Thom.*	Gospel of Thomas
Pss. Sol.	Psalms of Solomon	*Prot. Jas.*	Protevangelium of James

Barn.	Barnabas
1–2 Clem.	1–2 Clement
Did.	Didache
Diogn.	Diognetus
Herm. Man.	Hermas, Mandate
Sim.	Similitude
Vis.	Vision
Ign. *Eph.*	Ignatius, Letter to the Ephesians
Magn.	Ignatius, Letter to the Magnesians
Phld.	Ignatius, Letter to the Philadelphians
Pol.	Ignatius, Letter to Polycarp
Rom.	Ignatius, Letter to the Romans
Smyrn.	Ignatius, Letter to the Smyrnaeans
Trall.	Ignatius, Letter to the Trallians
Mart Pol.	Martyrdom of Polycarp
Pol. *Phil.*	Polycarp to the Philippians
Adv. Haer.	Irenaeus, Against All Heresies
De praesc. haer.	Tertullian, On the Proscribing of Heretics

F. Abbreviations of Names of Dead Sea Scrolls and Related Texts

CD	Cairo (Genizah text of the) Damascus (Document)
Hev	Naḥal Ḥever texts
Mas	Masada texts
Mird	Khirbet Mird texts
Mur	Wadi Murabbaʿat texts
P	Pesher (commentary)
Q	Qumran
1Q, 2Q, 3Q, etc.	Numbered caves of Qumran, yielding written material; followed by abbreviation of biblical or apocryphal book
QL	Qumran literature
1QapGen	*Genesis Apocryphon* of Qumran Cave 1
1QH	*Hôdāyôt (Thanksgiving Hymns)* from Qumran Cave 1
1QIsa[a,b]	First or second copy of Isaiah from Qumran Cave 1
1QpHab	*Pesher on Habakkuk* from Qumran Cave 1
1QM	*Milḥāmāh (War Scroll)*
1QS	*Serek hayyaḥad (Rule of the Community, Manual of Discipline)*
1QSa	Appendix A (*Rule of the Congregation*) to 1QS
1QSb	Appendix B (*Blessings*) to 1QS
3Q*15*	Copper Scroll from Qumran Cave 3
4QFlor	*Florilegium* (or *Eschatological Midrashim*) from Qumran Cave 4
4QMess ar	Aramaic "Messianic" text from Qumran Cave 4
4QPrNab	Prayer of Nabonidus from Qumran Cave 4
4QTestim	*Testimonia text* from Qumran Cave 4
4QTLevi	*Testament of Levi* from Qumran Cave 4
4QPhyl	Phylacteries from Qumran Cave 4
11QMelch	*Melchizedek* text from Qumran Cave 11
11QtgJob	*Targum of Job* from Qumran Cave 11

G. Abbreviations of Targumic Material.

Tg. Onq.	*Targum Onqelos*
Tg. Neb.	*Targum of the Prophets*
Tg. Ket.	*Targum of the Writings*
Frg. Tg.	*Fragmentary Targum*
Sam. Tg.	*Samaritan Targum*
Tg. Isa	*Targum of Isaiah*
Pal. Tgs.	*Palestinian Targums*
Tg. Neof.	*Targum Neofiti I*
Tg. Ps.-J.	*Targum Pseudo-Jonathan*
Tg. Yer. I	*Targum Yerušalmi I**
Tg. Yer. II	*Targum Yerušalmi II**
Yem. Tg.	*Yemenite Targum*
Tg. Esth I, II	*First or Second Targum of Esther*

*optional title

H. Abbreviations of Other Rabbinic Works

ʾAboṯ	*ʾAbot de Rabbi Nathan*	*Pesiq. R.*	*Pesiqta Rabbati*
ʾAg. Ber.	*ʾAggadat Berešit*	*Pesiq. Rab Kah.*	*Pesiqta de Rab Kahana*
Bab.	*Babylonian*		
Bar.	*Baraita*	*Pirqe R. El.*	*Pirqe Rabbi Eliezer*
Der. Er. Rab.	*Derek Ereṣ Rabba*	*Rab.*	*Rabbah* (following abbreviation for biblical book: *Gen. Rab.* [with periods] = *Genesis Rabbah*)
Der. Er. Zuṭ.	*Derek Ereṣ Zuṭa*		
Gem.	*Gemara*		
Kalla	*Kalla*		
Mek.	*Mekilta*		
Midr.	*Midraš*; cited with usual abbreviation for biblical book; but *Midr. Qoh.* = *Midraš Qohelet*	*Sem.*	*Semaḥot*
		Sipra	*Sipra*
		Sipre	*Sipre*
		Sop.	*Soperim*
Pal.	*Palestinian*	*S. ʿOlam Rab.*	*Seder ʿOlam Rabbah*
		Talm.	*Talmud*
		Yal.	*Yalquṭ*

I. Abbreviations of Orders and Tractates in Mishnaic and Related Literature.

ʾAbot	*ʾAbot*	*Nazir*	*Nazir*
ʿArak.	*ʿArakin*	*Ned.*	*Nedarim*
ʿAbod. Zar.	*ʿAboda Zara*	*Neg.*	*Negaʿim*
B. Bat.	*Baba Batra*	*Nez.*	*Neziqin*
Bek.	*Bekorot*	*Nid.*	*Niddah*
Ber.	*Berakot*	*Ohol.*	*Oholot*
Beṣa	*Beṣa* (= *Yom Tob*)	*ʿOr.*	*ʿOrla*
Bik.	*Bikkurim*	*Para*	*Para*
B. Meṣ.	*Baba Meṣiʿa*	*Peʾa*	*Peʾa*
B. Qam.	*Baba Qamma*	*Pesaḥ.*	*Pesaḥim*
Dem.	*Demai*	*Qinnim*	*Qinnim*
ʿEd.	*ʿEduyyot*	*Qidd.*	*Qiddušin*
ʿErub.	*ʿErubin*	*Qod.*	*Qodašin*
Giṭ.	*Giṭṭin*	*Roš. Haš.*	*Roš Haššana*
Ḥag.	*Ḥagiga*	*Sanh.*	*Sanhedrin*
Ḥal.	*Ḥalla*	*Šabb.*	*Šabbat*
Hor.	*Horayot*	*Šeb.*	*Šebiʿit*
Ḥul.	*Ḥullin*	*Šebu.*	*Šebuʿot*
Kelim	*Kelim*	*Šeqal.*	*Šeqalim*
Ker.	*Keritot*	*Soṭa*	*Soṭa*
Ketub.	*Ketubot*	*Sukk.*	*Sukka*
Kil.	*Kilʾayim*	*Taʿan.*	*Taʿanit*
Maʿaś.	*Maʿaśerot*	*Tamid*	*Tamid*
Mak.	*Makkot*	*Tem.*	*Temura*
Makš.	*Makširin* (= *Mašqin*)	*Ter.*	*Terumot*
Meg.	*Megilla*	*Ṭohar.*	*Ṭoharot*
Meʿil.	*Meʿila*	*T. Yom*	*Tebul Yom*
Menaḥ.	*Menaḥot*	*ʿUq.*	*ʿUqṣin*
Mid.	*Middot*	*Yad.*	*Yadayim*
Miqw.	*Miqwaʾot*	*Yebam.*	*Yebamot*
Moʿed	*Moʿed*	*Yoma*	*Yoma* (= *Kippurim*)
Moʿed Qat.	*Moʿed Qaṭan*	*Zabim*	*Zabim*
Maʿas. Š.	*Maʿaśer Šeni*	*Zebaḥ*	*Zebaḥim*
Našim	*Našim*	*Zer.*	*Zeraʿim*

J. Abbreviations of Nag Hammadi Tractates

Acts Pet. 12 Apost.	*Acts of Peter and the Twelve Apostles*
Allogenes	*Allogenes*
Ap. Jas.	*Apocryphon of James*
Ap. John	*Apocryphon of John*
Apoc. Adam	*Apocalypse of Adam*
1 Apoc. Jas.	*First Apocalypse of James*
2 Apoc. Jas.	*Second Apocalypse of James*
Apoc. Paul	*Apocalypse of Paul*
Apoc. Pet.	*Apocalypse of Peter*
Asclepius	*Asclepius 21–29*
Auth. Teach.	*Authoritative Teaching*
Dial. Sav.	*Dialogue of the Savior*
Disc. 8–9	*Discourse on the Eighth and Ninth*
Ep. Pet. Phil.	*Letter of Peter to Philip*
Eugnostos	*Eugnostos the Blessed*
Exeg. Soul	*Exegesis on the Soul*
Gos. Eg.	*Gospel of the Egyptians*
Gos. Phil.	*Gospel of Philip*
Gos. Thom.	*Gospel of Thomas*
Gos. Truth	*Gospel of Truth*
Great Pow.	*Concept of our Great Power*
Hyp. Arch.	*Hypostasis of the Archons*
Hypsiph.	*Hypsiphrone*
Interp. Know.	*Interpretation of Knowledge*
Marsanes	*Marsanes*
Melch.	*Melchizedek*
Norea	*Thought of Norea*
On Bap. A	*On Baptism A*
On Bap. B	*On Baptism B*
On Bap. C	*On Baptism C*
On Euch. A	*On the Eucharist A*
On Euch. B	*On the Eucharist B*
Orig. World	*On the Origin of the World*
Paraph. Shem	*Paraphrase of Shem*
Pr. Paul	*Prayer of the Apostle Paul*
Pr. Thanks.	*Prayer of Thanksgiving*
Sent. Sextus	*Sentences of Sextus*
Soph. Jes. Chr.	*Sophia of Jesus Christ*
Steles Seth	*Three Steles of Seth*
Teach. Silv.	*Teachings of Silvanus*
Testim. Truth	*Testimony of Truth*
Thom. Cont.	*Book of Thomas the Contender*
Thund.	*Thunder, Perfect Mind*
Treat. Res.	*Treatise on Resurrection*
Treat. Seth	*Second Treatise of the Great Seth*
Tri. Trac.	*Triparite Tractate*
Trim. Prot.	*Trimorphic Protennoia*
Val. Exp.	*A Valentinian Exposition*
Zost.	*Zostrianos*

Introduction to Colossians

Bibliography

Bandstra, A. J. "Did the Colossian Errorists Need a Mediator?" *New Dimensions in New Testament Study,* ed. R. N. Longenecker and M. C. Tenney. Grand Rapids: Zondervan, 1974, 329–43. **Bornkamm, G.** "The Heresy of Colossians." *Conflict at Colossae,* ed. F. O. Francis and W. A. Meeks. 2nd ed. SBLSBS 4. Missoula, MT: Scholar's Press, 1975, 123–45. Originally published as "Die Häresie des Kolosserbriefs." *TLZ* 73 (1948) 11–20. **Bruce, F. F.** *Paul. Apostle of the Free Spirit.* Exeter: Paternoster, 1977, 407–23. American edition, *Paul. Apostle of the Heart Set Free.* Grand Rapids: Eerdmans, 1977. **Bujard, W.** *Stilanalytische Untersuchungen zum Kolosserbrief als Beitrag zur Methodik von Sprachvergleichen.* SUNT 11. Göttingen: Vandenhoeck und Ruprecht, 1973. **Dibelius, M.** "The Isis Initiation in Apuleius and Related Initiatory Rites." *Conflict at Colossae,* ed. F. O. Francis and W. A. Meeks. 2nd ed. SBLSBS 4. Missoula, MT: Scholar's Press, 1975, 61–121. Originally published as *Die Isisweihe bei Apuleius und verwandte Initiations-Riten.* SHAW.Ph. 8/4. Heidelberg: Winter, 1917. **Duncan, G. S.** *St. Paul's Ephesian Ministry. A Reconstruction with Special Reference to the Ephesian Origin of the Imprisonment Epistles.* London: Hodder, 1929. **Francis, F. O.** "Humility and Angelic Worship in Col 2:18." *Conflict at Colossae,* ed. F. O. Francis and W. A. Meeks. 2nd ed. SBLSBS 4. Missoula, MT: Scholar's Press, 1975, 163–95. Originally published in *ST* 16 (1963) 109–34. ——— "The Background of EMBATEYEIN (Col 2:18) in Legal Papyri and Oracle Inscriptions." ibid. 197–207. **Guthrie, D.** *New Testament Introduction. The Pauline Epistles.* London: Tyndale, 1961. **Hooker, M. D.** "Were there False Teachers in Colossae?" *Christ and Spirit in the New Testament. Studies in honour of Charles Francis Digby Moule,* ed. B. Lindars and S. S. Smalley. Cambridge: University Press, 1973, 315–31. **Kümmel, W. G.** *Introduction to the New Testament.* Tr. H. C. Kee. 2nd ed. London: SCM, 1975. 17th American edition, Nashville: Abingdon, 1975. **Lähnemann, J.** *Der Kolosserbrief. Komposition, Situation und Argumentation.* SNT 3. Gütersloh: Mohn, 1971. **Lyonnet, S.** "Paul's Adversaries in Colossae." *Conflict at Colossae,* ed. F. O. Francis and W. A. Meeks. 2nd ed. SBLSBS 4. Missoula, MT: Scholar's Press, 1975, 147–61. Originally published as "L'étude du milieu littéraire et l'exégèse de Nouveau Testament: 4. Les adversaires de Paul à Colosses." *Bib* 37 (1956) 27–38; cf. also his article "L'Epître aux Colossiens (Col 2:18) et les mystères d'Apollon Clarien." *Bib* 43 (1962) 417–35. **Magie, D.** *Roman Rule in Asia Minor.* 2 vols. Princeton: University, 1950. **Marxsen, W.** *Introduction to the New Testament. An Approach to its Problems.* Tr. G. Buswell. Oxford: Blackwell's, 1968, 177–86. American edition, Philadelphia: Fortress, 1968. **Munn, G. L.** "Introduction to Colossians." *SWJT* 16 (1973) 9–21. **Percy, E.** *Die Probleme der Kolosser- und Epheserbriefe.* SHVL 39. Lund: Gleerup, 1946. **Polhill, J. B.** "The Relationship Between Ephesians and Colossians." *RevExp* 70 (1973) 439–50. **Ramsay, W. M.** *The Cities and Bishoprics of Phrygia.* Vol. 1. Oxford: University Press, 1895, 208–34. **Reicke, B.** "Caesarea, Rome and the Captivity Epistles." *Apostolic History and the Gospel. Biblical and Historical Essays presented to F. F. Bruce on his 60th Birthday,* ed. W. W. Gasque and R. P. Martin. Exeter: Paternoster, 1970, 277–86. American edition, Grand Rapids: Eerdmans, 1970. ———. "The Historical Setting of Colossians." *RevExp* 70 (1973) 429–38. **Schweizer, E.** "Zur neueren Forschung am Kolosserbrief (seit 1970)." *ThBer* 5 (1976) 163–91.

Colossae: The City and Its People

(a) *The City*

The ancient city of Colossae (the site of which was discovered in A.D. 1835) was situated in Phrygia on the southern bank of the river Lycus, a southern tributary of the Meander, which was famous for its many curves (hence the English word "meander" meaning "wander," "wind about"), and its fertile valley produced large crops of figs and olives. The site of Colossae is now deserted, but the town of Honaz (formerly a Byzantine fortress) lies three miles to the southeast.

Colossae (usually spelled Κολοσσαί, though later the spelling Κολασσαί occurs) lay on the early main road from Ephesus and Sardis to the Euphrates, and so finds mention in the itineraries of the armies of King Xerxes and Cyrus the Younger which marched along this road. Herodotus, in the fifth century B.C., speaks of Colossae as "a great city of Phrygia" (*History* 7.30.1), while in the following century the chronicler Xenophon described it as "a populous city, wealthy and large" (*Anabasis* 1.2.6). Its commercial significance was due to its wool industry. The wool was gathered from sheep which grazed on the slopes of the Lycus valley, and dyed a dark red color (Strabo, *Geography* 12.8.16) that was generally known as "Colossian" (Latin *colossinus:* Pliny, *History* 21.51).

Later the city declined considerably in importance, so that in Roman times, two generations before Paul, Strabo speaks of it only as a "small town" (*Geography* 12.8.13, *πόλισμα*). Colossae had been surpassed by Laodicea, ten miles to the west, and Hierapolis, twelve miles to the northwest, both in the same Lycus valley. These were mentioned by the apostle as places where Christians were to be found in close connection with those at Colossae (Col 2:1; 4:13, 15, 16). According to Strabo, Laodicea had developed into a flourishing city during the first century B.C. (12.8.16). Founded by Antiochus II (261–246 B.C.) who named it after his wife, Laodice, it had become—under Roman rule—the seat of a judicial district which was part of the province of Asia (Pliny, *History* 5.105). Not far away on the north side of the valley Hierapolis was also important in NT times, particularly because it was famous for its healing springs (Strabo, *Geography* 12.8.16).

Parts of the Lycus valley, especially Laodicea, were destroyed by earthquake in A.D. 60–61, according to Tacitus (*Annals* 14.27.1). Although Colossae is not mentioned it was probably damaged on the same occasion (cf. Reicke, *RevExp* 70 [1973] 430). Strabo expressly called the whole region a center of repeated earthquakes (*Geography* 12.8.16), and later Orosius commented that "in Asia three cities, Laodicea, Hierapolis and Colossae, have fallen by earthquakes" (*Historiae ad paganos* 7.7.12. It is not certain, however, whether this report refers to the same event which Tacitus records; Eusebius, *Chronicle* 215, dates this destruction in the ninth or tenth year of Nero).

Laodicea was soon restored without any outside assistance from Nero or the Romans, but Colossae never regained its place of prominence. If it was not destroyed in A.D. 60–61 then it may have suffered further seismic damage and was not rebuilt. There is some inscriptional and numismatic evidence that Colossae continued as a Roman city with its officials well into the Christian centuries (*Inscriptiones ad Res Romanes Pertinentes* 4.870; see Magie, *Rule,* 127, 986, and note Martin, *NCB,* 3). The present-day site is uninhabited and not yet excavated (note S. E. Johnson, "Unsolved Questions about Early Christianity in Anatolia." *Studies in New Testament and Early Christian Literature. Essays in Honor of Allen P. Wikgren,* ed., D. E. Aune [NovTSup 33; Leiden: Brill, 1972, 181–93] especially 185).

So by the time Paul wrote to the Christians living at Colossae the commercial and social importance of the town was already on the wane. What effect this might have had on the townspeople, or the Christians among them, we do not know. Last century Lightfoot (16) commented: "Without doubt Colossae was the least important church to which any epistle of St Paul is addressed"—and this may well be true.

(b) *The People of Colossae*

The three cities of Laodicea, Hierapolis and Colossae belonged to the proconsular province of Asia. It has been suggested that Colossae's population consisted mainly of indigenous Phrygian and Greek settlers. But in the early part of the second century B.C., according to Josephus (*Ant* 12. 147–53), Antiochus III brought two thousand Jewish families from Babylon and Mesopotamia and settled them in Lydia and Phrygia (Lightfoot, 19). So the Colossae of Paul's day seems to have been a cosmopolitan city in which differing cultural and religious elements mingled.

We know that the Jewish influence persisted in the neighborhood of Laodicea after the immigration of Jews in the second century B.C. Grave inscriptions found at nearby Hierapolis show that Jews had become part of the Asian culture (Martin, *NCB,* 3, citing evidence from Schürer). In 62–61 B.C. the Roman governor, Flaccus, prevented the Jews from sending to Jerusalem the temple tax which had been collected. He seized as contraband the sum of twenty pounds weight in gold from the district of Laodicea (and one hundred pounds of gold from the district of Apamea: Cicero, *pro Flacco* 28). Calculated at the rate of a half-shekel for each man (for women, children and slaves were exempted) this sum represents a Jewish male population of eleven thousand in the district of Laodicea (Lightfoot, 20; cf. Lohse, 9).

The Church at Colossae

The saints at Colossae, who are addressed as faithful brothers in Christ (1:2), were not converted through the ministry of Paul himself. This Christian community had come into existence during a period of vigorous missionary and evangelistic activity associated with Paul's Ephesian ministry (*c.* A.D. 52–55) recorded in Acts 19. But the apostle himself during his missionary work in Asia Minor had not reached Colossae in the upper valley of the Lycus (2:1; for a contrary view see Reicke, *RevExp* 70 [1973] 432, 433). His daily evangelistic "dialogs" held in the hall of Tyrannus in Ephesus were so effective that Luke can claim "all the residents of Asia heard the word of the Lord, both Jews and Greeks" (Acts 19:10). While the work was directed by Paul, he was assisted by several co-workers and through their ministry in various parts of the province of Asia churches were planted (for a recent detailed discussion of Paul and his colleagues in his apostolic band see W. H. Ollrog, *Paulus und seine Mitarbeiter. Untersuchungen zu Theorie und Praxis der paulinischen Mission* [WMANT 50; Neukirchen-Vluyn: Neukirchener, 1979]). The apostle was not able to visit all of these personally. Nevertheless they fell within the sphere of his apostolic ministry to Gentiles and he maintained warm personal contacts with them (cf. 1:24–2:5; Paul's ministry includes the Colossians: his sufferings are "for your sake," 1:24; his commission was "to you," 1:25; he is "for you . . . and for all who have not seen my face," 2:1; although absent in body, he is present in spirit, 2:5).

Among these churches planted in the province of Asia were the congregations at Colossae, Laodicea and Hierapolis. We have no firsthand information about the beginnings of these Christian communities except what may be derived from the letter to the Colossians itself. And it is to be inferred from the references to Epaphras in the letter (1:7, 8; 4:12, 13) that the congregations founded in these three cities were the fruit of his evangelistic endeavor. He was a native of Colossae (at 4:12 he is described as "one of you") through whom the Colossians had learned the truth of the gospel (1:7). He was engaged in the same struggle for the gospel as was Paul (cf. 4:13 with 1:29; 2:1) and this found particular expression in his urgent and unceasing intercessions for the Christians of the three towns of Colossae, Laodicea and Hierapolis. High tributes are paid to him by Paul: he is called "our beloved fellow-servant" and "a faithful minister of Christ" (1:7) who was Paul's representative ("on our behalf," *ὑπὲρ ἡμῶν*) in Colossae. The readers of this letter may thus be sure that the "truth" had faithfully been taught to them (Epaphras is called a *πιστός . . . διάκονος*, "a faithful minister") by one who is also described by the predicate of honor, "a servant of Christ Jesus" (4:12). Epaphras had come to visit Paul and, either voluntarily or because of his arrest by the authorities, had shared the latter's imprisonment (Phlm 23). So he was not free to return to the congregation when Paul's letter was sent. Instead it was entrusted to Tychicus (4:7, 8) who was commissioned also to bring news of the apostle's experiences in prison. No doubt the congregation would also wish to hear some encouraging news about Epaphras, their leader, especially as he would not be returning with Tychicus and Onesimus (4:9). Other members of the congregation were Philemon and his family (Phlm 1, 2) including Archippus (Col 4:17) and Philemon's runaway slave Onesimus (4:9; Philem 11) whom he hopes will be received by Philemon just as he, Paul, would be welcomed (Phlm 16, 17). (See the detailed relevant exegesis of these verses.)

There are many allusions to the pagan past of the letter's recipients suggesting that almost all of them were Gentile converts (Moule, 29, considers this can be established on the basis of four arguments: [1] it is suggested by 1:12, 21, 27, "where the terms are those of outsiders being brought inside." [2] There is a scarcity of OT allusions. [3] Distinctively Gentile vices are mentioned in 3:5–7. [4] There is a near lack of references to the matter of the reconciliation between Jews and Gentiles in the congregation; though note 3:11 and 4:11. (Cf. J. Bradley, "The Religious Life-Setting of the Epistle to the Colossians," *StBibT* 2 [1972] [d] 17–36, especially 19). They are reminded that once they had been utterly out of harmony with God, enmeshed in idolatry and slavery to sin: they were hostile to God in mind and godless in their actions (1:21). They are also said to have been spiritually dead because of their sins and "the uncircumcision of their flesh"—a statement which indicates they were both heathen and godless (2:13).

But Paul believed God had effected a mighty change in their lives: he had reconciled them to himself in an earthshattering event, namely, Christ's physical death on the cross (1:22); God had delivered them from a tyranny of darkness and transferred them into a kingdom in which his beloved Son held sway (1:13). They now possessed redemption and the forgiveness of their sins (1:14). Indeed, the assurance of the forgiveness of sins (which is an important motif in the letter: 1:14; 2:13; 3:13) is riveted to the readers' minds and consciences by means of graphic language: God had graciously forgiven (χαρισάμενος, 2:13) the Colossians all their trespasses. He had not only cancelled the debt, or signed IOU, but also destroyed the document on which it was recorded. This he did by blotting out the bond with its damning indictment against the readers and by nailing it to the cross when Christ died. Further, God stripped the principalities and powers, evil forces which had kept the Colossians in their evil grip, and divested them of their dignity and might. He exposed to the universe their utter helplessness leading them in Christ in his triumphal procession (2:13–15).

The Colossians now had a hope so secure that it was laid up for them in heaven (1:5; cf. v 23) where Christ was seated and where their thoughts and aspirations were to ascend (3:1–4). That hope, which focused on Christ himself (1:27), had been the subject of the apostolic announcement of Paul and his associates. When the gospel had first been preached by Epaphras to the Colossians it had taken up a firm place in their hearts and lives (1:5, 6). It had begun to bear fruit and to increase in their midst just as it was doing elsewhere throughout the world (1:6).

As Gentiles who had previously been without God and without hope they had been united to Christ in his death, burial and resurrection (2:11, 12; 2:20; 3:1, 3). He was the same person praised as the exalted Lord in creation and reconciliation in the magnificent hymn of chapter 1:15–20. He was none other than God's anointed one at the center of the mystery. That mystery formerly hidden for ages and generations had special reference to them as Gentiles for they were now included along with Jews on an equal footing as members of his body (1:26, 27). Thus they had his life within them and could look forward to the day when they would share in the fullness of his glory. His revelation as Son of God would be the time when they were manifested as the "sons of God" (3:4).

Because the congregation had received Christ Jesus the Lord as their tradition (παρελάβετε, 2:6) when they accepted the gospel at the hands of Epaphras, they are admonished to conduct their lives as those who have been incorporated into Christ. As they live under his lordship they are to abound in thanksgiving (note the references to this theme at 1:3, 12; 2:7; 3:15, 16, 17; 4:2), grateful to God for his mighty actions on their behalf (2:7). Since Christ Jesus was a more than adequate safeguard against the empty traditions of men, let them see to it that their way of life and thought conform continually to his teaching (2:6–8).

The picture is thus drawn of a Christian congregation which is obedient to the apostolic gospel. The report which Paul has received from Epaphras about the faith and love of the Colossian Christians are grounds for heartfelt thanksgiving to God (1:4–6). Epaphras has told the apostle of their "love in the Spirit" (1:8), and Paul writes in warm terms as he tells them he is delighted to learn of their orderly Christian lives and the stability of their faith in Christ (2:5).

The Occasion of the Letter

If the congregation's life and conduct are worthy of such praise what then is the occasion for sending the letter? No doubt one of the reasons for Epaphras' journey to meet with Paul and his willingness to share for a time the apostle's imprisonment (at Philem 23 he is described as a "fellow-prisoner") was his concern to inform him of the progress of the gospel in the Lycus valley and so encourage the apostle. But probably the main reason for his visit was to seek advice from Paul as to how to deal with the false teaching which had arisen in Colossae and which, if it was allowed to continue unchecked, would threaten the security of the church. Paul's letter is then written as a response to this urgent need. It is possible that Epaphras could not cope with the specious arguments and feigned humility of the false teachers and so needed the greater wisdom of the apostle. It has been suggested that Archippus had been left in charge of the work at Colossae, and he is mentioned in Colossians 4:17 as one who had received a ministry in the Lord, and in Philemon 2 as a "fellow-soldier" of Paul (cf. Guthrie, *Introduction,* 162).

The Threat to Faith and the "Colossian Heresy"

(a) *Introductory Remarks*

The letter to the Colossians has been described as "Paul's vigorous reaction to the news of the strange teaching which was being inculcated at Colossae" (Bruce, 165). The apostle became aware of the threatened danger and the need to rebut the error which lay at the heart of this strange aberration of the apostolic kerygma. So he warns the community, which is apparently unsuspecting and innocent, not to be misled by plausible but false arguments (2:4). They are to be on their guard lest they are kidnaped from the truth and led into the slavery of error (2:8). The congregation is urgently warned and admonished regarding the distinction between true and false teaching.

This erroneous teaching has normally been described as the "Colossian heresy" and the nature of it has been discussed for more than one hundred years since Lightfoot wrote his important commentary on Colossians in 1875. There is still considerable difference of opinion as to exactly what was this false teaching that threatened the peace and stability of the Colossian Christians and their near neighbors. (For a bewildering variety of opinion as to the identity of the opponents at Colossae see J. J. Gunther, *St. Paul's Opponents and Their Background. A Study of Apocalyptic and Jewish Sectarian*

Teachings [NovTSup 35; Leiden: Brill, 1973] 3, 4, who lists forty-four different suggestions of nineteenth and twentieth century NT scholars.)

(b) *Was There a "Colossian Heresy"?*

Nowhere in the letter does Paul give a formal exposition of the heresy, and its chief features can be detected only by piecing together and interpreting the apostle's positive counterarguments. In fact, it has recently been questioned by Hooker (*Christ,* 315–31) as to whether these counterarguments point to the existence of a "Colossian heresy" at all. Paul puts the Romans and Philippians on their guard against certain false teachings and wrong practices (Rom 16:17–20; Phil 3:2, 18, 19) without therefore implying that these practices had actually invaded the congregations in Rome and Philippi. Might he not be doing the same thing in Colossians? Hooker points out that, unlike the situation with the Galatians, there is no evidence that the church at Colossae had succumbed to distressing error (cf. 1:3–8; 2:1–5). It is argued that evidence is also lacking for the existence of false teaching with regard to Christ. She claims there were no such heretics in the Colossian community and that a more likely explanation of the situation is that young converts were under external pressure to conform "to the beliefs and practices of their pagan and Jewish neighbours" (*Christ,* 329). Paul's statements about the uniqueness and supremacy of Christ's work in creation and redemption (1:15–20) are a reminder that they need look nowhere else than to Christ for a completion of salvation and his exhortations are to be understood as general warnings.

Hooker's thesis contains much that is appealing: it has stressed again Paul's positive statements about the life and stability of the congregation (1:3–8; 2:5) and reminded us that there is nothing in Colossians like the strong indignation found in Galatians where Paul sees the very foundations of the faith being shaken. Further, Hooker has warned that in attempting to reconstruct the situation behind Paul's writings there is the danger of arguing in a circle (*Christ,* 319). Perhaps therefore one has to speak in terms of tendencies rather than a clear-cut system with precise and definite points. Nevertheless in our judgment her thesis has not taken sufficient account of the language of chapter 2:8–23, with its references to "fullness," specific ascetic injunctions (such as "Do not handle! Do not taste! Don't even touch!" v 21), its statements about the Colossian Christians being taken to task over food and holy days, and its unusual phrases which are best interpreted as catchwords of Paul's opponents (see the exegesis of 2:8–23). One also wonders whether her thesis really accounts for the emphasis on "realized eschatology" in the letter. Her contention, on the other hand, that the letter as a whole, especially chapter 1:15–20, is to be read as a polemic against the Jewish Torah ("both creation and redemption are completed in Christ because he has replaced the Jewish Law," and "Jesus Christ had indeed replaced the Torah as the revelation both of God's glory and of his purpose for the universe and for mankind. It is this fundamental truth which is expressed in Colossians . . . ," in *Christ,* 329, 331), is rather surprising in the light of the absence of terms such as "law" and "command" in the epistle (cf. H. Weiss, "The Law in the Epistle to the Colossians," *CBQ* 34 [1972] 294, and Schweizer, *ThBer* 5 [1976] 174).

(c) *Some Distinguishing Marks of the "Heresy"*

Although Paul gives us no formal exposition of the false teaching there are several crucial passages where he appears to be quoting slogans or catchwords of the opponents and these serve as invaluable clues in any attempt to understand the nature of what is being advocated at Colossae. To begin with the teaching was set forth as "philosophy" (φιλοσοφία, 2:8) based on venerable tradition (the term παράδοσις, "tradition," was used apparently to draw attention to the antiquity, dignity and revelational character of the teaching; Paul, however, rejects any suggestion of divine origin: it was the tradition of men, pure and simple) and was supposed to impart true knowledge and insight (2:18, 23).

The following phrases appear to be catchwords of the opponents which Paul quotes in his attack on the false teaching (for a detailed examination of these expressions see the relevant exegetical sections):

2:9 (cf. 1:19), "all the fullness" (πᾶν τὸ πλήρωμα)
2:18, "delighting in humility and the worship of angels" (θέλων ἐν ταπεινοφροσύνῃ καὶ θρησκείᾳ τῶν ἀγγέλων)
2:18, "[things] which he has seen upon entering" (ἃ ἑόρακεν ἐμβατεύων)
2:21, "Don't handle, don't taste, don't even touch" (μὴ ἅψῃ, μηδὲ γεύσῃ, μηδὲ θίγῃς)
2:23, "voluntary worship" (ἐθελοθρησκίᾳ), "humility" (ταπεινοφροσύνῃ), and "severe treatment of the body" (ἀφειδίᾳ σώματος).

In addition to these citations the apostle asserts that the false teachers took the members of the congregation to task over food regulations and with respect to holy days (2:16, 20, 21). Observance of these taboos in the "philosophy" was related to obedient submission to "the elemental spirits of the world" (τὰ στοιχεῖα τοῦ κόσμου, 2:8, 20), an enigmatic phrase that also appears in Galatians (4:3 cf. v 9; for a brief survey of the main lines along which this phrase has been interpreted see 129–132).

(d) *Interpreting These Distinguishing Marks*

How then are these unusual features to be understood? What was the nature or, if one cannot be too specific, what were the tendencies of the false teachers? No complete agreement has been achieved among scholars (Kümmel, *Introduction,* 339) concerning the nature of the teaching. Basically, however, it seems to have been Jewish. Evidence of this is seen in the part played in the "philosophy" by legal ordinances, food regulations, the sabbath, new moon, and other prescriptions of the Jewish calendar. Reference is made to circumcision (2:11) though it does not appear to feature as one of the legal requirements.

But what kind of Judaism? Was it some sort of "Jewish nonconformity" or "nonconformist Judaism," to borrow Matthew Black's recently popularized wider term (*The Scrolls and Christian Origins* [New York: Scribner's, 1961] 166; cited by Bruce, *Paul,* 416; note especially the latter's treatment of the "Colossian heresy," 412–17)? It does not seem to have been the more straightforward Judaism against which the Galatian churches had to be warned, a Judaism probably brought in by emissaries from Judea. Bruce (*Paul,* 413) suggests the Colossian heresy was "more probably a Phrygian development in which a local variety of Judaism had been fused with a philosophy of non-Jewish origin—an early and simple form of gnosticism." The synagogues in Phrygia seem to have been exposed to the influences of Hellenistic speculation and with these the tendencies to religious syncretism. Ramsay (*Cities*, 2. 637, *passim*) drew attention to the example—no doubt an extreme case—of a Jewish lady who was both honorary ruler of the synagogue and priestess of the imperial cult!

In the Colossian false teaching a special place was apparently given to angels, as agents in creation and in the giving of the law. One form of belief in angelic agency in creation appears in Philo (cf. H. Chadwick, "St. Paul and Philo of Alexandria," *BJRL* 48 [1965–66] 286–307, especially 303), another in Justin Martyr. The latter referred to certain Jewish teachers who took the words "let us make man" (Gen 1:26) and "as one of us" (Gen 3:22) to indicate "God spoke to angels, or that the human frame was the workmanship of angels" (Justin, *Dialogue* 62; cf. Bruce, *Paul*, 413).

The angelic agency in the giving of the law is mentioned by Paul in Galatians 3:19, as well as in Acts 7:53 and Hebrews 2:2, and it is attested in contemporary Jewish literature (cf. the earlier Jub 1:29 as well as the *Mek.* on Exod 20:18; *Sifre* on Num 12:5; and *Pesiq. R.* 21). In the Colossian false teaching these angels were to be placated by keeping strict legal observances. The breaking of the law incurred their displeasure and brought the lawbreaker into debt and bondage to them (cf. Col 2:12–15). These angels are included among the στοιχεῖα (a term already used with reference to angels at Gal 4:3, 9), and were "not only elemental beings but dominant ones as well—principalities and powers, lords of the planetary spheres, sharers in the divine plenitude (πλήρωμα) and intermediaries between heaven and earth" (Bruce, *Paul*, 414). Apparently they were thought to control the lines of communication between God and man. All this was presented as a form of advanced teaching for a spiritual elite. Epaphras had instructed the Colossian Christians only in the first steps and they were now being urged to press on in wisdom and knowledge to attain to true "fullness" (πλήρωμα). To do this they must follow a path of rigorous asceticism until finally they become citizens of that spiritual world, the realm of light.

In the following sections, although not intended as a history of research, the major scholarly contributions over the last hundred years to an understanding of the Colossian "philosophy" are examined. In this treatment I am particularly indebted to the survey of Francis and Meeks (*Conflict*, especially 209–218). We begin with:

(e) *Lightfoot: Essene Judaism of a Gnostic Kind*

Lightfoot (71–111; cf. 347–417) regarded the Colossian heresy as a form of Judaizing *gnōsis* which he traced back to the Essenes. He argued (a) that Essene Judaism was "gnostic," marked by the intellectual exclusiveness and speculative tenets of gnosticism (this term expresses "the simplest and most elementary conceptions" of theosophic speculation, shadowy mysticism and spiritual intermediaries; it does not, according to Lightfoot, refer to "a distinct designation of any sect or sects at this early date"; cf. Francis and Meeks,

Conflict, 209); (b) that this kind of Jewish thought and practice had established itself in this part of Asia Minor during the apostolic age; and (c) that the Colossian heresy was a type of gnostic Judaism, since it was clearly Jewish in its basis, and was marked by several distinctive features of gnosticism: an intellectual elite (with its insistence on wisdom and knowledge), cosmogonic speculation (with an emphasis on angelic mediation, the *πλήρωμα*, and so on), asceticism and calendrical regulations (cf. Bruce, *Paul*, 415).

More recently the discovery of the Qumran material with its points of contact in phraseology (e.g. "his body of flesh," *τῷ σώματι τῆς σαρκὸς αὐτοῦ*, at Col 1:22; cf. 2:11 and note 1QpHab 9:1, 2) and its references to a sect that observed a heterodox calendar, its sabbath regulations, food distinctions, asceticism, an insistence on wisdom and knowledge, involving a special understanding of the world, of angels, etc., have led some to consider that the Colossian philosophy was an offshoot of the teaching of the Qumran community. So W. D. Davies ("Paul and the Dead Sea Scrolls: Flesh and Spirit." *The Scrolls and the New Testament*, ed. K. Stendahl [New York: Harper, 1957] 166–69) maintained that there were clear allusions to the Qumran writings recognizable in the ascetic rules and the worship of the principalities and powers, while P. Benoit ("Qumran and the New Testament." *Paul and Qumran. Studies in New Testament Exegesis*, ed. J. Murphy-O'Connor [London: Chapman, 1968] 17) was of the opinion that circumcision, the exact observance of food laws and the festal calendar together with speculation about the angelic powers coincided with the views of the heterodox Jews living by the Dead Sea.

But in spite of the striking parallels one cannot identify the Colossian heresy as a variety of Essenism or of the Qumran doctrine. For example, we do not find in the letter to the Colossians any reference to an insistence on ceremonial washings, which seem to have played a significant role among the Essenes in general and at Qumran in particular. Baptism is mentioned in Colossians not as the true counterpart to heretical washings but in connection with the "circumcision made without hands" (Col 2: 11, 12; E. M. Yamauchi, "Sectarian Parallels. Qumran and Colossae," *BSac* 121 [1964] 141–52, after a careful assessment of the evidence from the scrolls, concluded that the Colossian heresy was not to be equated with Essene heterodoxy. Some of its features were quite dissimilar to Qumran's views, while others had greater affinities with the Gnostics of Chenoboskion; apparently the Colossian heresy reflected a stage of doctrinal evolution subsequent to Jewish heterodoxy and before the development of later Gnosticism).

(f) *Dibelius: A Pagan Mystery Cult*

One of the most influential contributions to an understanding of the Colossian heresy was that of Martin Dibelius in an essay which first appeared in 1917 (the English translation, "The Isis Initiation in Apuleius and Related Initiatory Rites," has been published in *Conflict*, 61–121). Beginning his investigation with the mystery cults Dibelius examined the unusual term *ἐμβατεύω* ("enter" found at Col 2:18; see the relevant exegesis of this verse) used to describe initiates entering the sanctuary so as to consult the oracle on completion of the rite. From the inscriptional data discovered in the sanctuary of

Apollo at Claros, Dibelius argued that the term signified mystery initiation. The Colossian Christians, without abandoning their Christianity, joined with their non-Christian teachers in a cultic life given over to the powers and were initiated into a cosmic mystery devoted to the elements (στοιχεῖα). The Colossian heresy was a Gnostic mystery; since the practice of this strange cult was independent of the church Dibelius considers this to have been an instance of pre-Christian Gnosticism.

Dibelius' preoccupation with ἐμβατεύω ("enter") in the above-mentioned inscriptions is the most significant factor in his reconstruction of the Colossian heresy. No importance is attached to the fact that the Clarion Apollo was an oracle sanctuary and no oracle is mentioned in Colossians. Also because Dibelius fixed his attention on the independent, pagan character of the cult he rejects any Jewish influence at Colossae (note the critique of Dibelius in *Conflict,* 210, 211, where it is also argued that Lohse [especially 127–31], while recognizing the Colossian allusions to apparent Jewish tradition, follows Dibelius' model faithfully. Accordingly, the regulations mentioned in chapter 2:21, etc. point neither to Essenism nor heretical Judaism but to a Gnostic or pre-Gnostic mystery cult: some Colossian Christians believed initiation and submission to the powers would perhaps open the way to Christ).

(g) *Bornkamm: A Syncretism of Gnosticized Judaism and Pagan Elements*

The important article of Günther Bornkamm, first published in 1948 and translated into English as "The Heresy of Colossians" (*Conflict,* 123–46) concluded that the Colossian false teaching was a pronounced syncretistic religion. Bornkamm adduced material from a wide range of religious movements in order to throw light on its various facets. He argued that the root of the heresy was to be found in a gnosticized Judaism, into which Jewish and Iranian-Persian elements, in addition to Chaldean astrological influences, had been uniquely synthesized and linked with the Christian faith. Inasmuch as Bornkamm understands the heresy as Gnosticism of a Jewish origin he is closer to Lightfoot than to Dibelius (Francis and Meeks, *Conflict,* 211; Conzelmann, 132, and H. M. Schenke, "Der Widerstreit gnostischer und kirchlicher Christologie im Spiegel des Kolosserbriefes," *ZTK* 61 [1964] 1–403, generally follow Bornkamm's reconstruction of the heresy; Conzelmann understands Gnosticism as a broad spiritual movement, not properly a religion, while both he and Schenke consider the Gnostic opponents in the church understood themselves to be Christians). His approach to the practice of a mystery, however, is similar to that of Dibelius, except that Bornkamm recognized the difficulty of Dibelius' presentation which located the source and actual practice of the heresy outside the church. Bornkamm therefore understood the mystery as being within the congregation. The heresy was a Christian error, the decisive characteristic of which was the opponents' teaching about the principalities and powers: Bornkamm postulates that the opponents gave Christ an integrated place among these powers. But Colossians does not say this (Francis and Meeks, *Conflict,* 212).

Further questions about this reconstruction have also been raised: granted the syncretistic nature of the religious situation in Phrygia (and Martin, *NCB,* 4, 5, has drawn attention to this with references to the cult of Cybele, the great mother-goddess of Asia, which flourished in Phrygia [cf. Strabo]; the widespread worship of Isis in Paul's day [cf. R. E. Witt, *Isis in the Graeco-Roman World*, London: Thames and Hudson, 1971] 130, 131); the linking of Iranian cosmology and astrology with the redemption-mystery of the religion of Mithras and its early arrival in the Asia Minor region (as well as the syncretistic Judaism already noted) one can legitimately ask whether such a composite religion as portrayed by Bornkamm actually existed. Even if some of Bornkamm's parallels to the Colossian situation are apt, should we suppose they are integrated in the way he has suggested? Francis and Meeks (*Conflict*, 212) point out that because models are not identical with the data, "they inevitably incorporate features not in the data"; Bornkamm postulates that the opponents gave Christ an integrated place among the powers, but Colossians says nothing of this. Bandstra (*Dimensions*, 330), for his part, suggests that the unusual nature of the syncretistic religion postulated by Bornkamm "results from a methodology in which inferences are made from the givens of the epistle that are not actually supported by the course of the argument in the epistle."

Lähnemann *(Kolosserbrief)* combined features of Lightfoot's model (Phrygian Judaism) with that of Dibelius (the mystery cult) although he excluded Gnosticism. So the Jewish community in the Lycus valley region provided the sectarian setting for a combination of factors similar to "Phrygian nature religion with its ecstatic rigorism, Iranian mythology regarding the elements, Greek wisdom and mystery religion" (Francis and Meeks, *Conflict*, 214). The opponents at Colossae were non-Christian who incorporated Christ into their *πλήρωμα*.

(h) *Lyonnet: Judaizing Syncretism*

Lyonnet, partly by way of response to Dibelius' reconstruction, considers it is unwise to build a whole theory of a pagan mystery at Colossae on the basis of one term, *ἐμβατεύω* ("enter"). Turning to the Qumran material one finds an interest in calendar, dietary regulations, visions and angels. He suggests that the expression "worship of angels" denotes the pattern of regulations of the moral life intended to honor the angels through whom the Mosaic law was given. Lyonnet rejects a pagan Gnostic background for the vocabulary of Colossians. Some terms (e.g. *πλήρωμα*, "fullness," and *σῶμα*, "body") are simply vocabulary familiar to Paul drawn from popular usage, while other terms (*ἀρχαί*, "rulers"; *ἐξουσίαι*, "authorities," etc.) have a Jewish background, as may be noted from comparable language in Galatians and 2 Corinthians. Lyonnet thus chooses a Jewish model over against a pagan one and this, according to Francis and Meeks (*Conflict*, 213) appears to presuppose a widely held view of early Christian history, namely, that Jewishness is to be identified with both temporal priority and doctrinal purity. Apparently because this theory appears to be self-evident Lyonnet does not give reasons as to why "the 'Jewish' *possibility* is more *probable* than the 'pagan'."

(i) *Francis: Jewish Christian Mystical Asceticism*

A fresh approach to this problem of the Colossian philosophy was made by Francis in his 1962 article on Colossians 2:18 (reprinted in *Conflict*, 163–

95; this was followed by a further paper, *Conflict,* 197–207). He examined the controversy as a whole, and especially this verse, "against the background of ascetic and mystic trends of piety" (*Conflict,* 166).

Francis demonstrated that *ταπεινοφροσύνη* (2:18, 23) was a term used by the Colossian opponents to denote ascetic practices (it was frequently employed in Jewish and Christian literature to denote fasting and other bodily rigors: see on 2:18) that were effectual for receiving visions of heavenly mysteries (*Conflict,* 167–71). Regarding the word *ἐμβατεύω* he argued it did not seem to denote "initiation" in the Claros inscriptions (as Dibelius had claimed) but that its specific significance in those inscriptions was impossible to determine. Instead the term was used broadly in the OT and the papyri with the connotation of "entering into possession of" something (for details see on 2:18), and that in conjunction with *ταπεινοφροσύνη* at Colossians 2:18 it had to do with some kind of heavenly entrance (*Conflict,* 171–76, 197–207).

Regarding the phrase *θρησκεία τῶν ἀγγέλων* ("worship of angels") although the dominant interpretation since Dibelius had understood this as an objective genitive, signifying the worship directed to angels, and was therefore taken to be evidence of a pagan feature in the heresy which must be syncretistic rather than entirely Jewish, Francis argued convincingly that the phrase ought to be taken as a subjective genitive, "the angels' worship (*sc.* of God)," so indicating that the entrance into heaven reached its climax in joining in the angelic worship of God. According to Francis and others who have developed his arguments such a liturgical climax could be parallelled in many Jewish/Christian sources of ascetic-mystical piety. These sources were also helpful in illuminating the concepts of "humility" and "entering" (*Conflict,* 176–81; cf. Bandstra, *Dimensions,* 331). If Francis is right in his understanding of this enigmatic phrase, and we consider a good case has been made out by him (see on 2:18), then the only reference used in support of the idea that the principalities and powers were actually worshiped by the false teachers at Colossae falls to the ground.

According to Bandstra's development of Francis' arguments a related Jewish tradition (as evidenced in 1QH, 4 Ezra, 2 Apoc Bar and the Apoc Abr) expressly affirmed that *"creation, present fellowship with God, and, in some instances, judgment, are the result of God's personal and unmediated action"* (Bandstra, *Dimensions,* 332, 333, his italics). At Qumran, for example, in addition to a fellowship with angels at the end-time, the members of the community believed themselves to be joined with the angels in common praise of God as part of their present experience (1QH 3:21–23; 11:10–14; cf. 1QS 11:7, 8; 4QDb). The elect have direct fellowship with the angels and the heavenly world without needing anyone as a mediator to bridge the distance between God and man. Bandstra carries the argument concerning Colossians 2:18 a step further (drawing in ascetic-mystical parallels to 2:2, 3 as well) and posits the hypothesis that the opponents at Colossae might have affirmed that a divine intermediary was not needed to achieve their mystical experiences; and that God, personally, by unmediated action, effected creation and gave them immediate understanding of the cosmic and redemptive mysteries. Angels would be important in such a system as God's messengers to give instructions concerning the requirements for and participation in the visionary experiences (*Dimensions,* 339). This kind of opposition could account for Paul's pointed insistence that Christ the Lord is mediator of creation and redemption. He is the one in whom all the invisible powers were created and who is head over them all.

Francis' presentation treats the error at Colossae within the bounds of Jewish-Hellenistic piety as marked out by Lightfoot, though he makes no use of Essene-Gnostic labels. The asceticism, cosmology and exclusiveness which Lightfoot isolated are taken up in Francis' model of Jewish ascetic-mystical piety. The preoccupation with mystery initiation stemming from Dibelius' reconstructions is rejected as resting on a mistake. Also, the almost universal assumption that the Colossian opponents worshiped angels is regarded as the repetition of an ancient error resting on meager, irrelevant evidence. At the same time observations made concerning correspondences between the text of Colossians and Hellenistic religious phenomena are not necessarily rejected—whether they are called Gnostic or not.

(j) *Concluding Observations*

In the midst of such a bewildering variety of hypotheses concerning the nature of the Colossian heresy (assuming it is even right to speak of a "Colossian heresy" at all) it might well be asked whether certainty is attainable. Many factors restrict our understanding. We are outsiders to the original communication. The writer could presuppose that the readers knew certain things. Others could be brought to their attention by the merest allusion. Some matters that are explicit may be peculiar to the relation between the writer and the Colossians.

But in spite of such qualifications (cf. Francis and Meeks, *Conflict,* 215–17) it does appear that recent scholarly work on the Jewish-Christian ascetic and mystical background has been helpful in illuminating the meaning of several of these difficult expressions in the polemical sections of Colossians (2:16–23). This is not to suggest, however, that (1) Paul's language (even when quoting the phrases of his opponents) has been fully comprehended, or that (2) the false teaching was simply Jewish without any admixture of pagan elements such as appear to have been prevalent in Phrygia.

In the light of these observations we turn to:

Paul's Handling of the Colossian Philosophy

Although one is not unmindful of a build-up in Paul's presentation in chapter 1 (and we shall have cause to return to this shortly), it is not until chapter 2:4 ("I am saying this in order that no one may deceive you with persuasive language") that the apostle *expressly* points to the dangers facing the congregation. He is aware of the methods employed by the false teachers and issues a strong warning to the Colossians to be on their guard (βλέπετε, 2:8) lest the proponents carry them away from the truth into the slavery of error (συλαγωγέω, to "carry off as booty," at 2:8 is both a rare word and a vivid one, showing just how seriously Paul regarded the evil designs of those seeking to influence the congregation): these spiritual confidence tricksters were trying to ensnare the congregation "through philosophy and empty deceit" (διὰ τῆς φιλοσοφίας καὶ κενῆς ἀπάτης, 2:8). Although the false teachers had set forth their philosophy as "tradition" (παράδοσις, 2:8), thereby drawing attention to its antiquity, dignity and revelational character, Paul rejects any suggestion of divine origin. It was a human fabrication (described as "the tradition *of men*") that stood over against the apostolic tradition which centered on "Christ Jesus as Lord."

Paul's reply to this "human tradition" (2:8) is to set over against it the tradition of Christ—not merely the tradition which stems from the teaching of Christ but that which finds its embodiment in him (at 2:6 the verb παρελάβετε, "received," is a semi-technical term to denote the receiving of a tradition, and here the apostle states the readers have received Christ as their tradition). He is the image of the invisible God (1:15), the one who incorporates the fullness of the divine essence (2:9). Those who are incorporated into him have come to fullness of life in him who is master over every principality and power. They need not seek, since they cannot find, perfection anywhere else but in him. It is in him, the one in whose death, burial and resurrection they have been united (2:11, 12), that the totality of wisdom and knowledge is concentrated and made available to his people—not to an elite only, but to all. Further, he is the sole mediator—and a mediator was certainly needed—between God and mankind.

The apostle's criticisms of the advocates of the Colossian philosophy with their false notions and aberrant behavior are trenchant, even devastating (2:16–23). Because of their false legalism the proponents failed to recognize God's good gifts and his purpose in giving them, namely, that all should be enjoyed and consumed through proper use (v 22). The things covered by the taboos were perishable objects of the material world, destined to pass away when used. The taboos themselves, which belonged to a transitory order (v 17), were merely human inventions that lay no claim to absoluteness but stood over against the revelation of the will of God (note the exegesis of "according to human commands and teaching," v 22). To place oneself under rules and regulations like those mentioned in verse 21 is to go back into slavery again—under the personal forces overthrown by Christ (v 20). As death breaks the bond which binds a subject to his ruler so dying with Christ severs the bond which bound the Colossians to the slavery of the principalities and powers. And they must not go back on that life-shattering event. Although the prohibitions (of which v 21 contains illustrations: "Don't handle, don't taste, don't even touch!") carry a reputation for wisdom in the spheres of voluntary worship, humility and severe treatment of the body, they were without any value whatsoever. Such energetic religious endeavors could not hold the flesh in check. Quite the reverse. These man-made regulations actually pandered to the flesh (v 23).

Regarding the false teachers themselves the apostle's words are just as severe: anyone who laid claim to exalted heavenly experiences or visions as a prelude to fresh revelations was puffed up. Such people apparently claimed that they were directed by the mind. "Yes," says Paul, "a mind of flesh!" If they boasted they were acquainted with divine "fullness," then all they were full of was their own pride (v 18)! Worst of all, the self-inflation and arrogance in these private religious experiences come from not maintaining contact with Christ, the head (v 19). No doubt those who sought to make inroads into the community presupposed that they were Christians. Indeed, how else could they have expected to have their views taken seriously? But they face the most serious of condemnations: they are severed from the very one who is the source of life and unity.

In his reply to the Colossian heresy Paul expounds the doctrine of the cosmic Christ more fully and systematically than in his earlier epistles. Hints certainly appear in Romans (8:19–22) and 1 Corinthians (1:24; 8:6; 2:6–10) but a range of points is spelled out in more detail in Colossians 1:15–20 and 2:13–15. The former is a magnificent hymnic passage in praise of Christ as the Lord in creation and reconciliation. Predicates and activities employed in the OT and Judaism of the personalized Wisdom of God are applied to the one who had been so ignominiously crucified only a few years before. Far from the angels playing a part in creation, Christ is the one through whom all things were created, including the principalities and powers which figured so prominently in the Colossian heresy. All things have been made in him as the sphere (*ἐν αὐτῷ*, 1:16) and through him as the agent *δι᾽ αὐτοῦ*, v 16). Indeed, he is unique for he is the ultimate goal of all creation (*εἰς αὐτόν*, v 16). And this magnificent passage emphasizes that even the cosmic principalities and powers, from the highest to the lowest, are all alike subject to Christ.

The hymn goes on to celebrate him as head of the new creation (vv 18–20): here too he is the "beginning," this time as the "first-born from the dead"; his is a primacy in resurrection. In the old creation he was the "head" of every principality and power (2:10) in the sense of being their author and ruler; in the new creation he is "head" of his body, the church, not simply in the sense of ruler or origin, but because he is so vitally united with his people that the life which they now live is derived from his life, that life which he lives as first-born from the dead.

It would be foolish for the Colossians to be misled by the false teachers into thinking it was necessary to obey the angelic powers through whom the law was given as though they controlled the lines of communication between God and man. That way was now controlled by Christ, the one mediator. The principalities and powers had held the Colossians in their grip through their possession of a signed IOU, a bond with its damning indictments. But God stripped these evil authorities, divesting them of their dignity and might, and had cancelled the bond, nailing it to the cross when Christ died. God exposed to the universe the utter helplessness of these principalities, leading them in Christ in his triumphal procession. He paraded these powerless powers so that all the world might see the magnitude of his victory (2:13–15).

Let those who through faith-union with Christ shared his death and resurrection not serve those elemental spirits which Christ had conquered. The Colossian heresy with all its taboos was "no syllabus of advanced wisdom; it bore all the marks of immaturity" (Bruce, *Paul,* 418). Why should those who had come of age in Christ go back to the apron strings of infancy? Why should those whom Christ had freed submit again to this yoke of bondage?

In his handling of the Colossian heresy Paul places his emphasis on realized eschatology (see especially on 2:12; 3:1–4). Within the "already-not yet" tension the stress falls upon the former, called forth by the circumstances of the letter. The Colossians have a hope laid up for them in heaven (1:5; cf. 3:1–4), they have been fitted for a share in the inheritance of the saints in light (1:12), having already been delivered from a tyranny of darkness and transferred into the kingdom of God's beloved Son (1:13). Not only did they die with Christ; they were also raised with him (2:12; 3:1; cf. v 3). The "already" of salvation needed to be asserted again and again over against those who were interested in "fullness" and the heavenly realm, but who had false notions about them, believing they could be reached by legalistic observances, a knowledge for the elite, visionary experiences and the like. The readers, therefore, were instructed that Christ had done all that was necessary for their salvation. They had died with Christ, been raised with him and given new life with him. Let them now zealously seek the things above (3:1, 2), that new order centered on the exalted Christ, and let them as a consequence show that true heavenly-mindedness meant they would be of the utmost earthly use (note the following injunctions of vv 5, 8, 12 and 3:18—4:1).

The Authenticity of the Letter

Up to this point it has been assumed that the letter to the Colossians was a genuine composition of Paul, written by him, or at least at his dictation, and sent out in his name. This view does not rule out the possibility of Paul utilizing other material, such as chapter 1:15–20 or even chapter 2:13–15 (for a discussion see the relevant exegetical sections). Not all, however, are convinced that the letter came from Paul's hand, either directly or indirectly, and their reasons are examined below (on the history of the problem see Percy, *Probleme,* 5–15, and Lähnemann, *Kolosserbrief,* 12–28).

The tradition that Colossians is a genuine Pauline epistle stands on good ground. The later Church fathers accepted it (Irenaeus, *Adv Haer* 3.14.1; Tertullian, *De Praescr Haer* 7; Clement of Alexandria, *Strom* 1.1) and there was no dispute over its authorship in the first decades, even if the allusions to the letter in the earlier part of the second century are not entirely clear. (It appears to have been used as early as Justin, *Dialogue* 85.2; 138.2.) Marcion included it in his canonical list, and it is also found in the Muratorian canon. The letter itself is thought to confirm this, as Paul's name appears at both the beginning (1:1) and the end (4:18).

The first significant denial of Paul's authorship in recent times came in 1838 when E. T. Mayerhoff claimed to have found in Colossians un-Pauline thoughts, evidences of disputation with the second century Cerinthus and a dependence on Ephesians. The main plank of F. C. Baur and the Tübingen school's theories was the alleged evidence that the heresy combated in the epistle was second-century Gnosticism. Accordingly the case for Pauline authorship was thought to have been disproved.

Although few scholars have followed the lead of Mayerhoff in his assertions about the letter's alleged dependence on Ephesians, F. C. Synge (*St. Paul's Epistle to the Ephesians: A Theological Commentary.* [London: S.P.C.K. 1941] 70–75) has (recently) championed the theory, regarding Colossians as a pale and inadequate imitation of Ephesians (which is considered a genuine Pauline letter). The style of Ephesians is said to be far superior to that of Colossians; in parallel passages (e.g. Eph 2:12, 13 and Col 1:20, 21) it is argued that the material of the former is more aptly suited to its context, while theological concepts such as "perfection" and "unity" are more primitive in Ephesians than in Colossians. But Synge's position fails to account for the many places where an advance in thought or a relationship of linguistic dependence can be more easily traced to Ephesians than to Colossians (cf. Polhill, *RevExp* 70 [1973] 441). Other hypotheses have been suggested to explain the relationship between the two letters: Ephesian dependence on Colossians (cf. Goodspeed, Mitton, Ochel, Beare), mutual interdependence (Holtzmann, Coutts), or that neither epistle is directly dependent on the other (Klijn)! (For an overview of the various hypotheses see Polhill, *RevExp* 70 [1973] 439–50.) But the question of the authenticity of Colossians must be decided on other grounds and so we turn to the two major issues in the discussion, the one literary, the other theological.

(a) *The Language and Style of Colossians*

Many of the formal features of Colossians show similarities with the other Pauline letters. The connections involve the structure of the epistle such as the introduction (1:1–2) and the conclusion (4:18), the thanksgiving prayer (1:3–8), connecting words and phrases which introduce instructional expositions and exhortatory conclusions (note the expression *θέλω γὰρ ὑμᾶς εἰδέναι* ["For I want you to know"], 2:1; and the uses of *οὖν* ["therefore"] at 2:6, 16; 3:1, 5, and elsewhere), as well as the list of messages and greetings (cf. 4:8, 10, 12, 15).

Many expressions used in Colossians show decidedly Pauline peculiarities of style (note esp. Percy, *Probleme,* 36–66, Kümmel, *Introduction,* 341, 342, Lohse, 84–91), for example, the superfluous use of *καί* ("and") after *διὰ τοῦτο* ("therefore," 1:9; cf. 1 Thess 2:13; 3:5; Rom 13:6, etc.); in phrases like *οἱ ἅγιοι αὐτοῦ* ("his saints," 1:26; cf. 1 Thess 3:13; 2 Thess 1:10) and *ἐν μέρει* ("in regard to," 2:16; cf. 2 Cor 3:10; 9:3); as well as in verbs such as *χαρίζομαι* meaning to "forgive" (2:13; 3:13; cf. 2 Cor 2:7, 10; 12:13). The similarities and points of contact extend into the theological terminology, such as the expressions "in Christ" (1:2, 4, 28), "in the Lord" (3:18, 20; 4:7, 17) or "with Christ" (2:12, 20; 3:1, 3); expositions about being united with Christ in baptism (2:11, 12); statements about being freed from the compulsive power of the regulations (2:14, 20, 21); concerning the contrast between the old and the new man (3:5–17); and also regarding the relation between the indicative and the imperative in the exhortations (3:5–17).

On the other hand, there are linguistic differences between Colossians and the other Pauline letters which are worthy of attention (see Lohse, 85–88, for details). In all there are thirty-four words appearing in Colossians but nowhere else in the NT, twenty-eight words which reappear in the NT but not in the other Pauline letters (not taking into account 2 Thess and the Pastorals), ten words which Colossians has in common only with Ephesians and a further fifteen appearing in Colossians and Ephesians as well as in the rest of the NT, but not in the other Pauline letters. Before coming to conclusions too quickly, several important factors need to be kept in mind. First, a good number of the words noted in these statistics appear either in the hymnic paragraph (though on the question of its authorship see 40–42) or in the interaction with the false teaching. It is not surprising, then, that unusual terms should appear either as catchwords of the Colossian "philosophy" or as part of the author's polemic. Second, Lohse (86) has drawn attention to compound words in Colossians which are to be compared with similar compounds in the other Pauline letters (e.g. ἀνταναπληρόω, 1:24; προσαναπληρόω, 2 Cor 9:12; 11:9). Further, it must be remembered that hapax legomena and other unusual expressions turn up in considerable numbers in the other Pauline letters (cf. Percy, *Probleme,* 17, 18; Galatians, for example, has thirty-one words appearing nowhere else in the New Testament). The nonappearance of certain Pauline theological terms such as "sin" (in the singular), "righteousness" and related words, "law," "salvation," "believe," etc. is not decisive. In other Pauline letters, occasionally one or more of these words does not appear or is strikingly infrequent: "righteousness" turns up in 1 Corinthians only at 1:30 and not at all in 1 Thessalonians. The verb "justify" does not occur in 1 Thessalonians, Philippians or in 2 Corinthians while "law" also is absent from 2 Corinthians. Likewise "salvation" does not appear in Galatians or in 1 Corinthians.

The absence of one or other word or concept may be due to the different subject matter being discussed in the particular letter. Schweizer (22; cf. Lohse, 87) considers it is quite peculiar that the very terms which could be expected to occur in a confrontation with legalistic doctrine are actually those which are missing: "sin" (in the singular), "righteousness," "justify," "believe" (an appropriate response might be that if these terms are so obvious in such a context why does not Paul's disciple [possibly Timothy, according to Schweizer] include them in his argument?).

Recent writers have drawn attention to the characteristic features of the letter's *style,* as distinct from its vocabulary (Lohse, 88–90; Bujard, *Untersuchungen;* cf. Percy, *Probleme,* 18: "the real problems concerning the form of the letter lie completely within the area of style"). Thus we note combined expressions belonging to the same stem ("strengthened with all power," 1:11; cf. 1:29; 2:11, 19), synonymous expressions ("praying and asking," 1:9; cf. 1:11, 22, 23, 26; 2:7; 3:8, 16; 4:12), series of dependent genitives ("the word of truth, of the gospel," 1:5; cf. 1:12, 13, 20, 24, 27; 2:2, 11, 12), examples of nouns attached to phrases by the preposition "in" (ἐν: "the grace of God in truth," 1:6; cf. 1:8, 12, 29 etc.) and a loosely joined infinitive construction ("to walk worthily of the Lord," 1:10; cf. 1:22, 25; 4:3, 6). Although similar usages can be cited from the chief Pauline letters they do not appear as frequently (cf. Schweizer, 22). Furthermore, it has been argued by Lohse (89) and others that Colossians is characterized by a liturgical hymnic style with its long sentences, made up of relative clauses, inserted causal phrases, participial phrases and further notes, some of which may be compared with material from the Qumran texts.

These stylistic pecularities, however, have been interpreted differently. Percy (*Probleme,* 43) considers that these features when compared with the rest of the Pauline letters have their "basis entirely in the peculiarity of the letter's content. This content, for its part, is clearly connected with the peculiarity of the situation which necessitated the letter" (cited by Lohse, 90; cf. Kümmel's conclusion, *Introduction,* 342: "On the basis of language and style . . . there is no reason to doubt the Pauline authorship of the letter"). Lohse (91) for his part, while concluding (on the grounds of theology) that "the author was a theologian decisively influenced by Paul" nevertheless admits that "on the basis of the observations made about the language and style of the letter, no final decision can yet be reached on the question of Pauline or non-Pauline authorship of the letter." Several recent continental scholars have been more negative in their judgment. So Schweizer (23, with special reference to Bujard's researches, *Untersuchungen*) concludes that a large number of carefully evaluated observations gives a uniform picture and depicts an author who, for all his dependence on Paul in vocabulary and thought, nevertheless argues differently from him. "The letter cannot have been written or dictated by Paul." Such a judgment in our view appears to be unduly negative and presupposes an almost infallible understanding of what Paul could or could not have done. It also does not really explain the close similarities between Colossians and the generally accepted Pauline letters, a point which Ollrog (*Paulus,* 220, 237) is painfully aware of but does not satisfactorily answer with his own thesis of authorship by one close to Paul, i.e. Timothy.

(b) *The Teaching of the Epistle*

For some scholars such as Lohse the supposed theological differences between Colossians and the generally accepted Pauline letters are decisive against the apostolic authorship of Colossians, even if the grounds of language and style were not. Earlier Mayerhoff believed that Colossians was full of non-Pauline ideas. F. C. Baur and the Tübingen school agreed with this judgment and cast further doubt on the apostolic authorship because this letter did not reflect the conflict between Jewish Christianity and Gentile Christianity which was the hallmark of the apostolic age. Further, it was argued that the letter's Christology belonged to a later period of church history when classical Gnostic influences had begun to exert themselves (on Baur's position see W. G. Kümmel, *The New Testament. The History of the Investigation of its Problems.* Tr. S. McLean Gilmour and H. C. Kee (London: SCM, 1972) 135–37 American edition [Nashville, TN: Abingdon, 1972], cited by Martin, *NCB,* 33). It has already been shown that one need not resort to supposed full-blown Gnostic influences of the second century as a reconstructed background to the heresy and its letter. If the Jewish background of an ascetic mystical kind is the most likely of the competing possibilities (see above xxxvi–xxxviii) then there is no need to look beyond the apostolic age and certainly Pauline authorship is not ruled out on this account.

More significant are the objections to Paul's authorship on the grounds that major differences exist between Colossians and the theology of the main Pauline epistles. These differences, it is asserted, are not limited to the passages that argue against the "philosophy," but also turn up in sections that are free of polemic. They may be examined under the following headings:

1. *Christology*

Lohse claims (178, 179) that Colossians develops its Christology on the basis of the Christ-hymn of chapter 1:15–20, and goes beyond the recognized Pauline statements of 1 Corinthians 8:6 and Romans 8:31–39 in its teaching that in Christ the entire fullness of deity dwells "bodily" (*σωματικῶς*, 2:9) and that he is the "head of every principality and power" (2:10). Certainly the hymnic passage (1:15–20) is central to the letter: the long prayer report of chapter 1:9–14 leads up to this paragraph in praise of Christ, while subsequent references in the epistle either echo some of its statements or are a spelling out of their implications. We judge that chapter 2:10 may be explained along these latter lines (there is no implication that "every principality and power" is a member of Christ's body; see the exegesis) while chapter 2:9 applies the words of the hymn (1:19) to the context of the Colossian heresy, making plain by the addition of the words "bodily" (*σωματικῶς*) the manner the entire fullness of deity dwells in Christ, i.e. in bodily form, by becoming incarnate (see on 2:9). The emphatic cosmic dimension of Christ's rule is a fuller and more systematic exposition of the theme of Christ's universal lordship, already made plain in earlier Pauline letters (cf. 1 Cor 8:6; 1:24; 2:6–10) and now spelled out in relation to and as a correction of the false teaching at Colossae. There is no need to postulate an author other than Paul as the source of such ideas.

2. *Ecclesiology*

The ecclesiology of Colossians is intimately connected with its Christology. This is nowhere more apparent than in the statement that Christ is the "head of the body" (*κεφαλὴ τοῦ σώματος*), that is, "the church" (*τῆς ἐκκλησίας*, 1:18). In the relevant exegetical section we have contended that *σῶμα* ("body") here did not originally refer to the cosmos and thus there is no need to look for Stoic antecedents as the source of the writer's ideas (see 48–50). In 1 Corinthians 12:12–27 and Romans 12:4, 5 Paul employs the body terminology and its constituent parts to refer to the mutual relations and obligations of Christians. In these earlier references the "head" (*κεφαλή*) of the body had no special position or honor; it was counted as an ordinary member (cf. 1 Cor 12:21). In Colossians (and Ephesians) there is an advance in the line of thought, from the language of simile (as in 1 Cor and Rom) to that of a real and interpersonal involvement. This advance may well have been stimulated by Paul's reflection on the issues involved, in the Colossian heresy (for details see on 1:18).

The term *ἐκκλησία* ("church") at chapter 1:18 is usually taken to refer to the people of God all over the world, the universal or world-wide church, where Christ here and now exercises his cosmic lordship (see for example E. Lohse, "Christusherrschaft und Kirche im Kolosserbrief," *NTS* 11 [1964–65] 203–216, especially 204–207). However, we have suggested below (57–61) against the majority opinion, that it is best to understand this as a reference to a heavenly assembly around the risen and exalted Christ (cf. Col 3:1–4; Eph 2:6). That heavenly gathering with Christ at its center is manifested here and now on earth. Hence the same word ἐκκλησία ("church") can be used of the local congregation at Colossae or even of a small house community (4:15, 16). The congregation in heaven finds its manifestation and becomes visible as the domain of Christ's rule where the saints and faithful brothers in Christ gather (1:2).

3. *Eschatology*

In the current discussion about the eschatology of Colossians several different arguments are used against an acceptance of the apostolic authorship of the letter. Since these have been treated at length in the relevant exegetical sections we shall simply summarize the salient points here.

Bornkamm (see on 1:5 and 3:4) alleged that ἐλπίς meaning the "object of hope" in chapter 1:5 was unusual in Paul ("hope" was normally regarded as signifying the subjective experience of the Christian like "faith" and "love"). Further, he detected in Colossians 1:26, 27 not hope in the sense of historical eschatology but a "gnostic spherical thought." However in neither chapters 1:26, 27 nor 3:4 are there spherical conceptions. Rather, there is evidence of a genuine eschatological tension. (It is perhaps not without significance that Bornkamm made no reference to Rom 8:24, 25—a passage in one of the main letters—where the connotation "object of hope" is certainly present [cf. Gal 5:5]; see the criticisms of Kümmel, *Introduction,* 344, and Martin, *NCB,* 34, 35.)

It is also alleged that eschatology in Colossians has receded into the background. Chapter 3:4 is said to contain the only explicit futuristic reference, and even here the "hidden-revealed" motif is without parallel in the earlier Pauline letters. Spatial concepts are thought to dominate at chapters 1:26, 27; 3:1–4; while none of the typically Pauline eschatological ideas—parousia, resurrection of the dead, judgment of the world—is encountered in Colossians. Further, it is pointed out that in this letter not only have believers died with Christ and been buried with him in baptism (2:11, 12), but also (unlike the genuine Pauline epistles), they are said to have been raised with him (2:12); God has made them alive together with Christ (2:13), raising them with him from the dead (3:1). The resurrection to new life has already occurred, so that the future event is no longer called the resurrection of the dead but the revelation of life in which the Christians already participate and which is still hidden with Christ in God (3:3, 4). The ethical "imperative" in Colossians as elsewhere in Paul is based on the "indicative"; however it is argued that in Colossians, but nowhere in the genuine epistles of Paul, the resurrection of Christians in the past or present is regarded as the basis of that imperative.

A more detailed examination of these contentions has been made at 168, 169). Suffice it to say at this point that there is an emphasis on realized eschatology in Colossians, called forth by the particular circumstances of the letter. In terms of the "already-not yet" tension the accent falls upon the former. But this is not to suggest that the "not yet" side of Paul's tension is absent. There is future eschatology at chapters 3:4, 6, 24 and, in our estimation, at 1:22, 28; cf. 4:11 (note the relevant exegetical sections). The "hidden-revealed" theme is a significant apocalyptic feature, while spatial concepts are used in the service of eschatology. The antithesis between eschatological and transcendent perspectives is a false one as both are found together in the undisputed Paulines and at Colossians 3:1–4. The apocalyptic notion of the resurrection from the dead is found at chapter 1:18 (see on this passage and 3:4) and in the undisputed Paulines the ideas of the resurrection from the dead and eschatological life are interchangeable (cf. Rom 4:17; 5:17, 18, 21; 8:11 etc.; see further on chapter 2:12). There is an eschatological motivation in Colossians; it may not be dominant but it is present nevertheless (the exhortation, "put to death, therefore, . . ." 3:5, is based on verses 1–4, the last of which has an eschatological emphasis). At the same time there are other grounds for exhortation in the generally accepted Pauline letters. In sum, the arguments against the Pauline authorship of Colossians based on a change in eschatology are inadequate. The differences of emphasis can be satisfactorily explained by the particular circumstances of the letter. There is no need to resort to a non-Pauline or post-Pauline authorship.

4. Tradition

The alleged differences between the theology of Colossians and that of the major Pauline letters in the above-mentioned areas of Christology, ecclesiology and eschatology—differences which are thought to pervade the non-polemical as well as the polemical parts of the letter—are ascribed to the emergence of a "Pauline school tradition" which was based probably in Ephesus. E. Käsemann ("A Primitive Christian Baptismal Liturgy," *Essays on New Testament Themes.* Tr. by W. J. Montague [London: SCM, 1964] 166, 167 American edition [SBT 41; Naperville, IL: Allenson, 1964]) focuses his attention on two further features of this tradition. First, the baptismal *homologia* or confession of faith. He maintains that the post-Pauline author of the epistle has taken over a pre-Christian hymn (1:15–20) and used it for his purposes by setting it within the framework of a Christian confession of faith, by surrounding it with baptismal motifs (1:13, 14, which he had, in fact, found already connected with the hymnic piece), and a pastoral admonition to remain true to the faith (1:21–23). The intention of the author's Christian use of the hymn was to combat heresy by a confession of faith shared by this community of the subapostolic age. Whatever else one may say about the overall approach, Käsemann's contentions that the hymn was originally a pre-Christian Gnostic text taken over in Christian usage in a baptismal liturgical reinterpretation have been rejected by contemporary New Testament scholarship, and with good reason (for details see below 37, 38, cf. 25 and note the critique of the view integral to Käsemann's argument that vv 12–14 were known in a prebaptismal context and served as an "introit" to the hymn).

The second feature of this post-Pauline tradition, according to Käsemann, is the adherence of the community "to the apostolic office as guardian of the truth. The apostolate expounds the truth of the Gospel, as the confession of faith fixes it" (*Essays,* 166, 167). It is not Paul who relates the confession and apostolate in this way; rather, it "is the voice of the subapostolic age."

Closely related to this presentation is the view of Marxsen (*Introduction,*

177–86) who argues that within the list of greetings in Colossians Epaphras' name is especially emphasized. One of the chief reasons for this document, which is "a kind of pastoral letter" (180), was to give an apostolic authorization to Epaphras whose teaching represents the mind of Paul. Now that the apostle is no longer alive Epaphras stands in an apostolic succession. The letter bears the marks of the "early catholicism" of the subapostolic age, according to Marxsen (note the remarks on 4:13). For Lohse (68) "Colossians certifies the gospel as the correct teaching by connecting it with the apostolic office."

However, serious questions have been raised about the grounds for such far-reaching reconstructions, and scholars such as Schweizer and Ollrog, who do not accept the direct Pauline authorship of Colossians, have made several pertinent criticisms. Both argue that of all the so-called deutero-Pauline letters Colossians stands most closely to Pauline theology. It is clearly an occasional letter written to a concrete church situation (cf. especially Lähnemann, *Kolosserbrief*). Colossians stands in a close relationship to the letter to Philemon. In both Paul is in prison (Col 4:3, 10, 18; Philem 1, 9, 10, 13, 23). The names of Paul and Timothy stand at the head of each letter (Col 1:1; Philem 1). Eight of the nine names mentioned in Philemon appear in Colossians. Clearly they are Paul's co-workers, and it just will not do with Lohse (177) to assert that the messages and greetings as well as particular details about fellow-workers of the apostle are used by the author of Colossians "to prove that his writing is an apostolic message" (Lohse adds: "In using Philemon's list of greetings and making it more vivid, he ensures that his letter will gain a hearing as a message from Paul"; Ollrog, *Paulus,* 238, 239, is critical of Lohse's methodology, claiming that the latter has not properly analyzed the epistolary situation of Colossians; rather, he has first decided that the theology reflected in the letter is post-Pauline, and then turned to the historical details such as the list of greetings to "confirm" his prior judgment that the Pauline school made literary use of Philemon). Both Schweizer (23–27) and Ollrog (*Paulus,* 241; cf. Lähnemann's arguments, *Kolosserbrief,* 181, 182) claim, with reference to the above-mentioned issue of tradition, that Colossians is not post-Pauline.

Finally the matter must be settled on the exegesis of chapters 1:7; 4:7–13 (see the relevant exegetical sections) and the important statement about Paul's commission to preach the gospel in chapters 1:23–2:5. The function of the latter passage is to spell out the content and purpose of Paul's ministry, a commission given to him in accordance with the gospel-plan of God to make known God's mystery among the Gentiles, and especially among the Colossians. He is a minister (*διάκονος*) of the gospel (1:23), just as are Epaphras (1:7; cf. 4:12, 13) and Tychicus (4:7). Against Lohse (68) it must be maintained that the gospel is not certified as correct teaching by its connection with the apostolic office. Quite the reverse. It is the gospel that gives the validity to Paul's commission: he is to serve that gospel and to proclaim it fully and effectively throughout the world (1:25, 26). His service of the gospel finds expression in suffering (1:24) and imprisonment, and while this is generally on behalf of Gentiles, to whom the mystery is now made known, it has particular reference to the Colossians (note the parallelism of 1:24–29 with 2:1–5).

This paragraph is not written to legitimize the gospel through the apostolic office of Paul, and then to assert (1:7; 4:7–13) the legitimation of Epaphras because of his relationship to Paul. Paul serves the gospel; so does Epaphras, and the apostle goes out of his way to show the equality of himself and his co-workers (*συνεργοί*) as ministers (*διάκονοι*) of that word. There is no attempt in these three passages (either singly or jointly) to give an apostolic authorization to Epaphras because he stands in an apostolic succession and his teaching represents the mind of Paul. There is no suggestion of ongoing authority or apostolic succession bound up with any single person.

In our estimation the so-called differences between Colossians and the generally accepted Pauline letters do not constitute sufficient grounds for rejecting the apostolic authorship of this epistle. Differences of emphasis there are, but these are best interpreted as being called forth by the circumstances at Colossae. It is not without significance that some of the most recent continental New Testament scholarship has recognized that the historical situation of Colossians, together with the theological answers provided for these difficult pastoral circumstances, stands very close to that of Paul (so Lähnemann, *Kolosserbrief*, 23–28, 177–83, Schweizer, 23–27, and Ollrog, *Paulus*, 219–31, 236–42). Rejecting a post-Pauline situation, the latter two scholars have suggested the differences between Colossians and the other epistles of Paul may be due to Timothy's authorship, or at least his active hand in the composition of the letter under Paul's authority. While it may not be necessary to resort to this suggestion, at this stage of NT research further understanding is needed as to what part Paul may have allowed his colleagues to play in the production of his letters.

The Place of Paul's Imprisonment

(a) *Introduction*

Four NT letters have been called the captivity Epistles: Colossians, Philemon, Ephesians and Philippians. As far as personal names are concerned Philemon, Colossians and Ephesians form a group by themselves. Colossians 4:7, 8 and Ephesians 6:21, 22 speak of Tychicus as a bearer of the two letters, and Dibelius-Greeven, (99; cf. Martin, *NCB*, 23) commenting on the latter passage indicates there is "the most extensive verbal contact" between the two epistles at this point. Tychicus had Onesimus as his companion on the journey to the Lycus valley, the same Onesimus mentioned in the note to Philemon who is returning, evidently at the same time (Phlm 12). Greetings are sent from practically the same people (Phlm 23; Col 1:7, 4:12–19) so that clearly Philemon and Colossians stand together (see above). The place of Archippus confirms this last point. He is addressed in Colossians 4:17 and encouraged to fulfill the ministry he has received in the Lord, while in the letter to Philemon he appears to be a member of Philemon's household (v 2).

On the other hand, Philippians stands somewhat apart. Except for Timothy all the rest of the personal names are different (the Epaphroditus of Phil 2:25; 4:18 is not to be identified with Epaphras), as are the travel plans. Further, Paul's future, as reflected in Philippians, was full of uncertainty.

His life was in the balance (1:20–24); he has no way of predicting the outcome of his trial, though on pastoral (1:24–26) and theological grounds (2:24) he hopes for his release. The possibility of being martyred for Christ was all too real (1:21; 2:17).

The other three prison epistles do not give any hint of this apprehensiveness about the future. The atmosphere of Colossians, by contrast, is calm. If the two letters come from the same imprisonment (and there is considerable difference of opinion over this) then we must assume that Paul's situation worsened considerably in the interval between the two letters.

Since early times attempts have been made to answer the question: where was Paul when the letter to the Colossians was written? The letter itself states that Paul was in bonds for the sake of the mystery of Christ (4:3), that Aristarchus, his fellow-prisoner, was with him (4:10), and that the congregation are asked to remember his imprisonment in prayer (4:18). Nothing is mentioned explicitly, however, as to where Paul was captive.

(b) *A Roman Imprisonment*

Until fairly recent times there was little doubt that Paul was in Rome when he wrote this letter. The "subscript" which was added at a later date asserts: "written from Rome by Tychicus and Onesimus" (K L etc.). Eusebius (*History*, 2.22.1) records that Paul was brought to Rome and that "Aristarchus was with him; whom also somewhere in his epistles he suitably calls a fellow-prisoner," a reference presumably to Colossians 4:10. This mention of Aristarchus agrees with the statement in Acts 27:2 from which it seems that he accompanied Paul all the way to Rome (see on Col 4:10).

Other factors which point to a Roman imprisonment when Paul wrote Colossians are:

(i) Paul's confinement in Rome is described by Eusebius as "without restraint" (borrowed from Acts 28:30) which suggests a measure of freedom that could account for the presence of co-workers and friends (4:7–17) and, if necessary, a scribe to engage in letter-writing for him.

(ii) The list of names which links Colossians with Philemon brings to our attention the case of Onesimus. Assuming he actually ran away and sought asylum in Paul's presence (see 266, 267), it is argued that fearful of being caught and punished he would seek anonymity in the imperial capital where he could safely disappear from public notice.

(iii) No other imprisonment in Acts seems a real alternative. Paul was in jail at Philippi (Acts 16:23–40) for one night only, and although he was held for two years at Caesarea (Acts 24:27) there are difficulties in assuming a Caesarean imprisonment when Paul might have written Colossians, as we have noted below. The suggestion of Rome is based on a known imprisonment of such a character as to allow the events reflected in Colossians to happen (note the mild restrictions mentioned in Acts 28:16, 30). Travel between Rome and the east was frequent and not so formidable a task as to make the communications implied in the prison epistles impossible (Moule, 24). Paul's joy over the triumph of the gospel throughout the whole world fits well in Rome (1:6, 23).

(iv) Bruce (*Paul*, 411, 412) considers a later imprisonment such as at Rome (rather than at Caesarea) to be more likely than an early imprisonment in Ephesus (dated *c.* A.D. 54–57). In default of more explicit evidence he claims that the progression in Pauline thought, notably in the conception of the church as the body of Christ, is an important criterion for the dating of Colossians. This letter "marks a more advanced stage in Paul's thinking on the subject than do 1 Corinthians and Romans." He adds that "it is difficult to date it [i.e. Colossians] during his Ephesian ministry, about the same time as 1 Corinthians and earlier than Romans. It follows that an Ephesian imprisonment is out of the question as the setting of Colossians" (411, 412). Rome is then preferred to Caesarea "on all counts" (Bruce, *Paul,* 411, is not unmindful of the danger of arguing in a circle, determining the development of Paul's thought from the order of his epistles, and then determining the order of his epistles from the development of his thought; Martin, *NCB,* 29, contends that arguments from the development of Paul's theological themes are not conclusive).

Nevertheless doubts have been raised over a Roman captivity as being the place from which the letter was sent (cf. Martin, *NCB,* 25, 26):

(i) The great distance between Colossae and Rome (some 1,200 miles) is a factor to be taken into account: Epaphras and Onesimus have already come to Paul, Tychicus and Onesimus are to return. Paul refers to these journeys, across land and sea, in a rather casual way.

(ii) Onesimus' escape to Rome in order to bury himself in the imperial city would have involved great risks and the possibility of capture on the long journey from Colossae. However, it must be remembered that other runaway slaves had traveled long distances with similar dangers in order to reach Rome.

(iii) Several scholars have noted that if Paul's hopes for a release from prison are granted he expects to visit Colossae (Phlm 22). This would involve a revision of an earlier intention to visit Spain (Rom 15:28) based on the conviction that his missionary and pastoral activities had been completed in the Eastern Mediterranean (Rom 15:23, 24). Now while Paul was known to change his plans, and was charged with inconsistency as a result (2 Cor 1:15–24), this change would seem to imply a shift in missionary strategy. (Also implied is the acceptance of the tradition deriving from Eusebius [*History,* 2.22, 2, 3] that Paul was released after the two years of detention in Rome, and Martin [*NCB,* 26] following others including G. Ogg, *The Chronology of the Life of Paul* [London: Epworth, 1968] 178–93 American edition, *The Odyssey of Paul* [Old Tappan, NJ: Revell] claims this is not certain.)

(iv) Further, if Paul is hoping for an early release (which seems to be implied in Philem 22), then his request, "prepare a guest room for me," is an unusual one given that he is about to undertake a 1,200-mile journey by sea and land before reaching Philemon's home.

(c) *A Caesarean Imprisonment*

The case for a Caesarean imprisonment has been advocated by scholars in recent times as the place where Colossians was composed (so Dibelius-Greeven, 52, Lohmeyer, 14, 15, Reicke, *History,* 277–82; and J. J. Gunther, *Paul: Messenger and Exile. A Study in the Chronology of His Life and*

Letters [Valley Forge: Judson, 1972] 98–112; cf. Kümmel, *Introduction*, 346–48). It is argued that Aristarchus' sharing of Paul's imprisonment (Col 4:10) can be harmonized with Acts 20:4; 24:23, while Tychicus who, according to Acts 20:4, had traveled with Paul to Jerusalem, might well have gone on with him to Caesarea. Onesimus is more likely to have wandered to Caesarea than to Rome, and it is possible he might have sought Paul's protection in the company of several Hellenistic Christians who were with Paul at Caesarea. Paul's request of Philemon for accommodation in Colossae (Phlm 22) is possible from Caesarea if he has not yet counted on an appeal to the emperor, or if as Reicke suggests he intended to visit Colossae on his way as a prisoner to Rome.

One serious question mark against the suggestion of a Caesarean imprisonment is that such a small city as Caesarea could hardly have been the home of active missionary work requiring such a large staff of Paul's co-workers of Gentile origin. It does not seem that this small harbor city was the center of vigorous propaganda as suggested in Colossians 4:3, 4 where Paul has freedom to speak. Nor is there any suggestion in Acts that Paul contemplated an early release once he had appealed to Caesar and his case was remitted to Rome.

(d) *An Ephesian Imprisonment*

In addition to Rome Ephesus was also named as the city in which Paul was in prison when he wrote to the community at Colossae. So the Marcionite prologue to the letter reads: "The apostle already in fetters writes to them from Ephesus." There is no explicit mention either in the Pauline epistles or in the Acts of the Apostles of an Ephesian imprisonment. However, advocates of this theory (which include Deissmann, Michaelis, and note especially Duncan, *Ministry;* cf. Martin, *NCB,* 26–32, and Ollrog, *Paulus,* 59 etc.) point out that evidence of imprisonments other than those recorded in Acts appears in 2 Corinthians 11:23 (while Clement of Rome, A.D. 96, mentions seven, *ad Cor* 5.6). In addition, several passages in the Corinthian letters which might have come out of a period of Paul's conflict in Ephesus tell us something of his deep troubles (1 Cor 4:9–13; 2 Cor 4:8–12; 6:4, 5; 11:23–25). First Corinthians 15:32 ("I fought with wild beasts," ἐθηριομάχησα), even if it is not to be taken literally, speaks of Paul enduring some life or death struggle at Ephesus. It has been conjectured that Paul may have been delivered because of his Roman citizenship. Second Corinthians 1:8 speaks of a severe trial (θλῖψις) in Asia, while the occasion on which Priscilla and Aquila risked their lives for Paul's sake (Rom 16:3, 4) is thought to have been at Ephesus.

If the possibility of such a captivity is allowed, then it is argued we can place Colossians more satisfactorily in this period of Paul's life, that is, during his extended stay at or near Ephesus, from the autumn of A.D. 54 to the late summer of A.D. 57 (cf. Ogg, *Chronology,* 134–38, who is followed by Martin, *NCB,* 27; others contend A.D. 52–55 are more likely dates). Duncan (*Ministry,* 111–15) fixes the occasion more precisely, attributing the imprisonment of Paul to a direct consequence of the Demetrius riot (Acts 19:23–41). This disturbance is dated in the late spring of A.D. 57, linking it with the festival in honor of the goddess Artemis during that year.

The arguments, then, used in favor of an Ephesian imprisonment as the setting of Colossians may be summarized as follows:

(i) The fact that Ephesus and Colossae were no more than one hundred miles apart is thought to explain more easily the movements described in the letter between the place of Paul's imprisonment and Colossae. Onesimus, it is claimed, is just as likely to have sought refuge in a metropolis, Ephesus, as in distant Rome (C. H. Dodd, *New Testament Studies* [Manchester: University, 1953] 95, argued, however, it was more likely that a fugitive slave, with his pockets lined at his master's expense, would make for Rome because it was distant rather than Ephesus because it was near).

(ii) If Paul was at Ephesus when he wrote Colossians and Philemon, then his request for a lodging at Colossae (Phlm 22) immediately after his release becomes more reasonable.

(iii) It is believed that the individuals mentioned in the two letters as relating to Paul in his confinement are more satisfactorily accounted for on this theory (cf. C. R. Bowen, "Are Paul's prison letters from Ephesus?" *AJT* 24 [1920] 112–35, 277–87; Duncan, *Ministry,* 156, and others favoring the Ephesian hypothesis; note Kümmel, *Introduction,* 347, against Lohse, 166).

(iv) Bowen ("The Original Form of Paul's Letter to the Colossians," *JBL* 43 [1924] 177–206) suggested Colossae had only recently been evangelized when Paul wrote to the church there. If this is correct then an extra reason is given for locating the letter during the period between Acts 19:10 and Paul's subsequent detention in or around Ephesus (Bowen's claim, however, is difficult to substantiate; see Guthrie, *Introduction,* 172).

Martin's conclusion (*NCB,* 30) is that "this apostolic letter belongs to that tumultuous period of Paul's life, represented in Acts 19–20, when for a brief space his missionary labours were interrupted by an enforced spell as a *détenu* near Ephesus."

To sum up. Of the three options, Ephesus and Rome have greater claims to being the place where Paul wrote Colossians and Philemon than Caesarea. The Ephesian hypothesis has many strong points in its favor and cannot be entirely ruled out since the evidence for Rome is not decisive. Certainly the latter hypothesis is built on a known imprisonment of such a character as to allow the events reflected in Colossians and Philemon to happen. The presence of Luke with Paul is supported by Acts, whereas the Ephesian ministry of the apostle does not occur in a "we" section and there is reasonable doubt whether Luke was with Paul during this period. Aristarchus was arrested in Ephesus (cf. Acts 19:29; Duncan, *Ministry,* 148–53, considers this points to an Ephesian imprisonment of Paul as the context of the letter, but this passage does not specifically mention an official arrest, only his seizure by mob violence), and it would seem from Acts 27:2 that he accompanied Paul to Rome (see on Col 4:10) and may well have shared to some extent his privations. Arguments based on development of thought must be used with caution, but there does seem to be some force to the contention that the theological expressions of Colossians belong to a later than an earlier period, and this would point in the direction of a Roman captivity. On balance we prefer this alternative.

If the Roman hypothesis is accepted then the most likely placing is fairly early in Paul's (first) Roman imprisonment, i.e. c. A.D. 60–61; those advocating the Ephesian alternative place it around A.D. 54–57, or on the earlier dating A.D. 52–55.

Analysis of Colossians

Chapter	1:1, 2	Introductory Greeting
	1:3–8	Thanksgiving: Faith-love-hope and the Gospel
	1:9–14	An Intercession for Knowledge and Godly Conduct
	1:15–20	Christ the Lord in Creation and Redemption
	1:21–23	Reconciliation Accomplished and Applied
	1:24–2:5	Paul's Mission and Pastoral Concern
	2:6–15	The Antidote to Error: Christ in All His Fullness
	2:16–23	Freedom from Legalism
	3:1–4	Seek the Things Above
	3:5–11	Put away the Sins of the Past
	3:12–17	Put on the Graces of Christ
	3:18–4:1	Behavior in the Christian Household
	4:2–6	Final Admonitions: Persistence in Prayer and Right Behavior toward Outsiders
	4:7–18	Personal Greetings and Instructions

Introductory Greeting (1:1, 2)

Bibliography

Berger, K. "Apostelbrief und apostolische Rede/Zum Formular frühchristlicher Briefe." *ZNW* 65 (1974) 190–231. **Deissmann, A.** *Bible Studies.* Tr. A. Grieve. Edinburgh: Clark, 1901. **Doty, W. G.** *Letters in Primitive Christianity.* Guides to Biblical Scholarship, NT Series. Philadelphia: Fortress, 1973. **Friedrich, G.** "Lohmeyers These über 'Das paulinische Briefpräskript' kritisch beleuchtet." *ZNW* 46 (1955) 272–74 and *TLZ* 81 (1956) 343–46. **Harder. G.** *Paulus und das Gebet.* NTF 1S, 10. Gütersloh: Bertelsmann, 1936. **Jewett, R.** "The Form and Function of the Homiletic Benediction." *ATR* 51 (1969) 18–34. **Lohmeyer, E.** "Probleme paulinischer Theologie. I. Briefliche Grussüberschriften." *ZNW* 26 (1927) 158–73. **Mullins, T. Y.** "Benediction as a NT Form." *AUSS* 15 (1977) 59–64. **Roller, O.** *Das Formular der paulinischen Briefe. Ein Beitrag zur Lehre vom antiken Briefe.* BWANT 4S, 6. Stuttgart: Kohlhammer, 1933. **Schenk, W.** *Der Segen in Neuen Testament. Eine begriffsanalytische Studie.* ThA 25. Berlin: Evangelische Verlagsanstalt, 1967. **Wiles, G. P.** *Paul's Intercessory Prayers: The Significance of the Intercessory Prayer Passages in the Letters of St Paul.* SNTSMS 24. Cambridge: University Press, 1974.

Translation

[1] *Paul, an apostle of Christ Jesus by the will of God, and Timothy our co-worker,*
[2] *To the saints and faithful brothers in Christ at Colossae: Grace and peace to you from God our Father.*

Form/Structure/Setting

Paul begins his letter to the Colossians in the usual way, mentioning author, recipients and a greeting. The Pauline prescript follows the oriental and Jewish model characterized by its twofold form: first, the name of the sender and that of the addressee(s); second, the greeting with its form of direct address: "peace be with you!" An example of this oriental model with its twofold structure, including a greeting in the form of a direct address, is the edict of Nebuchadnezzar which opens with the words "King Nebuchadnezzar to all peoples, nations and languages that dwell in all the earth: peace be multiplied to you! ([εἰρήνη ὑμῖν πληθυνθείη]" Dan 3:98 [4:1]; cf. *Apoc Bar* 78:2).

However consistent the *structures* of the address and greeting may be—and both verses 1 and 2 correspond to the outline used in all the Pauline letters—the creative variations in the opening formulae regarding authorship, where Paul adapts his description of himself and his credentials to the circumstances of each particular letter, the various phrases he employs to describe his Christian readers, and the theological content poured into the greetings all indicate that his prescripts are far from being stereotyped introductions to his epistles.

Comment

1. Παῦλος. Paul introduces himself to a Christian congregation that was not known to him personally (2:1) and which was founded through one of his colleagues—Epaphras—rather than by himself (1:4; 7–9). These points help to account for the distinctive features in the introductory greeting.

At the head of the letter is the name "Paul," used by the apostle in the Hellenistic-Roman world in place of the Jewish "Saul." Jews in the Greek-speaking areas took names which closely approximated to the sound of their Hebrew and Aramaic names, e.g. Silas:Silvanus; Jesus:Jason (cf. Deissmann, *Bible Studies,* 314, 315, and Lohse, 6).

ἀπόστολος Χριστοῦ Ἰησοῦ διὰ θελήματος θεοῦ. As in 2 Corinthians 1:1 Paul reserves the designation "apostle" for himself. Neither Timothy nor Epaphras who first brought the gospel to Colossae, is accorded this title. Paul alone was the Colossians' apostle, even though he had not previously visited them in person, for he had been independently and directly commissioned by the risen Lord. Timothy and Epaphras along with other loved and honored "fellow-servants" were Paul's lieutenants, commissioned to help in the task of proclaiming the gospel and planting churches. (At 1 Thess 2:6, 7, when Paul links Timothy and Silvanus with himself as "apostles of Christ," he appears to be using the term in a wider sense.)

Paul describes himself as an "apostle of Christ Jesus" in this introduction, not because there had been attacks made on his apostleship in Colossae, as there had been at Galatia and Corinth (cf. Gal 1:1, 10–12; 1 Cor 9:1–3; 2 Cor 10–13), but since he wished to establish his credentials at the outset. He will expose and refute the false teaching (cf. 2:4, 8) that had intruded into the life of the congregation, and underscore the rightness of Epaphras' instruction, given to this infant Christian community. So by the addition of this title Paul draws attention to the official character of his writing to the community. (For bibliographical information on apostleship see F. Hahn, "Der Apostolat im Urchristentum. Seine Eigenart und seine Voraussetzungen," *KD* 20 [1974] 54–77, J. A. Kirk, "Apostleship since Rengstorf: Towards a Synthesis," *NTS* 21 [1974–75] 249–64, and F. Agnew, "On the Origin of the Term *Apostolos,*" *CBQ* 38 [1976] 49–53.)

There is no suggestion of high-handedness on Paul's part when he styles himself an "apostle"; as such he belongs to Christ Jesus (Χριστοῦ Ἰησοῦ) and has been called to this ministry "through the will of God" (*διὰ θελήματος θεοῦ*), an expression that is tantamount to a declaration of God's unmerited grace, as well as a renunciation of personal worth (at 1:9 and 4:12 the "will of God" refers to that will which is to be fulfilled in the life of the Christian, whereas here it is the will of God which elects and which made Paul an apostle, cf. 2 Cor 1:1; Eph 1:1; 2 Tim 1:1). This calling in accordance with the divine purpose had special reference to his ministry to Gentile congregations (cf. Eph 3:1–13). As apostle he had authority to teach (cf. 1 Tim 2:7) and to deal pastorally with congregations in his care (2 Cor 13:10). As the letter unfolds we note Paul exercises his ministry in both teaching and pastoral care.

καὶ Τιμόθεος ὁ ἀδελφός. Paul associates Timothy with himself in the salutation (cf. the companion epistle, Philem 1 and contrast Eph 1:1) as he does in 2

Corinthians 1:1 and Philippians 1:1, and in the beginnings of the Thessalonian letters he names him along with Silvanus (1 Thess 1:1; 2 Thess 1:1). Those linked with Paul in his introductions are not joint authors of the letters. Their names probably appear alongside Paul's so as to indicate to the congregation that they too preach and teach the one true gospel (Lohse, 7).

Timothy was in Paul's company for much of his Ephesian ministry (cf. Acts 19:22; 2 Cor 1:1, etc.). Of all who were associated with the apostle's mission none held a more honored place than Timothy (note the tributes Paul pays to him at 1 Thess 3:2; 1 Cor 4:17; Phil 2:19–24, showing how much he valued his support). He is here described as a "brother" (ἀδελφός; cf. 2 Cor 1:1; 1 Thess 3:2; Phlm 1), which in this context means not so much "fellow-Christian" (though Timothy was obviously this, and the term has this meaning at v 2) as "co-worker" or "helper" (cf. E. E. Ellis, "Paul and his Co-Workers." *NTS* 17 [1970–71] 437–52, reprinted in *Prophecy and Hermeneutic in Early Christianity. New Testament Essays* WUNT 18; Tübingen: Mohr, 1978) 3–22; " 'Spiritual' Gifts in the Pauline Community." *NTS* 20 [1974] 128–44, reprinted in *Prophecy,* 23–44). He is elsewhere called a "minister" (διάκονος: 2 Cor 3:6 and 6:4 with reference to 1:1), "helper" or "fellow-worker" (συνεργός: Rom 16:21; 1 Thess 3:2; cf. 1 Cor 16:10) and a "good soldier of Christ Jesus" (2 Tim 2:3). The mention of Timothy in the superscription is an indication to the Colossians that Paul is not alone in his imprisonment. Martin (*NCB,* 44) makes the further suggestion that the mention of Timothy alongside Paul would be a useful buttress to his own teaching position and a denial that the letter was simply an expression of his own ideas.

2. *τοῖς ἐν Κολοσσαῖς ἁγίοις καὶ πιστοῖς ἀδελφοῖς ἐν Χριστῷ.* The recipients of the letter are now described in theological terms: "to the saints and faithful brothers in Christ at Colossae." The term "church" (ἐκκλησία) does not appear, but too much weight ought not to be placed on this since it is omitted from the prescripts of Romans, Philippians and Ephesians and in each of these instances ἅγιοι occurs instead. Further, the two expressions are not unrelated as 1 Corinthians 1:2 shows, for the words "the church of God (τῇ ἐκκλησίᾳ τοῦ θεοῦ) which is at Corinth" are in apposition to the following "those sanctified in Christ Jesus, called to be saints" (κλητοῖς ἁγίοις; cf. 2 Cor 1:1). Because the article is missing before "faithful brothers" (πιστοῖς ἀδελφοῖς) it has been argued that ἁγίοις should be connected with πιστοῖς as an adjective and rendered "holy and faithful brothers" (so NIV; cf. Moule 45). However, ἅγιοι always appears as a noun in the salutations of the letters and in our view this is how it is being employed here; it should therefore be translated "saints" or "holy ones."

The antecedents of this expression are to be found in the OT. Israel was God's holy people (Exod 19:6) chosen by him and appointed to his service. Having been brought into a covenant relationship with him, Israel was to be a holy nation because he is holy (Lev 11:44; 19:2; etc.). Christians are "saints" because of the new relationship they have been brought into by God through Jesus Christ. They are set apart for him and his service; as the people of his own possession they are the called and elect community of the end-time: they are "God's chosen ones, holy (ἅγιοι) and beloved" (3:12) whose lives are to be characterized by godly behavior.

The saints in Colossae (see earlier) are also designated "faithful brothers in Christ" (πιστοὶ ἀδελφοὶ ἐν Χριστῷ). While πιστός ("faithful") is used several times by Paul in Colossians to draw attention to the absolute reliability of his co-workers (1:7; 4:7, 9), here it has the sense of "believing," of being Christian (Bultmann, *TDNT* 6, 214; cf. Eph 1:1). The Colossians have placed their wholehearted trust in Jesus as Son of God, Lord and Savior. The expression "in Christ," however, does not point to him as the one in whom they have believed so much as the one in whom they, as brothers, have been brought together into a living fellowship (on the theme of incorporation in Christ see on 2:6–15).

χάρις ὑμῖν καὶ εἰρήνη ἀπὸ θεοῦ πατρὸς ἡμῶν. The opening greetings of Paul's letters (sometimes called benedictions or blessings) are stylized, remaining basically unchanged in wording throughout (cf. Wiles, *Prayers*, 108–114, and Mullins, *AUSS* 15 [1977] 59–64; cf. Roller, *Formular*, table 3). They have therefore been thought by some to be conventional adaptations from general epistolary usage or borrowed from some early Christian benediction. E. Lohmeyer "Probleme paulinischer Theologie. I. Briefliche Grussüberschriften," (*ZNW* 26 [1927], 158–73) argued that the *form* was dependent on Near Eastern epistolary antecedents while the *wording and content* represented a traditional early church formula used to introduce a service of worship. Friedrich (*ZNW* 46 [1955], 272–74), Schenk (*Segen*, 88–92) and others denied the liturgical borrowing on the grounds that neither Paul (cf. 1 Thess 1:1) nor the writers of the post-Pauline letters (1 Pet 1:2; 2 Pet 1:2; 2 John 3; Rev 1:4) preserved the formula always unchanged. Jewett (*ATR* 51 [1969], 18–34) located the origin of the NT benediction (particularly those found in the bodies of the letters) in "some portion of Early Christian worship which was intrinsically flexible—such as the sermon" (22).

Recently T. Y. Mullins (*AUSS* 15 [1977], 59–64), following an earlier suggestion of L. G. Champion (*Benedictions and Doxologies in the Epistles of Paul.* Oxford; privately published, 1934), argued that in the NT there was discernible a basic benediction form, of which the opening "grace to you and peace" was one type. The several types representing this form appeared in the LXX with its three basic elements of *wish, divine source* and *recipient* (2 Sam 24:23; Num 6:24–26; Ruth 2:4), and, according to Mullins, the NT form was patterned after that of the LXX, the OT of the Christian church.

But none of these sources fully explains both the *form* and the *content* of these epistolary greetings (cf. Wiles, *Prayers*, 108–14; Berger, *ZNW* 65, [1974], 191–207). The suggested substitution of χάρις and χαίρειν, a play on words involving a small syllabic addition, denotes a significant theological shift. There are important differences between each of these supposed antecedents and Paul's opening salutations.

We suggest that Paul himself was responsible for the exact character of the opening salutation, though no doubt some of the form and ingredients were suggested to him from epistolary and liturgical usage. As such the greeting would be thoroughly appropriate for his special use as an apostolic salutation and points to the range of blessings (grace and peace) needed by his readers in greater measure and which the letter was intended to convey.

"Grace" (χάρις) is a central theological concept that most clearly expresses Paul's understanding of Christ's work of salvation (cf. Rom 3:23, 24). Paul's message was the "gospel of the grace of God" (Acts 20:24; contrast Gal 1:6); it stood opposed to any idea of work or merit—indeed the idea of gift (free and unearned) was at the heart of this word (cf. Eph 2:8, 9). Grace, "favor toward men contrary to their desert," was attributed to God in his relations with sinful men (Rom 3:21–26; 4:4; 5:15; etc.), and to Christ (Rom 5:15; 1 Cor 16:23) inasmuch as the gracious attitude to men by God was also that of Christ (2 Cor 8:9; cf. Rom 5:8); and it was the work of Jesus, especially his death, that manifested God's grace (Rom 3:24; 5:2; Eph 1:6, 7). It was the basis of the whole work of salvation.

In certain circles, by the time Acts was written, early Christians were in the habit of placing one another under the grace of God, or of the Lord, as a form of farewell greeting. So members being sent on an important mission (Acts 14:26; 15:40) were commended to God's grace, while the elders of a congregation, during a solemn occasion of farewell, were commended "to the Lord and to the word of his grace" (Acts 20:32). In these contexts the theological meaning of "grace" is adapted to the immediate practical concerns for spreading the gospel (Acts 14:26; 15:40) or of standing fast under affliction (Acts 20:32).

Paul's use of χάρις in his greetings indicates a deep prayerful concern (the element of intercession is present in the greetings) for the readers. He desires that the Colossians may apprehend more fully the grace of God in which they already stand (cf. Rom 5:2); at the same time he is perhaps commissioning his readers "to renewed Christian living under grace appropriate to the immediate circumstances" (Wiles, *Prayers*, 111).

The second main word in the benediction, εἰρήνη, ("peace"), suggests a Jewish background (cf. Ezra 4:17; 5:7). In the LXX the epistolary greeting *šālôm* is rendered by εἰρήνη, while in Jewish prayer language generally, as well as in travel prayers in particular, there was a tendency to make requests for peace (cf. Harder, *Paulus*, 29; Str-B 1, 380–85).

εἰρήνη ("peace") in secular Greek (Foerster, *TDNT* 2, 400–402) indicated the antithesis to war, or the situation resulting from the cessation of war. It denoted the state of law and order from which the blessings of prosperity would arise.

In the LXX εἰρήνη was almost always used to translate the Hebrew *šālôm* which occurred more than 250 times in the OT. Unlike the Greek εἰρήνη the Hebrew term denotes not so much the opposite of war as of "any disturbance in the communal well-being of the nation" (Brown, *NIDNTT* 2, 777). So in the LXX under the influence of the Hebrew the Greek εἰρήνη acquires the sense of general well-being, the source and giver of which is Yahweh alone. *Šālôm* includes everything given by God in all areas of life (Foerster, *TDNT* 2, 402); cf. J. I. Durham, "*Šālôm* and the Presence of God." *Proclamation and Presence. Old Testament essays in honour of Gwynne Henton Davies,* ed. J. I. Durham and J. R. Porter, (London: SCM. 1970, 272–93 American edition [Richmond, VA: John Knox]). It covers well-being in the widest sense of the word, having a social dimension and is on occasion linked with righteousness (Isa 48:18; Ps 85:10).

εἰρήνη occurs ninety-one times in the NT, fifty-four of which occur in the Pauline corpus. Both as regards its form and content the idea of peace within the NT stands firmly in the LXX and Hebrew OT tradition. εἰρήνη may be used for harmony among men (Acts 7:26; Gal 5:22; Eph 4:3; James 3:18) and for the messianic salvation (Luke 1:79; 2:14; 19:42). The term can describe the content and goal of all Christian preaching, the message itself being called the "gospel of peace" (Eph 6:15; cf. Acts 10:36; Eph 2:17). The biblical concept of peace has to do with wholeness, particularly with reference to relationships. Peace as an order is established by the God of peace (1 Cor 14:33; cf. Rom 15:33; 16:20; Phil 4:9). Christ is the mediator of that peace (Rom 5:1; Col 1:20). Indeed, he himself is that peace (Eph 2:14–18).

Peace is mentioned regularly in the introductory benedictions by both Paul (Rom 1:7; 1 Cor 1:3; 2 Cor 1:2; Gal 1:3; Eph 1:2; Phil 1:2; Col 1:2; 1 Thess 1:1; 2 Thess 1:2; 1 Tim 1:2; 2 Tim 1:2; Tit 1:4; Philem 3) and other NT letter writers (1 Pet 1:2; 2 Pet 1:2; 2 John 3; Jude 2; Rev 1:4), and it featured in closing salutations (Rom 15:33; 16:20; 1 Cor 16:11; 2 Cor 13:11; Gal 6:16; Eph 6:23, cf. v 15; Phil 4:7, 9; 1 Thess 5:23; 2 Thess 3:16; Heb 13:20; 1 Pet 5:14; 2 Pet 3:14; 3 John 15). When Paul, therefore, prays for peace for the Colossians it is not simply a wish for spiritual prosperity; nor does it signify primarily an internal condition of contentment. His request is, rather, that they may comprehend more fully the nature of that relationship of peace which God has established with them.

ἀπὸ θεοῦ πατρὸς ἡμῶν. These two wide-ranging blessings of "grace" and "peace" are said to derive "from God our Father." As M. Barth aptly comments: "The giver determines the contents and value of the gift" (*Ephesians. Introduction, Translation, and Commentary on Chapters 1–3* [AB 34; Garden City, NY: Doubleday, 1974] 71). However, the form of the greeting here is unique for Paul in that the words "and from Christ Jesus our Lord" are not added. (The very uniqueness of the reading speaks in its favor; and in inferior texts scribes sought to make up the deficiency.) It is difficult to give any adequate reason for the omission (especially as Moule, 46, reminds us that the apostle moves to "a description of Christ in more exalted terms than in any of his other epistles"), and certainly mistaken to seek out theological reasons for such a shortening of the formula (so correctly Lohse, 11).

Explanation

Paul begins the letter to the Colossians in his customary way by mentioning his own name, along with that of his readers, and by offering a Christian greeting. He writes as an apostle—his letter has an official character about it—so establishing his credentials with a congregation that was unknown to him personally. Later he will deal with the theological and pastoral problems that had arisen at Colossae by exposing and refuting the false teaching that was beginning to make inroads into the community.

The readers are described by means of exalted language. They are God's holy people, chosen and set apart for him, and brothers who have been brought into a living relationship with Christ.

Paul's apostolic greeting indicates a deep prayerful concern for these readers that they may understand and appreciate more fully the grace of God in which they stand and the relationship of peace that God has established with them.

Thanksgiving: Faith-love-hope and the Gospel (1:3–8)

Bibliography

Bornkamm, G. "Die Hoffnung im Kolosserbrief. Zugleich ein Beitrag zur Frage der Echtheit des Briefes." *Studien zum Neuen Testament und zur Patristik. Erich Klostermann zum 90. Geburtstag dargebracht.* TU 77. Berlin: Akademie, 1961, 56–64. Reprinted in *Geschichte und Glaube 2. Gesammelte Aufsätze.* Vol. 4. BEvT 53. Munich: Kaiser, 1971, 206–213. **Bujard, W.** *Untersuchungen.* **O'Brien, P. T.** *Introductory Thanksgivings in the Letters of Paul.* NovTSup 49. Leiden: Brill, 1977, 62–104. ———. "Thanksgiving and the Gospel in Paul." *NTS* 21 (1974–75) 144–55. **Sanders, J. T.** "The Transition from Opening Epistolary Thanksgiving to Body in the Letters of the Pauline Corpus." *JBL* 81 (1962) 348–62. **Schubert, P.** *Form and Function of the Pauline Thanksgivings.* BZNW 20. Berlin: Töpelmann, 1939. **White, J. L.** *The Form and Function of the Body of the Greek Letter: A Study of the Letter-Body in the Non-Literary Papyri and in Paul the Apostle.* SBLDS 2. Missoula, MT: Scholar's Press, 1972. **Zeilinger, F.** *Der Erstgeborene der Schöpfung. Untersuchungen zur Formalstruktur und Theologie des Kolosserbriefes.* Vienna: Herder, 1974.

Translation

[3] *We always thank God, the Father of our Lord Jesus Christ,*[a] *when we pray for you* [4] *because we have heard of your faith in Christ Jesus and of the love which you show to all God's people.* [5] *Both spring from the hope which lies prepared for you in heaven; you heard about this hope before when the word of truth, the gospel,* [6] *first came to you. As it is producing fruit and increasing all over the world so it is among you also (and has done) since the day you heard and understood the grace of God in all its truth;* [7] *you learned this from Epaphras our dear fellow-servant who is a faithful minister of Christ on our behalf* [8] *and who has told us of your love in the Spirit.*

Note

[a] There are several variants to the reading *τῷ θεῷ πατρί κτλ.* ("to God the Father . . ."). D* G and Chrysostom insert *τῷ* ("the") before *πατρί* ("Father"), while ℵ' A I ψ and many other authorities insert *καί* ("and") instead, thus reading *τῷ θεῷ καὶ πατρί κτλ* ("to the God and Father . . ."). However, the more difficult reading, *τῷ θεῷ πατρὶ τοῦ κυρίου ἡμῶν Ἰησοῦ Χριστοῦ* ("to God, the Father of our Lord Jesus Christ"), is to be preferred. The rarity of the phrase argues in its favor and it is the reading from which the variants can be explained. An expression, quite as unusual, is found in chapter 3:17, *τῷ θεῷ πατρί*, "to God the Father"—again in the context of thanksgiving—where the manuscript evidence is even more decisive, cf. Moule, 48, 49.

Form/Structure/Setting

The second main section of the Pauline letter form (cf. Doty, *Letters*, 27–33) is the introductory thanksgiving paragraph. On occasion the more intimate letters of the Hellenistic period began with a thanksgiving to the gods for personal benefits received. Evidence of this comes from the beginning of the third century B.C. while the earliest extant papyrus letter in which εὐχαριστέω is used of thanksgiving offered to the gods is that written by Isias (in 168 B.C.) to her husband Hephaistion, begging him to come home. Examples become more numerous in the following centuries (see Schubert, *Form*, 158–79) so that a clear but simple pattern emerges: (1) thanks are offered to the gods (using either χάρις or εὐχαριστέω); (2) often there is an assurance that the gods are being petitioned regularly for the welfare or health of the readers; and (3) the reasons for the thanksgiving to the gods are mentioned—frequently because they are thought to have saved the writer or the reader from some calamity.

This *form* of introductory thanksgiving is also found in Hellenistic Judaism, as may be noted from the important paragraph, 2 Maccabees 1:10–13, where a letter from the Jews in Jerusalem to those living in Egypt is cited. As Schubert rightly pointed out, this example is functionally and structurally very close to the Pauline thanksgiving paragraph (*Form*, 117).

The apostle Paul adopted this Hellenistic epistolary *model*, frequently using it at the beginning of his letters as he expressed his gratitude to God, the Father of Jesus Christ, for what he had effected in the lives of these predominantly Gentile readers. While Paul was indebted to this epistolary convention he was no "slavish imitator" (Schubert, *Form*, 119) of any such literary form since his structures in these thanksgiving paragraphs are highly developed and sophisticated.

Furthermore, while the *structure* of the Pauline thanksgiving periods was Hellenistic there are good reasons for believing that the *contents* (apart from their specifically Christian elements) showed the influence of OT and Jewish thought. This point will be developed in the detailed exegetical notes below.

Two basic types of structure were noted in Paul's thanksgiving paragraphs: the first, which contained up to seven basic elements, began with the verb of thanksgiving and concluded with a ἵνα-clause (or its equivalent) which spelled out the content of the apostle's intercession for the readers. The second type was simpler in form. It also commenced with the giving of thanks to God (cf. 1 Cor 1:4) and concluded with a ὅτι-clause which noted the reason for this expression of gratitude (cf. Rom 1:8). (For a detailed discussion of these two main types as well as the mixed structures see Schubert, *Form*, 10–39, and O'Brien, *Introductory Thanksgivings*, 6–15.)

The introductory thanksgiving of Colossians is an example of the first type. It consists of the basic sevenfold structure commencing with (1) the verb of thanksgiving (εὐχαριστοῦμεν, "we give thanks," v 3), then (2) the personal object (τῷ θεῷ . . . , "to God," v 3) indicating the one who is thanked, (3) a temporal verb (πάντοτε, "always" v 3) denoting the frequency with which thanksgiving was offered, (4) a pronominal phrase (περὶ ὑμῶν, "for you," v 3), and (5) a temporal participle (προσευχόμενοι, "praying" v 3) which, because of an apparent digression in verses 6–8, is taken up and repeated in verse 9 as Paul moves to the content of his intercessory prayer. The sixth element (6) is the causal participial clause (ἀκούσαντες τὴν πίστιν ὑμῶν . . . , "because we heard of your faith," v 4) which spells out the ground for Paul's offering thanks to God. The final feature (7) of this thanksgiving form is the ἵνα-clause of verse 10 which indicates the content of the intercession for the Colossians. (Note Schubert's comparative chart, *Form,* 54–55.)

Yet, within this basic structure, verses 3–8 are still rather difficult to follow, for this single sentence contains seven participial expressions, four relative clauses, three *καθώς*-clauses and unusual prepositional and genitival expressions. Bujard, in his stylistic analysis, considered that there was no logical progression of thought, but rather an association of ideas (*Untersuchungen,* 80). Zeilinger, on the other hand, believed that after the mention of thanksgiving (v 3) and its ground (v 4) the remainder of the sentence could be divided into two sections: the first (vv 4*d*–6*a*) was balanced by two relative clauses beginning with *ἥν*, while the second was structured around three *καθώς*-clauses and their related *ἐν*-phrases (*Der Erstgeborene,* 34–36).

It is doubtful, however, whether such an analysis carries conviction and Bujard's comment about the association of ideas needs to be kept in view when giving an exegesis of the passage. Lohse rightly remarks that after the reason for thanksgiving has been set forth (*ἀκούσαντες . . . τὴν πίστιν ὑμῶν . . . καὶ τὴν ἀγάπην . . . διὰ τὴν ἐλπίδα,* vv 4–5*a*) several subordinate clauses are added: verse 5*b* (*ἣν προηκούσατε*) is related to the Colossians' hope, verse 6*a* refers to the world-wide scope of the proclamation (*καθὼς καὶ ἐν παντὶ τῷ κόσμῳ . . .*), while verses 6*b*–7 point back to the initial preaching to the Colossians by Epaphras (*καθὼς καὶ ἐν ὑμῖν,* v 6*b*; *καθὼς ἐμάθετε ἀπὸ Ἐπαφρᾶ,* v 7). See Lohse, 13, 14.

Comment

3. *εὐχαριστοῦμεν*. Paul writes "we give thanks" rather than "I give thanks." The plural is used (as in the Thessalonian correspondence: 1 Thess 1:2; 2:13, 3:9; 2 Thess 1:3; 2:13), not as an epistolary plural, nor because Paul stood at a distance from the Colossians, but since he was writing on behalf of Timothy and perhaps others as well as himself. When later in the same chapter he wishes to emphasize his own ministry as an apostle to the Gentiles and its eschatological significance, he changes to the first person singular (vv. 23–27, *οὗ ἐγενόμην ἐγὼ Παῦλος διάκονος . . . νῦν χαίρω κτλ.,* "of which I, Paul, became a minister . . . now I rejoice . . .").

It is also possible that the plural "we give thanks whenever we pray" may draw attention to the regular gathering together for prayer by Paul and his colleagues to give thanks to God for the Colossian Christians.

Some writers consider that thanksgiving was an activity engaged in because of personal benefits received and was therefore a descent from the lofty heights of praise. But although our English word "thank" means to express gratitude to a person for something received, and is therefore to some extent a man-regarding expression for praise, Paul's use of *εὐχαριστέω* ("I give thanks"), in the introductory paragraphs of his letters at least, is broader than this. For in each of these passages (though cf. v 12) Paul employs *εὐχαριστέω* consistently of thanksgiving for God's work in the lives of *others,* i.e. the readers, and *εὐλογητός* ("blessed," "be praised") for blessings in which *he himself* participated (2 Cor 1:3–5; Eph 1:3–12). Furthermore, when Paul employs *εὐχαριστέω* while the notion of gratitude is clearly present, the element of praise is not therefore absent. The corporate aspect of thanksgiving is often stressed by the apostle (2 Cor 1:11; Col 3:15–17).

We may suppose that Paul's report echoed his actual expression of gratitude and that, as he dictated his letter, thanksgiving to God once again welled up within him. (On the importance of thanksgiving in Colossians see 108, 205, 206.)

τῷ θεῷ πατρὶ τοῦ κυρίου ἡμῶν Ἰησοῦ Χριστοῦ. The apostle does not congratulate the Colossians. Instead he directs his prayer of thanksgiving to "God the Father of our Lord Jesus Christ." This phrase is different from the usual short formulation "I give thanks to God" (1 Cor 1:4, cf. 1 Thess 1:2; 2 Thess 1:3) and the more personal form "I give thanks to *my* God" (Phil 1:3; Phlm 4), and is somewhat reminiscent of Romans 1:8, "I give thanks to my God through Jesus Christ." At first sight the designation appears to be a stereotyped expression taken over from the worship of the early church, being employed in prayer with *εὐλογητός* (2 Cor 1:3; 11:31; Eph 1:3; cf. 1 Pet 1:3), *εὐχαριστέω* (Eph 1:17), as a summons to a doxology in Romans 15:6 and as the source of "grace and peace" in Philemon 3.

There is a textual problem as already noted and the more difficult reading (cited above) is to be followed and rendered as "God *who* is the Father of our Lord Jesus Christ" (Moule, 49). Paul expressed his gratitude to God in words that may have been used in early Christian worship but by omitting the article before *πατρί* he stressed that the God to whom thanksgiving was offered is the one whom Jesus reveals to us in his character as Father (1:2, 3, 12; 3:17).

πάντοτε . . . προσευχόμενοι. By means of the adverb "always" the apostle indicates the frequency with which he gave thanks. However, by using this term he was not referring to unceasing thanksgiving. To speak of prayer by this and similar terms (e.g. "continually," "at all times," "day and night") was part and parcel of the style of ancient letters, being a Jewish practice as well as a pagan one. A measure of hyperbole is also to be noted in these expressions. When Paul states he gave thanks "always" or "continually" he means that he regularly remembered them in his times of prayer: morning, noon and evening (the customary three hours each day), and whenever else he prayed. Here the adverb *πάντοτε* is further explained by *προσευχόμενοι* ("when we pray for you").

4. *ἀκούσαντες τὴν πίστιν ὑμῶν κτλ.* The basis for Paul's thanksgiving is expressed by means of this causal clause (cf. Phil 1:6; Phlm 5). He recalls the good reports that had been given to him about this congregation. *ἀκούσαντες*, by itself, does not indicate that Paul did not know the Colossians, but rather that he had received news about them via Epaphras who had referred to their "love in the Spirit," verse 8. We do know, however, from chapter 2:1–2 that the church was unknown to the apostle, even though individual members like Philemon had met him.

πίστιν . . . ἀγάπην . . . ἐλπίδα. The familiar Christian triad of faith-love-hope occurs within the causal clause. One or more elements of this formula were often a basis for the apostle's expression of gratitude to God (faith, love and hope: 1 Thess 1:3; faith and love: Eph 1:15 some manuscripts; 2 Thess 1:3; Phlm 5: faith: Rom 1:8). The triad appears elsewhere in the Pauline corpus (Rom 5:1–5; Gal 5:5–6; Eph 4:2–5), but may not have been the apostle's creation since it was also employed elsewhere in early Christian literature (Heb 6:10–12; 10:22–24; 1 Pet 1:3–8, 21–22; Barn 1:4; 11:8; Ign *Pol* 3:2–3). It seems to have been a sort of compendium of the Christian life current in the early apostolic church, and according to A. M. Hunter's suggestion (*Paul and his Predecessors* 2nd ed. (London: SCM, 1961, 33: American edition [Philadelphia: Westminster]) may have derived from Jesus himself. This passage could then represent Paul's own exegesis of the triad.

The "faith" of the Colossians is naturally mentioned first, for apart from it there would be no Christian existence (cf. Rom 10:9). This faith is "in Christ Jesus" (ἐν Χριστῷ Ἰησοῦ), an expression which does not denote the object to which their faith is directed but rather indicates the sphere in which "faith" lives and acts. The Colossian Christians live under the lordship of Christ Jesus for they have been incorporated into him. That is why they have been addressed as "the saints and faithful brethren *in Christ* at Colossae" (v 2). Some of the implications of living under this lordship will be spelled out in the later sections of the letter.

A faith which one may hear about (ἀκούσαντες; cf. ἀκούων, Phlm 5) and recount as Paul does here proves its reality by "working through love" (Gal 5:6). ἀγάπη is "the practical expression of care and concern" (Martin, *NCB*, 48) which is directed to all of God's holy people (the πάντας accentuates the breadth of the love; so Lohse, 17), i.e. Christians generally, particularly those at Colossae and in the other churches of the Lycus valley. It is through love that Christians serve one another (Gal 5:13) and the Colossians, according to Epaphras' reports, knew something of this service.

5. διὰ τὴν ἐλπίδα. The three elements of this summary of the Christian life are "not completely co-ordinated" (Bruce, 180). "Faith" and "love," grounds for Paul's thanksgiving, are based on "hope." The last is here emphasized and it clearly formed part of the apostolic message which the congregation had heard and accepted. Moule claims "it is remarkable that trust and love are described as dependent on ἐλπίς—the goal of Christian expectation" (49).

Both ἐλπίς ("hope") and its cognate verb ἐλπίζω ("hope") were used in the Pauline letters to denote the act of hoping as well as the objective content of the hope. Hope is oriented to that which is unseen in the future, the content of which is defined in various ways: salvation (1 Thess 5:8), righteousness (Gal 5:5), resurrection in an incorruptible body (1 Cor 15:52–55), eternal life (Titus 1:2; 3:7) and God's glory (Rom 5:2). On occasions in Paul the disposition of hoping is emphasized (Rom 4:18; 5:5; 12:12; 1 Cor 13:7), though Romans 8:24–25 shows that the term could be employed by the apostle in both ways within the one context (a point which Bornkamm, *TU* 77 [1961] 56–64, seems to have overlooked). In Colossians the concrete meaning is to the fore (so 1:23, 27, and the related ideas of 3:1–4), and in verse 5 ἐλπίς denotes "the content of hope," "that which is hoped for" (so Meyer, 256 and others). It already lies prepared (ἀποκειμένην) for them in the heavens, a phrase from common parlance denoting certainty (see Lohse, 17–18, for details). The Colossian Christians are assured that everything contained in their hope is kept for them in its right place—in heaven where no power, human or otherwise, can touch it. Though now hidden from men's view that hope, which is centered on Christ himself (he is ἡ ἐλπὶς τῆς δόξης, 1:27), will finally be revealed when he is revealed (3:4). That is why these believers in the Lycus valley are to direct their thoughts heavenward (3:1–4).

Their hope is clearly oriented toward the future, but because it is at this moment being kept safe for them (ἀποκειμένην is a present participle) it has present and immediate ramifications, not least as the basis for their ongoing faith and exercise of Christian love (ἔχετε is also a present tense). To suggest, with some of the older commentators that faith has to do with the past alone, love only with the present, and hope simply with reference to the future is to make a distinction that is not supported from this passage. (In Jewish apocalyptic literature God's future salvation was described as presently being reserved for the pious: 4 Ezra 7:14; 2 Bar 14:12. Cf. H.-W. Kuhn, *Enderwartung und gegenwärtiges Heil. Untersuchungen zu den Gemeindeliedern von Qumran* (SUNT 4; Göttingen: Vandenhoeck und Ruprecht, 1966, 181–88.)

Paul has gone out of his way to stress this third element of the triad, hope (Bornkamm, *TU* 77 [1961] 58). It is described as the content of the gospel or at least one of its significant elements (cf. 1:23, 27).

Why this emphasis? It is quite likely that "the false teachers at Colossae were intending to rob them (*sc.* the believers) of this aspect of the Christian message, possibly by denying any future dimension of Christian salvation" (Martin, *NCB*, 48). If this is so, then it was necessary for the apostle to underscore again the nature of their Christian hope, as originally taught by Epaphras. That Paul is stressing what is true over against the false teaching is further suggested by the statements about the gospel which immediately follow: it is true, universal, powerfully effective and is concerned with God's grace—phrases which probably contrast the Colossian error.

προηκούσατε ἐν τῷ λόγῳ τῆς ἀληθείας τοῦ εὐαγγελίου. The apostle was not telling the congregation anything new when he wrote about the heavenly hope. They had heard about it *before* (προ-ηκούσατε) when the gospel message was first proclaimed at Colossae by Epaphras (vv 7–8) and the congregation was founded (so Lohse, 18; Moule, 50, suggests it means "heard before the false teaching"). The phrase "the word of truth of the gospel" is best rendered with many commentators including Calvin: "the word of truth, which is the gospel." Schweizer (36, 37) and others rightly understand this against an Old Testament background where God's word, spoken and revealed to men, is "the word of truth." So the Psalmist prays "take not the word of truth . . . out of my mouth" (Ps 119:43; the term "hope" appears in the same context). God's word partakes of his character and is utterly reliable.

By describing the message as the "word of truth" (cf. Bultmann, *TDNT* 1, 244) a contrast with the false teaching of the Colossian heretics seems intended (against Hooker, *Christ*, 315–31). Their message, elements of which may be gleaned from the following passages of the letter, especially chapter 2, was not only misleading, but also a delusion. It was empty, false and vain (cf. 2:8 where it is described as κενῆς ἀπάτης, "empty deceit"). Here the "word of truth" is in apposition to the "gospel" for it was in the proclamation of the gospel that God's true word was announced.

6. Several features of that gospel are now set forth. First, it had made its triumphal progress, coming to the Colossian congregation (παρόντος εἰς

ὑμᾶς) and taking up a sure place in their lives (so Chrysostom and several recent commentators). Also, its progress at Colossae was at one (καθὼς καί) with its dynamic spread throughout the world (ἐν παντὶ τῷ κόσμῳ). As the gospel produced a vigorous and increasing fruit of Christian life and testimony at Colossae, so (καθὼς καί) it was doing the same throughout the world. In contrast to the false teaching with its restricted appeal this message was truly catholic (Lightfoot, 132, 133).

Ἐν παντὶ τῷ κόσμῳ. This phrase, along with similar universalistic passages (Rom 1:8; 10:18; 1 Thess 1:8) is not to be understood as a meaningless or "wild exaggeration" (as Scott, 16, claims). Certainly Paul did not mean that the whole world distributively, that is, every person under heaven, had been touched by the triumphal progress of the gospel. He has particularly in mind cities and towns, e.g. Damascus, Tarsus, Antioch, Corinth, Ephesus, etc., as centers from which the gospel moved further afield.

Bruce (181) claims that if Paul's language appears to have outstripped what had actually been accomplished at the time it was because he was indulging in prophetic prolepsis. It was with the eye of a true prophet that he described "the all-pervading course of the message of life rivalling that of the heavenly bodies of which the psalmist spoke: 'their sound went into all the earth, and their words unto the ends of the world' (Rom 10:18, quoting Ps. 19:4)."

καρποφορούμενον καὶ αὐξανόμενον. These participles, "bearing fruit and increasing," which refer to the continuing progress of the gospel echo OT language (against Ernst, 158). "To bear fruit and to grow" is a frequent combination used first of human reproduction (Gen 1:22, 28; cf. 8:17; 9:1, 7) and subsequently of Israel's population increase (Jer 3:16; 23:3). No metaphorical use of the phrase, however, occurs in the OT. It is always applied to people or animals. But in the parable of the sower (Mark 4) the seed, which is interpreted as the "word," bears fruit and increases in the lives of those who receive it rightly. Like the seed in the parable of the sower the word of the gospel bears fruit and grows. With Chrysostom and several modern commentators "fruit-bearing" is to be understood as a crop of good deeds (cf. Phil 1:11 where καρπός, "fruit," is found with this meaning), while the growth of the gospel points to the increasing number of converts.

καθὼς καὶ ἐν ὑμῖν. With the addition of the words "so among yourselves" (a second καθώς-clause, cf. Zeilinger, *Der Erstgeborene,* 35, 36) the writer's train of thought moves back from the world-wide aspect of the gospel's dynamic progress to the beginnings of the congregation at Colossae. This additional phrase is not an afterthought, as some commentators suppose, but reminds the Colossians in an objective way (Schweizer, 38) that they too shared in this world-wide action of God's word. They continued to grow "in spiritual character and in actual numbers" (Bruce, 181) from the time when they first heard and believed the gospel. This apostolic proclamation focused on the grace of God (on the centrality of "grace" in the initial proclamation at Colossae see Lähnemann, *Kolosserbrief,* 105, 106; cf. Acts 20:24). The Colossians both heard (ἠκούσατε) this message of God's gracious action in Christ and came to know (ἐπέγνωτε is an inceptive aorist, so Beare, 154) the reality of that grace when they were converted (R. Bultmann, *Theology of the New Testament.* Vol. 1. Tr. K. Grobel [NY: Scribner, 1952] 67).

ἐν ἀληθείᾳ ("in truth") has been taken by some commentators in an adverbial sense (= "truly") to mean that the Colossian Christians understood the message of God's grace "as it truly is," "untravestied" (Moule, 51). They did not receive some garbled version from their evangelist Epaphras which then needed to be supplemented by later teachers with their philosophy (2:8, 20). Other exegetes understand the phrase ἐν ἀληθείᾳ as a reference to the previous description of the gospel (e.g. Lohse, 20), corresponding to ἐν τῷ λόγῳ τῆς ἀληθείας "in the word of truth") of verse 5. On this view the apostle is stating that the congregation understood the apostolic message (λόγος) presented by Epaphras as "the truth," that is, "God's truth." It was not man-made, and since it centered on God's grace "it sets men free from superstition and bad religion" (Martin, *NCB*, 49).

Since this congregation knows the "word of truth" (v 5) and understood the "grace of God in truth" from the beginning, its Christian direction has already been set. It needs to come to a greater knowledge and understanding of God's will (1:9–10) and to know Christ more fully (2:2), in whom all the treasures of wisdom and knowledge are hidden.

Paul has gone out of his way here to stress the dynamic, indeed almost personal, activity of the gospel (see O'Brien, *NTS* 21 [1974–75] 144–55). In fact, the term εὐαγγέλιον ("gospel") and its synonyms μαρτύριον ("testimony"), λόγος ("word") and ὁ λόγος τοῦ θεοῦ ("word of God") occur frequently within Paul's introductory paragraphs and the majority of the references to these terms are bound up with Paul's actual thanksgivings for the churches, as they stand either in an immediate or a more distant causal relationship to the verb of thanksgiving. In one way or another the apostle's thanksgivings to God for his working in the lives of the readers are causally linked to the gospel or its right reception: so Paul is grateful for the Philippians' active participation (κοινωνία) in the gospel (1:5), that the *testimony* to Christ had been confirmed in the Corinthians' midst (1 Cor 1:6), and that the Thessalonians had been called through the gospel (2 Thess 2:14), and welcomed the word of God (1 Thess 2:13) when it came to them dynamically (1 Thess 1:5, 6).

It is a well-known fact that εὐαγγέλιον within the Pauline corpus is often used as a *nomen actionis* and this is the case in several instances where the noun appears within Paul's prayers of thanksgiving (Phil 1:5; Rom 1:9). The dynamic character of the gospel is accented in Paul's first introductory thanksgiving (1 Thess 1:5–6) where the manner of its coming was truly powerful, for it was not simply in word but also "in power and in the Holy Spirit and with full conviction."

A further point to be noted is that terms which are predicated of the gospel's activity—its coming (1 Thess 1:5), confirmation (1 Cor 1:6), or its bearing fruit and increasing (Col 1:6)—are employed with a slight change in meaning of the believers themselves. Fruit-bearing and increasing were marks of the gospel (Col 1:6). Paul then prays (see below) that fruit-bearing and increasing may be characteristics of the Colossians too—the fruit of good works and an increase in the knowledge of God (v 10)—that the dynamic of the gospel may characterize the lives of the Colossian believers themselves.

7. καθὼς ἐμάθετε ἀπὸ Ἐπαφρᾶ. A third "just as" (καθὼς) clause indicates how the Colossian Christians heard and understood the grace of God: they

learned (ἐμάθετε) the gospel from Epaphras. Usually Paul describes the acceptance of the gospel as "believing," "hearing" or "obeying" rather thar "learning," and the verb μανθάνω itself is found rather infrequently (for details see Rengstorf, *TDNT* 4, 406–12).

Masson (92) suggests, on the basis of the relative infrequency of the verb μανθάνω in Paul, that the apostle chose this verb intentionally so as to endorse Epaphras' ministry over against the new and pernicious, heretical teaching. The term "learned" (ἐμάθετε) probably indicates that Epaphras had given them systematic instruction in the gospel rather than some flimsy outline and that these Colossians had committed themselves as disciples to that teaching (cf. 2:6, 7).

The name Epaphras (Ἐπαφρᾶς) is a short form of Epaphroditus (Ἐπαφρόδιτυς), a very common name found frequently in inscriptions and the papyri of the period (BAG, 283). He is mentioned again at chapter 4:12, 13 and in Philemon 23 where he is described as Paul's fellow-captive (συναιχμάλωτος), meaning no doubt that he shared one of Paul's many imprisonments, possibly in Ephesus. (There is insufficient evidence for identifying him with the Epaphroditus of Phil 2:25; 4:18.) As a native of Colossae (ὁ ἐξ ὑμῶν, 4:12) he had been the evangelist of the Lycus valley where now there were flourishing churches—in Hierapolis and Laodicea as well as in Colossae. Epaphras had discharged his responsbilities faithfully (πιστός) and the presence of these congregations testified to the enduring character of his work (Bruce, 182).

τοῦ ἀγαπητοῦ συνδούλου ἡμῶν . . . πιστὸς ὑπὲρ ἡμῶν διάκονος τοῦ Χριστοῦ. The designations used of Epaphras, however, not only express the apostle's confidence in him. They also state significantly that he is Paul's representative in Colossae who has worked and who will continue to work in his place within the congregation. Epaphras is here described as "our beloved fellow-servant" while at chapter 4:12 he is called by the predicate of honor, a "servant of Christ Jesus" (δοῦλος Χριστοῦ Ἰησοῦ). In the OT "servant of God" was a title of honor to refer to those chosen by God and predestined for his service. Abraham (Ps 105:42), Moses (Ps 105:26; 2 Kings 18:12), David (2 Sam 7:5; Ps 89:4, 21) and others, especially the prophets (Amos 3:7), were God's servants. The last named were servants of the Word of the Lord who were to proclaim the message entrusted to them. In the NT an apostle was also a "servant of Christ Jesus" (Gal 1:10; cf. Rom 1:1). By styling Epaphras a "beloved fellow-servant" Paul draws attention to his reliable associate who guarantees to the church at Colossae that they received the true apostolic gospel.

Epaphras is also designated a "minister (διάκονος) of Christ." This term (διάκονος) originally denoted one who rendered service of a lowly kind (Beyer, *TDNT* 2, 91, 92) and was used in a variety of ways (cf. BAG, 184, 185) in the NT (at Rom 15:8 Christ himself is a "servant to the circumcision," διάκονος περιτομῆς; while at 2 Cor 11:23 and Eph 3:7 the apostle is a "minister" of Christ). Significantly in many of Paul's references it is one of a series of designations (cf. συνεργός, ἀδελφός, κοινωνός and ἀπόστολος) used of his associates in his missionary activity. The διάκονοι, according to Ellis (*NTS* 17 [1970–71] 438, 440), were a special class of co-workers who were active in preaching and teaching (cf. 1 Cor 3:5). So Timothy is a minister of God (1 Thess 3:2; 1 Tim 4:6) and so is Tychicus a minister in the Lord (Col 4:7; Eph 6:21). Epaphras has ministered on Paul's behalf (reading ὑπὲρ ἡμῶν, "on our behalf" with P46 ℵ* A B etc., rather than ὑπὲρ ὑμῶν, "on your behalf") and so the Colossians may be sure that the "truth" was faithfully taught to them (cf. H. Merklein, *Das kirchliche Amt nach dem Epheserbrief* [SANT 33; Munich: Kösel, 1973] 337–40, and E. Lohse, "Die Mitarbeiter des Apostels Paulus im Kolosserbrief," *Verborum Veritas. Festschrift für Gustav Stählin*, ed. O. Bocher and K. Haacker [Wuppertal: Brockhaus, 1970] 189–94).

8. ὁ καὶ δηλώσας ἡμῖν. More recently Epaphras had visited Paul in Rome and told him how the churches were faring. As apostle to the Gentiles Paul has a responsibility to the congregation at Colossae and no doubt he would be grateful for the reports given to him. Much of Epaphras' news was encouraging and although some aspects of the Colossians' church life were disquieting Paul for the moment dwells on those worthy of praise.

τὴν ὑμῶν ἀγάπην ἐν πνεύματι. This phrase indicates that the community's life was filled with a love generated by the Holy Spirit, enabling it to come to the help of all the saints (so Lohse, 23). No doubt these believers cherished a warm affection for Paul even though many had not met him personally (cf. 2:1). And the fact that they demonstrated this love in the Spirit toward Paul (as well as to others) would make it easier for him to exhort them about the dangers of the false teaching.

Explanation

In accordance with his usual custom Paul began his letter to the Colossians by reporting his thanksgiving to God for the faith and love of his readers. This faith which they have as men and women in Christ Jesus and the love they continue to show toward Christians around them are both based on a sure and certain hope that is kept for them in heaven where no power, human or otherwise, can touch it. Such a hope is centered on Christ himself (1:27) and was an essential element of the gospel Epaphras preached (cf. v 23). That gospel produced a vigorous and increasing fruit of Christian life and testimony at Colossae and was working in the same dynamic way throughout the rest of the world. Epaphras, as Paul's faithful co-worker, representative and minister of Christ, had diligently taught the Colossians that gospel. They may, therefore, be assured that they had been instructed in the "truth."

In this opening paragraph Paul begins to set the tone (which, incidentally, is not as warm as in the Philippian counterpart, 1:3–11) and introduce some of the themes that will be expanded in the rest of the letter. He does not attack the Colossian heresy as such. After all, he is reporting his thanksgiving to God. But Paul's positive descriptions of the gospel, the Colossians' response to it, and Epaphras' ministry all appear to be set over against something that is false. As the letter unfolds the nature of the error becomes more specific and clear.

At the same time by reporting that he gives thanks to God in connection with the faith, love and hope of the Colossians, and by mentioning the gospel and its world-wide fruitfulness together with the ministry of Epaphras, Paul instructs these Christian readers about those issues he considers vital. (On the didactic and exhortatory function of these introductory paragraphs, see below 29, 30.)

The mention of both the thanksgiving and the intercessory prayer which follows would no doubt help to strengthen the ties of fellowship between the apostle to the Gentiles and this congregation in the Lycus valley, most of whom he had come to know about through the reports of his colleague, Epaphras. In the offering of these prayers as well as in his telling them about it Paul clearly demonstrates his pastoral and apostolic concern for these Christians.

An Intercession for Knowledge and Godly Conduct (1:9–14)

Bibliography

Bornkamm, G. *Studien zu Antike und Urchristentum. Gesammelte Aufsätze.* Vol. 2. BEvT 28. Munich: Kaiser, 1959. **Deichgräber, R.** *Gotteshymnus und Christushymnus in der frühen Christenheit. Untersuchungen zu Form, Sprache und Stil der frühchristlichen Hymen.* SUNT 5. Göttingen: Vandenhoeck und Ruprecht, 1967. **Käsemann, E.** *Essays,* 149–68. **Montague, G. T.** *Growth in Christ. A Study in Saint Paul's Theology of Progress.* Fribourg, Switz.: Regina Mundi, 1961, 69–80. **O'Brien, P. T.** *Introductory Thanksgivings,* 62–104. **Schubert, P.** *Form.* **Zeilinger, F.** *Der Erstgeborene,* 36–39, 73–79.

Translation

[9] *For this reason, since the day we heard about you, we have not stopped earnestly praying for you that God may fill you with the knowledge of his will in all spiritual wisdom and understanding,* [10] *in order that you may lead a life worthy of the Lord and may please him in every way; bearing fruit in every good work, growing in the knowledge of God,* [11] *being strengthened with all power according to his glorious might so that you may show great endurance and patience, and joyfully* [12] *giving thanks to the Father, who has qualified you to share in the inheritance of the saints in the kingdom of light.* [13] *For he has rescued us from the tyranny of darkness and transferred us into the kingdom of the Son he loves,* [14] *in whom we have redemption, the forgiveness of sins.*

Form/Structure/Setting

The second major section of Paul's thanksgiving paragraph commences at verse 9, διὰ τοῦτο καὶ ἡμεῖς, ἀφʼ ἧς ἡμέρας ἠκούσαμεν κτλ. ("for this reason, since the day we heard about you"), and it spells out the content of his intercessory prayer report. The links between the thanksgiving and the intercession are strongly emphasized by: *(a)* the words διὰ τοῦτο καὶ ἡμεῖς . . . οὐ παυόμεθα ὑπὲρ ὑμῶν προσευχόμενοι . . . ("for this reason . . . we have not stopped praying for you"), verse 9, pick up and echo those of verse 3, εὐχαριστοῦμεν . . . πάντοτε περὶ ὑμῶν προσευχόμενοι ("we give thanks . . . always when we pray for you"; cf. Phil 1:9; 2 Thess 1:11 where a similar device is used to link the two sections); and by: *(b)* the repetition of terms and ideas already used in the thanksgiving: so, for example, "since the day" (vv 6, 9), "we heard" (vv 4, 9), "knowledge" (vv 6, 9, 10), "bearing fruit and increasing" (vv 6, 10), "giving thanks" (vv 3, 12), "the Father" (vv 3, 12), "the saints" (vv 4, 12), "spiritual" of verse 9 corresponds to "in spirit" of verse 8, while "the inheritance . . . in light" (v 12) may well overlap in meaning with ἐλπίς as the "object of hope" (v 5). It remains only to draw attention to the repeated use of "all" (πᾶς) in both sections (vv 4, 6, 9, 10, 11). "The resumption of these phrases and concepts clearly indicates that the thanksgiving and intercession are closely connected" (Lohse, 24).

After the main verb "we have not ceased to pray" (*οὐ παυόμεθα . . . προσευχόμενοι*, v 9) the content of the prayer is indicated by the *ἵνα*-clause: "that you may be filled . . ." (*ἵνα πληρωθῆτε*, v 9). An infinitive construction indicates the purpose for which the readers are to be filled with a knowledge of God's will, namely "to walk worthily of the Lord" (*περιπατῆσαι ἀξίως τοῦ κυρίου*, v 10) while the four participles which follow, "bearing fruit" (*καρποφοροῦντες*, v 10), "increasing" (*αὐξανόμενοι*, v 10), "being strengthened" (*δυναμούμενοι*, v 11) and "giving thanks" (*εὐχαριστοῦντες*, v 12), define more precisely what is involved in walking worthily of the Lord and pleasing him in all things. Each of the four participles is modified by a prepositional phrase, and so the whole paragraph may be structured as follows:

διὰ τοῦτο καὶ ἡμεῖς . . .
  προσευχόμενοι καὶ αἰτούμενοι . . .
  ἵνα πληρωθῆτε . . .
    περιπατῆσαι ἀξίως τοῦ κυρίου . . .

ἐν παντὶ ἔργῳ ἀγαθῷ	*καρποφοροῦντες*
	αὐξανόμενοι τῇ ἐπιγνώσει τοῦ θεοῦ
ἐν πάσῃ δυνάμει	*δυναμούμενοι*
μετὰ χαρᾶς	*εὐχαριστοῦντες . . .*

In verses 13 and 14 which are probably to be understood as an exposition of verse 12 (being fitted for God's inheritance in the realm of light meant that he had delivered them out of the realm of darkness, translated them into the kingdom of his beloved Son and given them redemption) two relative sentences occur (*ὃς ἐρρύσατο*, v 13, and *ἐν ᾧ ἔχομεν*, v 14), the first of which has two lines in contrasting parallelism:

13*a* *ὃς ἐρρύσατο ἡμᾶς ἐκ τῆς ἐξουσίας τοῦ σκότους*
13*b* *καὶ μετέστησεν εἰς τὴν βασιλείαν τοῦ υἱοῦ τῆς ἀγάπης αὐτοῦ.*

Not all commentators, however, are agreed that Paul's intercession extends to verse 14. A considerable and influential body of continental scholarly opinion is convinced that the prayer-report concludes with the words about patience and long-suffering in verse 11. *μετὰ χαρᾶς εὐχαριστοῦντες* ("joyfully giving thanks") introduces the community's confession of faith in Christ. On this view verses 12–20 are understood as a unit with verses 12–14 being regarded by Käsemann (*Essays*, 154, 155) and others as an introit to a baptismal liturgy (Bornkamm, *Studien*, 188–203, and N. A. Dahl, "Anamnesis. Mémoire et Commémoration dans le Christianisme primitif," *ST* 1 [1948] 86, 87, understand the hymnic confession in a eucharistic context). Our criticism of this division (cf. *Introductory Thanksgivings*, 71–75) is threefold: first, it is not at all clear why *εὐχαριστοῦντες* is to be separated from the preceding participles (which we have suggested define more precisely what it means "to walk worthily of the Lord") and understood as a summons or in an imperatival way. Second, although *εὐχαριστέω* was used in a wider sense than simply the giving of thanks for personal benefits received it is doubtful whether it was employed as a technical term to introduce a confession (cf. Bornkamm, *Studien*, 196,

197, and note Deichgräber's criticisms, *Gotteshymnus,* 145, 146). Third, Käsemann's particular view of the whole section being "an early Christian baptismal liturgy" is unproven. We do not know enough about early Christian liturgies to be able to make pronouncements with this certainty.

Paul's thanksgiving period extends from verses 3–14 (containing a thanksgiving report, vv 3–8, and an intercessory prayer report, vv 9–14). It does not have a well-rounded and clear-cut climax, but passes almost imperceptibly from the form of a prayer to that of a creed or hymn. Some of the terms and ideas of verses 12–14 may have been associated with baptism but in their present context are the basis of joyful thanksgiving to the Father.

Comment

9. *διὰ τοῦτο καὶ ἡμεῖς, ἀφ ἀφ' ἧς 'ἧς ἡμέρας ἠκούσαμεν κτλ.* "For this reason, since the day we heard about you . . ." Paul picks up the thread of his prayer-report of verses 3–5 and, as we have seen, goes out of his way to link the petition with the thanksgiving. The "we" (*ἡμεῖς*) stresses the identity of the ones who intercede with those who have given thanks. From the day he learned of their progress as Christians, the apostle not only offered constant thanksgiving to God the Father, he also added regular intercession for them. The word "asking" (*αἰτούμενοι*) is used synonymously with "praying" (*προσευχόμενοι*; cf, Mark 11:24, where the verbs have an exact parallel, "Whatever you ask in prayer [*προσεύχεσθε καὶ αἰτεῖσθε*], believe that you receive it, and you will"; against Meyer, 262, who understands the latter word to refer to general prayer), and together the two verbs probably indicate that the apostle along with his colleagues prayed to God with great intensity so that his request might be granted (Lohse, 25).

ἵνα πληρωθῆτε τὴν ἐπίγνωσιν τοῦ θελήματος αὐτοῦ. The content (*ἵνα*) of the petition is that God (the passive *πληρωθῆτε* shows it is he who supplies this knowledge in abundance) might fill the Colossian Christians with a perception of his will, which consists of an understanding of what is spiritually important. This would result in conduct that is pleasing to the Lord, i.e. a harvest of good deeds and growth in understanding (v 10). The power that would enable them to act in such a manner exercising patience and long-suffering would be derived from God's glorious might (v 11). At the same time, they would give thanks to the Father for an eternal inheritance, deliverance from the power of darkness, and the forgiveness of sins (vv 12–14). Thus, Paul's actual petition is for the discernment of God's will and the power to perform it (cf. Moule, 47; note Phil 1:9–11 as a parallel).

The ideas of "fullness," "abundance" or "riches" feature frequently in Paul's prayers (cf. 1 Cor 1:5; Phil 1:9; 4:19; 1 Thess 3:12; 2 Thess 1:3). The motif of "fullness" recurs frequently in this epistle (note the different terms used at 1:19, 24, 25; 2:2, 3, 9, 10; 4:12, 17), and it seems that the false teachers boasted that they offered the fullness of truth and spiritual maturity, while Epaphras had only instructed the Colossians in the first steps (Beare, 156). On the contrary, Epaphras had taught "the word of truth" (v 5) while Paul and his colleagues had consistently prayed (cf. 4:12) that the Colossians might receive fullness of blessing from God's gracious hand (note the passive πεπληροφορημένοι), and he indicates in the prayer that unfolds what that fullness is.

ἐν πάσῃ σοφίᾳ καὶ συνέσει πνευματικῇ. The readers are to be filled "with a knowledge of his will." The words which follow define what this means, i.e. the "perception of God's will consists in wisdom and understanding of every sort, on the spiritual level," to use Moule's paraphrase (53). These and the following words find clear OT parallels (on the Greco-Roman links see Lohse, 26, and Schweizer, 40). So "his will (τὸ θέλημα αὐτοῦ: Ps 103 [LXX 102]: 7; 143 [142]: 10), "knowledge" (ἐπίγνωσις), "wisdom and understanding" (σοφία καὶ σύνεσις), and their conjunction with πνεῦμα "spirit" turn up in the OT (cf. Exod 31:3; 35:31, 35: Deut 34:9; 1 Chron 22:12; Isa 11:2; etc., also the fourth benediction of the *Tefillah*), and are no doubt to be understood against this background (so Harder, *Paulus,* 118, 119, Lohmeyer, 32, 33). Furthermore, similar ideas appear in the writings of the Qumran community (for detailed parallels see Lohse, 25, 26). These three qualities of "knowledge," "insight" and "wisdom" were understood as gifts of God which he had imparted by his Spirit (1QS 4:3, 4; 1QSb 5:25) to the faithful members of the community.

"Knowledge" (ἐπίγνωσις) occurs twice in this intercessory request of Paul (vv 9, 10) while the cognate verb "know" was used in the thanksgiving as well (v 6). In fact, because the Colossians had *come to know* God's grace when they were converted (ἐπέγνωτε is probably an inceptive aorist), they might now be expected to grow in "knowledge," or "perception" as Moule (53) puts it.

"Knowledge" (ἐπίγνωσις) occurs as an important subject of Paul's intercessory prayers in each of the Captivity Epistles (Eph 1:17; Phil 1:9; Philem 6). L. Cerfaux (*Christ in the Theology of St. Paul.* Tr. G. Webb and A. Walker [New York: Herder, 1959] 402–438, especially 404) considered that the importance given to knowledge in these letters was due to its relationship to the "mystery." This mystery, which was Paul's gospel, had its accent on the salvation of Gentiles. It was in the churches of Asia that Paul became used to speaking of the gospel as a mystery, Cerfaux claims, and Christians were bound to advance in a knowledge of it. Such knowledge involved every facet of the Christian's life, hence the prayer that the Colossians might be "filled" with it. In addition to Cerfaux's suggestions, which do not adequately account for the appearance of "knowledge" in the prayers of Philippians (1:9) and Philemon (v 6), one needs to take note of Paul's own personal circumstances. In prison, aware that he might not be able to visit and strengthen the churches to which he wrote, he saw the need for them to increase in the knowledge of God and his will, and with this God's mystery, Christ. Also the requirements of the churches demanded a further exposition of the gospel to combat fresh dangers and heresies that were arising.

Paul's use of "knowledge" (ἐπίγνωσις) here might be by way of contrast with the much-canvassed *gnosis* of the false teachers. Heretical *gnosis* was speculative and theoretical while the knowledge for which the apostle prayed concerned the "will of God" (θέλημα θεοῦ; cf. Rom 12:2; Eph 5:17; 1 Thess 4:3; 5:18)—it was comprehensive and demanded an obedience visible in a person's actions. This perception of God's will consisted "in wisdom and understanding of every sort" (the πᾶς, "all," applies to both nouns), while the addition of πνευματικός ("spiritual"), in an emphatic position, indicates that both the wisdom and the understanding are on a spiritual level. As such they stood in sharp contrast to the wisdom of the false teachers, which at best was only a show (λόγος σοφίας, 2:23), an empty counterfeit calling itself "philosophy" (φιλοσοφία, 2:8). At the same time "spiritual" suggests that the full knowledge of God's will, for which Paul prays, comes through the insight God's Spirit imparts.

Later in the letter the apostle will have further things to say about wisdom and knowledge (ἐπίγνωσις 2:2; 3:10; σοφία 1:28; 2:3, 23; 3:16; 4:5; σύνεσις 2:2). He has prepared the way, in this intercessory prayer report, for further instruction on knowledge. At the same time it has been indicated that apart from the activity of God on their behalf (πληρωθῆτε), filling them with true discernment, they would not know as they ought to, nor grasp what he had to say in the following sections of the epistle. The prayer for knowledge *precedes* the exposition of Christ's lordship in creation and redemption (1:15–20), its ramifications (1:21–23) and the detailed interaction with the "philosophy" of the false teachers (2:6–23).

10. *περιπατῆσαι ἀξίως τοῦ κυρίου εἰς πᾶσαν ἀρεσκείαν.* Although there is perhaps greater emphasis on knowledge and wisdom in this petitionary prayer than in any other of Paul's letters (though cf. Eph 1:17–19; 3:16–19)—and this includes a strong intellectual element to enable them to combat error—in true Hebraic fashion it leads to right action and conduct. The Colossians are "to walk worthily of the Lord so as to please him in every way" (cf. Percy, *Probleme,* 126). περιπατῆσαι ("to walk") is an infinitive of purpose (this fits the context better than the suggestions that the infinitive is one of result, or of explanation), indicating that the knowledge for which Paul prayed was designed to lead to righteous behavior. Paul often characterizes the life and behavior of the Christian by this verb "walk" (περιπατέω: Gal 5:16; cf. v 25; Rom 6:4; 8:4; 14:15; 2 Cor 4:2; Eph 2:10; 4:1; 5:2, 15; Phil 3:17; etc.) and in this he is indebted to the OT (Seesemann, *TDNT* 5, 944. There are no parallels in classical Greek). The word is equivalent to the Hebrew *hālak/hithhallēk* which is found frequently in the Qumran texts to describe the activity of those who walk in "the ways of darkness" (e.g. 1QS 3:21), or, of those who showing themselves to be true sons of light walk before God in an upright manner (1QS 1:8). The latter "walk according to God's will" (1QS 5:10; 9:24; cf. Lohse, 27), refusing to please themselves (contrast CD 3:12). The Colossian Christians are to live in a manner that is worthy of the one whom they confess as Lord.

In secular Greek ἀρεσκεία ("pleasing") usually signified the behavior by which one sought to gain a favor, and therefore was most often employed with a negative connotation meaning "obsequiousness." However, it could also be used in a positive sense (cf. BAG, 105; Deissmann, *Bible Studies,* 224; MM, 75), and frequently in Hellenistic Judaism referred to what was "well pleasing to God" (especially Philo, *Spec Leg* 1.300; cf. Lohse, 27, 28). The cognate verb "to please" (ἀρέσκω) is found in Paul's letters on fourteen occasions, with reference to the necessity of pleasing God (or, of pleasing others as a result of one's obedience to God) rather than pleasing oneself (Rom

8:8; 15:1, 2, 3; 1 Cor 7:32; etc. Cf. BAG, 105). There is no doubt that in the context of this intercessory prayer, and in the light of the apostle's use of the cognate verb, *ἀρεσκεία* refers to pleasing the Lord (so rightly Schweizer, 41; against Foerster, *TDNT* 1, 456, and Lohmeyer, 34)—and that in all things.

καρποφοροῦντες . . . αὐξανόμενοι . . . δυναμούμενοι . . . εὐχαριστοῦντες. As mentioned above the four participles which follow, "bearing fruit" (v 10), "increasing" (v 10), "being strengthened" (v 11) and "giving thanks" (v 12), spell out more precisely what is involved in "walking worthily of the Lord." The first two, "bearing fruit and increasing," recall the words in Paul's thanksgiving about the powerful spread of the gospel (no distinction is intended between the middle voice, *καρποφορούμενον* of v 6 and the active here). It had borne fruit and spread throughout the whole world particularly at Colossae. But here in his intercessory prayer the apostle indicates that the words, with a slight change of meaning (cf. Moule, 51), are applied to the recipients of that gospel as well.

Some commentators consider that the two participles *καρποφοροῦντες* ("bearing fruit") and *αὐξανόμενοι* ("increasing") are to be held together (so Lohmeyer, 35, Beare, 157, Lohse, 29, and Martin, *NCB,* 52), and related to the source of progress in maturity. On this view, the bearing of fruit and increasing are effected through the knowledge of God and they become visible "in every good work" (cf. Schweizer, 42).

Our preference, however, is to see in the clauses an instance of the verbal arrangement of chiasmus *(abba),* so that *ἐν παντὶ ἔργῳ ἀγαθῷ* ("in every good work") is to be taken with *καρποφοροῦντες* ("bearing fruit"), while *τῇ ἐπιγνώσει τοῦ θεοῦ* ("in the knowledge of God")—a dative of reference—is joined to *αὐξανόμενοι* ("increasing"). Accordingly, Paul is asking God that the fruit of good works might appear in greater abundance in their lives—and this because of the seed sown in their midst (v 6)—while they continue to make progress in the knowledge of God. During their pagan days, the Colossians had expressed their hostility to God by "doing evil deeds" (*ἐν τοῖς ἔργοις τοῖς πονηροῖς,* 1:21; cf. 3:7). But now the fruit of good works (*ἐν παντὶ ἔργῳ ἀγαθῷ*) should appear in their behavior (cf. Rom 13:3; 2 Cor 9:8; Gal 6:10; Eph 2:10; 1 Tim 2:10; 5:10; 2 Tim 2:21; etc.). Since the participles which define the walking worthily are all in the present tense and stress the notion of progress, it is probably right to conclude that the Colossian Christians would receive further knowledge as they were obedient to the knowledge of God they had already received (Bruce, 186).

Paul's language in the intercessory prayer is reminiscent of the interpretation of the parable of the sower (in its Markan form: 4:1–9, 13–20). If the *Sitz im Leben* of the parable and its interpretation were the ministry of Jesus (and the arguments against this do not appear to be sufficiently weighty), then Paul's treatment could be a development of this, on the one hand applying the words to the gospel which he and his associate Epaphras preached (vv 6, 7), and on the other hand relating the terms to the recipients of that gospel, at the same time defining more precisely what was meant by each of the two ideas (on the application of dynamic verbs to the gospel and its recipients, see O'Brien, *NTS* 21 [1974–75] 144–55).

11. *ἐν πάσῃ δύναμει δυναμούμενοι κτλ.* The third clause "strengthened with

all power . . ." indicates how the conduct, worthy of the Lord, was to be achieved. The standards set before the Colossians were far higher than those of the false teachers. And nothing short of God's almighty power at work within them would enable them to live so as to please him in all things.

Two aspects of God's power are stressed by Paul in prayer contexts: first, that in calling and equipping him as an apostle to the Gentiles (cf. 1 Tim 1:12; 2 Cor 12:9); and secondly, that power of God which indwelt the Christian community enabling them to walk in a way that was pleasing to him (cf. Eph 1:18, 19). Here it is the latter which is in view.

God's power is a prominent motif in both Colossians and Ephesians (Col 1:29; 2:12; Eph 1:19; 3:7, 16, 20; 6:10). Here in his intercession, by heaping up several synonymous terms, Paul has accented (1) that it is nothing less than God's indwelling power which is required; (2) that "his glorious might" (τὸ κράτος τῆς δόξης αὐτοῦ; in the LXX κράτος occurs some fifty times, the overwhelming majority of which are references to the power of God) is more than adequate for the Colossians' needs; and, (3) that this strength will be provided as the varying circumstances are confronted (δυναμούμενοι; the present participle denotes the steady accession of strength).

God's mighty power will strengthen the community "for all endurance and long-suffering" (εἰς πᾶσαν ὑπομονὴν καὶ μακροθυμίαν), in the face of trials and opposition. ὑπομονή ("endurance"; the noun and its cognate verb ὑπομένω can be directed to God and so mean to "wait on him," or to the world connoting to "endure, be steadfast") signifies that kind of perseverance which enables one to hold the position already taken in battle against enemy attacks from without (Lohse, 30). By this "endurance" the Colossian community will stand firm in every respect (πᾶς goes with both nouns)—especially by holding out against the pressure of evil forces in the Lycus valley that would lead them astray as well as make them dispirited. This kind of endurance, however, does not derive from personal bravery or stoical fortitude. Rather, as in the OT and later Judaism (cf. Lohse, 30), it is seen to spring from God who is its source (cf. "the God of steadfastness," ὁ θεὸς τῆς ὑπομονῆς, Rom 15:5; this is a wish prayer). Thus he may be petitioned for it (as here; cf. 2 Thess 3:5), or thanked when it is evident in the lives of believers (1 Thess 1:3; cf. 2 Thess 1:4). At the same time Christians are summoned to endurance (cf. Rom 8:25; 15:4) and by it they prove their standing in the faith. With such endurance they persevere through suffering (2 Cor 1:6), as they direct their attention toward the final day (though cf. Martin, *NCB*, 53).

"Long-suffering" (μακροθυμία) in both Old and New Testaments is used of the patience of God and of his people—note especially Exodus 34:6, "The Lord, the Lord, a God merciful and gracious, *slow to anger* and abounding in steadfast love and faithfulness" (italics mine). Because of God's dealings with his people this word, which was not very significant in secular Greek, was given a new and unexpectedly profound importance, so that the human attitude of "long-suffering" (μακροθυμία) is now set in a new light. God's patience with his people means they ought to act in a similar manner toward others (cf. the parable of the wicked servant, Matt 18:23–35, and 1 Thess

5:14). "Long-suffering" is a fruit of the Spirit (Gal 5:22), unable to be produced from the individual's own resources.

The apostle thus prayed that the believers at Colossae, empowered by God's glorious might, would demonstrate "all patience and long-suffering" in the face of opposition, thereby showing that they had their hope set on him.

12–14. As already noted verses 12–14 bring us to the closing section of Paul's petitionary prayer-report rather than introduce a new section, the so-called introit to the hymn of verses 15–20, in which the community is urged to praise God with a thanksgiving.

It has been argued by Käsemann and others that the language and ideas of verses 12–14, which were not Pauline, "hark back . . . to the language of the LXX and revive many of its liturgical and cultic formulations" (*Essays*, 154, 155; note Schweizer, 44–50). The words, according to Käsemann, showed that the setting of the hymn (vv 15–20) was that of a baptismal liturgy (Bornkamm, *Studien*, 196, regarded vv 12–14 as the community's confession of faith offered at the eucharist; cf. Dahl, *ST* 1 [1948] 69–95).

It is possible that Paul, in his petitionary prayer-report, has selected terms and ideas that were current in early Christian worship. Käsemann may be right in noting that "deliver" (*ῥύεσθαι*), "transfer" (*μεθιστάναι*), "light" (*φῶς*), "share" (*μέρις*) and "lot" (*κλῆρος*) were known in a baptismal context (Schweizer, 49, admits this is difficult to prove; he prefers to call the language of v 12 "conversion terminology"). But the remembrance of being transferred from darkness to light, of receiving redemption and the forgiveness of sins would have been repeatedly the occasion for joyful thanksgiving. Further, if these motifs had been used in a baptismal context (and we have no certain means of knowing), and were in fact pre-Pauline, then it is quite understandable for Paul to *remind* the readers of these truths, so as to inculcate joyful thanksgiving to the Father. At the same time we may suppose that Paul has used these terms and ideas, with their unmistakable OT and Jewish ring, in his actual prayers for the Colossians. He is, after all, reporting his *prayer* in this epistolary style.

12. *μετὰ χαρᾶς εὐχαριστοῦντες τῷ πατρί*. The person to whom the Colossians are to offer joyful thanksgiving (*μετὰ χαρᾶς*, "with joy," is to be taken with *εὐχαριστοῦντες*, "giving thanks"; it preserves the balance of the three clauses in vv 11, 12, and is favored by Phil 1:4; see O'Brien, *Introductory Thanksgivings*, 93, 94, for further details) is "the Father" (*τῷ πατρί*). We have already noted at chapter 1:3 in *Paul's thanksgiving* the stress upon God in his character as Father. The same point is driven home at chapter 3:17, for it is to the Father that thanksgiving is to be given through the Lord Jesus Christ. Here the Father is praised because he has effected salvation and redemption in Christ.

τῷ ἱκανώσαντι κτλ. The grounds for this joyful thanksgiving are that the Almighty (*ὁ ἱκανός* is used in the LXX at Job 31:2 as a divine name, "the Almighty," and C. H. Dodd, *The Bible and the Greeks* [London: Hodder, 1935] 15, 16, suggested this OT passage had influenced Paul here and at 2 Cor 3:6) has fitted (*ἱκανώσαντι*, v 12) them for an eternal inheritance, delivered (v 13) them from a tyranny of darkness and transferred them into a kingdom in which his beloved Son holds sway. The aorist tenses point to an eschatology that is truly realized (i.e. God had *already* qualified [ἱκανώσαντι] the Colossians to share in the inheritance, he had *already* delivered [ἐρρύσατο] them from this alien power and had *already* transferred [μετέστησεν] them to his Son's kingdom), while by contrast, the present tense of verse 14, "we have" (ἔχομεν), stresses the continued results of the redemption wrought in the past.

εἰς τὴν μερίδα τοῦ κλήρου. This whole section, as has been noted, is full of OT echoes. "To share in the inheritance of the saints" recalls the promise, first given to Abram (Gen 13:14–17) and subsequently renewed to Israel (Num 26:52–56; 34:2, 13; Josh 19:9) that they would possess their inheritance as the tribes were apportioned the land of Canaan by lot. But the inheritance to which Paul refers belongs to a higher plane and a more lasting order than any earthly Canaan. (On the significance of the land of Canaan in the OT, Judaism and early Christianity see J. D. Hester, *Paul's Concept of Inheritance. A Contribution to the Understanding of Heilsgeschichte* [Edinburgh: Oliver and Boyd, 1968] and W. D. Davies, *The Gospel and the Land* [Berkeley: University of California, 1974]).

"Part, share" (μερίς) and "lot" (κλῆρος) were often used synonymously or together in the LXX (Deut 10:9; 12:12; 14:27, 29; 18:1; Josh 19:9; Isa 57:6; Jer 13:25), as were their Hebrew equivalents in the Qumran literature (1QS 11:7, 8; cf. 1QS 2:5; 1QH 11:11, 12; 1QM 1:1, 5; 13:5, 6; cf. E. Lohse, "Christologie und Ethik im Kolosserbrief," *Apophoreta. Festschrift für Ernst Haenchen,* ed. W. Eltester and F. H. Kettler [BZNW 30; Berlin: Töpelmann, 1964, 157–68] Reprinted in *Die Einheit des Neuen Testaments. Exegetische Studien zur Theologie des Neuen Testaments.* 2nd ed. [Göttingen: Vandenhoeck und Ruprecht, 1973] 249–61, esp. 258). Here we understand the phrase εἰς τὴν μερίδα τοῦ κλήρου as meaning "to have a share in the κλῆρος," i.e. the inheritance of God's people (so Moule, 55, and Bruce, 188). There are parallels in the biblical data (Deut 33:3; Ps 89:6; cf. 1 Thess 3:13) and the Qumran literature (especially 1QS 11:7, 8, where the motifs of inheritance, lot and holy ones are mentioned) to suggest that "holy ones" (οἱ ἅγιοι) here refers to angels, and many commentators take the expression in this way. The further point is added that the readers have their hope secure in God's presence ("in light") where the angels live. Paul, reflecting on his thought in chapter 1:5, is looking forward to a polemic against the cult of angels, which the false teachers were evidently practicing (2:18). So "at a single blow he dispels this veneration of the angelic powers by assuring the Colossians that they have attained a place shared by the angels (3:1)" (Martin, *NCB,* 54).

However, this interpretation of "holy ones" referring to angels is less likely than the view that God's people are being spoken about. The closely related passage of Acts 26:18 (the themes of "light," "darkness," "authority," "forgiveness of sins," "lot," and "holy ones" are common to both passages), where words are attributed to Paul, "those who are sanctified by faith in me" (ἐν τοῖς ἡγιασμένοις πίστει τῇ εἰς ἐμέ), can only refer to believers. Furthermore, as Schweizer (47) aptly notes all the other references to "holy ones" in this letter (1:2, 4, 22; particularly 1:26; 3:12) are to church members. κλῆρος τῶν ἁγίων is thus understood as a reference to the inheritance allotted to God's people (cf. Dibelius-Greeven, 8, and many English-speaking commentators). "In light" (ἐν τῷ φωτί) goes with the whole phrase that precedes, i.e. "to share in the inheritance of the saints." The point is that the inheritance for which the all-powerful Father had fitted them was in the realm of the light of the age to come. Unlike Canaan it belonged to a spiritual dimension, unable to be ravaged by war, famine or the like. For the Colossian Christians, most of whom were probably Gentiles by birth, this was good news indeed. They now had a share in God's inheritance with other believers, or to use the equivalent words of Paul's thanksgiving they had "a hope laid up in heaven" (v 5; cf. 3:1–4).

13. A further exposition of this remarkable change that God had effected at the time of the Colossians' conversion is spelled out in two corresponding lines (cf. Lohse, 36, and Zeilinger, *Der Erstgeborene,* 38; see above 19):

ὃς ἐρρύσατο ἡμᾶς ἐκ τῆς ἐξουσίας . . .
καὶ μετέστησεν εἰς τὴν βασιλείαν . . .

Negatively, God has delivered us (ἡμᾶς: note the change to the first person plural indicating that God's action has reference to other believers, including Paul, as well as to the Colossian Christians) from the tyranny of darkness and, positively, he has placed us under the rule of his beloved Son.

ὃς ἐρρύσατο κτλ. Deliverance from an alien power was an important theme in the OT (the Lord rescued his people from the hand of the Egyptians [Exod 14:30; Judg 6:9], from bondage [Exod 6:6] and from all her enemies [Judg 8:34]). The psalmists in particular loved to sing of the Lord's past deliverances, both national and personal, and on the basis of these prayed to him that he might deliver them from danger, sickness, death, enemies and hostile situations (Pss 33:18, 19; 79:9; 86:13; etc.). The influence of the Psalter on the later prayers of Judaism is quite marked (see the *Tefillah* where after the sixth petition for the forgiveness of sins there follow the words, "Look upon our affliction and plead our cause, and redeem us speedily for thy name's sake"; for Qumran parallels note 1QH 2:35; 3:19; cf. Deichgräber, *Gotteshymnus,* 80, 81). Most of the NT instances of the verb "to deliver" (ῥύομαι) appear in prayer contexts (Luke 1:74; Matt 27:43, the mocking words of the Jewish leaders to Jesus on the cross that God would not answer his cry for deliverance; though note 2 Pet 2:7, 9). So the Christian community prays to God "deliver (ῥῦσαι) us from the evil one" (Matt 6:13; cf. Luke 11:4) while it awaits its Lord "who delivers (τὸν ῥυόμενον) us from the wrath to come" (1 Thess 1:10 in a thanksgiving paragraph).

The inheritance for which the Colossians had been fitted was in the realm of light, a complete contrast to that tyranny under which they had once lived (ἡ ἐξουσία τοῦ σκότους; cf. Luke 22:52, 53) prior to their conversion (according to Lohse, 39, the contrast between the concepts of light and darkness for conversion to the God of Israel was already known in Hellenistic Judaism [Joseph and Asenath 8:9; 15:12]). Like a mighty king who was able to remove peoples from their ancestral homes and to transplant them (μετέστησεν; the same verb is used by Josephus [*Ant.* 9.235] of Tiglath-pileser's removal of the Transjordanian tribes to his own kingdom: μετέστησεν εἰς τὴν αὐτοῦ βασιλείαν; cf. 1 Cor 13:2 where the verb is used of transferring mountains) into another realm, God had taken the Colossians from the tyranny of darkness (Chrysostom aptly noted that "power" equals "tyranny" here), where evil powers rule (Luke 22:53) and where Satan's authority is exercised (Acts 26:18), transferring them to the kingdom in which his beloved Son held sway.

The notion of two realms to which human beings belong, which are characterized by the contrast of light and darkness, is found in the Qumran material: on the one side the lot of Belial and the sons of darkness (1QS 2:5; 1QM 1:1, 5, 11; 4:2; 13:2), on the other side the lot of the holy ones and the sons of light (1QS 1:9; 2:16; 11:7, 8; 1QH 11:11, 12).

This change of dominion so vividly described under the categories of "light" and "darkness" and which had taken place in the lives of the Colossians (together with other Christians including Paul—"us") at their conversion was "absolutely determinative for the life of the believer" (Lohse, 37; cf. 2 Cor 6:14; Eph 5:8; 1 Peter 2:9). They are now "children of light" (υἱοὶ φωτός, 1 Thess 5:5) and are to behave accordingly.

In the phrase "the kingdom (βασιλεία) of his beloved Son" we note one of the few New Testament references to the kingdom of Christ, an interim period between the resurrection of Jesus and the final coming of the kingdom of God. Paul seems to have distinguished two aspects of the heavenly kingdom in the phrases "kingdom of Christ" and "kingdom of God," the former referring to the heavenly kingdom in its present aspect, the latter concerning the final consummation (1 Cor 6:9, 10; 15:50; Gal 5:21; 2 Tim 4:1, 18; though some references have a more general significance: e.g. Rom 14:17; 1 Cor 4:20; Col 4:11).

14. *ἐν ᾧ ἔχομεν τὴν ἀπολύτρωσιν, τὴν ἄφεσιν τῶν ἁμαρτιῶν.* In the kingdom where God's Son holds sway there is redemption (ἀπολύτρωσις). This is equated with, or at least in apposition to, the forgiveness of sins, indicating, as Moule stated, "very clearly how entirely moral and spiritual the conception of the kingdom of God or of Christ was for the disciples of Christ" (58). Redemption, which connotes liberation from imprisonment and bondage, is not simply the object of hope (though cf. Rom 8:23; Eph 1:14; 4:30). It is here an existing reality, a present possession (reading ἔχομεν, "we have," which has the strongest manuscript support; cf. Büchsel, *TDNT* 4, 353), as often elsewhere in the Pauline writings (Rom 3:24; 1 Cor 1:30; Eph 1:7), and is "bound up strictly with the person of Jesus" (Büchsel, *TDNT* 4, 354). It is "in him" (ἐν ᾧ) that we possess it. God has made *him* to be our redemption (1 Cor 1:30; on the subject of redemption see L. Morris, *The Apostolic Preaching of the Cross.* 3rd ed. [London: Tyndale, 1965] 11–64: 1st American edition Grand Rapids: Eerdmans, 1955; D. Hill, *Greek Words and Hebrew Meanings. Studies in the Semantics of Soteriological Terms* [SNTSMS 5; Cambridge: University Press, 1967] 49–81).

τὴν ἄφεσιν τῶν ἁμαρτιῶν. The associated expression "the forgiveness of sins" does not occur frequently in Paul's writings. Normally he refers to "sin" (ἁμαρτία) in the singular, as a power which entered the world through Adam's action (Rom 5:12) and since then has tyrannized men until that power was broken by Christ's death on the cross (Rom 8:3; etc.). "Forgiveness of sins" is mentioned with reference to John's baptism (Mark 1:4), while in the Acts of the Apostles it is repeatedly cited as the content of salvation (Acts 2:38; 5:31; 10:43; 13:38; 26:18). Paul, in this context, may have been using a traditional expression to describe the blessings of forgiveness given in Christ (though cf. Percy, *Probleme,* 85, 86, who claims that this fits the context better than the distinctively Pauline terms of "justification," etc.). The linking of this motif with redemption may have been due to the specific problem at Colossae, for it is possible that the false teachers, like those of a later period to whom Irenaeus referred (*Heresies* 1.21, 2), distinguished between "the remission of sins" as the first stage received in baptism and "redemption" as the final stage coming from the divine Christ (so Bruce, 191, 192). It would be quite understandable why Paul would show that both were present realities experienced in God's Son.

With these words about redemption and the forgiveness of sins Paul's prayer shades off into the majestic hymn about the lordship of Christ.

Explanation

Having reported his thanksgiving to God for the faith and love of the Colossian Christians, Paul proceeds to spell out the content of his intercessory prayer for them. Basically his petition is for the discernment of God's will and the power to do it. He earnestly asks that God might fill the Colossians with a knowledge of his will so that they would possess true spiritual insight. This should lead to behavior fully pleasing to the Lord—namely, a crop of good deeds and growth in understanding. The power that would enable them to live in such a manner exercising patience and long-suffering could only come from above, that is, from God's glorious might. At the same time they are to give thanks to the Father for his mighty, gracious work in their midst: he has given them an eternal inheritance, delivered them from the power of darkness and transferred them into a kingdom where his beloved Son rules. Involved in this also were the blessings of redemption and the forgiveness of sins.

Paul's introductory thanksgiving paragraph of verses 3–14, of which the intercessory prayer forms an integral part, has a fourfold function:

(*a*) *epistolary*—it introduces major themes of the letter such as the universal spread of God's word, the gospel (in contrast to the limited circle of the Colossian heresy), the Christian hope, true wisdom and knowledge with a resulting behavior that pleases the Lord (in contrast to the false wisdom of the heretical teachers with its rigorous asceticism and show of humility), thanksgiving to the Father, deliverance from bondage, and so on. These themes are then expanded, sometimes by way of answer to the heresy, in the body of the letter. Stylistic features are foreshadowed in the passage, while the degree of intimacy of the letter can also be observed here. Paul does not know this church personally, and so does not write in the warm manner of the Philippian letter, for example.

(*b*) The *didactic* purpose is clearly in evidence. Important theological motifs occur in both the thanksgiving and the intercessory prayer, e.g. faith, love, hope, gospel, knowledge, God's will, wisdom and understanding, etc. It was the apostle's concern that these themes be fully grasped by the recipients, and he has expanded them in the body of the letter, so recalling the readers to truths already taught by Epaphras.

(c) The *exhortatory* function is also to be noted. Catechetical references to long-suffering (3:12; cf. 1:11), the putting on of love (3:14; cf. 1:4), the corporate giving of thanks to the Father (3:15–17; cf. 1:12), walking in the tradition they had received (2:6; cf. 1:10) and so behaving wisely to those "outside" (4:5) are prefigured in this introductory passage. At the same time the Colossians, knowing that Paul was interceding for them along the lines that he did, would have been encouraged to respond in the appropriate way.

(d) Finally, Paul, by his actual prayers and the recording of them (even if the reports are summaries of the prayers offered to God), demonstrated his *pastoral concern* for the readers. He desired that they might grow in spiritual knowledge in order to combat the dangers facing them. Such wisdom could only come from above, and we may suggest that Paul recognized that, apart from God's granting such insight, his teaching and exhortation in the words which were to follow would be of no avail.

Christ the Lord in Creation and Redemption (1:15–20)

Bibliography

The following is a select list of works chosen from the vast amount of secondary literature written on verses 15–20. Further bibliographical references will be found in these and other works noted at the relevant exegetical points. Commentaries which have not been included are listed.

Aletti, J. N. *Colossiens 1, 15–20. Genre et exégèse du texte Fonction de la thématique sapientelle.* AnBib 91. Rome: Biblical Institute, 1981. **Benoit, P.** "L'hymne christologique de Col 1, 15–20. Jugement critique sur l'état des recherches." *Christianity, Judaism and Other Greco-Roman Cults. Studies for Morton Smith at Sixty,* ed. J. Neusner. Part One. New Testament. SJLA 12. Leiden: Brill, 1975, 226–63. **Best, E.** *One Body in Christ. A Study in the Relationship of the Church to Christ in the Epistles of the Apostle Paul.* London: SPCK, 1955. **Burger, C.** *Schöpfung und Versöhnung. Studien zum liturgischen Gut im Kolosser- und Epheserbrief.* WMANT 46. Neukirchen: Neukirchener, 1975. **Burney, C. F.** "Christ as the APXH of Creation." *JTS* 27 (1926) 160–77. **Deichgräber, R.** *Gotteshymnus.* **Ernst, J.** *Pleroma und Pleroma Christi. Geschichte und Deutung eines Begriffs der paulinischen Antilegomena.* BU 5. Regensburg: Pustet, 1970. **Feuillet, A.** *Le Christ sagesse de Dieu d'après les épîtres pauliniennes.* Paris: Gabalda, 1966. **Gabathuler, H. J.** *Jesus Christus. Haupt der Kirche-Haupt der Welt. Der Christushymnus Colosser 1, 15–20 in der theologischen Forschung der letzten 130 Jahre.* ATANT 45. Zurich: Zwingli, 1965. **Gibbs, J. G.** *Creation and Redemption. A Study in Pauline Theology.* NovTSup 26. Leiden: Brill, 1971. **Hegermann, H.** *Die Vorstellung vom Schöpfungsmittler im hellenistischen Judentum und Urchristentum.* TU 82 Berlin: Akademie, 1961. **Jervell, J.** *Imago Dei. Gen 1, 26f im Spätjudentum, in der Gnosis und in den paulinischen Briefen.* FRLANT 76. Göttingen: Vandenhoeck und Ruprecht, 1960. **Käsemann, E.** "A Primitive Christian Baptismal Liturgy." *Essays,* 149–68. **Kehl, N.** *Der Christushymnus im Kolosserbrief. Eine motivgeschichtliche Untersuchung zu Kol 1, 12–20.* SBM 1. Stuttgart: Katholisches Bibelwerk, 1967. **Kim, S.** *An Exposition of Paul's Gospel in the Light of the Damascus Christophany. An Investigation into the Origin of Paul's Gospel.* University of Manchester: Unpublished Ph.D thesis, 1977. **Lähnemann, J.** *Kolosserbrief.* **Lyonnet, S.** "L'hymne christologique de l'Epître aux Colossiens et la fête juive du Nouvel An." *RSR* 48 (1960) 92–100. **McCown, W.** "The Hymnic Structure of Colossians 1:15–20." *EvQ* 51 (1979) 156–62. **Martin, R. P.** "An Early Christian Hymn (Col. 1:15–20)." *EvQ* 36 (1964) 195–205. **Michl, J.** "Die 'Versöhnung' (Kol 1, 20)." *TQ* 128 (1948) 442–62. **Münderlein, G.** "Die Erwählung durch das Pleroma. Bemerkungen zu Kol. i.19." *NTS* 8 (1961–62) 264–76. **Norden, E.** *Agnostos Theos. Untersuchungen zur Formengeschichte religiöser Rede.* 4th ed. Darmstadt: Wissenschaftliche Buchgesellschaft, 1956. **O'Brien, P. T.** "Col. 1:20 and the Reconciliation of all Things." *RTR* 33 (1974) 45–53. **O'Neill, J. C.** "The Source of the Christology in Colossians." *NTS* 26 (1979–80) 87–100. **Overfield, P. D.** "Pleroma: A Study in Content and Context." *NTS* 25 (1978–79) 384–96. **Pöhlmann, W.** "Die hymnischen All-Prädikation in Kol 1:15–20." *ZNW* 64 (1973) 53–74. **Sanders, J. T.** *The New Testament Christological Hymns. Their Historical Religious Background.* SNTSMS 15. Cambridge: University Press, 1971. **Schnackenburg, R.** "Die Aufnahme des Christushymnus durch den Verfasser des Kolosserbriefes." EKKNT Vorarbeiten 1. Neukirchen/Zurich: Neukirchener/Benziger, 1969, 33–50. **Schweizer, E.** "Die Kirche als Leib Christi in den paulinischen

Antilegomena." *TLZ* 86 (1961) 241–56. Reprinted in *Neotestamentica. Deutsche und englische Aufsätze, 1951–1963.* Zurich: Zwingli, 1963, 293–316. ———. "Kolosser 1, 15–20." EKKNT Vorarbeiten 1. Neukirchen/Zurich: Neukirchener/Benziger, 1969, 7–31. Reprinted in *Beiträge zur Theologie des Neuen Testaments. Neutestamentliche Aufsätze (1955–1970).* Zurich: Zwingli, 1970, 113–45. ———. *ThBer* 5 (1976) 163–191. ———. "Versöhnung des Alls. Kol 1, 20." *Jesus Christus in Historie und Theologie. Neutestamentliche Festschrift für Hans Conzelmann zum 60. Geburtstag,* ed. G. Strecker. Tübingen: Mohr, 1975, 487–501. **Vawter, B.** "The Colossians Hymn and the Principle of Redaction." *CBQ* 33 (1971) 62–81. **Vögtle, A.** *Das Neue Testament und die Zukunft des Kosmos.* Düsseldorf: Patmos, 1970. **Wengst, K.** *Christologische Formeln und Lieder des Urchristentums.* 2nd ed. SNT 7. Gütersloh: Mohn, 1972. **Zeilinger, F.** *Der Erstgeborene.*

Translation

15 *He is the image of the invisible God,*
The firstborn *over all creation,*
16 For *in him all things were created,*
In heaven and on earth,
Things visible and invisible,
Whether thrones or dominions, principalities or powers,
All things were created through him and for him;
17 And he *is before all things,*
And in him all things hold together.
18 And he *is the head of the body, the church.*
He is *the beginning,*
The firstborn *from the dead,*
In order that he might be pre-eminent in everything,
19 For *in him all the fullness was pleased to dwell,*
20 *And through him to reconcile all things to him,*
Whether things on earth or in heaven,
By making peace through his blood shed on the cross.

Form/Structure/Setting

(1) *Literary Form*

The weight of NT scholarly opinion today considers that Colossians 1:15–20 is a pre-Pauline "hymn" inserted into the letter's train of thought by the author. The preceding verses (12–14) are said to preserve the style of a confession (see above 19, 20) with its first person plurals ("we" and "us"), while the hymn itself makes no reference to the confessing community (all personal references are absent). Instead it asserts in exalted language the supremacy of Christ in creation and redemption. The immediately following words (vv 21–23) use the language of direct speech to apply themes from the hymn, especially that of reconciliation, to the Colossian community.

In describing the passage in this way it should be noted that the term "hymn" is not employed in the modern sense of what we understand by congregational hymns with metrical verses. Nor are we to think in terms of Greek poetic form. The category is used broadly, similar to that of "creed," and includes dogmatic, confessional, liturgical, polemical or doxological material (cf. Schweizer, 51, following Benoit, *Christianity*, 230, 231). The criteria are twofold: *(a) stylistic*—"a certain rhythmical lilt ascertainable when the passage is read aloud, a correspondence between words and phrases which are placed in the sentences in an obviously carefully selected position . . . the use of *parallelismus membrorum* (i.e. an arrangement into couplets); and traces of a rudimentary metre and the employment of rhetorical devices such as *homoeoteleuton*, alliteration, antithesis and *chiasmus*" (R. P. Martin, *Carmen Christi. Philippians ii. 5–11 in Recent Interpretation and in the Setting of Early Christian Worship* SNTSMS 4; Cambridge: University Press, 1967) 12, 13, and *(b) linguistic*—an unusual vocabulary, particularly the presence of theological terms, which is different from the language of the surrounding context (see R. P. Martin, "Aspects of Worship in the New Testament Church," *Vox Evangelica* 2 [1963] 6–32, especially 16–21, following the tests suggested by Stauffer; cf. Sanders, *Hymns*, 1–5).

So the presence of introductory relative clauses (ὅς ἐστιν, vv 15, 18), the positioning of words in such a way that lines and strophes may be arranged, chiasmus and *inclusio*, and unusual terms (which either do not appear elsewhere in the Pauline corpus or are used with a different meaning), are considered by the majority view as grounds for regarding this as a traditional hymnic piece.

Norden (*Agnostos Theos*, 250–54; cf. Gabathuler, *Jesus Christus*, 21–26) was the first scholar in recent times to subject the paragraph to a comprehensive form critical analysis and he sought to find in these verses "undoubtedly old traditional material" which he considered came originally from Jewish circles influenced by Greek ideas. Evidence of the latter was a Stoic "all"-formula (cf. 1:16, 17) and in a Platonic-type division of the cosmos into "things seen and things unseen." He noted two strophes or stanzas of unequal length (vv 15–18*a* and 18*b*–20). The first, beginning with "who is" (ὅς ἐστιν) of verse 15, treats the theme of Christ and creation, while the second, commencing with the same striking relative clause "who is" in verse 18, refers to Christ and the church. The term "firstborn" (πρωτότοκος) occurs in both stanzas (vv 15 and 18).

Since Norden's time continental scholars, in particular, have sought to determine the precise structure of this so-called hymnic paragraph. So, for example, Lohmeyer (40–68; cf. Gabathuler, *Jesus Christus*, 29–39), who described verses 13–29 as "the order of a primitive Christian worship service," which opened with a thanksgiving prayer (v 12), saw the hymn consisting of two strophes, each in seven lines (1:15–16*a*, 1:18–20) which were connected by a section of three lines (1:16*f*–17).

Käsemann (*Essays*, 149–68; cf. Gabathuler, *Jesus Christus*, 49–61) thought that the passage consisted of two strophes each with six lines (1:15–16, 1:18*b*–20), which were connected by 1:17–18*a*. But he, like many others since (see the lists in Benoit, *Christianity*, 238) regarded the words "the church" (τῆς ἐκκλησίας) of verse 18*a* together with those of verse 20*b*, "through the blood of his cross" (διὰ τοῦ αἵματος τοῦ σταυροῦ αὐτοῦ), as interpolations (for an assessment of Käsemann's presentation with special reference to his proposed origin of the hymn see 37, 38). According to Masson (104–107; cf. Gabathuler, *Jesus Christus*, 42–49) the parallelism was more Semitic than Greek and he sought to arrange the text in five strophes of four lines each on a supposed metrical basis (vv 15–16*b*, 16*c–f*, 17–18, 19–20*b*, 20*c–f*).

J. M. Robinson ("A Formal Analysis of Colossians 1:15–20," *JBL* 76 [1957] 270–87; cf. Gabathuler, *Jesus Christus*, 80–88; R. G. Hamerton-Kelly, *Pre-Existence, Wisdom and the Son of Man* [SNTSMS 21; Cambridge: University Press, 1973] 168–74) saw a close correspondence between the two stanzas with matching phrases and terms. However, to achieve this symmetry he has to delete from the existing text a number of phrases (the last clause of v 18 has been moved to the end of the second strophe, the first clause of the same verse loses its reference to the church, and the list of heavenly powers in v 16 is dropped). Robinson then reconstructs a hypothetical first draft of the hymn which the author of the epistle has taken over and supplemented, at the same time reinterpreting the meaning of the words.

E. Bammel ("Versuch zu Col 1:15–20," *ZNW* 52 [1961] 88–95; cf. Gabathuler, *Jesus Christus*, 118–21) contended that the hymn consisted of two strophes, each containing an elaborate chiastic parallelism and being introduced by "who is" (ὅς ἐστιν). However, his interpretation does not give sufficient emphasis to the parallel occurrence of "he is" (*αὐτός ἐστιν*) in verses 17 and 18. In addition, verses 17, 18*a* and 20 which contain teaching vital to the hymn are left unattached to the main structure (cf. Martin, *NCB*, 64).

Important and influential contributions to this ongoing debate (it is not possible in the brief compass of this note to examine all recent works on vv 15–20) have been made by Schweizer (note the bibliographical references to his writings in his recent commentary, 44–74). Observing the formal parallelism between verses 15 and 18 ("he is," ὅς ἐστιν, and "firstborn," πρωτότοκος), the repetition of "because in him" (*ὅτι ἐν αὐτῷ*, vv 16 and 19) and "all things through him" (*τὰ πάντα δι' αὐτοῦ*, vv 16 and 20), Schweizer arranged the hymn into two strophes (vv 15, 16 and 18*b*–20) between which stood a middle strophe *(Zwischenstrophe)* or stanza (vv 17–18*a*) that acted as a bridge (cf. Lähnemann, *Kolosserbrief*, 38). The first stanza consisted of three lines in which the cosmic Christ is praised as the Lord of creation, the One who brought the universe into existence and who directs its destiny. The middle stanza partly repeats the thought of Christ's preexistent activity and then proceeds to assert that he is the unifying principle which holds the universe together. The final strophe praises this cosmic Lord who embodies the divine "fullness" (*πλήρωμα*). As the risen One, he is God's agent in bringing the universe into harmony with God's purposes through reconciliation.

To secure an original hymn of perfect symmetry, with each stanza consisting of three lines and having a discernible rhythmical pattern, Schweizer omitted four phrases. These comments (v 16, "thrones or dominions or principalities or authorities"; v 18, "the church"; v 18, "that in everything he may be pre-eminent"; and v 20, "making peace by the blood of his cross") which exceed the rhythmical order and parallelism of the original hymn are, according to Schweizer, the author's own additions to a composition that was already in circulation prior to his writing the letter. He has thus corrected the theology of the hymn, for, with the exception of the first, these additions disagree with the theological conceptions of the original composition: at verse 16 "thrones or dominions or principalities or authorities" is a clarification of the statement, "all things in heaven and on earth," relating it to a special issue the letter addresses itself to, namely the subordination of all heavenly powers to Christ. The additional words of verse 18, "the church," reinterpret the hymn so as to rebut the false idea that Christ's body is to be identified with the world or that redemption was a merely physical or super-physical event. The third comment, "that in everything he might be pre-eminent," verse 18, is another reinterpretation in a Pauline sense, while in verse 20 the notion of reconciliation is corrected to that of making peace, i.e. pacification in the sense Roman emperors understood it. Finally, into a theology that focused exclusively on resurrection and exaltation the author introduces the Pauline stress on the cross as the reconciling act of Christ (v 20).

In spite of the increasing acceptance within certain circles of this reconstruction there seem to be considerable difficulties in the opinion of the present writer. If the author of Colossians made corrections to the hymn, as Schweizer has suggested, then why did he allow certain elements which were different from his own theology to remain? If reconciliation and pacification (v 20), to take but one example, are essentially different, why did he not remove the idea which did not fit in with his own view, especially as the formal structure of the hymn had been "ruined" anyway? To remove the so-called intruding elements ought not to have been difficult for the author of Colossians. Further, why is it necessary to consider "reconciliation" and "making peace" (including the notion of pacification) as essentially different (cf. Schweizer, *Neotestamentica*, 326)? In our judgment a more adequate exegesis can be given (see 55–57). But these questions only serve to raise the more general issue as to whether one can reasonably attempt to discover the original form of the hymn anyway. Lohse, 44, for example, has criticized the reconstructions of Robinson, Bammel and Schweizer on the grounds that: *(a)* their alterations meddle too much with the given text; *(b)* they have not provided sufficient evidence to make probable the hypothesis of two stanzas of exactly parallel structures (Schweizer's division of a middle strophe has been criticized on the grounds that v 16*c* with its ἔκτισται belongs to the preceding strophe as part of an *inclusio;* so Kehl, *Christushymnus,* 43, 44, and cf. Schnackenburg, EKKNT Vorarbeiten 1, 35); while *(c)* most of the phrases which are considered to be additions to an earlier shorter hymn are in fact statements which expand the meaning of the lines already plotted (cf. Pöhlmann's comments, *ZNW* 64 [1973] 53–74, with reference to the "all"-formula). Gabathuler (*Jesus Christus,* 125–31), at the end of his study on the history of research into chapter 1:15–20, concluded that there was still considerable uncertainty about the stylistic criteria. For example, when criteria of form and content differ, which take precedence? Or when different formal criteria lead to different results, which stylistic tests are to be followed?

In spite of the considerable amount of scholarly work carried out since Gabathuler's researches were published (1965), no consensus has been reached about the number and content of the stanzas in verses 15–20, or about possible Pauline or post-Pauline additions (cf. M. Wolter, *Rechtfertigung und zukünftiges Heil. Untersuchungen zu Röm 5, 1–11,* [BNZW 43; Berlin: Walter de Gruyter, 1978] 49; note the variations, and these do not include all possibilities, listed by Benoit, *Christianity,* 238). Even Lohse's conservative reconstruction (44, 45) with its two stanzas of unequal length which do not correspond to each other in all their details suggests, on stylistic grounds, that the latter strophe begins with the words of verse 18*b*, "He is the beginning, the firstborn from the dead" (ὅς ἐστιν ἀρχή, πρωτότοκος ἐκ τῶν νεκρῶν), so paralleling the opening statements of verse 15, "He is the image of the invisible God, the firstborn of all creation" (ὅς ἐστιν εἰκών . . . , πρωτότοκος πάσης κτίσεως). On this view the assertion of verse 18*a*, "He is the head of the body," forms a fitting climax to the first part of the poem (or at least the middle stanza) and refers to Christ's headship over the entire cosmos. But as the text stands this statement is a soteriological one. It is not certain that the words, "the church" (τῆς ἐκκλησίας), belonged to the original hymn; and although most recent writers regard the words as a redactional addition Kehl (*Christushymnus*, 93, 97), Hegermann (*Schöpfungsmittler*, 106) and Gibbs (*Creation*, 105; cf. Feuillet, *Christ*, 217–28) have argued that they are essential to the meaning of verse 18*a*.

No single reconstruction is completely convincing. Kümmel's comment (*Introduction*, 343) is worth quoting at length:

> . . . the numerous reconstructions of the hymn expanded by the author that have been undertaken since Lohmeyer's analysis have scarcely led to a really convincing result. Indeed, the assumption is not yet proved that a *hymn constructed according to a strict scheme* has been used and that accordingly every fragment of a sentence beyond the scheme must stem from the author of Col. What is far more likely is that the author of Col himself [whom Kümmel regards as Paul] has formed the hymn, utilizing traditional material . . .

(This is essentially the position of Dibelius-Greeven, Moule, Maurer and Feuillet, etc.)

It seems, therefore, better to speak of certain parallels, observed originally by Norden (note the subsequent treatments by Kehl, *Christushymnus*, 30–34, and Zeilinger, *Der Erstgeborene*, 39–43). So ὅς ἐστιν εἰκών ("he is the image," v 15) corresponds to ὅς ἐστιν ἀρχή ("he is the beginning," v 18); πρωτότοκος πάσης κτίσεως ("firstborn of all creation," v 15) is parallel to πρωτότοκος ἐκ τῶν νεκρῶν ("firstborn from the dead," v 18), while each of the relative clauses in turn is followed by a causal clause beginning with ὅτι ("because"): ὅτι ἐν αὐτῷ ἐκτίσθη ("because in him all things were created," v 16) and ὅτι ἐν αὐτῷ εὐδόκησεν ("because in him . . . was pleased," v 19). The cosmic dimensions of Christ's rule round out verse 16, εἴτε θρόνοι εἴτε κυριότητες εἴτε ἀρχαὶ εἴτε ἐξουσίαι ("whether thrones or dominions, principalities or powers"), and verse 20, εἴτε τὰ ἐπὶ τῆς γῆς εἴτε τὰ ἐν τοῖς οὐρανοῖς ("whether things on earth or in the heavens"). One may note the frequent use of πᾶς ("all") and the formal chiasmus in verses 16c and 20:

a τὰ πάντα ("all things")	*b* καὶ δι' αὐτοῦ ("and through him")
b δι' αὐτοῦ καί ("through him and")	*a* τὰ πάντα ("all things").

In verse 16 two examples of chiasmus occur. In the first, two lines are constructed chiastically in synonymous parallelism:

ὅτι ἐν αὐτῷ ἐκτίσθη τὰ πάντα
τὰ πάντα δι' αὐτοῦ καὶ εἰς αὐτὸν ἔκτισται·
"For in him all things were created
All things were created through him and for him."

In the second instance τὰ πάντα ("all things") is expanded and made more explicit with the words:

ἐν τοῖς οὐρανοῖς καὶ ἐπὶ τῆς γῆς
  τὰ ὁρατὰ καὶ τὰ ἀόρατα
"In the heavens and on earth,
things visible and invisible."

It has also been suggested that the repeated τὰ πάντα ("all things") and the verb ἔκτισται ("created") of the concluding line is an example of *inclusio* which binds the second chiasmus together.

Finally, the formal correspondence between verses 17 and 18 needs to be noted:

17 καὶ αὐτός ἐστιν πρὸ πάντων
18 καὶ αὐτός ἐστιν ἡ κεφαλή
"And he is before all things . . .
And he is the head . . ."

(2) *Background*

The possible backgrounds to these verses suggested by scholars have been remarkably varied. The following suggestions have been the most influential (cf. R. P. Martin, *Colossians: The Church's Lord and the Christian's Liberty* [Exeter: Grand Rapids, MI: 1972]; 1982 reprint, Palm Springs, CA 40–44):

(a) Käsemann (*Essays,* 149–68) thought that once the additions "the church" (τῆς ἐκκλησίας, v 18) and "through the blood of his cross" (διὰ τοῦ αἵματος τοῦ σταυροῦ αὐτοῦ, v 20), a mere eight words out of 112, were removed the hymn no longer displayed any specifically Christian characteristics. Originally it was a *pre-Christian Gnostic text* which dealt with the metaphysical and supra-historical drama of the Gnostic Redeemer. The hymn was taken over in Christian usage in a baptismal liturgical reinterpretation (integral to Käsemann's argument is the view that vv 12–14 were known in a pre-Pauline baptismal context and served as an "introit" to the hymn; for a critique of this see 19, 20) and finally cited by the author of Colossians in a refutation (!) of the Gnostic counter-movement at Colossae. For Käsemann creation and redemption were related constituents in the myth of the primeval man and Redeemer. He broke into the sphere of death as the pathfinder for those who belong to him. The purpose of the Redeemer's incarnation was to achieve an objective reconciliation—a reconciliation of the whole universe, i.e. of all the aeons that make up the cosmos. Such pacification (v 20) is neither personal nor moral. Instead, it constitutes a recognition on the part of these cosmic forces that the one aeon is Lord. The conflicting elements are pacified and the Redeemer announces universal peace.

Yet Käsemann's thesis is unconvincing for the following reasons: first, apart from his treatment of the strophes on stylistic grounds which is doubtful (note Gabathuler's criticisms, *Jesus Christus,* 52) even if it could be argued satisfactorily that the phrases in verses 18 and 20 were additions, there is the complex issue as to whether a Gnostic redemption saga has any bearing on our understanding of the New Testament message, and the legitimacy of appealing to second century documents for support. Second, several terms in the paragraph have an Old Testament ring about them, for example, the repeated references to the divine creation (vv 15, 16) and the verb *εὐδοκέω* ("be pleased," v 19) used in the OT of God's electing decree (Lohse, 45; see the exegesis below). Third, Schweizer and Lohse have correctly pointed out that the Christian character of the phrase *πρωτότοκος ἐκ τῶν νεκρῶν* ("the firstborn from among the dead," v 18) cannot be doubted. Indeed, the former contends that Käsemann's thesis of a pre-Christian hymn is "wrecked" by this phrase (Schweizer, *Neotestamentica,* 297, who is followed by Lohse, 45, and Pöhlmann, *ZNW* 64 [1973] 54; note especially the treatment of Kehl, *Christushymnus,* 88–93). The fourth and perhaps main criticism leveled against Käsemann's theory concerns the teaching about reconciliation. It is doubtful whether there is any non-Christian parallel to the Redeemer who comes to earth and unites God and man. Schweizer (*Neotestamentica,* 297) and others (cf. Pöhlmann, *ZNW* 64 [1973] 54, who consider that the attempt to find a pre-Christian original form of the hymn has now been given up by scholars) regard this as a distinctively Christian motif (the references in Codex *V* of the Nag Hammadi texts and the *Apoc Adam* which are thought to present an example of a redemption myth unaffected by the Christian story of Jesus are disputed as to their significance, cf. R. McL. Wilson, *Gnosis and the New Testament* [Oxford: Blackwell, 1968] 138, 139; American edition [Philadelphia: Fortress]).

(b) The second approach is to understand the hymn's religious message against the background of *Rabbinic Judaism.* Burney (*JTS* 27 [1926] 160–77) and W. D. Davies (*Paul and Rabbinic Judaism. Some Rabbinic Elements in Pauline Theology.* 2nd ed. London: SPCK, 1955, 150–52; 4th American edition [Philadelphia: Fortress, 1980] have been the chief exponents of this view. The former drew attention to the many similarities between the hymn and OT passages, particularly Proverbs 8 and Genesis 1 as interpreted by the rabbis with reference to Wisdom. Paul is thought to have given a meditative exposition on the opening words of the Bible *(bᵉrēšîṯ),* in which every possible meaning the rabbis were used to extracting from Genesis 1:1 ("in the beginning God created") and Proverbs 8:22 ("the Lord begat me in the beginning [*rēšîṯ*] of his way") was said to apply to the church's Lord. Thus, the need to call in extraneous, Hellenistic sources to explain the passage would be reduced if Burney's thesis is correct.

Although this approach has been criticized for assuming that Paul's opposition at Colossae sprang *solely* from a Jewish source (cf. Gabathuler, *Jesus Christus,* 28, 29) and that the theory is too ingenious (would a predominantly Gentile church have understood rabbinic methods of interpretation?), several positive points emerge. First, Burney and Davies are right in underlining the importance of the OT statements about creation as a background to the hymnic piece. Second, the significance attached to the Wisdom tradition in which Wisdom's function in creation is understood in Colossians 1:15–18 as being transferred to Christ is a point accepted by exegetes who have preferred to seek the background to the paragraph in Hellenistic Judaism (Pöhlmann, *ZNW* 64 [1973] 73, has shown that although the "all"-formula was frequently used in many prayer texts of the ancient world it did not appear often in the prayer traditions of early Rabbinic Judaism). So although Burney's detailed argument may be open to question, his drawing attention to OT parallels which clearly lie close at hand—rather than some uncertain parallels which have been claimed in Gnosticism, Stoicism and elsewhere—is commendable.

(c) The third general approach considers the background to Colossians 1:15–20 is to be sought in *Hellenistic Judaism.* This is the view of many continental scholars, especially Schweizer whose writings on this theme have been influential (cf. the references in his *commentary,* 44–74). The approach seeks to take seriously the character of the church as predominantly Gentile Christian and recognizes that the Jewish elements in the heresy which troubled the Colossians stemmed from the Dispersion. Schweizer considers that Colossians 1:15–20 may be part of a wider indebtedness of NT Christology to a type of Hellenistic Jewish speculation in which a central place was given to the Wisdom of God. The theology of the Christian group that created the hymn can be clearly seen from the many parallels to it found in the Wisdom literature. Christ is depicted as the pre-existent Mediator of creation and the One who holds together the cosmos, preserving the world from dissolution. The new point, made by the group which created the hymn, is that: "In Christ heaven and earth are reconciled again" (*Neotestamentica,* 325).

According to Schweizer the author of Colossians *corrected* the theology of the hymn in two ways: first, by inserting into the passage four additional comments (noted above in the section dealing with the literary form); second, in his commentary which follows (1:21–23) the author stressed that it is mankind, not nature, that is reconciled—and this through Christ's death on the cross.

We have already drawn attention to some of the considerable problems associated with Schweizer's suggestions about the author's "corrections" to the hymn (note Schnackenburg's pertinent question about additions or corrections, EKKNT Vorarbeiten 1, 37). It seems very unusual that the writer should allow certain elements which were different from his own theology to remain after he had corrected the hymn. Further, it is not at all certain that the author has varied the hymn's theology in the commentary immediately following the passage (1:21–23). In our judgment a more adequate explanation is possible (see the exegesis below). But Schweizer's point regarding the indebtedness of NT Christology to a general "Wisdom" background in Hellenistic Judaism may be correct, provided we keep in mind the following points: (i) a sharp distinction between Palestinian and Hellenistic Judaism, later reflected in the early church, can hardly be sustained in the light of recent research. Although this distinction has been axiomatic in some NT scholarly circles it has been rightly questioned by I. H. Marshall ("Palestinian and Hellenistic Christianity: Some Critical Comments," *NTS* 19 [1972–73] 271–87) and M. Hengel (in his magisterial work, *Judaism and Hellenism. Studies in their Encounter in Palestine during the Early Hellenistic Period,* Tr. J. Bowden [Philadelphia: Fortress, 1974]).

(ii) While the predicates of and activities ascribed to Wisdom in Hellenistic Judaism are akin to several of the statements made about Christ in Colossians 1:15–20 (see the detailed exegetical comments below) the differences ought not to be overlooked. There is, for example, no parallel in Jewish Wisdom literature (or in the rest of the extant Jewish materials for that matter) to the statement about Christ as the goal of creation: "all things have been created through him and *for him* (εἰς αὐτόν)," verse 16.

(iii) Further, while the statements about Wisdom—as the "image," "firstborn," etc., and the one through whom the universe was created—are understood in a quasi-personal way within the framework of Hellenistic Judaism, the one spoken of in our paragraph of Colossians is the living person, Jesus Christ, whom Paul had met face to face on the Damascus road. To the early Christians, as to Paul, Jesus Christ was the incarnate Wisdom of God.

If we suppose that the passage (along with several others in the NT: cf. Heb 1:1–4; John 1:1–18) gives evidence of an indebtedness to a general Wisdom background in the OT and Judaism, we still have to bear in mind that these predicates and activities ascribed to Wisdom came to be applied to Jesus of Nazareth, recently crucified and risen from the dead. How did this come about? The early Christians may have had the thought-forms provided by this Wisdom background but the application of these to Jesus Christ is still not explained by the background itself.

(3) *Authorship*

From what has already been written above, it is clear that the majority of recent writers think that the hymnic passage of chapter 1:15–20 is non-Pauline. (A minority including Lohmeyer, Percy, Dibelius, Maurer, Moule, Bruce, Feuillet, Kümmel and Caird take the paragraph to be Pauline.)

Two main arguments are advanced against the Pauline authorship of the hymn: first, a significant number of terms which do not appear elsewhere in the Pauline corpus, or which are used with a different meaning, turn up in the hymn (Lohse, 42, and Deichgräber, *Gotteshymnus,* 152, 153). So the Christological predicate εἰκὼν τοῦ θεοῦ ("image of God," v 15) occurs only in a formula-type sentence in 2 Corinthians 4:4. ὁρατός ("visible," v 16) is used only here in the NT while ἀόρατος ("invisible," vv 15, 16) is unusual (Rom 1:20; 1 Tim 1:17; Heb 11:27) and is never employed in contrast to ὁρατός ("visible"). θρόνοι ("thrones," v 16) appears nowhere else in Paul while κυριότης ("dominion," v 16) turns up only once more (Eph 1:21). The intransitive form of συνίστημι ("be established," v 17) is otherwise not used by Paul. In a Christological context Paul refers to Christ as ἀπαρχή ("firstfruits," 1 Cor 15:20) but never as ἀρχή ("beginning," v 18). πρωτεύω ("preeminent," v 18) and εἰρηνοποιέω ("make peace," v 20) are *hapax legomena* in the NT. The verb κατοικέω ("dwell," v 19) appears again only in Colossians 2:9 (which refers back to the hymn) and Ephesians 3:17, while ἀποκαταλλάσσω ("reconcile," v 20) only in Ephesians 2:16. Paul mentions the "blood of Christ" (v 20) only where he takes over traditional Christian expressions (Rom 3:25;

5:9; 1 Cor 10:16; 11:25, 27; cf. also Eph 1:7; 2:13), while the combination *αἷμα τοῦ σταυροῦ αὐτοῦ* ("blood of his cross," v 20) is without parallel.

But these observations do not present a convincing case against the Pauline authorship of verses 15–20 (note the critique of Kim, *Paul's Gospel*, 183–87). That the Christological predicate *εἰκὼν τοῦ θεοῦ* ("image of God") appears only in a formulalike sentence in 2 Corinthians 4:4 proves nothing (against Jervell's circular argument, *Imago*, 196, 197, 209; and Deichgräber, *Gotteshymnus*, 152, 153, who by asserting that *εἰκών* and *πρωτότοκος* are pre-Pauline and pre-Christian fails to ask who applied them to Christ for the first time: Paul or someone else before him? No one denies that *εἰκὼν τοῦ θεοῦ*, for example, is a predicate of Wisdom or appears in Gen 1:27). It was possible for Paul to have composed the confession that Jesus Christ is the *εἰκὼν τοῦ θεοῦ* ("image of God") and used it both in 2 Corinthians 4:4 and Colossians 1:15 (see below). Further, what does the observation about rare words—*ὁρατός, ἀόρατος, θρόνοι, κυριότητες, συνίστημι, κατοικέω, πρωτεύω* and *εἰρηνοποιέω*—prove? Was Paul incapable of using these words if the subject matter so demanded? Were there better or more natural terms at the writer's disposal if he needed to introduce these particular motifs (cf. Moule, 61, 62)? *ὁρατός* ("visible") and *ἀόρατος* ("invisible") are not strange words for one who uses the latter for the invisible nature of God in Romans 1:20. *θρόνοι* ("thrones") and *κυριότητες* ("dominions") are perfectly intelligible terms to have used if Paul, with special reference to the Colossian heresy, emphasizes that even the cosmic principalities and powers were created in Christ. The derivatives of the stem *καταλλαγ*—("reconcile")—occur only in Paul in the NT (Percy, *Probleme*, 86). The noun *ἀρχή* ("beginning") rather than *ἀπαρχή* ("first-fruits") is entirely fitting in a passage where the supremacy of Christ is emphasized and where the first creation and the new creation are paralleled, particularly as Christ is designated as the beginning of the new creation and the One who has initiated it by his resurrection. Again it is doubtful whether all the passages mentioning the blood of Christ are pre-Pauline (cf. Rom 5:9). But even if this were the case, Paul would presumably have made it his own and therefore could still have used it as such in the paragraph of verses 15–20. As in Romans 5:1–11 the motifs of reconciliation and peace are tied in with the blood of Christ for it is the means of atonement (cf. Rom 3:25).

The second argument against the Pauline authorship of Colossians 1:15–20 is based on structural grounds so that an original hymn, reconstructed according to rhythm, parallelism and strophic arrangement, has been taken over and reworked by the author of Colossians. But if our arguments above—about the uncertainty of the stylistic criteria, the number and content of the stanzas in verses 15–20, the possible Pauline additions, and thus the question of whether a hymn was constructed according to a strict scheme at all—are correct, then this argument too is not proven.

In other words, the case against the Pauline authorship is considerably more flimsy than its more ardent advocates would have us believe. We may thus ask: Is it impossible to imagine that Paul was using a hymn which he had earlier composed (so Feuillet, *Christ*, 246–73) with interpretative additions or expansions here and there (but not corrections or contradictions) in view of the situation of his readers, or expressing in an exalted hymnic style his beliefs about Christ in view of the situation of his readers and making use of some of their language? In our view one or other of these alternatives is more likely than that the hymn is pre-Pauline.

Recently Kim (*Paul's Gospel*, 173–339, especially 173–79) has argued that it was Paul who initiated the "identification" of Jesus with the divine Wisdom in the early church, and this as early as the first half of the '30s. He has pointed out that the designation of Christ as the *εἰκὼν τοῦ θεοῦ* ("image of God," 2 Cor 4:4; Col 1:15; cf. the almost synonymous *μορφὴ θεοῦ*, "form of God," Phil 2:6; Martin, *Carmen Christi*, 99–133, especially 107–120, and Kim, *Paul's Gospel*, 247–60) and the theme of Christians being conformed or transformed to the image of Christ appear explicitly only in Paul's letters of the NT (Rom 8:29; 1 Cor 15:49; cf. v 52; cf. Col 3:9; 10; Eph 4:24). In John (cf. the λόγος in chapter 1:1–18 becoming incarnate and revealing the Father: 12:45; 14:9; note too the statement that the children of God "shall be like him when he appears, for we shall see him as he is," 1 John 3:2) and Hebrews (note the Wisdom Christology of Heb 1:3 [cf. Wisd 7:26] where the Son is the "radiance [*ἀπαύγασμα*] of God's glory" and the "exact representation [*χαρακτήρ*] of God's nature"; cf. also the theme of Christians sharing the salvation, perfection and glorification pioneered by the Son: 2:10, 11; cf. 5:9; 6:20; 10:14; 12:2) the conceptual thought forms are similar to those of Paul, but the latter's actual expressions of Christ as the "image of God" and of the Christian's being conformed or transformed into that image are different.

Kim goes on to argue that Paul saw the exalted Christ in glory as the "image of God" and as the Son of God on the road to Damascus. This perception led him to conceive of Christ in terms of the personified Wisdom of God. Paul's Wisdom Christology was rooted in the Damascus revelation. The OT and Jewish backgrounds provided him with certain categories and thought-forms with which he could interpret the Damascus experience and produce his theology. (A similar argument has been used by Kim, *Paul's Gospel*, 392–97, to show that " 'reconciliation' is a distinctive Pauline theologoumenon to describe the purpose of the atonement God has wrought in Christ" [392], and more recently by R. P. Martin, *Reconciliation. A Study of Paul's Theology.* London: Marshall, Morgan and Scott. Atlanta, GA: John Knox, 1981.)

If these arguments are convincing so that Paul was the first to identify Christ with the *εἰκὼν τοῦ θεοῦ*, and the Wisdom of God according to an OT and Jewish background, then the case for the Pauline authorship of the hymn is considerably strengthened. In fact, the only other alternative possible, if Kim's arguments are correct, is that the hymn is *post-Pauline* (a point that critical scholars do not accept) and has been utilized by the post-Pauline author of Colossians for his own purposes in writing the letter. (See the introduction for our discussion of the authorship of Colossians.)

Comment

15. *ὅς ἐστιν εἰκὼν τοῦ θεοῦ τοῦ ἀοράτου.* The magnificent hymn in praise of Christ begins by asserting that he, the beloved Son, is "the image (*εἰκών*)

of the invisible God." The very nature and character of God have been perfectly revealed in him; in him the invisible has become visible. Both Old and New Testaments make it plain that "no one has ever seen God." The Fourth Evangelist, however, adds that "the only begotten Son, who is in the bosom of the Father, has made him known" (John 1:18). A similar statement is made elsewhere by Paul who, probably with the Damascus road experience in mind, asserts that "the light of the gospel of the glory of Christ, who is the image of God (εἰκὼν τοῦ θεοῦ)" had dawned upon him. The God whose creative Word in the beginning called light to shine forth from the darkness had now shone in his heart "to give the light of the knowledge of the glory of God in the face of Jesus Christ" (2 Cor 4:4, 6; cf. 3:18). The same point is made in another way by the writer to the Hebrews that Christ is the "radiance (ἀπαύγασμα) of God's glory and the very impress of his being" (Heb 1:3).

εἰκών ("image") is employed by Paul on a number of occasions not only with reference to Christ as the image of God (here and 2 Cor 4:4), but also regarding the corollary of the increasing transformation of the people of Christ into that same image by the power of the indwelling Spirit (2 Cor 3:18; cf. Col 3:10; Eph 4:24), so that at the end nothing remains of the earthly image in those who finally show forth the image of the heavenly man (1 Cor 15:49; Rom 8:29; cf. Bruce, *Paul,* 123; see above, where it is pointed out that linguistically, though not conceptually, Paul's use of "image" in this twofold way is unique in the NT).

Regarding Colossians 1:15, we are reminded of the OT where it is stated that man was made in God's image (Gen 1:26, 27) and for his glory (Isa .43:7). He is, the apostle states, "the image and glory of God" (1 Cor 11:7). Some have suggested it is difficult to separate Paul's depicting of the risen Christ as the second man, the last Adam, from his view of Christ as the image of God and the revealer of his glory (Bruce, *Paul,* 123). These two strands may well coalesce.

But Genesis 1 alone does not adequately explain the background to our phrase in Colossians 1:15 as Burney (*JTS* 27 [1926] 160–77) and others thought. On the other hand, attempts to understand the meaning of Paul's statement against an exclusively Greek background are not convincing either (see Feuillet, *Christ,* 166–75, for references). For although Plato had already called the cosmos the visible image of God (*Tim* 92*c*) and this notion was taken up elsewhere (cf. Lohse, 47), it does not explain the meaning of Paul's use of εἰκών here. Rather, as many scholars have argued, the Hellenistic-Jewish texts of Proverbs 8:22 and Wisdom 7:25 (cf. Kehl, *Christushymnus,* 52–81, especially 61–67, and Gibbs, *Creation,* 102, for references) provide a more convincing background to the meaning of "image." This term, used to refer to the divine revelation, was taken over in Hellenistic Judaism and transferred to "Wisdom." According to Proverbs 8:22, Wisdom was with the Lord at the beginning of his work, the creation of the world, while in Wisdom 7:25 the divine Wisdom which is personified, is described as the "image" (εἰκών) of God's goodness, i.e. the one who reveals the goodness of God.

Paul, in common with other NT writers (John 1:4; Heb 1:3), identified Christ with the Wisdom of God (see further Kim, *Paul's Gospel,* 173–339), ascribing to him certain activities which are predicated of personified Wisdom in the OT and Jewish literature.

As the first title of majesty, "image" emphasizes Christ's relation to God. The term points to his revealing of the Father on the one hand and his pre-existence on the other—it is both functional and ontological.

πρωτότοκος πάσης κτίσεως. If "image" (*εἰκών*) emphasizes Christ's relation to God, then the second title, "firstborn of all creation" (on the omission of the article before "creation" see Robertson, *Grammar*, 772, and BDF, para. 275[3]) designates his relationship to the creation. Stripped from its context and from other Pauline statements about Christ this phrase might be understood to include him among created things (as simply the "eldest" of the "family": at Rom 8:29 *πρωτότοκος* appears to be used in this inclusive sense).

But the context makes it plain that the title cannot refer to him as the first of all created beings since the immediately following words, which provide a commentary on the title (*ὅτι*), emphasize the point that he is the one by whom the whole creation came into being. Further, apart from the incompatibility of this thought with the teaching of Paul in general about the person and work of Christ, such an understanding is not required by the word *πρωτότοκος* ("firstborn") itself.

The term "firstborn" was frequently used in the LXX (130 times), mostly in genealogies and historical narratives, to indicate temporal priority and sovereignty of rank. Frequently "firstborn" was employed to denote one who had a special place in the father's love. So Israel is called "my beloved son" (*υἱὸς πρωτότοκός μου*, Exod 4:22), a phrase that expresses the particularly close relation between God and Israel. In Judaism the messianic king, as well as Israel, the patriarchs and the Torah are given this title of distinction (for references see Str-B 3, 256–58, 626; Michaelis, *TDNT* 6, 873–76).

Within the NT "firstborn" (*πρωτότοκος*), which occurs in the plural at Hebrews 11:28 and 12:23, always refers in the singular to Jesus Christ. In most of these contexts while priority of time is in view (Rom 8:29; cf. the parallel expressions in 1 Cor 15:20 and Acts 26:23; Rev 1:5) the notion of supremacy or priority of rank tends to dominate.

The title "firstborn," used of Christ here and in verse 18, echoes the wording of Psalm 89:27, where God says of the Davidic king: "I also will make him my firstborn, the highest of the kings of the earth." But as many have noted this title belongs to Jesus Christ not only as the Messiah of David's line, but also as the Wisdom of God (so Bruce, 194, 195, and Lohse, 48), a background we observed in connection with him as the "image of the invisible God." (For further references to Wisdom see Wilckens and Fohrer, *TDNT* 7, 465–526.)

While Jewish writers speculated about Wisdom by giving to it a quasipersonal status (it was present with God from all eternity, Wisd 9:9; sharing the divine throne, Wisd 9:4; existing before heaven and earth, and according to Philo was the "firstborn son," *πρωτόγονος υἱός*: *Conf Ling* 146; *Agric* 51; *Som* 1.215; the instrument "through whom the universe came into existence," *Fug* 109), the NT writers know that "whether they speak of this Wisdom expressly or only by allusion they are speaking of a living person, one whom some of them had met face to face. To them all, as to Paul, Jesus Christ was the incarnate Wisdom of God" (Bruce, 195).

As πρωτότοκος Christ is unique, being distinguished from all creation (cf. Heb 1:6). He is both prior to and supreme over that creation since he is its Lord.

16. *ὅτι ἐν αὐτῷ ἐκτίσθη τὰ πάντα.* The statement about Christ's unique position as "firstborn of all creation" is now given more explicit proof in the words: "*because* (ὅτι) in him all things were created." The passive form "were created" (ἐκτίσθη) indicates that God is the Creator, a point that is reiterated later in the verse when the clause is taken up again with the statement "all things were created [*sc.* by God] (ἔκτισται)through him and for him." In the first clause the aorist tense is employed to draw attention to the historical act, while the second reference uses the perfect to focus on creation's continuing existence. And the historical act of God "in him" establishes that Christ *is* (and "continues to be," so Schweizer, *Beiträge,* 123) the "firstborn of all creation."

The phrase "in him" (ἐν αὐτῷ) has occasioned some difficulty. Many commentators take the words in an instrumental sense. So Lohse (50) contends, for the following reasons, that they mean all things have been created "through him" (= δι' αὐτοῦ): first, the religious background, i.e. Jewish speculations about Wisdom, require that the phrase be regarded in this way. To treat it as referring to location, he claims, is possible only on the basis of a different history of religions background. Second, the parallel clause at the end of the verse with its phrase "through him" (δι' αὐτοῦ) is said to argue for this interpretation; while, third, the parallel statements from 1 Corinthians 8:6 ("through whom are all things," δι' οὗ τὰ πάντα) and John 1:3 ("all things were made through him," πάντα δι' αὐτοῦ ἐγένετο) are thought to support it.

Quite clearly the point about Christ as the Mediator of creation includes the notion of instrumentality. But is the phrase stating something more than this, going beyond even 1 Corinthians 8:6 and John 1:3? We agree with Haupt (30, 31; cf. Percy, *Probleme,* 69, 70) and Bruce (197) who suggest that the preposition "in" (ἐν) points to Christ as the "sphere" (cf. "in him" of v 19) within which the work of creation takes place. According to Haupt the phrase "in him" has the same force as in Ephesians 1:4; God's creation, like his election, takes place "in Christ" and not apart from him. On Christ depended (causally, so Meyer, 281) the act of creation so that it was not done independently of him (cf. Schweizer, *Beiträge,* 123–25).

Commentators have drawn attention to the affinities between Paul's language and Stoic terminology, notably the use of "all" (πᾶς) and the play on prepositions (ἐκ—εἰς—ἐν) by which the final unity of all that exists is expressed (Norden, *Agnostos Theos,* 240–50, 347, 348; see Lohse, 49, 50; and Schweizer, 61, for further references). So Norden and others have cited the statement of Marcus Aurelius, "O Nature . . . all things come from you, subsist in you, go back to you" (M. Aurelius, *Meditations* 4.23). Now it is one thing to note the linguistic affinities, another to argue that the meaning is the same or that Paul's thought is derived from Stoicism (Pöhlmann, *ZNW* 64 [1973] 53–74, has argued that the "all"-formula was used in many other traditions besides Stoicism, especially in Jewish ones; Bruce, 199, claims that to derive the "all" and prepositional constructions from Stoic formulations is to "pay more attention to the form of words than to their substance"). His ideas are very different from Stoic notions; for it is impossible in Paul to identify God with nature or some pantheistically conceived world-soul (cf. Kehl, *Christushymnus*, 103). And although it might have been possible for Paul, by using Stoic terms, to describe the creation as being called into existence through God's act—so providing a point of contact with those who had previously come from such a milieu—there is some difficulty with this because of the late dating of the linguistic parallels (Schweizer, 60, 61).

Rather, Paul's language is derived from Genesis 1 and the OT Wisdom literature (cf. Kehl, *Christushymnus*, 104–108), where Wisdom is styled the Creator's "master-workman" (Prov 8:30). For Paul, however, that "master-workman" is no longer a figure of speech, but the personal, heavenly Christ who had confronted him on the Damascus road.

ἐν τοῖς οὐρανοῖς καὶ ἐπὶ τῆς γῆς, τὰ ὁρατὰ καὶ τὰ ἀόρατα. The expression "all things" (*τὰ πάντα*) is expanded and depicted more clearly by two lines which are constructed chiastically in synonymous parallelism:

> *ἐν τοῖς οὐρανοῖς καὶ ἐπὶ γῆς*
> *τὰ ὁρατὰ καὶ τὰ ἀόρατα*
> "in heaven and on earth,
> things visible and invisible."

"Heaven" and "invisible" correspond as do "earth" and "visible." The expressions in the parallel lines embrace everything for there are no exceptions (Pöhlmann, *ZNW* 64 [1973] 58, 59, rightly points out that here is an example of *inclusio:* that is, the words *τὰ πάντα* are repeated in the concluding line so binding the chiastic structure together). All things have been brought into existence by the creative act of God in Christ.

εἴτε θρόνοι εἴτε κυριότητες εἴτε ἀρχαὶ εἴτε ἐξουσίαι. Probably with special reference to the Colossian heresy Paul now emphasizes that even the cosmic powers and principalities, which apparently received some prominence in that heresy, were created in Christ. Good or bad, all are subject to him as Creator. No doubt it is the hostile rather than the friendly powers Paul has particularly in view (although H. Schlier, *Principalities and Powers in the New Testament* [Questiones Disputatae 3; Freiburg: Herder, 1961] 14, 15, is of the opinion they are all wicked, hostile to God and Christ), as he endeavors to show the Colossians their proper place in relation to Christ (Bruce, 198). And the argument he develops in chapter 2 is that they were vanquished through that same Lord. None needs to be placated. They derive their existence from him, and they owe their obedience to him through whom they have been conquered (2:10, 15).

Here four classes of angelic powers are listed: "thrones" (*θρόνοι*) and "dominions" (*κυριότητες*, cf. 1 Cor 8:5), which were occasionally mentioned in Judaism among heavenly hosts of angels (2 Enoch 20:1; Test Levi 3:8), as well as "principalities" (*ἀρχαί*) and "powers" (*ἐξουσίαι*)—often named as supermundane beings and powers (for details see Lohse, 51). They probably represent the highest orders of the angelic realm. Whether the list is complete (here δυνάμεις, found in Rom 8:38; cf. 1 Cor 15:24; Eph 1:21, is missing) or the powers are arranged in a particular order is beside the point (Schlier, *Principalities,* 13, 14). From the highest to the lowest, all alike are subject to Christ. They were created *in* him, *through* him and *for* him.

Paul's teaching about Christ as the goal of all creation (εἰς αὐτόν is used of God at 1 Cor 8:6; cf. Percy, *Probleme,* 72, 73) finds no parallel in the Jewish Wisdom literature or in the rest of the extant Jewish materials for that matter. Martin (*NCB,* 58) aptly comments: "No Jewish thinker ever rose to these heights in daring to predict that Wisdom was the ultimate goal of all creation." And it needs to be remembered that the One of whom Paul speaks in this vein had recently been crucified as a common criminal in Jerusalem. However, he had risen victoriously from the dead and revealed himself to Paul as Son of God (Gal 1:15, 16). To him as goal the whole of creation, and therefore history as well, moved. It was the Father's intention that all things should be summed up in Christ (cf. Eph 1:10).

17. καὶ αὐτός ἐστιν πρὸ πάντων καὶ τὰ πάντα ἐν αὐτῷ συνέστηκεν· In a twofold statement about the preexistence and cosmic significance of Christ the teaching of verses 15 and 16 is reiterated (cf. Bruce, 220, and Benoit, *Christianity,* 228; on the importance of this verse see Hegermann, *Schöpfungsmittler,* 93, 94). There is no interest in the state or condition of the universe as such—only the concern to reassert the point about Christ's supremacy over the world. The first affirmation, "he is before all things" (αὐτός ἐστιν πρὸ πάντων), declares his temporal priority to the universe. Therefore one could not rightly say as Arius did that: "There was once when he was not" (ἦν ποτε ὅτε οὐκ ἦν). At the same time the statement implies his primacy over the cosmos (cf. Harris, *NIDNTT* 3, 1177) and points back to the earlier designation "firstborn of all creation." As the preexistent One (cf. John 8:58) he is Lord of the universe. Schweizer has made the interesting suggestion that the emphatic "he" (αὐτός) of this affirmation corresponds to the solemn "I" of the OT which refers to Yahweh himself (62).

τὰ πάντα ἐν αὐτῷ συνέστηκεν. Not only was the universe created in the Son as the sphere, by him as the divine agent, and for him as the goal; it was also established permanently "in him" alone, as the second affirmation, "in him all things are held together," asserts. He is the sustainer of the universe and the unifying principle of its life. Apart from his *continuous* sustaining activity (note the perfect tense συνέστηκεν) all would disintegrate.

Many have drawn attention to the similarities between this statement and the language of Platonic and Stoic philosophy where the term συνεστηκέναι (Plato, *Republic* 530a; Pseudo Aristotle, *Mund* 6; Philo, *Rer Div Her* 281, 311) was employed to denote the wonderful unity of the entire world (for further references see Hegermann, *Schöpfungsmittler,* 94, 95; Feuillet, *Christ,* 214; and Lohse, 52). While there are points of linguistic contact with Stoicism especially, and thus the language of the hymn may well have served as a bridge for those from such a background (cf. the similar function of λόγος in John 1), nevertheless Pauline thought is different from the pantheistically conceived world-soul of Stoicism. As Feuillet, Schweizer and others have noted, the parallels from Hellenistic Judaism, especially the LXX, are much closer. According to Wisdom 1:7, the Spirit "of the Lord, indeed, fills the whole world, and that which holds all things together (συνέχον τὰ πάντα) knows every word that is said" (*JB;* on the use of συνέχω rather than συνίστημι see Feuillet, *Christ,* 215), while Ecclesiasticus 43:26 states that "all things hold together by means of his word" (*JB;* ἐν λόγῳ αὐτοῦ σύγκειται τὰ πάντα). Martin (*NCB,* 59), following R. B. Y. Scott ("Wisdom in Creation: the *'Āmôn* of Proverbs viii.30." *VT* 10 [1960] 213–23), considers the thought is probably indebted to Proverbs 8:30 where Wisdom is called God's אמון, *'āmôn* (*RSV* "master workman"). Although Scott translates this as a "living link or vital bond" and suggests that Wisdom is regarded as a principle of coherence between God and his world, the appropriateness of his rendering has been questioned. For Paul, it is the Christ who has made himself known to the apostle who is the Sustainer and Unifier of the universe. As the Epistle to the Hebrews puts it, the Son of God through whom the worlds (αἰῶνες) were made sustains all things and bears them to their appointed end (φέρων . . . τὰ πάντα) by his powerful word (1:2, 3).

18. *καὶ αὐτός ἐστιν ἡ κεφαλὴ τοῦ σώματος, τῆς ἐκκλησίας.* With the mention of Christ as the head of the church, the hymn, according to Feuillet (*Christ,* 217), passes from a cosmological perspective to a soteriological one, a perspective that is maintained right to the end of the passage since this notion is of the utmost significance.

But not all commentators agree that verse 18*a,* at least as far as the original hymn was concerned, opens the soteriological section. The great majority of exegetes (see the list in Benoit, *Christianity,* 244) consider, on stylistic grounds, that the final strophe of the hymn commences with the words of verse 18*b,* "He is the beginning, the firstborn from the dead" (ὅς ἐστιν ἀρχή, πρωτότοκος ἐκ τῶν νεκρῶν), so paralleling the opening statement of verse 15, "He is the image of the invisible God, the firstborn of all creation" (ὅς ἐστιν εἰκὼν τοῦ θεοῦ τοῦ ἀοράτου, πρωτότοκος πάσης κτίσεως). On this view the statement of verse 18*a,* "He is the head of the body," forms a climax to the first part of the poem (or the middle strophe according to some) and refers to Christ's headship over the entire cosmos. The words "the church" (τῆς ἐκκλησίας) were added as a gloss by either Paul or the final redactor of the hymn (if the letter is regarded as coming from the Pauline school but not Paul himself) who has reinterpreted the cosmological statement along ecclesiological lines, thereby making his own significant contribution. Clearly the term "body" (σῶμα) in the original hymn was used to denote the whole cosmos, a usage which the majority believes to be paralleled in other writers from early times (for details see Ernst, *Pleroma,* 154–56, and Schweizer, *TDNT* 7, 1024–94).

According to Plato, the cosmos is a living being with a soul and pervaded by reason (*Tim* 31*b*,32*a*, etc.). The cosmos is a body that is directed by the divine soul which it follows as it is led (*Tim* 47*c*–48*b*). An Orphic fragment refers to Zeus as the "head" (κεφαλή) of the cosmos who with his power pervades the universe, the body (Fragment 168). In Stoic thought the cosmos is a living entity, the perfect σῶμα ("body") whose unity is everywhere given special emphasis. Created by God, it is governed by him as the world soul In fact, the cosmos is God himself (cf. Lohse, 53, 54).

Philo of Alexandria referred to the world of the heavens as a uniform body over which the Logos was set as head (*Som* 1.128). As the body of man needs the direction and guidance given by the head (*Spec Leg* 3.184), so too the "body" of the universe needs the eternal Logos which is its head to direct it (*Quaest in Ex* 2.117). So on the view that the words of the hymn are a cosmological assertion it is stated that Christ is the "head" (κεφαλή) who rules the "body" (σῶμα) of the cosmos. The universe is governed and held together by this head; it was founded and established in him alone.

There are, however, serious difficulties with this majority view. First, as has already been pointed out (see 35–37), the application of various stylistic criteria has not led to any consensus about the original structure of the hymn. Arguments from strophic balance have been shown to be so precarious that it is uncertain that the words "the church" could not have belonged to the original hymn. Most recent writers regard the words as a redactional addition but Kehl (*Christushymnus,* 93, 97: cf. Hegermann, *Schöpfungsmittler,* 106) and Gibbs (*Creation,* 105) have argued that they are essential to the meaning of verse 18*a.*

Second, it is by no means certain that "body" (σῶμα) originally referred to the cosmos. There is no parallel to this in the Pauline corpus where σῶμα is employed ninety-nine times. But on the other hand, and significantly, σῶμα is used to designate the church or local congregation as the body of Christ. At 1 Corinthians 12:12–27 where the apostle is concerned to impress on the Corinthian Christians that as fellow-members of that body they have mutual duties and common interests which must not be neglected, he asserts "you are the body of Christ and severally members of it" (v 27). Again at Romans 12:4, 5 where Paul focuses on the varieties of service the different members of the church render, in accordance with their respective gifts, he declares: "For as in one body we have many members, and all the members do not have the same function, so we, though many, are one body in Christ, and individually members one of another."

In these earlier letters, Paul employs the body terminology and its constituent parts to refer to the mutual relations and obligations of church members. Here the "head" (κεφαλή) of the body has no special position or honor; it is counted as an ordinary member (1 Cor 12:21; Best, *Body,* 113). In Colossians (and Ephesians) there is an advance in the line of thought so that the relationship which the church, as the body of Christ, bears to Christ as head of the body is treated. Many regard this difference as a valid argument against the identity of authorship (so, for example, Lohse, 55), but such a conclusion is unnecessary (see xlv). As Bruce (*Paul,* 421) has recently pointed out, the "advance from the language of simile in 1 Corinthians and Romans to the real and interpersonal involvement expressed in the language of Colossians and Ephesians may have been stimulated by Paul's consideration of the issues involved in the Colossian heresy." We have noted that Paul had repeatedly spoken of the church as the body of Christ. His headship over the church could easily be conceived as an organic relationship in which he exercised the control over his people that the head of a body exercises over its various parts. The living relationship between the members is thereby kept in view (so 1 Corinthians and Romans), while the dependence of the members on

Christ for life and power as well as his supremacy is reiterated against a heresy that called such matters into question.

If it is unnecessary to consider that the term "body" originally referred to the cosmos in the hymn then there is no need to look for Stoic antecedents as the source of the writer's ideas (Best, *Body*, 83; Bruce, *Paul*, 420, claims to do this is "an unwarranted exercise of the imagination"), even though there may be some linguistic parallels. Nor are the antecedents of Gnosticism, the Christian Eucharist, or rabbinic speculation on the body of Adam likely sources for this conception of the church as the body of Christ. A more fruitful line of inquiry, which was earlier mentioned by Best (*Body, passim*) is the OT concept of corporate personality, where an oscillation between the one and the many, the individual and the corporate can be traced. The notion is by no means strange to Paul for Christ and his people are so closely linked (concerning the notion of the corporate Christ see C. F. D. Moule, *The Origin of Christology* [Cambridge: University Press, 1977] 47–96) that on occasion he and they together can be called "Christ" (1 Cor 12:12). Further, we might well ask whether the notion was not indelibly impressed on Paul's mind when on the Damascus road he was addressed: "Saul, Saul, why do you persecute *me* (τί με διώκεις;)?" (Acts 9:4).

We consider, then, that it was Paul, rather than some unknown redactor, who is the originator of this way of expressing the church's vital union with Christ, the head (cf. Col 2:19). Using the Old Testament concept of corporate personality and by referring to "body" (σῶμα) and "head" (κεφαλή) as he does, he has made his own distinct contribution to NT Christology and ecclesiology. In the context headship over the body refers to Christ's control over his people as well as the dependence of all the members on him for life and power (cf. 2:19; for an important discussion on the meaning of κεφαλή as "origin" see S. Bedale, "The Meaning of κεφαλή in the Pauline Epistles," *JTS* 5 [1954) 211–15). As the body of Christ the church is vitalized by his abiding presence and his risen life.

τῆς ἐκκλησίας. (On the meaning of ἐκκλησία in Colossians, see 57–61).

ὅς ἐστιν ἀρχή, πρωτότοκος ἐκ τῶν νεκρῶν. The person who is head of the body, the church, is the *risen* Christ, for he is called the "beginning" (ἀρχή; this word, like πρῶτος, being absolute in itself does not require the definite article; it is most commonly omitted when ἀρχή occurs as a predicate: so Lightfoot, 155), and the "firstborn from the dead" (πρωτότοκος ἐκ τῶν νεκρῶν). The term ἀρχή ("beginning"; see Delling, *TDNT* 1, 479–84) has basically to do with primacy, whether in a temporal sense (Matt 19:4, 8; John 15:27; Acts 26:4; Heb 1:10; 2 Pet 3:4; 1 John 2:24, etc.) or with reference to authority and sovereignty (Rom 8:38; 1 Cor 15:24; Eph 1:21; 6:12, etc.). In Judaism both Wisdom and the Logos were called "the beginning" (cf. Prov 8:23; Philo, *Leg All* 1.43). At Colossians 1:18 when it is said of Christ that he is the "beginning," it does not mean he is the "beginning of God's creation" (ἀρχὴ τῆς κτίσεως τοῦ θεοῦ, Rev 3:14), or its first cause, points that might have applied in the first part of the hymn, but rather as the One who is "the firstborn from the dead" he is the founder of a new humanity. At Genesis 49:3 the two terms "firstborn" and "beginning" appear together to describe the firstborn as the founder of a people (cf. LXX Deut 21:17 and Rom 8:29).

The resurrection age has burst forth and as the first who has risen from among those who had fallen asleep (ἐκ τῶν νεκρῶν) he is the first-fruits who guarantees the future resurrection of others (1 Cor 15:20, 23).

ἵνα γένηται ἐν πᾶσιν αὐτὸς πρωτεύων. Because Christ is the "beginning" and the "firstborn" in resurrection as well as in creation he has therefore become (note the aorist γένηται) preeminent in all things. This was the divine intention as the purpose clause (ἵνα) makes plain. The words "be the first" (πρωτεύω) resume the double reference to "firstborn" (πρωτότοκος, vv 15 and 18), as well as the phrase "he is before all things" (v 17), while the expression "in all" (ἐν πᾶσιν) is linked with the frequently mentioned "all things" (τὰ πάντα). The hymn had previously asserted Christ's primacy in creation; it now mentions his primacy in resurrection. In both new creation and old the first place belongs to him alone (Michaelis, *TDNT* 6, 882). He *has become* preeminent "in everything."

19. ὅτι ἐν αὐτῷ εὐδόκησεν πᾶν τὸ πλήρωμα κατοικῆσαι. The reason for (ὅτι) this primacy of Christ over everything is now given: "in him all the fullness was pleased to dwell." Two main issues arise in this much disputed and frequently discussed verse: first, what is the subject of "was pleased" (εὐδόκησεν): God, Christ or "all the fullness"? Secondly, what does "all the fullness" (πᾶν τὸ πλήρωμα) mean? (For a detailed treatment of this verse with special reference to the meaning of πλήρωμα see Ernst, *Pleroma,* 72–94.)

Regarding the first question it is unlikely that the Son is the subject of "was pleased" for, although Ephesians 2:16 asserts that it is he who reconciles (at 2 Cor 5:18, 19 it is the Father), the phrase ἐν αὐτῷ (i.e. in Christ) seems to exclude the Son as the subject (Moule, 70). Many exegetes consider that "God" (ὁ θεός) should be supplied as the subject of the sentence, with the words "all the fullness . . . to dwell" (πᾶν τὸ πλήρωμα κατοικῆσαι) being taken as an accusative and infinitive construction: "God was pleased to let all the fullness dwell in him." This suggestion fits well with the masculine participle "making peace" (εἰρηνοποιήσας, v 20), while to insert the subject "God" is quite proper since the words εὐδοκία and εὐδοκέω (cf. θέλημα) are sometimes used absolutely to denote the good pleasure of God (Luke 2:14; Phil 2:13). On the other hand, it is grammatically possible to regard "all the fullness" (πᾶν τὸ πλήρωμα) as the subject, and if we understand the phrase as meaning "God in all his fullness" (see below) then the subsequent masculines, εἰς αὐτόν ("to him") and εἰρηνοποίησας ("having made peace"), may be explained as a construction according to sense, because πλήρωμα then stands for a masculine (Moule, 70, 71; Münderlein, *NTS* 8 [1961–62] 265, 266). On balance, this solution is preferred since it is not necessary to supply the missing subject, while at Colossians 2:9 in the following commentary on this passage πᾶν τὸ πλήρωμα τῆς θεότητος ("all the fullness of deity") is clearly the subject of the same verb κατοικεῖ.

Second, what does "all the fullness" (πᾶν τὸ πλήρωμα) mean? Various answers have been given depending in part on the history of religions background assigned to the notion. Some understand πλήρωμα as used in accord with the Gnostic (Valentinian) technical term (note, for example, Lightfoot's treatment of this view, 255–71). Certainly the idea of "fullness" played a significant role in the Gnosticism of the second century. The Valentinians referred to "pleroma" as the fullness of the emanations which came forth from God. It signified the uppermost pneumatic world in close proximity to God which in turn was separated from the cosmos by a boundary (for details see Ernst, *Pleroma,* 41–50; Lohse, 57). But according to Valentinian teaching God himself, "alone unbegotten, not subject to place or time" (Hippolytus, *Ref* 6.29.5), was distinguished from the heavenly fullness of emanations. Therefore others have argued that this understanding of the word "pleroma" cannot contribute anything to the explanation of Colossians 1:19 since in the hymn God himself is called "pleroma." The supposed parallels are later in time, while the Redeemer of Colossians does not leave the "pleroma" as in Gnostic thought when he makes the long descent to the world. Accordingly Paul was not indebted to Gnostic thought for his understanding of *πλήρωμα* (note the careful argument of Overfield, *NTS* 25 [1978–79] 384–96). But it is possible that he is undermining a cardinal point in the Colossian heresy which considered supernatural powers to be intermediaries between God and the world, the more so when it is considered that the phrase "*all the* fullness" is tautologous. Kehl's comment (*Christushymnus,* 119), that the "fullness" is not a "fullness" if it does not mean a totality, is apt. The additional words "all the" (*πᾶν τό*) may well be polemical.

The backgrounds in popular Stoicism (Dupont) and the Hermetic literature with the cosmos as the "fullness" do not provide an adequate basis for understanding Paul's use of the term in Colossians 1:19 and 2:9. Rather, as Moule (164–69), Kehl (*Christushymnus,* 116–25) and Gibbs (*Creation,* 107, 108) have pointed out there is no need to look beyond the OT for the source of Paul's ideas.

Three observations need to be made in this connection: first, the word *πλήρωμα* is employed in the OT (cf. Ernst, *Pleroma,* 22–30) in rather stereotyped expressions with an active meaning: the sea and its fullness (1 Chr 16:32; Ps 96:11; 98:7), the earth and everything in it (Ps 24:1; Jer 8:16; 47:2; Ezek 12:19; 19:7; 30:12), and the world with all it contains (Ps 50:12; 89:11). As yet, however, the term has not become a technical expression with a fixed and clearly defined meaning.

Second, in language akin to *πλήρωμα* the Old Testament recognizes that God himself (or his glory) fills the whole universe: so Jeremiah 23:24, " 'Do I not fill (*πληρῶ*) heaven and earth?' says the Lord," and Psalm 72:19, "may his glory fill (*πληρωθήσεται*) the whole earth" (cf. Isa 6:3; Ezek 43:5; 44:4, where the cognate *πλήρης* occurs). Obviously this notion, which draws attention to the immanence of God and his personal involvement in the world, is not to be understood along either pantheistic or dualistic lines.

Third, the verb "be pleased" (*εὐδοκέω*) which often appears in the OT to denote the good pleasure of God (Ps 44:3; 147:11; 149:4) is particularly used to designate divine election. Of special significance is the connection between God's choosing and his dwelling place. This conjunction repeatedly occurs and, on occasion, the same two verbs of Colossians 1:19, *εὐδοκέω* and *κατοικέω* are employed. Zion is "the mountain on which it pleased God to dwell" (*εὐδόκησεν ὁ θεὸς κατοικεῖν ἐν αὐτῷ*, LXX Ps 67:17; cf. LXX Ps 131:13, 14; Isa 8:18; 49:20, where the verb "elect," *ἐκλέγομαι*, replaces "be pleased")

As is well-known in Deuteronomic theology, the notion of the God of Israel choosing a place for himself where he wants his name to dwell repeatedly appears (Deut 12:5, 11; 14:23; 16:2, 6, 11; 26:2, etc.).

These three lines converge at Colossians 1:19 in the person of Christ (cf. Kehl, *Christushymnus,* 123, and Ernst, 171, and *Pleroma,* 84). He is the "place" (note the emphatic position of *ἐν αὐτῷ*) in whom God in all his fullness was pleased to take up his residence (the verb is the aorist infinitive *κατοικῆσαι*). All the attributes and activities of God—his spirit, word, wisdom and glory—are perfectly displayed in Christ (Bruce, 207). This is no temporary indwelling as the verb *κατοικέω* (in contrast to *παροικέω,* "sojourn") with its present tense at chapter 2:9 makes plain: "in him all the fullness of deity *dwells* (*κατοικεῖ*) bodily."

He is the one mediator between God and the world of mankind. The Colossian Christians need not fear those supernatural powers under whose control men were supposed to live, whether divine emanations, agencies or the like. God in all his divine essence and power had taken up residence in Christ.

20. *καὶ δι' αὐτοῦ ἀποκαταλλάξαι . . . τὰ ἐν τοῖς οὐρανοῖς.* With the statement about God's good pleasure in reconciling all things through Christ, the conclusion of the final strophe occurs, and the "high point" (so Kehl, *Christushymnus,* 125) of the hymn is reached.

The opening words of the paragraph have asserted that all things—the various heavenly bodies, thrones, lordships, principalities, powers and so on—were created in Christ, through him and for him. He is their Lord in creation. What is not spelled out, however, is what has happened to all things *since* creation (C.K. Barrett. *From First Adam to Last. A Study in Pauline Theology* [New York: Scribner's, 1962, 86]). Although there has been no previous mention of it, the presupposition is that the unity and harmony of the cosmos have suffered a considerable dislocation, even a rupture, thus requiring reconciliation (Lohse, 59; cf. Schweizer, 68, Schnackenburg, EKKNT Vorarbeiten 1, 38, Hegermann, *Schöpfungsmittler,* 103–105, and others). (On the problem of a disruption in nature within the thought of Hellenistic Judaism, see Schweizer, 68.)

The notion of reconciliation is certainly Pauline, appearing in the major letters (Rom 5:10, 11; 11:15; 2 Cor 5:18–20), even though the compound verb *ἀποκαταλλάσσω* ("reconcile") is unusual (cf. Eph 2:16 in addition to Col 1:20, 22) and is possibly a Pauline creation (Benoit, *Christianity,* 249). Also in each reference the ground of reconciliation lies in the gracious initiating activity of God (at Rom 5:8 the basis is the love of God, while Col 1:20 points to the divine good pleasure; cf. 2 Cor 5:18). The unusual feature of this passage is that it refers to the reconciliation of "all things" (*τὰ πάντα*) and that as a past event. Although 2 Corinthians 5:19 (cf. John 3:16 and similar passages) speaks of the reconciliation of the world (*κόσμος*), it is clear that it is the world of men which is in view. Further, it is argued that the freeing of creation from its bondage to decay so that it obtains the glorious liberty of the children of God (Rom 8:19–21) is a *future* eschatological event (Schweizer, *Beiträge,* 133).

Three related questions, therefore, arise: (a) What is the meaning of the phrase "to reconcile all things to him" (ἀποκαταλλάξαι τὰ πάντα εἰς αὐτόν)? (b) What is the relationship of this expression to the words which follow, "having made peace through the blood of his cross" (εἰρηνοποιήσας διὰ τοῦ αἵματος τοῦ σταυροῦ αὐτοῦ)? (c) Is it possible or even desirable to equate verse 20 with the notion of God's leading the evil powers in his triumphal procession at chapter 2:15?

The following views have been set forth as commentators have grappled with these questions: (1) Noting that the verb to "reconcile" properly applies to persons (except in the language of actuaries or logic) some exegetes consider the objects of reconciliation to be that which is reconcilable. On this view "all things" (τὰ πάντα) are concretized and explained by the additional phrases "whether things (εἴτε τά) upon the earth, or things (εἴτε τά) in the heavens." The first category is usually understood to denote the world of men which is reconciled, the second the world of angels (either the renewed subordination of the angels under Christ after his *kenosis*, so Michl, *TQ* 128 [1948] 442–62; or the reconciliation of the angels of the law which had been dethroned according to chapter 2:15, so B. N. Wambacq, " 'per eum reconciliare . . . quae in caelis sunt' Col 1, 20," *RB* 55 [1948] 35–42). For a critique of this see Vögtle, *Das Neue Testament*, 222.

(2) Kehl (*Christushymnus*, 163–65), refusing to understand ἀποκαταλλάξαι τὰ πάντα as denoting "an objective physical-metaphysical reconciliation of everything," examined the phrase against the background of God's glory filling the whole of creation. According to Romans 1:23, pagans "exchanged (ἤλλαξεν) the glory of the immortal God for images resembling mortal man or birds or animals or reptiles." This, according to Kehl, was the breach or rupture presupposed in Colossians 1. It had occurred in man, not in creation. Reconciliation, therefore, involved the healing of this breach. "The ἀποκαταλλαγή of Colossians 1:20 is the reversal of the exchange of Romans 1:23" (160). But in spite of its many insights Kehl's approach has been criticized for its narrow anthropocentric slant. It has been argued that he appears to oversimplify and limit the meaning of the text with its utterances on the cosmic rule and peace-making work of Christ (cf. M. Barth, *CBQ* 30 [1968] 110; cf. Wolter, *Rechtfertigung*, 55).

(3) According to another view, reconciliation has to do with the subjection, that is, the pacification of the cosmic powers. "All things" (τὰ πάντα) does not include the world of men but denotes the cosmic forces as the object of God's reconciling activity. Since all of these powers are evil (so Schlier, *Principalities*, 14, 15) they need to be brought into subjection to Christ as head. They are "pacified" through him (cf. Col 2:14, 15) and cosmic peace is once again restored. However, if Kehl's view was open to the criticism of wrongly limiting "all things" to the world of men, this approach is open to a similar charge of incorrectly narrowing the text to the cosmic powers, and while this viewpoint has the great merit of seeking to relate chapter 2:15 to the climactic words of the hymn, it does not in the end adequately explain the meaning of "all things" (τὰ πάντα).

(4) Lohse's view (59–61) is that the universe ("all"), which suffered a considerable disturbance, has now been reconciled through the Christ-event. Heaven and earth have been returned to their divinely created and determined order and this has occurred through the resurrection and exaltation of Christ. The

universe is again under its head, and cosmic peace—a peace which according to some apocalyptic expectations would only occur at the end time—has returned. Lohse, along with the majority of recent commentators, regards the phrase "through the blood of his cross" (v 20) as an interpretative addition to the original hymn by the author of the epistle. "Peace has not been established in an other-worldly drama but rather in the death of Jesus Christ" (60). The principalities are stripped of their power (cf. 2:14, 15) and the reconciliation of all things has taken place. This word is then addressed to the recipients of the letter, for the message of reconciliation which pertains to the whole world applies to them as well (vv 21–23).

(5) The approach of F. Mussner (*Christus, das All und die Kirche. Studien zur Theologie des Epheserbriefes* *[TTS 5; Trier: Paulinus, 1955]), following the view of Gewiess (cf. Vögtle, *Das Neue Testament,* 227–29), considers the emphasis of the passage lies elsewhere. Instead of underscoring the words "all things" (τὰ πάντα) in the sentence, and then determining what categories are included (e.g. How can the cosmos as an impersonal entity be reconciled? Does the reconciliation concern men with God, men with angels, men with one another, or fallen angels with God, etc.?) this approach considers our attention should be directed to the one who effects the reconciliation. The significant question is not, "*Who* or *what* is reconciled?" but "Who is the mediator of reconciliation?" and the answer given is "Christ alone" (Mussner, *Christus,* 71). In the first strophe of the hymn the centrality of Christ is asserted and the "all"-formula is employed so as to elicit praise for Christ as the Mediator and Lord of creation. He is also the focus of attention in the second strophe, verses 18*b*–20, and the "all"-formula serves to point decisively to him once again. He and only he is the Mediator of reconciliation. The statement of verse 20, "whether things upon the earth, or things in heaven," which is in apposition to "all things," does not contradict this view, it is argued, since the words do not provide a detailed breakdown of the objects of reconciliation. The redactor of the hymn is only interested in men as the objects (hence the application in vv 21–23), while the omission of any reference to a cosmic fall is in keeping with the author's intention of focusing his interest on Christ. Vögtle (*Das Neue Testament,* 227–29), who has recently championed this view, claims Schweizer's emphatic statement about the reconciliation of all things being understood as an "exclusively Christological assertion" (*Beiträge,* 134) approximates to his own position.

But granted that the passage, in a magnificent fashion, emphasizes Christ's supremacy in every sphere, clearly asserting that he alone is the Mediator of reconciliation, this same text does in fact mention the objects or beneficiaries of this reconciliation, first generally ("all things") and then rather more specifically ("whether on earth or in heaven"). To ask "Who or what has been reconciled?" may not be the primary question, but it is a legitimate question nevertheless since the text itself encourages us to look for an answer. Further, to suggest with Vögtle, on the basis of the application in verses 21–23, that the "redactor" is only interested in men as objects, overlooks the fact that many truths of a Christological kind asserted in the hymn are not directly applied to the readers. We ought, however, not to conclude that these were therefore unimportant.

(6) The "reconciliation of all things" ought to be understood, in our judg-

ment, with Lohse (59) to mean that the "universe has been reconciled in that heaven and earth have been brought back into their divinely created and determined order . . . the universe is again under its head and . . . cosmic peace has returned."

Although Schweizer and others reject the suggestion, it is best to understand "reconciliation" as expanded in the following words—"having made peace through the blood of his cross." If, on Schweizer's view, the author made corrections to the hymn, why did he allow certain elements, which were different from his own theology, to remain? If reconciliation and pacification are essentially different why did not the author remove the idea which did not harmonize with his own view? (Cf. O'Brien, *RTR* 33 [1974] 45–53, against Schweizer, *Neotestamentica,* 326, 327.)

The peace which Christ has brought may be "freely accepted, or . . . compulsorily imposed" (Bruce, 210), for when Paul speaks of reconciliation on this wide front he includes the notion of "pacification." If, as many commentators suggest, verse 20 is to be understood in the light of God's triumph in Christ over the principalities and powers (2:15)—though the meaning of Christ's reconciling work ought not to be limited by these words of chapter 2:15 since it is broader than the pacification of the principalities and powers, applying to the world of men, indeed the whole cosmos as well—then these are certainly not depicted as gladly surrendering to God's grace but as "submitting against their wills to a power which they cannot resist" (Bruce, 210). In other words, they have been pacified—a notion that was not strange to those living in the Mediterranean region under Roman rule of the first century A.D. Yet "pacification" of or victory over these powers, presumed to be hostile toward God or Christ, does not mean they are done away with or finally destroyed. It is evident that they continue to exist, inimical to man and his interests (cf. Rom 8:38, 39; Barrett, *Adam,* 86). Nevertheless they cannot finally harm the person who is in Christ, and their ultimate overthrow in the future is assured (1 Cor 15:24–28; see on Col 2:15).

Paul affirms that this universal reconciliation has been brought about, not in some other-worldly drama, but through something done in history, the death of Jesus Christ upon the cross. Further at chapter 2:14, 15 it is asserted that God, in Christ, destroyed the "certificate of indebtedness" that stood over against the Colossian Christians, nailing it to the cross, and also vanquished the principalities and powers leading them in his triumphal procession.

W. Michaelis (*Versöhnung des Alls. Die frohe Botschaft von der Gnade Gottes* [Bern: Siloah, 1950]) argued on the basis of Colossians 1:20, Ephesians 1:10, etc., that because God's eternal plan and purpose was reconciliation then nothing in his creation would finally or ultimately be lost. Yet can verse 20 be taken to mean that Paul looked for the ultimate reconciliation to God of all people and, indeed, of hostile spiritual powers as well? The cosmic reconciliation has to do with *τὰ πάντα,* including everything in its scope. The reconciliation of the principalities and powers is in mind. They are one category whatever others are included. Yet these forces are shown as submitting against their wills to a power they cannot resist. They are reconciled through subjugation (cf. 1 Cor 15:28), and Christ's victory has reduced them to the position of "weak and beggarly elements" (cf. Gal 4:9). Though they are included within the reconciliation, theirs is no glad surrender to the Lord of the cosmos. Similarly it cannot be assumed from verse 20 that all sinful men have freely accepted the peace effected through the death of Christ. Like the principalities and powers, might not that peace have to be imposed compulsorily, at least on some?

Although all things will *finally* unite to bow in the name of Jesus and to acknowledge him as Lord (Phil 2:10, 11), it is not to be assumed that this will be done gladly by all. For as the words following the hymn (Col 1:21–23) indicate, the central purpose of Christ's work of making peace has to do with those who have heard the Word of reconciliation and gladly accepted it. To assert that verse 20 points to a universal reconciliation in which every man will finally enjoy celestial bliss is an unwarranted assumption.

A Note on the Term ἐκκλησία in Colossians and Philemon

(1) *ἐκκλησία in the Greek city-state*

The term *ἐκκλησία* ("assembly"), derived from *ἐκ-καλέω* ("call out," a verb used for the summons to the army to assemble), is attested from the time of Euripides and Herodotus onward (fifth cent. B.C.) and denoted the popular assembly of the full citizens of the *πόλις* or Greek city-state. During this period it met at regular intervals, though the term in cases of emergency could describe an extraordinary gathering. Every citizen had the right to speak and to propose matters for discussion. The term *ἐκκλησία*, centuries before the translation of the OT and the time of the NT, was clearly characterized as a political phenomenon; it was the assembly of full citizens, functionally rooted in the Greek democracy, an assembly in which fundamentally political and judicial decisions were taken. The *ἐκκλησία* (as distinct from the *δῆμος* ["people, populace, crowd"] which was continuous) was only regarded as existing when it was actually assembled.

(2) *ἐκκλησία in the LXX, Josephus and Philo*

In the translation of the LXX the Greek word *ἐκκλησία* ("assembly") occurs about one hundred times, of which twenty-two are in the Apocrypha. It represents the Hebrew *qāhāl* ("assembly") some seventy-three times (but never *ᶜēdâh*, "congregation"; frequently *qāhāl* is rendered by the Greek *συναγωγή*, "place of assembly"; W. J. Dumbrell, *The Meaning and Use of Ekklesia in the New Testament with Special Reference to its Old Testament Background.* University of London: Unpublished M.Th. thesis, 1966, 1–26, especially 3, argued that although *qāhāl* and *ᶜēdâh* have the same basic meaning of a convened meeting, the latter "represents the people as a national unit, whether assembled or not . . . while *qāhāl* represents the people as summoned, convened or assembled for some special purpose"). The Hebrew term *qāhāl* and its Greek equivalent *ἐκκλησία* could describe assemblies of a less specifically religious or nonreligious kind, for example the gathering of an army in preparation for war (1 Sam 17:47; 2 Chron. 28:14) or the "coming together" of an unruly and potentially dangerous crowd (Ps 26 [LXX 25]: 5; Ecclus 26:5). However, particularly significant are those instances of *ἐκκλησία* (rendering *qāhāl*) which denote the congregation of Israel when it assembled to hear the Word of God on Mt. Sinai, or later on Mt. Zion where all Israel were required to assemble three times a year. Sometimes the whole nation appears to be involved, as on those occasions when Moses is addressing the people prior to their entry into the promised land. In this connection Deuteronomy 4:10 may be cited. Recalling the scene at Sinai, Moses reminded the Israelites of "the day when you stood before the Lord your God in Horeb, when he said to me, 'Assemble the people before me to hear my words.' " The parallel is even clearer in the LXX which uses the word *ἐκκλησία* and its cognate *ἐκκλησιάζω*: "the day of the church when the Lord said to me, 'Form the people into a church before me' " (cf. Deut 9:10; 18:16; 31:30; 8:35 [LXX 9:2]; Judg 20:2, etc.). At other times it is only the chief representatives that seem to be present, as with the congregation of tribal heads, or patriarchal chiefs, at Solomon's dedication of the Temple in Jerusalem (1 Kings 8:14, 22, 55, etc.).

Josephus also used the word frequently (some forty-eight times, of which eighteen are LXX quotations), always of a gathering. These vary in character, e.g. religious, political and spontaneous assemblies are mentioned (Josephus *Ant* 4.309; *Life,* 268; *JW* 1.654, 666). Philo employs the term some thirty times, all but five of which are in quotations from the LXX. These five appear in a classical Greek sense.

The term, then, in the Greek and Jewish world prior to Paul meant an assembly or gathering of people; it did not designate an "organization" or "society." Although it had no intrinsically religious meaning and could refer to meetings that were quite secular in character, of special significance are those occurrences of *ἐκκλησία* in the LXX which refer to the congregation of Israel when it assembled to hear the Word of God.

(3) *ἐκκλησία in the New Testament*

The word *ἐκκλησία* turns up 114 times in the NT and over half of these occur in Paul (sixty-two instances; and other occurrences are: Matthew, three; Acts, twenty-three; Revelation, twenty; non-Pauline epistles, six). Whether the Christian use of *ἐκκλησία* was first adopted from Jewish or Gentile usage is a disputed point. I. H. Marshall ("New Wine in Old Wine Skins: V. The Biblical Use of the Word 'Ekklēsia,' " *ExpTim* 84 [1972–73] 359–64) after an examination of the alternatives, contends that the most satisfactory explanation for the Christian employment of the term is "ultimately connected with the Jewish use in the LXX" (362). (On the question as to why the early Church did not use *συναγωγή*, "gathering-place, place of assembly," to describe itself—James 2:2, is the one exception though even here *ἐκκλησία* occurs—if it was choosing a designation from the LXX, W. Schrage, " 'Ekklesia' und 'Synagoge.' Zum Ursprung des urchristlichen Kirchenbegriffs," *ZTK* 60 [1963] 178–202, argued the former was avoided because of its close links with the Jewish law and because it had come to be used of Jewish buildings. Although these reasons are possible, it must be remembered that *ἐκκλησία* denoted a "meeting" or an "assembly," rather than an "organization" or a "society," and this is how the term is used in the NT.)

(a) PAULINE USES IN THE EARLIER LETTERS

Other occurrences of the term *ἐκκλησία* ("assembly") in the NT all postdate Paul's usage of the word and therefore it is necessary to determine the meaning he attaches to it in the various contexts. His first use occurs at 1 Thessalonians 1:1 in his greetings to the Christians at Thessalonica: "Paul, Silas and Timothy. To the church of the Thessalonians (*τῇ ἐκκλησίᾳ Θεσσαλονικέων*) in God the Father and the Lord Jesus Christ." The term is employed in the same way as in Greek and Jewish circles, that is, like other assemblies in the city, it is described as "a gathering of the Thessalonians." But it is distinguished from the regular political councils by the addition of the words "in God the Father," and from the regular synagogue meetings by the use of the term *ἐκκλησία* and the additional phrase "in the Lord Jesus Christ" (so correctly R. Banks, *Paul's Idea of Community. The Early House Churches in Their Historical Setting* (Grand Rapids, MI: Eerdmans, 1980) 43; note the same ascription at 2 Thess 1:1). From the closing remarks of the letter it is clear Paul has in mind an actual gathering of the Thessalonian Christians. So he requests that his letter "be read to all the brethren" and that they "greet all the brethren with a holy kiss" (1 Thess 5:26, 27).

In the two Thessalonian letters reference is made to "the churches (*ἐκκλησίαι*) of God" (2 Thess 1:4) and "the churches of God in Judea" (2:14). Other epistles such as Galatians (1:2), the two letters to the Corinthians (1 Cor 7:17; 11:16; 14:33, 34; 2 Cor 8:19, 23, 24; 11:8, 28; 12:13) and Romans (16:4, 16) also employ the plural when more than one church is in view (the only exceptions are the distributive expression "every church," 1 Cor 4:17, and the phrase "the church of God," 1 Cor 10:32, in a generic or possibly localized sense). So reference is made to "the *churches* in Galatia (Gal 1:2; 1 Cor 16:1), "the *churches* of Asia" (1 Cor 16:19), "the *churches* in Macedonia" (2 Cor 8:1), and "the *churches* of Judea" (Gal 1:22). This suggests that the term was only applied to an actual gathering of people, or to a group that gathers when viewed as a regularly constituted meeting (Banks, *Idea*, 43). Although we often speak of a group of congregations collectively as "the church" (i.e. of a denomination) it is doubtful whether Paul (or the rest of the NT) uses *ἐκκλησία* in this collective way. Also the notion of a unified provincial or national church appears to have been foreign to Paul's thinking. An *ἐκκλησία* was a meeting or an assembly. This primary sense of "gathering" comes out clearly in 1 Corinthians 11–14 where expressions such as "when you assemble in church" (1 Cor 11:18) and "to speak in church" (14:35; cf. vv 4, 5, 12, 19, 28) turn up. It is of particular significance that at the beginning of the two Corinthian letters (1 Cor 1:1; 2 Cor 1:1; cf. 1 Cor 10:32, 11:22 and Rom 16:16), the church is described as belonging to the one who brought it into existence (that is, God), or the one through whom this has taken place (that is, Christ). Such an *ἐκκλησία* was not simply a human association or a religious club, but a divinely created entity (cf. Banks, *Idea*, 45).

Paul's reference in Galatians (1:13: cf. also 1 Cor 15:9; Phil 3:6) to his original persecution of "the church of God" does not contradict this suggestion since the expression may signify a reference to the church at Jerusalem before it was distributed into a number of smaller assemblies in various parts of Judea, or that it was as the believers met together that the arrests were made—their gathering together provided evidence of their Christian associations (Banks, *Idea*, 44).

(b) ἐκκλησία IN THE LATER LETTERS

Our term ἐκκλησία turns up five times in Colossians and Philemon and is used in three separate though related, ways: *(a)* at Colossians 4:16 the word is employed in its customary sense of an "assembly," that is, at Laodicea. As in the earlier instances so here too an actual gathering is in view: after Paul's letter to the Colossians has been read aloud in the assembly, they are to pass it, or perhaps a copy, on, so that it may be read in the congregation at Laodicea (the expression παρ' ὑμῖν, "among you," is virtually equivalent to ἐν . . . ἐκκλησίᾳ, "in . . . the assembly"). *(b) In two references* ἐκκλησία designates a "house-church": so at Colossians 4:15 reference is made to "Nympha and the church that is in her house (καὶ τὴν κατ' οἶκον αὐτῆς ἐκκλησίαν)," while at Philemon 2 it is clear that Philemon's house was used as a meeting-place in Colossae ("the church that meets in your house," τῇ κατ' οἶκον σου ἐκκλησίᾳ). Paul has already used the word ἐκκλησία in this sense of a "house-church" (Rom 16:5; 1 Cor 16:19, BAG, 241; for further details see on Col 4:15).

Of particular significance are the two instances in Colossians 1 where ἐκκλησία has a wider reference than either a local congregation or a house-church: at verse 18 it is stated that Christ is "the head of the body, that is, the church," while in verse 24 a similar expression is employed in the context of Paul's sufferings ("on behalf of his body, which is the church"). Most commentators interpret these developed references in Colossians (and the similar instances in Ephesians) of the "universal church" which is scattered throughout the world. But there are two serious criticisms that may be levelled against this view: first, the term ἐκκλησία can no longer have its usual meaning of "gathering" or "assembly," since it is difficult to envisage how a world-wide church could assemble, and the term ἐκκλησία must be translated in some other way to denote an organization or society. Second, the context of chapter 1:15–20 which is moving on a heavenly plane suggests it is not an earthly phenomenon that is being spoken of in verse 18, but a supernatural and heavenly one. Earlier in the letter it has been mentioned that the readers have already been fitted for a share in the inheritance of the saints in the kingdom of light, and have been transferred from a tyranny of darkness to a kingdom in which God's beloved Son holds sway (1:12–14). On the one hand, the Colossians are obviously members of an earthly realm (note the exhortations of 3:4–4:6), and the apostle looks forward to their being presented as "holy, irreproachable and blameless" before God on the last day (1:22). On the other hand, they are described as presently existing in a heavenly realm. Since they have been raised with Christ they are to seek the things that are above where Christ is, seated at God's right hand (3:1). Because they live with Christ in this heavenly dimension (note that Christ who is their life is already in heaven, vv 3, 1) they are assured that when he appears they will also appear with him in glory (v 4). Such thoughts are not entirely new: in Galatians, Paul had already drawn a contrast between the children of the "present Jerusalem" and those who belong to the "Jerusalem above" (Gal 4:25–27). Later, in his letter to the Philippians, the idea is developed with reference to heavenly citizenship: the Philippian Christians who are alive on earth are at the same time members of a heavenly community (Phil 3:19, 20). "Membership in this heavenly community, together with all the benefits that accompany it, was as continuing an affair as membership in the Roman commonwealth"(Banks, *Idea,* 53).

Later references in Ephesians are thought to point in this same direction: it is expressly mentioned that God "made us alive with Christ, . . . raised us up with him and seated us in the heavenly realms in Christ Jesus" (2:5, 6). The same readers of this circular letter have been "blessed . . . in the heavenly realms with every spiritual blessing in Christ" (1:3). Again reference is made to Christ's headship over the "church" (ἐκκλησία) which is his body (1:22, 23). If the term ἐκκλησία is to be understood here as "church" taking place in heaven then this would mean that Christians participate in it as they go about their ordinary daily tasks. They are already gathered around Christ which is another way of saying that they now enjoy fellowship with him. Further references (3:10, 21; 5:23, 25, 27, 29, 32) have been taken in the same way.

If the term ἐκκλησία does point, on some occasions at least, to a heavenly entity then one may well ask what is its relationship to the local congregations (or even house-churches) which are styled ἐκκλσίαι? Certainly local gatherings are not *part* of the heavenly church any more than they are part of an alleged universal church. Paul consistently refers to *the* church which meets in a particular place. Even when there are several gatherings in a single city (e.g. at Corinth) the individual assemblies are not understood as *part* of the church in that place, but as *one* of "the churches" that meet there. This suggests that each of the various local churches are manifestations of that heavenly church, tangible expressions in time and space of what is heavenly and eternal.

(For further references to secondary literature on ἐκκλησία, "assembly, congregation, church," in addition to those already noted, see: Marshall, *ExpTim* 84 [1973], 359–64, and Coenen, *NIDNTT* 1, 305–7.)

Explanation

The language of prayer and thanksgiving shades off at the end of chapter 1:14, with its reference to the forgiveness of sins, into a magnificent hymnic passage in praise of Christ as the Lord in creation and reconciliation. It begins with a series of predicates and activities employed in the OT and Judaism of the personalized Wisdom of God which are applied to the One who had been so ignominiously executed only a few years before.

The first statement spells out his relationship to God, the second to creation. As the "image of the invisible God," Christ is the preexistent One who has revealed the very nature and character of God. He is both prior to and supreme over creation, for he is its Lord. All things have been created in him as the sphere and through him as the agent. Yet the passage tells us more: Christ is unique, for he is the ultimate goal of all creation (no parallel assertion was ever made of Wisdom in the OT or Jewish literature).

Probably with special reference to the Colossian heresy the hymn emphasizes that even the cosmic principalities and powers, from the highest to the lowest, are all subject to Christ. It could not rightly be said that: "There was once when he was not," for the passage asserts that he is both prior to the universe and supreme over it. Further, that universe was established in him alone; apart from his continuous sustaining activity all would disintegrate.

Passing from a cosmological perspective to a soteriological one, Paul affirms that Christ is the head of the body, that is, the church. That headship, pointing to an organic and living relationship with his people, denotes his control over them and their total dependence on him for life and power. It is the risen Christ who is this head; as the beginning and firstborn in resurrection he is the founder of a new humanity. The hymn had previously asserted his primacy in creation; now it mentions his primacy in resurrection. He has therefore become preeminent in everything.

The reason for this primacy is then spelled out: Christ is the one in whom God in all his fullness was pleased to take up residence. His spirit, word, wisdom and glory are perfectly displayed in Christ. Further, this was no temporary indwelling as the hymn and the subsequent commentary on it (2:9) make plain.

Although there has been no previous mention of it, the presupposition is that the unity and harmony of the cosmos have suffered a dislocation, even a rupture, so requiring reconciliation. It was God's good pleasure to reconcile all things through Christ. Heaven and earth have been brought back to their divinely created and determined order. The universe is under its Lord and cosmic peace has been restored. Reconciliation and making peace (which includes the notion of pacification) are used synonymously to describe the climactic work of Christ effected on the historical plane in and through his death on the cross.

To speak of this paragraph as a Christological digression or even as an excursus is misleading for it is to suggest that the hymn does not really belong to its context. Whatever previous existence the passage may have had (and whether it was composed by Paul or not), it is clearly central to the context in which it currently stands, and the task of the exegete is to explain its meaning within this framework and not some hypothetically reconstructed context. Paul's lengthy prayer leads up to the hymn, while the words which immediately follow take up phrases and ideas from it and apply the truths to the readers. Indeed, the paragraph undergirds the whole letter; remove it and a serious dislocation occurs.

The language is majestic. In the opening lines the writer has drawn on a Wisdom background from the OT and Judaism, applying predicates and activities to Christ. Stylistic features such as repetition, parallelism, chiasmus and *inclusio* (see p. 32–37) have all been employed in order to praise Christ as the Lord in creation and reconciliation. Some of the language, e.g. his lordship over the principalities and powers, appears to touch on the heresy of the false teachers.

In the words immediately following the hymn, themes, such as reconciliation, are applied to the readers: Christ's mighty reconciling work had special reference to the Colossians who had previously been alienated from God and at enmity with him. Later in the letter other motifs are touched upon or expanded further (cf. 2:9). But not every statement is directly applied to the recipients.

It is difficult to ascertain, perhaps impossible, how much the Colossians knew of the language and concepts contained in the hymn prior to their reception of the letter. We are told that they had accepted Christ Jesus the Lord as their tradition (2:6, 7), and in the light of Paul's praise of the teaching ministry of his colleague, Epaphras (1:7; cf. 4:12, 13), we may assume that what was asserted in the hymn was not inconsistent with the instruction previously given in the gospel. However, we do know what Paul expected his readers to understand *now* (chapter 2 will deal with some of the ramifications of this). Further, these majestic words in praise of Christ may well have become the basis for their own praises and thanksgivings, offered both corporately as they met together and privately.

Reconciliation Accomplished and Applied (1:21–23)

Bibliography

In addition to the literature cited in the bibliography to chapter 1:15–20 the following are noted:

Dahl, N. A. "Form-Critical Observations on Early Christian Preaching." *Jesus in the Memory of the Early Church.* Minneapolis: Augsburg, 1976, 30–36. **Tachau, P.** *"Einst" und "Jetzt" im Neuen Testament. Beobachtungen zu einem urchristlichen Predigtschema in der neutestamentlichen Briefliteratur und zu seiner Vorgeschichte.* FRLANT 105. Göttingen: Vandenhoeck und Ruprecht, 1972.

Translation

21 *You also, who once were alienated from God, hostile in mind and doing evil deeds,* 22 *he has now reconciled*[a] *in Christ's physical body through his death, in order to present you holy, blameless and innocent in his sight—* 23 *provided that you persevere in the faith, established and firm, and not shifting away from the hope held out in the gospel. This is the gospel that you heard and which has been proclaimed to every creature under heaven, and of which I, Paul, have become a servant.*

Notes

[a]The more difficult reading, the passive ἀποκατηλλάγητε ("you were reconciled"), which creates a harsh anacoluthon after ὑμᾶς in verse 21, is followed by some textual critics. Metzger, *Textual Commentary,* 622, notes that this reading which is attested by diversified and early witnesses (B Hilary Ephraem and, in effect, P[46] and 33) can account for the rise of the other readings as attempts to mend the syntax of the sentence (cf. Lightfoot and Lohmeyer).

On the other hand, Lohse (64) argues that preference ought to be given to ἀποκατήλλαξεν, the best attested textual reading (ℵ A C D[c] K vg syr, etc.), which was altered at a very early stage to the passive so as to strengthen the direct address to the community. Clearly the conflicting textual phenomena are difficult to resolve.

Form/Structure/Setting

This short section of three verses, situated between the hymn and Paul's statement about his apostolic task, returns to the language of direct speech. The introductory words *καὶ ὑμᾶς* ("and you"), which are emphatic in both the original Greek and the English translation, mark a new beginning in which the author interprets and applies statements of the hymn to the readers.

By means of a short, traditional rhetorical form (*ποτέ*, "once," v 21; *νυνί*, "now," v 22) a sharp contrast is drawn between the reader's pre-Christian and pagan past on the one hand, and their present standing in Christ on the other (Tachau, *Einst*). The two contrasting statements may be set out as follows (cf. Zeilinger, *Der Erstgeborene,* 43):

v. 21*a*	καὶ ὑμᾶς:	ποτε ὄντας	ἀπηλλοτριωμένους . . .
b			ἐν τοῖς ἔργοις . . .
22*a*		νυνὶ δὲ	ἀποκατήλλαξεν
b			ἐν τῷ σώματι . . .

A purpose clause—(v. 22*c*, commencing with παραστῆσαι, "to present") is dependent on the latter part of the ποτέ-νυνί construction, thereby indicating why such a form has been employed (see the exegetical notes below), while a lengthy conditional sentence with its positive (v 23*a*, εἴ γε ἐπιμένετε . . . , "provided that you continue . . .") and negative formulations (v 23*b-c*, καὶ μὴ μετακινούμενοι . . . , "and not moved . . ."), which is a demand to continue in the faith, rounds out the section.

Three themes of the paragraph in praise of Christ (1:15–20) are taken up and related to the readers: (a) the catchword "to reconcile" (ἀποκαταλλάξαι, v. 20) in the words "you also . . . he has now reconciled" (ἀποκατήλλαξεν, vv 21, 22), (b) this reconciliation has been effected through Christ's death (compare v 20 with v 22), and (c) since Christ's rule encompasses all things, for everything has been *created* in him (ἐν αὐτῷ ἐκτίσθη τὰ πάντα, v 16), then the gospel is to be, indeed already has been, preached to every *creature* under heaven (ἐν πάσῃ τῇ ὑπὸ τὸν οὐρανόν, v 23).

There is a correspondence between verses 20*b* and 22*b*:

εἰρηνοποιήσας . . .
ἀποκατήλλαξεν . . .

Further, the purpose of verse 22*c* ("to present you holy and without blemish and unreprovable before him"), expressed in cultic language, is akin to the petitionary prayer of verse 10 ("to walk worthily of the Lord unto all pleasing"). Zeilinger (*Der Erstgeborene,* 44) has also noted that the themes of faith, hope, hearing the gospel and its dynamic spread, which have already appeared as significant theological themes in Paul's thanksgiving (vv 4–6) are reiterated at the conclusion of this short section (v 23).

Comment

21. καὶ ὑμᾶς. cf. Ephesians 2:1. The opening words, "and you," stand in an emphatic position in Paul's sentence as he indicates that the central purpose in Christ's reconciling work has to do with the Christian readers at Colossae. It is not simply that what has occurred on a cosmic scale just happens to relate to them by way of application. Rather, this congregation is designated as the "goal" (Lohse, 62) toward which the event encompassing heaven and earth is directed. It has special reference to them, designed to reconcile those who were once alienated and at enmity with God, and to put them on a firm footing of faith and hope.

ποτέ (v 21) . . . νυνὶ δέ (v 22). By means of a short rhetorical form often employed in primitive Christian proclamation (see Bultmann, *Theology* 1, 105, 106; Dahl, *Jesus,* 33; and especially the full treatment by Tachau, *Einst*) a sharp contrast is drawn between the readers' pre-Christian past and their present standing in Christ: "you were once . . . but now you are . . ." This schema appears almost exclusively in the epistolary literature of the NT (though cf. Acts 17:30) and is found in doctrinal, paraenetic or personal contexts (Gal 1:23: cf. 1 Tim 1:13; Philem 11). It is frequently employed by Paul (Rom 5:8–11; 7:5, 6; 11:30–32; 1 Cor 6:9–11; Gal 1:23; 4:3–7, 8–10; Col 2:13; 3:7) but is used by other NT authors as well (1 Pet 2:10, 25; cf. Heb 12:26). The wonder of the salvation that has been experienced is contrasted with the lost situation from which God has delivered them. The past condition is mentioned first (ποτέ) by either terms relating to sin (Rom 5:8–11; 7:5), ethical practices, or alienation from God and his people (Col 1:21; Eph 2:1). However, the gravity of their previous condition serves to magnify the wonder of God's mercy. The past is recalled not because the emphasis falls upon it, but to draw attention to God's mighty action—here in the reconciling death of his Son—on the readers' behalf. Their response ought to be one of loving gratitude that shows itself in a determination to continue in the faith (vv 22, 23).

ὄντας ἀπηλλοτριωμένους . . . τοῖς πονηροῖς. Reconciliation, as we have seen with reference to verse 20, presupposes estrangement. Paul therefore describes that former condition of the Colossians in a threefold way. Tachau (*Einst,* 103) suggests that the latter two statements, "enemies in your mind" and "doing evil deeds," define more precisely in an active way the meaning of the first, "once you were alienated":

(a) ὄντας ἀπηλλοτριωμένους. "once you were alienated." The perfect passive participle means "were estranged" (i.e. from God), while the addition of *ὄντας* expresses "still more forcibly the persistence of the . . . state of things" (BDF, para. 352; cf. Burton, para. 155). The Colossians were once continuously and persistently out of harmony with God (cf. Eph 4:18 for the passive voice of the same verb), a statement that could only describe former Gentiles (cf. Eph 2:12 where the estrangement is put in terms of relationships with God's people: "alienated [ἀπηλλοτριωμένοι] from the commonwealth of Israel and strangers to the covenants of promise"). As such they did not serve God; rather, they were enmeshed in idolatry and slavery to sin.

(b) ἐχθροὺς τῇ διανοίᾳ. While the term "enemy" is on occasion employed in a passive sense meaning "hated" (so Rom 11:28; cf. Bultmann, *Theology* 1, 286) here the word *ἐχθροί* is best understood in an active sense (so Foerster, *TDNT* 2, 814) because of the following *τῇ διανοία*, to denote a conscious antagonism to the only true God, i.e. "hostile in mind." As his opponents, they act in open enmity toward him with reference to their thinking (*τῇ διανοίᾳ* is probably a dative of reference; against Meyer, 309, who regards it as a causal dative) and in their total conduct (*ἐν τοῖς ἔργοις πονηροῖς*). The word "mind" (*διάνοια*) which was a very common term in Greek prose was employed in the LXX usually as a translation of *lēḇ,* ("heart": Gen 8:21; 17:17; 24:45; 27:41; Exod 28:3, etc.; cf. Behm, *TDNT* 4, 965, for further references). Both it and the Greek *καρδία* ("heart") were often related in the LXX (*διάνοια* was also used with reference to emotions [Lev 19:17; Isa 35:4], acts of will [Exod 35:22, 26; Deut 29:17] or the totality of man's spiritual nature [Gen 8:21; Deut 4:39]—just like *καρδία*), even interchangeable, and in the NT the two terms were repeatedly employed together to designate the thinking and

mentality of man (Luke 1:51; Heb 8:10; 10:16; see Behm, *TDNT* 4, 966). This word "mind" (διάνοια) can have either a positive or a negative meaning depending on the context. Here it is clearly the latter connotation which is in view: the Colossian Christians prior to their conversion were estranged and hostile to God in their thinking, in their cast of mind (cf. Eph 2:3; 4:18).

(c) ἐν τοῖς ἔργοις τοῖς πονηροῖς. This kind of thinking naturally finds visible expression in active behavior (Tachau, *Einst,* 103). Godlessness naturally leads to evil actions. The expression "evil work(s)" does not occur frequently in the NT (John 3:19; 7:7; 1 John 3:12; 2 John 11; also 2 Tim 4:18), although similar expressions are to be found: "the works of darkness" (*ἔργα τοῦ σκότους*: Rom 13:12; Eph 5:11), "the works of the flesh" (*ἔργα τῆς σαρκός*: Gal 5:19) and "dead works" (*ἔργα νεκρά*: Heb 6:1; 9:14, etc.; cf. Bertram, *TDNT* 2, 645, and Harder, *TDNT* 6, 557). These phrases denote the actions of the unbelieving world, which belong to the ways of darkness rather than the ways of light, and which ultimately lead to death. When living as unconverted Gentiles the readers had offended God by their wicked ways, a term which, according to Martin (*Lord,* 56), suggests a combination of idolatry and immorality (cf. Rom 1:18–32).

22. *νυνὶ δὲ ἀποκατήλλαξεν.* Having painted a grim picture of the Colossians' pre-Christian and pagan past Paul proceeds to describe the turning point when God acted mightily on their behalf: "now he has reconciled you." There is a textual problem in the word "reconciled." See earlier 64. However, the general sense is clear and on either reading it is plain (i) that the Colossians *have been reconciled* to the one with whom they had previously been at enmity (cf. Wolter, *Rechtfertigung,* 54, 59–62), (ii) that this could only be achieved through divine intervention; and (iii) that attention is focused upon the crucial event which marks the turning point for them, namely Christ's death.

At first sight the aorist tense pointing to Christ's death is rather surprising, for this would suggest, if the time note is pressed, that the Colossians were reconciled to God long before they were historically at enmity with him, or even born! The issue, however, is to be understood in the light of Paul's eschatology, particularly his and the rest of the New Testament's teaching on the two ages. Like the dying and rising with Christ motif, the verb in the indicative is used to denote the decisive transfer of the believers from the old aeon to the new which has taken place in the death of Christ (cf. R. C. Tannehill, *Dying and Rising with Christ. A Study in Pauline Theology* [BZNW 32; Berlin: Töpelmann, 1967], 74). The focus of attention here (as well as in the other "once . . . now" passages) is not simply on what took place in the historical experience of Christ, but also on what happened in the actual life experience of these believers (see especially the discussion of R. B. Gaffin, *The Centrality of the Resurrection. A Study in Paul's Soteriology* [Grand Rapids: Baker, 1978] 41–44). But clearly the death of Christ is the basis, the decisive event by which they are reconciled (cf. Tachau, *Einst,* 114, 115).

ἐν τῷ σώματι τῆς σαρκὸς αὐτοῦ διὰ τοῦ θανάτου. God has reconciled us (so Lohse, 64, and Martin, *NCB,* 67; against Bruce, 211, 212, and Ernst, 181) "in his (*sc.* Christ's) body of flesh, through his (this is the significance of the article *τοῦ*) death." The preposition *ἐν* ("in") signifies not the place of death (see Dibelius-Greeven 22) but is instrumental indicating that Christ's physical body (note the similar expression σῶμα τῆς σαρκός at 2:11 and the discussion 116, 117) was the means by which reconciliation was effected (cf. Abbott, 226). The expression "his body of flesh" appears to be rather heavy. It was evidently a Hebraism meaning "physical body" and has an exact verbal equivalent in the Qumran literature (1QpHab 9:2: "And they inflicted horrors of evil diseases and took vengeance upon his (*sc.* the wicked priest's) body of flesh"; for further examples in Greek see Lohse, 64). The addition "of flesh" (τῆς σαρκός) characterizes the body as the physical body of Jesus which was subject to suffering (cf. R. H. Gundry, *SŌMA in Biblical Theology with Emphasis on Pauline Anthropology* [SNTSMS 29; Cambridge: University Press, 1976] 239), and it is quite likely that this "insistence on the true incarnation of our Lord was a necessary corrective to the tendency of the Colossian heresy" (Bruce, 212). The whole phrase makes plain that the reconciliation of the Colossians was accomplished by one who was truly incarnate (against a docetic understanding of Jesus' historical life) and who really died (διὰ τοῦ θανάτου; against a gnostic interpretation which glossed over his death as unreal). "The phrase is heavily loaded with polemical overtones" (Martin, *NCB*, 67).

παραστῆσαι ὑμᾶς . . . God effected the reconciliation of the Colossians with a particular end in view: to present them holy, blameless and irreproachable before him. (It is possible that the aorist infinitive παραστῆσαι may look back to εὐδόκησεν, i.e. "it was his good pleasure . . . to present you," but the nearer verb ἀποκατήλλαξεν, assuming this is the correct reading, because of its closer proximity and the break at v 21, "and you," is the more likely.) Cultic terminology is employed in this statement. So the words "holy" (ἅγιος) and "blameless" (ἄμωμος) are used to describe the unblemished animals set apart for God as OT sacrifices (LXX of Exod 29:37, 38; cf. Heb 9:14; 1 Pet 1:19). Furthermore, the verb παραστῆσαι ("to present") was, on occasion, employed of presenting a sacrifice (Rom 12:1; cf. Lev 16:7; see BAG, 633). Lightfoot therefore concluded that these expressions, together with the prepositional phrase κατενώπιον αὐτοῦ ("before him"), pointed to the bringing of the Colossians in the here and now as sacrifices into God's presence for approval. God is thus regarded not as a judge but as the "examiner" (μωμοσκόπος) who inspects the sacrifices to make sure they are unblemished (Lightfoot, 160, 161).

It is doubtful, however, whether thoughts of sacrifice are really present in this clause at all. The last term "irreproachable" (ἀνέγκλητος), which probably determines the meaning of the other two (so Abbott, 229), does not belong to the context of cultic statements. It was a judicial word (which came to be used in everyday speech more generally, as the papyri show: cf. MM, 40, 41) denoting a person or thing against which there could be no ἔγκλημα and which was "free from reproach," "without stain" (Grundmann, *TDNT* 1, 356, 357). Likewise the verb παραστῆσαι ("to present") was often employed in legal language with the meaning "to bring another before the court" (some take 1 Cor 8:8, and 2 Cor 4:14 in this way; cf. 2 Cor 11:2; Rom 14:10; 2 Tim 2:15). If the judicial overtones are present in the clause then Paul is asserting that the purpose of God's work of reconciling the readers through Christ's death was that they should be irreproachable when they finally stand before him (cf. Rom 14:10). As men and women who are forgiven and reconciled they are declared blameless (cf. Rom 8:33, 34), without fault or stain (the terms "holy" and "blameless" appear to have lost any cultic overtones at Eph 1:4; 5:27; Phil 2:15; Jude 24) on the occasion of the Great Assize. At 1 Corinthians 1:8 where the same word ἀνέγκλητος points to the irreproachability of the Corinthians (cf. O'Brien, *Introductory Thanksgivings,* 126–30) the Parousia is mentioned explicitly: "on the day of our Lord Jesus Christ." The same time note is meant here with the phrase "before him" (κατενώπιον αὐτοῦ, cf. Hegermann, *Schöpfungsmittler,* 194, 196; there is no justification within this context for the view of D. M. Stanley, *Christ's Resurrection in Pauline Soteriology* [AnBib 13; Rome: Pontifical Biblical Institute, 1961] 209, that: "Paul is probably thinking of the presentation of the Colossian church in the Eucharistic liturgy"!). These words of verse 22 prepare the way for a similar understanding of Paul's aim in his ministry, namely "to present (παραστήσωμεν, the same verb, appears) every man perfect in Christ," verse 28, i.e. acceptable to God at his tribunal on the final day (Rom 14:10). God's work of reconciliation in Christ had as its goal the fitness and preparedness of his people for the Parousia. Paul's ministry, in which he worked mightily, had the same aim in view—the ultimate perfection of the Colossians in Christ.

23. A lengthy conditional sentence with its positive (v 23a) and negative (v 23*b-c*) formulations, setting forth a demand to continue in the faith, rounds out the section.

εἴ γε. The prospect of the Colossians' standing irreproachable before him at the Great Assize is conditional upon their remaining firmly founded and established in the faith. The Greek construction εἴ γε, translated "provided that," does not express doubt. Although the same expression in Galatians 3:4 may leave "a loophope for doubt" (J. B. Lightfoot, *The Epistle of Paul to the Galatians,* 2nd American reprint edition. Grand Rapids, MI: Zondervan, 1957, 135), the other Pauline references (2 Cor 5:3; Eph 3:2; 4:21 and Rom 5:6, if the text of B is followed) according to Lightfoot (161), Thrall (*Particles,* 87, 88, 90) and Martin (*Lord,* 58, 59) would appear from their contexts to denote confidence. So the words in this sentence may be paraphrased: "At any rate if you stand firm in the faith—and I am sure that you will," words with which Thrall (*Particles,* 88) rightly compares chapter 2:5, "rejoicing to see your order and the firm stability of your faith in Christ." But continuance is the test of reality. If it is true that the saints *will* persevere to the end, then it is equally true that the saints *must* persevere to the end. And one of the means which the apostle uses to insure that his readers within the various congregations of his apostolic mission do not fall into a state of false security is to stir them up with warnings such as this.

ἐπιμένετε τῇ πίστει τεθεμελιωμένοι καὶ ἑδραῖοι. The call is to steadfastness in the face of the danger of being drawn away from the apostolic gospel. ἐπιμένω with the dative case is used figuratively several times by Paul, meaning "continue," "persist (in)," "persevere" (cf. Rom 6:1; 11:22, 23; 1 Tim 4:16). "The faith" in this context is another description for the apostolic gospel rather than the subjective response of the Colossians to that gospel.

Paul's terms "stable and steadfst" (τεθεμελιωμένοι καὶ ἑδραῖοι) are metaphors of strength and security used in connection with a house (cf. Matt 7:24–27).

Both the foundation (the noun θεμέλιον is akin to this verb) ought to be well established and the structure firm (ἑδραῖος). In the OT the verb "establish" (θεμελιόω) was used to describe: (a) God's founding activity in creation (LXX Pss 8:4: 23:2; 101:26; Isa 48:13; 51:13, 16; etc.), and (b) the establishing of his city on Mt. Zion (LXX Ps 47:9; Isa 14:32; 44:28; Hag 2:18; Zech 4:9; 8:9; etc.; see Lohmeyer, 72, and Lohse, 66). The Qumran community regarded itself as God's house (1QS 5:6; 7:17; 8:7, 8; 9:5, 6; 1QH 6:25–27; 7:8, 9; see O. Betz, "Felsenmann und Felsengemeinde [Eine Parallele zu Mt 16:17–19 in den Qumranpsalmen]," *ZNW* 48 [1957] 49–77, for further examples cf. B. Gärtner, *The Temple and the Community in Qumran and the New Testament* [SNTSMS 1; Cambridge: University Press, 1965] 16–46, and R. J. McKelvey, *The New Temple. The Church in the New Testament* [OTM 3; Oxford: University Press, 1969] 46–53). The NT writers often take up the thought of the Christian community as a holy building of God (sometimes specifically the temple: 1 Cor 3:10, 11, 17; Eph 2:20; 1 Tim 3:15; 1 Pet 2:4–10; cf. Matt 16:17–19), stressing different motifs: e.g. the unity of the building, its holiness, it is the place where God's Spirit dwells, and so on. That community as God's building has a sure foundation, Jesus Christ (1 Cor 3:10, 11; Eph 2:20; 2 Tim 2:19), and as a house is erected with strong supports and buttresses (cf. 1 Tim 3:15 where the cognate ἑδραίωμα points to the local congregation as the "bulwark" of the truth). Paul's summons to steadfastness is needed in time of discouragement and stress (Martin, *NCB*, 68; cf. 1 Cor 15:58) and reappears in Christian vocabulary when the church has to withstand the attacks of heretics (Ignatius, *Eph* 10:2, perhaps echoing the words in Colossians, "Be steadfast in the faith"; Polycarp, *Phil* 10:1).

καὶ μὴ μετακινούμενοι. The same idea is now put negatively (according to Winer, para. 55.1a the use of μή implies that this clause is conditioned by the preceding; cf. Abbott, 227), though it is defined more precisely by the following words: "not constantly shifting (present tense) from the hope of the gospel." The verb μετακινέω, meaning "shift," "remove," is used figuratively (in the OT there are several places where it means "be put to flight," e.g. LXX Deut 32:30) as Paul calls his readers not to shift from the fixed ground of the Christian hope—that hope which was the content of the gospel (εὐαγγελίου is a subjective genitive).

τοῦ κηρυχθέντος . . . ὑπὸ τὸν οὐρανόν. As the themes of reconciliation and the saving significance of Christ's death are taken up from the hymn of verses 15–20 and applied to the readers, so too the note of universalism is reiterated. Paul has already said that the gospel was "bearing fruit and increasing in all the world" (1:6). He now asserts that, since Christ's rule in both creation and reconciliation encompasses all things (vv 15–20), the gospel which announces that lordship is directed to the whole world (cf. H. Kasting, *Die Anfänge der urchristlichen Mission. Eine historische Untersuchung* [BEvT 55; Munich: Kaiser, 1969] 138, 139). In fact, it *has already been preached* (κηρυχθέντος) to every creature (ἐν signifies the location where the preaching takes place: Matt 3:1; 11:1; 24:14; Acts 9:20; Gal 2:2; while πάσῃ κτίσει here means "all humankind": a similar phrase occurs at Mark 16:15 in the context of world mission, cf. Foerster, *TDNT* 3, 1029; Schweizer, 78; the expression ὑπὸ τὸν οὐρανόν does not appear elsewhere in Paul but accords well with the Greek OT: Gen

1:9; 6:17; 7:19; Exod 17:14; etc.). But in what sense has the gospel of hope been proclaimed to all humankind? It certainly does not mean that every individual has heard the message. Nor, on the other hand, do we agree with Dibelius-Greeven (22) that the statement is to be regarded as a rhetorical exaggeration. Rather, along the lines of chapter 1:6 Paul has particularly in mind cities and towns from which the gospel moved further afield (see above 13).

Also, by referring to the universal scope of the gospel, Paul shows it is *the* authentic message. "The catholicity of the gospel is a token of its divine origin and power" (Bruce, 213). It stands in stark contrast to the heretical teaching with its appeal to a select group of initiates (cf. Masson, 109).

οὗ ἐγενόμην ἐγὼ Παῦλος διάκονος. Having begun his thanksgiving report at verse 3 with the plural "*we* give thanks"—so writing on behalf of Timothy and perhaps others as well as himself—Paul now wishes to emphasize his own ministry as closely bound up with God's gracious plan for the world and so he emphatically turns to the singular: "of which (*sc.* gospel) I, Paul, became a minister."

It has been argued by some recent interpreters (notably Käsemann, *Essays,* 166, 167, and Lohse, 67) that when the title "minister of the gospel" is here applied to Paul it is the voice of the subapostolic age looking back to him as the guarantor of the apostolic office. So a later generation is in these words asserting that the Pauline gospel has binding validity because of its apostolic character. But such a reading of the situation fails to come to grips with: *(a)* the glaring omission of the significant term "apostle" (ἀπόστολος) which would have uniquely served this supposed intention of the post-Pauline writer (cf. Ernst, 182, and Martin *NCB,* 68, 69), *(b)* the fact that Paul, in his major letters, uses the word διάκονος of himself, as well as his colleagues, particularly when he wishes to stress that both he and they are on the same footing as servants through whom God works (notably 1 Cor 3:5). That the phrase "minister *of the gospel*" does not occur in the chief Pauline letters is of no real significance since it is clear in these epistles that such ministers are servants of the Word who preach and teach the gospel anyway (cf. 2 Cor 3:6 with 2:17 and 4:2; note Ellis, *NTS* 17 [1970–71] 441–45).

Rather, Paul appears to be making a different point in this context, namely that the message which focuses on the lordship of Christ and the reconciliation wrought by him is the mighty gospel of which he has been privileged to become a servant. He of all people has become a minister of that gospel. In the wider context of the letter by styling himself a διάκονος Paul is demonstrating that he is on the same level as Epaphras and Tychicus (1:7; 4:7), his trusted fellow-workers (cf. 1 Cor 3:5) who are thereby commended as true exponents of that gospel at Colossae.

Explanation

The message of Christ's peace-making work, which involves the reconciliation of the cosmos, has particular reference to the Colossian Christians. These readers who are now addressed directly (v 21, "and you") are reminded of their pre-Christian past when they were enemies, alienated from God and his people. The gravity of their previous situation sets in bolder relief God's gracious and mighty action of reconciling them to himself. That reconciliation which was effected in history at great cost—the death of his Son on the cross—had as its goal the fitness and preparedness of his people for the final day when they will stand before him.

Continuance, however, is the test of the reality of their faith. Like a building set on a sure foundation and erected with strong supports and buttresses they are to remain true to the gospel, and not to shift from the fixed ground of their Christian hope. The claim of Paul's gospel (which focused on this hope) to be the authentic message is attested by its universal appeal. No class or group is to be excluded from hearing it since it speaks of Jesus' lordship in creation and redemption. In fact, this message about God's plan for the world, which Paul is privileged to serve as a minister, has already been preached in towns and cities of the empire and is well on the way to being proclaimed throughout the Mediterranean world.

Paul's Mission and Pastoral Concern (1:24–2:5)

Bibliography

Bandstra, A. J. *Dimensions,* 329–43. **Bauckham, R. J.** "Colossians 1:24 Again: The Apocalyptic Motif." *EvQ* 47 (1975) 168–70. **Bowers, W. P.** "A Note on Colossians 1:27a." *Current Issues in Biblical and Patristic Interpretation. Studies in Honor of Merrill C. Tenney Presented by His Former Students,* ed. G. F. Hawthorne. Grand Rapids: Eerdmans, 1975, 110–14. **Brown, R. E.** *The Semitic Background of the Term "Mystery" in the New Testament.* FBBS 21. Philadelphia: Fortress, 1968. **Dahl, N. A.** *Jesus,* 30–36. **Kamlah, E.** "Wie beurteilt Paulus sein Leiden? Ein Beitrag zur Untersuchung seiner Denkstruktur." *ZNW* 54 (1963) 217–32. **Kremer, J.** *Was an den Leiden Christi noch mangelt. Eine interpretationsgeschichtliche und exegetische Untersuchung zu Kol. 1, 24b.* BBB 12. Bonn: Hanstein, 1956. **Lührmann, D.** *Das Offenbarungsverständnis bei Paulus und in paulinischen Gemeinden.* WMANT 16. Neukirchen-Vluyn: Neukirchener, 1965. **Montague, G. T.** *Growth in Christ,* 81–85. **Pfitzner, V. C.** *Paul and the Agon Motif.* NovTSup 16. Leiden: Brill, 1967. **Reumann, J.** "OIKONOMIA—Terms in Paul in Comparison with Lucan *Heilsgeschichte.*" *NTS* 13 (1966–67) 147–67. **Trudinger, L. P.** "A Further Brief Note on Colossians 1:24." *EvQ* 45 (1973) 36–38. **Yates, R.** "A Note on Colossians 1:24." *EvQ* 42 (1970) 88–92. **Zeilinger, F.** *Der Erstgeborene,* 44–49, 82–115.

Translation

24 *Now I rejoice in my sufferings for your sake, and I fill up in my flesh what is still lacking in regard to Christ's afflictions, for the sake of his body, which is the church.* 25 *I have become its minister in accordance with the commission God gave me concerning you to preach the word of God fully and effectively—* 26 *the mystery that was kept secret for ages and generations, but has now been disclosed to the saints.* 27 *To them God chose to make known among the Gentiles the glorious riches of this mystery, which is Christ in you, the hope of glory.* 28 *We proclaim him, warning and teaching everyone with all wisdom, so that we may present everyone perfect in Christ.* 29 *To this end I labor, striving with all the energy he so powerfully works in me.*

2:1 *I want you to know how greatly I strive for you, for those at Laodicea, and for all who have not met me personally.* 2 *My purpose is that they may be strengthened in heart and instructed in love, so that they may have the whole wealth of full understanding and thus know the mystery of God, namely Christ,* 3 *in whom all the treasures of wisdom and knowledge have been stored up.* 4 *I am saying this in order that no one may deceive you with persuasive language.* 5 *For even if I am absent from you in body, I am present with you in spirit, and I rejoice to see your orderly life and the stability of your faith in Christ.*

Form/Structure/Setting

Paul's statement that he is the servant of the gospel (v 23) provides the transition to this following section in which he describes his suffering as an apostle and its relationship to his God-given task (vv 24, 25). His message is the public proclamation of the mystery, now revealed, which focuses on Christ as the hope of the Gentiles (vv 26, 27). As apostle, therefore, he works energetically, seeking systematically to teach and warn everyone with the aim of presenting everyone perfect in Christ (vv 28, 29). This activity, in which he engages on a universal scale, particularly applies to the congregations at Colossae and elsewhere in the Lycus valley where he was unknown. Because of his commission Paul is able to instruct and strengthen these Christians (2:1–5).

The whole paragraph which deals with Paul's ministry to the churches (1:24–2:5) may be divided into two sections: 1:24–29 and 2:1–5. While there are one or two instances of parallelism (which are noted below) the sentences in both sections cannot be divided easily. In the first paragraph Paul begins with the first person singular (*χαίρω, ἀνταναπληρῶ*, v 24), changes to the plural at v 28 (*ἡμεῖς καταγγέλλομεν*), and then reverts to the singular in the last verse (*κοπιῶ ἀγωνιζόμενος*, v 29).

V 24 may be divided into two parts of unequal length, each of which commences with a finite verb in the first person singular (*χαίρω . . . ἀνταναπληρῶ*) and is then followed by prepositional phrases commencing with *ἐν* (*ἐν τοῖς παθήμασιν . . . ἐν τῇ σαρκί μου*) and *ὑπέρ* (*ὑπὲρ ὑμῶν . . . ὑπὲρ τοῦ σώματος αὐτοῦ*). The additional words in the second half, however, mean that the sentence is not perfectly balanced.

Zeilinger (*Der Erstgeborene*, 44–46) understands the paragraph in a circular fashion with the twofold statement of the mystery (vv 25*d*–27) at the center and items 1, 5, and 2, 4 corresponding:

1. The suffering of the apostle (v 24)
2. The apostle's task (v 25*a–c*)
3. The mystery (vv 25*d*–27)
4. The carrying out of the task (v 28)
5. The toil and labor of the apostle (v 29).

Such a division, however, is a little too neat, for although Zeilinger's headings are apt enough there is not the circular correspondence he suggests.

The second section is made up of three sentences of unequal length: the first extends to verse 3, the second comprises verse 4, the third verse 5. Commencing with a well-known literary form "I want you to know" (*θέλω . . . ὑμᾶς εἰδέναι*) Paul indicates how great is the conflict in which he is engaged on behalf of the Colossians and others:

ἡλίκον ἀγῶνα ἔχω
ὑπὲρ ὑμῶν
καὶ τῶν ἐν Λαοδικείᾳ
καὶ ὅσοι οὐχ ἑόρακαν τὸ πρόσωπόν μου ἐν σαρκί.

The purpose of this strenuous effort is indicated by means of a *ἵνα* clause (v 2), which then leads on to a further statement about the mystery which is centered on Christ. A relative clause (*ἐν ᾧ* expands this indicating that in him alone exist true "wisdom" and "knowledge" (v 3). A warning note is sounded (τοῦτο λέγω) so that (ἵνα) the community may not be led astray by the high-sounding words of the deceivers (v 4). The danger to the congregation is a serious one. Paul is distant. He cannot be on hand to speak directly to the community but he is present with it in spirit—note the synthetic parallelism of verse 5a and b:

εἰ γὰρ καὶ τῇ σαρκὶ ἄπειμι
ἀλλὰ τῷ πνεύματι σὺν ὑμῖν εἰμι.

Finally, by means of two participles (χαίρων, βλέπων) Paul indicates he is pleased with the Colossians' orderly Christian life and the stability of their faith.

Comment

24. This verse has been an exegetical crux since earliest times as Kremer (*Leiden Christi*) has shown in his history of the exegesis of the passage. It appears to express ideas that go beyond Paul's statements elsewhere and which seem to have no parallel in the rest of the NT. Several questions immediately arise: What are Paul's sufferings and how can they be an occasion for rejoicing? In what sense can these sufferings be for the body of Christ (ὑπὲρ τοῦ σώματος αὐτοῦ), or for the Colossians (ὑπὲρ ὑμῶν), a congregation which he had neither evangelized nor visited? Then, what is meant by the phrase "Christ's afflictions"? How can it be meaningfully said that something is "lacking" in these afflictions, and in what way can Paul (or other Christians if it applies to them) fill this deficiency? We shall endeavor to answer these questions in the exegesis that follows.

νῦν χαίρω ἐν τοῖς παθήμασιν ὑπὲρ ὑμῶν. Having spoken about the worldwide preaching of the gospel of which he has been privileged to become a servant (v 23), Paul states that he rejoices in his sufferings for the Colossians. By using the first person singular, "I rejoice" (χαίρω), which naturally follows on from verse 23, he contrasts the previous plurals "we give thanks" (εὐχαριστοῦμεν, v 3) and "we do not cease to pray for you" (οὐ παυόμεθα ὑπὲρ ὑμῶν προσευχόμενοι, v 9). What follows, then, has particular reference to him. The "now" (νῦν) points not so much to Paul's actual imprisonment (as Abbott, 228, and Masson, 109, suppose), which is not specifically mentioned until chapter 4:3, but to the present time when Christ's lordship is proclaimed universally in the gospel and when he, Paul, is privileged to suffer as a servant of that gospel and for the Colossians.

The word πάθημα, meaning "suffering," "affliction," or "misfortune," was used from the time of the Greek tragedians onward to denote that which befell a man and had to be accepted by him. The term does not appear in the LXX (though kindred words such as πάσχω do) while in the NT (apart from Heb 2:9) it is always used in the plural (for details see Michaelis, *TDNT* 5, 930–35). Apart from the rare meaning of "passion," "impulse" (at Gal 5:24; Rom 7:5) its usual sense is "suffering" (Rom 8:18; 2 Cor 1:5–7; Phil 3:10; Col 1:24; 2 Tim 3:11; Heb 2:9, 10; 10:32; 1 Pet 1:11; 4:13; 5:1–9).

Paul uses the word to designate the afflictions in which all Christians participate as part of the sufferings of Christ (Rom 8:18; 2 Cor 1:5–7; cf. Phil 3:10). Here, however, because of the context ἐν τοῖς παθήμασιν refers to Paul's own sufferings (some manuscripts, ℵ³ 81 etc., add μου, "my," but the meaning is plain enough without this explanatory addition; the definite article denotes the sufferings actually experienced, the ones Paul knows about), bound up with the special significance of his calling to minister to Gentiles through the world-wide preaching of the gospel (cf. Bauckham, *EvQ* 47 [1975] 168–70). So we note the emphatic singulars ("I rejoice," "I fill up") and the references to his ministry as a servant (vv 23, 25) deriving from the particular stewardship given to him by God (v 25), the content of which was to fulfill the word of God, i.e. the mystery (vv 25, 26).

Elsewhere Paul refers to suffering (by various terms including θλῖψις, ἀσθένεια, etc.; see Kamlah, *ZNW* [1963] 217–32, and Schweizer, 81–86, and the literature cited there) as integral to his apostolic ministry (1 Cor 4:9–13; 2 Cor 11:23–33; 12:9, 10; 13:4 and Gal 6:17) and as such it was tied in with the clear proclamation of the gospel (2 Cor 4:4–6 with vv 7–18; 5:18–21 with 6:1–11; cf. 1 Thess 1:5, 6; 3:3, 4 and Acts 14:22). For him the conjunction of suffering with his apostolic ministry of the gospel was no new thing; he had been forewarned by Christ at the very beginning when he was called to preach him among the Gentiles: "I will show him how much he must suffer [note the δεῖ of divine necessity] for the sake of my name" (Acts 9:16).

Second Corinthians 1:3–11 provides an important parallel to Colossians 1:24 for in both passages the terms θλῖψις and πάθημα appear. In the former paragraph where Paul tells the Corinthians of the excruciating nature of his affliction (θλῖψις) in Asia (v 8), he indicates that this sort of distress he experiences (v 4, ἐπὶ πάσῃ τῇ θλίψει ἡμῶν; v 6, θλιβόμεθα) is part and parcel of the sufferings of the Messiah (τὰ παθήματα τοῦ Χριστοῦ, v 5). The Corinthians too share in the same messianic woes (vv 6, 7) even though the precise nature of their affliction was different from that of Paul (for a more detailed treatment see O'Brien, *Introductory Thanksgivings*, 244–50). At Colossians 1:24 the two terms "sufferings" (παθήματα) and "afflictions" (θλίψεις), though synonymous, are reversed. The former denotes the sufferings actually experienced by Paul in his apostolic labors; the latter is employed in the enigmatic phrase "the afflictions of Christ" (αἱ θλίψεις τοῦ Χριστοῦ), the meaning of which is discussed below.

The words ὑπὲρ ὑμῶν ("for your sake"; on the meaning of ὑπέρ see BDF, para. 231) have occasioned some difficulty (how could Paul's sufferings be for a congregation which he had neither evangelized nor visited?) and so have been connected with the verb χαίρω: "I rejoice . . . over you." But the phrase ὑπὲρ ὑμῶν naturally attaches to ἐν τοῖς παθήμασιν to mean "(I rejoice) in my sufferings for your sake," with particular reference to the Colossian Christians (Moule, 79, claims that the words "for your sake," while strictly applying to the Colossians or the Lycus valley churches must not be confined to them since they are representative of others; this is possible though the ὑμᾶς naturally follows on from the second person plurals of vv 21–23 ["you were alienated . . . but now he has reconciled you," etc.], and these certainly apply to the Colossians and other Lycus valley Christians. More significant for Moule's contention is that ὑπὲρ ὑμῶν is parallelled by ὑπὲρ τοῦ σώματος αὐτοῦ. The wider reference is to be seen in this latter phrase, not the former).

The first clause (v 24*a*) does not state in what way Paul's sufferings are for the Colossians (ὑπὲρ ὑμῶν). This issue can only be settled by reference to the following words (v 24*b*) which clarify and explain more closely the meaning of verse 24*a* (the καί is explicative: so Lohse, 69, and Zeilinger, *Der Erstgeborene,* 83):

καὶ ἀνταναπληρῶ τὰ ὑστερήματα τῶν θλίψεων τοῦ Χριστοῦ κτλ. This may be translated literally as: "And in my flesh I complete what is lacking in Christ's afflictions for the sake of his body, that is, the church." The significance of the statement is by no means clear and it has occasioned a considerable amount of comment and discussion. Our method will be to examine the critical phrases in the clause, noting several alternative interpretations, before suggesting the lines along which we judge the meaning is to be sought.

τὰ ὑστερήματα τῶν θλίψεων τοῦ Χριστοῦ. The Greek may be rendered by "what is lacking in Christ's afflictions," and the following are some of the more significant interpretations (cf. Kremer, *Leiden Christi*) that have been suggested:

(1) H. Windisch (*Paulus und Christus. Ein biblisch-religionsgeschichtlicher Vergleich.* [Leipzig: Heinrich, 1934] 236–50) took the phrase to mean that there was still something lacking in the vicarious sufferings of Christ which must be supplied by the apostle. Paul bore away the sufferings "which Christ could not carry away completely" (244). This view has been largely abandoned by recent scholars, and with good reasons. Paul, like the other NT writers, regarded the death of Jesus as the means by which reconciliation was truly and uniquely accomplished. To go no further than Colossians itself Paul states that because of Christ's death on the cross all our trespasses have been forgiven (2:13, 14; cf. 1:12–14, 19–22). In addition to this, it has been correctly pointed out by Staab, Schweizer and others that nowhere else in the NT is the phrase "Christ's afflictions" used of his redemptive act or general experience of suffering. Instead, Paul uses the concepts "blood," "cross" and "death" to refer to that act of redemption.

(2) A popular view in seventeenth and eighteenth century Protestant interpretation was to understand the genitive τοῦ Χριστοῦ as objective (or as a *genitivus auctoris*) so that the phrase meant suffering "for the sake of Christ." It was argued that this was consistent with Pauline thought (cf. 2 Cor 4:10, 11), while Acts 9:16 records how much Paul will suffer for the sake of Christ's name. So, with this perspective, the exegetical difficulties are said to disappear. Paul is not speaking of completing or filling up the sufferings of Jesus; instead, he is suffering for Christ's sake. The difficulty with this approach, however, is that it does not really explain the phrase "what is lacking" (τὰ ὑστερήματα), nor does it indicate how the apostle can "fill up" these sufferings.

(3) Another line of approach that was popular among some early interpreters was to understand τοῦ Χριστοῦ as a genitive of quality referring to the sufferings of Paul "which resemble those of Christ." Greek commentators such as Photius and Theodoret adopted this line as did Pelagius on the Latin side, and it appears to have been revived during the nineteenth century by Meyer, von Soden and Abbott. Paul's sufferings were similar to the distresses

experienced by Christ; Christ's afflictions "are regarded as the type of all those that are endured by His followers on behalf of the church" (Abbott, 232). But again it may be asked: In what sense can one meaningfully speak of a lack in Christ's afflictions, and how is Paul able to remedy such a deficiency?

(4) A fourth approach which has been very influential in times past is the Christ-mysticism view. All that Paul does and suffers happens in mystical union with Christ (cf. Gal 2:20). The "afflictions of Christ" are those sufferings experienced in mystical fellowship with him. Deissmann and Schmid, two exponents of this theory, held that the words applied to Paul alone, while Schneider and Dibelius thought they referred to the whole church. Advocates of the Christ-mysticism approach considered that Paul could write in this way without bringing into question or reducing the suffering of Christ on earth. This mystic union with Christ in his dying and resurrection (supposedly supported by Phil 3:10) in some way or other conferred a benefit on the church. Lohmeyer's criticisms (76–79; cf. Percy, *Probleme*, 128–34) of this view, however, are still trenchant. He finds difficulty with the word ὑστερήματα ("what is lacking") claiming that in "a 'mystical suffering in accordance with Christ' either the entire suffering of Christ is present and 'what is lacking' is never perceptible, or else the personal suffering of faith remains separate from the exemplary sufferings of Christ" (Lohmeyer, 77; cf. Lohse, 69, 70). In other words, it seems incomprehensible how, in the light of this intimate communion of suffering, there could be a measure of afflictions which still lacked something.

(5) Clearly any satisfactory explanation of the passage (as Best, *Body*, 136, notes) must take the words τὰ ὑστερήματα seriously without suggesting that Christ's sufferings were insufficient to redeem, and explain why Paul's sufferings can be linked with those of the Messiah, at the same time indicating why he should rejoice in his sufferings for the sake of Colossians. Several scholars (including Best, *Body*, 136, Moule, 76, Lohse, 70–72, Martin, *NCB*, 70, and Zeilinger, *Der Erstgeborene*, 82–94; note, however, the criticisms of Ernst, 184, 185) consider a more fruitful line of inquiry into the meaning of "Christ's afflictions" is the OT and Jewish background with its apocalyptic conception of the afflictions of the end time, the woes of the Messiah. The presence of the definite article "*the* afflictions of Christ" (τῶν θλίψεων τοῦ Χριστοῦ) suggests a definite or well-known entity such as the birth-pangs of the Messiah (cf. Kremer, *Leiden Christi*, 168). Since the immediate context contains references to other concepts which have an apocalyptic ring (the mystery previously hidden but now revealed, v 26; "the riches of the glory of this mystery," v 27; "God's mystery," 2:2; and "in whom all the treasures of wisdom and knowledge are hidden," 2:3) it is considered that the attempt to find such associations in this disputed phrase is appropriate.

The term θλῖψις ("affliction") which stands in the LXX for several Hebrew terms that more or less denote the distresses of life in various nuances gained its theological significance from the fact that it predominantly signified "the oppression and affliction of the people of Israel or of the righteous who represent Israel" (Schlier, *TDNT* 3, 142; cf. Zeilinger, *Der Erstgeborene*, 84). Israel constantly experienced "affliction" (θλῖψις) in its history, for example, the oppression in Egypt and the affliction of the exile, both important events of salvation history (Exod 4:31; Deut 4:29; 28:47–68; Judg 6:9; 10:6–16; 1 Sam 10:18, 19; 2 Kings 19:3), while the righteous in Israel, according to the Psalms, were afflicted too (Pss 9:10; 12:5; 22:5; 31:7; 33:7, 18, etc.). In addition to this continual visitation of the chosen people by God, according to Daniel 12:1 there belongs also a future *ἡμέρα θλίψεως* ("There is going to be a time of *great distress,* unparalleled since nations first came into existence," JB; cf. Hab 3:16; Zeph 1:15). So Schlier (*TDNT* 3, 142) concludes: "The judgment fulfilled in the history of Israel will be totally revealed in the eschatological *θλῖψις*."

Jewish apocalyptic writing, with its doctrine of the two ages ("the present age" and "the coming age"), frequently pictured the disasters and catastrophes coming upon the world (cf. Dan 12:1) as a prelude to the end-time which would usher in the coming anointed ruler of God. Plagues, war, famine and the like will fall upon mankind, and even God's people will be called upon to suffer (for examples see Str-B 4, 977–86). When these horrors and cosmic disorders reach their climax, their appointed limit, the advent will come. The afflictions of these last days are called the "woes of the Messiah" (Hebrew *ḥebᵉlô šel māšîaḥ* = *ἡ ὠδὶν τοῦ Χριστοῦ* [cf. Matt 24:8; Mark 13:8; Paul's expression *αἱ θλίψεις τοῦ Χριστοῦ*, "the afflictions of the Christ/Messiah," is synonymous and equivalent) as they immediately precede the arrival of the anointed ruler of God. They are the travail out of which the messianic age is born. God has set a limit to these sufferings, prescribing a definite measure for the afflictions which the righteous and the martyrs must endure (1 Enoch 47:1–4; 2 Baruch 30:2).

The NT's teaching concerning the end-time is not unrelated to these Jewish apocalyptic conceptions. God has set the measure and extent of these afflictions, thereby limiting them (Mark 13:19–24 and parallels). However, the NT significantly modifies this apocalyptic concept of the messianic woes: *(a)* it is not some unknown figure who will appear at the advent: it will be the Son of Man on the clouds of heaven who is none other than the crucified and risen Lord Jesus. The sorrows to be endured will usher in his glorious appearing for judgment and salvation. *(b)* With the death and resurrection of the Lord Jesus Christ the "coming age" has been inaugurated. The present age continues so that Christians live in the overlap of the two aeons. The woes of the Messiah, the afflictions of Christ, have already begun and when their appointed limit has been reached the coming age will be consummated and this present evil age will pass away.

All Christians participate in these sufferings; through them they enter the kingdom of God (Acts 14:22; cf. 1 Thess 3:3, 7). Suffering with Christ is a necessary prerequisite to being glorified with him (Rom 8:17, *εἴπερ συμπάσχομεν ἵνα καὶ συνδοξασθῶμεν*). But none of these afflictions is able to separate the believer from the love of God in Christ Jesus (Rom 8:38, 39). They ultimately lead to hope and glory (Rom 5:3), and there is the assurance given that such afflictions of the present time (Rom 8:18, *τὰ παθήματα τοῦ νῦν καιροῦ*) are not worth comparing with that glory to be revealed.

ἀνταναπληρῶ τὰ ὑστερήματα . . . The term *ὑστέρημα* ("need," "want," "deficiency," BAG, 849; cf. Wilckens, *TDNT* 8, 592–601) was used of the absence of a person to whom one is attached (1 Cor 16:7; Phil 2:30), and of a deficiency in a specific situation (1 Thess 3:10). The presence of the definite article τά suggests the phrase "what is lacking in Christ's afflictions" refers to something well-known (so Lohse, 71; Zeilinger, *Der Erstgeborene*, 89) and agrees with the apocalyptic notion of a definite measure of affliction to be endured in the last days. As God had set a definite measure in time (cf. 4 Ezra 4:36, 37; Gal 4:4) and the limit of the tribulations at the end (cf. Mark 13:5–27) so there is a definite measure of suffering that is to be filled up. That limit of the messianic woes has not yet been reached. There are still deficiencies (τὰ ὑστερήματα) which Paul through his sufferings is in the process of completing.

Though the precise significance of ἀντί in the verb ἀνταναπληρόω ("complete") is not certain (it has been taken to mean "in quick succession," or "instead," "for someone else" [cf. BAG, 72]; Lightfoot, 162, 163, after a comparison of classical and Hellenistic Greek occurrences rendered the verb "I fill up on my part," "I supplement," arguing that the preposition "signifies that the supply comes from an *opposite quarter* to the deficiency"; while Schweizer, 84, and Moule, *Idiom Book*, 71, suggest it may anticipate the force of the ὑπέρ which follows), the simplest interpretation is to regard the prefix as suggesting correspondence, i.e. the supply corresponds to the deficiency so that the filling up *replaces* the lack (cf. Bruce, 215).

The apostle, through the sufferings which he endures in his own flesh (ἐν τῇ σαρκί μου refers to his bodily sufferings, or as Schweizer, *TDNT* 7, 136, puts it: "the reference is to the physical existence of the apostle as this is exposed to affliction"; cf. Gal 6:17: ἐν τῷ σώματί μου; 2 Cor 4:10 and 12:7), contributes to the sum total of these eschatological afflictions. By helping to fill up this predetermined measure Paul brings the end, the dawning of the future glory, so much closer (Lohse, 71).

ὑπὲρ τοῦ σώματος αὐτοῦ. (On the background and meaning of the "body of Christ" see on v 18). In verse 24*a* the apostle had indicated that his sufferings were "for your sake" (ὑπὲρ ὑμῶν, a reference as we have seen to the Colossians and their Lycus valley Christian neighbors). Here Paul's statement is parallel (note the repeated ὑπέρ) though the designation is wider. His contributing to the sum total of the messianic afflictions, through his service and suffering bound up with his calling as an apostle or minister to the Gentiles, is on behalf of Christ's body. By filling up what was lacking of a predetermined measure of afflictions which the righteous must endure, Paul also reduces the tribulations other believers, especially these Gentile Christians at Colossae, are to experience. The more of these sufferings he personally absorbed, as he went about preaching the gospel, the less would remain for his fellow Christians to endure.

Though presently exalted in heaven Christ continues to suffer in his members, and not least in Paul himself. This was driven home to him on the Damascus road when Christ said to him: "Why do you persecute *me*?" (Acts 9:4). Up until this moment, Paul had been actively engaged in making Christ suffer in the person of his followers in Judea. But from now on he would suffer for Christ's sake (Acts 9:16, cf. Acts 13:47, quoting Isaiah 49:6, where not only is the Servant's mission of enlightenment among the nations to be carried on by Paul [and Barnabas], but also the Servant's sufferings are borne by him [Bruce, 216]) or, to use an equivalent expression, for the sake of his body, the church (Col 1:24).

ὅ ἐστιν ἡ ἐκκλησία. (See introduction 57–60.)

25. *ἧς ἐγενόμην ἐγὼ διάκονος κατὰ τὴν οἰκονομίαν τοῦ θεοῦ . . . τὸν λόγον τοῦ θεοῦ.* Paul was known as a "minister" (*διάκονος*, cf v 23) in the Gentile communities. This appointment was "in accordance with the commission of God" given to him (*κατὰ τὴν οἰκονομίαν τοῦ θεοῦ τὴν δοθεῖσάν μοι*, a somewhat unusual expression since Paul normally speaks of the "grace" of God that is given to him: Rom 12:3; 15:15; 1 Cor 3:10; Gal 2:9; cf. A. Satake, "Apostolat und Gnade bei Paulus," *NTS* 15 [1968–69] 96–107).

οἰκονομία (see Michel, *TDNT* 5, 151–53) is employed in the Pauline corpus to denote either (1) Paul's administration of his apostolic office (1 Cor 9:17; cf. 4:1 where he describes himself as one of the stewards [*οἰκονόμοι*] of God's mysteries), or (2) God's administration of the world and salvation (Eph 1:10; 3:9; cf. 3:2). In the earlier references Paul is the *οἰκονόμος* (1 Cor 4:1), having been entrusted with a commission (*οἰκονομία*; 1 Cor 9:17); he is not able to withdraw from this solemn responsibility, but must fulfill it obediently. He is a steward of the mysteries of God (1 Cor 4:1) and it is naturally expected of him that he be found trustworthy (4:2; cf. Luke 16:2). In the later Pauline texts the emphasis is upon God's *οἰκονομία*. (This need not necessarily imply that the earlier epistles come from a time when Paul had no notion of a divine plan of salvation; so rightly Reumann, *NTS* 13 [1966–67] 155–66.) Most examples of the *οἰκονομία* terminology in Paul occur in close proximity to the word "mystery" (*μυστήριον*: the only exception being 1 Cor 9:17) suggesting that the latter was important for understanding the meaning of *οἰκονομία*.

At Colossians 1:25 this nuance of God's plan, which is administered by him, is most likely for the following reasons: (a) *οἰκονομία τοῦ θεοῦ* had this general sense in the Hellenistic world; (b) the genitive *τοῦ θεοῦ* which is subjective supports this interpretation; and (c) *κατά* ("according to") suggests the notion of a plan in this context (so Reumann, *NTS* 13 [1966–67] 163).

At the same time, since the apostle speaks of the *οἰκονομία* as "given to me" some commentators have concluded that the phrase must be interpreted exclusively of Paul's office or activity, his assignment rather than God's plan which can hardly be said to be given. Perhaps the way forward is to understand that what is given to Paul is insight into that plan, a suggestion probably confirmed by verse 26 with its statement about the mystery being revealed to him and others. If we allow the meaning of "office" to be attached, then it must be done with Dibelius' comment (24) in mind: "the office stems from the plan." The double sense seems to be intended as Masson and Reumann have pointed out: Paul says, "I am a minister according to the plan of God, the execution of which has been conferred upon me in that which concerns you" (Masson, 111, 112; cf. Reumann, *NTS* 13 [1966–67] 163, and Moule, 80).

If this double sense is intended in verse 25 then the passage stands at an important pivotal point between the earlier and later references. In all three examples in Ephesians (1:10; 3:2, 9–10) *οἰκονομία* has to do with God's gospel-plan or mystery, together with its divine administration, while Ephesians 3:2, like Colossians 1:25, also deals with the role given to Paul in this, namely the making of the mystery known (1:9). (On the meaning of οἰκονομία see in addition to the works noted above: M. Bouttier, "Remarques sur la conscience apostolique de St. Paul," *OIKONOMIA. Heilsgeschichte als Thema der Theologie,* ed. F. Christ [Hamburg—Bergstadt: Reich, 1967] 100–108; A. van Roon, *The Authenticity of Ephesians,* [NovTSup 39; Leiden, Brill, 1974] 175, 176; and C. C. Caragounis, *The Ephesian* MYSTERION. *Meaning and Content* [ConB, New Testament Series 8; Lund: Gleerup, 1977] 97, 98).

The Colossians are bound up with that ministry of Paul, and indeed the very gospel-plan of God, since it is for their benefit (εἰς ὑμᾶς). His ministry as apostle to the Gentiles vitally concerns them (cf. vv 26–29), and that is why he can style himself a "minister of the church," even though most of the members of the congregation do not know him personally. This expression is therefore not as unusual (Schweizer, 86) as some think (bearing in mind that Paul employs a variety of expressions to describe his ministry: he is a minister of God, 2 Cor 6:4; a minister of Christ, 2 Cor 11:23; and of the new covenant, 2 Cor 3:6), and not "obviously in tension with v. 23," as F. Hahn contends (*Mission in the New Testament.* Tr. F. Clarke [London: SCM, 1965] 146 American edition [SBT 47; Naperville, IL: Allenson, 1965]; see further Merklein, *Amt,* 337–40).

πληρῶσαι τὸν λόγον τοῦ θεοῦ. For Paul the content of that stewardship, the task to be performed (cf. Percy, *Probleme,* 128; Abbott, 233, rightly observes that the aorist infinitive πληρῶσαι is not one of design, but is explanatory, indicating the content of the οἰκονομία; against Meyer, 325) was "to complete the word of God." A form of this same verb πληρόω (i.e. ἀνταναπληρόω) has just been used of filling up the deficiencies in the Messiah's afflictions; now it is employed with reference to the Word of God. The verb πληρόω covers a wide range of meanings: "to fill, make full, fulfill, complete or finish" (BAG, 670–72). Here it carries the sense of "doing fully," or "carrying to completion" the divine commission (see also Acts 14:26 of completing a piece of missionary work, Acts 12:25 of a mission of assistance, Col 4:17 of a ministry received in the Lord, and Luke 9:31 of the way of Jesus to the cross; cf. Acts 13:25; Rev 3:2; for further references note Delling, *TDNT* 6, 286–98).

The nearest parallel to our text is Romans 15:19, where Paul, in A.D. 57, claims that he has "brought to completion" the preaching of the gospel (πεπληρωκέναι τὸ εὐαγγέλιον, lit. "fulfilled the gospel") of Christ in the area between Jerusalem and Illyricum. Some scholars, such as R. Asting (*Die Verkündigung des Wortes im Urchristentum* [Stuttgart: Kohlhammer, 1939] 138) consider this latter passage could mean that Paul has brought the gospel to its "fulfillment," to its destiny among the Gentiles; while J. Munck (*Paul and the Salvation of Mankind.* Tr. F. Clarke [London: SCM, 1959]; American edition [Richmond, VA: 1959] 48) going a step further, connects Romans 15:19 and Colossians 1:25 with 2 Timothy 4:17 ("that through me the message might be fully proclaimed [πληροφορέω], and that all the Gentiles might hear") in connection with the bringing in of the "fullness (πλήρωμα) of the Gentiles" (Rom 11:25). J. H. Schütz (*Paul and the Anatomy of Apostolic Authority* [SNTSMS

26; Cambridge: University Press, 1975] 47) commenting on Romans 15:19, makes the interesting suggestion that fulfilling the gospel describes not the finishing of an assignment, but rather the way in which Paul has executed his task: fully, in word and deed, with signs and wonders, etc. He has set in motion forces by which Christ wins obedience from the nations. Whether this suggestion is likely in the context of Romans 15:19 is an open question, since it is bound up, in part, with Schütz's views about "gospel" and "authority." However, he has rightly drawn our attention to the notion of an effective and dynamic preaching of the gospel on the part of the apostle (note in the context of Rom 15:19 the terms "power," "signs" and "wonders"), and his comments give us a clue to the meaning of the shorter expression in Colossians 1:25. The Word of God is "fulfilled" not simply when it is preached in the world (so many commentators including Lohse, 73), but when it is dynamically and effectively proclaimed in the power of the Spirit (cf. 1 Thess 1:5, 6; it is to this end that Paul prays and requests his friends to intercede for him: cf. Eph 6:18–20; Col 4:2–4; 2 Thess 3:1–3) throughout the world, and accepted by men in faith (Percy, *Probleme,* 128; Bruce, 217). Like God's Word of old (Isa 55:11) it is dynamic, achieving the very purpose for which it has been sent forth. Obviously this has particular reference to Gentiles, as Asting, Munck and others have pointed out, since they are specifically mentioned in the immediate context (note especially v 27; cf. Eph 3:8).

Paul's comission to make the Word of God fully known has led to the ministry of that Word, through his associate Epaphras, at Colossae and thus made the Colossians beneficiaries of his apostolic commission, even though he had not visited them in person.

26. *τὸ μυστήριον . . . τοῖς ἁγίοις αὐτοῦ.* The message (*λόγος τοῦ θεοῦ*) which Paul was to "fulfill" is now defined as "the mystery." By means of a "revelation pattern" that may well have been used in primitive Christian preaching (so Dahl, *Jesus,* 32, 33; cf. Bultmann, *Theology* 1, 105, 106, and Lührmann, *Offenbarungsverständnis,* 124–33) a contrast, using antithetic parallelism, is set forth: the mystery that was once hidden has now been revealed (cf. Rom 16:25–27; 1 Cor 2:6–10; Eph 3:4–7, 8–11).

The word *μυστήριον* ("mystery") was employed in a variety of contexts in the Greek world and Hellenism: from the many ancient pagan mystery cults whereby *τὰ μυστήρια* figured as the cultic rites in which the destinies of a god were portrayed by sacred actions before the devotees so as to give them a part in the fate of the god and thus attain to salvation (*σωτηρία*); to the mysteries in philosophy, the secret teachings that had as their aim the vision of the divine; on to the mysteries in secular usage, and Gnosticism which presupposed and fostered a process of intermingling and reinterpreting the ancient mystery cults (for details see R. Reitzenstein, *Hellenistic Mystery-Religions. Their Basic Ideas and Significance.* Tr. J. E. Steely [Pittsburg: Pickwick, 1978]; Bornkamm, *TDNT* 4, 802–13; Caragounis, *Mysterion,* 1–22).

Contemporary biblical scholarship, however, has rightly rejected the earlier views of the history of religions which saw the background to the Pauline use of *μυστήριον* in the ancient pagan mystery cults (on the decline of the history of religions school generally see M. Simon, "The *religionsgeschichtliche Schule,* fifty years later," *RelS* 11 [1975] 135–44). Instead, recent research has focused attention on the Old Testament and Judaism (including Qumran), particularly the wisdom literature and apocalyptic material (so, for example, Bornkamm, TDNT 4, 813–17; Brown, *Background,* 1–30; Zeilinger, *Der Erstgeborene,* 94–115, among others), and Brown is able to demonstrate that "the NT writers, particularly Paul, had in this [Semitic] background all the raw material they needed for the use of 'mystery' without venturing into the pagan religions" (32).

The term *μυστήριον* ("mystery") corresponds to the Aramaic רז, *rāz* ("secret"), frequently found in the Book of Daniel (2:18, 19, 27, 28, 29, 30, 47 [twice], which denotes "an eschatological mystery, a concealed intimation of divinely ordained future events whose disclosure and interpretation is reserved for God alone" (Bornkamm, *TDNT* 4, 814, 815; cf. Brown, *Background,* 8). God discloses to his seers "the things that must come to pass" for it is only he "who reveals mysteries" (*ὁ ἀποκαλύπτων μυστήρια* LXX Dan 2:28, 29). According to the Qumran community God had revealed to the speaker of the Thanksgiving Hymns (probably the Teacher of Righteousness) "wonderful mysteries" which he is then able to interpret to others (1QH 1:21; 2:13; 4:27–29). These mysteries like those revealed in Daniel, have to do with God's purpose to be realized at the end-time.

The word *μυστήριον* ("mystery") appears in Paul's corpus of letters on some twenty-one occasions and the passages having the closest links with Colossians 1:26, 27 are 1 Corinthians 2:6–10 and Romans 16:25–27 (Zeilinger, *Der Erstgeborene,* 98–102; cf. Brown, *Background,* 52–56). Here mystery does not have to do with some future event that lies hidden in God's plan, but refers to his decisive action in Christ in the here and now (cf. Schweizer, 88). In fact, the content of the mystery—note it is singular—is Christ himself, the hope of glory for these Gentile Christians (v 27). This mystery formerly hidden is now disclosed (1 Cor 2:7; cf. Rom 16:25 where *φανερόω* is also used). The phrase *ἀπὸ τῶν αἰώνων καὶ ἀπὸ τῶν γενεῶν* ought not to be understood with Dibelius-Greeven (24), of the principalities and powers from whom the mystery was hidden (cf. 1 Cor 2:8), but has its normal temporal significance meaning "from (*ἀπό* = "since") ages and generations of the past" (so most commentators).

A dramatic turn of events has occurred (*νῦν δέ*) so that what was previously hidden has now been disclosed by God (the passive *ἐφανερώθη* points to the divine activity while the content of this mystery is spelled out in the following verse). Paul normally describes the word "mystery" in terms of its disclosure or its being made known: so it is found along with "revelation" (*ἀποκάλυψις*) at Romans 16:25; Ephesians 3:3; and with the verbs "reveal" (*ἀποκαλύπτω*) 1 Corinthians 2:10; Ephesians 3:5; "make known" (*γνωρίζω*) Romans 16:26; Ephesians 1:9; 3:3, 5; Colossians 1:27; and "manifest" (*φανερόω*) Romans 16:26; Colossians 1:26.

The recipients of this disclosure are "his saints" (*οἱ ἅγιοι αὐτοῦ*), a phrase that denotes neither "angels" (Lohmeyer, 82), nor a limited circle of "charismatics" (Käsemann, noted by Lohse, 75), nor "the Pentecostal community of Jerusalem" (L. Cerfaux, *The Church in the Theology of St. Paul.* Tr. G. Webb and A. Walker [New York: Herder, 1959] 130–40), but believers, those who have already been described as the "saints (ἅγιοι) and faithful brothers in Christ" (1:2), and are later called "God's chosen ones, holy (ἅγιοι) and beloved" (3:12; cf. Bornkamm, *TDNT* 4, 821; Lähnemann, *Kolosserbrief*, 47; Lohse, 75). They are not some select group of initiates, but are those who have heard and received the word of God, for it is in the effective preaching and teaching of the gospel that the revelation of the mystery takes place (cf. 1 Cor 2:1, 7; 4:1; Eph 3:8, 9; 6:19), a point that emerges from an examination of those contexts where "mystery" stands in apposition to one or other of the gospel terms: e.g. Colossians 4:3, "Word" (λόγος) and "mystery" (μυστήριον); and Romans 16:25 where the phrases "according to my gospel (εὐαγγέλιον) and the preaching (κήρυγμα) of Jesus Christ" are parallel to the words "according to the revelation of the mystery" (κατὰ ἀποκάλυψιν μυστηρίου).

27. *οἷς ἠθέλησεν ὁ θεὸς γνωρίσαι.* The usual way of taking this clause is in terms of God wishing to make known the mystery to the saints. The verb "make known" (γνωρίσαι) resumes the "revealed" (ἐφανερώθη) of v 26, while the recipients of this knowledge are "the saints," i.e. Christians generally (the antecedent of οἷς is τοῖς ἁγίοις). The additional point being made in v 27 concerns the immense greatness of this mystery, the content of which is succinctly stated as "Christ in you, the hope of glory."

Bowers, however (*Issues*, 110–14), has put forward an interesting alternative. He suggests that the relative οἷς ("to whom") should be regarded as an accusative οὕς (having been attracted to the dative case of its antecedent τοῖς ἁγίοις, a common enough phenomenon in the NT), and this functions as the subject of the infinitive γνωρίσαι ("make known"). The resultant translation would be: verses 26, 27, ". . . to his saints, who God willed should make known how rich is the splendor of this mystery among the Gentiles," and the effects of this rendering would be: *(a)* "make known" (γνωρίσαι) denotes not an elaboration of the mystery's disclosure just mentioned in v 26*b*, but a reference to its proclamation; *(b)* "the saints" are the agents of this making known rather than the recipients (the mystery has already been manifested to them according to v 26); and *(c)* "among the Gentiles" (ἐν τοῖς ἔθνεσιν) indicates the audience who hear this proclamation by the saints.

The second alternative overcomes the difficulty of the first, where the Greek seems to suggest that the recipients of this "revelation" are different from the subjects of it (i.e. the content of the μυστήριον is the risen Christ's dwelling in you Gentiles). Bowers's view is that "the saints" are the agents in making known the mystery to Gentiles since it concerns the latter. D. W. B. Robinson ("Who Were the Saints?" *RTR* 22 [1963] 45–53), had already made this distinction, believing that "the saints" denoted the first Jewish believers who, having received the revelation, were to be instrumental in its proclamation to Gentiles.

On balance it seems that while the second alternative has much in its favor the grammatical point about an attraction of the relative from a dative to an accusative case is difficult to prove. We therefore prefer the usual interpretation. Further, while the passage does not state explicitly (as do 1 Cor 2:10 and Eph 3:3) that Paul received the revelation of the mystery, and so may seem to give the impression that the mystery was revealed directly to God's saints (v 26), the context clearly implies that in Paul's (and his colleagues') preaching the mystery is revealed to believers.

τί τὸ πλοῦτος τῆς δόξης τοῦ μυστηρίου . . . ἡ ἐλπὶς τῆς δόξης. Several features of this mystery are now set forth: first, it is magnificent in every way being characterized by "glory" (*δόξα*). The heaping together of dependent genitive constructions is characteristic of Colossians (cf. Bujard, *Untersuchungen,* 156, 157, though it is not necessary to draw from this feature his conclusions about the authorship of the letter) and here we have a further example in the expression "the riches of the glory of this mystery." (Paul is particularly given to the use of *πλοῦτος* with a following genitive: Col 2:2; Rom 2:4; 9:23, a close parallel to this text; 2 Cor 8:2; Eph 1:7; 2:7; 3:8.)

πλοῦτος ("riches") is for Paul a term "to denote the being of Christ, the work of God in Christ, and the eschatological situation of Christ's community" (Hauck-Kasch, *TDNT* 6, 328, 329). In the Corinthian correspondence the wealth of the Christian life was often expressed by this word *πλοῦτος* and its cognates, while elsewhere the apostle spoke of God's or Christ's wealth (Rom 2:4; 9:23; 10:12; 11:33; Phil 4:19). The Corinthians certainly exaggerated the spiritual wealth they possessed (note the irony of 1 Cor 4:8), failing to recognize the source (2 Cor 8:9), its terms of reference (2 Cor 4:7), that it had been brought by a mere poverty-stricken apostle (2 Cor 6:10), and that its possession ought to have resulted in a deep-seated compassion for others (2 Cor 8:2, 7).

In Colossians and Ephesians the "wealth of God" is a prominent idea pointing to the lavish bestowal of his blessings in Christ (cf. Col 2:2, note the synonymous term "treasures" used at v 3; Eph 1:7, 18; 3:8, 16). Here at Colossians 1:27 "riches" and "glory" are used together to point to the immense greatness of the mystery (the two terms are often mentioned together in the OT: cf. LXX Gen 31:16; 1 Kings 3:13; 1 Chron 29:28; etc.). Perhaps by employing the term "glory"—*δόξα* was chosen by the LXX translators to render the Hebrew כבוד, *kābôd,* the usual word for the splendor or glory of God—the apostle wished to emphasize that this wonderful mystery partook of the character of God himself.

ἐν τοῖς ἔθνεσιν. The second feature of this mystery is that God graciously purposed to make it known "among the Gentiles" for it had special reference to them. The prophets of the OT looked forward to the saving purpose of God in which Gentiles along with Israelites would be embraced within its scope (note Paul's quotations in Rom 15:9–12 to this effect; see also, for example, Isa 49:6). The manner in which that purpose would come to fruition—by the incorporation of both Jews and Gentiles into the body of Christ—was not made known. That had remained a mystery until the time of its fulfilment, and Paul, as apostle to the Gentiles and first steward of this mystery, has the privilege of unfolding its wonder to his readers. Non-Jews are included along with Jews on an equal footing as members of Christ's body, and it was Paul's great joy, as well as his divinely imposed obligation, to be the agent of making known "the glorious riches of this mystery among the *Gentiles*" (for an expansion of this see Eph 3:2–12; Bruce, 218, 219). Here of all places the wealth of God was lavished in a wonderful way.

ὅ ἐστιν Χριστὸς ἐν ὑμῖν. Thirdly, the content of this mystery Paul assures his readers is "Christ is *in you,* [Colossians], the hope of glory." These words add to what has previously been asserted: (a) Christ is at the center of God's mystery. The μυστήριον focuses on him as its content. (b) While the mystery has been proclaimed or made known *among* the Gentiles (ἐν τοῖς ἔθνεσιν) it has been believed by the Colossians (cf. 1 Tim 3:16 where the "mystery" refers to Christ not only preached among the Gentiles *but also* "believed in the world"). Christ had been preached to them by Epaphras and they had received him as Lord (2:6). Christ therefore was "in them" (not simply "*among* them" which is an appropriate translation of the preposition ἐν in the clause γνωρίσαι . . . ἐν τοῖς ἔθνεσιν; but here the ἐν ὑμῖν is more specific than ἐν τοῖς ἔθνεσιν, having particular reference to the Colossian readers, and with the verb ἐστιν points to Christ's indwelling in them as Gentile believers (Bruce, 219, against Lohse, 76).

As members of his body they had his life within them. They therefore had a sure hope that they would share in that fullness of glory yet to be displayed on the day of "the revealing of the sons of God" (Rom 8:19; cf. 5:2; Col 3:4; 1 Thess 2:12; 2 Thess 1:10; 2:14). (The "mystery" of Ephesians is not as different from Colossians as some, including Mitton, *Ephesians,* 86–88, and Dibelius-Greeven, 24, 83–85, have suggested; it is not simply God's acceptance of the Gentiles, but also includes their incorporation, along with Jewish believers, into the community of the Messiah, cf. v 24.)

28. ὃν ἡμεῖς καταγγέλλομεν νουθετοῦντες . . . διδάσκοντες. Paul reverts to the plural "we" (cf. v 9) as he describes his ministry and that of his colleagues, particularly those coworkers like Epaphras who had brought the gospel to Colossae (vv 7, 8). He employs three related verbs to describe this activity, and each is in the present tense so pointing to the habitual practice of his coworkers and himself:

(a) The first verb "proclaim" (καταγγέλλω) is a weighty one occurring only in Acts and Paul (cf. Schniewind, *TDNT* 1, 70–72) becoming almost a technical term for missionary preaching since it was normally used of the gospel itself or some element in it. So the gospel (1 Cor 9:14), the mystery of God (1 Cor 2:1), and the Word of God (Acts 13:5; 17:13; cf. 15:36) are "proclaimed," while sometimes Christ (Phil 1:17, 18), his death (1 Cor 11:26) and resurrection (Acts 4:2), as well as the forgiveness of sins (Acts 13:38), were the significant elements in the apostolic announcement. At Romans 1:8 Paul indicates that with the diffusion of the gospel throughout the known world went the report of the Roman believers' faith (on the significance of this see O'Brien, *Introductory Thanksgivings,* 207–9). Here at Colossians 1:28 the Christ who is "proclaimed" is the one at the center of God's mystery, i.e. Christ in you (Gentiles). He is the sum and substance of Paul's message.

(b) The public proclamation of Christ as Lord is explained and developed in the following words about admonition (νουθετοῦντες) and instruction (διδάσκοντες), for it is through the teaching and warning of every man that the proclamation of Christ is carried out (this is the relationship of the two participles to the finite verb καταγγέλομεν, "we announce"; so Lohse, 77, following Schniewind, *TNDT* 1, 72). Clearly for Paul and his colleagues evangelistic and missionary outreach was not effected by some superficial presentation

of the saving message about Christ to the world, but rather was prosecuted through warning and intensive teaching in pastoral situations. (It is unnecessary to see here, as does Hahn, *Mission,* 146, a sharp dichotomy between evangelistic and church proclamation.) The verb νουθετέω ("admonish," "warn," "instruct"), together with its cognate noun νουθεσία ("admonition"), had to do with setting the mind of someone in proper order, correcting him or putting him right (cf. Behm, *TDNT* 4, 1019–22). It occurs mostly in the exhortatory contexts of Paul's writings within the New Testament having to do with general admonition given to new Christians (Acts 20:31 of Paul's ministry at Ephesus; cf. 1 Cor 10:11) as well as more specific instruction such as the training of children within the Christian family (Eph 6:4). Paul uses the term of a ministry of admonition, criticism and correction, whether by himself, as at Corinth (1 Cor 4:14), or by church leaders as at Thessalonica (1 Thess 5:12). On occasion, reference is to the disciplining of those who held false beliefs (Titus 3:10), while both 1 Thessalonians 5:14 and Colossians 3:16 show that the term could be used of members of the Christian community admonishing one another.

(*c*) Paul and his colleagues are also involved in intensive teaching (διδάσκοντες), for it is through this activity, too, that Christ is proclaimed. In Colossians, as Rengstorf and others have observed, there is an emphasis on teaching. All Christians are to teach and admonish one another in psalms, hymns and spiritual songs (3:16 where διδάσκω and νουθετέω are again used together; cf. the similar conjunction in Plato, *Prot* 323D, Dio Chrysostom, *Or* 32.27 and Plutarch *Aud* 46B; for details see Behm, *TDNT* 4, 1019, 1020). The congregation is to remain firm in the faith just as they had been taught to do (καθὼς ἐδιδάχθητε, 2:7) when they were first instructed through the apostolic gospel (1:28). The ongoing teaching of the apostolic band referred to here has been given "in all wisdom" (ἐν πάσῃ σοφίᾳ), a phrase that may stand over against the Colossian heretics who boasted of their superior wisdom with its speculative knowledge of the higher worlds. By contrast Paul in the proclamation of Christ brings all wisdom within the reach of all.

πάντα ἄνθρωπον. The expression "every man" occurs three times in verse 28, being repeated to emphasize, on the one hand, the universality of the gospel as taught by Paul and his coworkers, and to contrast the intellectual exclusiveness of the false teachers on the other (Abbott, 235). "There is no part of Christian teaching that is to be reserved for a spiritual elite. All the truth of God is for all the people of God" (Bruce, 219). At the same time Paul does not write the plural "all (men)" (πάντες [ἄνθρωποι]) which would also have pointed to the universality of the message. The singular is used to show that each person individually (ἄνθρωπος is generic) was the object of the apostle's care. This was consistent with his regular practice, for elsewhere he describes his apostolic work in terms of the individual care of souls, e.g., 1 Thessalonians 2:11, 12: "For you know how, like a father with his children, we exhorted *each one of you* (ἕνα ἕκαστον ὑμῶν) and encouraged you and charged you to lead a life worthy of God, who calls you into his own kingdom and glory" (RSV). Paul lays strong emphasis in these passages (cf. Acts 20:20) on the personal character of his work and the fact that at Colossians 1:28 he deliberately returns to the plural verbs ("*we* proclaim, warning . . .

and teaching") suggests that his colleagues who ministered with him had followed his example. One could not have been a member of this apostolic band for long without realizing that Paul, like his Master, cared for the ultimate well-being of *individual* men and women.

ἵνα παραστήσωμεν πάντα ἄνθρωπον τέλειον ἐν Χριστῷ. The goal of this Christ-centered instruction, Paul's preaching and teaching, is "that we may present every man perfect in Christ." This is similar to the end God had in view in reconciling the Colossians through the death of his Son, verse 22: to present them (the aorist of the same verb παρίστημι is used) holy, blameless and irreproachable before him (see 68, 69). God's work of reconciliation in Christ and Paul's active ministry have the same end in view, namely, the perfection of each man in Christ on the final day (Rom 14:10).

The term τέλειος ("perfect," "whole") appeared in a variety of contexts in the Hellenistic world (for details see P. J. Du Plessis, ΤΕΛΕΙΟΣ. *The Idea of Perfection in the New Testament* [Kampen: Kok, 1959] 36–121) to denote unblemished sacrificial animals (Homer *Il,* 1, 66), a person who has reached the limit of his professional abilities and the cosmos which contains all kinds of living creatures. The word was also employed to designate the "perfect" man in Greek philosophy (Delling, *TDNT* 8, 69–72), but whether it was also a technical term for initiates in the Hellenistic mystery religions is disputed (cf. Reitzenstein, *Mystery-Religions,* 150, 432, BAG, 809, and the literature cited there). It is just possible that the letter to the Colossians opposes those who claimed to have the experience of being filled with supernatural wisdom and divine power and as such were regarded as "perfect" (τέλειοι); cf. Lightfoot, 168, 169, and Lohse, 78.

τέλειος is attested twenty times in the OT (often rendering, שלם, *shālēm* or תמים *tāmîm*) to denote that which is whole, perfect or intact. It is used of the heart which is wholly turned to God (1 Kings 8:61; 11:4), and of the man who has bound himself fully to him (Gen 6:9; cf. Deut 18:13). In the Qumran material the Hebrew term *tāmîm* is understandably colored by the OT. Those who are perfect *(tāmîm)* are those who keep God's law wholly and so walk perfectly in his ways (1QS 1:8; 2:2). Members of the community are also called "the perfect" (1QS 8:20). The contexts in which *tāmîm* ("perfect") appears in the Qumran writings show clearly that the reference is to a total fulfillment of God's will through keeping all the rules of the community (Delling, *TDNT* 8, 73).

The relationship of perfection to the will of God is found explicitly in Paul at Romans 12:2 as well as by implication in other NT writings (cf. Matt 5:48 in the context of the Sermon on the Mount; James 1:4, 25; 3:2). The two notions are specifically related at Colossians 4:12 where Paul mentions that his colleague, Epaphras, has prayed that the readers might "stand perfect and fully assured in all the will of God" (ἵνα σταθῆτε τέλειοι καὶ πεπληροφορημένοι ἐν παντὶ θελήματι τοῦ θεοῦ).

When the apostle speaks of presenting every man "perfect" or fully grown in Christ, as in verse 22 (see 68, 69), he has the Parousia in mind (so Bruce, 220, and Pfitzner, *Paul,* 109; against Lohse, 78, 79, who takes it as a reference to the present, and Du Plessis, *Perfection,* 199, who regards παραστήσωμεν as an ingressive aorist denoting Paul's "purpose to introduce people to Christ").

Although he is aware of the real progress in faith and love (v 4) the readers have already made, as a true pastor Paul will not be satisfied with anything less than the full Christian maturity of every believer. There are to be no exceptions, since his aim is that each one (*πάντα ἄνθρωπον*) should reach perfection. However, this will be fully realized only on the last day, for only then will they, like the Thessalonian Christians, be completely sanctified (1 Thess 5:23; cf. 3:13).

29. *εἰς ὃ καὶ κοπιῶ ἀγωνιζόμενος*. With the prospect of their full perfection in Christ on the last day in view, Paul expends all his energies in the exercise of his ministry. His apostolic tasks were not completed with the conversion of men and women. This was only the beginning and the end would not be reached until the day of Christ when the quality of his ministry would be tested (Bruce, 221).

With vivid metaphors Paul indicates how he exerts himself on behalf of the Colossians and other Gentiles like them (the singular is used again in v 29 to describe his own labors, but this implies no adverse comment on the ministry of others for he was aware of their faithful labor on behalf of the various communities: 1 Thess 5:12; 1 Cor 16:16; Rom 16:6).

κόπος, a word used in secular Greek of "a beating," "weariness" (as though one had been beaten) and "exertion," was the proper word for physical tiredness induced by work, exertion or heat (see A. von Harnack, "*Κόπος* (*Κοπιᾶν*, *Οἱ Κοπιῶντες*) im frühchristlichen Sprachgebrauch," *ZNW* 27 [1928] 1–10, and Hauck, *TDNT* 3, 827–30). It denoted severe labor and, together with its cognate *κοπιάω* was used in the New Testament of: (1) work in general, such as manual labor (2 Cor 6:5; 11:27; Eph 4:28); and (2) Christian work in and for the community. Under the latter heading *κοπιάω* could describe Paul's apostolic ministry (1 Cor 4:12; 15:10; Gal 4:11; Phil 2:16; Col 1:29; cf. *κόπος* 1 Thess 2:9; 3:5; 2 Thess 3:8; 2 Cor 11:23), as well as the toil of other Christians (1 Thess 5:12; 1 Cor 16:16; Rom 16:6, 12; cf. *κόπος* 1 Cor 3:8; 15:58; 2 Cor 10:15). These cognate words were key terms used of Paul's pastoral efforts in some of his earliest correspondence (note the references in 1 and 2 Thessalonians), and in Colossians 1:29 the emphasis is on the great effort expended by one who labors unceasingly for the congregation's welfare.

ἀγωνίζομαι ("fight," "struggle," "engage in a contest," BAG, 15), perhaps even a stronger term than the preceding, could denote a physical conflict in which weapons were used (John 18:36; cf. 2 Macc 8:16) and an athletic contest (1 Cor 9:25). Pfitzner, *Paul,* 109, 110, claims that at verse 29 this verb (a participle *ἀγωνιζόμενος*) is qualified by *κοπιῶ* (the finite verb), and not vice versa, so that both words designate the intense labor and effort of Paul toward the one goal of presenting every man perfect in Christ. So the translation "striving" (denoting a metaphorical usage) is to be preferred to any reference to struggle or conflict (cf. 1 Tim 4:10 where a similar expression is found: *εἰς τοῦτο . . . κοπιῶμεν καὶ ἀγωνιζόμεθα*, "to this end we toil and strive"). Pfitzner concludes that, although a conscious reference to the athletic contest is hardly present, the verb *ἀγωνίζομαι* still carries with it the original coloring of striving after a specific aim or goal (see further on *ἀγών*, 2:1).

κατὰ τὴν ἐνέργειαν αὐτοῦ τὴν ἐνεργουμένην ἐν ἐμοὶ ἐν δυνάμει. It has already been noted (see 24) that God's power is a prominent motif in Colossians and Ephesians (Col 1:11; 2:12; Eph 1:19; 3:7, 16, 20; 6:10) denoting that might which he exercised when he raised Christ from the dead and by which he now works in and through the lives of his apostle and people (see on v 11).

While Paul works, earnestly expending all his energies in the prosecution of his ministry, he gladly acknowledges that the strength for such unremitting labor comes from above (cf. Schweizer, 90), an acknowledgment he underscores by heaping up synonyms for power and might in this context (note the similar feature in 1:11, Eph 1:19; 3:7, 16, 20; 6:10). *ἐνέργεια* means "power to work effectively," having appeared in many different writers from the pre-Socratic period onward. In the NT it always denotes supernatural power, twice of an evil activity which parodies the work of Christ and lays claim to divine honors (2 Thess 2:9, 11), but mostly of the exercise of divine power (Eph 1:19; 3:7; Phil 3:21; Col 2:12). The preposition *κατά* ("according to") is on occasion found in Paul's petitions and thanksgivings (cf. Phil 4:19; Eph 1:19; 3:16) as well as other contexts where God's power, grace or glory are seen as the source of blessing to the recipient. At the same time, the supply corresponds to the riches of the divine attribute and is more than adequate for the needs (cf. Harder, *Paulus,* 45).

The cognate verb *ἐνεργέω* ("be at work," "work," "be effective"; see Bertram, *TDNT* 2, 652–54, and N. Baumert, *Täglich Sterben und Auferstehen. Der Literalsinn von 2 Kor 4, 12–5, 10* [SANT 84; Munich: Kösel, 1973] 267–83) may here be a middle voice (so BAG, 265, among others), but is more probably a passive (K. W. Clark, "The Meaning of *ἐνεργέω* and *κατεργέω* in the New Testament," *JBL* 54 [1935] 93–101; J. A. Robinson, *St. Paul's Epistle to the Ephesians,* 2nd edition [London; Macmillan, 1904] American edition [Grand Rapids: Kregel, 1979] 245–47) indicating that the strength is powerfully (*ἐν δυνάμει* is best understood adverbially) wrought within him (*ἐν ἐμοί*). The present tense of *ἐνεργουμένην* ("is being effected") parallels *κοπιῶ ἀγωνιζόμενος* ("I toil, working hard"). As Paul strives, so God continues to work mightily within him (cf. 1 Cor 15:10). If one asks the question: "Where is God powerfully at work?" then in this context the answer would be: "Where Paul toils energetically." That is why he is able to say: "I can do all things in him who strengthens me" (*πάντα ἰσχύω ἐν τῷ ἐνδυναμοῦντί με,* Phil 4:13).

2:1 *θέλω γὰρ ὑμᾶς εἰδέναι.* In the previous paragraph (1:24–29) Paul spoke in general terms of his apostolic service. His ministry to the Gentile congregations included the Colossians (vv 24, 25). Now he turns to them in direct personal address (*ὑμᾶς*), with the aim of strengthening the bond between the Colossian believers, whom he had not met previously, and himself. By means of a form used in the letter-writing convention of his day he wishes to instruct them in an important matter. (Cf. T. Y. Mullins, "Disclosure. A Literary Form in the New Testament," *NovT* 7 [1964] 44–50, who has termed this a "Disclosure form." Other examples are Rom 1:13; 11:25; 1 Cor 10:1; 11:3; 12:1; 2 Cor 1:8; 1 Thess 4:3). The content of that instruction or "disclosure" appears in the following words: *ἡλίκον ἀγῶνα ἔχω.* The cognate verb *ἀγωνιζόμενος* ("striving") has already been used (v 29) of Paul's energetic pastoral activities on behalf of those congregations he had founded. He now states that he is engaged in a similar conflict (ἀγών) for the sake of those who had not heard the gospel from his lips, viz. those at Colossae (ὑπὲρ ὑμῶν), the neighboring city of Laodicea (τῶν ἐν Λαοδικείᾳ) and at other places in the Lycus valley (καὶ ὅσοι οὐχ ἑόρακαν κτλ.), including, no doubt, those at Hierapolis (cf. 4:13), who apparently were converted through the ministry of Epaphras.

But what was the precise nature of this conflict? Lohmeyer (89, 92) argued that the verb "strive" (ἀγωνιζόμενος), used at verse 29, and the cognate noun "conflict" (ἀγών) were almost technical terms for martyrdom. Accordingly he used these verses to support his thesis that the letter to the Colossians, like that to the Philippians, was permeated with the thought of martyrdom. Paul wrote to the Colossians in conscious awareness of his fate as a martyr. This view, however, has not commended itself to NT scholars. There is no mention in the entire letter to the Colossians (nor in Philippians for that matter) of martyrdom, whether in the case of Paul himself or of his readers. Further, both ἀγών and ἀγωνίζομαι were not used by Paul as technical terms for martyrdom.

A second view, set forth by Pfitzner (*Paul*, 109–12, 126–29), is to understand Paul's conflict as his struggle for the gospel or the faith. It involves in the first place untiring toil and labor, an intense wrestling and struggle for the spread, growth and strengthening of the faith as the goal of his mission. Further, the thought of a continual struggle *against opposition* is not far distant when Paul speaks of his ἀγών. Suffering is often involved so that when he refers to his "struggle on your behalf" this is akin to his statement of verse 24 about his "sufferings for your sake" (παθήματα ὑπὲρ ὑμῶν). Others may participate in Paul's missionary activity. In fact, several passages (Col 4:12, 13; 1 Thess 2:2) reveal an extension of this struggle for the gospel to include the activity of his coworkers as well as to members of a whole congregation (Phil 1:27–30; cf. Rom 15:30–32) facing special trial and of whom it can be said they "share the same *conflict*" (τὸν αὐτὸν ἀγῶνα ἔχοντες, Phil 1:30). According to Pfitzner's interpretation, Paul's conflict is not to be limited to his inner struggles for the sake of his readers, whether it be his intercessory prayers on their behalf (cf. ὑπὲρ ὑμῶν), or his inner turmoil of some kind. Rather, this expenditure of his energies—through his concerns, his prayers (cf. 4:12 regarding Epaphras' ministry of intercession) and by his letters—are to be understood within the wider struggle for the spread of the gospel and of the faith. His inner conflicts and concerns, then, are part of that wider ἀγών itself.

2. ἵνα παρακληθῶσιν αἱ καρδίαι αὐτῶν. The purpose of this apostolic activity is to strengthen the readers' hearts. The παρακαλέω word-group had a wealth of meanings in the Greek world of Paul's day, including "to call someone to oneself," "to beseech," "to ask" (sometimes in prayer), "to exhort," and "to comfort" (see Schmitz-Stählin's fine article in *TDNT* 5, 773–99). On occasion in the NT, the verb served to denote missionary proclamation (2 Cor 5:20; cf. 1 Thess 2:3 and on this note A. Grabner-Haider, *Paraklese und Eschatologie bei Paulus. Mensch und Welt im Anspruch der Zukunft Gottes* [NTAbh, NS 4; Münster: Aschendorff, 1968] 33–44) and as a kind of formula to introduce pastoral administration (on the use of the παρακαλέω-formula see C. J. Bjerkelund, *Parakalô. Form, Funktion und Sinn der parakalô-Sätze in den paulinischen Briefe*

[Bibliotheca Theologica Norwegica 1; Oslo: Universitetsforlaget, 1967]). While the translation "comfort" is perfectly legitimate in many contexts (see O'Brien, *Introductory Thanksgivings*, 241–47, for an examination of this "consolation" theme in 2 Cor 1 in the light of its rich OT background), and is preferred here by Lohse (80), Schmitz-Stählin (*TDNT* 5, 797) and others, such a rendering appears to be too weak (cf. Bruce, 223, and Zeilinger, *Der Erstgeborene*, 108). The verb implies more than "comfort" and ought to be rendered "strengthen" (cf. v 4, the context of which supports this rendering). In Colossians there is no mention of, or allusion to, distresses or persecutions that would have elicited consolation or comfort as the object of the apostle's energetic activities. What made Paul concerned was the readers' danger of being carried away by the heretical teaching. Consequently their hearts needed to be strengthened (note the parallel in 2 Thess 2:16, 17 where *παρακαλέω* is used, with reference to the addressees' hearts, synonymously with *στηρίζω*, "strengthen"). "Heart" (*καρδία*) is employed in its customary OT sense denoting the inner life of the person, the center of his personality, understood as the source of will, emotion, thoughts and affections.

συμβιβασθέντες ἐν ἀγάπῃ. A good case has been made for rendering this phrase as "being instructed in love," so referring to the loving admonition given to the community. Several commentators (including Dibelius-Greeven, 25, 26, Scott, 36, and Montague, *Growth in Christ*, 82) have adopted this line. The verb *συμβιβάζω* does, on occasion, carry this didactic meaning outside the Bible (for examples in Aristotle, Philo, etc. see Delling, *TDNT* 7, 763) while all ten LXX instances mean "instruct," "make known," "teach," and refer exclusively to authoritative direction (cf. Exod 4:12, 15; 18:16; Lev 10:11; Deut 4:9; Judg 13:8; etc. Isa 40:13 is cited by Paul with the meaning "instruct" at 1 Cor 2:16). The same connotation occurs at Acts 9:22 and 19:33. Further, Scott observed that Paul's preoccupation in Colossians was less the issue of unity than that his readers be enlightened in their faith over against heretical teachings and practices (the Vulgate seems to have caught this point with its rendering "*instructi in caritate*"). Also this interpretation suits the immediate context with its strong emphasis on "knowledge," "understanding" and "wisdom." *ἐν ἀγάπῃ* then refers less to Paul's love for the readers—as though they were "charitably instructed"—than to love in its full breadth of meaning, as the foundation of the Christian life (cf. Eph 3:17). (Note the discussion of Montague, *Growth in Christ*, 82.)

The majority view, however, takes the verb *συμβιβάζω* in the sense of "unite," "knit together," a meaning equally well known from ancient times (cf. Herodotus 1.74.3, Thucydides 2.29.6, and Plato, *Prot* 337E; cf. Delling, *TDNT* 7, 763), and which Paul gives it in verse 19 and Ephesians 4:16. In this sense (taking *ἐν* instrumentally) love binds them all together (as some interpret 3:14 where love is called the "bond of perfection," *σύνδεσμος τῆς τελειότητος*), and from the union that results they would attain to full understanding and knowledge.

The issue is a finely balanced one and while most argue that the translation "being knit together" is preferable in the light of the later verses in Colossians, our inclination, because of the immediate context, is in favor of the sense "taught," "instructed."

καὶ εἰς πᾶν πλοῦτος κτλ. Martin, *NCB*, 75, aptly remarks: "There is an appeal to clear-sighted appreciation of theological truth in the second part of the verse." The object toward which Paul's instruction moves (εἰς) is a deeper understanding of the divine mystery, while the stress on the superabundance of such knowledge is signified through the accumulation of synonyms (cf. Percy, *Probleme,* 25, 26, and Bujard, *Untersuchungen,* 147–50).

As at chapter 1:9, 10 "insight" (σύνεσις) and "knowledge" (ἐπίγνωσις) are linked to express the concern of the apostle for the community. Here he goes out of his way to emphasize the abundant fullness of this σύνεσις ("insight" or "understanding" implies, as at 1:9, the capacity to distinguish the true from the false) by connecting the words "riches" (πλοῦτος; cf. the comments at 1:27) and "fullness" (πληροφορία). The latter term can mean "full assurance," "certainty" (BAG, 670), and this is its connotation at 1 Thessalonians 1:5 (and also in non-Christian literature, so Delling, *TDNT* 6, 310). If this is the correct rendering here, then Paul has introduced the note of assurance or certainty which was important for the Colossians in the face of false doctrines: either Paul desires that their judgment be exercised with full certainty (so Abbott, 239, on the grounds that σύνεσις has an intransitive sense and means "the faculty of judging") or, more likely, he is looking for the conviction which results from insight (as Moule, 86, Turner, *Syntax,* 211, and Montague, *Growth in Christ,* 83, take it).

On the other hand, it is equally possible that πληροφορία means "fullness" (so among others Lohse, 81, and van Roon, *Ephesians,* 246), is tautologous with "riches" (πλοῦτος) and, together with the additional word "all" (πᾶν), underscores in an emphatic manner the rich fullness of this insight.

εἰς ἐπίγνωσιν τοῦ μυστηρίου τοῦ θεοῦ, Χριστοῦ. From the abundance of this understanding Paul turns to speak of the uniqueness of its object. The two phrases introduced by the preposition εἰς ("to") are parallel, though the second emphatically points out the special object toward which the σύνεσις is directed (Meyer, 342; Abbott, 239): it is the "knowledge of God's mystery, of Christ." (On the meaning of ἐπίγνωσις see on 1:9 where the parallel expression, "that you may be filled with the knowledge of his will [τὴν ἐπίγνωσιν τοῦ θελήματος αὐτοῦ]," occurs.)

The Greek editions of the NT show that the textual witnesses are divided over the exact wording of the last phrase (note the bewildering variety of alternatives in the United Bible Societies edition of *The Greek New Testament,* edited by K. Aland and others). However, the reading τοῦ μυστηρίου τοῦ θεοῦ, Χριστοῦ (RSV "[knowledge] of God's mystery, of Christ") appears to have been original. It asserts that the Christ proclaimed among the nations and who is the hope of glory for these Gentile readers (cf. 1:27) is the content of the divine mystery. This text is plainly to be preferred because of the strong external testimony (being supported by P^{46} B Hilary). Also, because of the difficulty of this reading it gave rise to manifold alterations. Later scribes attempted to clarify the sense by their changes and additions, but each of them can be explained as variants of this original text (for a brief note see Metzger's *Textual Commentary,* 622, and for a more detailed treatment cf. his volume *The Text of the New Testament. Its Transmission, Corruption and Restoration.* 2nd ed. [New York/London: Oxford University Press, 1968, 236–38]).

The knowledge of which Paul speaks is personal. Christ himself is God's mystery revealed, the Christ with whom these Colossian readers had become one (Bruce, 224). There could be no appreciation of divine wisdom apart from this personal knowledge of him.

3. *ἐν ᾧ εἰσιν πάντες οἱ θησαυροὶ τῆς σοφίας καὶ γνώσεως ἀπόκρυφοι.* The person whom the readers are to know more fully is Christ in whom (*ἐν ᾧ*; rather than "in it," i.e. the mystery, which is more distant from the relative pronoun and less likely to be the antecedent on contextual grounds) all the treasures of wisdom and knowledge have been stored up. "Wisdom" (*σοφία*) and "knowledge" (*γνῶσις*), conjoined under the one definite article (*τῆς*), are virtually regarded as a single entity, as they are elsewhere in Jewish literature (LXX Ecclus 1:16–18; 2:26; 7:13; 9:10; cf. 1QS 4:3, 22; 1QH 1:18, 19; CD 2:3). Significantly, the two terms are linked at Romans 11:33 and again conjoined with the notion of wealth (*πλοῦτος*; cf. Col 1:27; 2:2) as Paul praises God for the manner in which his magnificent sovereign purposes for mankind have been effected with the bestowal of his unmerited mercy on Jews and Gentiles alike: "O the depth of the riches and wisdom and knowledge of God."

The term "treasure" (*θησαυρός*) was employed in the LXX not only of material wealth (Josh 6:19, 24; Prov 10:2; etc.), but also of spiritual goods, e.g. at Isaiah 33:6 wisdom and the fear of God are called "treasures" (Hauck, *TDNT* 3, 137). Paul asserts here, rather unusually, that all these treasures of wisdom and knowledge (the *πάντες* rules out all exceptions) which exist (*εἰσιν*) lie "hidden" (*ἀπόκρυφοι* indicates the manner of that existence; Lohmeyer, 94, and Lohse 82). At first sight this statement seems to run counter to chapter 1:26 where it was indicated that the mystery, previously hidden (*ἀποκεκρυμμένον*), has now (*νῦν δέ*) in a dramatic turn of events been disclosed by God. However, the treasures are "hidden" (*ἀπόκρυφοι*) not in the sense that they are "kept concealed," which is the significance of the perfect passive participle *ἀποκεκρυμμένον*, but that they exist (*εἰσιν*) being "deposited" or "stored up" in Christ (cf. Zeilinger, *Der Erstgeborene,* 111). To search for other sources of knowledge apart from him is a useless enterprise.

According to Lohse, 82, Jewish apocalyptic writings occasionally used the image of a hidden treasure in order to challenge men and women to pursue right knowledge (cf. 1 Enoch 46:3). Here Paul is encouraging the readers to look to Christ as the only "place" where the treasures of wisdom and knowledge are to be found.

In the hymn of chapter 1:15–20 Christ has been identified with the Wisdom of God, ascribing to him activities which are predicated of personified Wisdom in the OT and Judaism. Here, by stating that all of God's stores of wisdom and knowledge are hidden away in him, the apostle is indicating again in an overwhelmingly impressive way that "Christ has become to Christians all that the Wisdom of God was, according to the Wisdom Literature, and more still" (Moule, 86). Because he holds this exalted position there is good reason to encourage these Christians of the Lycus valley to turn to him for all God's stores of insight, understanding, wisdom and knowledge.

It has been argued by some that since the expression "the treasures of wisdom and knowledge" was not a common one in the Pauline corpus and as the exact phrase does not occur in the OT, it may well have been borrowed from the vocabulary of the opposition at Colossae. To be more specific verse 3 is sometimes understood as supporting the Gnostic character of the opposition. Lightfoot, for example, took this view claiming that Paul, in employing ἀπόκρυφοι, again adopts "a favourite term of the Gnostic teachers, only that he may refute a favourite doctrine" (172). Davies, whose basic thesis is that the "essential ideas" lying behind Paul's proclamation are derived from Judaism, nevertheless states that the apostle asserts the truth of verse 3 "with a side-glance at the shibboleths of Gnosticism" (*Paul*, 173), while Hauck argues that it is "not impossible that the expression chosen in Col 2:3 . . . is influenced by current Gnostic terminology" (*TDNT* 3, 138; cf. also Bradley, *StBibT* 2 [1972] 22). However, the supposed parallels to Gnostic literature adduced by Hauck refer to "treasures of light" rather than to treasures of wisdom and knowledge. There is, therefore, little direct evidence to support the Gnostic character of the expression used (cf. Bandstra, *Dimensions*, 340, 341).

Others have turned to the OT and Jewish milieu as a more likely source for Paul's ideas. So Martin (*NCB*, 76) considers that the whole cluster of terms and motifs "suggest a conscious indebtedness to the figure of wisdom in Proverbs 2:3ff." (cf. Ecclus 1:25 and Isa 45:3 LXX). Paul is making an appeal to Jewish sources partly because the false teaching at Colossae on its Jewish side (it was a fusion of Jewish and pagan elements) was insisting that Jesus Christ was only one mediator and one source of revelation among many.

J. Dupont (*Gnosis. La connaissance religieuse dans les épîtres de saint Paul* [Paris: Gabalda, 1949] 16–18) had previously drawn attention to the appearance here of terms used by Judaism concerning the law (Isa 33:5, 6; cf. Bar 3:15–4:1; Ecclus 24:23 and 2 Apoc Bar 44:14; 54:13). The Jews were confident that in the law they possessed all the treasures of wisdom (σοφία), and to this the idea of knowledge (γνῶσις), apparently introduced by Judaizing elements, was attached. According to Dupont (who is followed by Montague, *Growth in Christ*, 84, 85), Paul unites the two expressions, substitutes Christ for the law, and shows that the only ἐπίγνωσις ("knowledge") a Christian should seek is to be found in the mystery of Christ. Clearly, on Dupont's reconstruction, the Jewish elements of the false teaching at Colossae are those which draw the apostle's immediate fire here.

Bandstra (*Dimensions*, 339–43) has taken the discussion further by arguing that the close parallels to Paul's phraseology of verse 3 in 2 Apoc Bar (esp. 44:14 and 54:13 where "treasures of wisdom" appears) provide additional evidence for the basically Jewish character of the opposition at Colossae. In the former passage, which is definitely eschatological with its reference to the "new world," "the world to come," "promised time," etc., Baruch suggests that the possession of the treasures of wisdom and understanding, designated for those who shall receive the inheritance of the promised time, can be secured if the elders follow Baruch's advice and instruct the Israelites to remain true to the law. But Paul affirms that the place where the treasures of wisdom and knowledge are to be found is in Christ and in him alone. Bandstra agrees with Francis' claim (*Conflict*, 163–95) that the ascetic-mystic literature provides the most helpful background for understanding the opposition reflected in chapter 2:18, a background that provides the closest parallels to chapter 2:2, 3. The opposition at Colossae, basically a danger from without, may have come from "a conventicle of Jewish mystical ascetics who affirmed that knowledge of God's mysteries came to a person quite apart from any divine mediator" (343). Christ was not really necessary in order to know God's eschatological and cosmic mysteries.

4. Now for the first time Paul *expressly* points to the danger facing the church (Schweizer, 95; Martin, *NCB*, 76).

τοῦτο λέγω. These words have been taken: (1) prospectively, referring to what follows. Accordingly the statement may be regarded as commencing a new paragraph in which Paul begins to confront the opposition more directly: so Moule, 88, who understands the *ἵνα* in an imperatival sense: "What I mean is this, don't let anyone . . ." Cf. Bruce, 224, and Bjerkelund, *Parakalô*, 182, 183, who regards the phrase as equivalent to a *παρακαλέω*-sentence commencing a new section.

It is preferable, however, to interpret the words (2) retrospectively, referring to what has immediately preceded, for the following reasons: *(a)* the so-called parallels to the prospective use of *τοῦτο λέγω*, viz. Galatians 3:17 and 1 Corinthians 1:12, do not contain the *ἵνα* clause; *(b)* there is no example in the NT of an imperatival *ἵνα* following a *τοῦτο λέγω* construction, while John 5:34 encourages the retrospective interpretation: "I say these things in order that (*ταῦτα λέγω ἵνα*) you may be saved"; *(c)* the *γάρ* ("for") in chapter 2:5 is much more difficult to justify on the first view (as Moule, 88, rightly concedes) since Paul's words here about being absent in body but present in spirit pick up the thought of verse 1, so binding verses 1–5 together (note Bandstra's careful treatment, *Dimensions*, 340). The translation is therefore: "I am saying this in order that no one . . . ."

παραλογίζηται ἐν πιθανολογίᾳ. "[That no one] may deceive you with persuasive language." The verb, meaning "deceive," "delude" (BAG, 620), is used in the New Testament only here and at James 1:22 which refers to the self-deception of those who are hearers of the word but not doers (the term appears in the LXX and later Greek writers, cf. BAG, 620 and MM, 487). This deception is effected "by plausible (but false) arguments" (BAG, 657). *πιθανολογία* means "persuasive speech," "art of persuasion" (so Plato) and here it is being used in an unfavorable sense.

Paul has said these things (vs 1–3, especially v 3) to warn the Colossian community not to give in to the beguiling speech of the false teachers (against Hooker, *Christ*, 317, who does not agree that the Colossians are in such imminent danger). Their behavior and manner are so different from the true messenger of the gospel whose proclamation is "not in plausible words of wisdom, but in demonstration of the Spirit and power" (1 Cor 2:4; cf. Lohmeyer, 95).

5. *εἰ γὰρ καὶ τῇ σαρκὶ ἄπειμι*. Although (the combination *εἰ καί* has a concessive sense here, see Thrall, *Particles*, 79) Paul is absent from the Colossian community, he is aware that the danger facing them is a real one. That is why he is at pains to warn them (the *γάρ* links with the preceding and gives the basis for speaking such words: see on v 4 and note Dibelius-Greeven, 26). If he were present at Colossae he would deal with this menacing situation in person; but his imprisonment prevents him from being with them "in

the flesh" (here the meaning of σάρξ "flesh" is the same as σῶμα "body" and denotes bodily existence: so Meyer, 346, Schweizer, *TDNT* 7, 136, and most others; Moule, *Idiom Book*, 46, renders the dative with the adverb "physically").

ἀλλὰ τῷ πνεύματι σὺν ὑμῖν εἰμι. Even if he is absent in body *yet* (cf. 1 Cor 4:15; 9:2; 2 Cor 4:16; Rom 6:5; etc.; BDF, para. 448[5]; on the formula-type character of the phrase "absent in body, present in spirit" see G. Karlson, "Formelhaftes in den Paulusbriefen," *Eranos* 54 [1956] 138–41, for further examples from ancient epistolary literature; cited by Lohse, 83) he is present in spirit. Paul's sense of being "spiritually present" with his fellow-Christians at a distance was extremely strong and vivid. The clearest and most remarkable example is recorded at 1 Corinthians 5:3–5, where he speaks of himself as being present in spirit (παρὼν δὲ τῷ πνεύματι) in the assembly at Corinth, while living at Ephesus, in order to take part in a disciplinary action. In that case his presence was assured to a congregation with which he was well acquainted. Here he gives the same assurance to a church he had not previously visited, while his presence was for "a much happier purpose" (Bruce, 225).

But *how* did Paul envisage his spirit as being present with the Colossians or the Corinthians? Regarding the latter context (1 Cor 5:3–5) the expression "in spirit" (τῷ πνεύματι) suggests something more than that they were present in his thoughts and prayers, however true this may have been. Paul states that he is present with them, not that they are with him. Certainly at 1 Corinthians 5:4 it is a real presence, not simply that he agrees with their verdict, for he writes, "When you and my spirit are assembled." He clearly conceived of his spirit's presence in a place far removed from where his body stood. Otto may be right when he states: "In all reality and without hesitation he believed that he was capable of operating spiritually at a distance" (cited by J. D. G. Dunn, *Jesus and the Spirit. A Study of the Religious and Charismatic Experience of Jesus and the First Christians as Reflected in the New Testament* [Philadelphia: Westminster, 1975] 73), but this does not tell us much, while Dunn's hint that it was due to the power of a charismatic personality makes the reference too narrow. Best's suggestion (*Body*, 59) is nearer the mark. Commenting on the Corinthian passage, he affirms that Paul is present with the Corinthians since both live with Christ. Because Best takes the idea of Christ as an inclusive or corporate personality seriously, he envisages the presence of the whole personality whenever a "part" of it is acting. Paul is truly at Corinth and Colossae not because his πνεῦμα is to be "regarded as the gift of the Spirit of God which has been given to him, which denotes his authority, and which also exerts an influence beyond his physical presence" (so Schweizer, *TDNT* 6, 436), but since the Spirit of God has united both him and the Colossians to Christ. Because both live with Christ, he is present in spirit with them.

χαίρων καὶ βλέπων κτλ. These words indicate by way of summary how the Colossian community was faring, and the description is a positive one. The two participles χαίρων and βλέπων are best taken together and rendered "rejoicing to see" (with Bengel 2, 459, Robertson, *Grammar*, 426, 427, BDF, para. 471[5], etc., against Meyer, 347, who considers that χαίρων refers to

Paul's joy *at the fact* that he is with them spiritually, while βλέπων adds to the thought by indicating what is perceived). Obviously because of Paul's physical absence βλέπω is used figuratively meaning "perceive," "note" (cf. Rom 7:23; 2 Cor 7:8; Heb 2:9; 10:25).

Two interesting terms are employed in this positive description of the church's condition: τάξις ("order") and στερέωμα ("firmness," "steadfastness"), both of which could appear in military contexts, the former denoting the positions which soldiers occupy (cf. Xenophon, *Anabasis* 1.2.18; the Qumran community called itself a camp and its order was to be maintained at all costs: 1QS 10:25; cf. 4:4; 1QM 3:1, where the Hebrew equivalent of τάξις is used; cf. Bertram, *TDNT* 7, 614), the latter describing a bulwark or fortification (1 Macc 9:14; cf. Bertram, *TDNT* 7, 609–14). So some have pressed the military metaphor in this context. For Lohmeyer, "The apostle is 'with them' as a field commander standing before his troops and arranging the ranks for battle once more" (95), while Martin (*NCB*, 76, 77) interprets the words of Paul to mean that he viewed with approval their steadfast intent to close ranks and stand firm, without yielding to erroneous propaganda from an intruding enemy (cf. Moule, 89).

An examination of the different occurrences of these two terms in a variety of contexts (Classical Greek writers, the LXX, papyri and patristic material) shows that from earliest times τάξις and στερέωμα did not necessarily have a military nuance but only assume one from their respective contexts (Abbott, 243; cf. Dibelius-Greeven, 26; the lexicons of BAG, MM, Hatch and Redpath, and Lampe draw attention to a variety of instances where there is no military meaning). Further, the context here does not suggest the positioning of troops for battle. Both concepts are employed in a more general sense so that τάξις denotes the well-ordered Christian behavior of the community (cf. 1 Cor 14:40) which previously had not been disturbed by sectarian divisions nor forsaken by its readers, while στερέωμα describes the "firmness" or solidarity of their faith in Christ (τῆς εἰς Χριστὸν πίστεως ὑμῶν; cf. Acts 16:5; 1 Peter 5:9). This faith, which was dynamic in character (cf. Bultmann, *TDNT* 6, 212, who correctly points out that πίστις can frequently denote the living and dynamic aspect of faith rather than the mere fact of it, for example, 2 Cor 10:15; Phil 1:25) was firmly founded because it was directed to Christ alone (εἰς Χριστόν), and as long as they held fast to him no temptation would overcome them. Well might Paul be joyful (χαίρων) as he was given this description by Epaphras of the believing community at Colossae.

The praise given to the congregation suggests that, although it was troubled by false teachers (who were hardly an external threat only, as W. Foerster, "Die Irrlehrer des Kolosserbriefes," *Studia Biblica et Semitica. Prof. Th. C. Vriezen dedicata* [Wageningen: Veenman and Zonen, 1966] 72, 73, and Lähnemann, *Kolosserbrief*, 43, indicate), the church was still basically sound in the faith, preserving the apostolic message and persisting in it. The heresy had not achieved anything like real success (cf. 2:4, 8, 20) though it may well have encroached on a section of the Christians, threatening to disrupt others. On the basis of their adherence to the apostolic gospel, with its center being Christ Jesus as Lord, the apostle is now able to attack the heresy which has been enticingly presented (v 4).

Explanation

Having stated that he is a servant of the gospel (v 23) Paul describes his suffering and its relation to his God-given task (v 24, 25). He rejoices in his sufferings on behalf of the Colossians for they are part and parcel of the afflictions of Christ, the messianic woes that usher in the end-time. The more sufferings he personally absorbed—as he was engaged in his apostolic task of preaching the gospel—the less would remain for these fellow Christians to endure. He was currently filling up what was left over of the full quota of these messianic afflictions.

Though now exalted in heaven, Christ continues to suffer in his members, not least in Paul himself. Prior to his conversion, Paul had been actively engaged in making Christ suffer in the person of his followers in Judea (cf. Christ's words to him: "Saul, Saul, why do you persecute *me?*" [Acts 9:4]). But from now on he would suffer for Christ's sake (Acts 9:16) or for the sake of his body, the church.

Paul's ministry, a commission given to him in accordance with the gospel-plan of God, was to proclaim the Word of God dynamically and effectively throughout the world. The message itself was none other than God's mystery (previously hidden but now revealed), a message that was truly glorious, for here the wealth of God was lavished in a wonderful way; it was a message God had graciously purposed to make known among the Gentiles since it had special reference to them; and, it focused on Christ as the one who indwelt the Colossians.

Paul worked energetically proclaiming Christ as Lord. This he did by systematic and intensive teaching and admonition. His pastoral and apostolic tasks were not finished with the conversion of men and women. This was only the beginning and the end would not be reached until the day of Christ when the quality of his ministry would be tested. So he strove energetically for the cause of the gospel as God continued to work mightily through him, and he made it his aim to present every man perfect in Christ on the final day.

What was true of Paul's struggle for the sake of the gospel generally had reference to the Colossians and other Lycus Valley Christians as well. He desired that their lives might be strengthened and this would occur as they came to a deeper understanding of Christ, God's mystery revealed, the one in whom all the treasures of wisdom were available.

Now, for the first time (2:4), Paul expressly mentions the danger facing the church. He warns the Colossian community not to give in to the persuasive but deceptive speech of the false teachers. Though he is physically absent from them he is present in spirit and he wants to encourage them with the good reports he has heard; he is delighted to learn of their orderly Christian life and the stability of their faith in Christ.

The Antidote to Error: Christ in All His Fullness (2:6–15)

Bibliography

Bacchiocchi, S. *From Sabbath to Sunday. A Historical Investigation of the Rise of Sunday Observance in Early Christianity.* Rome: Pontifical Gregorian University, 1977, 339–62. **Bandstra, A. J.** *The Law and the Elements of the World. An Exegetical Study in Aspects of Paul's Teaching.* Kampen: Kok, 1964. American edition, Grand Rapids, MI: Eerdmans, n.d. **Beasley-Murray, G. R.** *Baptism in the New Testament.* London: Macmillan, 1962. ———. "The Second Chapter of Colossians." *RevExp* 70 (1973) 469–79. **Benoit, P.** "Corps, tête et plérôme dans les épîtres de la captivité." *RB* 63 (1956) 5–44. **Blanchette, O. A.** "Does the *Cheirographon* of Col 2:14 Represent Christ Himself?" *CBQ* 23 (1961) 306–12. **Blinzler, J.** "Lexikalisches zu dem Terminus τὰ στοιχεῖα τοῦ κόσμου bei Paulus." *Studiorum Paulinorum Congressus Internationalis Catholicus.* 2 vols. Rome: Pontifical Biblical Institute, 1963. 2.429–43. **Bornkamm, G.** *Conflict,* 123–45. ———. "Baptism and New Life in Paul. Romans 6." *Early Christian Experience.* Tr. P. L. Hammer. London: SCM, 1969, 71–86. American edition, New York: Harper and Row, 1969. **Bruce, F. F.** *Tradition Old and New.* Exeter: Paternoster, 1970. American edition, Grand Rapids, MI: Zondervan, 1970. **Carr, W.** "Two Notes on Colossians." *JTS* 24 (1973) 492–500. **Cullmann, O.** "The Tradition." *The Early Church,* ed. A. J. B. Higgins. London: SCM, 1956, 59–99. **Ernst, J.** *Pleroma.* **Halter, H.** *Taufe und Ethos. Paulinische Kriterien für das Proprium christliche Moral.* Freiburg: Herder, 1977. **Hanson, A. T.** *Studies in Paul's Technique and Theology.* London: SPCK, 1974. **Lohse, E.** "Ein hymnisches Bekenntnis in Kolosser 2, 13c–15." *Mélanges Bibliques en hommage au R. P. Béda Rigaux,* ed. A. Descamps and A. de Halleux. Gembloux: Duculot, 1970, 427–35. Reprinted in *Einheit,* 276–84. **Martin, R. P.** "Reconciliation and Forgiveness in Colossians." *Reconciliation and Hope. New Testament Essays on Atonement and Eschatology presented to L. L. Morris on his 60th Birthday,* ed. R. Banks. Exeter: Paternoster, 1974, 104–124. American edition, Grand Rapids, MI: Eerdmans. 1974. **Moule, C. F. D.** *Origin.* **Schille, G.** *Frühchristliche Hymnen.* 2nd. ed. Berlin: Evangelische Verlagsanstalt, 1965. **Schnackenburg, R.** *Baptism in the Thought of St. Paul. A Study in Pauline Theology.* Tr. G. R. Beasley-Murray. New York: Herder, 1964. **Schweizer, E.** "Christianity of the Circumcised and Judaism of the Uncircumcised. The Background of Matthew and Colossians." *Jews, Greeks and Christians. Religious Cultures in Late Antiquity. Essays in Honor of William David Davies,* ed. R. Hamerton-Kelly and R. Scroggs. Leiden: Brill, 1976, 245–60. ———. "Die 'Elemente der Welt.' Gal 4, 3.9; Kol 2, 8.20." *Verborum Veritas. Festschrift für Gustav Stählin zum 70. Geburtstag,* ed. O. Bocher and K. Haacker. Wuppertal: Brockhaus, 1970, 245–59. Reprinted in *Beiträge,* 147–63. **Seeberg, A.** *Der Katechismus der Urchristenheit.* Leipzig: A. Deichertschen, 1903. Reprinted as TBü 26. Munich: Kaiser, 1966. **Tannehill, R. C.** *Dying.* **Wegenast, K.** *Das Verständnis der Tradition bei Paulus und in den Deuteropaulinen.* WMANT 8. Neukirchen-Vluyn: Neukirchener, 1962. **Weiss, H.** *CBQ* 34 (1972) 294–314. **Wengst, K.** *Formeln.* **Williamson Jr., L.** "Led in Triumph. Paul's Use of Thriambeuō." *Int* 22 (1968) 317–32.

Translation

[6] *So then, just as you received Christ Jesus as Lord, continue to live in him,* [7] *rooted and built up in him, established in the faith as you were taught, and overflowing with thanksgiving.*[a]

[8] *See to it that no one takes you captive by means of a hollow, deceptive philosophy,*
which depends on mere human tradition, derived from the elemental powers of the
world and not from Christ. [9] *For in him the whole fullness of deity dwells in bodily*
form, [10] *and you have been filled in him who is the head over every power and*
authority. [11] *In him you were also circumcised with a circumcision not made with*
hands, in the putting off the body of flesh, by the circumcision of Christ. [12] *You*
were buried with him in baptism; in him you were also raised with him through
faith in the power of God who raised him from the dead. [13] *When you were dead in*
your sins and in the uncircumcision of your sinful nature, God made you alive with
Christ. He forgave us all our trespasses, [14] *having canceled the IOU which, because*
of the regulations, was against us and stood opposed to us; he took it away, nailing
it to the cross. [15] *Having stripped the principalities and powers of their authority*
and dignity God exposed their utter helplessness for all to see, leading them in his
triumphal procession in Christ.

Notes

[a] Although the reading *ἐν αὐτῇ ἐν εὐχαριστίᾳ* has strong manuscript support [B D[c] H K *Byz Lect*, some of the versions, etc.] it is probably a copyist's assimilation to 4:2, while the alternate reading *ἐν αὐτῷ* is probably a subsequent modification because of the preceding phrase *ἐν αὐτῷ· ἐν εὐχαριστίᾳ* appears to have been the original reading; cf. Metzger, *Textual Commentary*, 622.

Form/Structure/Setting

As he begins his interaction with the "philosophy" (*φιλοσοφία*) of the false teachers, the apostle admonishes the addressees to continue in the teaching they had received and to remain immovable in their faith (2:6, 7). These two verses, which summarize much of what has preceded (Lähnemann, *Kolosserbrief*, 49) and which lay the foundation for the attack on the Colossian heresy that follows, contain an introductory subordinate clause (v 6*a*, *ὡς οὖν παρελάβετε τὸν Χριστὸν Ἰησοῦν τὸν κύριον*, "so then, just as you received Christ Jesus as Lord") and a longer principal clause (vv 6*b*, 7) consisting of an imperative, three participial expressions joined by *καί* ("and"), a parenthesis and a concluding participial expression (Zeilinger, *Der Erstgeborene*, 50; cf. Bujard, *Untersuchungen*, 74–76, 80–86, regarding the literary style of vv 6–15):

6*b* *ἐν αὐτῷ περιπατεῖτε*
7*a* *ἐρριζωμένοι*
b *καὶ ἐποικοδομούμενοι ἐν αὐτῷ*
c *καὶ βεβαιούμενοι τῇ πίστει*
d *—καθὼς ἐδιδάχθητε—*
e *περισσεύοντες ἐν εὐχαριστίᾳ.*
("live in him
rooted
and built up in him
and established in the faith
—as you were taught—
overflowing with thanksgiving.")

At verse 8 the community is confronted with the first of several warnings that will demand of it clear, unequivocal decisions. The imperative βλέπετε ("beware") is followed by what is, in effect, a sentence of prohibition and by using two sets of prepositional phrases in synonymous parallelism the means by which the false teachers intend to carry out their plan to ensnare the congregation is mentioned:

8b διὰ τῆς φιλοσοφίας
c καὶ κενῆς ἀπάτης
d κατὰ τὴν παράδοσιν τῶν ἀνθρώπων
e κατὰ τὰ στοιχεῖα τοῦ κόσμου.
("through philosophy
and empty deceit
according to the tradition of men
according to the elemental powers of the world.")

The conclusion of the verse is brief and pungent, presenting a sharp antithesis to what has immediately preceded: *καὶ οὐ κατὰ* Χριστόν ("and not according to Christ").

Verses 9 and 10, in which language from the hymn is taken up (*ἐν αὐτῷ κατοικεῖ πᾶν τὸ πλήρωμα κτλ.*) spell out why (*ὅτι*) the "philosophy" of the false teachers is "not according to Christ." Two reasons are given in separate clauses, linked by *καί* ("and"), where there is a play on *ἐν αὐτῷ* ("in him") and *πλήρωμα* ("fullness"):

ὅτι ἐν αὐτῷ κατοικεῖ πᾶν τὸ πλήρωμα τῆς θεότητος σωματικῶς.
καὶ ἐστὲ ἐν αὐτῷ πεπληρωμένοι,
ὅς ἐστιν ἡ κεφαλὴ πάσης ἀρχῆς καὶ ἐξουσίας.
("For *in him* the whole *fullness* of deity lives in bodily form, and you have been *filled in him*,
who is the head over every power and authority.")

Paul continues (vv 11, 12) the theme of incorporation in Christ. Having mentioned that the readers have been "filled in him," he elaborates on this by asserting that they have participated in Christ's death, burial and resurrection:

ἐν ᾧ καὶ περιετμήθητε περιτομῇ ἀχειροποιήτῳ . . .
συνταφέντες αὐτῷ . . .
ἐν ᾧ καὶ συνηγέρθητε . . .
("In him you were also circumcised with a circumcision not made with hands,
you were buried with him . . .
in him you were also raised . . ."

Verse 13 marks a change in the section. There is a switch in the subject from "you" to "he"; God has made you who were dead to be alive with Christ. Again a sharp contrast is drawn between the readers' pre-Christian past (*καὶ ὑμᾶς νεκροὺς ὄντας . . . τῆς σαρκὸς ὑμῶν*, "also you who were dead . . .") and their present standing in Christ, brought about by God's action (*συνεζωοποίησεν ὑμᾶς σὺν αὐτῷ*, "he made you alive together with him").

In the latter half of the verse there is a further change to "us" and "our" from "you" (i.e. from the second person to the first), and several scholars have concluded that verses 13*c*–15, in which traditional Christian formulations appear, are a fragment of a confession constructed in hymnic phrases which the author appropriated, since it clearly expressed for him the essential connection between the forgiveness of sins and victory over the principalities and powers (so Lohse, 106, 107; also *Einheit*, 276–84; cf. Martin, *Reconciliation*, 1974, 116–24).

Schille (*Hymnen*, 31–37; cf. Lohmeyer, 100–102) had previously argued that a redeemer or baptismal hymn underlay verses 9–15 but this view has been rejected even by those who detect hymnic elements in verses 13–15. Verses 9, 10*b* are not the beginning of a hymn (the ὅτι is causal, not recitative) but rather an explanatory resumption of chapter 1:15–20 (note the critiques of Deichgräber, *Gotteshymnus*, 167–69, and Lohse, *Einheit*, 277–79). Wengst too (*Formeln*, 186–94) assumed that verses 13–15 were based on a continuous traditional piece. However, to demonstrate that the hymn consisted of three verses each containing three lines (vv 13, 14, 15) he is obliged to change the text (the "you" was originally "we" and the expression "the uncircumcision of your flesh" is dropped out), but these adjustments are not convincing.

Lohse's structuring of the passage has the merit of drawing to our attention the relationship of the participles to the finite verbs in verses 14 and 15 (ἐξαλείψας . . . ἦρκεν . . . προσηλώσας, "having canceled . . . he took away . . . nailing"; and ἀπεκδυσάμενος . . . ἐδειγμάτισεν . . . θριαμβεύσας, "having disarmed . . . he made a spectacle . . . leading in his triumphal procession"), but this does not commit us to a hymnic confession underlying verses 13*c*–15. The linguistic argument is two-edged. For if the passage contains words that occur either rarely or nowhere else in the NT (cf. Lohse, 106) then it is unusual to speak of the author adopting "traditional formulations." The problem of the source of these expressions remains, and it might as well have been Paul as some unknown disciple—at least he does use the verb θριαμβεύω (2 Cor 2:14; he is the only NT writer to have done so).

Nevertheless verses 13*c*–15 are difficult to structure; in verse 13 a contrast is drawn: καὶ ὑμᾶς νεκροὺς ὄντας . . . συνεζωοποίησεν, "and you who were dead . . . he made alive." The participle χαρισάμενος which introduces the statement about the forgiveness of sins is probably causal (though some have suggested it is explanatory, see the exegesis below), while each of the two finite verbs in verses 14 and 15 is preceded and followed by a participle (see above).

It remains to draw attention to the "in Christ (him)" motif which runs like a scarlet thread through the whole passage (the significance of which is assessed below): ἐν αὐτῷ ("in him," vv 6, 7, 9, 10, 15); ἐν ᾧ ("in whom," vv 11, 12; cf. αὐτῷ, "him," v 12, and σὺν αὐτῷ, "with him," v 13). That the paragraph should begin with this important phrase ἐν αὐτῷ and end on a similar note suggests we have an example of *inclusio*, i.e. the text closes on the same note as its beginning.

Comment (2:6, 7)

In the paragraph commencing with verse 6 we come to the heart of the letter (cf. Dibelius-Greeven, 26). Here Paul gives a careful exposition of his teaching (sometimes drawing on traditional materials) for purposes of positive instruction and by way of a corrective to the false teaching. Verses 6 and 7 occupy a pivotal position: (a) they set forth the positive instruction that serves as a basis for the attack on the Colossian heresy, and this is because (b) they summarize much of what has preceded: so the Christological statement, "Christ Jesus the Lord," draws attention to the one who is at the center of the mystery (1:27) and the subject of the magnificent hymn (1:15–20), who is Lord over all; the notion of incorporation ("in him") is reiterated as is the thought of being grounded in the faith (v 7; cf. 1:23). The significant motif of teaching (to which may be joined the kindred theme of tradition), verse 7, focuses our attention again on the initial instruction in the gospel by Epaphras (1:6, 7), while the ideas of "walking" (v 6) and "abounding in thanksgiving" (v 7) tie in with Paul's intercessory prayer for the readers (1:10, 12), namely that they may walk (*περιπατέω*) worthily of the Lord and give joyful thanksgiving to the Father. In the space of a few brief words the apostle encapsulates many of the important ideas already spelled out in the letter, drives them home to the hearts of his readers by means of an "indicative-imperative" formulation and prepares to confront them with sharp alternatives (v 8) that will demand of them clear unequivocal decisions.

6. *ὡς οὖν παρελάβετε τὸν Χριστὸν Ἰησοῦν τὸν κύριον.* With the connective particle "then" (*οὖν*) a transition is made to a new section. The writer uses an "indicative-imperative" form (cf. 2:20; 3:1–4; Rom 15:7; Gal 5:25; Phil 2:5) to introduce the subject of tradition, for when Paul says that his readers have "received" (*παρελάβετε*) Christ Jesus as their Lord he is not simply reflecting on their personal commitment to Christ (though this is no doubt included), but he uses the semitechnical term specifically employed to denote the receiving of something delivered by tradition.

Early Christianity took over from rabbinic Judaism the idea of transmitting and safeguarding a tradition (the verbs "receive," "accept," *παραλαμβάνω*, and "transmit," *παραδίδωμι*, correspond to the rabbinic terms *qibbēl* and *māsar*). The classic Jewish exposition occurs in the "Sayings of the Fathers" which scribal legend had traced back to Moses: "Moses received the Torah from Sinai and delivered it to Joshua, and Joshua to the elders, and the elders to the prophets, and the prophets delivered it to the men of the Great Synagogue" (*m. 'Abot* 1:1). Primitive Christian tradition, however, was not connected with the authority of famous teachers, but was concerned ultimately with its source, "from the Lord" (1 Cor 11:23). Paul regularly reminded his congregations in the Gentile mission of the traditions he handed over to them, the content of which appear to have comprised three main elements: *(a)* a summary of the gospel, particularly the death and resurrection of Christ, expressed as a confession of faith (1 Cor 15:1–5; 1 Thess 2:13); *(b)* various deeds and words of Christ (1 Cor 11:23–26; 7:10, 11; 9:14); and *(c)* ethical and procedural rules (1 Cor 11:2; 1 Thess 4:1; 2 Thess 3:6). (On the subject of tradition see Cullman, *Church*, 59–99; Bruce, *Tradition*, 29–38; J. I. H. McDonald, KERYGMA *and* DIDACHE. *The articulation and structure of the earliest Christian message* [SNTSMS 37; Cambridge: University Press, 1980] 101–125; cf. Wegenast, *Verständnis*, 121–30, who, however, considers *παραλαμβάνω* at v 6 refers not to the acceptance of the apostolic tradition but to the baptized person's coming under the lordship of Christ [128]).

The Colossians have received Christ himself as their tradition. The expression τὸν Χριστὸν Ἰησοῦν τὸν κύριον is not an allusion to sayings of Jesus communicated as directions for right conduct (though cf. 1 Cor 7:10, 11; 9:14), as Cullmann, in *Church*, 64, suggested but is an early credal confession "Jesus Christ is Lord" (cf. Rom 10:9; 1 Cor 12:3; Phil 2:11). No doubt it summarizes the tradition delivered to the Colossians in Epaphras' initial evangelism which focused on the person of Christ Jesus (note 2 Cor 4:5). Whether "Christ" (τὸν Χριστὸν) was here understood as a title or not is a disputed point (Moule, 89, 90, claims it is difficult not to give it the force of a title; so also Turner, *Syntax*, 167; against Lohse, 93, who regards it as joined to "Jesus" to form a double name). Certainly the definite article "the" (τὸν) before "Lord" (κύριον) makes this term emphatic and probably as Foerster, *TDNT* 3, 1090, has suggested, gathers up all that Paul has previously said about Christ in Colossians. The one whom the Colossians received as their tradition is the center of God's mystery (1:27, 2:2), and the Lord in both creation and reconciliation (1:15–20). He is Lord absolutely (1 Cor 8:5, 6), not just one among many.

ἐν αὐτῷ περιπατεῖτε. With this summons, "continue to live in him," the apostle moves from the indicative to the imperative. For Paul there is no hiatus between believing and behaving. As Lohse (93) puts it: "Christology and ethics are intimately conjoined." The metaphor of walking (cf. the comments on 1:10) is frequently employed by Paul, deriving ultimately from an OT and Jewish background, to characterize the Christian's life and behavior (see Gal 5:16; Rom 14:15; 2 Cor 4:2, etc.). He has already interceded for his readers (1:10) that they might *live* (περιπατῆσαι) in a manner worthy of the one whom they confess as Lord, by pleasing him in all things. Having prayed to that end he now exhorts them along similar lines. His pastoral activity of praying did not obviate the necessity for exhortation. Indeed, the latter may well have been one of the means used by God to bring about the answers to Paul's petitions.

Since the Colossians had begun the Christian life by submitting to Christ Jesus as Lord they were now (the "as," ὡς, of the first clause may be balanced with the corresponding "so" but the meaning is clear enough without the οὕτως being supplied; cf. Seeberg, *Katechismus*, 169; BAG, 897, under section II) to go on living (the imperative περιπατεῖτε is a present tense) under that lordship as those incorporated into him (for a recent study on the "in Christ" and "in the Lord" phrases with special reference to the notion of incorporation see Moule, *Origin*, 47–96, and the literature cited there). They are to understand more and more about the consequences of his supremacy (Masson, 120). This would mean a rejection of rival loyalties, especially of alien principles (Martin, *Lord*, 73).

7. At chapter 1:10, in Paul's intercessory prayer for the Colossians, four participles ("bearing fruit," "increasing," v 10; "being strengthened," v 11; and "giving thanks," v 12) directly followed the verb "to walk" (περιπατῆσαι) and defined more precisely what was involved in walking "worthily of the Lord." Here also a series of four participles, "rooted" (ἐρριζωμένοι), "built up" (ἐποικοδομούμενοι), "established" (βεβαιούμενοι) and "abounding" in thanksgiving (περισσεύοντες ἐν εὐχαριστίᾳ) indicate what is meant by walking (the same verb περιπατεῖτε is used) in him. Perhaps it is not coincidental

that in both passages the imagery of a tree is employed (at 1:10 the notion of bearing the fruit of good works is in view, while here the idea of being firmly rooted is to the fore), as well as the theme of thanksgiving which appears as the last of the series in each section. In his pivotal passage the apostle instructs the readers as to what is involved in true Christian behavior before proceeding to deal with the false teaching.

ἐρριζωμένοι καὶ ἐποικοδομούμενοι ἐν αὐτῷ καὶ βεβαιούμενοι τῇ πίστει. The first three participles belong together though as Lightfoot (174) noted there is a rapid transition of metaphor. Having spoken of a path on which one is to walk (v 6) Paul moves to the language of horticulture ("rooted"), then to an architectural metaphor ("built up") and finally on to an image of the law-court ("established," "confirmed"). Each of these participles is in the passive voice probably pointing to the divine activity. Whatever responsibilities to Christ the readers had, and these were many, they were not to lose sight of the fact that God had been at work in their midst. It was he who had rooted them in Christ and was presently building them up in him, thereby consolidating them in the faith.

(1) *ἐρριζωμένοι.* The verb *ῥιζόω* ("cause to take root"; in the LXX "take root") appears in the NT only here and at Ephesians 3:17, though in both cases the building metaphor is linked. The perfect tense, in contrast to the three following participles which are all in the present, is significant and denotes a settled state (so most commentators): the readers have been firmly rooted in Christ (the *ἐν αὐτῷ* qualifies *ἐρριζωμένοι* as well as *ἐποικοδομούμενοι*) and they are to conduct their lives asccording to this beginning.

(2) *ἐποικοδομούμενοι.* Repeatedly in ancient literature the images of being rooted and built up are linked with reference to buildings (for references see Maurer, *TDNT* 6, 990). Here, as at 1 Corinthians 3:6–11, the metaphors are joined so as to describe the solid foundation upon which believers' lives are to be based. The original figurative meaning of both verbs is not to be pressed since the expression is determined by the conception of the thing signified, i.e. the being in Christ and walking in him (so rightly Meyer, 351; the first metaphor lost much of its original figurative meaning by its conjunction with the second anyway, while the image of the building only goes so far: Paul has written neither *ἐπ' αὐτόν*, 1 Cor 3:12, nor *ἐπ' αὐτῷ*, Eph 2:20, which would have been in harmony with this latter participle, but *ἐν αὐτῷ*, "in him").

(3) The words *καὶ βεβαιούμενοι* ("and being established") *continue* the notion of the readers' consolidation in the faith (the *καί* is epexegetical, expanding on the meaning of the previous words, while the tense of the verb is present). *βέβαιος* and its cognates were used as technical terms in the papyri to speak of guaranteeing legal contracts (cf. Deissmann, *Bible Studies,* 104–9, MM, 107, 108). Schlier (*TDNT* 1, 600–603) and others, therefore, have been inclined to see a technical legal sense in most of the NT occurrences of these terms. This is doubtful in the four passages (1 Cor 1:8; 2 Cor 1:21; Heb 13:9 and here) where the verb is employed of confirming persons. Rather, we are reminded of the Psalter (41:12; 119:28), and it is possible that Paul was influenced by this source, where the Lord is said to strengthen his needy ones in their distress (cf. Harder, *Paulus,* 70, and BAG, 138).

Although the whole phrase (βεβαιούμενοι τῇ πίστει) could be taken as a reference to the Colossians' being progressively reinforced in their Christian *conviction* (or *trust*), as Moule, 90, suggests, in the light of the parenthesis that immediately follows ("as you were taught") and the parallel reference at chapter 1:23 it is better to understand "faith" (πίστις) as that which is the object of belief, the content of the teaching which Epaphras had faithfully passed on to them. It was this *faith* they were to continue in (at 1:23 note the active voice), for it was only by this *faith* (perhaps τῇ πίστει is a dative of relation, but the meaning is not significantly altered if we take it as instrumental) that they would be consolidated (the corresponding passive referring to God's activity; cf. 1 Cor 1:8).

περισσεύοντες ἐν εὐχαριστίᾳ. Thanksgiving is referred to no fewer than six times (seven if ἐν [τῇ] χάριτι of 3:16 is included in the count) in the space of four short chapters of Colossians (1:3, 12; 2:7; 3:15, 16, 17; 4:2; see O'Brien, *Introductory Thanksgivings*, 62–67). This is the first explicit exhortatory reference (at 1:12 in the context of Paul's intercessory prayer there is an implied exhortation to the giving of thanks: see 30). The clear indication is that joyful thanksgiving is to characterize the lives of these readers, no doubt bearing in mind all the mighty things God had done on their behalf.

In the pagan world of Paul's day, although thanks to the gods were expressed publicly (as evidenced in inscriptions), the public only shared in the thanksgiving from the outside, as it were, so that the action was in effect a private affair. In Colossians the corporate nature of thanksgiving is in view at least by implication here and explicitly at chapter 3:15–17. εὐχαριστέω and its cognates in the NT mean to "give thanks" and not simply to "be grateful." This is not to say with Bornkamm (*Studien*, 188–203), Käsemann (*Essays*, 154) and Lohse (32, 94) that the verb has acquired almost a technical significance meaning to "confess Christ in the liturgy," so that Paul is here exhorting the readers to praise the Lord in hymnic confessions, especially 1:15–20 (see O'Brien, *Introductory Thanksgivings*, 71–75).

Explanation (2:6, 7)

Verses 6 and 7 occupy a pivotal position in the letter. They serve as the basis of Paul's interaction with the Colossian heresy (vv 8–23) having summarized much of what has already been written in the epistle. The focus of attention is upon "Christ Jesus as Lord" whom the Colossians received as their "tradition" when they accepted the gospel at the hands of Epaphras. This Christ Jesus is none other than the Lord of all, in both creation and redemption (1:15–20), and he is the center of God's mystery (1:27; 2:2). By means of an indicative-imperative form the readers, who have had many of the important ideas driven home to their hearts, are admonished to conduct their lives as those who have been incorporated into Christ. They have been securely rooted in him, they are progressively being built up in Christ as they are reinforced in the faith they had been taught. As they live under Christ's lordship they are to abound in thanksgiving, grateful to God for his mighty actions for them. Christ Jesus was a more than adequate safeguard against the empty traditions of men. Let them see that their way of life and thought conform continually to his teaching.

Comment (2:8–15)

8. *βλέπετε μή τις ὑμᾶς ἔσται ὁ συλαγωγῶν.* By means of a strong warning (*βλέπετε* here means: "beware," "be on your guard," BAG, 143; other examples are: Mark 13:9; Phil 3:2; 2 John 8) the congregation is alerted to the dangers touched upon in verse 4. They are to be on guard *lest* (normally the expression is *μή*, etc. with the subjunctive: 1 Cor 8:9; 10:12; Gal 5:15; cf. Mark 13:5; Acts 13:40; Heb 12:25; but here the future indicative is employed: BDF para. 369[2]; Moule, *Idiom Book,* 139; Moulton, *Grammar,* 192, understands it as a cautious assertion meaning "perhaps," but the contexts suggest it is stronger than this) anyone carry them off as booty or spoil. Although no one is named (Bruce, 230, suggests Paul possibly had one particular teacher in view; cf. Masson, 121) both writer and readers would have been able to identify the person(s) concerned (cf. Lightfoot, 176, on this use of the indefinite *τις*). The verb *συλαγωγέω* is a rare word—appearing nowhere else in the NT—probably meaning "carry off as booty" or "as a captive" (so BAG, 776; cf. Lightfoot, 176) rather than "rob" or "despoil." Accordingly the word is used figuratively of carrying someone away from the truth into the slavery of error. The term is a vivid one and shows how seriously Paul regarded the evil designs of those trying to influence the congregation.

διὰ τῆς φιλοσοφίας καὶ κενῆς ἀπάτης. The method (*διά*) by which these spiritual confidence tricksters might ensnare the community is through using "philosophy and empty deceit." The term "philosophy" (*φιλοσοφία*) which occurs only here in the NT (the cognate *φιλόσοφος*, "philosopher," is used of the Epicureans and the Stoics at Acts 17:18), carried a wide range of meanings describing all sorts of groups, tendencies and viewpoints within the Greek and Jewish worlds (Michel, *TDNT* 9, 172–88), from the Greek pursuit of knowledge and wisdom to the sects of Hellenistic Judaism which sought to present themselves as "philosophies" (so Philo designated the Torah as "the ancestral philosophy [*ἡ πάτριος φιλοσοφία*]," *Leg* 156; "the philosophy according to Moses [*ἡ κατὰ Μωϋσῆν φιλοσοφία*]," *Mut* 223; while Josephus described the Pharisees, Sadducees and Essenes as the three philosophies [*τρεῖς φιλοσοφίαι*] within Judaism, *Bell* 2.119; *Ant* 18.11; for details see Bornkamm, *Conflict,* 140).

As Bornkamm (*TDNT* 4, 808–10) and Lohse (95) have pointed out, various religious groups sought to convince men that they were imparting philosophy. Even those who practiced magic called themselves "philosophers" as they sought by rights, initiations and magical spells to capture the allegiance of men.

Paul no doubt adopted the term here because it was used by the false teachers themselves to refer to their own teachings in a positive way (cf. Wilckens, *TDNT* 7, 523). But by the addition of the words "and empty deceit" (*καὶ κενῆς ἀπάτης*: the use of the one preposition *διά* and the absence of the definite article before the second noun *ἀπάτης* show that the apostle is describing this particular philosophy and making no comment on philosophy in general, a point already noted by Clement of Alexandria, *Strom* 6.8.62; cf. Bengel 2, 460) he exposes it as a hollow sham, having no true content, seductive and misleading (ἀπάτη can describe the seduction which comes from wealth, Mark 4:19; the deceitfulness of sin, Heb 3:13; wicked deception generally, 2 Thess 2:10 or deceptive desires, Eph 4:22; cf. BAG, 81). As "deceitful" it stands opposed to the gospel, "the word of *truth*" (1:5), and to "wisdom and knowledge" (2:3), while the designation of it as "empty" (κενή) sets this philosophy in sharp contrast to the mystery and its "glorious *riches*" (τὸ πλοῦτος τῆς δόξης, 1:27), and Christ in whom all the *treasures* (θησαυροί) of wisdom and knowledge are hidden (2:3).

κατὰ τὴν παράδοσιν τῶν ἀνθρώπων. The false teaching is next described with reference to its source—"the tradition of *men*." The teaching of the Greek philosophers, from Plato onward, was passed on from teacher to pupil (e.g. *Theaet* 36, 198b). Further, the "philosophy" to which the mysteries referred was also preserved by means of sacred tradition, so that in the initiation rites the devotee received the holy teaching or "sacred word" (ἱερὸς λόγος) through which the divine revelation came. Later Gnostics used the term παράδοσις ("tradition") of the authoritative teachings which, as revelation, were to be preserved and passed on (for detailed examples see Delling, *TDNT* 4, 12, Wegenast, *Verständnis*, 123–26, and Lohse, 95, 96). The importance of tradition in Judaism, described in the *m.'Abot* as "a fence around the law" (3:14), has already been noted (see 105).

It is not possible from an examination of this phrase alone (ἡ παράδοσις τῶν ἀνθρώπων) to determine the precise content of the "tradition." The words might be Jewish or Gentile or both. At Mark 7:8 the same phrase refers to Pharisaic expositions of the Jewish law, while at 1 Peter 1:18 (πατροπαράδοτος) it is probably Gentile (though some have argued that this too is Jewish). In both places the vanity or emptiness of such traditions is stressed (Bruce, 231). A decision regarding the content at Colossians 2:8 can only be made by reference to other parts of the letter. But the manner in which the words are introduced here does suggest that the false teachers had set forth their "philosophy" as "tradition" (παράδοσις), thereby pointing to its antiquity, dignity and revelational character (cf. Michel, *TDNT* 9, 186). Paul, however, rejects any suggestion of divine origin. This was a human fabrication standing over against the apostolic tradition which centered on "Christ Jesus as Lord." Its false content was "according to the elements of the universe and not according to Christ."

κατὰ τὰ στοιχεῖα τοῦ κόσμου καὶ οὐ κατὰ Χριστόν. See the following note on στοιχεῖα τοῦ κόσμου where it is argued, with the majority of recent commentators, that the phrase denotes the "elemental spirits of the universe," the principalities and powers which sought to tyrannize over the lives of men (cf. 2:10, 15). The phrase probably held an important place in the syncretistic "tradition" of the philosophy. The apostle sets a stark contrast: whatever is in accordance with these demonic, personal powers stands over against Christ, the one at the center of the apostolic tradition, and the person who embodies God's mystery.

9. ὅτι ἐν αὐτῷ κατοικεῖ πᾶν τὸ πλήρωμα τῆς θεότητος σωματικῶς. Paul continues

his polemical thrust as he makes plain to the readers why (ὅτι) the "philosophy" of the false teachers is "not according to Christ" (the ὅτι is causal, though it is not attached to the βλέπετε of v 8 as if to give the reason for the warning; the view of Schille, *Hymnen,* 31–37, especially 31, that it is a recitative ὅτι introducing a hymnic piece is rightly criticized by Deichgräber, *Gotteshymnus,* 167–69; cf. Lähnemann, *Kolosserbrief,* 115; on the question of a hymn in vv 9–15 see above). He focuses attention on the centrality of Christ, whom the readers are to follow unswervingly, by resuming the phrase "in him" (ἐν αὐτῷ) of verse 7 and repeating it as a theme in the following verses (Lohse, 99). In fact it runs like a scarlet thread through this whole section, verses 9–15: "in him" (ἐν αὐτῷ) the entire fullness of deity dwells bodily (v 9); "in him" (ἐν αὐτῷ) you are filled (v 10); "in whom" (ἐν ᾧ) you have been circumcised (v 11); "with him" (αὐτῷ συν-) you have been buried, "in whom" (ἐν ᾧ) you also have been raised with him (v 12); God has made you alive "with him" (σὺν αὐτῷ, v 13); and he has led the principalities and powers in triumphal procession "in him" (ἐν αὐτῷ, v 15).

In this statement of verse 9, words from the earlier hymn (1:19) are taken up and applied (but not "corrected" as some, such as Lähnemann, *Kolosserbrief,* 115, suppose) with reference to the Colossian heresy: note the repetition of ἐν αὐτῷ ("in him") in an emphatic position, the verb κατοικέω ("dwells") and πᾶν τὸ πλήρωμα ("all the fullness"). The high Christological statement serves as the basis for the application to the particular needs of the congregation. Here, we note several significant points: (1) κατοικέω ("dwells") is used in the present tense; (2) the genitive "of deity" (τῆς θεότητος) more precisely determines the meaning of "fullness," while (3) the addition of σωματικῶς ("bodily") indicates the manner in which the fullness dwells in Christ.

Although there was some doubt at chapter 1:19 as to whether πᾶν τὸ πλήρωμα ("all the fullness") was the subject of the verb εὐδόκησεν ("was pleased") no such ambiguity exists here: πᾶν τὸ πλήρωμα is the subject of κατοικεῖ so indicating that the entire fullness of deity dwells in Christ. As noted above, the expression "the *entire* (πᾶν τό) fullness" is tautologous and this suggests Paul is writing polemically to underscore the point that the "pleroma" is to be found exclusively in Christ (on the meaning of πλήρωμα see 51–53).

τῆς θεότητος. The additional words "of deity" specify *what* dwells in Christ in its entire fullness. θεότης ("deity"), is the abstract noun from ὁ θεός ("God") and is to be distinguished from ἡ θειότης ("divine nature," "quality"), the abstract from θεῖος ("divine," Rom 1:20; Wisd 18:19; cf. Lightfoot, 179, who illustrates the difference between the two nouns in Plutarch's *Moralia*). The former is *deitas,* the being God, i.e. the divine essence or Godhead; the latter is *divinitas,* i.e. the divine quality, godlikeness (Meyer, 358). Meyer adds: "Accordingly, the *essence* of God, undivided and in its whole fullness, dwells in Christ in His exalted state, so that He is the essential and adequate image of God (i. 15), which He could not be if He were not possessor of the divine essence."

Some recent exegetes have objected to the traditional exegesis of this phrase claiming that the deity of Jesus Christ is not to be interpreted in static, ontological categories such as those of "substance" or "essence," but in soteriological and eschatological thought forms that refer to God's working in Christ. It is true that in the immediate context the notion of fullness as being imparted to the readers is in view (so v 10). However, the reception of salvation, described in verse 10 as being filled in him alone, becomes meaningful only if he is the one in whom the plenitude of deity is embodied. If the fullness of deity does not reside in him then the Colossians' fullness would not amount to much at all—the very point Paul is making over against the errorists' teaching on fullness. Further, a functional Christology presupposes, and finds its ultimate basis in, an ontological Christology (Harris, in *NIDNTT,* 3, 1193).

κατοικεῖ . . . σωματικῶς. As distinct from chapter 1:19 where the aorist εὐδόκησεν κατοικῆσαι ("was pleased to dwell") occurs, here the present tense κατοικεῖ ("dwells") indicates that the whole fullness of God resides in the resurrected and exalted Christ (cf. Schweizer, 108). The adverb of manner σωματικῶς indicates how the fullness of deity dwells in Christ, but there is considerable difference of opinion as to its meaning. Moule (92–94), for example, has listed five options:

(i) "as an organized body," i.e. the totality of the Godhead is "not distributed through a hierarchy of beings," but is gathered into one "organism" in Christ.
(ii) "expressing itself through the Body [of Christ, i.e. the Church]."
(iii) "actually"—in concrete reality, not in mere seeming.
(iv) "in essence."
(v) "assuming a bodily form," "becoming incarnate."

View *(i)* suits the hypothesis that Paul had taken the term πλήρωμα from the vocabulary of the false teachers, but is not wholly dependent on it, if the "philosophy" at Colossae taught that the divine attributes were spread throughout the many heavenly powers of which Christ was one. But there are some doubts as to whether this was actually taught. Further, to express the organization in Christ of all these powers by a single adverb, Moule (93) rightly claims, is doubtful. Caird (191) points out that this view, at least in the form presented by Lohmeyer, requires us to understand "body" as the universe (which is contrary to Pauline usage) and "fullness of deity" as lordship over that universe—but "fullness of deity" must mean more than this.

(ii) puts too much weight on a single adverb, however attractive the view might be otherwise (Moule, 93, and Caird, 191; after a careful assessment Best, *Body,* 120, concludes that the Body of Christ metaphor is not in view here). Even its presentation by Benoit (*RB* 63 [1956] 5–44) and subsequent development at the hands of Burger (*Schöpfung,* 89), who understands it as an abbreviated expression connoting "the new creation," is open to the same criticism (cf. Ernst, *Pleroma,* 101, 102).

(iv) Moule claims is improbable if intelligible.

This leaves us with *(iii)* and *(v)*. The former is strongly advocated by Caird who understands it, not of Paul combating some sort of docetic Christology such as was later associated with Gnosticism but, "in the light of v 17, where σῶμα ('body') is used to denote the solid reality of the new age in contrast with the shadowy anticipations of it in the legal systems of the age that is past" (192). Jervell's arguments (*Imago,* 223, 224, followed by Lohse, 100) are essentially the same. View *(v)* which had the strong support of Lightfoot (180; note Moule's treatment, 93, 94) runs into some difficulty with the present tense κατοικεῖ ("dwells"; one might have expected a perfect, though Moule 93, raises the possibility as to whether the present is being used here as a Greek perfect tense, representing the continuance in the present of some state begun previously). Bruce, 232, comments that the adverb σωματικῶς refers not to the incarnation as such, but to Christ's complete embodiment of the πλήρωμα.

A final decision between *(iii)* and *(v)* is difficult. Lohse, 100, 101, is no doubt right when he claims that the author chose the word "bodily" in order to relate his statements to the term "body" (σῶμα). But which "body"? That referred to in chapter 2:17, the "body" as opposed to the "shadow," or the incarnate "body," cf. chapter 1:22, for example? On the whole we are inclined to the last view *(v)* and understand the statement as meaning that the fullness of deity dwells in Christ "in bodily form."

10. καὶ ἐστὲ ἐν αὐτῷ πεπληρωμένοι. Paul's thought continues in a statement that is correlative with verse 9: from the fullness of deity that dwells in the exalted Christ follows the infilling of the Colossian Christians. There is clearly a play on the word "fullness" here (v 9 πλήρωμα, v 10 πεπληρωμένοι), though the tense of the verb (a perfect) points to a continuing state as the result of some prior action, and the passive voice suggests the readers have been filled *by God.* The language and word order again draw attention to the motif of incorporation—it is in union with Christ alone that they possess this fullness already.

The apostle does not define the content with which these believers are filled; there are no accompanying nouns (in the genitive or accusative cases) as might normally be expected. To suggest that the reference is to the "fullness of deity" is unlikely on grammatical grounds apart from asserting too much. Elsewhere Paul often employs this language of fullness to describe godly qualities or graces that he either desires or prays for with reference to believers (Rom 15:13, "joy and peace"; Phil 1:11, "the fruit of righteousness"; 4:19, "every need"; and in Colossians itself, 1:9, "the knowledge of his will"; cf. Eph 3:19, where the prayer is that the readers may be filled "in the direction of [εἰς] all the fullness of God"); or in some sense he is convinced they already possess (Rom 15:14, "knowledge"). Here, unless we insert some comprehensive expression such as "you have come to fullness of life in him" (RSV; Martin, *NCB,* 80, 81; cf. Caird, 192), and assume the Colossians are so filled, it is better to understand Paul as meaning "you are filled in him" (Burger, *Schöpfung,* 90, prefers "you are infilled in him"). As such he is affirming the presence of salvation among them. Perhaps as Dibelius-Greeven, 29, have suggested, Paul is employing a slogan the false teachers were adopting when they spoke of "fullness of life" to their followers, and asserting by way of contrast that it is only in Christ that the Colossians have been filled. This could explain the use of the unusual expression.

It has already been made plain that the Colossian Christians are to conduct their lives in the light of God's gracious work in their midst (1:9–14; cf.

2:6, 7). The possession of all things in Christ in no way absolved them from the need for continual growth (an error into which some of the Corinthians had fallen: note the biting irony of 1 Cor 4:8, "Already you are filled! Already you have become rich!" Cf. Phil 3:12–14). However, there was little danger that the Colossians would misunderstand Paul's realized eschatology in this way (cf. Caird, 192; Schweizer, 109). Theirs was the opposite temptation of thinking that "fullness" was beyond their grasp unless they took sufficient account of the spiritual powers and followed a strict discipline of ritual and ascetic observance.

ὅς ἐστιν ἡ κεφαλὴ πάσης ἀρχῆς καὶ ἐξουσίας. The readers need not pay their respects to the principalities and powers. For the one in whom they are complete is Lord and Master of such beings. While in apocalyptic thought the final overthrow of evil forces was not expected until the end of the present age (cf. Rev 19:11–16) here the present rule of Christ is emphasized. These words hark back to the language of the hymn where Christ is said to be creator of all powers and authorities (1:16) as well as their sustainer (1:17). He is "head" over the principalities and powers for God has divested them of all authority in him (2:15). Although they continue to exist, inimical to man and his interests (cf. Rom 8:38, 39) their final defeat is inevitable (cf. 1 Cor 15:24–28).

By directing his attention to the present rule of Christ (*ὅς ἐστιν ἡ κεφαλή*; the textual variant *ὅ ἐστιν* is probably due to assimilation to what was a common expression, 1:24, 3:14; certainly the relative clause refers to Christ, not the "fullness"; cf. BDF, para. 132[2], Lohse, 101, and Schweizer, 109) Paul may well have been asserting an emphasis that was needed at Colossae, for as has been suggested it is possible that the spirit-powers (perhaps even angelic beings) were adopted by the false teachers as mediators, so giving to inferior members an allegiance due only to the head.

When calling Christ the "head" (*κεφαλή*) over all rule and authority Paul stops short of designating the cosmic powers a "body" (*σῶμα*) organically united under Christ's rule (against Dibelius-Greeven, 29, and Lohmeyer, 107). Nowhere in Pauline teaching is the cosmos called Christ's body; rather the church is so described (1:18, 24) and through it alone is the cosmos to be brought into unity with him (Eph. 1:10; 3:10).

11. Paul continues the theme of incorporation in Christ. He has already mentioned, by means of a perfect tense (v 10, *ἐστέ . . . πεπληρωμένοι*), that the believers have been filled in him (*ἐν αὐτῷ*). He now elaborates on this describing their participation in Christ's death, burial and resurrection with a series of aorist tenses: "in whom you were circumcised" (*περιετμήθητε*, v 11), "you were buried with him" (*συνταφέντες*, v 12), "in him you were raised with him" (*συνηγέρθητε*, v 12), and "he made you alive with him" (*συνεζωοποίησεν*, v 13).

ἐν ᾧ καὶ περιετμήθητε περιτομῇ ἀχειροποιήτῳ. (On *ἐν ᾧ καί* see v 12). While the death, burial and resurrection themes are commonly related to the motif of union with Christ in Paul's letters (Rom 6:3–6; 7:1–6; 8:17; 2 Cor 1:3–9; 4:7–14; 5:14–17; 7:3; 13:4; Gal 2:19, 20; 6:14, 15; Eph 2:5, 6; Phil 3:9–11; Col 2:20; 3:1–4, 9, 10; 1 Thess 4:14; 5:10; cf. especially Tannehill's treatment, *Dying*) the sudden introduction of circumcision in this context is unusual.

Several have claimed that its presence here can only be accounted for because of its being advocated by the false teachers (cf. Lightfoot, Williams, Beasley-Murray, Caird, etc.). Paul's choice of language here would be particularly apt if circumcision was one feature of that syncretism being inculcated upon the congregation (Bruce, 234, 235). If so, we might have expected, as in Galatians, some direct condemnation of the practice, but in verses 16–23 there is no reference to it. Schweizer (110, 111; cf. *Jews, Greeks and Christians,* 250) claims that the references to circumcision and uncircumcision in verses 11 and 13 have been "spiritualized" and are not directed polemically against any particular practice of the false teachers. Lohse (102), on the other hand, suggests that circumcision at Colossae was not considered to be a sign of the covenant that required obedience to the OT law. Rather, it was understood as a sacramental rite by which a person entered the community and gained salvation. But there is no contemporary evidence for this and we cannot say with certainty why Paul introduced the circumcision motif at this point (cf. Halter, *Taufe,* 609).

The verb *περιτέμνω* meaning to "cut (off) around" (BAG, 652) occurred frequently in the LXX as a ritual technical term to denote physical circumcision, an outward sign of the covenant between Yahweh and his people (cf. Gen 17:10–14, 23–27; Exod 4:25; 12:44, 48; Lev 12:3, etc.). Within the OT the term came to be used in a transferred and ethical sense pointing to the "circumcision of the heart" (cf. Deut 10:16; Jer 4:4; Ezek 44:7) in which Israel was to give evidence of its true circumcision by complete obedience to the commandments of the Lord, the covenant God. The OT did not suggest, however, that this spiritual circumcision was to replace or be a substitute for physical circumcision. 1QS 5:5, "[Each man] shall circumcise in the community the foreskin of evil inclination and of stiffness of neck that they may lay a foundation of truth for Israel, for the community of the everlasting covenant" (Vermes' translation), shows that in the NT period a figurative and spiritualized view of circumcision was not unknown within the framework of Palestinian Judaism (Meyer, *TDNT* 6, 79). Here true circumcision was understood eschatologically (cf. Schweizer, 110), since it served as the basis for the everlasting covenant.

The apostle speaks of the Colossians being circumcised "with a circumcision not made with hands" (*περιτομῇ ἀχειροποιήτῳ*; by characterizing their circumcision in this way it is immediately distinguished from what is elsewhere meant by circumcision, cf. Meyer, 363). The adjective *χειροποίητος* ("made with hands") was employed in the LXX to denote idols (Lev 26:1; Isa 2:18; at 16:12 it is applied to an idol's sanctuary), false gods (Isa 11:9) or images (Lev 26:30); it therefore described the gods as made with men's hands and which stood over against the living God. In all of its NT occurrences *χειροποίητος* ("made with hands") is used to set forth the contrast between what is constructed by man and the work of God (Lohse, *TDNT* 9, 436; cf. Mark 14:58; Acts 7:48; 17:24; Eph 2:11; Heb 9:11, 24). To speak of something "not made with hands" (*ἀχειροποίητος*) is to assert that God himself has created it: so the heavenly house to which Paul refers (2 Cor 5:1), that will be given to each one of us at death, is "not made with hands," that is, it is wholly a divine creation; similarly the temple that Jesus said he would erect within three days is "not made with hands" (Mark 14:58). When Paul at Colossians 2:11 speaks of a circumcision "not made with hands" (ἀχειροποίητος) he sets in antithesis Jewish circumcision (which was done by the hand of man) with the work of God which the readers had experienced. God himself had decisively effected the change from the old life to the new (a point that is further underscored by the passive verbs used in the paragraph to signify the divine activity: περιετμήθητε, συνταφέντες, συνηγέρθητε; cf. συνεζωοποίησεν, the subject of which is God), a theme which the apostle emphatically struck at chapter 1:21, 22. The precise nature of this circumcision can only be suggested in the light of the following phrases, particularly the parallel reference to the "circumcision of Christ." By way of anticipation we understand this latter phrase as a reference to Christ's death, and the words "you were circumcised" to mean "you died," that is, in his death.

ἐν τῇ ἀπεκδύσει τοῦ σώματος τῆς σαρκός. This is a key phrase in the argument of verses 11 and 12 and the meaning given to it determines the answers to several other questions raised by the passage. On the whole scholars have ranged themselves in adherence to two main lines of interpretation:

(1) The first view understands the phrase in the light of the Pauline teaching on the "flesh" (σάρξ) to mean "putting off the old nature" (cf. Col 3:9). Accordingly, "body of flesh" is equivalent to "the body of this death" (τὸ σῶμα τοῦ θανάτου τούτου, Rom 7:24) or "the body of sin" (τὸ σῶμα τῆς ἁμαρτίας, Rom 6:6). The imagery is said to relate to baptism (cf. Gal 3:27, for an example of similar symbolism, namely, of baptism and putting on Christ) so that the stripping off of the old nature, which is said to occur in baptism, is then described as a spiritual counterpart of circumcision. It is further argued that such a use of τῆς σαρκός, which is virtually equivalent to the adjective "sensual," is paralleled in the same chapter, verse 18, "by his sensual mind" (νοῦς τῆς σαρκός). Exponents of this view concede that the almost identical expression, "in the body of his flesh" (ἐν τῷ σώματι τῆς σαρκὸς αὐτοῦ, 1:22), which points to Christ's physical body, has a different meaning from the reference here, the significant omission being the word "his" (αὐτοῦ). (Lähnemann, *Kolosserbrief,* 121, 122, and Zeilinger, *Der Erstgeborene,* 144, 145, do endeavor to relate the two references while insisting on their basic difference of meaning). According to this interpretation (which normally understands the following phrase "the circumcision of Christ" as meaning "the circumcision which Christ gave," that is, Christian circumcision which is baptism, see below) Paul is saying that Christians do not need to submit to circumcision, for baptism has now replaced it. (With some variations see the comments of Lohse, 103, Zeilinger, *Der Erstgeborene,* 144, 145, Schnackenburg, *Baptism,* 68, and Caird, 192–94.)

(2) The second approach takes the phrase "in putting off the body of flesh" as a reference to the death of Christ (so Moule, 95, 96, Beasley-Murray, *Baptism,* 152, 153, cf. *RevExp* 70 [1973] 474, 475, and Gundry, *Sōma,* 40–42), thereby squaring with the earlier mention of his death at chapter 1:22, "the body of his flesh" (ἐν τῷ σώματι τῆς σαρκὸς αὐτοῦ). This interpretation has the added advantage of providing a plausible explanation of verse 15, namely that in Christ's death God divested (ἀπεκδυσάμενος, the cognate verb to the rare ἀπέκδυσις) the principalities and powers, leading them in his triumphal procession.

Assuming the two phrases, "in the stripping away of the body of flesh" and "in the circumcision of Christ," are construed alike (by regarding the two genitives as objective), then the meaning is that the body of flesh was stripped off when Christ was circumcised, that is, when he died; the whole statement is "a gruesome figure for death" (Beasley-Murray, *Baptism*, 152). Here is a circumcision which entailed not the stripping off of a small portion of flesh but the violent removal of the whole body in death.

But several objections have been leveled against this approach: first, the absence of any noun or pronoun such as "his" (*αὐτοῦ*) means that the expression "the body of flesh" belongs to the subject of the clause, i.e. believers who have been circumcised (*περιετμήθητε*). It is argued that the phrase is different in meaning from the earlier reference "in the body of *his* flesh," (1:22). But the omission (which Lohse, 103, and Caird, 193, consider to be serious) may have occurred because "the identification of the baptized with Christ is regarded as so close as to render a specifying pronoun out of place," Moule, 95, or because the words "of Christ" in the following phrase made clear whose body of flesh is stripped off in circumcision (so Gundry, *Sōma*, 41).

Second, the idea of stripping off the physical body at death is said to smack of dualism and contradict Paul's theology of resurrection (Caird, 193). However, it is possible that the term *ἀπέκδυσις* ("putting off"), perhaps even a Pauline coinage, was chosen by him to underscore the point that Christ's death was a violent and gruesome one, and to say no more than this. This language is clearly metaphorical, like the statements about being clothed and unclothed at death to which Caird refers (2 Cor 5) in his criticisms of this view. On the whole we prefer the second alternative and understand the phrase as pointing to Christ's violent death.

ἐν τῇ περιτομῇ τοῦ Χριστοῦ. In our view, then, the "circumcision of Christ" is not his circumcision as a Jewish infant of eight days old (Luke 2:21); nor is it the "circumcision which belongs to Christ," understood as a Christian circumcision in tacit contrast to the circumcision which belongs to Moses and the patriarchs, and therefore a periphrasis for baptism (though many exegetes take it this way). It is better to regard the statement as denoting the circumcision that Christ underwent, that is, his crucifixion, of which his literal circumcision was at best a token by way of anticipation (cf. Bruce, 234). By interpreting the phrase in this way as denoting Christ's death and not as a synonym for baptism, verse 11 is then seen to provide a consistent application of the symbolism of circumcision, and it is not until the clause "buried with him in baptism" (v 12) is reached that the baptismal language actually begins (cf. Beasley-Murray, *Baptism*, 153).

The primary elements of the apostolic gospel were: "Christ died for our sins . . . he was buried . . . he was raised . . ." (1 Cor 15:3, 4). These same elements are clearly discernible in Colossians 2:11, 12 (on the above interpretation) as Paul uses first the language of circumcision (v 11), then that of baptism (v 12): Christ's body was stripped off in his death, he was buried and he was raised. Here the believers' participation in those saving events is also asserted (cf. Rom 6:3, 4): you died in his death (that is, you were circumcised in his circumcision; this language takes the place of *συσταυρόω*, "crucify together with," or some similar verb which would conform to the συν-verbs that follow, so Tannehill, *Dying*, 49), you were buried with him and raised with him.

12. συνταφέντες αὐτῷ ἐν τῷ βαπτισμῷ. If the believers at Colossae were circumcised in Christ's circumcision, that is, they died in his death, then it immediately follows that they "were buried with him in baptism" (the textual support of βαπτισμῷ, a "washing," "dipping," P[46] B D* etc., is as strong as that for βαπτίσματι, the Christian term meaning "baptism." The former word is less common and therefore more likely to have been changed by copyists to the latter, cf. Metzger, *Textual Commentary*, 623). συνθάπτω ("bury with") which appears only at Romans 6:4 and here in the NT is used in a figurative sense of the believer's being buried with his Lord in baptism (BAG, 789). As the burial of Christ (1 Cor 15:4) set the seal upon his death, so the Colossians' burial with him in baptism shows that they were truly involved in his death and laid in his grave. It is not as though they simply died *like* Jesus died, or were buried *as* he was laid in the tomb (for a survey and critique of this popular view, with special reference to Rom 6, see Beasley-Murray, *Baptism*, 131–46). Rather, they died with him on the cross and were laid in his grave (cf. Beasley-Murray, *RevExp* 70 [1973] 475). The burial proves that a real death has occurred and the old life is now a thing of the past. Those who have been buried with Christ "through baptism into death" (Rom 6:4) can no longer go on living as slaves to sin.

ἐν ᾧ καὶ συνηγέρθητε. Not only did the readers die with Christ in his death and were buried with him in baptism. They were also raised with him in resurrection. Having previously set forth the negative side, the apostle now turns to the positive (cf. J. D. G. Dunn, *Baptism in the Holy Spirit* [London, SCM, 1970] 154: American edition [SBT, 2nd Ser. 15; Naperville, IL: Allenson, 1970]), and does so in a statement that is particularly strong, so underlining this aspect of the apostolic kerygma: *(a)* the finite verb συνηγέρθητε, as distinct from the preceding participle, receives the emphasis (so Lohse, 104, Lähnemann, *Kolosserbrief*, 122, and Schweizer, 112); *(b)* the expressions which expand this note of resurrection are full; and *(c)* the theme of new life is taken up in verse 13. Several features of this resurrection description are to be observed:

(1) The Colossians have been raised *with Christ*. A strong case has been made out by Beasley-Murray (*Baptism*, 153, 154; cf. *RevExp* 70 [1973] 476), who is followed by others (English-speaking exegetes have often taken this line: cf. Abbott, 251, 252, Scott, 45, etc. and note the RSV, NEB, TEV), in favor of taking ἐν ᾧ as "in which," that is, as a reference to baptism, and so he translates the verse as: "Buried with Him in baptism, in which you were also raised with Him through faith in the working of God" (*Baptism*, 154). He considers that the statement "you were raised with him" (συνηγέρθητε) is more naturally regarded as set in parallelism with "you were buried with him" (συνταφέντες αὐτῷ), the latter words "with him" (αὐτῷ) binding the two verbs together. Also to read the words ἐν ᾧ as "in him" (rather than "in which[baptism]") Beasley-Murray argues is to cause a separation between the two elements of baptism, with the result that Paul is asserting that the believer is buried with Christ in baptism but raised with him in some other way. So he contends it is simpler and more natural to refer the relative pronoun to its immediate antecedent, namely, "in baptism."

Our preference, however, in spite of these arguments is to take it as pointing to Christ ("in whom"; cf. Lohmeyer, 108, Schnackenburg, *Baptism*, 69, Lohse, 104, Grundmann, *TDNT* 7, 792) and stating that we were raised with him. Attention has already been drawn to the theme of being "in Christ." The expressions "in him" and "in whom" are used again and again throughout the paragraph to show that the Colossians are complete in Christ alone. It is therefore more consistent with the rest of the passage to interpret ἐν ᾧ as "in him," rather than "in it" (i.e. baptism), particularly as the same expression at verse 11, ἐν ᾧ καί, can only refer to Christ and is rendered "in *him* also." Further, it is not clear why the theme of baptism ought to be carried through consistently to the second half of the verse as Beasley-Murray contends (*RevExp* 70 [1973] 476). In the light of the exegesis above (which is in part indebted to Beasley-Murray), baptism is not linked with the death of Jesus—the circumcision imagery serves this purpose. At best baptism would refer to only two of a total three elements, that is, Christ's burial and resurrection, but not his death (in Rom 6 baptism is tied in with the death and burial). Finally, although the expression "in him" may seem rather unusual when joined to a verb prefixed by συν- (συνηγέρθητε, "you were raised with") Ephesians 2:6 places "with" and "in Christ" next to each other in the same way: "and raised us up with him and made us sit with him in the heavenly places in Christ Jesus" (καὶ συνήγειρεν . . . ἐν Χριστῷ Ἰησοῦ). Because the reference there is specifically to Christ Jesus, rather than to a personal pronoun that could be rendered "him" or "it," there is no ambiguity.

Some have allowed thoughts concerning baptism to dominate their exegesis of the passage: first, by interpreting the statements about circumcision in verse 11 as equivalent to or an explanation of baptism, and second, by wishing to interpret the baptismal motif as applying to both parts of verse 12. Instead it is the dying and rising with Christ theme that is central to the passage: dying with him in his death is spelled out in verse 11 by means of circumcision terminology; being buried with him in baptism is then asserted in verse 12*a*, while being raised with Christ through faith receives the emphasis in the latter half of this verse. Of the three elements the accent falls on the first and third, namely, the death and resurrection (rather than the burial in baptism), for it is these statements that commence with the emphatic "in him also" (ἐν ᾧ καί), which employ a finite verb rather than a dependent participle (περιετμήθητε and συνηγέρθητε) and which are taken up, though in a somewhat different way, in verse 13. Baptismal statements are not developed in the passage.

(2) The resurrection of the Colossians with Christ has *already* taken place: it is described by means of an aorist tense συνηγέρθητε ("you were raised"). This is not to suggest that the eschatology of Colossians is fully realized (see on 3:1–4); the future element is mentioned as the revelation of that life which is currently hidden in Christ with God (3:3, 4), not as the resurrection of the dead.

It is sometimes said (cf. E. Grässer, "Kol 3,1–4 als Beispiel einer Interpretation secundum homines recipientes," *ZTK* 64 [1967] 139–68, especially 147, 148) that Colossians (here and at 3:1) and Ephesians (cf. 2:5, 6), in speaking of Christians as *already raised* with Christ, are at variance with the "genuine"

Pauline letters where their resurrection remains a hope for the future (cf. 2 Cor 4:14; Phil 3:11). Romans 6:5–8 is said to have particular relevance here: "If we have been united with him in his death, we will certainly also be united with him in his resurrection . . . But if we have died with Christ, we believe that we shall also live with him."

Now it may be that the notion of the believer's participation in the risen life of Christ finds clearer expression here at Colossians 2:12 (cf. 3:1 and Eph 2:6) than elsewhere in Paul's letters. But that is not to suggest it is absent from the earlier epistles or that someone else is responsible for the Colossians phraseology so giving clearer expression to the apostle's central thought than Paul himself could give! (Cf. Bruce, 236).

Whether we regard the future tenses of Romans 6:5, 8 as logical futures (if A is true, then B will also be true) rather than real ones, or not (Caird, 194, regards them as logical futures, while Tannehill, *Dying,* 10–12, rejects the suggestion), it is clear that in Romans 6:11, 13, where Paul bids his readers present themselves as alive to God, the apostle believes that they as Christians enjoy a new sort of life here and now (G. M. Styler, "The Basis of Obligation in Paul's Christology and Ethics," *Christ and Spirit in the New Testament. Studies in Honour of Charles Francis Digby Moule,* ed. B. Lindars and S. S. Smalley [Cambridge: University Press, 1973] 181–83; cf. Moule, *Origin,* 124; on Rom 6 see Bornkamm, *Experience,* 71–86, and Schnackenburg, *Baptism,* 30–61). For as Caird (194) pointedly asks: How could Christians be expected to "walk in newness of life" (Rom 6:4), to conduct their lives on the assumption they are "dead to sin and alive to God in Christ Jesus" (6:9), or to behave "as men who have been brought from death to life" (6:13) if they are still dead and buried with no hope of resurrection before the last trumpet? Styler (*Christ,* 182, 183) also draws attention to 2 Corinthians 4:10, 11 which refers to the experience of the resurrection in this present earthly life (cf. 2 Cor 13:4), as well as Galatians 2:19, 20 which speaks not of "the final sharing of the risen life of Christ" but a real sharing in the here and now of that life "in the flesh."

Although it is only in Colossians and Ephesians that the apostle speaks of having been raised with Christ as a past event, these references in the earlier epistles presume the present experience of the resurrection life in Christ (Beasley-Murray, *Baptism,* 155). The differences of language may partly be accounted for because of the different circumstances that called forth the letters. At Romans 6, in seeking to answer the question: "Shall we continue in sin that grace may abound?" (v 1), the apostle asserts that the believer is no longer a slave to sin because he has been crucified with Christ. He has been freed from the dominion of this slave driver. He participates in the new life now and is to *walk* in that newness of life. The emphasis of the passage falls upon the believer counting himself dead to sin, not letting sin reign in his mortal body, presenting himself to God, surrendering his members to him as instruments of righteousness, and so on. To have asserted that one had already been raised with Christ in the context of Romans 6 might have led to a smug self-satisfaction or triumphalism (as in the case of 1 Cor 4:8, "Already you have been filled! Already you have become rich!") because it was thought that since salvation had already been given fully and completely in the present there was nothing left to do but to glory in it (cf. Tannehill, *Dying*, 10–12).

But this was not the danger at Colossae. The false suggestion was that the believers were not complete in Christ. They needed to follow a strict discipline of ritual and ascetic observance and to take sufficient account of the spiritual powers if they were to proceed along the path to perfection, to "fullness of life." Against this the apostle asserts that the Colossian Christians had already been raised with Christ (cf. Schnackenburg, *Baptism*, 71).

(3) This is not to suggest, however, that the Colossians are being encouraged to fall into a fanatical enthusiasm of the kind mentioned in 2 Timothy 2:18 with its catchcry: "The resurrection has already taken place" (*ἀνάστησιν ἤδη γεγονέναι*), and the implication that all eschatology has been fully realized. Resurrection with Christ means that those who have been raised with him have been raised through faith in God's power (*ἐνέργεια* is here the object of faith, cf. Eph 1:19–21; on the meaning of *ἐνέργεια* see on 1:29), that same power which brought Christ back from the dead and which energizes them and maintains the new life within them. In fact, the new life is nothing less than Christ's resurrection life imparted to all the members of his body (Bruce, 236).

13. With the words of this verse the standpoint changes. No longer is the Christian viewed as having been united with Christ in his death, burial and resurrection; rather, he is seen from the position of having been truly dead in trespasses and sins in those earlier days of his paganism, but now made alive by God in Christ. The movement of thought (cf. Dibelius-Greeven, 31, Lohmeyer, 113, Zeilinger, *Der Erstgeborene*, 168) is indicated by the change in subject from "you" to "he," that is, to God (note the specific mention in v 12, "*God* who raised him [Jesus] from the dead") who has mercifully acted in his Son. Nevertheless there is a connection with the preceding in that the nature of the resurrection life is explained in what follows (cf. Schweizer, 113).

καὶ ὑμᾶς νεκροὺς ὄντας . . . συνεζωοποίησεν ὑμᾶς σὺν αὐτῷ. As at chapter 1:21, 22 (see 64–66) a sharp contrast is drawn between the readers' pre-Christian past and their present standing in Christ (in the earlier instance the *ποτέ*, "once," and the *νῦν*, "now," were specifically mentioned; see Tachau, *Einst*, 84–87, cf. Conzelmann, 144, and Burger, *Schöpfung*, 98). Again the wonder of the salvation that has been experienced is contrasted with the lost situation from which God has freed them. The past is recalled not because the emphasis falls upon it (here the previous condition is described by means of a participle, "being dead," *ὄντας*, the action of God by the finite verb, "he made alive," *συνεζωοποίησεν*), but to draw attention to the wonder of God's quickening the Colossians with Christ.

Terms akin to those used in verses 11 and 12 are employed here though with different meanings: e.g. "dead" (*νεκρούς*, cf. *ἐκ νεκρῶν*, v 12, and the idea of dying with Christ, v 11), "uncircumcision," (cf. v 11, "you were circumcised with a circumcision not made with hands"), the repetition of "flesh" (*σάρξ*, cf. v 11) and "quickened" (cf. "you were raised with," v 12).

Paul proceeds to describe the former condition of the Colossians: *καὶ ὑμᾶς νεκροὺς ὄντας κτλ.* (Note the fuller treatment in Eph 2:1–6.) Apart from the literal use which denotes physical death (e.g. Rom 14:9; cf. Bultmann, *TDNT* 4, 892–94), terms for death are used by the apostle to speak of being united with Christ in his death (cf. v 20). In addition, the adjective "dead" (νεκροί) is employed figuratively to describe the state of being lost or under the dominion of death (note the present participle, "being" ὄντας). It is sometimes called spiritual death and denotes a state of alienation or separation from God caused by sin (the description is not simply proleptic, "liable to eternal death," as Meyer suggested in his comment on Eph 2:1 ([*Critical and Exegetical Hand-book to the Epistle to the Ephesians.* Tr. M. J. Evans and W. P. Dickson (New York: Funk and Wagnalls, 1884] 92), but points to the present condition of those apart from Christ as being without spiritual life).

τοῖς παραπτώμασιν καὶ τῇ ἀκροβυστίᾳ τῆς σαρκὸς ὑμῶν. This wretched and culpable condition had been caused by their trespasses and sinful nature (the datives *τοῖς παραπτώμασιν* and *τῇ ἀκροβυστίᾳ* are probably causal, cf. Rom 11:20; so BDF, para. 196; Lightfoot, 184, von Soden, 48, Williams, 94, Lohse, 107, Zeilinger, *Der Erstgeborene,* 168; at the same time it is likely that the words are descriptive of their previous circumstances: cf. Moule, 97; some early scribes [cf. P^{46} A C etc.], by inserting the preposition ἐν, "in," apparently understood it this way). *παράπτωμα* ("false step," "transgression," "sin," so BAG, 621; cf. Michaelis, *TDNT* 6, 170–73), a term occurring rather frequently in Paul (elsewhere in the NT at Matt 6:14, 15 [some MSS], and Mark 11:25), is one of several words for sin which particularly emphasizes the deliberate act of disobedience with its fateful consequences. In the LXX the noun, like the cognate verb *παραπίπτω* ("fall beside," "go astray," "err," "sin"), was used for words expressing conscious and deliberate sinning against God ("rebellion," Job 36:9; Ezek 14:11; 18:22; "unfaithfulness," Ezek 14:13; 15:8; 18:24; 20:27; "injustice," Ezek 3:20; 18:26). Paul in Romans 5:15–18, 20 employs the term in the singular to describe Adam's disobedience (the actual sin of Gen 3 is in view) through which sin entered the world (Rom 5:12). "Trespasses" (in the plural) describe the actions by which all men rebel against God (Rom 5:16; 2 Cor 5:19; cf. Gal 6:1), and for which Christ was given up to death (Rom 4:25) in order that we might receive forgiveness of them (2 Cor 5:19; Eph 1:7; and Col 2:13).

If the first term points to the acts of rebellion against God as a cause of spiritual death then the second, which is closely conjoined, indicates that the lives of those outside of Christ are in a state of permanent disobedience. They live in the uncircumcision of their flesh (*τῇ ἀκροβυστίᾳ τῆς σαρκὸς ὑμῶν*). *ἀκροβυστία* ("uncircumcision"; cf. Schmidt, *TDNT* 1, 225, 226), which occurs some twenty times in the NT, is found only in Paul, apart from Acts 11:3. He often uses the word to designate pagans (Rom 2:25–27; 3:30; 4:9–12; 1 Cor 7:18, 19; Gal 2:7; 5:6; 6:15; Eph 2:11; Col 3:11), and in this context the term which stands in contrast to the language of verse 11 ("in him also you were circumcised in a circumcision not made with hands," see above 114–116) since verse 13 describes their pre-Christian condition while the earlier reference speaks of the change wrought in Christ, is to be understood in two senses. First, there is a reference to their being physically uncircumcised: the Colossians were Gentiles. But this of itself did not mean that they were spiritually dead. Physical "uncircumcision" was a *symbol* of their spiritual alienation from God and his covenant of grace (Eph 2:11, 12; cf. Moule, 97, Schweizer, 114, Caird, 194, 195); they were both heathen and godless (Lohse, 107).

συνεζωοποίησεν ὑμᾶς σὺν αὐτῷ. But the uncircumcision of these Gentiles has been removed by the "circumcision not made with hands" (2:11) in the death of Christ, and God has made them alive with him (note the aorist *συνεζωοποίησεν; ὑμᾶς* is repeated for the sake of emphasis [it has the adequate support of ℵ* A C K 81 614 etc.]; its omission from some manuscripts was probably due to its being thought by scribes to be superfluous while its replacement with *ἡμᾶς* in P46 B 33 etc. was probably to bring it into line with the following *ἡμῖν*. In other words, it is the reading which explains the others; cf. Metzger, *Textual Commentary*, 623). *ζωοποιέω* ("make alive," "give life to") was used as a simple synonym for *ἐγείρω* ("raise") when describing the eschatological raising from the dead (cf. 1 Cor 15:22 with Rom 8:11; Bultmann, *TDNT* 2, 874, 875). Only here and in Ephesians 2:5 is the compound *συζωοποιέω* ("make alive together with") to be found, though the additional phrase "with him" (*σὺν αὐτῷ*; on the meaning of the expression "with Christ" see 169–171) indicates that the prefix here is important. The Colossians have come to life with Christ, who was dead and rose again; their new life, then, is a sharing in the new life which he received when he rose from the dead. It is only in union with him that death is vanquished and new life, an integral part of God's new creation, is received. Further, the following words make plain that the giving of this life is an act of pure grace (*χαρισάμενος*) since it is related to the forgiveness of sins.

χαρισάμενος ἡμῖν πάντα τὰ παραπτώματα· The suggestion that verses 13*c*–15 were a fragment of a confession formulated in hymnic phrases is discussed in the preceding section ("Form," 104). Those who have advocated this consider that the forgiveness of sins is thematic standing at the beginning of the confession (so Lohse, 106, also his article in *Einheit*, 276–84; note Martin's variation on this *Reconciliation*, 1974, 117). However true this suggestion about a confessional statement may be, the words concerning forgiveness are to be interpreted in their immediate context and this has to do with new life in Christ.

God has made you alive together with him because he has forgiven us all our sins (the relationship of the participle *χαρισάμενος*, "having forgiven," to the finite verb *συνεζωοποίησεν*, "he made alive with," is causal; Abbott, 254, von Soden, 49, cf. Meyer, 373; however, Grundmann, *TDNT* 7, 792, understands the participle as explanatory of the preceding). Because he had remitted all (*πάντα*) our sins the cause of spiritual death was done away. "Whether a man is morally and spiritually dead or alive depends on his relationship with God, the one source of life; and the relationship, once severed by sin, can be restored only by forgiveness" (Caird, 195).

χαρίζομαι ("give freely or graciously as a favor"; with the dative of the person and the accusative of the thing = "remit," "forgive," "pardon") is employed here and at Ephesians 4:32 of God's forgiving men, while at Colossians 3:13 (cf. 2 Cor 2:7, 10; 12:13; Eph 4:32) it is used of men's forgiving one another (cf. Conzelmann, *TDNT* 9, 397). Perhaps its use here (since it is the only occasion in Paul where the full expression to "forgive trespasses" is found) may be due to the fact that it is a suitable verb for the cancellation of a debt (cf. Luke 7:42, 43; BAG, 876, 877).

The change of person from "you" to "us" (ἡμῖν) indicates that Paul, along with other Jewish Christians, as well as the readers who were Gentile believers, alike had been "forgiven."

14. *τὸ καθ' ἡμῶν χειρόγραφον τοῖς δόγμασιν ὃ ἦν ὑπεναντίον ἡμῖν.* God has not only removed the debt; he has also destroyed the document on which it was recorded. *χειρόγραφον* denotes a "document," especially a "note of indebtedness" written in one's own hand as a proof of obligation (cf. BAG, 880, and Lohse, *TDNT* 9, 435). This meaning is well-attested in both the Jewish and Greco-Roman world (for details see Lohse, *TDNT* 9, 435). A common thought in Judaism was that of God keeping accounts of man's debt, calling in the debt through angels and imposing a just judgment based on the records kept in the ledger (cf. Rabbi Akiba's illustration of God as a shopkeeper, *m. 'Abot* 3:20).

The image is derived from legal practice about debts, but the precise application in Colossians 2:14, partly occasioned by some grammatical difficulties in the text, is not patently clear. Certainly there is no sure reference to (1) a pact or handwritten certificate of indebtedness between Adam and the devil in which man commits himself to a life of sin and death in exchange for benefits Satan gives him. Some of the church fathers took this view, and it has been revived in modern times (cf. G. Megas, "Das χειρόγραφον Adams. Ein Beitrag zu Kol 2:13–15," *ZNW* 27 [1928] 305–320, for evidence; on the history of the exegesis of the passage see E. Best, *A Historical Study of the Exegesis of Col 2, 14*. Rome: unpublished thesis, 1956).

(2) Another line of interpretation has been to regard the χειρόγραφον not as a document of human guilt with regard to the Mosaic law but as an indictment presented at the heavenly court. Bandstra (*Law*, 158–63) drew attention to a use of χειρόγραφον in an anonymous Jewish apocalypse (ascribed to the first century B.C.) where the word designates the book held by an accusing angel in which the seer's sins are recorded, and regarding which he asked that they might be blotted out. Developing a suggestion of Blanchette (*CBQ* 23 [1961] 306–312), Bandstra agreed there was an early Jewish-Christian interpretation which identified the χειρόγραφον with Christ himself. Accordingly, in Colossians 2:14 reference is made to our body of flesh which Christ took on himself and in which our sins were condemned (cf. 2 Cor 5:21; Gal 3:13; 4:4; Rom 8:3). He took this body on himself in order to blot it out on the cross. Martin (*Reconciliation*, 1974, 121, 122) claims that additional support for this interpretation comes from the *Gospel of Truth* (20:22–28) where reference is made to Jesus taking or wearing a body as his own, and as being nailed to the cross where he affixed the ordinance of the Father to that cross. Both Bandstra and Martin tie in this interpretation with the unusual word "divest" (ἀπεκδύομαι, v 15; 3:9; cf. 2:11). In "putting off" the body of flesh (2:11) Christ also divested himself of the principalities and powers. The evil powers had attacked Christ since he had assumed in his body the χειρόγραφον, the charge-list of guilt (Martin, *Reconciliation*, 1974, 122), and so they accused him as though he was a sinner. However, he stripped off (ἀπεκδυσάμενος, v 15) their hold and overcame them.

This ingenious interpretation, if correct, would solve some of the exegetical problems of the passage. But certain difficulties remain: first, in the light of the widespread use of χειρόγραφον as a certificate of indebtedness signed by men over against a single instance of a heavenly book, doubt is raised about the application of the term to an angelic indictment. Also χειρόγραφον becomes the heavenly charge-list, then the body of flesh and finally Christ, or at least the body which Christ takes upon himself. The term is meant to signify too many things at once.

(3) Our preference is to understand χειρόγραφον as the signed acknowledgment of our indebtedness before God. Like an IOU it contained penalty clauses (see Job 5:3; Philem 19). The Jews had contracted to obey the law, and in their case the penalty for breach of this contract meant death (Deut 27:14–26; 30:15–20). Paul assumes that the Gentiles were committed, through their consciences, to a similar obligation, to the moral law in as much as they understood it (cf. Rom 2:14, 15). Since the obligation had not been discharged by either group the "bond" remained against us (καθ' ἡμῶν).

The term "regulation" (δόγμα) is employed in a variety of ways in the NT to denote a "decree" of Caesar Augustus concerning the enrollment (Luke 2:1; cf. Acts 17:7), and the "decisions" (plural δόγματα) of the Jerusalem council (Acts 16:4). At Ephesians 2:15 the plural δόγματα denotes the individual statutes of the commandments of the Mosaic law (in Hellenistic Judaism the commandments of God were called δόγματα: 3 Macc 1:3; 4 Macc 10:2, and for further references in Josephus and Philo cf. Kittel, *TDNT* 2, 230–32). Here the term may be translated "binding statutes" or "legal demands" (regarding its relationship to the cognate δογματίζεσθε see on v 20). The dative case τοῖς δόγμασιν is probably: (a) *causal,* "because of the regulations," so indicating why the bond or certificate of indebtedness has a case against us (Lohse, 109, 110, Bacchiocchi, *From Sabbath,* 350, and Schweizer, 116, as well as some earlier exegetes who supplied the participle "written" to complete the sense), rather than *(b)* one of *obligation,* i.e. the bond placed us under an obligation to keep the regulations (J. A. T. Robinson, *The Body. A Study in Pauline Theology* [SBT 5; London: SCM, 1952] 43; C. F. D. Moule, "Death 'to Sin,' 'to Law,' and 'to the World'; a Note on certain Datives," *Mélanges Bibliques en hommage au R. P. Béda Rigaux,* ed. A. Descamps and A. de Halleux [Gembloux: Duculot, 1970] 371, 372; Caird, 195, who translates the clause: "our undischarged commitment to the decrees of the law . . ."), or *(c)* a dative of *accompaniment,* "the bond, decrees and all" (Bruce, 237; cf. Harris, in *NIDNTT* 3, 1199). (Percy's view, *Probleme,* 88, 89, which connects the dative τοῖς δόγμασιν with the following clause ὃ ἦν ὑπεναντίον ἡμῖν, so that the meaning is "the handwriting that was against, which by virtue of the ordinances [i.e. the law of Moses] testified against us," states the reason why the "bond" could make its enmity against us effective; this suggestion has the merit of dealing with the apparently superfluous words "which was against us," but is rather awkward to construe in spite of the parallels he presents.)

The words "which was against us" (ὃ ἦν ὑπεναντίον ἡμῖν) need not be regarded as an awkward addition (by the author of Colossians [so Lohse, 109] or by Paul [Martin, *Reconciliation,* 1974, 121]) to an already existing original text. The earlier phrase "against us" (καθ' ἡμῶν) "emphasizes the brute fact of indebtedness, while the latter ὑπεναντίον ἡμῖν stresses the active hostility produced by this fact" (Harris, *NIDNTT* 3, 1199). Such a distinction gains support from the meaning of ὑπεναντίος ("opposed," "contrary," "hostile," BAG, 838) for in the LXX it occurs often as a designation for enemies (Gen 22:17; 24:60; Exod 1:10; 15:7; 23:27, etc.; cf. Lohmeyer, 118, who is followed by Lohse, 110).

ἐξαλείψας . . . καὶ αὐτὸ ἦρκεν ἐκ τοῦ μέσου προσηλώσας αὐτὸ τῷ σταυρῷ. God has not only forgiven us all our sins but he also utterly removed the signed acknowledgment of our indebtedness. The removal of the debt is signified by ἦρκεν ἐκ μέσου and this is further elaborated in two figures: *(a)* he blotted it out, and *(b)* he nailed it to the cross (A. Deissmann, *Paul. A Study in Social and Religious History*. Tr. W. E. Wilson. 2nd ed. [London: Hodder and Stoughton, 1926], 172, considered that the papyrus debt-records illustrate the popular appeal of this double metaphor; the bond is first blotted out and then canceled).

αἴρω ("lift up," "pick up") can be used of removal by force, even by killing (BAG, 24). Here the expression (αἴρω ἐκ μέσου) which was common in Greek (1 Cor 5:2; for extrabiblical instances, cf. BAG, 24, and Lohse, 110) signifies the decisive removal of the "certificate of indebtedness" (the change from the aorist tense to the perfect points to the permanence of the removal). This taking away was effected through blotting it out (ἐξαλείψας; cf. Jeremias, *TDNT* 1, 185, 186). ἐξαλείφω means to "rub out," "wipe away" and so obliterate from sight, as writing on wax or other written records were removed (at Acts 3:19 it is used of blotting out sins, in Rev 3:5 of a name from the Book of Life). God has wiped the slate clean and given a fresh start. An OT antecedent is Isaiah 43:25 (LXX): "I am the one who wipes out (ἐξαλείφων) your iniquities and I will not remember them" (cf. LXX Ps 50:1; Jer 18:23, etc.).

That "certificate of indebtedness" was removed when God nailed it to the cross (προσηλώσας αὐτὸ τῷ σταυρῷ). A. Deissmann (*Light from the Ancient East*. Tr. L. R. M. Strachan [New York: Doran, 1927] 332, 323. Reprinted [Grand Rapids: Baker, 1978]) considered the verb "nailed" referred to a common custom of cancelling a bond or other agreement by crossing it out with the Greek cross-letter X. But there is no mention here of crossing out the "bond"; the Greek word for this action is χιάζω, and the word σταυρός does not suggest the X shape (cf. Bruce, 238), while "there seems to be no evidence for the alleged custom of cancelling a bond by piercing it with a nail" (Moule, 99). The metaphorical language is not to be pressed. God has canceled the bond by nailing it to the cross—this is a vivid way of saying that because Christ was nailed to the cross our debt has been completely forgiven. (There may also be an allusion to the custom of affixing to the cross the "inscription" [ἐπιγραφή] bearing the crime of the evildoer, Mark 15:26. God nails the accusation against us to the cross of Jesus, just as his accusation had been nailed there.)

15. ἀπεκδυσάμενος τὰς ἀρχὰς καὶ τὰς ἐξουσίας κτλ. If verses 13 and 14 speak in graphic terms about the forgiveness of sins and the removal of our signed acknowledgment of indebtedness, then verse 15 refers to God stripping the

principalities and powers, "whose possession of the damning indictment kept us in their grip" (Bruce, 239), of their authority and dignity.

In the early church and among many recent commentators it was thought that Christ rather than God is the subject of the sentence (for earlier references see Lightfoot, 187–89, and more recently Bruce, 238, 239, rather cautiously Martin, *NCB*, 86, 87, and Hanson, *Studies*, 8–10, etc.). For this to be correct there must have been a change of subject in the middle of the sentence (Hanson sees the transition occurring at ἐξαλείψας; Lightfoot postpones it till ἦρκεν) since in verse 13 God is explicitly the one who gave life to the Colossians with Christ. Nevertheless this interpretation has the merit of retaining the same meaning for the key term ἀπεκδύομαι ("put off") in Colossians 2 and 3 (cf. 3:9 and ἀπέκδυσις at 2:11) as Beasley-Murray (*Baptism*, 161) concedes.

At chapter 3:9 the middle voice of this verb (ἀπεκδυσάμενοι) denotes "putting off," as of clothes. The Greek fathers thought that at chapter 2:15 Christ divested himself of the principalities and powers. These hostile forces had clung to him on the cross like an alien garment (Lightfoot, 188, who agreed with this general view of the Greek fathers commented: "The powers of evil, which had clung like a Nessus robe about his humanity, were torn off and cast aside for ever"). The Latin fathers in response to the question, "What did Christ strip himself of?" answered: "the flesh" (cf. v 11, "in the putting off of the body of flesh"), since the flesh was the means by which the evil powers could exercise their tyranny over man (cf. Robinson, *Body*, 41: "The dying Jesus, like a king, divests Himself of that flesh, the tool and medium of their power, and thereby exposes them to ridicule for their Pyrrhic victory." On this view "principalities and powers" is governed by "displayed" but not by "stripped off"). Scott (*Christianity according to St Paul* [Cambridge: University Press, 1927] 34–36) combined these two early interpretations understanding that Christ stripped off from himself the evil forces which attacked him and that he did so by divesting his flesh, since it was the latter, his frail humanity, which the evil powers assaulted. But Colossians 2:15 does not hint at the suggestion that Christ was clothed with the "principalities and powers," nor is it to be inferred that these beings are identical with the "body of flesh."

In NT Greek there was a tendency to substitute the middle voice for the active in certain verbs (BDF, para. 316 (1) list ἀπεκδύομαι as one example of this tendency; cf. Robertson, *Grammar*, 804, 805). Perhaps, therefore, the best way to resolve the exegetical difficulty is to regard ἀπεκδυσάμενος as a middle voice with an active sense (="strip"), so indicating that God stripped the principalities and powers, utterly divesting them of their dignity and might (Lohmeyer, 119, argued that the imagery was not drawn from the battlefield where an army is "disarmed" [RSV, cf. Oepke, *TDNT* 2, 319, and BAG, 83] but from a royal court in which public officials are degraded by being stripped of their dignity; cf. Martin, *NCB*, 87, Schlier, *TDNT* 2, 31, and Lohse, 112. However true this may be, the context of Colossians 2:15 demands that we understand the removal of power or authority which the principalities exercised over the lives of men by holding the certificate of indebtedness in their grip).

This interpretation retains the same subject throughout (it must be pointed out, however, that many who consider Christ is the subject of the action of divesting remind us that such a transition is possible for Paul since it was God in Christ who was at work in the redemptive events; we ought not to separate the action of the Father from that of the Son: so Bruce, 239, E. Larsson, *Christus als Vorbild. Eine Untersuchung zu den paulinischen Tauf- und Eikontexten* [ASNU 23; Uppsala: Gleerup, 1962] 85, Hanson, *Studies*, 10, 11), while allowing the final words of the paragraph ἐν αὐτῷ to be rendered "in him," rather than "in it (i.e. the cross)," so being consistent with the earlier references in the section, verses 6–12, where the words "in him" and "in whom" sound like a refrain.

ἐδειγμάτισεν ἐν παρρησίᾳ. Having divested the principalities and powers of their dignity and authority on the cross, God exposed to the universe their utter helplessness. δειγματίζω occurs on only one other occasion in the Greek Bible, at Matthew 1:19, where it is found with reference to Joseph not wishing to cite Mary publicly and thus expose her (cf. BAG, 172; Schlier, *TDNT* 2, 31; on the possible OT background to the verb in this passage see Hanson, *Studies*, 1–12). Here the term means not to "make an example" of them (which would be παραδειγματίζω), but to "show them in their true character." By putting them on public display God exposed the principalities and powers to ridicule (cf. Meyer, 383). This open manifestation of their being divested of dignity and authority only serves to demonstrate more clearly the infinite superiority of Christ (so Schlier, *TDNT* 5, 883, 884, with reference to the significance of ἐν παρρησίᾳ; cf. Lohse, 112).

θριαμβεύσας αὐτοὺς ἐν αὐτῷ. The word θριαμβεύω occurs only here and at 2 Corinthians 2:14 in the NT. The image behind this verb is that of a tumultuous procession through the streets of Rome to celebrate a military victory (note Williamson's careful examination of the texts, *Int* 22 [1968] 317–32; and for a colorful account of a triumph see his lengthy quotation of Plutarch's *Aemilius Paulus*, 32–34, on pp. 322, 323). The term ought to be translated: (1) to "enjoy a triumphal procession" or "celebrate a victory" (as distinct from "triumphing" or "triumphing over," for these terms convey the idea of winning a victory, while the texts point to a Roman celebration, not the victory itself), when θριαμβεύω is used absolutely or followed by a prepositional phrase; or (2) to "lead as a conquered enemy in a victory parade," when followed by a direct personal object (as at 2 Cor 2:14 and Col 2:15). (Recently R. B. Egan, "Lexical Evidence on Two Pauline Passages," *NovT* 19 [1977] 34–62, argued at some length that the meaning "reveal" yields good sense in both Pauline instances of the verb θριαμβεύω; in our judgment, however, the case is not proven: first, it is doubtful whether this meaning of the term was sufficiently early and widespread for Paul to have used it in this way and for his two groups of readers at Corinth and Colossae to be in no doubt about its meaning. Further, the meaning "reveal" does not fit the Colossians context as well as the other rendering.)

At 2 Corinthians 2:14 Paul is a prisoner in a triumphal procession. He is a slave in the triumph but paradoxically as a privileged captive, as a "slave of Christ." There is no extant evidence to suggest that the expression could apply to a victorious soldier or subordinate officer in a triumphal procession (cf. Williamson, *Int* 22 [1968] 325, 326, and Delling, *TDNT* 3, 160). In the Colossians reference, however, the victims are true enemies. The "principalities and powers" who have been conquered and are drawn along in God's triumphal procession are not related to God or Christ as Paul and other Christians are. God parades these powerless "powers" and "principalities" to make plain to all the magnitude of the victory (Lohse, 112). Their period of rule is finished; they must worship and serve the victor. These authorities are not depicted as gladly surrendering but as submitting against their wills to a power they cannot resist. They have been pacified (1:20), overcome and reconciled, yet not finally destroyed or appeased. They continue to exist, opposed to man and his interests (Rom 8:38, 39). But they cannot finally harm the person who is in Christ, and their ultimate overthrow, although in the future, is sure and certain (1 Cor 15:24–28).

A Note on the "Elements of the Universe" (στοιχεῖα τοῦ κόσμου)

The phrase the "elements of the world" (*στοιχεῖα τοῦ κόσμου*) appears three times in Paul's letters (Col 2:8, 20; Gal 4:3; at v 9 the parallel expression *τὰ ἀσθενῆ καὶ πτωχὰ στοιχεῖα*, "the weak and beggarly elements," is used) and while it is of considerable importance for an understanding of the heresy propounded by the false teachers at Colossae, and the apostle's answer to that false teaching, its meaning has been disputed since earliest times as Bandstra has shown in his history of the exegesis of these passages (*Law*, 5–30, especially 5–12).

The noun *στοιχεῖον*, which was probably derived from *στοῖχος* (originally a military term meaning a "row"), had the connotation a "member of a row or series." The earliest known reference was to a "shadow" by which time was reckoned (fifth-fourth cent. B.C., Aristophanes in *Ecclesiazusae*, 651, cited by Bandstra, *Law*, 31). *στοιχεῖον* was essentially a "formal" word, similar to the English word "element" and capable of taking on new sets of meanings when applied to different contexts. So in Aristotle it connoted "letters" or "phonemes" of language, "notes" in a musical scale, "elementary principles" or "rules" in politics, geometrical and mathematical "propositions" basic to the proof of other propositions, and so on.

"Element" was a common word in the language of the philosophers particularly when they spoke of the matter or the elements out of which everything was formed. So Plato referred to the "primary elements (*στοιχεῖα*) of which we and all else are composed" (*Theaet* 201*e*). Zeno defined an element as "that from which particular things first come to be at their birth and into which they are finally resolved." "Earth" (*ὕλη*), "fire" (*πῦρ*), "water" (*ὕδωρ*), and "air" (*ἀήρ*) are then mentioned as the four elements which constitute everything (Diogenes Laertius 7:136, 137). This meaning of "element" was widely known in the Hellenistic philosophical schools and was current in Hellenistic Judaism (4 Macc 12:13; Wisd 7:17; 19:18, etc. Cf. Lohse, 97, for references), though as one might expect in the latter it was given a distinctive theological twist: Philo, *De Cher* 127, "the four elements" (*τὰ τέσσαρα στοιχεῖα*) are the "material" (*ὕλη*) from which God fashioned the universe.

At this point it is necessary to note that during the nineteenth and twentieth centuries, scholars, in seeking to understand Paul's use of this phrase "the elements of the world" (*τὰ στοιχεῖα τοῦ κόσμου*) in Galatians and Colossians, have presented three major lines of interpretation as they have borne in mind that: *(a)* the meaning of *στοιχεῖον* varies considerably according to its contexts (much the same as the English word "element"); *(b)* Paul uses the phrase in polemical contests; *(c)* the errors combated in Galatians and Colossians while containing some similarities (references to Jewish regulations, and a relapse from the freedom of Christianity into some dogmatic system) are different at significant points; and *(d)* in Galatians 4 both Jews and Gentiles outside of Christ are under the "elements" (vv 3, 9). With individual variations the following are the main lines (cf. Bandstra, *Law,* 15–30):

(1) The first approach takes its cue from *στοιχεῖον* as an "element" or "principle" and understands the phrase in question as the "principles of religious teaching or instruction," which are usually associated with the immaturity of humanity prior to Christ. The main differences in this general approach are whether *στοιχεῖα* points to the Jewish law alone (so de Wette), or to principles common to both Jewish and Gentile religion (Meyer, B. Weiss, Lightfoot), and whether *κόσμος* ("world") denotes the whole of humanity outside of Christ or the external material world.

Among twentieth century exponents of this view Ewald drew attention to the extra-Christian world's deficiency in knowledge. *στοιχεῖα* denoted the "elements of knowledge" which represented the age of minority. Burton, after a lengthy note in his commentary on Galatians, concluded the phrase meant "the rudimentary religious teachings possessed by the (human) race," a view similar to that of Strack-Billerbeck. Moule admitted that in this context of Colossians although belief in demonic powers was present, because of the absence of evidence outside the NT for this meaning of the term *στοιχεῖα* until later times, he preferred the rendering "elementary teaching"—that teaching by Judaistic or pagan ritualists, "a 'materialistic' teaching bound up with 'this world' alone, and contrary to the freedom of the Spirit" (Moule, 92; cf. BAG, 768, 769, which lists "fundamental principles" as a possible meaning of the phrase in both Galatians and Colossians).

Bandstra's own view which falls within this general approach begins with the meaning of *στοιχεῖον* as "inherent component." Inextricably bound up with this is the notion of "power" or "force." The term *κόσμος* is not understood in the sense of "universe" (as most moderns take it here) but denotes "that whole sphere of human activity which stands over against Christ and His salvation, not considered first of all as inherently and structurally evil, but . . . which is ineffectual for overcoming sin and . . . for bringing salvation" (*Law,* 57). The *στοιχεῖα* are the basic components of this area of activity—they are, Bandstra concludes after an exegetical examination of Galatians 4 and Colossians 2, the *law* and the *flesh.* These were the "two fundamental cosmical forces" which held Jews and Gentiles alike in bondage and from which men and women needed to be freed by Christ's death. Some of the phrases in the Colossians paragraph seem to have been chosen to cover both Jewish and pagan items: so "tradition of men" is "not necessarily to be limited to [the] Jewish tradition of the fathers, but could include all sorts of tradition common to mankind" (*Law,* 70), while "philosophy" probably includes a reference to the Mosaic law but is broader than this.

Bandstra's approach, which interprets the *στοιχεῖα* as the "law" and the "flesh" (unregenerate human nature), two elemental forces in the world operating before Christ and apart from him, could be seen as being in line with Paul's general teaching. However, several comments may be made: *(a)* his case has been worked out with special reference to Galatians and has not paid sufficient attention to the distinctive features in Colossians. *(b)* It is hardly correct to speak of the "law" and the "flesh" as the basic structural entities outside of Christ. *(c)* The real weakness of this approach which interprets *στοιχεῖα* as "elements" in the sense of "principles" is that Paul speaks of them in a rather personal fashion (at Gal 4:3, 9 they seem to be conceived of as angelic powers), and in contexts where other personal beings or forces are referred to (at Col 2:10, 15, demonic principalities desire to exercise their tyranny over men). *(d)* Finally, this line does not pay sufficient attention successively to the developing evidence (admittedly some is second century A.D. material) from Jewish sources indicating a belief in angels governing and being active in the forces of nature, the other evidence to show that similar ideas were present in contemporary pagan and syncretistic religions, and the importance of the spirit world in NT thought generally.

(2) A second interpretation has been called the "cosmological" view. The term *κόσμος* ("world") in the phrase *τὰ στοιχεῖα τοῦ κόσμου* was understood to refer to the material, visible world while *στοιχεῖα* denoted the elemental parts of that world. Zahn, for example, argued that Paul understood by the expression "nothing but the *κόσμος* itself, and this as composed of manifold material elements" while Kögel considered that being bound to material things was the point of comparison between the observance of the Jewish law and the practices of pagan religions.

Recently Schweizer (*Jews, Greeks and Christians,* 249–55; cf. his commentary, 100–107) has argued that since all the parallels to the phrase *τὰ στοιχεῖα τοῦ κόσμου* ("the elements of the universe") outside the NT do not designate anything other than the elements earth, water, air and fire (cf. Blinzler, *Studiorum,* 438–41) it is difficult to understand it differently in Colossians 2:8 and 20. A connection between the term "elements" and stars or their deities, spirits or demons cannot be found before the second century A.D. Philo proves that his readers were expected to understand the term in its normal physical understanding without any overtones pointing to their demonic character (*Her* 140; *Abr* 162, etc.), while the total absence of the phrase in all the Pauline (or post-Pauline) lists of powers, thrones, authorities, principalities, dominions, and so on argues, according to Schweizer, in this same direction. The phrase would be expected at Colossians 1:16; 2:10 or 2:15 if it denoted demons. Schweizer further suggested that the Colossian "philosophy" had been influenced by Pythagorean ideas in which cosmic speculation had already been ethicized (see the introduction on the nature of the Colossian philosophy). The elements exercise power in much the same way that the law does (note the points of contact with Bandstra's view above). Because the impure soul cannot ascend to the highest divine element it would be driven back to the lower elements, to the air, the sea, and the earth. So, purification of the soul by abstinence from meat, and so on, was a matter of life and death, and became a kind of slavery to innumerable legalistic demands.

(3) The majority of commentators this century have understood the "ele-

ments of the world" in Galatians and Colossians as denoting spiritual beings, regarded as personal and active in the physical and heavenly elements. From early times the stars and powers thought to control the universe were worshiped and given offerings. Later in the Hellenistic period this homage was justified by pointing out that man was fashioned from the same elements of the cosmos.

The term στοιχεῖα was applied, as we have seen, to the physical components of the universe—earth, fire, water and air (Philo, *Quis* 134; cf. 2 Pet 3:10, 12). In Hellenistic syncretism the teaching about the elements was "mythologized" so that they were thought to be under the control of spirit powers. Along with the stars and heavenly bodies these were described as personal beings believed to control man's destiny. At a later time the *Testament of Solomon* can describe the "elements" as the "cosmic rulers of darkness" (8:2), while the stars whose constellations controlled the universe and in particular man's fate were also styled "elements" (στοιχεῖα; Ps-Calisthenes 1, 12, 1). Men must not only possess knowledge about these elements but also reverence these principalities and powers submitting to the rules and regulations imposed on one's life. (Because of contextual considerations in Col 2, Lohse, 99, and others have argued that too much weight should not be placed on the lack of explicit usage of τὰ στοιχεῖα as "elemental spirits" in the pre-Pauline writings.)

Although in Judaism worship was offered to the one true God, increasing prominence was given to angels. Jewish apocalyptic literature had already associated angels closely with the heavenly powers. According to Jubilees 2:2 each of the elements had its own angel to rule over it, while in 1 Enoch 60:11, 12 reference is made to the spirits of the various natural elements (cf. 1 Enoch 43:1, 2; 80:6; 2 Enoch 4:1, 2, etc.). Three times in the NT (Acts 7:53; Gal 3:19 and Heb 2:2) the Jewish tradition regarding the angelic mediation of the law (absent from the Pentateuchal account of the law-giving) is mentioned, and in Galatians 4:3 some close connection between (or identification of) these angels and the στοιχεῖα is required.

It is probable that in the syncretistic teaching being advocated at Colossae these στοιχεῖα were grouped with the angels and seen as controlling the heavenly realm and man's access to God's presence. One way they could be placated was by rigorously subduing the flesh so as to gain visionary experiences of the heavenly dimension and to participate in their angelic liturgy (see the discussion on 2:18). By this the devotees gained fullness of salvation, reached the divine presence and attained the esoteric knowledge which accompanied such visions. Christ had in effect become just another intermediary between God and man.

Explanation (2:8–15)

After admonishing the readers to continue in the teaching they had received when they accepted "Christ Jesus the Lord" as their "tradition" and to remain immovable in their faith (vv 6 and 7), Paul confronts the community with the first of several warnings: they are to be on guard lest they be carried away from the truth into the slavery of error. The means these spiritual confidence tricksters would use to ensnare the community was their particular "philosophy" (v 8) that was seductive and misleading. It gave all the appearance of having authority, dignity and revelation on its side, but was really a tool in the hands of the principalities and powers (vv 10, 15), those demonic personal forces which sought to tyrannize over the lives of men. Worst of all it stood diametrically opposed to Christ.

Taking up language from the hymn of chapter 1:15–20 the apostle spells out why (v 9) the philosophy of the false teachers is not according to Christ. Two reasons are given: first, this Christ is the one in whom the whole fullness of the Godhead dwells bodily. Only in him is fullness to be found. It is not to be attained by groveling before the elements of the universe or by observing their regulations. Second, the readers have *already* been "filled" in Christ, the same person in whom the fullness of Deity dwells and the One who is ruler and master over every principality and power.

Paul elaborates on the theme of the Colossians' being filled in Christ by describing their participation in his death, burial and resurrection with a series of past tenses: you were circumcised in his circumcision, i.e. you died in his death, you were buried with him in baptism and you were raised with him in his resurrection. The apostolic message, as evidenced in 1 Corinthians 15:3–5, spoke of Christ's death, burial and resurrection; here the same elements are spelled out with reference to the Colossians' incorporation into those salvation history events. The resurrection of the Colossians with Christ has already taken place. The suggestion of the false teachers was probably that the believers were not complete in Christ. They needed to follow a strict discipline of ritual and ascetic observance, as well as taking sufficient account of the spiritual powers if they were to proceed along the path to "fullness of life." Against this the apostle asserts that the believers of this congregation in the Lycus valley had already been raised with Christ.

Those who had once been spiritually dead in their trespasses and sinful nature God had made alive. The Colossians had come to life with Christ who was dead and rose again. Their new life, then, was a sharing in the life which he received when he rose from the dead. God had forgiven them as Gentiles, along with Paul and other Jewish Christians, all their trespasses. Indeed, he had not only canceled the debt but also destroyed the document on which it was recorded. This he did by blotting out the bond with its damning indictment against us and nailing it to the cross when Christ died. Further, he stripped the principalities and powers, who had kept us in their grip through their possession of this document, divesting them of their dignity and might. God exposed to the universe their utter helplessness leading them in Christ in his triumphal procession. He paraded these powerless "powers and principalities" so that all the world might see the magnitude of his victory.

But these spiritual powers had not been annihilated. In that triumphal procession they were visible. They continue to exist, inimical to man and his interests (Rom 8:38, 39). Nevertheless they are powerless figures unable to harm the Christian who lives under the lordship of Christ. How foolish is it then for the Colossians to think, as the false teachers want them to, that they needed to grovel before these weak and beggarly elements as though they controlled the lines of communication between God and man.

Christ is the one whom they received as Lord. Let them continue to live in him, for he is the one in whom the entire fullness of Godhead dwells, the one in whom they have been made full, the person in whom they have been incorporated in death, burial and resurrection. It is in him that they have been raised and given new life. What really matters then is Christ and Christ alone.

Freedom from Legalism (2:16–23)

Bibliography

Bandstra, A. J. *Dimensions,* 329–43. *Law.* ———. **Beasley-Murray, G. R.** *RevExp* 70 (1973) 469–79. **Bornkamm, G.** *Conflict,* 123–45. **Carr, W.** *JTS* 24 (1973) 492–500. **Dibelius, M.** *Conflict,* 61–121. **Francis, F. O.** *Conflict,* 163–207. **Hanssler, B.** "Zu Satzkonstruktion und Aussage in Kol 2, 23." *Wort Gottes in der Zeit. Festschrift für Karl Hermann Schelkle zum 65. Geburtstag,* ed. H. Feld and J. Nolte. Düsseldorf: Patmos, 1973, 143–48. **Hollenbach, B.** "Col. ii. 23: Which Things lead to the Fulfilment of the Flesh." *NTS* 25 (1978–79) 254–61. **Hooker, M. D.** *Christ,* 315–31. **Kehl, N.** "Erniedrigung und Erhöhung in Qumran und Kolossä." *ZKT* 91 (1969) 364–94. **Lähnemann, J.** *Kolosserbrief,* 125–49. **Reicke, B.** "Zum sprachlichen Verständnis vom Kol. 2, 23." *ST* 6 (1952) 39–53. **Schweizer, E.** *Beiträge,* 147–63. ———. *ThBer* 5 (1976) 163–91. **Zeilinger, F.** *Der Erstgeborene,* 56–60, 125–34.

Translation

16 *Therefore, do not let anyone pass judgment on you with regard to food and drink or concerning a religious festival, a new moon celebration or a sabbath day.* 17 *These are a shadow of the things that were to come; the reality, however, is found in Christ.* 18 *Let no one condemn you, delighting in humility and the angelic worship [of God], which*[a] *he has seen upon entering. He is puffed up with idle notions from his unspiritual mind,* 19 *and he does not hold fast to the head, from whom the whole body, nourished and held together by its joints and ligaments, grows with a growth that is from God.* 20 *Since you died with Christ from the control of the elemental spirits of the world, how can you, as if you still lived in a worldly way, voluntarily place yourselves under the regulations:* 21 *"Do not handle! Do not taste! Do not even touch!"?* 22 *These are all destined to perish with use, for they are based on human commands and teachings.* 23 *Such regulations actually lead—though having a reputation for wisdom in the spheres of voluntary worship, humility and*[b] *severe treatment of the body, without any value whatsoever—to the gratification of the flesh.*

Notes

[a] The reading ἁ ("which") is strongly supported by $\mathfrak{P}^{46}$ and good representatives of the Alexandrian and Western types of text (ℵ* A B D* etc.). On the insertion of the negative "not" (οὐκ or μή) due to a failure to understand Paul's idiom, and on the number of conjectural emendations see the exegetical comment below.

[b] The καί ("and") was omitted by $\mathfrak{P}^{46}$ B 1739 Origen^{lat} and other Fathers, and this is strong and early external evidence. Accordingly ἀφειδίᾳ σώματος is not the third in a series of datives after ἐν ("in") but is an instrumental dative ("by severe treatment of the body") qualifying the previous prepositional phrase. On the other hand, the omission may have been accidental since it is found in ℵ A C D^{gr} H 33 81, etc.

Form/Structure/Setting

This lengthy and involved section, which follows hard upon the positive exposition of God's work in Christ and the Colossians' union with him in his death, burial and resurrection, springs out of (οὖν, "therefore") what has preceded (see Lohmeyer, 96, and Lähnemann, *Kolosserbrief*, 136). The short warning about the "philosophy" in verse 8 is developed in the further injunctions of this paragraph. There are formal analogies between the expression μὴ οὖν τις ὑμᾶς ("Therefore do not . . . anyone . . . you") and the opening words of verse 8, βλέπετε μή τις ὑμᾶς ("See to it that no one . . . you"), while verse 18 continues with a similar introductory formula, μηδεὶς ὑμᾶς . . . ("let no one [condemn] you").

The first sentence (vv 16, 17) opens with a warning μὴ οὖν τις ὑμᾶς κρινέτω ("Therefore do not let anyone pass judgment upon you"). Five areas covered by the prohibition are then enumerated and the first three of them are introduced by the preposition ἐν ("in," that is, "with reference to"):

> <u>ἐν</u> βρώσει καὶ <u>ἐν</u> πόσει,
> ἢ <u>ἐν</u> μέρει ἑορτῆς ἢ νεομηνίας ἢ σαββάτων.
>
> "with regard to food or drink,
> or concerning a religious festival, a new moon celebration
> or a sabbath day."

Verse 17, which spells out the reason for Paul's attack is constructed as a sharp antithesis. The first clause is the criticism, the second the Christological contrast:

> ἅ ἐστιν σκιὰ τῶν μελλόντων,
> τὸ δὲ σῶμα τοῦ Χριστοῦ.
>
> "These are a shadow of the things that were to come;
> the reality, however, is found in Christ" (NIV).

In verse 18 with a similar introductory formula to that of verse 16 the apostle refutes one of the claims of the false teachers voiced in the Colossian community: μηδεὶς ὑμᾶς καταβραβευέτω ("let no one condemn you"). The words which immediately follow, θέλων ἐν ταπεινοφροσύνῃ . . . ἐμβατεύων ("delighting in humility . . . entering"), which are attached grammatically to καταβραβευέτω ("let [no one] condemn") are best understood as quotations from catchwords of the "philosophy" (see the relevant comment) and indicate the basis of the opponents' haughty manner. The two participial clauses which follow, εἰκῇ φυσιούμενος . . . ("puffed up without reason . . ." v 18) and οὐ κρατῶν τὴν κεφαλήν . . . ("not holding fast to the head," v 19) are Paul's severe criticisms of the false teachers. The remainder of verse 19 is a relative clause (ἐξ οὗ . . . , "from whom") dependent on κεφαλή ("head") which speaks of the growth of the whole body. By means of two prepositions ἐκ ("from") and διά ("through") both the source of the sustenance by which the body lives and the channels through which the nourishment comes are mentioned.

In the strongly polemical section of verses 20–23 the apostle begins with a conditional clause to remind his readers that they were united with Christ in his death (cf. v 11), and to show that this death severed the bond which bound them to the "elemental spirits of the world": εἰ ἀπεθάνετε σὺν Χριστῷ ἀπὸ τῶν στοιχείων τοῦ κόσμου (the introductory εἰ does not express doubt but means "if as is the case," "since"; cf. 3:3). The second half of the sentence, in which the application is made, consists of a rhetorical question and a rebuke: *τί ὡς ζῶντες ἐν κόσμῳ δογματίζεσθε;* ("How then can you conduct your lives as if you still lived in a worldly way?").

Three negative regulations, examples of the kinds imposed by the principalities and powers, are then quoted by Paul as he ridicules his opponents with biting irony: *μὴ ἅψῃ μηδὲ γεύσῃ μηδὲ θίγῃς* ("Do not handle! Do not taste! Do not even touch!" v 21). By means of two relative clauses several criticisms of these kinds of regulations are made: *ἅ ἐστιν πάντα εἰς φθορὰν τῇ ἀποχρήσει,* . . . (v 22, "all of which are destined to perish through use . . ."), and *ἅτινά ἐστιν . . . πρὸς πλησμονὴν τῆς σαρκός* (v 23, "which things [actually] lead to the gratification of the flesh"). Strictly speaking the first clause with its relative *ἅ* "which") makes an objective statement about the regulations, while the second with its relative of quality *ἅτινα* ("which sort of things") characterizes and condemns the precepts of verse 21 and others like them. The prepositional phrase within the first clause (which echoes the wording of Isaiah 29:13 LXX), *κατὰ τὰ ἐντάλματα καὶ διδασκαλίας τῶν ἀνθρώπων* ("according to the regulations and doctrines of men") points out that these taboos are merely human inventions. Within the second relative clause a lengthy parenthesis is found (for a detailed justification of this see the comment on *λόγον μὲν ἔχοντα σοφίας ἐν ἐθελοθρησκίᾳ καὶ ταπεινοφροσύνῃ καὶ ἀφειδίᾳ σώματος, οὐκ ἐν τιμῇ τινι*) ("though having a reputation for wisdom in the spheres of voluntary worship, humility and severe treatment of the body, without any value whatsoever"). The parenthesis consists of a concessive clause *λόγον μὲν ἔχοντα κτλ.* ("though having a reputation . . ."). Prohibitions of the kind mentioned in verse 21 carry a reputation for wisdom in the spheres mentioned (note the preposition *ἐν*, "in," qualifies the three following nouns which are linked by *καί*, "and"). The second clause within the parentheses is subordinate to the concessive clause and is Paul's comment: *οὐκ ἐν τιμῇ τινι* ("without any value whatsoever").

Comment

Bad theology leads to bad practice. The false notions about the person and work of Christ, which are corrected in the positive affirmations of chapter 2:8–15, have their inevitable corollary in these unusual aberrations on the practical side (Martin, *NCB,* 89). Masson (130) has aptly entitled this section "A Defence of Christian Liberty," for in it the apostle points out that since God has divested the principalities and powers of their authority and dignity in Christ (and Paul has already said that Christ is head over all of these principalities, 2:10) then those who have been united in him are free from the constraints of the "elemental spirits of the universe." The evil powers which are seen to be behind the false practices and regulations (2:20) have been defeated and publicly disgraced in Christ. The Colossians are not to be impressed by those who boast of their own experiences and arrogantly pass disparaging judgments on the readers in connection with various ordinances.

As many commentators have indicated our knowledge of the Colossian "heresy," which at best is fragmentary and indirect, is derived mostly from this passage (see the fuller discussion on the nature of the false teaching in the Introduction, xxx–xxxviii). The section is written in a polemical style and filled with allusions to the teaching and catch-words of the philosophy. However, some of the sentences are tightly constructed (cf. vv 18, 21 and 23) so that it is not always clear when the writer has taken words over from the opponents and used them polemically, or when the phrases are his own formulation.

16. *μὴ οὖν τις ὑμᾶς κρινέτω*. "Therefore, do not let anyone pass judgment on you." The *οὖν* ("therefore") links this passage with the preceding (cf. 2:6; 3:1). The evil powers have been signally defeated in Christ (v 15). The Colossians are not to observe the following customs and rituals as obligatory for this would be to acknowledge the continuing authority of the powers through whom these regulations are mediated, the very powers which had been overthrown. *κρίνω* in this context is used of the judgment which people customarily pass upon the lives and actions of their fellow men (BAG, 452), so trying to influence them, and it means to "take one to task" (Lightfoot, 191), "pass judgment on" (Rom 2:1, 3; 14:3, 4, 10, 13; 1 Cor 10:29; etc.). *μή τις* (as in v 8) rather than *μηδείς* ("no one"), may point to definite persons Paul has in mind (von Soden, 52, Abbott, 263). Also the present imperative *μὴ . . . κρινέτω* ("do not . . . let judge") probably implies that this sitting in judgment was already being done by some. But *whoever* it is that tries to act in this way is behaving falsely.

This taking the Colossians to task occurred in two main areas: *(a)* with respect to *food: ἐν βρώσει καὶ ἐν πόσει* ("about what you eat or drink"), and *(b)* regarding *holy days: ἐν μέρει ἑορτῆς ἢ νεομηνίας ἢ σαββάτων* ("with regard to a religious festival, a new moon celebration or a sabbath day").

ἐν βρώσει καὶ ἐν πόσει ("about what you eat or drink"; lit. "with regard to food and drink"). Paul is probably not referring directly to the OT food laws since the Torah contained no prohibitions respecting drinks, except in a few special cases (e.g. of priests ministering in the tabernacle, Lev. 10:9; of liquids contained in unclean vessels, Lev 11:34, 36; and of Nazirite vows, Num 6:3; on *βρῶσις*, "eating," "food," see Behm, *TDNT* 1, 642–45, and on *πόσις*, "drinking," "drink," note Goppelt, *TDNT* 6, 145–48). Nor is he directing attention to abstentions similar to those enjoined in the apostolic letter of Acts 15:23–29 in which Gentiles without compromising their Christian liberty were to behave considerately to their "weaker brethren" of Jewish birth. Rather, these are more stringent regulations of an ascetic nature apparently involving the renunciation of animal flesh and of wine and strong drink, after a Nazirite fashion. They follow from the demand of "severe treatment of the body" (v 23), whereby abstinence from certain food is required (v 21; cf. 1 Tim 4:3).

There are various reasons why abstinence from food and drink was practiced in the ancient world: the belief in the transmigration of souls might prevent a person from eating meat. Some practiced asceticism since it was bound up with their views of purity. Others thought that by fasting one served the deity, came closer to him or prepared oneself for receiving a divine revelation, a point that is important in the light of verse 18 (see Behm, *TDNT* 4, 924–35, especially 926, where the relevant Hellenistic texts are noted). T e observance of taboos and sacred times in the Colossian "philosophy" seems to have been related to obedient submission to the "elemental spirits of the universe" (cf. v 20).

The apostle lays down the principle of Christian liberty: don't let anyone sit in judgment on you. In writing to Corinth and Rome, where Christians had scruples about food and drink as well as the observance of holy days, Paul introduces the further principle which might impose a voluntary limitation on one's Christian liberty, i.e. "the strong" should go out of their way to avoid offending the tender consciences of "the weak" or scrupulous (Rom 14:1–15:13; 1 Cor 8–10). But at Colossae the scrupulous were threatening to impose their rigid principles on the rest of the congregation. Christian liberty needed to be asserted in the light of false attempts to undermine it.

ἐν μέρει ἑορτῆς ἢ σαββάτων. The injunction continues: "[don't let anyone take you to task] with regard to a religious festival, a new moon celebration or a sabbath day." The Greek phrase *ἐν μέρει,* denoting a category, comes to be used with a technical meaning "in the matter of," "with regard to" (cf. 2 Cor 3:10; 9:3, and note the extrabiblical examples listed in BAG, 506), and it is followed by three nouns (in the genitive case). The terms "festival" (*ἑορτή*), "new moon" (*νεομηνία*) and "sabbath" (*σάββατα*) often occur in the OT to describe special days dedicated to God (LXX Hos 2:13; Ezek 45:17; 1 Chr 23:31; 2 Chr 2:3; 31:3). For Israel the keeping of these holy days was evidence of obedience to God's law and a sign of her election among the nations. At Colossae, however, the sacred days were to be kept for the sake of the "elemental spirits of the universe," those astral powers who directed the course of the stars and regulated the order of the calendar. So Paul is not condemning the use of sacred days or seasons as such; it is the wrong motive involved when the observance of these days is bound up with the recognition of the elemental spirits.

On the question as to what were the main influences on the Colossian "philosophy," Jewish or pagan, and the possible links between the false teaching and nonconformist Judaism, as evidenced at Qumran, see the survey of scholarly opinion in the Introduction.

17. *ἅ ἐστιν σκιὰ τῶν μελλόντων, τὸ δὲ σῶμα τοῦ Χριστοῦ.* "These are a shadow of the things that were to come; the reality, however, is found in Christ" (NIV). The ground for Paul's attack is now given (the clause is an epexegetical relative one, supplying the basis for what has just been said; so rightly Meyer, 386). They must not be judged in these matters *because* they all belonged to a transitory order.

The contrast between outer appearance and the real substance was taught in Plato (especially the famous image of the cave in his *Republic,* 514a–518b) and frequently taken up in Hellenistic times. True being belongs to the realm of ideas and not to the shadows which they cast in this world and which are perceived by our senses (cf. Lohse, 116). *σκία* ("shadow") and *εἰκών* ("form," "image") were the two terms most frequently used to describe the contrast, though on occasion *σῶμα* ("body") was employed in place of *εἰκών* ("form," "image") for true reality as distinct from mere appearance (Lohse, 116; cf. Zeilinger, *Der Erstgeborene,* 160, 161). (For examples see Philo, *De conf ling* 190, *De migr Abr* 12, etc.; cf. Schulz, *TDNT* 7, 394–97. In Josephus there is the oft-quoted example of Archelaus appearing in Rome to petition the emperor for the shadow [σκία] of rule when he had already appropriated the body [σῶμα], *JW* 2.28.)

There are, however, two significant differences between the Platonic and Philonic use of this "shadow/substance" contrast and that of Paul. The first difference is an eschatological one. At Colossians 2:17 the first member of the contrast σκία ("shadow"; not "outline" or "sketch" as some earlier commentators suggested, which would be σκιαγραφία or σκιαγράφημα) is qualified by τῶν μελλόντων (lit. "of the coming things"). The antithesis is not set within the framework of a timeless metaphysical dimension but is understood as a contrast between the two ages (Schulz, *TDNT* 7, 398; Schweizer, 120): "shadow" is used not so much in the Platonic sense of a copy of the heavenly and eternal "idea" as in the sense of a foreshadowing of what is to come. At Hebrews 10:1 the same point is made (by means of the terms σκία, "shadow" and εἰκών, "image") where the writer is thinking more especially of the law concerning matters of priesthood and sacrifice in relation to the wilderness tabernacle and the Jerusalem temple (on the differences between Philo and Hebrews regarding time and eschatology see R. Williamson, *Philo and the Epistle to the Hebrews* [ALGHJ 4; Leiden: Brill, 1970] 142–59). The expression "the things to come" (τὰ μέλλοντα) does not refer to what lies in the future from the standpoint of the writer (as Meyer, 387, argued), so pointing, for example, to the time of the Second Coming, for then the σκία ("shadow") would not have been superseded and the ordinances referred to would retain their importance. Rather, the expression is to be interpreted from the period when the legal restrictions of verse 16 were enjoined; it is future from the standpoint of the OT (cf. Williams, 105, Lähnemann, *Kolosserbrief*, 136, and Schweizer, 120). Christ has arrived. The substance has already come. The regulations belonged to a transitory order, and have lost all binding force. Hence the RSV translation "a shadow of the things to come" is ambiguous, if not misleading; better is the NIV rendering "a shadow of the things that were to come."

The second difference is Christological: the "substance belongs to Christ" (τὸ δὲ σῶμα τοῦ Χριστοῦ). σῶμα, perhaps of the body that casts a shadow, in contrast to σκία ("shadow"), comes to be used of "the thing itself," "the reality" (BAG, 799), or "the substance." This is not the sense in which the term is used elsewhere in the letter, and attempts have been made to understand σῶμα τοῦ Χριστοῦ here as the "body of Christ." Lohse (117) for example, argues that since σῶμα is employed rather than the more frequently used alternative εἰκών ("image") the author obviously wants to emphasize this term "body" once again. He adds: "The reality which exists solely with Christ is shared only by those who, as members of the body, adhere to the head (2:19)." This statement is correct, but whether it springs out of the phrase in question or has to be read back into it is the issue. Lohmeyer (123) went further than other commentators in seeing a reference to the cosmic body of Christ but this is unlikely (see above 48–50). Benoit (*RB* 63 [1956] 12; cf. Zeilinger, *Der Erstgeborene*, 161) claims that the term σῶμα is being used not simply to signify "substance." Had Paul meant only this he would have written τὸ δὲ σῶμα ὁ Χριστός ("the substance is Christ"—a nominative case; cf. Schweizer,

121, who thinks the nominative was probably original, but there is no manuscript evidence to support this). Instead, the present expression is elliptical and when written fully reads: *τὸ δὲ σῶμα ἐστιν τὸ σῶμα τοῦ* Χριστοῦ ("the substance is the body of Christ"). According to Benoit *σῶμα* thus has two meanings: (1) "reality" as opposed to shadow, and (2) the resurrected body of Christ, that is the church.

Although many recent writers (cf. Moule, 103, Martin, *NCB*, 91, 92) have understood *σῶμα τοῦ* Χριστοῦ as denoting the body of Christ, one wonders whether the double reference is necessary. On this view *σῶμα* requires to be understood as appearing twice, as well as having two different meanings. But the sentence can be understood more simply by referring it to the shadow/substance contrast alone (cf. Bruce, 245, who claims that the attempts to interpret the phrase of the "body of Christ" are unsatisfactory, while Best, *Body*, 121, asserts we must not fall into the error of assuming that "every time Paul uses this word he gives to it its theological undertone—unless it cannot be explained without that undertone").

Christ and his new order are the perfect reality to which these earlier ordinances pointed. These prescriptions of days gone by were but a shadow. They have lost any binding force. Since the reality is here, the things of the shadow no longer constitute a norm for judgment (Bandstra, *Law*, 92).

18. This verse has been described as one of the most contested passages in the NT, presenting great difficulties in language and content (Percy, *Probleme*, 143). However, the researches of Francis (*Conflict;* and subsequently Kehl, *ZKT* 91 [1969] 364–94, and Bandstra, *Dimensions*, 329–43) have helped to throw light on the possible background to the passage as well as the meaning of some of the more difficult terms in it. Although there is still considerable difference of opinion about the details (note the Introduction, xxxvi–xxxviii), the general drift of Paul's thought is reasonably clear. In our exegesis we shall restrict our discussion to the more likely possibilities, and in particular attention will be given to Francis' two articles: "Humility and Angelic Worship in Col 2:18," *ST* 16 (1963) 109–34, *Conflict*, 163–195, and "The Background of EMBATEYEIN (Col 2:18) in Legal Papyri and Oracle Inscriptions," *Conflict*, 197–207.

μηδεὶς ὑμᾶς καταβραβευέτω. As in verse 16, though with different words, the apostle refutes one of the claims the opponents made at Colossae: "let no one condemn you." The main verb *καταβραβεύω* is rarely found in Greek literature (BAG, 409). It has been thought here to retain the primary sense of the simple verb *βραβεύω*, to "act as umpire or one who gives the prize" (see Stauffer, *TDNT* 1, 637–39). The force of the word would then be to "deprive," "disqualify" or "encroach upon another's interest." However, it is probably better, with many modern commentators, to understand it as meaning to "condemn," and so is equivalent to *κατακρίνω* (cf. F. Field, cited by Pfitzner, *Paul*, 156).

A series of dependent participial clauses follows: *εἰκῇ φυσιούμενος* ("puffed up without reason") and *οὐ κρατῶν τὴν κεφαλήν* . . . ("not holding fast to the head") are Paul's negative evaluations of the false teachers. The words that immediately follow the warning, *θέλων ἐν ταπεινοφροσύνῃ* . . . *ἐμβατεύων*, indicate the basis for their position and haughty manner. These phrases "delighting in humility," "worship of angels," and "which he has seen upon entering" are therefore best understood as quotations from catchwords of the "philosophy" rather than Paul's critical or ironical remarks about their behavior (cf. Lohse, 117, 118, Francis, *Conflict,* 167–85; against Percy, *Probleme,* 169, who took the entire clause as a critical remark).

θέλων ἐν. The expression is akin to the Hebrew *ḥāpēṣ bᵉ*, to "delight in" (1 Sam 18:22; 2 Sam 15:26: 1 Kings 10:9; 1 Chr 28:4; Pss 111:1; 146:10) and so refers to those practices in which the advocates of the philosophy took pleasure (cf. Lightfoot, 193, Moule, 104, Schrenk, *TDNT* 3, 45, Percy, *Probleme,* 145–47; this seems more likely than the view that *θέλων* meaning "willfully" is an adverbial absolute modifying *καταβραβευέτω*: "let no one willfully disqualify you," so Dibelius-Greeven, 34, and A. Fridrichsen, "ΘΕΛΩΝ Col 2:18," *ZNW* 21 [1922]135–37). Francis, *Conflict,* 167, renders the expression "being bent upon" (RSV "insisting on").

ἐν ταπεινοφροσύνῃ καὶ θρησκείᾳ τῶν ἀγγέλων: "In humility and angelic worship [of God]." (The two nouns *ταπεινοφροσύνη* and *θρησκεία* are joined by the one preposition *ἐν* and thus closely linked.) The Greek word *ταπεινοφροσύνη* is normally used in the NT in a good sense of the Christian grace of "humility" (cf. 3:12; Phil 2:3; 1 Pet 5:5). Most exegetes have therefore thought that here a false humility is being spoken about and have suggested that it is to be understood in the light of the following phrase, "worship of angels" (so Meyer, 393, Lightfoot, 194, Abbott, 268, and Scott 54). However, if the term was employed by the opponents it must carry some sense such as "mortification" or "self-denial." Can we be more specific than this? Lohse, 118, contends that the two occurrences of the term (vv 18 and 23), both in the context of worship, point to the eagerness and docility with which a person fulfills the cultic ordinances (="readiness to serve"). He understands this not so much of a disposition as of cultic conduct.

Francis (*Conflict,* 167–71) has taken a different line. He has argued that the term was used extensively in Jewish and Christian literature to denote fasting and other bodily rigors (note in Col 2:16–23 the references to food and drink, and severity to the body, point to fasting). These ascetic practices in Jewish mystical-pietistic literature were effectual for receiving visions of the heavenly mysteries. Francis claims that though the technique of "humility" (a prerequisite for receiving visions) was widespread in the Hellenistic world, *ταπεινοφροσύνη* receives this application only in Jewish/Christian sources (notably Hermas, *Vis* 3, 10, 6; *Sim* 5, 3, 7, Tertullian, Philo, *Som* 1.33–37; *Mos* 2.67–70; *QE* 2.39; 1 and 2 Enoch, 4 Ezra, 2 and 3 Apoc Bar, etc.; for references see *Conflict,* 167–71). On Francis' view, which seems likely (see Introduction, xxxvi–xxxviii), the apostle is stating that the advocates of the Colossian "philosophy" delighted in ascetic practices as a prelude to the reception of heavenly visions.

θρησκείᾳ τῶν ἀγγέλων. The phrase has normally been taken (with the genitive being regarded as objective) to denote "the worship directed to the angels." *θρησκεία* ("worship"; cf. Acts 26:5; James 1:26, 27) can be used in either a positive or a negative way, depending on the particular context (Schmidt, *TDNT* 3, 157, 158). This statement concerning angel-worship seems to go beyond speculation about angels present in the Jewish schools and denotes an actual cult of angels. The principalities and powers might have been in view but Paul here refers to angels as a class (according to Bruce, 247, this is the natural inference from the definite article "the" before "angels," τῶν ἀγγέλων). There is little evidence for the worship of angels among the Jews (cf. A. L. Williams, "The Cult of Angels at Colossae," *JTS* 10 [1909] 413–38, Percy, *Probleme,* 149–55, and Carr, *JTS* 24 [1973] 496–500), and so it is argued that the expression is evidence of the syncretistic character of the "philosophy" at Colossae. It was Jewish mixed with pagan elements. The angels determined the course of the cosmos and with it man's circumstances. Men submitted to the angels in the cult by performing the prescribed acts and by fulfilling the regulations laid down (so Lohse, 118, representing the majority view).

Francis (*Conflict,* 176–81; cf. Carr, *JTS* 24 [1973] 499, 500), on the other hand, has argued that the phrase (taking the genitive as subjective) denotes "the worship which the angels perform." Using a wide range of sources representing what he terms ascetic-mystic piety Francis drew attention to the many descriptions of angelic worship. So the Ascension of Isaiah 7:13–9:33 has a sevenfold description of the angelic worship which the visionary sees; the Testament of Levi 3:4–8 details the liturgical climax of Levi's entry into heaven (note Rev 4, 5 which records John's vision of the heavenly liturgy). Participation in the angelic worship is detailed in several sources: so Isaiah participates in the worship of the fifth, sixth and seventh heavens (*Asc Isa* 7:37; 8:17; 9:28, 31, 33), while the daughters of Job praise and glorify God in an angelic tongue (Test Job 48–50). Frequently the Qumran literature refers to the members of the community as priests who offered sacrifice (=the Qumran way of life) not only before Yahweh but also *in communion with* the angels (cf. 1QSb 4:25, 26; 1QH 3:20–22, etc.; note Kehl, *ZKT* 91 [1969] 383–92). Francis thus claims that these texts provide a better background to understanding the "worship of angels" than does the "syncretistic" view—the initiate is enraptured and participates in the heavenly worship of God performed by the angels.

Martin (*NCB,* 94), following Lohse (119), claims that there is "a fatal objection" to Francis' view, namely, this reading "fails because of v 23 where 'self-chosen worship' (ἐθελοθρησκία) specifically characterizes the concept 'worship' (θρησκεία) as performed by men" (Lohse, 119). But the term ἐθελοθρησκία ("self-made religion," perhaps "would-be religion," BAG, 218) presents no obstacle to the second interpretation of the phrase since the term does not specify a cult performed by men. It says no more than that the advocates of the "philosophy" "chose/aspired to/gave pretence of some worship . . . We could say, if we accepted Lohse's translation, that the Colossians chose for themselves the worship performed by the angels" (Francis, *Conflict,* 182). Accordingly, the false teachers claimed to have joined in the angelic worship of God as they entered into the heavenly realm and prepared to receive visions of divine mysteries.

ἃ ἑόρακεν ἐμβατεύων (lit. "which he has seen upon entering"). The third quotation from the catchwords of the "philosophy" is not patently clear, and its precise significance turns on the meaning of *ἐμβατεύων.* Because of the difficulty of reducing the phrase to intelligible terms all sorts of changes have been suggested: (1) one of the earliest attempts to make sense of the expression was to insert a negative: hence AV "intruding into those things which he hath *not* seen." The negative μή which denies the reality of the experience claimed was due to a failure to understand Paul's idiom (cf. Bruce, 246, Metzger, *Textual Commentary*, 623); and (2) conjectural emendations (see Bruce's full note page 248, n. 93) which appear to be variations of Lightfoot's proposal to read κενεμβατεύω, "tread the air." None of these suggested emendations carries conviction.

ἐμβατεύω means to "set foot upon," "enter" (a place, city, sanctuary, etc.); "come into possession of"; "enter into a subject," i.e. investigate it closely (cf. BAG, 254; Preisker, *TDNT* 2, 535). The major attempts to unravel the meaning of the phrase (as distinct from unhelpful conjectures) are as follows:

(a) In the light of the connotation of ἐμβατεύω to "approach something in order to investigate it" (cf. 2 Macc 2:30; Philo, *De plant 80)* Preisker (*TDNT* 2, 535, 536) argued the phrase meant: "what he had seen in a vision, he tried to investigate" (in order to gain deeper insight into divine mysteries). On this view Paul is refuting the earnest quest for knowledge which characterized the "philosophy" at Colossae (and elsewhere, cf. 2 Tim 3:7; 2 John 9). According to Preisker the false teachers waited for moments of ecstatic vision and then entered by painful investigation into what had been seen in ecstasy.

(b) The dominant interpretation takes its point of departure from the use of ἐμβατεύω ("enter") as a technical expression in the mystery religions to describe the initiates entering the sanctuary so as to consult the oracle on completion of the rite (cf. S. Eitrem, "ΕΜΒΑΤΕΥΩ. Note sur Col 2, 18," *ST* 2 [1948] 90–94). First William Ramsay (in a communication to the *Athenaeum* in 1913; for details see Bruce, 249) and then Dibelius (*Conflict*, 61–121) drew attention to the inscriptional data from the sanctuary of Apollo at Klaros. From this evidence Dibelius argued that the time of entering was the climax of the initiation while the inner sanctuary, or possibly the oracle grotto, is the place one entered. Building on this fixed use of the term ἐμβατεύω ("enter") as one element in the mystery rite, it was assumed that in the Colossian "philosophy" certain cultic rites were performed. Our expression ἃ ἑόρακεν ἐμβατεύων (translated "as he has had visions of them during the mystery rites") indicates that the one upon whom the initiation rites were performed, experienced the vision of cosmic secrets. Cultic rites were actually performed in order to worship the "angels" and the "elements of the universe." Because of their teaching and greater experiences the followers of the philosophy were boastful, considering themselves to be superior to the members of the congregation (cf. Lohse's reconstruction, 118–21, which follows Dibelius' presentation closely). Critics of Dibelius have noted that the two situations are not parallel (cf. Lyonnet, *Bib* 43 [1962] 417–35, and *Conflict*, 147–61; Schweizer, 123, 124, claims the linguistic parallels are uncertain) but exponents of the view argue that this does not overthrow Dibelius' basic model.

(c) Rejecting the view that the mystery language or practice had penetrated the church at Colossae, it has been argued that ἐμβατεύω does not have the uniform technical significance that Dibelius and others claimed for it. Francis, first in his article "Humility and Angelic Worship in Col 2:18" (*Conflict*, 163–95) but more fully in "The Background of ΕΜΒΑΤΕΥΕΙΝ (Col 2:18) in Legal

Papyri and Oracle Inscriptions" (*Conflict,* 197–207; the criticisms of Francis by Lohse, 118–20, and Martin, *NCB,* 94, 95, do not take into account this development in the latter article), questioned whether the verb had the precise significance Dibelius gave to it. The term was used broadly in the OT (cf. Josh 19:49, 21) and the papyri to denote the "entering into possession of" something, particularly the possession of property (in the legal papyri over a period of six centuries from the third century B.C. it had this significance). In Joshua the giving of the land constituted the fulfillment of God's promises. To possess the land was to "have a portion in the Lord" and so to "have the right to worship him" (cf. Josh 22:24–26). Francis argues that the unexpressed object of ἐμβατεύων ("entering") in Colossians is "*not* a plot of ground, but it *is* a portion in the Lord" (*Conflict,* 199; cf. the tribe of Levi which received no land but their portion was still the Lord God of Israel). So he holds that the entering here is "the heavenly realm" (*Conflict,* 197; he also notes that certain of the fathers explicitly employed ἐμβατεύω with heaven as its object; cf. Nemesius of Emesa, *De Nat Hom* Matt, 63–65). Though drawing on a different history of religions background Bousset argued that Colossians 2:18 could be explained with reference to the heavenly journey of the soul, while Nock suggested the term "may indicate some claim to special knowledge obtained on a visionary entry into heaven" (A. D. Nock, "The Vocabulary of the New Testament," *JBL* 52 [1933] 131–39, especially 133). Recently Carr (*JTS* 24 [1973] 492–500) has produced additional evidence to that of Francis for this meaning of ἐμβατεύω ("enter") in mystical asceticism. He claims that Colossians 2:18 is concerned with visions and with the encountering of the divine in real religious experience. It is the heavenly sanctuary where the worship conducted by the angels (Carr also understands θρησκείᾳ τῶν ἀγγέλων as a subjective genitive) occurs and this appears in the mind of the worshiper. So it was not the mystery language or practice which was penetrating the church at Colossae. Rather, it was a similar problem to what was encountered elsewhere: "claims to spiritual superiority validated by claims to higher religious experience through mystical-ascetical piety" (Carr, *JTS* 24 [1973] 500; cf. Bandstra, *Dimensions,* 329–32).

Although we may agree with Schweizer (124) that we know too little about the specific background at Colossae to be certain as to the precise meaning of this phrase, we consider a stronger case has been made for the third view *(c).* Dibelius' approach *(b)* has serious weaknesses (he builds too much on ἐμβατεύω as a technical expression), while the first view *(a)* though possible is not as cogent as the approach of Francis and others (note the Introduction).

Whatever the precise spiritual experiences the proponents claimed to have passed through, their exploitation of these experiences to their own advantage stands in contrast to Paul's apologetic account of the unusual things that happened to him when he "was caught up to Paradise. He heard inexpressible things, things that man is not permitted to tell" (2 Cor 12:4, NIV; cf. Bruce, 250).

εἰκῇ φυσιούμενος ὑπὸ τοῦ νοὸς τῆς σαρκὸς αὐτοῦ. If in the earlier phrases Paul has quoted from the catchwords of the philosophy, then with these words he presents the first of two devastating criticisms: "his unspiritual mind puffs him up with idle notions" (NIV). Being puffed up (φυσιόω in the passive means to "become puffed up," "become conceited," BAG, 869) was a standing and characteristic danger of the Corinthians (all the NT references to the word, apart from Col 2:18, occur in the Corinthian correspondence: 1 Cor 4:6, 18, 19; 5:2; 8:1; 13:4; 2 Cor 12:20). It took various forms: boasting against Paul, moral indifference (5:2) and exalting oneself above another (4:6). The apostle states that "knowledge puffs up" (8:1) and its proponents are conceited. At Colossae whoever laid claims to these exalted and heavenly experiences was puffed up. The cause of this conceit was "the mind of his flesh" (ὑπὸ τοῦ νοὸς τῆς σαρκὸς αὐτοῦ), an unusual expression (though cf. Rom 8:7, "the mind [φρόνημα] that is set on the flesh") that means the attitude and outlook which are characteristic of the old nature, dominated by the flesh. The νοῦς (cf. Behm, *TDNT* 4, 950–60) is that aspect of a man's mentality which when enlightened can distinguish between good and evil, as well as recognize and respond to the claims of God (Rom 7:21–25; 12:2). It may be controlled by the old nature as long as one goes on living κατὰ σάρκα, "according to the flesh." Perhaps the proponents boasted (εἰκῇ means "without cause") they were directed by the mind (ὑπὸ τοῦ νοός); Paul's answer is, yes. But a mind of the flesh! (τῆς σαρκός is a possessive or characterizing genitive). Bornkamm (*Conflict*, 140; cf. Martin, *NCB*, 92) suggested they were boasting of their acquaintance with divine "fullness" and being full of knowledge (γνῶσις), when all they are full of is their own pride!

19. καὶ οὐ κρατῶν τὴν κεφαλήν. "And not holding fast to the head." The second criticism is even more devastating: the self-inflation and pride in these private religious experiences come from not maintaining contact with Christ, the head. κρατέω—a verb employed in a variety of ways (sometimes of arresting [Matt 14:3; 21:46] or of seizing a person forcibly [Matt 12:11; 18:28])—is used here of "holding fast to someone" and so remaining closely united to him (cf. Mark 7:3; 2 Thess 2:15; Rev 2:13, 14, 15; note BAG, 448; Michaelis, *TDNT* 3, 910–12; the antithesis is ἀφίημι, to "let go," cf. LXX Song of Sol 3:4, "I held fast [ἐκράτησα] to him and would not let him go" [οὐκ ἀφήσω]). The false teacher's behavior shows he is not keeping a close hold of Christ (Best, *Body*, 126); in fact, it is evidence of his rejecting the head (the negative οὐ, instead of μή, with the participle is equivalent to an affirmative sentence meaning "he is letting go of, or rejecting," Zerwick, *Greek*, 148; cf. Dibelius-Greeven, 36, BDF, para. 430[3]). No doubt those who sought to make inroads into the community presupposed that they were Christians (Percy, *Probleme*, 142). Indeed, how else could they have attempted to make these inroads? But they face the most serious of condemnations: they are severing themselves from the very one who is the source of life and unity.

The "head-body" relationship is employed again in this passage (cf. 1:18). Since he is Lord over all, Christ is described at chapter 2:10 as "head of every power and principality" (though these powers are not said to be part of his body). Here at chapter 2:19 the two metaphors have to do with his headship over the church. Dibelius-Greeven (36) argued along similar lines in their exposition of chapters 1:18 and 2:10, that "body" denoted the cosmos here and "head" the rule over every principality and power. The false teachers hold to the members of the cosmos-body (i.e. to the principalities and powers) instead of Christ as the head. But this line of interpretation introduces un-

Pauline elements into the argument (cf. Percy, *Probleme,* 382–84; Bruce, 251; cf. Robinson, *Body,* 66) and the view is rejected as being inadequate (σῶμα does not refer to the cosmos in Pauline thought: cf. Merklein, *Amt,* 29, 30, and Bedale, *JTS* 5 [1954] 214).

κεφαλὴν ἐξ οὗ πᾶν τὸ σῶμα κτλ. "The head from whom the whole body . . . ." Although he is not explicitly named it is clear that Christ is that head (cf. E. D. Roels, *God's Mission. The Epistle to the Ephesians in Mission Perspective* [Franeker: Wever, 1962] 107). As such he (the concentration on Christ is so strong in the text that the masculine relative pronoun "from whom," ἐξ οὗ, is used although the word "head," κεφαλή, in Greek is feminine gender; noted by many commentators including Schweizer, 125) is both the source (ἐκ, "from," signifies source, while διά, "through," denotes the channels through which the nourishment, etc., come) of the sustenance by which the body lives as well as the source of unity through which it becomes an organic whole (Best, *Body,*127). There is no explicit mention of direction by the head. It might be argued, however, that headship implies this. Further, the suggestion in the immediate context is that each part of the body will function properly only as it is under the control of the head. If it acts independently the consequences can be very serious. The false teachers are in great peril and each member of the congregation should heed the apostle's warning.

The human body provides the analogy for Paul's description, and the image used here corresponds to ancient physiology (note the evidence from ancient medical writings in Lightfoot, 196–98): ἁφαί are the "joints" (lit. the "points of contact," akin to ἅπτομαι, "touch") while σύνδεσμοι are the "ligaments" (cf. BAG, 785; Fitzer, *TDNT* 7, 856–59) which provide nourishment (ἐπιχορηγέω, though understood by Robinson [*Ephesians,* 186, 187] with reference to Eph 4:16, as "furnished," or "equipped," is better taken as "provided," "supplied" [Lightfoot, 198, and note Moule's discussion, 107]; on this rendering, however, the physiology is not to be pressed as though the joints and ligaments were strictly the channels of supply) and "unite" the members of the body (on the various meanings of συμβιβάζω, here used figuratively meaning "unite," "knit together," see 2:2). With his illustration about the ligaments, nerves or muscles as we would call them, Paul indicates that the body is constantly supplied (note the *present* participles) with energy and nourishment by the head, and is held together as a unity by that head alone (at Eph 4:16 the emphasis is upon the vital cohesion and union of the parts with each other, here it focuses on the continuous dependence on the head). The physiological language is metaphorical; the joints and ligaments are not to be understood with Masson (198), commenting on Ephesians 4:1–16 of ministers, who are distinct from ordinary church members, or with Schnackenburg of office bearers ("Christus, Geist und Gemeinde [Eph 4:1–16]," *Christ and Spirit in the New Testament. Studies in honour of Charles Francis Digby Moule,* ed. B. Lindars and S. S. Smalley [Cambridge: University Press, 1973] 290; cf. Merklein, *Amt,* 114, 115; so rightly Schweizer, 126).

πᾶν τὸ σῶμα . . . αὔξει τὴν αὔξησιν τοῦ θεοῦ. The whole body (πᾶν τό shows that no member is to be excluded) which is totally dependent on the head to nourish and unify it is said (lit.) to "increase with the increase of God." αὐξάνω (and αὔξω), meaning to "cause to grow," in later Greek came to be used intransitively of to "grow," "increase" (John 3:30; Acts 6:7; Eph 4:15; BDF, paras. 101, 309[2]; BAG, 121). The expression "the growth of God" (τὴν αὔξησιν τοῦ θεοῦ) is probably, with many recent exegetes, to be understood as an accusative of content (so BDF, para. 153[1], F.-J. Steinmetz, *Protologische Heils-Zuversicht. Die Strukturen des soteriologischen und christologischen Denkens im Kolosser- und Epheserbrief.* [FTS 2; Frankfurt: Knecht, 1969] 128; Lohse, 122; cf. Matt 2:10; Eph 2:4). But what does the genitive "of God" (τοῦ θεοῦ) mean? And how are we to understand the nature of the growth: in size or in perfection? Because Christ, the head, is the source (ἐξ οὗ) of the increase then the words "of God" must describe its nature, i.e. it is a divine type of growth. So the increase comes from Christ and its quality is divine (Best, *Body,* 128). This suggests that its growth is in terms of perfection. But does this growth include a numerical increase, both the inward and the outward (as Steinmetz, *Heils-Zuversicht,* 128, argues; Merklein, *Amt,* 94, refers to it as "intensive-ethical" and "extensive")? Schweizer, with explicit reference to this passage, considers that mission as a salvation historical phenomenon derives from the notion of the growth of the body. In other words, growth for him must include numerical increase (*Neotestamentica,* 301, cf. 327, 328; Merklein, *Amt,* 94, endorses this pointing out that such a growth is a particular interest of Colossians, cf. 1:6, 10, where the same verb "grow," αὐξάνω, is found, and especially 1:26, 27). However, without wishing to deny the importance of the worldwide spread of the gospel (1:6) or the significance of making the mystery known to Gentiles (note especially 1:24–29), the immediate context has nothing to do with numerical increase; it is concerned with growth in perfection (at 1:6 the increase is numerical, while at 1:10 it is a growth in perfection: the mere mention of the term "increase" does not mean that both notions are necessarily included). Paul here is drawing a contrast between the divine growth of the whole body (πᾶν τὸ σῶμα) and the individual growth of the Colossian false teachers (Best, *Body,* 128). In fact, theirs is not a growth at all; it is a vain puffing up by their fleshly minds (v 18). The believer cannot grow to perfection alone. The "growth of God" only occurs as the "ultimate result" of the body's union with the head; the nourishment and unity which come through the joints and ligaments "are only intermediate processes" (Best, *Body,* 128, following Lightfoot, 198).

The application to the Colossian situation is plain: the false teacher who does not depend on the head has no contact with the source of life and nourishment, and does not belong to the body. The community must realize that they must remain in living union with Christ as the head. Let them not be drawn off or enticed away by the appeal of the false teachers to their heavenly experiences.

20. Paul had already told his readers that they were united with Christ in his death (v 11). He now takes this up and applies it with special reference to their circumstances.

εἰ ἀπεθάνετε σὺν Χριστῷ ἀπὸ τῶν στοιχείων τοῦ κόσμου. Because the Colossians have died with Christ on the cross (the εἰ does not express doubt, but means "if, as is the case," "since"; note 3:3 and cf. BDF, para. 372), then that death severed the bond which bound them to the "elemental spirits of the world." Paul normally uses the dative case after the verb "die" (ἀποθνήσκω) of the person or thing from which one is separated by death (e.g. Gal 2:19, he died to the law [νόμῳ], while at Rom 6:2, he speaks of having died to sin [τῇ ἁμαρτίᾳ; cf. BAG, 91]). Here the preposition translated "to" really means "from," that is, "out of the control of" (BDF, para. 211, consider ἀπό is used here for a genitive of separation with the added thought of alienation). Robinson (*Body*, 43) has caught the sense well with his rendering: "Ye died with Christ out from under the elements of the world." As death breaks the bond which binds a subject to his ruler so dying with Christ severs the bond that bound the Colossians to the slavery of the principalities and powers (on the meaning of τὰ στοιχεῖα τοῦ κόσμου see 129–132).

τί ὡς ζῶντες ἐν κόσμῳ δογματίζεσθε. The application is made by means of a rhetorical question and a rebuke (cf. Martin, *NCB*, 96): "How can you, as if you still lived in a worldly way, voluntarily place yourselves under the regulations?" κόσμος ("world," in the phrase ἐν κόσμῳ) is interpreted by exegetes in various ways, depending on their understanding of the "elements of the world" (τὰ στοιχεῖα τοῦ κόσμου). So Schweizer (126, 127) argues that the two expressions mean the same thing, while Bandstra (*Law*, 69) contends the reference is to "the world of mankind, the whole sphere of human activity." On the view that the "elements" denote personal forces such as the principalities and powers it is best to take the phrase as describing the situation in which the world dominates a person's existence, the old way of life (Caird, 200, renders the phrase by "worldly").

δογματίζω means to "represent and affirm an opinion or tenet," "establish or publish a decree," "proclaim an edict" (Kittel, *TDNT* 2, 231; cf. LSJ, 441, and Lohse, 123). It is akin to δόγμα ("decree," "ordinance") used in the plural at chapter 2:14 of the regulations with their penalty clauses associated with the signed acknowledgment of our indebtedness before God. Here the restrictive regulations have particular reference to ordinances of taste and touch (v 21 lists three of them), though we should not suppose that the verb is specifically limited to these. The passive voice of the verb carries the notion of "allowing oneself to be . . ." (some older grammarians took the verb as a middle voice with much the same significance, so Robertson, *Grammar*, 807, "probably direct middle"; Abbott, 272, cf. Turner, *Syntax*, 57), so that a literal rendering is "let yourself be regulated" (BDF, para. 314; cf. 1 Cor 6:7). The point is that the Colossians were in danger of falling victim to the false teaching and of voluntarily placing themselves under the regulations imposed by these powers (Hooker, *Christ*, 317, considers that the admonition does not mean the Colossian Christians have already submitted to the regulations). This was tantamount to reverting to the slavery previously experienced in their pagan past (cf. Gal 4:3, 8, 9).

21. *μὴ ἅψῃ μηδὲ γεύσῃ μηδὲ θίγῃς.* "Do not handle! Do not taste! Do not even touch!" Paul quotes three examples of the sorts of regulations imposed by the principalities and powers. They are all negative and admit of no exceptions (note the OT apodictic laws). It has been suggested that, because of the form in which the regulations are cited here, Paul is ridiculing his opponents (so Lohse, 123, who cites Chrysostom with approval: "Mark how he makes sport of them, *handle not, touch not, taste not,* as though they were keeping themselves clear of some great matters") attributing to them a total withdrawal from all worldly contacts (Caird, 200).

The three verbs appear to deal with regulations concerning food and drink (cf. v 16). However, the first and last words are virtually synonymous (cf. LXX Exod 19:12) and it is difficult to pinpoint any distinction between them. Bauer (BAG, 102, 103) suggested as a possibility that ἅπτομαι could be translated to "eat something" (like our "touch food"). Accordingly, the three prohibitions would form an anticlimax: "Do not eat, do not taste, do not touch!" But ἅπτομαι has a more general meaning than "eat" and this suggestion is unlikely. On the basis of it being used with a sexual connotation (cf. 1 Cor 7:1, "It is good for a man not to touch a woman," γυναικὸς μὴ ἅπτεσθαι), R. Leaney proposed that the false teachers forbade sexual relations ("Colossians ii. 21–23. [The use of πρός]," *ExpTim* 64 [1952–53] 92). But this is unlikely for the following reasons: first, nowhere else in this letter is there the slightest hint of a prohibition of sexual relations (the false teachers of 1 Timothy 4:3 forbade marriage but there γαμέω, "marry," is used). Second, when ἅπτομαι is employed with this connotation the object of the verb makes plain that this is meant (cf. Gen 20:4, 6; Prov 6:29; 1 Cor 7:1). The verb by itself can apply to a wide range of areas. Third, the immediately following words (v 22, "These are all destined to perish with use") suggest material objects such as food and drink are in view: verse 22*a* does not apply if sexual relations are meant.

If as Lightfoot (201) and others have suggested ἅπτομαι can have a somewhat stronger connotation than the rather colorless word θιγγάνω and means to "take hold of" something with a view to possessing it (Lohse, 123) then the threefold prohibition could refer to defilement incurred through the sense of touch, though in different degrees: "Handle not, nor yet taste, nor even touch."

22. Several criticisms of the false teachers' approach are set forth by the apostle: (1) ἅ ἐστιν πάντα εἰς φθορὰν τῇ ἀποχρήσει. The things covered by the taboos are perishable objects of the material world, destined to pass away when used (the expression ἐστιν εἰς denotes appointment = "is destined for"; cf. Acts 8:20; 2 Pet 2:12: so Oepke, *TDNT* 2, 428). Paul is probably thinking especially, but not exclusively, of food (cf. Harder, *TDNT* 9, 102). φθορά refers to the "physical dissolution" (Abbott, 274) of such things in their natural use (ἀπόχρησις, "consuming," "using up," so BAG, 102; although the term can have, on occasion, the connotation "abuse," this does not fit the present context where the reference is to physical objects being used in a proper and ordinary manner). If these objects are transient and perishable then the proponents of the "philosophy" lack a true sense of proportion by making them issues central to their teaching. Matters of food and drink are of no consequence as far as godliness is concerned (Rom 14:17; 1 Cor 6:13)—particularly when a test case is made of their abstinence or enjoyment (Martin, *Lord,* 96; for Paul overindulgence that leads to gluttony and drunkenness is another question, 1 Cor 5:9; Eph 5:18, as is food offered to idols, 1 Cor 8). (See R. J. Austgen, *Natural Motivation in the Pauline Epistles.* 2nd ed. [Notre Dame: University Press, 1969] especially chapter v, "Natural Motivation and Dietary Practices," 98–117.) There may be the further point, as Lohse, 124, has suggested, that because of their false legalism the proponents failed to recognize God's good gifts and his purpose of giving them, namely, that all without exception (πάντα) should be consumed through proper use.

(2) κατὰ τὰ ἐντάλματα καὶ διδασκαλίας τῶν ἀνθρώπων. Paul's second indictment is that these taboos are merely human inventions: they are "according to the regulations and doctrines of men." Behind the phrase lies the wording of Isaiah 29:13 (LXX) which reads: "But in vain do they worship me teaching the commandments and doctrines of men" (ἐντάλματα ἀνθρώπων καὶ διδασκαλίας). In the original context the prophet complains that Israel's religion is not a personal knowledge of God but a set of conventional rules learned by rote. The text was cited by Jesus in the Gospels (Mark 7:7; cf. Matt 15:9) in his dispute with the Pharisees and scribes about the "tradition of men" (ἡ παράδοσις τῶν ἀνθρώπων), by which the Jews had nullified the word of God. That tradition is likened to the "commandments and doctrines of men," an interesting juxtaposition for in Colossians 2 the same two expressions are employed: verse 8, "the tradition of men" (ἡ παράδοσις τῶν ἀνθρώπων), and this text. The second reference may be regarded as a "concretizing" of the earlier phrase, i.e. the tradition of men finds concrete expression in man-made commandments and teachings.

ἐντάλματα ("commandments") occurs only three times in the NT (Matt 15:9; Mark 7:7; Col 2:22), each of which is an echo of the Isaiah text (29:13). In the Colossians reference it is closely linked with διδασκαλίαι ("teachings," by means of the one definite article). The plural in the LXX is significant since it suggests a multiplicity of human teachings that lay no claim to absoluteness but stand over against the revelation of the will of God (cf. Rengstorf, *TDNT* 2, 161). Paul brings out the same point here about the ordinances being merely human with his emphasis on the last part of the phrase, τῶν ἀνθρώπων: "You died *with Christ* and yet receive orders *from men!*" These taboos of human origin frustrate the pure teaching of God with its liberating message.

23. (3) Paul continues his attack on the false teaching. The verse is not entirely clear as to its structure and meaning for it is not always certain when the apostle is quoting from catchwords of the opponents or making his own comments (cf. Moule, 108–10, Masson, 137, and Schweizer, 128). Some exegetes, assuming that the text was corrupted very early, sought to reconstruct it by means of conjectural emendations and additions (Nestle wanted to begin a new sentence with "severity" [ἀφειδία in the nominative case], cf. von Dobschütz; B. G. Hall, "Colossians II. 23," *ExpTim* 36 (1924–25) 285, considers that "forgetting" was original, while others would add a line; for details see Lohse, 125, n.88). But none of these can claim any manuscript support since the manuscript tradition has retained the "obscurities" intact! In our estimation the most satisfactory explanation of the ambiguities is that presented by Reicke (*ST* 6 [1952] 39–53; cf. Bengel 2,466) and supplemented with additional arguments by Hollenbach (*NTS* 25 [1978–79] 254–61). The punctuation and rendering are as follows:

ἅτινά ἐστιν—λόγον μὲν ἔχοντα σοφίας ἐν ἐθελοθρησκίᾳ καὶ ταπεινοφροσύνῃ καὶ ἀφειδίᾳ σώματος, οὐκ ἐν τιμῇ τινι—πρὸς πλησμονὴν τῆς σαρκός.

"Which things lead—though having a reputation for wisdom in the spheres of voluntary worship, humility and severe treatment of the body, without any value whatsoever—to the gratification of the flesh."

On this interpretation ἐστιν, (translated "are" because of the plural subject *ἅτινα*, "which things") is not joined with *ἔχοντα* ("having") to form a periphrastic present tense, but rather stands alone as the predicate of the main clause, which is *ἅτινά ἐστιν . . . πρὸς πλησμονὴν τῆς σαρκός* ("which things [actually] lead to the gratification of the flesh"). The conjunction *μέν* ("though") appears as the second word in its clause (*λόγον μὲν ἔχοντα κτλ.* "though having a reputation . . ."), its normal position in the Pauline epistles and marks a subordinate clause as being concessive in relation to its main clause. It should, therefore, be translated as "though" (cf. Rom 7:25*b;* 8:10). Parallels to the construction *ἐστιν πρός* signifying "lead to" are to be found at John 11:4, "This disease will not lead to (*οὐκ ἐστιν πρός*) death," and at 1 Corinthians 14:26, "May everything be done in such a way that it may lead to edification (*πρὸς οἰκοδομὴ γινέσθω*)."

(Hollenbach, *NTS* 25 [1978–79] 255, has demonstrated in detail that "virtually every occurrence of *μέν*, regardless of its function, is immediately after the first word of the grammatical unit to which the *μέν* pertains"; the exceptions he adequately explains: *μέν*, "on the one hand," "though," would normally be followed by the correlative *δέ*, "on the other hand": Lightfoot, 203, has pointed out that such suppressions were common enough in classical writers, e.g., Plato, and he claims that here an exact correlative is found in a new form *οὐκ ἐν τιμῇ τινι*, "without any honor," cf. Moule, 108, BDF, para. 477[2], [3], Robertson, *Grammar*, 1152, and Lohse, 126. Reicke, *ST* 6 [1952] 43, argued it was an example of *μέν*, *solitarium*, not an elliptical correlative, which appears absolutely like *μήν*, "indeed," "and yet," cf. Lähnemann, *Kolosserbrief*, 147. It seems best, however, to consider that the *δέ* would normally have occurred after the first word of the clause to which the concessive clause is subordinate, i.e. after *ἅτινα*, "which things"; but since the concessive clause is embedded within the main clause by the time the *μέν* was written the proper place to insert *δέ* was already past—hence the omission, so Hollenbach, *NTS* 25 [1978–79] 260.)

ἅτινα ("which things," cf. Gal 4:24; 5:19; Phil 3:7), a relative of quality, points back not so much to "the commandments and teachings" (*τὰ ἐντάλματα καὶ διδασκαλίας*, v 22) as Masson (137) supposed, but to the precepts or regulations included under *δογματίζεσθε* ("you let yourselves be regulated"), of which verse 21 contains illustrations (Williams, 115): "Handle not, don't taste, don't even touch!" Verse 22 with its relative *ἅ* ("which") makes an objective statement about the regulations, whereas this remark (*ἅτινα*, "which sort of things") characterizes and condemns not only the particular precepts of verse 21 but also others falling within the same category (Lightfoot, 203).

λόγον μὲν ἔχοντα σοφίας. Prohibitions of this kind carry a reputation for wisdom. *λόγον ἔχω* means to "have the reputation of," "be considered as" (on other connotations see Lightfoot, 203, 204), with *λόγος* signifying "reputation," "credit" (LSJ, 1059). It is employed to denote that which has no substance to it and stands in contrast to *ἀλήθεια*, "truth" (it is synonymous with *μῦθος*, "rumor," "fable," cf. Stählin, *TDNT* 4, 770; Chrysostom aptly remarked: "neither the power, nor the truth"). Even though the regulations have the reputation for wisdom they lack the reality. This wisdom is only a facade (note the play on *φιλοσοφία*, "philosophy," 2:8 and *σοφία*, "wisdom"); true wisdom is to be found in Christ alone (2:3; cf. 1:9, 28; 3:16) for he is the wisdom of God (1:15–20). Zeilinger (*Der Erstgeborene,* 128, 129) has recently contended that in the phrase, "having the appearance of wisdom," there is a deliberate polemic on the part of the author against a Jewish view (cf. Bar 4:1–4) which regarded the preexistent Torah (= Wisdom, *σοφία*) as the ground of all things; humility, reverencing of angels and the practice of ascetic severity leads ultimately to the possession of wisdom, the resurrection of the dead and with them the possession of life in the coming age. Against this the author argues that salvation from Christ is already objectively present—in Christ the gift of the eschaton has already been given.

ἐν ἐθελοθρησκίᾳ καὶ ταπεινοφροσύνῃ καὶ ἀφειδίᾳ σώματος. The false teachers' reputation for wisdom was acquired "in the sphere of (*ἐν*, so Williams, 116, Schweizer, 128; Meyer, 410, regards the preposition as instrumental) voluntary worship, humility and severe treatment of the body." *ἐθελοθρησκία*, a term which does not occur in Greek before Paul, is rendered by the RSV as "rigor of devotion" (BAG, 218, "self-made religion," it cannot, however, be rendered in this way if Paul, as we contend, is actually quoting a catchword of the philosophy). At least three areas of meaning may be in view for compounds formed with *ἐθελο-*(BDF, para. 118[2], who regard this as modelled after *φιλο-*, consider the first element governs the second, *θρησκεία*): *(a)* voluntariness, e.g. "voluntary servitude" (*ἐθελοδουλεία*; MM, 181, think *ἐθελοθρησκία* is a Pauline coinage on the analogy of this word); *(b)* interest, including delight or endeavor, e.g. "aiming at fashion" (*ἐθελάστειος*); and *(c)* pretense, as in "would-be philosopher" (*ἐθελοφιλόσοφος*, so Francis, *Conflict,* 181). In all cases the separate nuances point to the action of the will in different circumstances (hence BDF's point about the first element of the compound governing the second, para. 118[2]). If this term, along with the other two, was used by Paul's opponents, then it presumably meant that they had freely chosen the cult in which they participated. It corresponds to *θρησκεία τῶν ἀγγέλων* of verse 18 which we have rendered the "worship which the angels perform" (see above 142, 143). Here the term *ἐθελοθρησκία* does not specify that it is worship performed by men (as Lohse, 119, and Martin, *NCB,* 94, suggested in their criticism of Francis, *Conflict,* 176–81), only that it is a freely chosen worship. If Paul did not coin the word but took it over from the "philosophy" then it is "a sarcastic borrowing from his opponents' language" (W. L. Knox, *St Paul and the Church of the Gentiles* [Cambridge: University Press, 1939, 171] cited by Martin, *NCB,* 98). The apostle regards this worship as freely chosen but wrong!

ταπεινοφροσύνῃ. See above on verse 18 (142) where it is suggested that the term has to do with fasting and other bodily rigors. Ascetic practices such as these were a kind of "humility technique" and regarded as effective for receiving visions of the heavenly mysteries. The false teachers' reputation for wisdom was acquired in this sphere also.

ἀφειδίᾳ σώματος. The advocates of the "philosophy" described their way of life as "severe (lit. "unsparing," akin to *φείδομαι*) treatment of the body" (BAG, 124), an expression that denotes a rigorous and austere way of life particularly with reference to the ascetic activity required by the regulations (cf. 1 Tim 4:3, "who forbid marriage and enjoin abstinence from foods"). By means of fasting and abstinence they thought to prepare themselves for divine fullness and the reception of visions. Yet this too was nothing more than the mere appearance of wisdom (λόγον . . . σοφίας).

οὐκ ἐν τιμῇ τινι. "Without any value whatsoever." On the basis of the above-mentioned explanation this clause is regarded as subordinate to the preceding words and is Paul's comment. Whether the exponents of the "philosophy" employed the word τιμή ("honor," "value") as a slogan or not, the apostle's assertion that the practice of these false teachers, though having a reputation for wisdom in the sphere of voluntary worship, humility and severe treatment of the body, is of no value whatsoever.

Although many commentators link the words οὐκ ἐν τιμῇ τινι, "without any value whatsoever," with what immediately follows πρὸς πλησμονὴν τῆς σαρκός, "for the satisfaction of the flesh," as comprising one clause, this involves several difficulties: the position of οὐκ, "not," is irregular and we would have expected it to precede ἐστιν, "is"; the meaning of the whole clause, and especially τιμή, is obscure; there is no precedent for ἐν τιμῇ, "with honor," as a complement of ἐστιν, "is"; nor of τιμή ("honor") occurring with a following πρός ("for"); and none of the attested meanings of τιμή seems to fit the context. Note the attempts of Lightfoot, 204–206, Moule, 108–110, and Lohse, 126, 127, and see Hollenbach's critique, *NTS* 25 (1978–79) 258, 259.

ἅτινά ἐστιν . . . πρὸς πλησμονὴν τῆς σαρκός. The following are the most significant attempts to explain the meaning of this clause. Our preference is for the third suggestion:

(1) Many of the early fathers regarded the latter phrase as a further description of the Colossians' ascetic practices. They equated σάρξ ("flesh") with σῶμα ("body"), took it in a positive sense and understood the phrase to mean "legitimate bodily satisfaction." On this ancient interpretation the false teachers do not indulge the body, that is, they do not show it the respect given by God. They deprive it rather than satisfy it (cf. Delling's presentation, *TDNT* 6, 133). However, several difficulties with this interpretation ought to be noted: *(a)* the links with the phrase "severe treatment of the body" (ἀφειδία σώματος) are awkward (so Moule, 109); *(b)* πλησμονή can hardly be rendered "reasonable wants" or "legitimate bodily satisfaction" in the light of σάρξ ("flesh," cf. v 18) which appears to stand in contrast to σῶμα ("body") in the preceding clause and ought to be understood in Paul's usual sense of "lower nature," the old Adam-nature in its rebellion against God (Bruce, 256, and BAG, 673). *(c)* On this ancient view the apostle's criticism is much too soft. He is not timidly remarking that the regulations fail because they do not hold the body in sufficient honor. Rather, this legalistic way of life leads only "to the satisfaction of the flesh."

(2) Lightfoot (204–206, cf. Moule, 108–110), who interpreted the final phrase in conjunction with the preceding words (see above), rendered the Greek of the clause as "yet not really of any value to remedy indulgence of the flesh." Apart from the difficulties already mentioned about this conjunction of phrases, the rendering of πρός as "against," in the sense of combating, is unusual and does not read as easily as the following view.

(3) The Colossian proponents' legalistic way of life leads only to the satisfaction of the flesh. πλησμονή ("satisfaction," "gratification," BAG, 673, Delling, *TDNT* 6, 131–34), which appears only here in the NT, occurred some twenty-

eight times in the LXX. It was frequently used in a good sense to denote "satisfaction," especially with food and drink, and other types of enjoyment (of satisfaction by nourishment: Exod 16:3, 8; Lev 25:19; 26:5; Ps 77:25; Hag 1:6; of the gifts of God which satisfy: Deut 33:23); but the term also occurred in a bad sense to denote "excess" or "satiety" which led to sin and apostasy from the Lord (Ezek 39:19; Hos 13:6). Probably behind Paul's use of πλησμονή there is a play on the word "fullness." The false teachers were concerned about "fullness of life." The aim and goal (πρός) of all their efforts—the observance of the strict regulations, the reverence and respect paid to the principalities and powers—was satisfaction. But all that was satisfied was "the flesh" (τῆς σαρκός). Their energetic religious endeavors could not hold the flesh in check. Quite the reverse. These man-made regulations actually pandered to the flesh.

Explanation

In a paragraph that is polemical in style and filled with allusions to the teaching and catch-words of the philosophy Paul sets out what is, in effect, a charter of Christian freedom. False notions about "fullness," and the person and work of Christ, which are corrected in Paul's positive affirmations of chapter 2:8–15, have as their corollary these strange aberrations on the practical side. The apostle's criticisms are devastating as he trains his guns first on the practices and the false notions lying behind them, then on the false teachers themselves.

The Colossians ought not to be taken to task by the adherents of the "philosophy" over matters of food, drink or holy days. Their stringent regulations of an ascetic nature which follow from the demand for "severe treatment of the body" (v 23) are a shadow of the things that were to come. Christ and his new order are the perfect reality to which these earlier ordinances pointed forward. The rigorous prescriptions of the false teachers have no binding force. The reality has already come and the things of the shadow no longer constitute a norm for judgment.

In writing to Corinth and Rome, where Christians had scruples about food and drink as well as the observance of holy days, Paul introduces the principle of Christian liberty, namely, "the strong" should go out of their way to avoid offending the tender consciences of "the weak" or scrupulous (Rom 14:1–15:13; 1 Cor 8–10). This, however, was not the issue at Colossae: the scrupulous were threatening to impose their rigid principles on the rest of the congregation. Christian liberty needed to be asserted in the light of false attempts to undermine it.

Further, if the Colossians were to fall victims to the false teaching and voluntarily placed themselves under rules and regulations, imposed by the principalities and powers, such as "Do not handle! Do not taste! Do not even touch!" this would be to go back into slavery again, a servitude to the very principalities of the universe from which they had been freed when they died with Christ in his death. The matters covered by the taboos were perishable objects of the material world, destined to pass away when used. These taboos were merely human inventions, "the commandments and doctrines of men," which frustrated the pure teaching of God with its liberating message. Although the prohibitions (of which v 21 contains illustrations) carry a reputation for wisdom in the spheres of voluntary worship, humility and severe treatment of the body, they were without any value whatsoever.

Concerning the false teachers the apostle's words are just as severe. Those who laid claim to exalted heavenly experiences or visions as a prelude to fresh divine revelations were puffed up. They may have claimed that they were directed by the mind; but it was a mind of flesh. Theirs was the attitude and outlook which were characteristic of the old nature, dominated by the flesh. If they boasted of their acquaintance with divine "fullness" and knowledge, then all they were full of was their own pride! Worst of all those who took the Christians at Colossae to task, using their own private religious experiences as the basis of their authority, were in fact rejecting Christ as their head, the one who is the source of life and nourishment by which his body lives, and the source of unity through which it becomes an organic whole. The advocates of the false teaching face the most serious of condemnations: they are severed from the very one who is the source of life and unity. The application to the Colossians is plain: let them not be drawn off or enticed away by the appeal of the false teaching.

Seek the Things Above (3:1–4)

Bibliography

Dupont, J. ΣΥΝ ΧΡΙΣΤΩΙ. *L'union avec le Christ suivant saint Paul.* Paris: Desclée de Brouwer, 1952, 39–47. **Grässer, E.** *ZTK* 64 (1967) 139–68. **Lincoln, A. T.** *The Heavenly Dimension. Studies in the Role of Heaven in Paul's Thought with Special Reference to His Eschatology.* University of Cambridge: Unpublished Ph.D. thesis, 1977, 198–217. **Merk, O.** *Handeln aus Glauben. Die Motivierungen der paulinischen Ethik.* Marburger Theologische Studien 5. Marburg: Elwert, 1968, 201–204. **Moule, C. F. D.** " 'The New Life' in Colossians 3:1–17." *RevExp* 70 (1973) 481–93. **Schnackenburg, R.** *Baptism,* 67–73. **Schrage, W.** *Die konkreten Einzelgebote in der paulinischen Paränese.* Gütersloh: Mohn, 1961. **Wulf, F.** " 'Suchet, was droben ist, wo Christus ist, sitzend zur Rechten Gottes!' (Kol 3, 1)." *GuL* 41 (1968) 161–64, **Zeilinger, F.** *Der Erstgeborene,* 60–63, 147–51.

Translation

[1] *Since then you were raised with Christ, seek the things above, where Christ is, seated at God's right hand.* [2] *Set your minds on the things above, not on earthly things.* [3] *For you died, and your life is hidden with Christ in God.* [4] *When Christ, who is our*[a] *life, is revealed, then you also will be revealed with him in glory.*

Notes

[a] Throughout Colossians there is some doubt about the correct reading between the first and second person plurals (cf. 1:7; 2:13 and this text). Here it is possible that *ἡμῶν* ("our"), which is supported by B D^{c} H K 326 syr^{p,h} cop^{sa} etc., was altered by scribes to *ὑμῶν* so as to bring it into line with the second person pronouns throughout verses 1–4. However, the reading *ὑμῶν* ("your") has considerably stronger manuscript support, including P^{46} and good representatives of both the Alexandrian and Western text types (ℵ C D* F G P 31 81 it vg cop^{bo} etc.; cf. Metzger, *Textual Commentary,* 624). Accordingly, if *ὑμῶν* ("your") was the original reading the change to *ἡμῶν* ("our") may have been due to faulty hearing or because the copyist wished to maintain the point that Christ is the life of Christians generally and not simply of those at Colossae. On balance it seems more likely that the reading "our life" (*ἡ ζωὴ ἡμῶν*) was the original text and was altered very early to conform to the second person style of this section of the letter.

Form/Structure/Setting

The short section of four verses commencing with the words *εἰ οὖν συνηγέρθητε τῷ Χριστῷ* ("since therefore you were raised with Christ") serves as an important transition piece in the letter (cf. Grässer, *ZTK* 64 [1967] 146, Lähnemann, *Kolosserbrief,* 30, 31, Zeilinger, *Der Erstgeborene,* 60–62, Schweizer, 130, 131). On the one hand, it rounds off what has been said previously serving as the conclusion to the author's polemic against the "philosophy" of the false teachers (2:8–23) and presenting the true alternative to that teaching (Zeilinger, *Der Erstgeborene,* 61). On the other hand, it marks a new beginning spelling out programmatically the inferences of the preceding for the walk of believers (Lähnemann, *Kolosserbrief*, 30). So the οὖν ("therefore," v 1, cf. vv 5, 12) indicates that what follows is connected with the train of thought previously developed (cf. the similar function of the conjunction at Rom 12:1; Eph 4:1). By means of the introductory συνηγέρθητε ("you were raised with," v 1) the apostle takes up the συνηγέρθητε ("you were raised with") and the συνεζωοποίησεν ("he made you alive together with") of chapter 2:12, 13, at the same time preparing for the summons to "put on the new man" of chapter 3:12. With the ἀπεθάνετε ("you died," v 3) Paul harks back to the ἀπεθάνετε σὺν Χριστῷ ἀπὸ τῶν στοιχείων τοῦ κόσμου ("you died with Christ from the elemental spirits of the universe," 2:20), and picks up ideas expressed in chapter 2:11–13 ("you were circumcised . . . in the circumcision of Christ . . . you were buried with him"), at the same time providing the basis for the imperative in the exhortatory section νεκρώσατε ("put to death," 3:5). The τὰ ἄνω ("the things above," vv 1, 2) which designates the transcendent heavenly realm at the center of which is the exalted Christ is perhaps a summary expression reiterating the points made in chapters 1 and 2 about the lordship of Christ (cf. 1:15–20; 2:6, 10), at the same time providing the point of orientation for the new man (3:10). τὰ ἐπὶ τῆς γῆς ("earthly things," v 2), whatever else it involves, clearly refers back to chapter 2:20–23 and designates the instruction and practice of the false teachers. At the same time the phrase is picked up and used generally to describe the catalog of vices (3:5). Like chapter 2:6, 7 these four verses stand at an important pivotal point in the letter.

Structurally the section may be divided into two parts: verses 1, 2, and verses 3, 4 (note Zeilinger's analysis, *Der Erstgeborene*, 60–62). Verse 1 contains three clauses, an introductory conditional clause εἰ οὖν συνηγέρθητε τῷ Χριστῷ ("if [= since] then you were raised with Christ"), a principal clause with its imperative τὰ ἄνω ζητεῖτε ("seek the things above") and an indirect question (in its present form it is an adverbial clause of place), οὗ ὁ Χριστός ἐστιν ἐν δεξίᾳ τοῦ θεοῦ καθήμενος ("where Christ is, seated at the right hand of God"). Verse 2 contains two imperatival clauses set in a short antithesis:

τὰ ἄνω φρονεῖτε
μὴ τὰ ἐπὶ τῆς γῆς
"Set your mind on things above
not on earthly things."

Unlike the earlier antitheses of chapter 2:8, 16 and 17, 18 and 19, where the negative statement or injunction occurs first and is followed by its positive contrasting assertion, here the positive exhortation is spelled out first.

The second part of the section, verses 3 and 4, is joined to the preceding (γάρ, "for," v 3) and provides the basis for the earlier exhortations. In verse 3 the orientation is toward the past, while in verse 4 it is directed to the future (note the verbs used: v 3, ἀπεθάνετε, "you died," and κέκρυπται, "has been hidden"; v. 4, φανερωθῇ, "is manifested," i.e. in the future, and φανερωθήσεσθε, "you will be manifested"). Yet the two verses may be paralleled as follows (cf. Zeilinger, *Der Erstgeborene*, 61, 62):

v. 3a ἀπεθάνετε γὰρ
b καὶ ἡ ζωὴ ὑμῶν
c κέκρυπται σὺν τῷ Χριστῷ
d ἐν τῷ θεῷ

v. 3a "For you died
b and your *life*
c is hidden *with* Christ
d *in* God."

4a ὅταν ὁ Χριστὸς φανερωθῇ
b —ἡ ζωὴ ἡμῶν—
c τότε καὶ ὑμεῖς σὺν αὐτῷ φανερωθήσεσθε
d ἐν δόξῃ

4a "When Christ appears
b —our *life*—
c then you also will appear *with* him
d *in* glory."

Comment

The major hortatory section of the letter begins with Paul's reminder that the Colossians not only died with Christ in his death (2:20, cf. vv 11, 12) but they were also raised from the dead with him (2:12, συνηγέρθητε). This short paragraph of four verses also concludes the "doctrinal" section of the epistle for it rounds out what has previously been said by the apostle against the "philosophy" of the false teachers (2:8–23) presenting the true alternative to that teaching: since you have shared in Christ's resurrection your aims, ambitions, in fact your whole outlook, are to be centered in him, in that place of highest honor where God has exalted him. Chapter 3:1–4, like the earlier short section chapter 2:6, 7, serves as an important bridge passage in the epistle, drawing together themes previously mentioned (2:11, 12, 13, 20), at the same time setting forth the theological foundation (the "indicative") for the exhortation (the "imperative") that follows.

Although Paul is not dealing directly with the catchwords of the false teachers it is possible that the positive expressions set forth in verses 1–4 show that the controversy is still in view (Grässer's contention, however, that all the formulations are polemically directed is difficult to prove, *ZTK* 64 [1967] 151; for a more cautious approach see Lähnemann, *Kolosserbrief,* 53).

1. εἰ οὖν συνηγέρθητε τῷ Χριστῷ. With the assertion, "since, therefore, you were raised with Christ," the apostle consciously sets forth the positive counterpart to chapter 2:20, "since you died with Christ" (the εἰ οὖν is resumptive of εἰ in 2:20, while the εἰ [= "since"] no more suggests doubt here than it did in the earlier reference, a point which incidentally is confirmed by 3:3 ἀπεθάνετε γάρ, "for you died," cf. Williams, 121, and Delling, *TDNT* 7, 686). He does not finish with the negative statement that Christians have been set free from the rule of the evil powers, but presses on to make the positive assertion about their being raised with Christ together with its implications. What follows then is connected with the train of thought previously developed (cf. Lohse, 132; the οὖν "therefore" [cf. vv 5, 12], functions as in Rom 12:1; Eph 4:1): you have been raised with Christ for new life. συνηγέρθητε ("you were raised") picks up the same word from chapter 2:12 (cf. v 13, "he [God] made you alive together with him [Christ]") while the definite article τῷ, "the" (before Χριστῷ, "Christ," an instance of the article of renewed mention), makes plain that it is in union with the same person with whom they died (ἀπεθάνετε σὺν Χριστῷ, 2:20) that they have been raised. Again it is noted that the Colossians' resurrection with Christ is described as a past act (see

the discussion at 2:12; the aorist tense, συνηγέρθητε, does not indicate that the author is advocating perfectionism, as Grässer, *ZTK* 64 [1967] 161, claims). If their death with him severed the links that bound them to the old order, then their resurrection with him established links with a new and heavenly order (Bruce, 258).

τὰ ἄνω ζητεῖτε. Because the readers have been raised with Christ, their lives are to be different: they have no life of their own since their life is the life of Christ. So their interests must be his interests. In Romans 6 the imperatives are based on the past death with Christ (vv 2–4); here the admonition is grounded in their past resurrection with him (cf. Tannehill, *Dying,* 47, and Schweizer, 131). The apostle had previously been at pains to point out that the Colossian readers had been "filled in him [Christ]." (For a discussion of the emphasis on a "realized eschatology" in this letter see 119–121.) This did not mean, however, that all things had been consummated or that the eschaton had already arrived. The future element is mentioned in this paragraph: their new life was currently hidden with Christ in God (v 3) but awaited its manifestation at the Parousia (v 4); while the exhortation with its ongoing responsibility to "seek the things above" presupposes that they are not yet perfect (Zeilinger, *Der Erstgeborene,* 149).

ζητέω, a term which has a wide range of meanings like the English word "seek" (see BAG, 339), has particular reference to the orientation of man's will (Greeven, *TDNT* 2, 893), which can be directed to unprofitable aims (Rom 10:3; 1 Cor 1:22) or to worthwhile ends (Rom 2:7). Here the readers are told to look upward so as to receive clear direction for their conduct. The present imperative shows that a continuous ongoing effort is required, something that would not occur naturally. Paul employs ζητεῖτε as a direct command only here (it turns up as an indirect one at 1 Cor 10:24; cf. 1 Cor 14:12; 10:33; 13:5; Phil 2:21; 1 Thess 2:6), so its force may be to provide a positive counterpart to the false teachers' energetic activity in "seeking" visionary experiences (cf. Lincoln, *Dimension,* 202; Grässer, *ZTK* 64 [1967] 151, asserts that both imperatives "seek" and "consider" correspond antithetically to the activities of the false teachers who with their asceticism, visions, and so on, sought to be free from the spiritual powers—activities which the author calls ζητεῖν τὰ ἐπὶ τῆς γῆς, "to seek what is on earth").

The imperative that follows from the present possession of Christ's resurrection life is phrased in spatial terms (cf. Grässer, *ZTK* 64 [1967] 154–59, Steinmetz, *Heils-Zuversicht,* 30, 31, 43, 44, and Lincoln, *Dimension,* 200–206): "Seek *the things above*" (τὰ ἄνω ζητεῖτε). Paul has already used the term "heaven(s)" (οὐρανός: in the plural at 1:5, 16, 20; note the singular at 1:23; cf. 4:1), and here in verses 1 and 2 the plural expression "the things above" (τὰ ἄνω) replaces it. This phrase (a substantive use, cf. Robertson, *Grammar,* 547, Turner, *Syntax,* 14) does not occur elsewhere in the Pauline letters though reference is made to "the Jerusalem which is above" (ἡ ἄνω Ἱερουσαλήμ, Gal 4:26) and the "upward call" (ἄνω κλῆσις, Phil 3:14). The spatial contrast is not a metaphysical one—as though God and Christ belong to the upper realm but have nothing to do with the lower which is evil because it is physical and material. Paul elsewhere uses the term γῆ ("earth") and ἐπίγειος ("earthly") without strong negative overtones (cf. 1 Cor 15:47; 2 Cor 5:1,

2; Phil 2:10) but in Colossian ... between heaven and earth is ethical ... with the earth being regarded as the special theater of sin (in the light of Gen 3:17, "cursed is the ground" [ἐπικατάρατος ἡ γῆ], it is understandable that the earth should be regarded as the primary setting of fallen creation; cf. Lincoln, *Dimension,* 204–207, who further claims that Paul's opponents were positively obsessed with "the things above," and the apostle by using this term outclasses his opponents on their own ground, not completely disparaging their concern with the heavenly realm but rather redirecting it, at the same time exposing its false premises about contacting this realm through legalistic external observances and the like; Paul turns the tables on his opponents "by taking over spatial terminology in order to point to the exclusiveness and completeness of Christ. . . . For Paul there could be no going beyond the one in the supreme position in heaven at God's right hand" [206]).

The OT itself had already used spatial terminology of heaven and earth, ascending and descending, etc. (cf. Gen 11:5; Exod 19:20; 24:9, 10; Ps 14:2; Ezek 1:26; Dan 7:13), while the notion of an upper world was common in apocalyptic and Hellenistic Judaism (cf. Schweizer, 103). In rabbinic Judaism the contast between the two ages ("the present age" and "the coming age") is paralleled by the notion of the lower and upper worlds (Cf. *b. Ḥag.* 2.1, "My fathers gathered treasures for below, I gathered treasures for above . . . my fathers gathered treasures in this world, and I gathered treasures for the future world," Str-B 1, 395, 977; cf. 2, 116, 133, 430, 431), and in the Qumran literature the predominantly ethical contrast between light and darkness had similar spatial connotations between the upper and lower realms (cf. Lincoln, *Dimension,* 201). Paul is thus employing spatial categories in a qualitative manner (Zeilinger, *Der Erstgeborene,* 149) to describe two spheres which correspond to the eschatological schema of the two ages. Here *τὰ ἄνω* stands for the heavenly world and the new aeon. It has to do with what is ultimately essential, transcendent and belonging to God (Moule, 111) and although "seeking the things above" has a definite ethical significance (as the apostle makes plain later) *τὰ ἄνω* is not to be defined solely with reference to ethical categories. The Colossian Christians have already participated in the world to come, the powers of the new age have broken in upon them, they already participate in the resurrection life of Christ. Thus their aims, ambitions, indeed their whole orientation is to be directed to this sphere.

οὗ ὁ Χριστός ἐστιν ἐν δεξιᾷ τοῦ θεοῦ καθήμενος. The basic reason for seeking the heavenly realm is that this is "where Christ is." Grammatically this clause spells out the place and character of *ἄνω* ("above," cf. Schweizer, 132), but it also provides the ground and motivation for the Christians seeking the things above (von Soden, 58). Paul is not indicating an interest in some cosmic geography, nor is he encouraging the pursuit of "that which is above" for its own sake. The significance of this realm, closely related to the sphere of resurrection existence, is that the exalted Christ is at its center.

The phrase *ἐν δεξιᾷ τοῦ θεοῦ καθήμενος* ("seated at God's right hand"; with most commentators *ἐστιν,* "is," should not be connected with *καθήμενος,* "seated," so making a periphrastic tense, but separated from the participle by a comma; there are two dependent clauses, cf. 2:3 and the similar comment regarding εἰσιν . . . ἀπόκρυφοι) is an allusion to Psalm 110:1. Paul takes up the Christological interpretation of this psalm, which was common in the early church, to speak of Christ's session at God's right hand and so to define further the realm above which is to be the goal of the Colossians' striving (cf. J. Daniélou, "La Session à la droite du Père," *Studia Evangelica*. ed. K. Aland and others [TU 73; Berlin: Akademie, 1959] 689–98, D. M. Hay, *Glory at the Right Hand. Psalm 110 in Early Christianity* [SBLMS 18; Nashville: Abingdon, 1973], M. Gourges. *A la droite de Dieu* [Paris: Gabalda, 1978] 57–63, and W. R. G. Loader, "Christ at the right hand—Ps. cx. 1 in the New Testament," *NTS* 24 [1977–78] 199–217).

Christ's ascension to the right hand of God was an essential and regular element in the early apostolic preaching, finding echoes throughout the NT (Acts 2:33–35; 5:31; 7:55, 56; Rom 8:34; Eph 1:20; Heb 1:3, 13; 8:1; 10:12; 12:2; 1 Pet 3:22; Rev. 3:21). This goes back to the messianic interpretation of Psalm 110:1: "The Lord says to my Lord: 'Sit at my right hand, till I make your enemies your footstool.' " Jesus claimed these words for himself when he was brought before the Sanhedrin in Jerusalem (Matt 26:64; Mark 12:36; Luke 20:41–44). After his resurrection and ascension the apostolic announcement was that this enthronement had taken place. Christ ruled from the right hand of God and would continue to do so until all his enemies had submitted to him (1 Cor 15:25).

According to Hay (*Glory*, 15) some thirty-three quotations of or allusions to Psalm 110 (vv 1 and 4) are scattered throughout the NT (seven more may be found in other Christian writings produced before the middle of the second century). These occur in contexts: *(a)* that point to Jesus or Christians being seated at the right hand of God (Rom 8:34; Eph 1:20; 2:6; Col 3:1; Mark 14:62; Matt 26:64; Luke 22:69; Acts 2:33–35; 5:31; 1 Pet 3:22; Rev 3:21; Heb 1:3, 13; 8:1; 10:12; 12:2), *(b)* where Psalm 110:1 is used in support of Christological titles such as "Lord" (Acts 2:33–36; Mark 16:19), "Son of Man" (Mark 14:62; Matt 26:64; Luke 22:69; Acts 7:56; cf. Barn 12:10, 11), "Son of God" (Heb 1:3, 13; cf. 1 Cor 15:25, 28; 1 Clem 36:4) and "Son of David" (Mark 12:35–37; Matt 22:41–45; Luke 20:41–44; cf. Barn 12:10, 11), *(c)* where affirmations are made about the subjection of the powers to Christ (1 Cor 15:25; Eph 1:20; Heb 10:12, 13; 1 Peter 3:22; Rev 3:21; cf. I Clem 36:5, 6; Pol *Phil* 2:1; Apoc Pet 6), and *(d)* where statements are made in connection with Jesus' intercession and priestly office (Rom 8:34; cf. Heb 7:25 and possibly 1 Pet 3:22). Colossians 3:1, which is an allusion to Psalm 110:1 rather than a quotation, does not stress the movement of the exalted one (cf. Steinmetz, *Heils-Zuversicht*, 85; in Acts 2:33–36; 5:31 the references in Hebrews, and Rev 3:21 the interest is concentrated on the past moment of exaltation, though each passage assumes the continuance of the exaltation into the present and the future, so Hay, *Glory*, 90). Instead, the accent falls on the present fact of his exaltation (the participle καθήμενος, "seated," as distinct from the imperative or finite verb, describes a state or condition; Christ is, according to Steinmetz, *Heils-Zuversicht*, 85, the "constantly exalted one").

The apostles were aware that they were using figurative language when they spoke of Christ's exaltation to the right hand of God. They no more thought of a literal throne at the literal right hand of God than we do. Ancient Jews and Gentiles alike commonly regarded the right side and a position at the right hand side as symbolic of honor or good fortune (Hay, *Glory*, 90, cf. 52–58). When the psalm was employed by early Christian writers it was to "articulate the supreme glory, the divine transcendence, of Jesus through whom salvation was mediated" (Hay, *Glory*, 155). At Colossians 3:1 the phrase alluded to in the psalm, "seated at the right hand of God" (ἐν δεξιᾷ τοῦ θεοῦ καθήμενος) points to the centrality and supremacy of Christ in the heavenly realm. Or to put it another way the apostle alludes to the psalm in order to describe the realm above in terms of the exalted Christ. This heavenly realm centers around the one with whom they have been raised. Since he is in a position of supreme authority no principality or power can prevent their access to this realm and to God's presence. They are thus to keep on aiming at that which is above and him who is at its center.

2. τὰ ἄνω φρονεῖτε, μὴ τὰ ἐπὶ τῆς γῆς. In the light of Christ's heavenly supremacy Paul repeats his summons: "Consider that which is above, not that which is on earth." Here the verb is different (φρονεῖτε in place of ζητεῖτε, v 1) and the exhortation is heightened by the contrast μὴ τὰ ἐπὶ τῆς γῆς ("not that which is on earth"; so Lincoln, *Dimension*, 203). φρονέω (one of several words derived from the stem φρην-) appears no fewer than twenty-three times in Paul out of a total of twenty-six occurrences in the NT. As a rather neutral term it acquires its proper meaning from its immediate context and covers a range such as to "think," "judge," and "give one's mind to" (cf. Goetzmann, in *NIDNTT* 2, 616). However, several of the Pauline contexts (e.g. Rom 8:5–8 where the cognate φρόνημα ["way of thinking," "aim"] also occurs) make it plain that the way one thinks is intimately related to the way one lives (whether as a Christian in the Spirit and by faith, or in the flesh, in sin and in spiritual death). "A man's thinking and striving cannot be seen in isolation from the overall direction of his life; the latter will be reflected in the aims which he sets himself" (Goetzmann, in *NIDNTT* 2, 617). φρονέω thus expresses not simply an activity of the intellect, but also a movement of the will; it has to do with aims and the motives underlying them. So in addition to the range of meanings mentioned above, to "set one's mind on," "be intent on," and "be minded or disposed" (cf. BAG, 866) must also be included (the AV/KJV rendering "set your affection" is misleading today since it gives the impression the verb primarily has to do with a person's emotional state). The apostle exhorts the Roman Christians not to consider themselves too highly but to think with sober judgment and in accordance with the measure of faith God has given them (Rom 12:3, note the fourfold use of φρονέω words: ὑπερφρονέω, "be haughty," "consider oneself too highly," σωφρονέω, "be sensible or reasonable," "keep one's head," and φρονέω twice); elsewhere he admonishes his readers to "be of the same mind" (Rom 12:16; 15:5; 2 Cor 13:11; Phil 2:2; 4:2; cf. Gal 5:10; Phil 3:15), an injunction that is not intended to squash independent thinking by Christians or to prevent them from having different opinions on secondary matters, but is to exhort them to be at one in basic aim, direction and orientation of their behavior. If the AV/KJV rendering of Philippians 2:5 expresses the correct interpretation of this disputed passage ("Let this mind be in you, which was also in Christ

Jesus"; Martin, *Carmen Christi*, 290, 291, etc., following Käsemann, prefers a "kerygmatic" interpretation to an exemplary one; for a restatement and endorsement of the latter view, that is the "ethical" interpretation, see C. F. D. Moule, "Further Reflexions on Philippians 2:5–11," *Apostolic History and the Gospel. Biblical and Historical Essays Presented to F. F. Bruce*, ed. W. W. Gasque and R. P. Martin [Exeter: Paternoster, 1970] 264–76, especially 269, 270, American edition [Grand Rapids, MI: Eerdmans, 1970]; cf. I. H. Marshall, "The Christ-Hymn in Philippians 2:5–11," *TB* 19 [1968] 104–127, and M. D. Hooker, "Philippians 2:6–11." *Jesus und Paulus. Festschrift für Werner Georg Kümmel zum 70. Geburtstag*. 2nd ed., ed. E. E. Ellis and E. Grässer [Göttingen: Vandenhoeck und Ruprecht, 1978] 151–64) then Christ's self-abasement is the model for a similar attitude by Christians, while Romans 12:2 (cf. v 3) suggests that this considering is accompanied by the "renewal of the mind" (*ἀνακαίνωσις τοῦ νοῦς*, cf. Lohse, 133). *φρονεῖτε* at Colossians 3:2 is an admonition to be heavenly minded instead of earthly minded. Like its previous counterpart *ζητεῖτε* ("seek"; Meyer, 418, 419, has argued with some justification that *φρονεῖτε* is more comprehensive than *ζητεῖτε*, expressing not only the striving but also the whole bent of thought and disposition) it is addressed to the whole congregation. Obedience to the injunction requires that great effort be made. The overtones of sober consideration and firm purpose may also be present, perhaps over against visionary experiences of heavenly mysteries.

The sharp contrast between "that which is above" (*τὰ ἄνω*) and "that which is on earth" (*τὰ ἐπὶ τῆς γῆς*; it has been argued that the latter expression preceded by the negative *μή*, "not," defines more precisely the former phrase, Lohse, 133) is given a strong ethical content, as the following section (i.e. vv 5–7) makes plain. Schweizer (133; cf. Lincoln, *Dimension*, 203), who argues that the "above" and "on the earth" are not properly topographical definitions but rather signify spheres in which a person may live (note Phil 3:19 where Paul accuses his opponents of having their "minds set on earthly things [*οἱ τὰ ἐπίγεια φρονοῦντες*]" and of making a god out of their belly, in contrast to those whose citizenship is in heaven [*πολίτευμα ἐν οὐρανοῖς*]), rightly claims that this contrast closely resembles that which Paul describes elsewhere as the spheres of the "flesh" and the "Spirit." At Romans 8:5, 6, using both *φρονέω* and the cognate *φρόνημα* ("way of thinking," "mind[= set]," though here = "aim," "aspiration," "striving," so BAG, 866), a similar sharp antithesis in categories of "flesh" and "Spirit" is presented: "Those who live according to their sinful nature have their minds set on what that nature desires (*τὰ τῆς σαρκὸς φρονοῦσιν*); but those who live in accordance with the Spirit have their minds set on what the Spirit desires (*τὰ τοῦ πνεύματος* [*φρονοῦσιν*]). The mind of sinful man is death, but the mind controlled by the Spirit is life and peace" (NIV). Paul does not repudiate living "in the flesh" when he means living "in the body," that is, as a human being on earth. As such, flesh is part of God's good creation. Rather, he rejects the orientation of life toward the flesh, that old order to which the Christian no longer belongs.

3. *ἀπεθάνετε γὰρ καὶ ἡ ζωὴ ὑμῶν κέκρυπται κτλ.* The grounds for (*γάρ*; it does not simply mean "in effect," so Zeilinger, *Der Erstgeborene*, 147, following Hugedé, 162) Paul's admonition to consider the things above, not those on

earth, are twofold: (1) you died to that old order, and (2) your new life is hidden with Christ in God. ἀπεθάνετε should be rendered "you died" for it points back to the specific occasion of their union with Christ in his death (rather than "you have died," RSV or "you are dead"); it picks up the statement of chapter 2:20, "you died (ἀπεθάνετε) with Christ from the elemental spirits of the universe" and harks back to the ideas expressed in chapter 2:11, 12, "you were circumcised . . . in the circumcision of Christ . . . you were buried with him," at the same time providing the basis for the imperative in the exhortatory section, "put to death" (3:5). This death with Christ involves a dying to the elemental spirits and by implication to what has been designated τὰ ἐπὶ τῆς γῆς ("the things on earth"), the content of which is spelled out, in part at least, in chapter 2:16–23 with its references to ascetic regulations, visionary experiences and the like.

But the Colossians are exhorted to think on the things of heaven not only because they died with Christ to the old order, but also (καί) because they have been raised with him and participate in his resurrection life. The apostle frequently used the terms "life" (ζωή) and to "live" (ζάω: cf. ζωοποιέω, to "make alive," "give life to") to describe the life of the age to come which will be received on the final day and which through the resurrection of Christ from the dead has become for the believer a present reality (ζωή: Rom 6:4, 22, 23; 8:2, 6, 10; 2 Cor 4:10, 11, etc.; ζάω: Rom 1:17; 6:11, 13; 8:13; 2 Cor 13:4; Gal 2:19, 20, etc.; cf. ζωοποιέω: Rom 8:11). Here at Colossians 3:3, 4 both present and future aspects are linked: at verse 3 the life (described as the believer's own life, ἡ ζωὴ ὑμῶν) is already present, bound up with Christ, though in a hidden way (cf. Steinmetz, *Heils-Zuversicht,* 30); at verse 4 the future note is struck when it is asserted that this life (which is so closely related to Christ that he himself can be called the believer's life, ἡ ζωὴ ἡμῶν [see notes]) will be manifested for what it really is at the Second Coming (Grässer, *ZTK* 64 [1967] 161, 162, considers the reference is exclusively to future life, but apart from the fact that v 3 speaks of its present existence, albeit in a hidden way, the assertion at 2:13 that God had already made the Colossians alive with Christ, together with the statements of their having been raised with him in the past [2:12; 3:1], shows that the apostle has a present aspect in view as well as a future manifestation; cf. Bultmann, *TDNT* 2, 861–75).

κέκρυπται σὺν τῷ Χριστῷ ἐν τῷ θεῷ. The verb *κέκρυπται* ("hidden") is a perfect tense, in contrast to the preceding aorist, ἀπεθάνετε ("you died," drawing attention to the specific occasion of their death with Christ), and stresses the ongoing and permanent effects: your life has been hidden with Christ in God and it remains that way. This is sometimes taken to mean that the new life of Christians in Christ is a secret to the unconverted (and in part even to themselves; note Bengel's oft-quoted statement: "The world knows neither Christ nor Christians, and Christians do not even fully know themselves," 2, 467) so that it remains unrevealed until the end. Moule, 112, raises the question as to whether some connection with the ἀπόκρυφοι ("stored up") of chapter 2:3 is in view. Christ is the storehouse of all God's secrets including the believer's new life. He is "above" and since the Christian's life is hidden with him then it is already in heaven (as Tannehill, *Dying,*

48, rightly comments: "the life of the believer is already a heavenly life"; cf. Mussner, *Christus,* 93, who notes that since this life is inseparable from the person of the Exalted One then it belongs to the transcendent realm). Ephesians 2:6, by asserting explicitly that Christians have been seated with Christ in the heavenlies, simply brings out what has already been implied here in Colossians 3:3, 4 (cf. A. T. Lincoln, "A Re-Examination of 'The Heavenlies' in Ephesians," *NTS* 19 [1972–73] 473, 474). (Regarding the choice of this verb κέκρυπται some have suggested there may be an allusion to the pagan idea that death indicates a man is "hidden" in the earth—dead and gone; Christians claim that they are hidden indeed, but in Christ, cf. Moule, 112, and Schweizer, 133; others have thought the term may have been called forth by a desire on the part of the proponents of the false teaching to refer to the notion of hiddenness, for a secret knowledge belonging only to the initiated, cf. 1:26, 27; 2:2, 3; so Lincoln, *Dimension,* 208, 209.)

The believer's life is said to be hidden σὺν τῷ Χριστῷ ἐν τῷ θεῷ ("with Christ in God"). The expression "in God," the very antithesis to what is material and visible, is used rather rarely by Paul and the only precise parallels to the believers being "in God" are 1 Thessalonians 1:1 and 2 Thessalonians 1:1 (at Rom 2:17; 5:11 it is the rejoicing [καυχάομαι] in God which is in view; cf. 1 Thess 2:2 and Eph 3:9). The phrase "in God" modifies both "life" (ζωή) and the immediately preceding words "with Christ" (σὺν τῷ Χριστῷ; elsewhere in the Pauline letters this phrase [using the preposition by itself; it is different with verbs compounded with σύν] occurs only of future existence, cf. Moule, *RevExp* 70 [1973] 485; on the meaning of this expression see the following note): our life is hidden with Christ because we died with him and have been raised with him to new life; "in God" because Christ himself has his being in God and those who belong to Christ have their being there too (cf. Bruce, 261; Grundmann, *TDNT* 7, 785). Centered in God means that the hidden life is secure, unable to be touched by anyone.

4. Our heavenly life will be fully manifest in all its glory when Christ who embodies it appears at his Parousia. We too who share his life will share his glorious epiphany. What is now secretly present shall be revealed when Christ shall appear.

ὅταν ὁ Χριστὸς φανερωθῇ, ἡ ζωὴ ἡμῶν. Paul's statement is striking and vivid. He does not insert any conjunction such as καί ("and") or δέ ("but"), with the result that the very abruptness of the expression helps to underline the assurance of the hope more vividly (Williams, 124; cf. Abbott, 249, Bengel 2, 467, and Meyer, 422). The temporal note is struck (cf. the balancing of the two clauses ὅταν . . . . τότε, "when . . . . then") in a context where spatial categories have been employed, and the significance of this chronological assertion is not to be watered down as some have suggested (see below 168, 169; Steinmetz, *Heils-Zuversicht,* 30, wrongly considers that the time note is not strong in ὅταν, but he fails to give the balancing τότε, where there is a stress on future consummation, its due weight).

For the fourth time in as many verses the name "Christ" (ὁ Χριστός) appears (cf. v 2, τῷ Χριστῷ, ὁ Χριστός; v 3 τῷ Χριστῷ). The pronoun "he" (or "him") would have been more natural but less emphatic (so Lightfoot, 208; cf. Williams, 124) as Paul goes out of his way to emphasize that true Christian existence is found "with Christ" alone. The verb φανερόω ("reveal," "make known," "show," BAG, 852, 853; cf. Bultmann/Lührmann, *TDNT* 9, 3–6) which the apostle often employs synonymously with ἀποκαλύπτω ("reveal"; cf. Rom 1:17 and 3:21 on the revelation of God's righteousness in Christ, and Eph 3:5 with Col 1:26 on the revelation of the mystery hidden for ages), does not speak of a manifestation that has already taken place as in chapter 1:26 (against Brown, in *NIDNTT* 3, 322), but refers rather to the Parousia when the veil will be drawn back so that what is hidden from our eyes will shine in bright light (Lohse, 134). This term often denotes in Paul the revelation that takes place in the proclamation of the gospel or the mystery (Rom 3:21; 16:26; 2 Cor 2:14; 11:6; Col 1:26; cf. 4:4). Here, however, it has to do with the future manifestation of Christ himself (cf. 1 John 2:28; 3:2) and of believers (φανερωθήσεσθε) on the final day (cf. 1 Cor 4:5 with reference to the future judgment where φανερόω points to the making known of what is currently hidden) in contrast to the present hiddenness (κέκρυπται and φανερωθῇ/φανερωθήσεσθε stand in sharp contrast to each other, as both their meanings, "hide," "make known," and tenses indicate).

So closely is the cause of Christ identified with that of his people that he is said to be their life (ὁ Χριστός . . . ἡ ζωὴ ἡμῶν). The words mark a twofold development on the previous statement (cf. Lightfoot, 208): first, it is not simply that the life is said to be shared with Christ: "the life *is* Christ." Second, if the reading "our life" (ἡ ζωὴ ἡμῶν) is original (see the note above 157), then the apostle has gone out of his way to include himself and other believers among the recipients of this mighty blessing. When writing to the Philippians he could say, "For to me to live is Christ" (Phil 1:21; cf. Rom 8:2, 10; 2 Cor 4:10; Gal 2:19, 20). But he did not regard this as true only of himself. Christ is the life of all who are united to him by faith, who are members of his body. Whoever belongs to him has passed from death to life, to use Johannine language (John 5:24, 25; 11:25, 26; cf. 1 John 5:12).

τότε καὶ ὑμεῖς σὺν αὐτῷ φανερωθήσεσθε ἐν δόξῃ. Christ is now enthroned in heaven at God's right hand. When he appears at the end of days at the Parousia, it will become plain that his own are with him. The day of the revelation of the *Son* of God will be the day of the revelation of the *sons* of God (the position of σὺν αὐτῷ lays stress on the closeness of the relation of "you" and "him," as well as keeping ἐν δόξῃ in a position of final emphasis, so Williams, 124), as Paul makes plain with his "then" (τότε which is emphatic pointing to the same time or occasion specified in the ὅταν clause, i.e. when Christ is revealed), the additional words "you also" (καὶ ὑμεῖς) and his selection of the same verb "reveal" (φανερόω) to apply to the believers themselves as well as to Christ. That manifestation will take place "in glory" (ἐν δόξῃ). "Glory" was a characteristic theme in apocalyptic thought where it was closely associated with heavenly existence as it is also in Paul's writings. The future manifestation in glory predicted here for the believer has particular reference to his sharing Christ's likeness (cf. 1 John 3:2, "we know that when he appears, we shall be like him, for we shall see him as he is"), and to receiving the glorious resurrection body. It was this same hope to which the apostle directed the Philippians' attention: "Our citizenship is in heaven. And we eagerly await a Savior from there, the Lord Jesus Christ, who, by the power that enables him to bring everything under his control, will transform our lowly bodies so that they will be like his glorious body (*σῶμα τῆς δόξης αὐτοῦ*)" (Phil 3:20, 21 NIV; cf. 1 Cor 15:42, 43; 2 Cor 5:1, 2).

It has been argued that this is the only *explicit* futuristic eschatological reference in Colossians (there are hints at 3:24 and 4:11) and that this use of the "hidden—revealed" motif is without parallel in the earlier Pauline letters. Spatial concepts are said to dominate at chapters 1:26, 27; 3:3, 4, while none of the typically Pauline eschatological ideas—Parousia, resurrection of the dead, judgment of the world—is encountered in Colossians. It is further alleged that in chapter 1:5, 23 and 27 "hope" is no longer chronologically conceived but has become an otherworldly quality of hope (cf. especially Bornkamm, *Geschichte und Glaube* 2, 206–213). Grässer (*ZTK* 64 [1967] 165) considers that Paul's dialectic of eschatological existence has been replaced by a dialectic of transcendent existence. No longer does the author, like Paul, speak in the language of apocalyptic about a resurrection of the dead but instead refers to "life" as the eschatological gift (*ZTK* 64 [1967] 161). Further, to assert that someone has been raised with Christ, of necessity means there can be no future resurrection. Meanwhile Lohse, while not endorsing all of the above-mentioned arguments, regards the changed eschatology of Colossians as one of the reasons for his decision against Pauline authorship. Eschatology has receded into the background. In Colossians the basis for exhortation is baptism, while eschatological themes provide the motivation in Paul (Lohse, 180).

By way of response we have already noted that there is an emphasis on realized eschatology in Colossians. In terms of the Pauline "already—not yet" tension the accent falls upon the former, called forth no doubt by the particular circumstances of the letter (see xxx–xli, 120). But this is not to suggest that the "not yet" pole in Paul's tension is absent. There is future eschatology at chapter 3:4 and 6 (a reference to the future eschatological wrath of God), 24 (where the reception of a future inheritance is in view) and in our estimation at chapter 1:22 and 28 where the presentation of every man as perfect at the Parousia is in mind (see above, 68, 69, 89, 90; Steinmetz, *Heils-Zuversicht*, 31, 32, notes traces of future eschatology in 4:11 also). The "hidden—revealed" motif and the concept of glory (note *ἐν δόξῃ* at v 4) are both significant apocalyptic features (cf. 1:26, 27 where the "hidden—revealed" theme is used of the mystery that has now been made known), while spatial concepts ("above," "on earth") are used in the service of eschatology. To speak of a heavenly realm was meaningful in a Hellenistic syncretistic environment while categories such as this were already at hand in the thought world of Jewish apocalyptic. Paul had previously employed such motifs in his earlier letters and they are used in Colossians to draw attention to the two ages: "this age" and "the age to come" (cf. Zeilinger, *Der Erstgeborene*, 149). Grässer's antithesis (*ZTK* 64 [1967] 165) between eschatological and transcendent perspectives is a false one since both are found together in the undisputed Paulines and at Colossians 3:1–4. Further, the apocalyptic notion of a resurrection from the dead is found at chapter 1:18 in the title ascribed to Christ, "firstborn from the dead" (*πρωτότοκος ἐκ τῶν νεκρῶν*, cf. 1 Cor 15:20), and even if the author is taking over traditional material (for the various arguments see 40–42) it is clear that he is giving the terminology his approval. Verse 18 can only be adequately understood of Christ's primacy in resurrection (see the detailed exegesis 50, 51). In the undisputed Paulines the notions of the resurrection from the dead and eschatological life are interchangeable (so Rom 4:17; 5:17, 18, 21; 6:22, 23; 8:11; 1 Cor 15:45), and Grässer's remark (*ZTK* 64 [1967] 161) that whoever has been raised with Christ will not participate in a future resurrection shows he fails to come to grips with the "already—not yet" tension.

Against Lohse it may be argued that there is an eschatological motivation in Colossians; it may not be the dominant one but it is present nevertheless. The exhortation, "put to death, therefore, . . ." (*νεκρώσατε οὖν*, 3:5), is based on verses 1–4 (not simply v 3) and the last of these has an eschatological emphasis (compare 3:6; 2:4; and 4:5). At the same time there are other grounds for exhortation in the generally accepted Pauline letters. The question is simply one of emphasis. There was good reason for Paul stressing what God had done in uniting the readers with his Son (the aspect of realized eschatology or the "already" of the tension) as the basis for ethical exhortation in Colossians. "Against those who were removing the basis of Christian living away from grace and toward legalistic observances, knowledge, visionary experiences, Paul insists that God has *already* done everything necessary in Christ" (Lincoln, *Dimension,* 217; note his careful analysis on 212–17; for a critique of Bornkamm's understanding of "hope" in Colossians see above xlvi, 11, and regarding the arguments against the Pauline authorship of the letter because of the realized eschatological emphasis see xlvi–xlvii).

A Note on the Expression "With Christ"

The phrase "with Christ" (*σὺν Χριστῷ*) occurs in the Pauline letters far less frequently than the formula "in Christ" (*ἐν Χριστῷ*), appearing on only twelve occasions (four of which are in Colossians: 2:13, 20; 3:3, 4). The expression "to be with Christ" (*σὺν Χριστῷ εἶναι*) turns up once at Philippians 1:23, though related statements do appear: "we shall be with the Lord" (*σὺν κυρίῳ ἐσόμεθα,* 1 Thess 4:17), and "we shall live together with him" (*σὺν αὐτῷ ζήσωμεν,* 5:10). Apart from the references in Colossians, five further expressions using different verbs are to be found: "he [God] will bring with him [Jesus]" (*σὺν αὐτῷ,* 1 Thess 4:14), "he will raise us with Jesus" (*σὺν Ἰησοῦ,* 2 Cor 4:14), "we will live with him" (*σὺν αὐτῷ,* 13:4), "since we died with Christ" (*σὺν Χριστῷ,* Rom 6:8), "how will he not also, along with him, graciously give us all things?" (*σὺν αὐτῷ,* 8:32). A brief glance at these references shows that no single expression completely agrees with any other, but that the preposition *σύν* ("with") was suited to express intimate personal union with Christ, the Lord, Jesus or him in various contexts (rather than *μετά,* "with," which was more suited to indicate close association or attendant circumstances, e.g. 1 Thess 3:13; cf. Harris, in *NIDNTT* 3, 1206, 1207). Because of this variety several have argued it is incorrect to speak of "with Christ" (*σὺν Χριστῷ*) as a *formula.* Rather it is a *motif* or theme which can be expressed in a number of different ways (so Tannehill, *Dying,* 87, 88, Lohse, 104, 105; cf. J. Gnilka, *Der Philipperbrief* [HTKNT 10/3; Freiburg: Herder, 1968] 76, against Grundmann, *TDNT* 7, 782).

In addition to these prepositional phrases Paul employs a number of words compounded with σύν ("with") which describe the believer's close union with Christ, the most important of which are: συσταυρόω ("crucify together with," Rom 6:6; Gal 2:20), συνθάπτω ("bury with," Rom 6:4; Col 2:12), σύμφυτος (an adjective meaning "grown together," deriving from συμφύομαι, Rom 6:5), συζάω ("live together with," Rom 6:8; 2 Tim 2:11), συγκληρονόμος ("co-heir," Rom 8:17; cf. Heb 11:9; 1 Pet 3:7), συμπάσχω ("suffer with," Rom 8:17), συνδοξάζω ("glorify with," Rom 8:17), σύμμορφος ("having the same form as," Rom 8:29; Phil 3:21) and συμμορφίζω ("confer the same form," Phil 3:10). For full details see Grundmann, *TDNT* 7, 786, 787.

To be with Christ or with the Lord (Phil 1:23; 1 Thess 4:17) refers to the future and signifies the perfection which is to come (Dupont, ΣΥΝ ΧΡΙΣΤΩΙ, 39–47, etc., has distinguished two phases: "being or living with the Lord" [1 Thess 4:17; 5:10] emphasizes believers' sharing in the eschatological blessings of the kingdom enjoyed by Christ since his resurrection, while in Phil 1:23 ["being with Christ"] and 2 Cor 5:8 ["dwelling with the Lord"] the emphasis falls on intimate fellowship with the King in his kingdom [cf. Harris, in *NIDNTT* 3, 1207]). However, by means of some of the compound words the apostle points out that this intimate personal union with Christ is already a present reality (on the relationship of the statements ["with Christ," "with the Lord," etc.] that point to the future and those speaking about the present, particularly in the light of possible backgrounds to the notion, see Schnackenburg, *Baptism*, 170–77, and the literature cited by Lohse, 104, note 76). The believer has already been united with Christ in his death and resurrection. So according to Romans 6 we were "buried with him" (v 4), "united with him in his death" (v 5), and "our old self was crucified with him" (v 6). Verse 8 asserts "we will live with him," while later in the same letter Paul speaks about a union with Christ that comes to be known through suffering, but which the Christian endures in view of the future glory: "if indeed we share in his sufferings in order that we may also share in his glory" (εἴπερ συμπάσχομεν ἵνα καὶ συνδοξασθῶμεν, 8:17).

In Colossians Paul frequently uses the phrase "with Christ." As we have noted elsewhere, consistent with the emphasis on realized eschatology, this expression "with Christ"—the "already" of salvation speaks of the union with Christ in his death and resurrection which has already occurred. So the readers were buried with Christ in baptism (συνταφέντες αὐτῷ, 2:12), and were made alive together with Christ (συνεζωοποίησεν σὺν αὐτῷ, 2:13); they died with him to the elemental spirits of the universe (ἀπεθάνετε σὺν Χριστῷ, 2:20), were raised with him (συνηγέρθητε, 3:1) and as a result their life is hidden with him in God (κέκρυπται σὺν τῷ Χριστῷ, 3:3). On the other hand, the future note is not completely absent. The "not yet" of salvation is in view at chapter 3:4 where it is stated: "When Christ, who is our life, appears, then you also will appear with him (σὺν αὐτῷ φανερωθήσεσθε) in glory."

The phrase "with Christ" is not a formula like the expression "in Christ," but is a motif used in a variety of ways to express the intimate personal union of the believer with Christ. The expression "to be with Christ" (Phil 1:23) or its equivalents (1 Thess 4:17; 2 Cor 4:14; 13:4) looks forward to the future when the destiny of Christians, after death or after the Parousia, is in view. When the preposition σύν ("with") is compounded with certain verbs it relates to past events and resulting present experiences so that this close union with Christ is already a present reality. Both the phrase and related verbs are employed in Colossians to describe the death and resurrection with Christ as a past event and the resulting new existence for the Christian: it is his life with Christ. Like Christ's life it is hidden in God. What Christians await is the appearance of Christ, that is, his emergence from concealment and their own manifestation with him (σὺν αὐτῷ, 3:4) in glory. It is not called the resurrection of the dead, but the manifestation of the hidden life (Grundmann, *TDNT* 7, 785, 786).

Explanation

This short paragraph, in which the apostle exhorts the Colossians to pursue those things that belong to the heavenly realm where Christ reigns, occupies an important pivotal position in the letter (cf. the similar function of 2:6, 7). Containing both indicatives and imperatives it concludes the section where Paul attacks the "philosophy" of the false teachers, providing the true alternative to the erroneous teaching. It is possible that the positive expressions set forth in chapter 3:1–4 show the controversy is still in view as Paul draws together themes previously mentioned (2:11–13, 20). At the same time the theological foundations (the "indicative") for the admonitions (the "imperative") that follow (3:5–4:6) are set forth.

The grounds for Paul's admonition to aim at the things above, not those on earth, are twofold (v 1, 3): first, the Colossians died to that old order with its elemental spirits (2:20), its ascetic and enslaving regulations, visionary experiences and useless will-worship. Second, as those who have already been raised with Christ they now participate in his resurrection life. So their lives are to be different. Their interests are to be centered on Christ; their minds, aims, ambitions, in fact their whole outlook, are to be centered on that heavenly realm where he reigns and where their lives truly belong. The continuous ongoing effort required for such a cast of mind does not come automatically. That realm above is to be sought diligently (and in contrast to any false seeking of heavenly experiences by the advocates of the Colossian "philosophy") for this is where Christ is, seated as king in the place of honor.

For the moment their heavenly life remains hidden, secure with Christ in God. Their new life as Christians in Christ is not visible to others and, in some measure, is hidden from themselves. It will only be fully manifest when Christ, who embodies that life, appears at his Parousia. Indeed, the day of the revelation of the *Son* of God will be the day of the revelation of the *sons* of God. That manifestation will take place "in glory" for it will involve the sharing of Christ's likeness and the receiving of the glorious resurrection body.

In Colossians, as we have already noted, there is an emphasis on realized eschatology. Within the "already—not yet" tension the stress falls upon the former, called forth by the circumstances of the letter. The basis for seeking or setting the mind on the heavenly realm, at the center of which is the exalted Christ, is God's mighty action in uniting the readers with Christ in his death and resurrection. The "already" of salvation needed to be asserted repeatedly over against those who were interested in the heavenly realm but who had false notions about it, believing it could be reached by legalistic observances, knowledge, visionary experiences and the like. Ultimately the doctrine of grace was at stake. The readers, therefore, needed to be instructed that they had died with Christ, been raised with him and had been given new life with him. He had done all that was necessary. So they were zealously to pursue the things of that new order, centered on the exalted Christ.

But if the "already" pole received the emphasis, the "not yet" of salvation still needed to be mentioned, and here in verse 4 we find a clear future reference. Christ was currently hidden from sight. So too were their lives, for they were hidden with him. The final day would come when he would appear; and they would appear with him—they would be like him, clothed with the resurrection body.

Put Away the Sins of the Past (3:5–11)

Bibliography

Bouttier, M. "*Complexio Oppositorum:* sur les Formules de 1 Cor. xii. 13; Gal. iii. 26–8; Col. iii. 10, 11." *NTS* 23 (1976–77) 1–19. **Easton, B. S.** "New Testament Ethical Lists." *JBL* 51 (1932) 1–12. **Jervell, J.** *Imago,* 231–56. **Kamlah, E.** *Die Form der katalogischen Paränese im Neuen Testament.* WUNT 7. Tübingen: Mohr, 1964. **Larsson, E.** *Christus,* 188–223. **Merk, O.** *Handeln,* 204–212. **Moule, C. F. D.** *RevExp* 70 (1973) 481–93. **Schnackenburg, R.** "Der neue Mensch—Mitte christlichen Weltverständnisses (Kol 3, 9–11)." *Schriften zum Neuen Testament. Exegese in Fortschritt und Wandel.* Munich: Kösel, 1971, 392–413. **Schrage, W.** *Einzelgebote.* **Schweizer, E.** "Die Sunde in den Gliedern." *Abraham Unser Vater. Juden und Christen im Gespräch über die Bibel. Festschrift für Otto Michel zum 60. Geburtstag,* ed. O. Betz, M. Hengel and P. Schmidt. AGSU 5. Leiden: Brill, 1963, 437–39. ———. "Gottesgerechtigkeit und Lasterkataloge bei Paulus (inkl. Kol und Eph)." *Rechtfertigung. Festschrift für Ernst Käsemann zum 70. Geburtstag,* ed. J. Friedrich, W. Pöhlmann and P. Stuhlmacher. Göttingen: Vandenhoeck und Ruprecht, 1976, 461–77. ———. "Traditional ethical patterns in the Pauline and post-Pauline letters and their development (lists of vices and house-tables)." *Text and Interpretation. Studies in the New Testament presented to Matthew Black,* ed. E. Best and R. McL. Wilson. Cambridge: University Press, 1979, 195–209. **Vögtle, A.** *Die Tugend- und Lasterkataloge im Neuen Testament, exegetisch, religions- und formgeschichtlich untersucht.* NTAbh 16. Münster: Aschendorff, 1936. **Wibbing, S.** *Die Tugend- und Lasterkataloge im Neuen Testament und ihre Traditionsgeschichte unter besonderer Berücksichtigung der Qumrantexte.* BZNW 25. Berlin: Töpelmann, 1959. **Zeilinger, F.** *Der Erstgeborene,* 63–66, 151–60.

Translation

5 *Therefore put to death what belongs to your earthly nature: sexual immorality, impurity, lust, evil desire and covetousness which is idolatry.* 6 *Because of these things the wrath of God is coming.*[a] 7 *You too used to walk in these ways in the life you once lived.* 8 *But now put them all away: anger, rage, malice, slander and filthy language from your lips.* 9 *Stop lying to one another since you have put off the old man with his practices,* 10 *and have put on the new man which is being renewed in knowledge after the image of his creator.* 11 *Here there is no longer Greek and Jew, circumcised and uncircumcised, barbarian, Scythian, slave and free, but Christ is all and in all.*

Notes

[a] ἐπὶ τοὺς υἱοὺς τῆς ἀπειθείας. Although there is widespread and early testimony supporting the longer reading which includes these words "upon the sons of disobedience" (ℵ A C D F etc., most miniscules, it vg cop^bo and several other versions) it is likely that they represent an intrusion into the text from Ephesians 5:6, and were omitted by P46 B cop^sah and several of the fathers. The phrase is a Hebraism, meaning "disobedient people" and denotes those whose lives are characterized by defiance of the law of God (contrast 1 Pet 1:14, "children of obedience").

Form/Structure/Setting

If the preceding paragraph (3:1–4) serves as an important transition piece in the letter, functioning as the conclusion to Paul's polemic against the "philosophy" of the false teachers and presenting a true alternative to that teaching, then this paragraph begins the lengthy paraenetic section of chapters 3:5–4:6. Four distinctive catchwords of early Christian catechesis are found at the head of their respective paragraphs: "put to death" (3:5–11; cf. also "put off," v 8); "put on" (3:12–17); "be subject" (3:18–4:1) and "watch and pray" (4:2–6).

The first of these, verses 5–11, has been called the "negative paraenesis" (Zeilinger, *Der Erstgeborene,* 63) since it contains the injunctions νεκρώσατε ("put to death," v 5) and ἀπόθεσθε ("put off," v 8) together with two catalogs of vices (v 5, 8). The first injunction with its οὖν ("therefore"), νεκρώσατε ("put to death") and τὰ μέλη τὰ ἐπὶ τῆς γῆς ("the members which are on earth") is designed to recall what has been previously written (see the comment on v 5). As the particular objects of the imperative "put to death" five vices are listed (grammatically they are in apposition to τὰ μέλη τὰ ἐπὶ τῆς γῆς, "[your] earthly members"):

v 5: πορνείαν —ἀκαθαρσίαν
πάθος —ἐπιθυμίαν
καὶ τὴν πλεονεξίαν ἥτις ἐστὶν εἰδωλολατρία.
v 5: sexual immorality —impurity
lust —evil desire
and covetousness which is idolatry.

The last πλεονεξία ("covetousness") is specially emphasized by the addition of καί ("and"; it is not used to separate the others in the list), the presence of the definite article τήν ("the"; the article does not appear before the other nouns) and the relative clause ἥτις ἐστὶν εἰδωλολατρία ("which is idolatry"). Three further relative clauses with verbs in the indicative mood follow, and they describe the pagan past of the readers in relation to the vices previously mentioned (vv 6, 7).

By means of the "once-now" antithesis (see on 1:21, 22 and 2:13) the Colossians are shown how they ought to behave now in contrast to their past (vv 7, 8). This schematic form is used to tie in the second catalog of vices with the first (the antecedent of ἐν οἷς, "in which," v 7, is the first list of vices, v 5, while τὰ πάντα, "all," v 8, is the object of the second imperative and is defined more precisely by the second catalog). (On the chiastic structure of the two sentences see below 186). Once again five sins are mentioned: they stand in apposition to τὰ πάντα, "all," and as in the first list so here also the last member is specially emphasized by an addition:

v 8: νυνὶ δὲ ἀπόθεσθε καὶ ὑμεῖς τὰ πάντα
ὀργήν —θυμόν
κακίαν —βλασφημίαν
αἰσχρολογίαν ἐκ τοῦ στόματος ὑμῶν.

v 8: "But now put them all away,
anger —rage
malice —slander
filthy language from your lips."

The opening words of verse 9 continue the series of imperatives and they are most naturally connected with the preceding themes of "slander" and "abusive language": *μὴ ψεύδεσθε εἰς ἀλλήλους* ("Stop lying to one another"). Two parallel aorist participial clauses give the twofold reason for this abandonment of evil ways:

v 9: *ἀπεκδυσάμενοι τὸν παλαιὸν ἄνθρωπον*
σὺν ταῖς πράξεσιν αὐτοῦ
v 10: *καὶ ἐνδυσάμενοι τὸν νέον τὸν ἀνακαινούμενον*
εἰς ἐπίγνωσιν κατ᾽ εἰκόνα τοῦ κτίσαντος αὐτόν.
v 9: "(Since) you have put off the old man
with his practices,
v 10: and have put on the new man which is being renewed
in knowledge in the Creator's image."

According to verse 11 within this realm of the new man (*ὅπου*, "where") the barriers that divided people from one another are abolished. A strong negative (*οὐκ ἔνι*, "there is not") is followed by four pairs of subdivisions of the human family, the first two of which are linked by *καί* ("and"). Finally, the concluding triumphant words contrast (*ἀλλά*, "but") the centrality of Christ with the divisions that separate people in the world (note the emphasis of the statement which falls on the last word *Χριστός*, "Christ"):

v 11: *ὅπου οὐκ ἔνι*
Ἕλλην καὶ Ἰουδαῖος,
περιτομὴ καὶ ἀκροβυστία
βάρβαρος —Σκύθης
δοῦλος —ἐλεύθερος,
ἀλλὰ [τὰ] πάντα καὶ ἐν πᾶσιν Χριστός.
v 11: "where there is no
Greek or Jew,
circumcised or uncircumcised,
barbarian —Scythian,
slave —free;
but Christ is all and in all."

Comment

The exhortations to "seek the things above" and to "set the mind on the things above" find concrete expression and application in the following imperatives: "put to death" (*νεκρώσατε*, v 5), "put away" (*ἀπόθεσθε*, v 8; cf. "do not lie," *μὴ ψεύδεσθε*, v 9), and "put on" (*ἐνδύσασθε*, v 12). Being heavenly minded does not mean living in the clouds! The believer who obeys the apostolic injunction to aim at the things above will be involved in an ongoing spiritual warfare here below as he or she puts to death sinful propensities and pursuits, and allows the new nature to find outward expression in a godly life. Because they are new persons in Christ they are to live like new persons. Having exposed and refuted the claims of a false asceticism (2:20–23), the apostle now strongly urges a positive line of self-control that is opposed to indulgence (vv 5–8) and affirms a life style that is consistent with Christ himself, the image of the Creator (vv. 10, 11; cf. Martin, *NCB*, 102).

5. *νεκρώσατε οὖν τὰ μέλη τὰ ἐπὶ τῆς γῆς* "Put to death, therefore, whatever belongs to your earthly nature" (NIV). The wording of Paul's first injunction in this paraenetic section is designed to recall what he has written previously in the earlier part of the letter: "therefore" (*οὖν*) harks back to the general context of chapters 2:20–3:4, in particular verses 3 and 4 where the theological basis is set forth (cf. Lohmeyer, 135; Zeilinger, *Der Erstgeborene*, 63; W. Nauck, "Das *οὖν*-paräneticum," *ZNW* 49 [1958] 134, 135), "put to death" (*νεκρώσατε*) recalls the union with Christ in his death (2:20; 3:3; cf. 2:11, 12), "the things on earth" (*τὰ ἐπὶ τῆς γῆς*) picks up the language of verse 2, "[do not set your mind on] the things on earth," while "members" (*μέλη*) is best understood against the background of "the body of sin" (*τὸ σῶμα τῆς σαρκός*, 2:11) which has been stripped off in the circumcision of Christ. Paul's imperative is based upon the previous indicatives which spell out what God has done in his Son the Lord Jesus Christ.

νεκρόω ("put to death"; cf. BAG, 535; Bultmann, *TDNT* 4, 894), which is used in a literal sense at Romans 4:19 and Hebrews 11:12 (both in the perfect passive with reference to Abraham, meaning "worn out," "as good as dead"), is employed figuratively by Paul here (so most commentators, cf. Bultmann, *TDNT* 4, 894; regarding the figurative use of the adjective "dead," *νεκρός*, see on 2:13; so also Luke 15:24, 32; Rom 6:11; 7:8; 8:10; Eph 2:1, 5; Col 2:13; Heb 6:1; 9:14; James 2:17, 26; Rev 3:1; and as a substantive: Matt 8:22; Luke 9:60; John 5:25). This is similar to his use of "count yourselves dead to sin" (*λογίζεσθε ἑαυτοὺς νεκρούς*) at Romans 6:11 (cf. the indicative "you put to death," *θανατοῦτε*, Rom 8:13): in the Colossian injunction the aorist tense points to a decisive initial act which introduces a settled attitude (as expressed by the present tense in Romans).

That which is to be put to death is somewhat unusually described: "the members which are upon earth" (*τὰ μέλη τὰ ἐπὶ τῆς γῆς*), and these are set in apposition to a list of five vices commencing with "fornication" (*πορνείαν*). *μέλος* ("member," "part," "limb," BAG, 501, 502; cf. Horst, *TDNT* 4, 555–68, Schütz, *NIDNTT* 1, 229–32, and Schweizer, *Abraham*, 437–39) was employed in the ancient world with a wide range of meanings and applications, being used in secular Greek of the "member of the body" (so Homer with reference to both men and animals: *Od* 18, 70; 24, 368), an "organ" (in relation to thought, so Parmenides, *Fr* 16, 3), or in the sense of a "melody" or "song" (in Plato, *Rep* 3, 398d). In the LXX the term denotes the bodily members of men (e.g. Judg 19:29; Job 9:28) and animals (e.g. Exod 29:17) as well as signifying a song or melody (either a song of pleasure: Ecclus 32:6, or a lament: Ezek 2:10; Mic 2:4; *μέλος* is not used in this sense in the NT). Within the NT the word is employed literally of various parts of the human body (so Matt 5:29, 30; Rom 6:13, 19; James 3:6, etc.). But Paul is not here referring to the actual members of the human body (as Meyer, 423, thought) nor does he mean quite the same thing as Jesus intended when he spoke of cutting off the offending hand or foot, or plucking out the offending eye if entrance into life could not otherwise be gained (Matt 5:29, 30; 18:8, 9; Mark 9:43–47). The point seems clear from the catalog of vices which is set in apposition to the word "members."

Yet the conjunction of this list with the term "members" is rather abrupt and various attempts have been made to ease the difficulty. Lightfoot (209), for example, placed a period after "earth" (γῆς) and regarded the following nouns ("fornication, uncleanness . . ." πορνείαν, ἀκαθαρσίαν κτλ.) as "prospective accusatives" governed by a verb such as "put off" or "put away" (ἀπόθεσθε) as in verse 8. Accordingly, Paul intended to make these accusatives directly dependent on the verb "put off," but he introduced the intervening clauses which led to a change in the construction of the sentence. Although such breaches are not uncommon in Paul, had he intended this he would probably have placed the imperative before the list of nouns (cf. Bruce, 267, though note Moule, 116). In order to remove the difficulty, Masson proposed that "the members" be understood as a vocative and refer to Christians as limbs of Christ's body (142; he appealed to BDF, para. 147[2] in support; cf. Turner, *Insights*, 104, 105). But this suggestion has not commended itself to scholars (it has been argued that such an absolute use of "members," μέλη, would be possible only if their membership in the body of Christ was made plain in the immediate context: so Dibelius-Greeven 41, Bruce, 268).

Lohse agreed it was hardly possible to interpret "members" here as man's bodily members. Instead, he regarded it as a reference to a traditional form of expression: in Iranian thought a man's members were his good or bad deeds out of which his heavenly self was constituted and so his other-wordly fate was decided (137, following Richard Reitzenstein. Note his *Mystery-Religions*, 338–51. Cf. Dibelius-Greeven, 41, Conzelmann, 150). Five virtues and five vices are mentioned in each instance in the Iranian tradition. Two catalogs of vices (3:5, 8) and the list of virtues (3:12) are based on this enumeration. Without being conscious of the history of religions connections (much less the myth of the two cosmic "men" with their five members, as Käsemann argued) the author, according to Lohse, used "members" in this traditional way and adopted the existing fivefold schema to spell out in his exhortations the kind of life demanded of the Christian.

But there is no need to look to Persian analogies (see the treatment below). Paul is moving wholly within OT and Jewish categories (cf. Schweizer, *Abraham*, 437–39, who has claimed that the close juxtaposition of "members" and "sin," in which sins were localized in the members, can be paralleled in Jewish texts such as 2 *Apoc Bar* 49:3, "these entrammelling *members*, which are now involved in *evils*, and in which *evils* are consummated," [Charles' translation]; see further his *Commentary*, 138). At Romans 6:13, 19 the apostle points out that the readers' bodily members can be offered, on the one hand, to sin as instruments of wickedness and impurity, or, on the other, to God as instruments of righteousness and holiness. At chapter 7:23 of the same letter he refers to the "law of sin which is in my members" (ἐν τοῖς μέλεσίν μου). In Colossians 3:5 Paul goes further and practically identifies the readers' members with the sins those members committed. They had been used as instruments of sin in the old life (this is the point of the qualifying phrase "which are upon earth," τὰ ἐπὶ τῆς γῆς; it has nothing to do with the Greek view whereby the spirit or soul of each man already lives "above," while the members in which sin still works are said to be held fast "below"; cf. Philo, *Det Pot Ins* 85, who considered the feet of man were rooted on earth while his mind and senses were already linked with the circuits of air and heaven). So the term "members" (μέλη) comes to be extended beyond its ordinary sense to comprehend "the various kinds of sin which were committed by their means and in which the 'flesh' (the old nature) expressed itself actively" (Bruce, 268). Here the practices and attitudes to which the readers' bodily activity and strength had been devoted in the old life is in view (Moule, 115, who regards the whole phrase, τὰ μέλη τὰ ἐπὶ τῆς γῆς, as "meaning 'your limbs as put to earthly purposes,' the use of your limbs [or organs] for sensuality," cf. 1 Cor 6:15, and note Gundry, *Sōma*, 42, who arrives at much the same conclusion when he states: "we should probably treat 'the members' as a figurative expression for sins which constitute the earthly 'old man' [v 9]"). A similar extension of meaning can be seen with reference to the related term "body" (σῶμα): "the body of sin" (Rom 6:6), "this body of death" (7:24), and "your body is dead because of sin" (8:10). In these references it is not simply the physical body that is in view; rather σῶμα denotes "the whole personality organized for, and geared into rebellion against God" (Robinson, *Body*, 31).

Putting to death those members which partake of the old nature is not the same as "mortification of the flesh" traditionally understood, for as Moule, 114, has pointed out this latter phrase during its long history has acquired certain associations, often standing for self-inflicted bodily pain through flagellation as practiced by ascetics, or for "self-denial" in the form of abstaining from what one enjoys so as to gain control over the body or acquire merit. But true "mortification" in the context of Colossians 3:5 has to do with a transformation of the will, a new attitude of the mind (cf. Rom 6:11), "a radical shifting of the very centre of the personality from self to Christ, such that 'death' to selfishness is by no means too strong a description" (Moule, 115).

πορνείαν, ἀκαθαρσίαν, πάθος, ἐπιθυμίαν κακήν, καὶ τὴν πλεονεξίαν κτλ. Five sins are identified with the earthly members: fornication, impurity, lust, evil desire and covetousness in general—a movement from the outward manifestations of sin to the inward cravings of the heart, the acts of immorality and uncleanness to their inner springs.

This is the first of two catalogs of vices, the second series of five appears in verse 8, "anger, rage, malice, slander, filthy language" (NIV), and it is then followed by a list of five graces, verse 12, "compassion, kindness, humility, gentleness and patience" (NIV) which the readers are to put on like new clothing.

A Note on the New Testament Ethical Lists

(1) *Background*

Lists of virtues and vices meet us in the NT, particularly in the writings of Paul (Rom 1:29–32; 1 Cor 5:9–11; 6:9, 10; Gal 5:19–23; Phil 4:8; 1 Tim 3:1–13; Titus 1:5–9; 1 Pet 4:3, etc.). They were a common form among pagan moralists and, at least as far as the vices were concerned, in the antipagan polemic of Jewish propagandists. Some have argued that these lists in the NT were indebted to Jewish proselyte catechism as the church took over lists of ethical qualities required by its self-understanding as a neo-levitical community (so P. Carrington and G. Klein). This suggested origin has been challenged recently, particularly by those who have traced the genesis of such lists to Stoicism (Easton, *JBL* 51 [1932] 1; Vögtle *Lasterkataloge*) or to Iranian influences, mediated through sectarian Judaism, such as the Qumran community (Wibbing, *Lasterkataloge*). But Christian borrowing from Stoicism was limited; there is no Stoic parallel to Paul's identification of virtues with the "fruit of the Spirit" (Gal 5:22, 23); the four cardinal virtues (wisdom, manliness, self-control, righteousness) and corresponding vices (folly, cowardice, intemperance, injustice) are not present in the NT catalogs (cf. Wibbing, *Lasterkataloge,* 86); and several of the so-called virtues in the NT lists were regarded as vices in Stoicism. So, for example, "humility" (ταπεινοφροσύνη) was a term of opprobrium in Greek thought (Grundmann, *TDNT* 8, 2), while in the Qumran literature (1QS 5:3, 4;cf. 1QS 2:24; 4:3, 4; 5:25) and in Paul (cf. Phil 2:3; Col 3:12) it denoted the "practice of living together in community before God in such a way that other people are given a dignity and respect as they too are seen in God's sight . . . The 'humility' of Christ becomes a model" (Martin, *NIDNTT* 3, 928).

Kamlah *(Form)* varied Wibbing's suggestion of an Iranian origin of the NT catalogs by distinguishing two forms, a "descriptive" catalog which closed with a promise of salvation and a threat of destruction (e.g. Gal 5:19–23), partly based on the *lex talionis,* "destruction to the destroyer" (cf. E. Käsemann, "Sentences of Holy Law in the New Testament." *New Testament Questions of Today.* Tr. W. J. Montague [London: SCM, 1969] 66–81), and a "paraenetic" one, a putting off of the old life as a prelude to putting on the new (e.g. Col 2:20–3:17), which he traced to the Hellenistic syncretism of the mystery cults. However, Schroeder (*IDBSup,* 546) has argued against this on the ground that the NT lists manifest the ethical dualism of the OT particularly the apocalyptic promises and threats which contain lists of blessings and curses (Deut 27–30)—note the closing appeal: "See, I have set before you this day life and prosperity, death and destruction . . . blessing and curses. Now choose life" (30:15, 19; cf. Jer 21:8; Ezek 18:5–9, 15–17).

Virtues and vices recur in the "Two Ways" scheme, found in *Didache* 1–5; Barn 18–20 and Hermes, *Man* 6:1; cf. Ignatius, *Magn* 5; 2 Clem 4. It has been suggested that underlying this is the Jewish proselyte catechism with its way of light and way of darkness, governed by the spirits of truth and error (Test Levi 19:1; Test Judah 20:1; and especially 1QS). The contrast of men walking in two ways is typically an OT one (Ps 1:6; 16:11; 119:33;

Deut 5:33; 11:22; Josh 22:5; Prov 8:13; Jer 21:8; Zech 1:4; cf. Martin, *NIDNTT* 3, 929).

(2) *Characteristics of Paul's Ethical Lists*

Several features of the Pauline catalogs are to be noted: *(a)* it is evident that considerable variety exists in both their form and content. No hypothetical original list appears to have existed (Easton, *JBL* 51 [1932] 7); there is too much variety, not only in the number of items but also in their sequence, to suggest there were fixed general rules for their logical construction (Wibbing, *Lasterkataloge,* 81–83; cf. Kamlah, *Form,* 176, who claims they were multiform regarding both their content and form).

(b) However, it is going too far to say that the sins or virtues listed have little or nothing to do with the contexts in which they appear (cf. Lohse, 137, 138); the items specifically mentioned are often significant or exemplary (cf. Col 3:5, 8 and note below) and may change according to the situation (Schweizer, *Rechtfertigung,* 476). In most cases they are not full or exhaustive catalogs, a point that is made specifically at the conclusion of the list of vices in Galatians 5:19–21, ". . . envy, drunkenness, orgies, *and the like*" (καὶ τὰ ὅμοια τούτοις).

(c) Paul's lists of vices are frequently set within the framework of God's judgment and the final day: so evildoers, the unrighteous and those who practice such sins will not inherit the kingdom of God, according to 1 Corinthians 6:9, 10, Galatians 5:21 and Ephesians 5:5; while Romans 1:29–31 indicates that those who commit these transgressions or encourage others to do the same deserve death. Following the list of pagan vices at Colossians 3:5 the apostle goes on to assert that on account of these things the wrath of God falls (v 6).

(d) These catalogs are not to be understood in a moralistic sense or as some kind of new law so that the avoidance of the sins or the exercise of the virtues listed would lead to the achievement of righteousness or the acquiring of merit. Rather, they describe the walk of the Christian (Rom 1:29–31 is a catalog of pagan vices). So the persons who clothe themselves with the graces of Christ, such as compassion, kindness, humility, and so on, are addressed as "God's chosen people, holy and dearly loved" (Col 3:12). They have already been raised with Christ (3:1, 3), and have put on the new man (v 10). The graces produced in their lives are the fruit of God's Spirit (Gal 5:22–23; cf. Eph 5:8–11; James 3:13–18, esp. v 18; Matt 7:16–20; Kamlah, *Form,* 182, claims that the influence of Ps 1:3 is discernible in these passages). Similarly, they are to reject pagan ways, such as fornication and idolatry, from their pre-Christian past (Col 3:5; cf. 1 Cor 6:9, 10; 1 Pet 4:3, "For you have spent enough time in the past doing what pagans choose to do—living in debauchery, lust, drunkenness, orgies, carousing and detestable idolatry" [NIV]) because they have already been united with Christ in his death (Col 2:11, 12, 20; 3:3). Getting rid of a repulsive collection of habits (as one might cast aside old clothes) such as anger, quick temper, malice together with slander and foul talk is to be effected because they have stripped off (ἀπεκδυσάμενοι) the "old man" that they once were, together with the practices he loved to indulge in (3:8, 9). Obedience to the apostolic injunctions to

reject sin and be clothed with the graces of Christ is necessary for men and women who are in a new relationship with God through Christ and have become part of God's new creation (Wibbing, *Lasterkataloge,* 123–27).

Comment

The five sins listed are those which belonged to their pagan past (v 7). These were vices for which the Jews especially reproached the pagans (cf. Wisd 14 and note Easton, *JBL* 51 [1932] 1–12, who has drawn attention to the presuppositions of the Hellenistic Jewish apologetics which he considers are visible in the NT lists of virtues and vices).

πορνεία ("prostitution," "unchastity," "fornication," of every kind of unlawful sexual intercourse, BAG, 693) which is mentioned first in the list is always emphatically forbidden. Paul regularly brings to the attention of Gentile Christians the incompatibility of *πορνεία* and the kingdom of God. It is the first of the works of the flesh (Gal 5:19) from which believers are to abstain (1 Thess 4:3) or shun (1 Cor 6:18), since no "sexually immoral person" (*πόρνος*) will inherit the kingdom of God (1 Cor 6:9; cf. 5:9–11; Eph 5:5). The term *πορνεία* carries several shades of meaning in the NT, ranging from extramarital sexual relationships (1 Thess 4:3) to marriages contracted with partners within illicit degrees of kinship (so probably Acts 15:20, though see M. Simon, "The Apostolic Decree and its Setting in the Ancient Church," *BJRL* 52 [1969–70] 437–60, who understands the decree as a condensed code of levitical purity based mainly on Lev 16–18, but also as regards mixed marriages, on Exod 34:15–16; *πορνεία* should be understood as a general term including all sorts of sexual impurities). It denotes any kind of illegitimate sexual intercourse (cf. BAG, 693; Hauck/Schulz, *TDNT* 6, 579–95; Reisser, *NIDNTT* 1, 497–501; this however has been questioned by B. Malina, "Does *Porneia* Mean Fornication?" *NovT* 14 [1972] 10–17; note, however, J. Jensen, "Does *Porneia* Mean Fornication? A Critique of Bruce Malina." *NovT* 20 [1978]: 161–84, who argues that the term and its cognates in the NT describe wanton sexual behavior including fornication) and the word-group was employed in the LXX (rendering the Hebrew *zānâh*) to denote unchastity, harlotry, prostitution and fornication (Gen 34:31, 38:15; Lev 19:29; Deut 22:21). In later rabbinic literature, *z*^e^*nûṯ*. (= *πορνεία*) was understood as including not only prostitution and any kind of extramarital sexual intercourse (*'Aboṯ* 2:8) but also all marriages between relatives forbidden by rabbinic law (cf. Str-B 2, 729, 730). Incest (Test Rub 1:6; Test Jud 13:6; cf. Lev 18:6–18) and all kinds of unnatural sexual intercourse (e.g. Test Ben 9:1) were regarded as fornication (*πορνεία*). One who surrenders to it indicates ultimately that he has broken with God (Wisd 14:27, 28; cf. Reisser, *NIDNTT* 1, 499). In contrast to the loose living that prevailed in the Hellenistic world the NT, and in particular Pauline, teaching requires unconditional obedience to the prohibition against "fornication" (cf. Vögtle, *Lasterkataloge,* 223–25, Hauck/Schulz, *TDNT* 6, 593, 594, and Lohse, 138).

ἀκαθαρσία ("impurity," i.e. moral uncleanness, though on occasion it described ceremonial impurity: Matt 23:27; cf. Num 19:13) which occurs frequently with *πορνεία* ("fornication") and denotes immoral sexual conduct, underscores Paul's injunction (according to Schweizer, 143 and *Rechtfertigung*, 475, the meaning of the first member, πορνεία, is developed through the following three). "Impurity" like "fornication" is a work of the flesh (Gal 5:19) and incompatible with life in the Spirit (1 Thess 4:7, 8, "For God did not call us to be impure [ἐπὶ ἀκαθαρσίᾳ] but to live a holy life . . . he who rejects this instruction does not reject man but God, who gives you his Holy Spirit"; 2 Cor 12:21; Rom 1:24; Eph 5:3, 5; cf. Hauck, *TDNT* 3, 427–29). Like the other members of this list it points to the immoral state of the pre-Christian life, to the behavior of the man whose actions are determined by his commitment to his natural lusts; and yet it was all too easy for Gentile converts to slip back into pre-conversion ways—hence the admonition.

πάθος ("passion") was used by the Stoics to describe the person who allowed himself to be dominated by his emotions, and therefore could not attain "tranquility" (ἀπάθεια; cf. Vögtle, *Lasterkataloge*, 208–210). In the NT references, all of which occur in Paul (Rom 1:26; Col 3:5 and 1 Thess 4:5), it does not turn up in this Stoic sense; rather it denotes shameful passion which leads to sexual excesses (1 Thess 4:5; the vices of homosexuality at Rom 1:26; note Michaelis, *TDNT* 5, 928).

ἐπιθυμία ("desire," "longing") was employed in a positive fashion to describe a variety of aims including the longing to see a Christian congregation (1 Thess 2:17) or the desire to depart and be with Christ (Phil 1:23; cf. Luke 22:15; the verb "desire," ἐπιθυμέω, can also be used in a good sense: Matt 13:17; Luke 17:22; 1 Tim 3:1; Heb 6:11; 1 Pet 1:12; cf. Büchsel, *TDNT* 3, 168–71). Here the desire is characterized negatively with the addition of the adjective "evil" (κακήν) so that it describes wicked concupiscence (Büchsel, *TDNT* 3, 170, 171, points out that the noun and the verb usually indicate evil desires which may then be expanded with reference to the object of the longing: Matt 5:28, a woman; Mark 4:19, other things; 1 Cor 10:6, evil things; or the direction: Gal 5:17, against the Spirit; or the vehicle or origin: Rom 1:24, the heart; Rom 6:12, the body; Gal 5:16; Eph 2:3; 1 John 2:16; 2 Pet 2:18, the flesh, and so on). Evil desire is a manifestation of the sin which dwells in the natural man and which controls him. It reveals his carnality (Gal 5:16, 24), his separation from God and his subjection to divine wrath (Rom 1:18–24).

The final member of the list "covetousness" (πλεονεξία, lit. "a desire to have more," so meaning "greediness," "insatiableness," "avarice," BAG, 667; see Delling, *TDNT* 6, 266–74, and Selter, *NIDNTT* 1, 137, 138) is especially accented as a gross sin: "and that chief vice, covetousness which is idolatry" (so BDF, para. 258[1], who note, "the addition of the relative clause ἥτις etc. occasions the use of the article by making the preceding noun definite"; cf. Zeilinger, *Der Erstgeborene*, 64; Schweizer, 143, 144). It breaks the sequence by turning attention from sexual vices to the more general sin of greed (Martin, *NCB*, 103). In some contexts, of course, covetousness can have sexual overtones (cf. the cognate πλεονεκτέω at 1 Thess 4:6; the noun was used by Plato and Aristotle to include sexual desire), but normally it refers to the sin of acquisitiveness, the insatiable desire to lay hands on material things. The word group appears only occasionally in the LXX, occurring chiefly in the denunciations and warnings of the prophets about dishonest gain and the enrichment of the politically powerful by means of violence (Jer 22:17; Ezek 22:27; Hab 2:9). The ungodly and thoroughly bad character of covetousness comes out in the LXX references (cf. 2 Macc 4:50). Accordingly, the psalmist prays that he may be preserved from it (Ps 119:36 [LXX 118:36]). Even in the Greco-Roman world covetousness was repudiated; there was no place for it in a just and equitable society.

The NT warns again and again about the sin of covetousness, particularly as a means of security (Luke 12:15, "Watch out! Be on your guard against all kinds of greed [*ἀπὸ πάσης πλεονεξίας*]"). In the catalogs of vices covetousness is the mark of a life which lacks the knowledge of God (Rom 1:29; cf. 1 Cor 5:10, 11; 6:10, 11; Eph 5:3). Its presence along with other kinds of wickedness is evidence, according to Paul, of the power of sin in the ravaging of human relationships (Delling, *TDNT* 6, 272) and a sign that God has given men and women over to a depraved mind (Rom 1:28). For Christians involved in the ministry of God's Word there is a particular danger of covetousness. The temptation to abuse one's position and to exploit the preaching of God's Word for personal gain was a danger from which the early church did not escape. Paul refutes the suggestion that he and his co-workers had exploited anyone at Corinth, desiring to enrich themselves by their ministry (cf. the cognate *πλεονεκτέω*, "cheat," "defraud," used at 2 Cor 7:2 and 12:17). In his missionary work at Thessalonica, as elsewhere, he was free not only from self-seeking motives (1 Thess 2:4, 5) which might have been hidden behind an unselfish activity (v 3) but also from covetousness; when he preached he had no ulterior purpose of enriching himself ("nor did we put on a mask to cover up greed [*οὔτε ἐν προφάσει πλεονεξίας*]," v 5; cf. Delling, *TDNT* 6, 273). Although the charge could not stick in the case of Paul, for it was wholly unfounded, there were others who abused their position to satisfy their greed: Paul's opponents at Corinth are described as "peddlers of God's word" (*καπηλεύοντες τὸν λόγον τοῦ θεοῦ*, 2 Cor 2:17), while according to 2 Peter 2:3, 14 the false teachers exploited the congregation, being motivated by their greed for material gain—in fact, they are said to be experts in greed! But it was not only those involved in the ministry of God's Word who were open to the tempation of covetousness. Paul's exhortation here in verse 5 is addressed to *all* the readers. Like immorality and impurity, covetousness is to be put to death by *all* who died and rose with Christ.

The danger of covetousness is stressed emphatically because it is so closely related to idolatry: rather suprisingly the former is equated with the latter (*τὴν πλεονεξίαν ἥτις ἐστὶν εἰδωλολατρία*). The two sins stood together in Jewish exhortations and were condemned as part of the horrors of paganism. According to the Testament of Judah (19:1) greed seized control of a man, led him away from God and held him captive in idolatry: "The love of money leads to idolatry; because, when led astray through money, men name as gods those who are not gods." Elsewhere in Jewish thought greed was soundly condemned (by Philo, *Spec leg* 1:23–27; cf. Delling, *TDNT* 6, 270; for rabbinic examples see Str-B 3, 606, 607; and note the negative judgment on possessions in the writings of the Qumran community: 1QpHab 6:1; 8:11, 12; 1QS 10:19, 11:2, etc.). Since a man can serve only one master, God or mammon, but not both (Matt 6:24), then if he sets his heart on wealth, he adores false gods and abandons the one true God (Lohse, 139; Schweizer, *Text*, 200, aptly remarks: "When man has lost God, he is at the mercy of all things, because his own covetousness takes the place of God"). Instead of setting his aims and whole orientation on the things above, at the center of which is the exalted Christ, he is seeking the things below. He worships and serves the creature rather than the Creator (Rom 1:25). The apostle's words in Romans 7:7, 8 indicate how the commandment revealed to him the special deadliness of this subtle sin. Perhaps it is the more dangerous because it may assume so many respectable forms.

6. *δι' ἃ ἔρχεται ἡ ὀργὴ τοῦ θεοῦ [ἐπὶ τοὺς υἱοὺς τῆς ἀπειθείας]*. These are the things for which men and women will be punished with divine retribution. Several of the NT lists of vices conclude with a reference to God's judgment on sin. So in his great arraignment of the pagan world at Romans 1:18–32, the apostle sets his lengthy catalog of vices within the context of God's wrath (v 18) and concludes that men who practice such things deserve death (v 32). At 1 Thessalonians 4 when dealing with the related issues of sexual immorality (*πορνεία*, v 3) and covetousness (*πλεονεκτέω*, v 6), Paul states that the "Lord will punish men for all such sins" (v 6), while at the conclusion of a list of vices in 1 Corinthians 5:13, the note of God's judgment is struck again. A similar motif appears at 1 Corinthians 6:9, 10 and Galatians 5:21 (cf. Eph 5:5, 6) in conjunction with these catalogs, this time in terms of people who live in a pagan way not inheriting the kingdom of God. The serious note of God's judgment on those who practice these vices was written to Christian congregations and served as a solemn reminder of what would have happened to them had they continued to live in their former pagan ways. And indirectly, if not explicitly, an added reason is set forth for avoiding these sins, for putting to death the members upon earth.

The expression "the wrath of God" (*ἡ ὀργὴ τοῦ θεοῦ*) turns up in both Old and New Testaments to describe God's holy anger against sin and the judgment that results (cf. 1 Thess 1:10; 2:16; note especially the treatment of Stählin, *TDNT* 5, 419–47, who recognizes that although *ὀργή* in most NT passages is the divine work or judgment of wrath [cf. Rom 2:5; 3:5; 12:19, etc.] the idea of an actual attitude of God cannot be disputed in many NT verses, any more than this is possible in the case of "love" or "mercy." In sum, the NT, like the Old, presents *ὀργή* as "both God's displeasure at evil, His passionate resistance to every will which is set against Him, and also His judicial attack thereon" [425]). Unlike the wrath ascribed to pagan deities of the ancient world this phrase and its equivalents denote neither God's vindictive anger nor his outbursts of passion (the term *θυμός*, "passion," "wrath," "rage," turns up at Rom 2:8 with reference to the wrath of God but it is used synonymously with *ὀργή*; the occasional heaping up of such terms [Rom 2:8, 9; cf. Rev 16:19] serves not to describe unbridled and hence unrighteous revenge, but to enhance the shattering impression of the reality of the divine wrath, cf. Stählin, *TDNT* 5, 422). Many of the Pauline passages speak about "wrath" (*ὀργή*) without the qualifying genitive "of God" ([*τοῦ*] *θεοῦ*: Rom 2:5 [twice], 8; 3:5; 4:15; 5:9; 9:22 [twice]; 12:19; 13:4, 5; Eph 2:3; 1 Thess 1:10; 2:16; 5:9; contrast Rom 1:18; Eph 5:6; Col 3:6 where the qualifying genitive appears). Accordingly the suggestion has been advanced that "wrath" in Paul is an autonomous entity alongside God, either as an independently operating though personified force, or as a *principle* of retribution that is not to be associated closely with the personality of God. Concerning the former alternative it was argued that this personification of "wrath" was prefigured in the OT when reference was made to the instruments of wrath together with the many figurative impressions of the sending, coming and passing of wrath (e.g. Isa 10:6; 26:20; cf. Isa 63:5: "Then my fury helped me;" see Stählin, *TDNT* 5, 414, 424, for references). Judaism developed the line still further and this "absolute" view in the NT is a continuation of this development. C. H. Dodd was an energetic exponent of the latter, though closely related, alternative. He points out that Paul never uses the verb to "be angry" with God as subject, and claims that wrath meant "not . . . the attitude of God to man, but . . . an inevitable process of cause and effect in a moral universe" (*The Epistle of Paul to the Romans* [London: Hodder, 1932] 23; cf. G. H. C. Macgregor's essay, "The Concept of the Wrath of God in the New Testament," *NTS* 7 [1960–61] 101–109).

However, against both variations it needs to be argued, first, that in the above-mentioned references "the wrath" (ἡ ὀργή) and "wrath" without the article (ὀργή) decisively point to God's holy anger (just as εὐδοκία, "good pleasure," and ϑέλημα, "will," can be used without qualification of the good pleasure or will of God). Second, one cannot on the basis of several figurative references personify wrath over against God himself (see below). In both Old and New Testaments it is indissolubly related to God (cf. H. C. Hahn, *NIDNTT* 1, 107–13). Third, the wrath of God is not to be set in sharp contrast with the love and mercy of God. It is so often asserted that if God is truly love he cannot be angry. But wrath and love are not mutually exclusive. In the NT as well as in the Old, in Jesus as in the prophets and apostles the proclamation of God's mercy is accompanied by the preaching of his wrath. A holy God does not stand idly by when men act unrighteously, transgress the law, show disdain to him as their creator or spurn his love and mercy. He acts in a righteous manner punishing sin in the present and especially on the final day. Yet God also acquits the guilty, and only the person who understands something of the greatness of his wrath will be mastered by the greatness of his mercy. The converse also is true: only he who has experienced the greatness of God's mercy can understand something of how great that wrath must be (Stählin, *TDNT* 5, 425).

7. You used to practice these same vices on account of which God's wrath is coming; in fact, your lives were characterized by them. At verses 7 and 8 the "once-now" antithesis is repeated (see on 1:21, 22 and 2:13, and note Tachau, *Einst*, 123–25) as the readers (cf. the emphatic "and you," v 7) are shown how they ought to behave now in contrast to their past. In the two earlier contexts (1:21, 22 and 2:13) the antithetical statements described their previous lost condition and their present standing in Christ. Here, however, the "once-now" antithesis functions rather differently. The past behavior is characterized by the indicative mood (περιεπατήσατε, "you walked" and ἐζῆτε, "you lived," v 7), but instead of following this with another indicative to describe their present standing the apostle employs an imperative "put away" (ἀπόϑεσϑε, v 8; cf. Rom 6:15–23; 7:4–6; Gal 4:8–11; Eph 5:8) to spell out

their new responsibilities in Christ. At the same time the two catalogs of vices (vv 5, 8) are joined together through the "once-now" schema (the antecedent of ἐν οἷς, "in which," v 7, is the first list of vices, v 5, while τὰ πάντα, "all," v 8, is defined more precisely by the second catalog) in two sentences which are constructed chiastically (cf. Tachau, *Einst*, 124):

	ἐν οἷς καὶ ὑμεῖς	περιεπατήσατέ
		ποτε . . .
	νυνὶ δὲ ἀπόθεσθε	καὶ ὑμεῖς τὰ πάντα
lit.	"In which also you	walked once, . . .
	but now put away	(you also) them
		all."

ἐν οἷς καὶ ὑμεῖς περιεπατήσατέ ποτε "you too used to walk in these ways." If Paul has been drawing upon traditional lists of vices (see above) then he is applying them to the readers (hence καὶ ὑμεῖς, "you also"), reminding them of their pre-Christian past (so Vögtle, *Lasterkataloge*, 19, Jervell, *Imago*, 235, Lohse, 140, Martin, *NCB*, 104; ἐν οἷς is neuter, "in which," if the shorter reading of v 6 is followed [see the note above, 173], and designates the vices of v 5 on account of which God's wrath comes; if, however, one reads "upon the sons of disobedience" [ἐπὶ τοὺς υἱοὺς τῆς ἀπειθείας] of v 6 then ἐν οἷς would be masculine meaning "among whom"; the shorter reading is preferred for the reasons given). The Colossians had conducted their lives (on the verb περιπατέω, "walk," a favorite Pauline metaphor, drawn from the OT and Jewish tradition, for a way of life see above on 1:10 and 2:6) by doing evil deeds (cf. 1:21). Their outward behavior corresponded with their established attitudes and sentiments (Caird, 205; the ὅτε ["when"] clause expands on the preceding: the imperfect tense of the verb ζάω, "live," draws attention to a continuing state with its fixed attitudes, while ἐν τούτοις, "in them," is more emphatic and condemnatory than the expected ἐν αὐτοῖς, so Lightfoot, 211), and they were dead in their sins (cf. 2:13).

8. νυνὶ δὲ ἀπόθεσθε καὶ ὑμεῖς τὰ πάντα κτλ. But a change has occurred, (on the "once-now" antithesis see on v 7; cf. Stählin, *TDNT* 4, 1121) and they are to discard their old repulsive habits like a set of worn-out clothes. ἀποτίθημι meaning to "put away" was used literally with reference to clothes at Acts 7:58 (cf. 2 Macc 8:35; Jos *Ant* 8, 266) and in a metaphorical and ethical sense at Romans 13:12; Ephesians 4:22, 25; Hebrews 12:1; James 1:21; and 1 Peter 2:1. For the representation of behavior or character as a garment see Job 29:14; Psalm 35:26; 109:29; 132:9; Isaiah 11:5; 59:17; 61:10; Romans 13:12, 14; and 1 Thessalonians 5:8. The notion is extended to the putting off of the old (terrestrial) body and the putting on of the new (celestial) one (in 1 Cor 15:53, 54; 2 Cor 5:2–4; cf. Bruce, 271). In Colossians 3 although there is no specific reference to having put off the old man until verse 9, the object of the putting aside in verse 8 is a totality (τὰ πάντα) and best understood as a reference to the entire sinful nature (cf. Kamlah, *Form*, 183, and Lohse, 140; at Heb 12:1; James 1:21; 1 Pet 2:1 the same verb "put off" is joined to "all"). The readers (καὶ ὑμεῖς underscores the contrast with what they once were) are to put aside everything that was done in connection with the old man.

ὀργήν, θυμόν, κακίαν, βλασφημίαν, αἰσχρολογίαν ἐκ τοῦ στόματος ὑμῶν. The content of this "all" (*τὰ πάντα*) is spelled out in the fivefold catalog of vices (which may have been taken over from traditional material, as many suggest but which were entirely relevant to the concrete situation addressed, cf. Moule, *RevExp* 70 [1973] 488); "all" looks forward prospectively to the list of five vices which follow (so Moule, 118, though cf. his article, *RevExp* 70 [1973] 488; Zeilinger, *Der Erstgeborene,* 64, and Lohse, 140, rather than referring *back* to all the evils just mentioned in v 5 and adding a further characterization of them in terms of other sins [cf. Lightfoot, 212, Williams, 128, Meyer, 429]). The sins to be put off are anger, quick temper, malice and the language which accompanies these things, slander and foul talk. (Commentators like Caird, 205, who consider the phrase "from your mouth" belongs to the verb "put away" rather than with the last noun in the list regard all five vices as forms of intemperate speech; but there are difficulties with this view: first, "wrath" and "passion," as well as "evil," have to be restricted to sins of the tongue, cf. Williams, 128; and, second, the expression "from your mouth" is distant from the verb "put away".)

ὀργή ("wrath") and *θυμός* ("anger") go together and although Stoic thinkers distinguished the two, the one denoting a more or less settled feeling of hatred, the other a tumultuous outburst of passion (for references see Lightfoot, 212), there appears to be little difference between them here: as outbursts of temper they are destructive of harmony in human relationships (cf. Büchsel, *TDNT* 3, 168; Moule, 118) and both must be put away (cf. Eph 4:31). (On the almost totally negative appraisal of human anger in the NT see Stählin, *TDNT* 5, 420, 421; note the exception at Eph 4:26, "If you are angry, be careful not to sin".) The rage of anger (plural *θυμοί*) belongs to the "works of the flesh" (Gal 5:19, 20) and ought not to be found among Christ's people (2 Cor 12:20).

Along with these, "malice" (*κακία*) is to be removed since it is an evil force that destroys fellowship. The term is a general one (cf. BAG, 397, Grundmann, *TDNT* 3, 482–84) ranging from "trouble" (with no moral implications, Matt 6:34), to a definitely culpable attitude of "wickedness." It might denote a single iniquity such as the grasping desire of Simon Magus (Acts 8:22) or be used more generally for the evil men do to one another. Martin includes it as one of the sins of speech (*NCB,* 104, 105; he claims that at 1 Cor 5:8; 14:20; Rom 1:29 and Eph 4:31 it depicts the havoc to human society wrought by evil-speaking), though it is possible to regard it here as "malice," that is, the deliberate intention to harm which is subsequently expressed in evil speech such as "slander" and "abusive language."

βλασφημία ("slander," "defamation," "blasphemy," BAG, 143; cf. Beyer, *TDNT* 1, 621–25) in biblical Greek most frequently referred to "speech against God," for even when the object of the attack was human, it was usually in some sense as God's representative (2 Kings 6:22; 19:4; Isa 52:5; Ezek 35:12, 13; 2 Macc 8:4; 9:28; 10:4, 34; cf. Moule, 118; Währisch/Brown, *NIDNTT* 3, 341, 342). In NT times "blasphemy" was directed immediately against God (Rev 13:6; 16:11, 21), against the name of God (Rom 2:24; 1 Tim 6:1; Rev 16:9), against the word of God (Tit 2:5), against Moses and God, and so against the bearer of the revelation in the law (Acts 6:11; Beyer, *TDNT* 1, 622, 623). In nonbiblical Greek the term often meant "abuse" or "slander," and probably has this sense of defamation of human character here in an ethical list rather than to a curse directed against God (so many recent commentators including Martin, *NCB*, 105, Lohse, 140, and Schweizer, 145; Beyer, *TDNT* 1, 624, on the other hand, claims that the predominantly religious connotation of blasphemy against God is present in the lists of offenses even when it is not explicitly mentioned: Mark 7:22; Matt 15:19; Eph 4:31; Col 3:8; 1 Tim 6:4; 2 Tim 3:2; this presumably could arise when Christians were under persecution or in the company of derisive non-Christians). Accordingly, it covers any type of vilifying of man, either by lies or gossip. The Christian is commanded to "slander no one" (Tit 3:2).

The last of the five vices, αἰσχρολογία ("foul talk") like its counterpart in the previous list ("covetousness," v 5), is especially emphasized this time by the additional words "out of your mouth" (cf. Zeilinger, *Der Erstgeborene*, 44; some commentators take the phrase as applying to both "slander" and "foul talk," so for example Abbott, 283; others, as we have noted above, link the phrase with the verb "put off"). αἰσχρολογία occurs only here in the NT but outside the Bible covers the ideas of obscene speech or abusive language (Lightfoot, 212, who supposes that the two notions of "filthiness" and "evil-speaking" are included here; cf. BAG, 25). Such language ought to be stopped before it comes out of their mouths.

9. You used to tell lies to one another as though it was the natural thing to do; don't do it any more (this is probably the significance of the present imperative, so Bruce, 272, though cf. Moule, *Idiom Book*, 20, 21). μὴ ψεύδεσθε εἰς ἀλλήλους continues the series of imperatives and is most naturally connected with the preceding notions of "slander" and "abusive language." As Martin (*NCB*, 105) rightly points out this injunction does not come as an anticlimax. The "social effects of untrustworthy promises and pledges are enormous." The expression "to one another" (εἰς ἀλλήλους) shows that the exhortation has particular reference to believers in their relations within the Christian community. This, of course, in no way suggests that Christians could take the question of truth less seriously when speaking to outsiders. The apostle is simply asserting that in their regular contact with fellow-believers they must speak "the truth, the whole truth and nothing but the truth."

The twofold reason for this abandonment of evil ways is now given: (1) you have put off the old man with his practices (v 9), and (2) you have put on the new man . . . (v 10). Many exegetes consider that the two aorist participles ἀπεκδυσάμενοι ("having put off," v 9) and ἐνδυσάμενοι ("having put on," v 10) are to be understood in an imperatival sense, so that in effect Paul is continuing his appeal begun with the injunction, "Don't lie." Accordingly, the readers are urged to give up the old nature with its habits and to replace it by putting on the new man. Grammatically this interpretation is possible (cf. Merk, *Handeln*, 205), and the use of the participle for the imperative was a genuine Hellenistic development (Moulton, *Grammar* 1, 180–83), with instances in the NT (e.g., Rom 12:9) while examples of this phenomenon were common enough in rabbinic usage (as D. Daube has demonstrated, cf. his "Participle and Imperative in 1 Peter," in E. G. Selwyn, *The First Epistle of St Peter* [London: Macmillan, 1947] 467–88; note also E. Lohse, "Paränese und Kerygma im 1. Petrusbrief," *ZNW* 45 [1954] 75, 76, and his commentary, 141). However, the alternative view of treating the two verbs as true participles which describe the past event, in which the readers have already put off the old nature and put on the new, as the basis for the abandonment of evil ways, is preferable since it is more in keeping with Paul's teaching elsewhere in Colossians (the parallel passage in Ephesians 4:22–24 supports the imperatival translations though the point being made there, using infinitives rather than participles, is somewhat different). In the paraenetic sections of Colossians the apostle grounds his exhortations in what has already occurred to the readers when they were incorporated in Christ (2:6, 7 and 2:16–3:4; Jervell, *Imago,* 236, has argued this point forcibly; cf. Abbott, 283; Masson, 143; Larsson, *Christus,* 198; Maurer, *TDNT* 6, 644; Merk, *Handeln,* 205; and Martin, *NCB,* 106). Paul often refers back to the readers' life-changing event; he does so by means of an aorist participle or an aorist indicative (1:6, 7, 13, 22; 2:6, 7, 11–15, 20; 3:1, 3). It is therefore natural to regard these participles of verses 9 and 10 in a similar light, indicating that the readers had stripped off the old man when baptized into Christ's death and put on the new man. Verse 12 with its exhortation to put on the graces of Christ (or God) is then grounded in the fact that they had put on the new man.

The picture of putting on and putting off a garment was widespread in the ancient world and was employed in the mystery religions with reference to the action of initiation. The putting on of the garment consecrated the initiate so that he was filled with the powers of the cosmos and shared in the divine life. In Gnostic texts the donning of the garment indicates that redemption had come, a redemption that would be subsequently perfected (so Käsemann noted by Lohse, 141). But the background of the expression "putting off the old man" and "putting on the new man" was neither Gnosticism nor the mystery religions. The clothing metaphor was common in Hebrew and Greek writings, but not with "man" as an object. (Against the background of initiation into the Isis-mysteries as described by Apuleius in his *Metamorphoses* XI, 23f. and cited by Lohse, 141, three objections have been raised: *(a)* none of the parallels cited is pre-Christian; *(b)* most parallels belong to a different sphere of ideas; and *(c)* a literal parallel, i.e., putting on or putting off a "man," has not yet been found). In the OT the notion of being clothed with moral and religious qualities is found, e.g. strength (Isa 51:9; 52:1), righteousness (Ps 132:9; Job 29:14), majesty (Ps 93:1), honor and majesty (Ps 104:1; Job 40:10), and salvation (2 Chron 6:41), cf. dishonor (Ps 109:29) and cursing (Ps 109:18); while the rabbinic literature refers to clothing with spiritual and ethical qualities, e.g. the Torah clothes with humility and reverence (*'Abot* 6:1; cf. Str-B 2, 301, for further references), which are analogous to Colossians 3:12 and 3:8 (for a discussion see P. W. van der Horst, "Observations on a Pauline Expression," *NTS* 19 [1972–73] 181–87.)

So the Pauline expression is without an exact literal parallel. Also the terms "the old man" (τὸν παλαιὸν ἄνθρωπον) and "the new (man)" (τὸν νέον) do not simply describe an individual's condition (e.g. one's old, bad character and the new, Christian character), but also carry corporate associations denoting an old and a new order of existence (Moule, 119, 120; cf. Tannehill, *Dying,* 25, 50–54; Martin, *NCB,* 107; Jervell, *Imago,* 240, states that "no parallel to this unique concept has been found in non-Christian sources" [cf. 240–48 for his detailed treatment]; neither in Gnostic texts nor in Judaism was there any idea of an antithesis between the old and the new man—see below.) The "old man" here, as in Romans 6:6 and Ephesians 4:22, designates the whole personality of man when he is ruled by sin. At the same time it signifies his belonging to the old humanity in Adam (cf. Larsson, *Christus,* 197, and Zeilinger, *Der Erstgeborene,* 197). Verse 9 speaks of the old man "with his deeds" (*σὺν ταῖς πράξεσιν αὐτοῦ*) being stripped off. These "practices" (on *πρᾶξις* see BAG, 697, 698; Maurer, *TDNT* 6, 642–44) evidently include the two lists of vices in verses 5 and 8. The connection between the old man and these vices is expressed in another way at verse 5 where the list of vices stands in apposition to the "members on earth" (*τὰ μέλη τὰ ἐπὶ τῆς γῆς*; cf. Tannehill, *Dying,* 50). Fornication, covetousness and the like are "members" of the old man (just as the virtues of v 12 might aptly be styled "members" of the new man). Since the old man and his practices have been put off in Christ's death, the readers are to have no truck with false speaking or any of the other repulsive habits mentioned.

10. *καὶ ἐνδυσάμενοι τὸν νέον.* The new man has been put on in place of the old. The Greek adjective *νέος* ("new"; cf. BAG, 535, 536; Behm, *TDNT* 4, 896–901) stands in contrast to *παλαιός* ("old") and means the same as the synonym *καινός* ("new"; cf. BAG, 394; Behm, *TDNT* 3, 447–54; older exegetes [notably R. C. Trench, *Synonyms of the New Testament,* Grand Rapids: Eerdmans, 1969 = 1880, 219–25] regarded *νέος* primarily as a temporal adjective meaning "young" while *καινός* had qualitative connotations: as "new" it actually supplants the old and calls it into question in a qualitative manner. But these distinctions are difficult to maintain: both terms can imply a qualitative as well as a temporal significance; here *τὸν νέον* is followed by a compound of *καινός—τὸν ἀνακαινούμενον,* "which is being renewed"—and may have been chosen simply for the sake of stylistic variety; in the parallel passage of Eph 4:23, 24, conversely the verb contains *νέος* and the adjective is *καινός*; cf. R. A. Harrisville, "The Concept of Newness in the New Testament," *JBL* 74 [1955] 69–79; Larsson, *Christus,* 200; Moule, 119).

To another group of Christians Paul states: "as many of you as were baptized into Christ did put on Christ" (Gal 3:27; note the corresponding imperative of Rom 13:14, "put on the Lord Jesus Christ"). Here the "new man," like its opposite "the old man," has a twofold significance—singular and corporate. On the one hand, it has an individual reference, designating the new nature which the Colossians had put on and which was continually being renewed (the present participle *ἀνακαινούμενον* indicates an ongoing process; cf. Rom 12:2) in accordance with the Creator's image. The point about the renewal of the new man is to be compared with what Paul says about the "inner man" (*ὁ ἔσω ἄνθρωπος*) of 2 Corinthians 4:16 which is also being renewed from day to day (*ἀνακαινοῦνται*). According to Ephesians 3:16, through a similar process the addressees are strengthened with power by God's Spirit "for the inner man" (*εἰς τὸν ἔσω ἄνθρωπον*; cf. Rom 7:22). On the other hand, the expression, "the new man," has a corporate reference designating the new humanity in Christ. Just as the "old man" is what they once were "in Adam," the embodiment of unregenerate humanity, so the "new man" is what they now are "in Christ," the embodiment of the new humanity. Verse 11 with its statements about the abolition of racial, religious, cultural and social barriers underscores this corporate aspect (cf. Schnackenburg, *Schriften*, 392–411; and for forceful statements in favor of this corporate emphasis see Robinson, *Body*, 58–67, and Tannehill, *Dying*, 25). The renewal refers not simply to an individual change of character but also to a corporate recreation of humanity in the Creator's image. Christ is the "new man" whom the Colossians have put on. He is the second Adam, the head of a new creation (cf. 2 Cor 5:17; Gal 6:15).

τὸν ἀνακαινούμενον εἰς ἐπίγνωσιν κατ' εἰκόνα τοῦ κτίσαντος αὐτόν. Grammatically it seems best to regard the prepositional phrase κατ' εἰκόνα τοῦ κτίσαντος αὐτόν ("after the image of its Creator") as modifying τὸν ἀνακαινούμενον ("which is being renewed"; cf. Larsson, *Christus*, 198; this is preferable to its being attached to ἐπίγνωσιν, "knowledge": for a discussion of this and other alternatives see Jervell, *Imago*, 248, 249, and Merk, *Handeln*, 205). Accordingly, the image of the Creator serves as the model or archetype for the renewal of the new man—a renewal that has in view the readers' progressive increase in true knowledge (Eph 4:24 speaks of the creation of the new man but not, as does Col 3:10, of its constant renewal).

κατ' εἰκόνα τοῦ κτίσαντος αὐτόν. "After the image of its Creator." Even though this phrase is not an explicit Scripture citation one cannot miss the allusion to Genesis 1:27, where the first Adam is said to have been created by God "in his own image" (κατ' εἰκόνα θεοῦ). However, the first Adam is now regarded as the "old man" that has been discarded so that the believer may put on the new man. Although Chrysostom and some modern writers regarded the words τοῦ κτίσαντος as designating Christ as the Creator it is, in fact, a description of God (cf. Eph 4:24 where it is stated that the new man is created κατὰ θεόν, lit. "according to God," or as the RSV puts it "after the likeness of God"; in the Pauline material as well as in the rest of the NT God is the subject of κτίζω, "create": Rom 1:25; Eph 3:9; cf. 1 Cor 11:9; Eph 2:10; 4:24; 1 Tim 4:3; Matt 19:4; Mark 13:19; 1 Pet 4:19; Rev 4:11; 10:6; while in Col 1:16, as we have already shown, God is the logical subject of the passive verb "created," ἐκτίσθη and ἔκτισται; cf. Moule, 120, Jervell, *Imago*, 249, 250, G. Delling, "Partizipiale Gottesprädikationen in den Briefen des Neuen Testaments," *ST* 17 [1963] 25, Merk, *Handeln*, 207, Lohse, 143, and Martin, *NCB*, 107). However, to say that the new man is being renewed "according to the image of God," in the light of the hymnic paragraph where Christ is praised as the εἰκών ("image") of God (1:15; see 42–44) and Paul's Christological teaching elsewhere (Rom 8:29; 1 Cor 15:49; 2 Cor 4:4; and Phil 2:6) means that God's recreation of man "is *in the pattern of Christ*, who is God's Likeness absolutely" (Moule, 120). This is not at variance with the apostle's statements elsewhere which speak of the Christian's transformation *into* the image of Christ (Rom 8:29; 1 Cor 15:49; 2 Cor 3:18; Phil 3:21), for while the former makes it clear that the redeemed become the "new man" or καινὴ κτίσις ("new creation") to whom the image of God—which Adam lost—has been restored, the latter denotes that this restoration of the divine image is nothing other than their transformation into the image of Christ (Kim, *Paul's Gospel*, 406, cf. 295, 296). The expression "him that created *him*" (*αὐτόν* refers to the "new man") does not imply that Christ personally is a created being even though he is the new man whom believers have put on: "the new man who is created is the new personality that each believer becomes when he is reborn as a member of the new creation whose source of life is Christ" (Bruce, 273; cf. Larsson, *Christus,* 209).

εἰς ἐπίγνωσιν ("in knowledge") occurs here in an absolute sense as in Philippians 1:9: "that your love may abound more and more with knowledge and all discernment." The renewal of the new man has in view (cf. von Soden, 61) the readers' progressive increase in the ability to recognize God's will and command (cf. Col 1:9; see Lohse, 143), something which the old man did not possess. This true knowledge leads to a conduct that is in conformity with the Creator's will.

11. Within this new humanity (*ὅπου*, a particle denoting place, is here employed figuratively to denote the circumstances or presupposition of what has gone before = "in the realm of the new man," Dibelius-Greeven, 42) the barriers that divided people from one another—racial, religious, cultural and social—are abolished (Lightfoot, 214, claims that *οὐκ ἔνι* means: "Not only does the distinction not exist, but it *cannot* exist"; cf. Martin, *NCB,* 108; for a contrary view see Abbott, 285). The theological reason is that "all were baptized into the one body—Jews or Greeks, slaves or free" (1 Cor 12:13). Elsewhere in the Pauline letters similar subdivisions of the human family are listed: e.g. Galatians 3:28, where Paul states that for those who have been baptized into Christ and put on Christ "there is neither Jew nor Greek, there is neither slave nor free, there is neither male nor female; for you are all one in Christ Jesus" (cf. Rom 1:14). Here the teaching of Galatians is repeated and expanded, no doubt in accordance with the needs of the Colossian readers (so Lightfoot, 214, 215, Jervell, *Imago,* 251, and Martin, *NCB,* 108; against Lohse, 143, who regards the verse as traditional; Bruce, 275, suggests that the choice of antitheses in Gal 3:28 is made with "a view to overthrowing the threefold privilege which a pious Jew recalls morning by morning when he thanks God that He did not make him a Gentile, a slave or a woman"). Further, the list of social distinctions mentioned throws light on the kind of frictions the Christian faith had to overcome (Moule, 121).

Ἕλλην καὶ Ἰουδαῖος, περιτομὴ καὶ ἀκροβυστία. "Greek and Jew, circumcised and uncircumcised." Greeks and Jews are mentioned first in the series to describe the whole of humanity (cf. 1 Cor. 1:24; 10:32; 12:13; Gal 3:28; Greeks are mentioned as the outstanding representatives of the Gentiles; on the "Jew" in Paul see Gutbrod, *TDNT* 3, 380–82, and on "Greek" Windisch, *TDNT* 2, 512–16). Normally the Jews appear first as an expression of their privileged place in salvation history. Here the order is reversed, probably because the majority of the readers were Gentile Christians (cf. 1:21, 22; 2:13). In Christ the old distinction between Jew and Gentile was abolished—a remarkable achievement of the gospel. So "circumcision" (Meyer, *TDNT* 6, 82, 83; Hahn, *NIDNTT* 1, 307–12) and "uncircumcision" (Schmidt, *TDNT* 1, 225, 226) have lost their meaning; it is the "new creation" (*καινὴ κτίσις*, Gal 6:15) that really counts (in both Galatians and Colossians it was necessary for Paul to underscore the abolition of the distinction between Jew and Gentile in the light of the Jewish stamp of the teaching he was countering, so Bruce, 275).

βάρβαρος, Σκύθης. "Barbarian, Scythian." The list of terms overlaps somewhat. "Barbarian" (Windisch, *TDNT* 1, 546–53) and "Scythian" (Michel, *TDNT* 7, 447–50) are not contrasted like "Greek" and "Jew," or "bondman" and "freeman." Rather, they stand over against "Greek" when the latter is used in its cultural sense. The "barbarian" (cf. Rom 1:14; 1 Cor 14:11; Acts 28:2, 4) is the non-Greek, who did not speak that language (the Greeks themselves divided mankind into two main categories—Greeks and barbarians). Yet Paul's apostolic ministry was directed to them both (Rom 1:14, "I am under obligation to both Greeks and barbarians ["Ελλησίν τε καὶ βαρβάροις]"). The "Scythian" represents the lowest kind of barbarian who was probably also a slave; the term was applied to tribes around the Black Sea from which was drawn a wretched slave class (Lightfoot, 216, cf. BAG, 758; Michel, *TDNT* 7, 449, 450, suggests the possibility of the Scythian being mentioned separately from the barbarian because of some special situation at Colossae; but against this see Lohse, 144). Josephus (*Ap* 2, 269) said: "they are little better than wild beasts" (they were occasionally figures of fun in Greek comedy because of their uncouth ways and speech, cf. Bruce, 276). But the gospel breaks down these cultural barriers, overcoming the offense which a Scythian might give to another's natural sensibilities.

δοῦλος, ἐλεύθερος. "Slave, free." Likewise "in the realm of the new man" (Dibelius-Greeven, 42) distinctions of social position are irrelevant. A slave in the ancient world was, legally speaking, not a person but a piece of property, "a living tool" according to Aristotle (see below regarding Paul's treatment of Onesimus). But in the Christian community the slave as well as the freeman was the brother for whom Christ died. The apostle is not speaking about some natural equality of all persons nor about a morality that is binding on all. When in Galatians 3:28 he says that in Christ "there is no male or female" he does not mean that the distinctive functions or capacities of men and women are abolished, for they like Greeks and Jews, slaves and free, continue to live in the various roles the word assigns them (see Bouttier, *NTS* 23 [1976–77] 1–19). But in Christ there is no inferiority of the one sex to the other, or one class to another; men and women of completely diverse origins are gathered together in unity in Christ through a common allegiance to their Lord. There is no difference in spiritual status between them.

ἀλλὰ [τὰ] πάντα καὶ ἐν πᾶσιν Χριστός. The concluding triumphant words, "but Christ is all and in all," contrast the centrality of Christ with the divisions that separate people in the world. Similar expressions are found at 1 Corinthians 15:28 ("that God may be all in all") and Ephesians 1:23 ("the fullness of him who fills all in all") where, in the former at least and possibly also the latter, the relationship of God himself to the cosmos is in view. Here, however, the phrase is applied to Christ. The *καί* ("and") suggests that both halves of the phrase are important (note Eph 4:6). The first half states in an emphatic way that Christ is "absolutely everything" (see Moule, 121, 122), or "all that matters," while the words he is "in all" (*ἐν πᾶσιν*), which in the light of the preceding statement of verse 11a should probably be regarded as masculine (rather than neuter), mean that he permeates and indwells all members of the new man, regardless of race, class or background (cf. Schnackenburg, *Schriften*, 408, and Zeilinger, *Der Erstgeborene*, 159; note however Lohse, 145). Christ lives in those who believe (cf. Col 1:27; Gal 2:20; 4:19).

Explanation

Paul's previous exhortations to the Colossians to aim at the things above (3:1–4), which were based on their union with Christ in his death and resurrection, find concrete expression and application in the further injunctions which follow: "put to death" (v 5), "put away" (v 8; cf. "do not lie," v 9) and "put on" (v 12). The first of these imperatives ("put to death") recalls the union with Christ in his death (2:20; 3:3; cf. 2:11, 12): because they have died with him, then they are to put to death whatever belongs to their earthly nature. Five sins are identified with these earthly members as the apostle describes first the outward manifestations of sin ("sexual immorality" or "fornication") and then the inward cravings of the heart ("ruthless greed"), the acts of immorality and uncleanness and then their inner springs. Here Paul employs the first of two catalogs of vices, similar to those found among pagan moralists and in the anti-pagan polemic of Jewish propagandists (the second series of five appears in verse 8, while five graces, which the readers are to put on like new clothing, follow in verse 12). Here, as often elsewhere, the list of pagan sins is set within the context of God's judgment: "on account of such the wrath of God is coming" (v 6). By means of a preaching form, the "once-now" antithesis of verses 7 and 8, the readers are shown how they ought to behave now in contrast to their pagan past. They are to discard their old repulsive habits of improper speech like a set of worn-out clothes. The twofold reason for this abandonment of evil ways is that: *(a)* they have already put off the old man with his practices (v 9), and *(b)* have put on the new man which is being renewed in the Creator's image (v 10). The expressions, the old man and the new, carry both individual and corporate connotations: the former designates the whole personality of man when he is ruled by sin, at the same time signifying his belonging to the old humanity in Adam. The latter also has an individual reference, designating the new nature which the Colossians had put on and which was continually being renewed in accordance with the creator's image. At the same time the new man has a corporate reference, denoting the new humanity in Christ. Within this realm of the new man there is no inferiority of one class to another; men and women of completely diverse origins are gathered together in unity in Christ, sharing a common allegiance to their Lord. Christ is all that matters; he permeates and indwells all members of his body, regardless of race, class or background.

Put on the Graces of Christ (3:12–17)

Bibliography

Jervell, J. *Imago,* 249–256. **Larsson, E.** *Christus,* 210–23. **Merk, O.** *Handeln,* 210–14. **Schrage, W.** *Einzelgebote.* **Zeilinger, F.** *Der Erstgeborene,* 66–68. (See also the bibliography to 3:5–11 concerning the New Testament lists of sins and graces.)

Translation

12 *Therefore, as God's chosen ones, holy and dearly loved, clothe yourselves with*
heartfelt compassion, kindness, lowliness, gentleness and longsuffering. 13 *Bear with*
one another and forgive each other if one has a complaint against another; as the
Lord[a] *has graciously forgiven you, so you should also forgive one another.* 14 *In*
addition to all these graces put on love which is the bond that leads to perfection.
15 *Let Christ's peace rule in your hearts. It was also to this peace that you were*
called in one body. And be thankful. 16 *Let the Word of Christ*[b] *dwell in you richly*
as you teach and admonish one another in all wisdom by means of Spirit-inspired
psalms, hymns and songs, singing thankfully to God[c] *with your whole being.* 17 *And*
whatever you do in word or deed, do everything in the name of the Lord Jesus,
giving thanks to God the Father[d] *through him.*

Notes

[a] The reading *κύριος* ("Lord") which has the strong support of P[46] as well as the best witnesses of both the Alexandrian and Western texts (A B D* G it[d,g] vg etc.) was interpreted, quite correctly, by copyists as Χριστός ("Christ"). But the latter is not the original reading; nor are the other variants (*θεός*, "God," and *θεὸς ἐν* Χριστῷ, "God in Christ") which seem to be scribal assimilations to Ephesians 4:32 (Metzger, *Textual Commentary,* 625; cf. Moule, 123, and Lohse, [1]48).

[b] In place of the unusual expression "the Word of Christ," several witnesses substitute the more customary "the Word of God" or "the Word of the Lord." In addition Χριστοῦ ("of Christ") has the strong support of P[46] ℵ[c] B C[2] D G etc.

[c] The Textus Receptus in accordance with Ephesians 5:19 reads *τῷ κυρίῳ* ("to the Lord"). But the early and widespread manuscript evidence is in favor of *τῷ θεῷ* ("to God": P[46] ℵ A B C* D* etc.).

[d] The unusual expression of *τῷ θεῷ πατρί* ("to God the Father"), which has widespread support P[46] (apparently) ℵ A B C 81 etc., was emended by copyists who inserted *καί* ("and") to bring it into line with Ephesians 5:20 (note 1:3 and 12).

Form/Structure/Setting

With the introductory imperative of verse 12, *ἐνδύσασθε* ("put on"), which governs the sentence structure to verse 13c, the positive exhortation begins; it stands in contrasting parallelism with the preceding section, verses 5–11, which also began with an aorist imperative (*νεκρώσατε*, "put to death"), the conjunction *οὖν* ("therefore") and a list of five items. This positive exhortatory material naturally falls into two sections: *(a)* verses 12–14, and *(b)* verses

15–17. In the former the imperatival sentence contains a fivefold catalog of virtues (v 12) which stands in contrast to the fivefold vice catalog of the preceding paragraph (vs 5, 8). The imperative is continued in the two parallel participial clauses (v 13*a*, ἀνεχόμενοι ἀλλήλων, "forbearing one another," and v 13*b*, χαριζόμενοι ἑαυτοῖς, "forgiving each other") with which is linked a conditional sentence (v 13*c*, ἐάν τις πρός τινα ἔχῃ μομφήν, "if one has a complaint against another"). The remainder of verse 13, with its balancing καθώς . . . οὕτως construction ("as . . . so") sets forth the motive for mutual forgiveness—the activity of the Lord who has first forgiven them. Finally, verse 14, which appears to be dependent on the introductory imperative, ἐνδύσασθε ("put on" of v 12), speaks of ἀγάπη ("love") as the bond that leads to perfection. The structure may be set forth as follows:

12*a* ἐνδύσασθε οὖν ὡς ἐκλεκτοὶ τοῦ θεοῦ · · ·
b σπλάγχνα οἰκτιρμοῦ
c χρηστότητα—ταπεινοφροσύνην
d πραΰτητα—μακροθυμίαν
13*a* ἀνεχόμενοι ἀλλήλων
b καὶ χαριζόμενοι ἑαυτοῖς,
c ἐάν τις πρός τινα ἔχῃ μομφήν.
d καθὼς καὶ ὁ κύριος ἐχαρίσατο ὑμῖν—
e οὕτως καὶ ὑμεῖς.
14*a* ἐπὶ πᾶσιν δὲ τούτοις τὴν ἀγάπην,
b ὅ ἐστιν σύνδεσμος τῆς τελειότητος.
12*a* "Clothe yourselves, therefore, as God's chosen ones . . .
b heartfelt compassion
c kindness—lowliness
d gentleness—longsuffering
13*a* Bear with one another
b and forgive each other,
c if one has a complaint against another.
d As the Lord has graciously forgiven you—
e so you too (should forgive).
14*a* In addition to all these (put on) love,
b which is the bond that leads to perfection."

The second section, comprising verses 15–17, stands as a unity. Verse 15 contains three clauses each of which is, in effect, introduced by καί ("and"): a cohortative clause, καὶ ἡ εἰρήνη τοῦ Χριστοῦ βραβευέτω . . . (v 15*a*, "and let the peace of Christ rule . . ."); a dependent relative clause, εἰς ἣν καὶ ἐκλήθητε (v 15*b*, "into which also you were called . . ."); and a short, independent imperatival clause, καὶ εὐχάριστοι γίνεσθε (v 15*c*, "and be thankful"). Verse 16, like the preceding verse, commences with a cohortative clause, ὁ λόγος τοῦ Χριστοῦ ἐνοικείτω . . . ("let the word of Christ dwell . . ."). It is followed by three participles διδάσκοντες, νουθετοῦντες and ᾄδοντες ("teaching," "admonishing" and "singing"). The concluding verse contains a relative clause (πᾶν ὅ τι, "whatever") with a condition inserted (ἐὰν ποιῆτε, "if you do"), a principal clause (πάντα (ποιεῖτε) ἐν ὀνόματι . . ., "do all in the name of . . .") and a participial construction (εὐχαριστοῦντες τῷ θεῷ . . ., "giving thanks to God . . ."). Verses 15–17 may be structured as follows:

15*a* καὶ ἡ εἰρήνη τοῦ Χριστοῦ βραβευέτω . . .
b εἰς ἣν καὶ ἐκλήθητε . . .
c καὶ εὐχάριστοι γίνεσθε
16*a* ὁ λόγος τοῦ Χριστοῦ ἐνοικείτω . . .
b ἐν πάσῃ σοφίᾳ διδάσκοντες καὶ νουθετοῦντες . . .
c ἐν τῇ χάριτι ᾄδοντες . . .
17*a* καὶ πᾶν ὅ τι ἐὰν ποιῆτε . . .
b πάντα ἐν ὀνόματι τοῦ κυρίου ' Ιησοῦ
c εὐχαριστοῦντες τῷ θεῷ πατρὶ δι 'αὐτοῦ.
15*a* "And let Christ's peace rule . . .
b into which also you were called . . .
c And be thankful.
16*a* Let the word of Christ dwell in . . .
b in all wisdom teaching and admonishing . . .
c singing with thanksgiving . . .
17*a* And whatever you do . . .
b [do] all in the name of the Lord Jesus
c giving thanks to God the Father through him.
(cf. Zeilinger, *Der Erstgeborene*, 66–68).

Comment

12. ἐνδύσασθε οὖν. As God's chosen ones who have already put on the new man (v 10) they must don the graces which are characteristic of him. In the preceding paragraph the apostle had set forth the negative requirements in the admonitions "put to death" (v 5) and "put off" (v 8); here he spells out the positive exhortation which, like the injunction of verse 5 with its οὖν ("therefore"), follows as a direct consequence (οὖν, "therefore") of what has previously been said. The graces with which they are to be clothed are those qualities predicated of God or Christ (note the treatments of Larsson, *Christus*, 210–20, and Jervell, *Imago*, 251, 252). It is, thus, not unusual that Paul should exhort the Roman Christians to "put on (ἐνδύσασθε) the Lord Jesus Christ" (Rom 13:14). The imperative ἐνδύσασθε ("put on"), like its counterpart in verses 5 (νεκρώσατε, "put to death") and 8 (ἀπόθεσθε, "put off") is an aorist tense signifying a decisive initial act which introduces a settled attitude (Schweizer, 153).

ὡς ἐκλεκτοὶ τοῦ θεοῦ, ἅγιοι καὶ ἠγαπημένοι. "As elect of God, holy and beloved." The members of the congregation are addressed by means of exalted titles: they are the chosen, holy and beloved people of God. These descriptions are important not only because they were used of Israel as God's own possession—and as Lightfoot, 219, claimed are now transferred to the Colossians as the new people of God—but also since they are designated of Christ, thereby underlining the point of their similarity to and identification with him, features that are all the more significant in a context where they are encouraged to put on his graces. ἐκλεκτός ("chosen," "elect"; BAG, 242, Schrenk, *TDNT* 4, 181–92; cf. G. Delling, "Merkmale der Kirche nach den Neuen Testament," *NTS* 13 [1966–67] 305) was employed in the LXX of men of God in salvation history (Num 11:28; Ps 105:23, etc.), the land of Palestine (Jer 3:19; Zech 7:14), the city of Jerusalem (Tob 13:13) and Israel as the people of God (Isa 43:20; 65:9, 15, 23; Pss 104:43; 105:5, etc.; cf. Schrenk, *TDNT* 4, 182, 183). Although the word-group (including ἐκλέγομαι, "choose," and ἐκλεκτός, "chosen") occurs relatively infrequently in the New Testament (in Paul ἐκλεκτός, "elect," "chosen," is found at Rom 8:33; 16:13; Col 3:12; 1 Tim 5:21; 2 Tim 2:10; and Titus 1:1; ἐκλογή, "election," at Rom 9:11; 11:5, 7, 28; and 1 Thess 1:4; and ἐκλέγομαι, "choose," at 1 Cor 1:27, 28 and Eph 1:4) in comparison with the LXX (where ἐκλέγομαι, "choose," and ἐκλεκτός, "elect," turn up 245 times), ἐκλεκτός is used of Christ as the "elect one" (Luke 23:35; cf. 9:35; John 1:34; 1 Pet 2:4, 6) as well as of the Christian community: "But you are a chosen race (γένος ἐκλεκτόν), a royal priesthood, a holy nation, God's own people," 1 Peter 2:9.

Believers are "God's elect" (ἐκλεκτοὶ θεοῦ) against whom he will never lay any charge for it is he who justifies them (Rom 8:33). This term, together with others akin to it (e.g. the καλέω group with reference to "calling"), emphasizes the gracious initiative of God in drawing men and women to himself (the Qumran community regarded itself as the assembly of the chosen ones: 1QpHab 10:13, "God's elect"; cf. 5:4; 1QH 14:15; 4QpPs 37.2.5, "the community of his elect"). The parallel terms ἅγιοι ("holy") and ἠγαπημένοι ("beloved") are best taken as predicates of ἐκλεκτοί ("elect"; against Lohmeyer, 145, ἐκλεκτοί does not designate the heavenly "communion of saints" and so the "angels," and ὡς, "as," is not meant to distinguish Christians from them as another group; rather it simply emphasizes the Colossians' identity with the elect; so Larsson, *Christus*, 210, Lohse, 146, Martin, *NCB*, 109): his choice souls are those whom he has set apart for himself and placed his love upon them (so Abbott, 286, Procksch, *TDNT* 1, 107; cf. Delling, *NTS* 13 [1966–67] 305, and Lohse, 146). Again it is important to note that ἅγιος ("holy"; see on chap. 1:2) is employed of Jesus as the "Holy One" (Mark 1:24; Luke 4:34; John 6:69; cf. Acts 4:27, 30) while ἀγαπητός ("beloved," is akin to the sparsely used ἀγαπημένος which appears at 1 Thess 1:4 and 2 Thess 2:13 in the context of election and describes Christians as "beloved by God") turns up in the Gospels as a messianic designation for Jesus (Matt 3:17 and parallels; 12:18; 17:5 and parallels).

σπλάγχνα οἰκτιρμοῦ, χρηστότητα, ταπεινοφροσύνην, πραΰτητα, μακροθυμίαν. "Heartfelt compassion, kindness, lowliness, gentleness, longsuffering." In verses 5 to 8 two catalogs were listed, each enumerating five vices that were to be put away with the old man. Now five virtues, which are not strictly opposites of the preceding vices, are to be put on. These are elsewhere designated as the graces and actions of God or Christ. σπλάγχνα οἰκτιρμοῦ means "heartfelt compassion" (BAG, 561; lit. "bowels of compassion," οἰκτιρμοῦ is a genitive of quality) and appears first. οἰκτιρμός (Bultmann, *TDNT* 5, 159–61, Esser, *NIDNTT* 2, 598) in the LXX is predicated first and foremost of God who is described as "compassionate": he has acted graciously and compassionately on behalf of his people (LXX Pss 24:6; 50:1; 102:4; 144:9; cf. Neh 9:19, 27, 28, etc.; the plural is normally used, perhaps partly to describe concrete acts of compassion [so BDF, para. 142; Robertson, *Grammar*, 408], but no doubt due to the influence of the Hebrew *raḥ^{a}mîm* as well; there is no difference in meaning with the singular. Also cf. LXX Exod 34:6; 2 Chron 30:9; Neh 9:17, 31; Pss 85:15; 102:8; 110:4; 144:8; Joel 2:13; and Jon 4:2, where the adjective οἰκτίρμων, "compassionate," "merciful," makes the same point about God's gracious actions). In the Qumran literature "mercies" (Hebrew *raḥᵃmîm*) first of all describe God's compassion (1QS 1:22; 1QH 1:31; 1QM 11:4) though as in the OT the term can also refer to the godly person who lives according to God's will (note especially 1QS 4:3 in a list of virtues describing the behavior of the new people of God; cf. 2 Chron 30:9; Ps 106:46). οἰκτιρμοί ("mercies") in the NT describes God's compassion: at Romans 12:1 it denotes his concrete acts of mercy in his Son, while at 2 Corinthians 1:3 as the "Father of mercies" (πατὴρ τῶν οἰκτιρμῶν) he is the "compassionate Father" (a genitive of quality), and the "Father from whom all compassion comes" (a genitive of origin), cf. O'Brien, *Introductory Thanksgivings*, 241, 242; note also Luke 6:36; James 5:11.

σπλάγχνον (almost always in the plural, meaning literally "inward parts," BAG, 763; cf. Köster, *TDNT* 7, 548–59, Esser, *NIDNTT* 2, 599, 600) comes to be used figuratively of the seat of the emotions, i.e. the "heart." In fact, like other anthropological terms the word is found in Paul for the whole man, expressing strongly and forcefully what concerns the personality at the deepest level, especially in his capacity of loving (Köster, *TDNT* 7, 555; note the references in Philemon, vv 7, 12, 20). The few references to σπλάγχνα and the cognate verb σπλαγχνίζομαι ("have pity," "feel sympathy") in the LXX occur mostly in the later books where there is no Hebrew original. The predominant meaning "merciful," "show mercy," is found in the Testaments of the Twelve Patriarchs and this prepares the way for the NT usage. The love of God is signified in these Testaments by both noun (TLevi 4:4, TZeb 8:2; TNapht 4:5) and verb (TZeb 8:1). The NT tendency is to employ both terms of God or Christ. So in the Synoptics the verb σπλαγχνίζομαι describes (a) the attitude of Jesus as it characterizes the divine nature of his acts (Matt 9:36; 14:14; Mark 1:41; 9:22; Luke 7:13), and (b) the actions of key persons in three of Jesus' parables (Matt 18:27; Luke 10:33; 15:20) who make the unbounded mercy of God visibly plain, while at Philippians 1:8 where the noun is employed (ἐν σπλάγχνοις Χριστοῦ Ἰησοῦ, "with the affection of Christ Jesus"), Christ is seen to be "the source of the love that embraces and lays claim to the apostle's whole personality" (Esser, *NIDNTT* 2, 600; cf. Phil 2:1; and Luke 1:78, "through the tender mercy [διὰ σπλάγχνα ἐλέους] of our God"). In this context of Colossians the joint expression means "a compassionate heart" or "merciful compassion" (it is not necessary to posit a literary dependence on "affection and compassion" [σπλάγχνα καὶ οἰκτιρμοί] of Phil 2:1; the almost identical phrase "heart of mercy" is used at Luke 1:78; cf. TZeb 7:3).

χρηστότης, ("goodness," "kindness," "generosity," BAG, 886; Weiss, *TDNT* 9, 483–92; Beyreuther, *NIDNTT* 2, 105, 106) is a quality which God himself demonstrates in concrete actions. Both noun and cognate adjective (χρηστός, "good," "kind") are favorite words in the LXX for expressing the abundance of his goodness which he displays to his covenant people—indeed to all men as his creatures. His constant mercy and readiness to help are essential themes of the psalms (e.g. Pss 25[LXX 24]:7; 31[30]:19; 65[64]:11; 68[67]:10; 85[84]:12) as well as in the prophets where the kindness of God is all the more amazing in the face of his people's sin (Jer 33[LXX 40]:11;

cf. 24:2, 3, 5). In the Qumran literature the sect expected its members to show mercy to one another thereby reflecting the kindness each had received from God (1QH 7:30; 10:16; 11:6, 9, 31; 12:21; 13:16 with 1QS 4:3). The predominant number of NT references to the word-group appear in the Pauline letters (the adjective χρηστός, "kind," "good," occurs at Matt 11:30; Luke 5:39 and 6:35; all other instances are in Paul) where the apostle turns repeatedly to the incomprehensible kindness of God: χρηστότης denotes God's gracious attitude and acts toward sinners. He desires the salvation of the sinner, not his death (Rom 11:22; Eph 2:7; Tit 3:4), while his kindness and forbearance are designed to lead the impenitent to repentance (so Rom 2:4). As a response to God's merciful kindness the person who has put on the new man, the Lord Jesus Christ, is to show kindness to others. This does not come naturally; nor can it be produced from one's innate ability. Along with "patience" it is a fruit of the Spirit (Gal 5:22), and according to 1 Corinthians 13:4 is a direct outworking of love (itself a fruit of the Spirit): "love is patient and kind."

ταπεινοφροσύνη has already been used twice in the letter (2:18, 23) by the Colossian opponents to denote "mortification," "self-denial" or even ascetic practices such as fasting that were a prelude to receiving visions of the heavenly mysteries (see 142, 153). Here, however, it signifies the grace of "lowliness," "humility" (BAG, 804; cf. Grundmann, *TDNT* 8, 21–23, Esser, *NIDNTT* 2, 259–64). It is well-known that in profane Greek literature the term occurs on only a few occasions, and then usually in a derogatory sense of servility, weakness or a shameful lowliness. In the OT although the noun ταπεινοφροσύνη ("humility") is lacking, ταπεινός ("lowly," "humble") and its cognates turn up about 270 times. Particularly significant are those references to the Lord's acting in history to bring down the proud and arrogant and to exalt the lowly: (a) the prophets express it in warnings of judgment (Amos 2:6, 7, 13; 8:6, 7; cf. Isa 2:9, 11, 17; 5:15; Zeph 2:3; 3:12, etc.), (b) the historical books spell it out with reference to events (Judg 4:23; 6:15; 1 Sam 1:11, 16; 7:13; 2 Sam 22:28, etc.), (c) the psalmists express the theme in their prayers (Pss 10:17, 18 [LXX 9:38, 39]; 25:18 [24:18]; 31:7 [30:8], etc.), while (d) in proverbs of the wisdom literature "humility" is spoken of as the fruit of experience and as a rule of life (Job 5:11; Prov 3:34; 11:2; 15:33, in some manuscripts "humility" is parallel with "the fear of the Lord"; 16:2, 19, etc.; for further references see Esser, *NIDNTT* 2, 260, 261). In the NT ταπεινοφροσύνη signifies the "lowliness" with which one serves Christ (Acts 20:19) or is submissive to other Christians (Eph 4:2; Phil 2:3; 1 Pet 5:5). The pattern or model is Jesus who invited people to come to him as the one who is "meek and lowly (ταπεινός) in heart" (Matt 11:29). The twin themes of humiliation and exaltation, noted in the OT material, come to their clearest expression in the hymn of Philippians 2:6–11 where it is stated that Jesus humbled himself (ἐταπείνωσεν ἑαυτόν, v 8) even to death on a cross and God exalted him (v 9), bestowing on him the name above every name. The hymn provides the basis for the preceding exhortation (2:1–5), and Christ's action in humbling himself is the pattern for believers who, in humility (τῇ ταπεινοφροσύνῃ, v 3), are to esteem others better than themselves and to be concerned about others' welfare (v 4).

πραΰτης ("gentleness," "humility," "meekness," BAG, 699; cf. Hauck/Schulz, *TDNT* 6, 645–51, Bauder, *NIDNTT* 2, 256–59) turns up in the Pauline writings of the NT some eight times (1 Cor 4:21; 10:1; Gal 5:23; 6:1; Eph 4:2; Col 3:12; 2 Tim 2:25; Tit 3:2; in addition it occurs at James 1:21; 3:13; 1 Pet 3:15) but the cognate adjective πραΰς ("meek," which is found at Matt 5:5; 11:29; 21:5; 1 Pet 3:4) does not appear in Paul. Like the earlier terms this word-group needs to be understood against an OT background. In the LXX our terms were used to designate the poor in Israel, those without landed property, many of whom were victims of unscrupulous exploitation (Isa 32:7; Ps 37:14; Job 24:4). The "poor" (Heb'*ānî*) are the defenseless, those without rights, who are oppressed, cheated and exploited (cf. Pss 9, 10). However, Yahweh is the God of those without rights (Pss 25:9; 149:4; 34:2); he comforts those who find no mercy from their fellow-men (Isa 29:19; Job 36:15) and will finally reverse all that is against them (Isa 26:6; Ps 37:11; 147:6). The term "poor" comes to be applied to those who in deep need humbly seek help from Yahweh alone (e.g. Ps 40:17; Zeph 2:3; 3:12; Isa 41:17, etc.). At Zechariah 9:9 the term πραΰς ("meek") is a title of honor given to the Messiah. "Meekness" is one of the marks of Jesus' rule. He fulfills the role of the messianic king who brings salvation without using force (Matt 21:5 = Zech 9:9), describing himself as "meek" (πραΰς, Matt 11:29). Paul mentions the "meekness of Christ" (πραΰτης · · · τοῦ Χριστοῦ, 2 Cor 10:1) as characteristic of Jesus' behavior toward men during his life on earth, and exhorts the Corinthians on the basis of this example. "Meekness" is to characterize the lives of Christians in relation to fellow-believers who have sinned (Gal 6:1, 2, by bearing one another's burdens they "fulfill the law of Christ"; 2 Tim 2:25, cf. 1 Cor 4:21), as well as outsiders (Tit 3:2; cf. Phil 4:5). It is a fruit of the Spirit (Gal 5:23) standing in lists of graces as a concrete expression of Christian love (cf. 1 Tim 6:11; 1 Pet 3:4). This gentleness is not to be confused with weakness (as contemporary Hellenistic thought understood it), but contains the elements of (a) a consideration for others, and (b) a willingness to waive one's rights (cf. Martin, *NCB*, 111).

μακροθυμία. (In addition to the treatment at chap. 1:11 see Horst, *TDNT* 4, 374–87, Falkenroth and Brown, *NIDNTT* 2, 768–72). It denotes that "long-suffering" which endures wrong and puts up with the exasperating conduct of others rather than flying into a rage or desiring vengeance (cf. L. H. Marshall, *The Challenge of New Testament Ethics* [London: Macmillan, 1947] 294, cited by Martin, *NCB*, 111).

Each of the five graces with which God's elect are to be clothed show how Christians should behave in their dealings with others, particularly with fellow-believers.

13. The exhortation continues with the two participles ἀνεχόμενοι ("bear with") and χαριζόμενοι ("forgive"; on the imperatival use of the participle see on 3:9), while the reason or justification for such a conciliatory attitude is: "the Lord has forgiven you." The exercise of forbearance (ἀνέχομαι means "endure," "bear with," "put up with," so BAG, 65) by Christians toward "one another" (ἀλλήλων, in the genitive case after a verb of emotion, so BDF, para. 176[1]; Robertson, *Grammar*, 508, indicates that putting up with other members of the congregation is in view) results from their being clothed

with "longsuffering" (μακροθυμία, v 12; according to Lohmeyer, 146, the five-fold list of v 12 is a unity which is tied in with the two admonitions of v 13). That forbearance is to be continual (the verb ἀνέχομαι has a linear connotation while the present tense shows it is ongoing) and reciprocal (cf. Eph 4:2; see also 2 Cor 11 where the note of mutual forbearance is struck several times: vv 1 [twice], 4, 19, 20; cf. Falkenroth and Brown, *NIDNTT* 2, 765, 766). In addition, believers' relationships (although it is possible Paul has in mind a concrete situation in the Colossian church, the reference is probably more general; cf. Lohse, 147, 148, and Martin, *NCB,* 112) with each other (ἑαυτοῖς; older commentators drew a distinction here between ἀλλήλων, "one another," and ἑαυτοῖς, "each other," although the significance of the distinction varied; but there does not seem to be any difference in meaning: the change is for the sake of stylistic variety, cf. BDF, para. 287, and Robertson, *Grammar,* 690) should be characterized by mutual forgiveness. χαρίζομαι ("give freely or graciously as a favor," "give" = "remit," "forgive," "pardon," BAG, 876, 877, and note Conzelmann, *TDNT* 9, 372–402) is not the common word for remission or forgiveness (which is ἀφίημι, "cancel," "remit," or "pardon"), but one of richer content emphasizing the gracious nature of the pardon (at Luke 7:42 in our Lord's parable of the two debtors the AV renders the word "frankly forgave"; it is found elsewhere in the Pauline corpus of God's gracious giving or forgiving at Rom 8:32; 1 Cor 2:12; Gal 3:18; Eph 4:32; Phil 1:29; 2:9; Col 2:13; note also 2 Cor 2:7, 10; 12:13; Philem 22). The present tense of the verb (χαριζόμενοι) makes it plain that this forgiveness is to be unceasing, even unwearying (a point which Jesus himself taught when instructing his disciples that forgiveness ought to be "until seventy times seven," Matt 18:22; cf. vv 21–35), while the conditional sentence, "if one has a complaint against another" (ἐάν τις πρός τινα ἔχῃ μομφήν), recognizes that within the congregation there will be grounds for grievance from time to time (μομφή, "blame," "cause for complaint," BAG, 527, cf. Grundmann, *TDNT* 4, 571–74, appears only here in the Greek Bible, occurring elsewhere only rarely and in poetry). "One against another" (τις πρός τινα) is a general reference suggesting that legitimate complaints might be directed by any member of the community against any other. But whenever these grievances arise the readers are to forgive.

The ground and motivation for this response are of the highest order: "as the Lord has forgiven you, so you should also forgive one another" (καθὼς καὶ ὁ κύριος ἐχαρίσατο ὑμῖν οὕτως καὶ ὑμεῖς. The two halves of this sentence, as noted above, are balanced by an "as . . . so" construction (καθὼς καί . . . οὕτως καί) which is paralleled elsewhere in Paul's letters (Rom 15:7, 8; Eph 5:2, 25, 29; cf. Rom 15:3; Mark 10:45; 1 Pet 2:21; 3:18). This is part of what has been described as his "conformity"-teaching in which the full impact of Christ's sacrifice on the cross is set forth as a paradigm of the life style to which the believer "conforms"—it is not simply Christ's human life which is a model to be imitated by following in his earthly steps (the "imitatio" of later piety). Cf. Dahl, *Jesus,* 34, 35, and Martin, *NCB,* 112. Because Christ has forgiven us we ought to forgive one another. κύριος ("Lord") is the better attested reading (see above) and refers to Christ himself rather than God (so Lohse, 148, against Ernst, 228, and Merk, *Handeln,* 211, who incorrectly appeals to 1:10 in support of the view that κύριος is a reference to "God"). It is a singular expression, however, for usually it is God who is said to forgive: so Colossians 2:13 and the parallel passage, Ephesians 4:32, "God in Christ forgave you." Clearly Christ's mighty work of reconciliation (1:22) is the basis on which that forgiveness of sins is provided. And here the apostle reproduces Jesus' insistence on the close connection between divine forgiveness of us and our forgiveness of others (cf. the Lord's Prayer, Matt 6:12 and Luke 11:4).

14. Finally, "love" is the crowning grace which the new man has to put on as part of his distinctive dress (ἀγάπην, "love," is another object of the imperative ἐνδύσασθε, "put on," v 12). If each of the graces previously mentioned was seen to be characteristic of God or Christ then this is preeminently so of ἀγάπη ("love"), as a concordance will quickly show, and one needs only to refer to 1 Corinthians 13:4 in support for this statement about love so clearly reflects the character of Christ (Larsson, *Christus,* 221, 222). "Above all" (ἐπὶ πᾶσιν δὲ τούτοις) may convey the idea of "on top of all the other 'articles of clothing' " (so Moule, 123. BDF, para. 235[3], and Robertson, *Grammar,* 605, agree that here the preposition ἐπί with the dative means "in addition to"). Elsewhere the apostle asserts that "love" is the motive power of faith (Gal 5:6); according to 1 Corinthians 13:13 it is the supreme Christian grace, while at Romans 13:9, 10 all the commandments are summed up in the one commandment, "you shall love your neighbor as yourself." "Love" is the fulfilling of the law (πλήρωμα νόμου) because it does nothing but good to a neighbor.

But what is meant by the explanatory clause, "[love] which is the bond of perfection (σύνδεσμος τῆς τελειότητος)"? (The explanatory phrase ὅ ἐστιν, "which is," as a special idiom is used without much regard to the gender or number of either antecedent [ἡ ἀγάπη] or predicate [σύνδεσμος], so Robertson, *Grammar,* 411, 703, and BDF, para. 132[2]; note also 1:24, 27; 2:10, 17.) The word σύνδεσμος (a "bond" that holds something together [so BAG, 785] is used of the sinews of the body at Col 2:19) has been taken by some as the link which unites and binds together all the previously mentioned graces of verse 12, so producing the fullness of Christian living. It is the "perfect bond" (τῆς τελειότητος, "of perfection," is regarded as a qualitative or descriptive genitive) which joins all the other virtues to form an organic unity. Commentators who advocate this line point out that the Pythagoreans regarded "friendship" (φιλία) in much the same way. It was much more highly honored than any other quality being called the "bond of all the virtues" (σύνδεσμον . . . πασῶν τῶν ἀρετῶν, Simplicius' saying in *Epictet,* p. 208; cf. Plato, *Polit* 310a for σύνδεσμος ἀρετῆς, "the bond of virtue," which Fitzer, *TDNT* 7, 859, claims has formal similarities with Col 3:14. Note also BAG, 785, Moule, 123, 124, and Bruce, 281). But it is doubtful whether this is what the apostle meant. Nowhere else does he regard love as a uniting force linking other virtues, and this thought is not found in other NT statements about love. In addition, questions have been raised about the relevance of the extrabiblical parallels (Du Plessis, *Perfection,* 201, rightly notes that Paul was not a champion of a hierarchy of virtues, of which he conceived love to be the supreme or dominating principle; cf. Percy, *Probleme,* 407, and

Schmauch, 80–82). Consequently an alternative interpretation has been proposed, that is, to regard the genitive "of perfection" (τῆς τελειότητος) as one of purpose, so meaning that love is the bond that leads to perfection (A. Fridrichsen, "Charité et perfection. Observation sur Col. 3, 14," SO 19 [1939] 41–45, Percy, *Probleme,* 407, Dibelius-Greeven, 44. Several consider the genitive to be objective, but the significance is the same = "the bond which produces perfection," so BDF, para. 163, Turner, *Syntax,* 212, Delling, *TDNT* 8, 79, Du Plessis, *Perfection,* 201, Larson, *Christus,* 221. For a full discussion see Schmauch, 80–82). Love binds together the members of the congregation (rather than the graces previously mentioned) into unity in the body of Christ (the variant reading τῆς ἑνότητος, "of unity," though secondary, captures the apostle's thought) so producing perfection (Lohse, 149). Paul is concerned with the readers' corporate life and the perfection he sets before them is not something narrowly individual. It is attained only as Christians, in fellowship, show love to one another. It is by this love, one of the graces of Christ, that his body is built up.

15. From love Paul passes on to peace (at Eph 4:3 peace rather than love is the "bond," σύνδεσμος, in which the unity of the Spirit is to be maintained), and in so doing leaves behind the motifs of the old man and the new which have been central to the thought of the chapter from verse 9 on. The prayer for peace frequently turns up in Paul's letters (e.g. Phil 4:7, "the peace of God, which surpasses all understanding, will keep your hearts and minds in Christ Jesus"; cf. the opening and closing epistolary greetings [see above], and Gal 6:16; 2 Thess 3:16; note also Rom 16:20; 2 Cor 13:11; Phil 4:9; 1 Thess 5:23; and see Wiles, *Prayers*). Here peace occurs in an exhortation to the readers (not a prayer as Lohse, 149, claims) to let Christ's peace hold sway in their lives as they relate to one another (note the context of vv 11, 13 and 14). The distinctive phrase "the peace of Christ" (ἡ εἰρήνη τοῦ Χριστοῦ) designates that peace which he both embodies and brings (cf. John 14:27). As the "Lord of peace" (κύριος τῆς εἰρήνης; elsewhere God is called the "God of peace," Rom 15:33; 16:20; 1 Cor 14:33; 2 Cor 13:11; Phil 4:9; 1 Thess 5:23) he gives peace to believers (2 Thess 3:16); indeed, he himself is that peace (Eph 2:14).

βραβεύω which occurs only here in the NT (at Col 2:18 the compound καταβραβεύω,"condemn," is used) originally referred to the function of the umpire (βραβευτής) who presided over and presented prizes at the games (evidence for this comes from the time of Euripides, fifth century B.C.; cf. Stauffer, *TDNT* 1, 637, 638, BAG, 146, Pfitzner, *Paul,* 155, Field, *Notes,* 196). But there is considerable evidence to show that the verb was normally used in the more general sense of "judge," "decide," "control," or "rule" (BAG, 146; for examples see Field, *Notes,* 196; against Lightfoot, 221, who presses the point about Christ's peace acting as umpire: "the idea of a *decision* and an *award* is prominent in the word"). ἐν ταῖς καρδίαις ὑμῶν, "in your hearts," does not point to some private and inward peace of the soul or some peaceful disposition of spirit. Rather, "heart" is being employed in its customary OT sense to denote the center of one's personality as the source of will, emotion, thoughts and affections (cf. Behm, *TDNT* 3, 611–13, see on 2:2). The peace of Christ is to hold sway over the whole of the readers' lives as they relate to one another (cf. D. Wiederkehr, *Die Theologie der Berufung in den Paulusbriefen* [Studia Friburgensia, NS 36; Freiburg, Schweiz: Universitätsverlag, 1963] 196; the phrase "in your hearts" is picked up in v 16 with the words "in you," ἐν ὑμῖν); Christ himself is to be present and ruling in their midst.

εἰς ἣν καὶ ἐκλήθητε ἐν ἑνὶ σώματι. "Into which also you were called in one body." Since the Colossians are said to have been called into the peace of Christ (and that through the gospel), then the latter expression must designate the realm or sphere in which the new man now lives. So Foerster (*TDNT* 2, 414) calls it "a kingdom in which the believer is protected" (cf. Lohse, 150). As such it is almost equivalent to salvation (see Masson, 146, and E. Biser, "Die Idee des Friedens nach den paulinischen Gefangenschaftsbriefen," *GuL* 27 [1954] 165–70). ἐν ἑνὶ σώματι, "in one body," indicates not the purpose of the believers' calling but the manner or mode (Masson, 147, Schmauch, 82; cf. Turner, *Syntax*, 264): it is to the peace of Christ that they were summoned "as members of a single body" (Moule, 124). Because the phrase contains neither definite article (τῷ, "the") nor explicit reference to Christ (Χριστοῦ or αὐτοῦ, "his") it must in the first instance be interpreted to mean "inasmuch as you belong to a single organism" (Moule, *Origin*, 76), denoting the unity of the group, the local congregation at Colossae (Moule, *Origin*, 76,77, interprets the parallel passage of Eph 2:15, 16 along similar lines as denoting one, coherent organism, "in a single body"). Accordingly, those who have been reconciled to God (1:20, 22), who have peace with him through Christ, should manifest that peace among themselves. But is there more than a passing reference to the body metaphor, more than an allusion to communal life? It is possible, as most commentators suppose, that Paul implies Christ's body is this organism and it is depicted as the place of peace (Ernst, 228, claims that the linking of the motifs of peace and body reminds one of the Colossian hymn, 1:15–20. Christ is the head of the body and the origin of peace and reconciliation. What is seen there in a world-wide context, he claims, is here actualized for a special church and its problems). In it men and women are reconciled to one another and to God: it is the sphere of redemption (Best, *Body*, 154; cf. W. Bieder, *Die Berufung im Neuen Testament* [ATANT 38; Zürich: Zwingli, 1961] 77–79; Schweizer, 156, in the light of the earlier references [1:18, 24; 2:19], understands the phrase as referring to the body of Christ, although he does concede that it could refer simply to the unity of the group).

καὶ εὐχάριστοι γίνεσθε. "And be thankful." Once again in the letter the note of thanksgiving is struck (cf. 1:3, 12; 2:7; 3:17; 4:2). The Greek refers not simply to a grateful attitude or a thankful disposition (so the rendering "be grateful" does not quite get the point), though this is obviously included. Within the Pauline letters the εὐχαριστέω word-group regularly denotes gratitude that finds outward expression in thanksgiving; there is an emphasis in Paul on the public aspect of thanksgiving. By mentioning what God has graciously done in his Son other Christians are encouraged to praise him also; and as thanksgivings abound so God is glorified (2 Cor 4:15; cf. 1:11; on this theme see P. T. O'Brien, "Thanksgiving within the Structure of Pauline Theology," *Pauline Studies in Honour of Professor F. F. Bruce*, ed. D. A. Hagner and M. J. Harris [Grand Rapids: Eerdmans, 1980] 50–66). From this general exhortation (cf. also v 17; see below for the view that v 15*b* is a sort of rubric to the next topic of catechetical instruction) it is clear that thanksgiving is an integral part of the Christian life (εὐχάριστος, "thankful," occurs only here and at Prov 11:16 in the Greek Bible; the imperative γίνεσθε, lit. "become," rather than ἐστε, "be," according to Meyer, 446, draws attention to the "constant striving after this exalted aim as something not yet attained"; cf. Abbott, 290); indeed the regular offering of thanks to God is almost synonymous with being a Christian (see A. Hamman, *La Prière. I. Le Nouveau Testament* [Tournai: Desclée, 1959] 291, 292). By contrast, pagans who possess the raw materials of the knowledge of God, as his creatures were bound to render glory and thanksgiving to him as their creator (Rom 1:21), i.e. to recognize his lordship and live in grateful obedience. But they were destitute of that thanksgiving which the knowledge they possessed should have drawn forth (cf. the ἀχάριστοι, "ungrateful," of 2 Tim 3:2 which describes the character of men in the last days), and the original image of God was defaced (Merk, *Handeln*, 213). Here at verse 15 the grounds for thanksgiving are not spelled out, though previously in the letter the readers were encouraged to praise God for having delivered them from a tyranny of darkness and transferred them into the kingdom of his beloved Son (1:12–14). Elsewhere in Paul's letters, while the grounds for the giving of thanks are manifold, the great emphasis falls upon the mighty work of God in Christ bringing salvation through the gospel. God's activity in creation is, on occasion, mentioned as a basis for the expression of gratitude (cf. Rom 1:21 and the thanksgivings said over food: Rom 14:6; 1 Cor 10:30; 1 Tim 4:3, 4). But the majority of the Pauline references are in the context of God's grace given in Christ (1 Cor 1:4; cf. 2 Cor 9:15 with 8:9; Rom 1:8; 2 Cor 1:11; Eph 1:16; Phil 1:3, etc.). At Colossians 3:15 such thanksgiving, which is inculcated upon those who are in one body, will be offered as the readers "sing psalms, hymns and spiritual songs" (v 16). However, it will not be restricted to these corporate occasions (at v 17 the giving of thanks to God as Father is to be the accompaniment of every activity), as it is to be offered "under all circumstances" (ἐν παντί, 1 Thess 5:18), being the appropriate response of those who are filled with God's Spirit (Eph 5:18–20).

16. As the Colossians were exhorted to let the peace of Christ rule their lives (v 15), so now they are admonished to let the Word of Christ (ὁ λόγος τοῦ Χριστοῦ is parallel to ἡ εἰρήνη τοῦ Χριστοῦ, "the peace of Christ") dwell richly among them. The expression, "the Word of Christ" (ὁ λόγος τοῦ Χριστοῦ), is used here instead of "the Word" (ὁ λόγος, 4:3), "the Word of God" (ὁ λόγος τοῦ θεοῦ, 1:25) or "the Word of the Lord" (λόγος κυρίου, 1 Thess 4:15; 2 Thess 3:1). The change from "of God" or "of the Lord" may have been due to the Colossian situation; certainly the present expression is in keeping with the rest of the letter with its emphasis on the person and work of Christ (von Soden, 64, and Abbott, 290). While the genitive "of Christ" (τοῦ Χριστοῦ) might be subjective indicating that Christ himself is the speaker when his word is proclaimed (cf. Lightfoot, 222, Meyer, 447, Bruce, 283), it is probably objective referring to the message that centers on Christ, that Word of truth or gospel (ὁ λόγος τῆς ἀληθείας τοῦ εὐαγγελίου, 1:5; cf. Gal 1:7; 1 Cor 9:12; 2 Cor 2:12) which came to the Colossians and

took up a firm place in their lives from the time Epaphras first preached it to them. As such it is normative and ought to control their lives.

That Word is to dwell richly in their midst. ἐνοικέω ("live in," "dwell in," "indwell"; so BAG, 267) appears only in a metaphorical sense in the New Testament (all six occurrences are in the Pauline corpus). So God himself will dwell among his people (2 Cor 6:16 citing Lev 26:11, 12), and the Holy Spirit dwells in believers (Rom 8:11 [cf. v 9]; 2 Tim 1:14; cf. 1 Cor 3:16). Not only the Word of Christ but also faith (2 Tim 1:5) may be said to dwell among God's own (contrast Rom 7:17 regarding the indwelling sin). ἐν ὑμῖν has been taken to mean "in your hearts" (so Lightfoot, 222, who understands the statement to refer to "the presence of Christ in the heart as an inward monitor"), "among you" (Masson, 147; cf. Schrage, *Einzelgebote,* 91) or "in you," that is, "in your *church* . . . , as a *whole,* being compared to a house, in which the word has the seat of its abiding operation and rule" (Meyer, 448; cf. Abbott, 290). Bruce, 283, claims that Paul would not have wished to be pinned down too firmly to the alternatives of either "within you" (as individual Christians) or "among you" (as a Christian community). He does add, however, that "if one of the two had to be accepted, the collective sense might be preferred in view of the context." πλουσίως ("richly," "abundantly") describes the manner of the Word's indwelling. Elsewhere in the epistles this adverb is found in statements which describe God's gracious and rich bestowal of his gifts: at 1 Timothy 6:17 it is used of "God who richly (πλουσίως) furnishes us with everything to enjoy," in contrast to the "rich in this world"; while at Titus 3:6 the Holy Spirit is "poured out upon us richly (πλουσίως) through Jesus Christ our Savior," and in 2 Peter 1:11 an "entrance into the eternal kingdom of our Lord and Savior Jesus Christ will be richly (πλουσίως) provided." Here in Colossians πλουσίως ("richly") appears within an exhortation: the gospel is to have its gracious and glorious way in their lives. If the double reference of ἐν ὑμῖν ("within you" and "among you") is in view then this rich indwelling would occur when they came together, listened to the Word of Christ as it was preached and expounded to them (see Schrage, *Einzelgebote,* 91, Ernst, 229, and Schweizer, 157) and bowed to its authority. By this means Christ's rule would be exercised in their lives. As the Spirit of God indwells believers (Rom 8:9, 11; 2 Tim 1:14; cf. 1 Cor 3:16) so the "Word of Christ" should reside among them in rich abundance, producing great blessing (cf. Ernst, 229, and Lohse, 150).

ἐν πάσῃ σοφίᾳ διδάσκοντες καὶ νουθετοῦντες ἑαυτούς κτλ. As the word of Christ richly indwells the Colossians, so by means of its operation they will "teach and admonish one another in all wisdom by means of psalms, hymns and spiritual songs" (this lengthy clause gives a modal definition of the preceding, so Meyer, 448). "Teaching and admonishing" (διδάσκοντες καὶ νουθετοῦντες; some exegetes consider that these dependent participles occur with an imperatival force, so Lightfoot, 222, Lohse, 150, etc.; if they are taken as true participles then the nominative plurals following the subject ὁ λόγος τοῦ Χριστοῦ, "the word of Christ," are constructed according to sense, so Turner, *Syntax,* 230, cf. Meyer, 448, and note the similar instance at 2:2—either way the teaching and admonition in all wisdom arise from the indwelling of the word, cf. Delling, *TDNT* 8, 498, Ernst, 229, and Dunn, *Jesus,* 237) were previously mentioned as activities of Paul and his co-workers, for it was by such instruction and admonition that the public proclamation of Christ as Lord was effected (see on 1:28). Here, however, it is the members of the congregation (so most commentators including Behm, *TDNT* 4, 1022 [cf. Rom 15:14; 1 Thess 5:14], but contrast Schrage, *Einzelgebote*, 137) who teach and admonish one another (*ἑαυτούς*, "yourselves," which does not really differ from *ἀλλήλους*, "one another," being reflexive in a reciprocal sense [so Robertson, *Grammar*, 690, BDF, para. 287, Turner, *Syntax*, 43], binds the two participles together). The phrase "in all wisdom" (*ἐν πάσῃ σοφίᾳ*) is attached to the following words indicating the manner in which the teaching and admonition are to occur (although Lightfoot, 221, 222, argued that the phrase, on the basis of 1:9; Eph 1:8; 5:18, 19, should be taken with the preceding clause [cf. AV, RV], the other alternative is favored by the sense of 1:28, where teaching and admonition occur in all wisdom, and it is balanced by *ἐν χάριτι ᾄδοντες*, "singing with grace or thankfulness," so ARV, RSV, NEB, NIV; cf. Bruce, 283, Lohse, 151, Schweizer, 157), that is, in a thoughtful and tactful manner (Bruce, 283; see also Bratcher and Nida, 90).

The motif of wisdom (*σοφία*) turns up on several occasions in Colossians: so Paul prays that the Colossians might be filled with a knowledge of God's will, and the perception of that will consists in wisdom (*ἐν πάσῃ σοφίᾳ*) and understanding of every sort, on the spiritual level (1:9). At chapter 1:28 the apostolic ministry of admonition and teaching is effected "in all wisdom" (*ἐν πάσῃ σοφίᾳ*). In Christ all the treasures of wisdom and knowledge have been stored up (2:3), while by contrast the taboos which the false teachers propounded were merely human inventions having only the appearance of wisdom (2:23, *λόγον . . . σοφίας*). At chapter 4:5 "wisdom" has to do with practical and realistic behavior in Christians' dealings with those outside the congregation. Here at chapter 3:16 it is possible that the phrase "in all wisdom" (*ἐν πάσῃ σοφίᾳ*), as at chapter 1:28, stands in contrast to the heretics' claim to wisdom. At the same time this true wisdom, for which Paul had previously prayed, shows itself in a practical way: the teaching and admonition are given in a thoughtful and tactful manner.

ψαλμοῖς, ὕμνοις, ᾠδαῖς πνευματικαῖς. This mutual instruction and warning are to take place "by means of psalms, hymns and spiritual songs." The ARV punctuates the sentence along these lines (cf. also the AV and RV) although the RSV renders the Greek "and as you sing psalms and hymns and spiritual songs with thankfulness in your hearts to God" (cf. NIV) so linking these three nouns with the following participle *ᾄδοντες* ("singing"). It is not patently clear as to which is the correct interpretation and commentators are as divided on the point as the versions (so, for example, Delling, *TDNT* 8, 498, Lohse, 136, 151, Schweizer, 153, and Bartels, *NIDNTT* 3, 675, link the noun with the following participles, while Meyer, 448, Lightfoot, 222, Percy, *Probleme*, 395, and Bruce, 283, 284, opt for the other alternative). Our preference for joining "psalms, hymns and spiritual songs" with "teaching and admonishing one another" is for the following reasons: *(a)* the two participial clauses *ἐν πάσῃ σοφίᾳ διδάσκοντες* . . . ("in all wisdom teaching . . .") and *ἐν* (*τῇ*) *χάριτι ᾄδοντες* . . . ("with thanksgiving [or grace] singing . . .") are symmetrically balanced with their prepositional phrases (both commencing with *ἐν*, "in,") at the head of each clause and the participles immediately following (cf. Meyer, 448). By contrast the other alternative with ψαλμοῖς κτλ. being attached to the following involves an overweighting of the final participial clause (a criticism noted by Bruce, 284). *(b)* The RSV rendering necessitates the insertion of "and" before "singing" (ᾄδοντες, cf. NIV) but this does not appear in the original (cf. Schweizer, 157, against Delling, *TDNT* 8, 498). *(c)* The parallel passage in Ephesians 5:19 (which interestingly enough the RSV renders as "addressing [λαλοῦντες)] one another in psalms and hymns and spiritual songs, singing and making melody to the Lord with all your heart") gives the same general sense as our interpretation. *(d)* The objection that mutual teaching and admonition would not take place in such psalms, hymns and spiritual songs is not valid. If the apostle had in mind antiphonal praise or solo singing for mutual edification in church meetings (Bruce, 284) then mutual instruction and exhortation could well have been possible. Further, recent study of NT hymnody (note the bibliography to 1:15–20 and see also R. P. Martin, "Approaches to New Testament Exegesis," *New Testament Interpretation. Essays on Principles and Methods,* ed. I. H. Marshall [Exeter: Paternoster, 1977] 235–41 American edition (Grand Rapids, MI: Eerdmans, 1977) has shown that within early Christian hymns both didactic and hortatory elements featured.

It is not possible to distinguish sharply between each of the three terms "psalms," "hymns" and "songs" (so most recent writers, cf. Schlier, *TDNT* 1, 164, and note Lohse's treatment, 151; against Lightfoot, 222, 223). ψαλμός ("song of praise," "psalm," BAG, 891; cf. Delling, *TDNT* 8, 489–503, and Bartels, *NIDNTT* 3, 668–76) is employed by Luke of the OT psalms (Luke 20:42; 24:44; Acts 1:20; 13:33) though it came to be used more generally of a song of praise (1 Cor 14:26; Eph 5:19) of which the OT psalms were probably regarded as spiritual prototypes (on the basis of the original meaning of ψάλλω to "pluck [hair]," "twang" a bow-string, and then "pluck" a harp or any other stringed instrument, some have thought that ψαλμός inevitably meant a song sung to the accompaniment of a stringed instrument; but this restriction is unnecessary, cf. Bruce, 284, and Delling, *TDNT* 8, 499). At 1 Corinthians 14:26 ψαλμός may be a newly coined "song of praise" prompted by the Spirit and sung with thankful rejoicing by a member of the congregation. Bartels (*NIDNTT* 3, 671, 672) suggests that such songs of praise "will include free compositions as well as repeated liturgical fragments . . . , and also new Christian songs (which may well have been modelled on the Psalms of the OT and of later Judaism . . .), such as we know from the wording of the various songs of Rev." ὕμνος, a general term in Biblical literature, denotes any "festive hymn of praise" (LXX Isa 42:10; 1 Macc 13:51; cf. Acts 16:25; Heb 2:12) though in its two NT occurrences it refers to an expression of praise to God or Christ (here and Eph 5:19). ᾠδή ("song," BAG, 895) is used in the NT of the song in which God's acts are praised and glorified (cf. Rev 5:9; 14:3; 15:3). Although firm distinctions cannot be drawn between the terms nor can an exact classification of NT hymns be made on the basis of the different words (so Delling, *TDNT* 8, 499, and *Worship in the New Testament.* Tr. P. Scott [London: Darton, Longman and Todd, 1962] 86, 87, and Martin, *NCB,* 116) taken together these three words "psalms," "hymns" and "songs" describe "the full range of singing which the Spirit prompts" (Lohse, 151; while the adjective πνευματικαῖς "prompted by the Spirit," consistent with Greek usage, agrees grammatically with the last term ᾠδαῖς, "songs," it refers to all three nouns). As the word of Christ indwells the members of the community and controls them so they teach and admonish one another in Spirit-inspired psalms, hymns and songs (whatever the precise musical form is, see W. S. Smith, *Musical Aspects of the New Testament* [Amsterdam: Have, 1962]).

ἐν [τῇ] χάριτι ᾄδοντες ἐν ταῖς καρδίαις ὑμῶν τῷ θεῷ. These words may specify another result of the rich indwelling of the word of Christ (Meyer, 450, prefers this interpretation in which the clause is taken as co-ordinate with the preceding), or they may denote the attitude or disposition which is to accompany the previously mentioned instruction and admonition, that is, as the Colossians teach one another in psalms, hymns and songs inspired by the Spirit, so they are to sing thankfully to God with their whole being (on this view the participial clause ἐν [τῇ] χάριτι ᾄδοντες, "singing gratefully," is subordinate to the preceding; note the discussions of von Soden, 64, and Abbott, 292). Although it is difficult to be certain, our preference is for the latter since it links the singing with the teaching through song. If the participial clauses had been co-ordinate one might have expected a καί, "and," to have been inserted. From the context it is clear that both the instruction and the disposition which should accompany it arise from the rich indwelling of the Word.

The expression ἐν τῇ χάριτι could mean "gratefully" (i.e. with thanksgiving), "by the grace (of God)" or "in the (realm of God's) grace," (cf. Moule, 125, 126), and the presence or absence of the article τῇ ("the"), about which the manuscripts are divided, does not finally settle the issue (so Moule, 125, 126, and *RevExp* 70 [1973] 493; against Lohse, 152, who contends that the definite article specifies χάρις as "God's bestowal of grace which gives life to the believers. The phrase ἐν [τῇ] χάριτι reminds the readers of *sola gratia* (by grace alone) which is the sole basis of existence and creates the realm in which the Christian life can exist and develop." Cf. Dibelius-Greeven, 45, and Schmauch, 82). Each of these renderings falls within the range of meanings of χάρις ("grace"; cf. BAG, 877, 878, and Schweizer, 158) and perhaps one ought not to distinguish between them too sharply. However, since the note of thanksgiving is an important theme in the section, appearing at verses 15 and 17, it is just possible that thankfulness, our proper response to God's grace, is in view once again. ἐν ταῖς καρδίαις ὑμῶν does not specify an inward disposition as though the apostle is speaking of silent worship in contrast to "with your voices." As in verse 15 καρδία ("heart") is employed to refer to the whole of one's being. "Man should not only praise God with his lips. The entire man should be filled with songs of praise" (Lohse, 151).

17. The paragraph with its injunctions is summed up (cf. Bujard, *Untersuchungen*, 98) in an exhortation that is universal in scope, covering every aspect of life; it is by no means "colorless" as Lohmeyer, 151, claims. There are few exhortations in the NT which are as comprehensive as this one (cf. 1 Cor 10:31, "So whatever you eat or drink or whatever you do, do it all for the glory of God"). Every activity is to be done in obedience to the Lord Jesus and accompanied by the giving of thanks to God through him. If the

rich indwelling of the Word of Christ in the readers' lives should be manifest in mutual teaching and admonition, as the Colossians gratefully sing to God, then it should also (*καί*) show its dynamic presence in this comprehensive way.

πᾶν ὅ τι ἐὰν ποιῆτε ἐν λόγῳ ἢ ἐν ἔργῳ. This first clause, "whatever you do, in word or deed," is an absolute nominative (cf. Meyer, 452, 453; Abbott, 292, and Lohmeyer, 151) placed at the beginning for rhetorical emphasis and it stands syntactically independent. The expression "whatever" (*πᾶν ὅ τι ἐάν*, a Semitic phrase according to K. Beyer, *Semitische Syntax im Neuen Testament* [SUNT 1; Göttingen: Vandenhoeck und Ruprecht, 1962] 169, BDF, para. 466[3], and Lohse, 152) introduces this clause and is picked up again with the word "everything" (*πάντα*), which begins the main clause. In this way the point is strongly driven home that the Christian's whole life must be lived in obedience to the Lord Jesus. "In word or deed" (*ἐν λόγῳ ἢ ἐν ἔργῳ*) explains the first term "all" (*πᾶν*) so making plain that the injunction ought not to be limited to the context of worship (there is no intention in this comprehensive injunction to restrict the meaning of "word" and "deed" to the liturgical practices of "preaching" and the Lord's Supper). In all his activities the believer ought to render "spiritual worship" (Rom 12:1, 2. Cf. E. Käsemann, "Worship in Everyday Life: a note on Romans 12," *New Testament Questions of Today*, 188–95).

πάντα ἐν ὀνόματι κυρίου Ἰησοῦ. "(Do) everything in the name of the Lord Jesus." The verb in this principal clause has to be supplied, but it is clear from the context that it should be the imperative *ποιεῖτε*, "Do" (so most commentators who rightly prefer it to the participle *ποιοῦντες*; the following participle *εὐχαριστοῦντες*, "giving thanks," is then dependent on the imperative). "In the name of the Lord Jesus" (*ἐν ὀνόματι κυρίου Ἰησοῦ*) is used elsewhere in the context of baptism (Acts 10:48). The whole content of salvation revealed in Jesus is comprised in his name (Acts 4:12; 1 Cor 6:11). Belief in the name of Jesus, i. e. his messianic mission (John 3:18), is God's command (1 John 3:23; 5:13), so that anyone who believes in that name receives the forgiveness of sins (Acts 10:43; 1 John 2:12), has eternal life (John 20:21; 1 John 5:13) and escapes the judgment (John 3:18). The formula "in the name of Jesus" is used with reference to God giving the Holy Spirit (John 14:26) and the offering of thanks (Eph 5:20). Jesus' disciples perform miracles and acts of compassion in his name (Luke 10:17; Mark 8:38, 39), while Paul was able to admonish through the name of the Lord Jesus (2 Thess 3:6; 1 Cor 1:10), and give judgment in that name (1 Cor 5:4) as one commissioned and authorized by him (so Bietenhard, *NIDNTT* 2, 654; for further details see his treatment in *TDNT* 5, 270–81). Here at Colossians 3:17, "The whole life of the Christian stands under the name of Jesus," as Bietenhard has aptly put it (*TDNT* 5, 274. Lohse, 152, Martin, *NCB*, 117, and others have drawn attention to the rabbinic parallel, credited to Rabbi Jose [*c.* A.D. 100]: "Let all thy deeds be done for the sake of Heaven" [lit. "in the name of heaven"; Danby's translation]). In becoming a Christian the believer calls upon Jesus as Lord (Rom 10:9, 10) and comes under the authority of Christ. He belongs wholly to him; thus everything he says or does ought to be in the light of the fact that Jesus is his Lord. His behavior should be entirely consistent with Jesus' character (Merk, *Handeln,* 214, following Schrage, *Einzelgebote,* 240, 241, claims that this singular expression, "in the name of the Lord Jesus," is a reference to the historical Jesus), and this will occur as the word of Christ richly indwells him and other members of the congregation (v 16).

εὐχαριστοῦντες τῷ θεῷ πατρὶ δι' αὐτοῦ. Thanksgiving is to be the accompaniment of every activity (this clause provides an accompanying definition, "while you at the same time give thanks . . ."; cf. Meyer, 453), being offered to the Father through Christ. We have already noted elsewhere in Colossians that thanksgiving is offered to God in his character as Father (see on 1:3, 12; and note W. Marchel, *Abba, Père! La prière du Christ et des chrétiens.* 2nd ed. [AnBib 19A; Rome: Pontifical Biblical Institute, 1971] 190–97). Once again such praise is to ascend to him though here it is specifically mentioned as "through the Lord Jesus" (*δι' αὐτοῦ,* i.e. the one in whose name all things are to be said and done; cf. Eph 5:20, "giving thanks in the name of our Lord Jesus Christ to God the Father"). Lohse (153, following Oepke, *TDNT* 2, 68, 69) rejects the notion that Jesus Christ is here thought of as the one who mediates thanks to God (on the ground that the formula "through Christ" is never linked with verbs of asking) and asserts that the phrase "gives pregnant expression to the constitutive significance of Christ for the whole of the Christian life" (Oepke, *TDNT* 2, 69, cited by Lohse, 153; he also makes reference to W. Thüsing, *Per Christum in Deum. Studien zum Verhältnis von Christozentrik und Theozentrik in den paulinischen Hauptbriefen.* 2nd ed. [NTAbh, NS 1; Münster: Aschendorff, 1969] 164–237, who treats the relevant passages from the major Pauline epistles along similar lines). So Lohse asserts: "Christ is the Lord who provides the basis and sets the goal for the life of believers."

However, without wishing to deny that the ultimate ground for the giving of thanks in Paul's letters is the mighty work of God in Christ bringing salvation through the gospel (O'Brien, *Studies,* 50–66, especially 62), here the basis is not spelled out (H. Greeven, *G bet und Eschatologie im Neuen Testament* [Gütersloh: Bertelsmann, 1931] 180, considers Paul's short form of exhortation to thanksgiving, in which the grounds are not expressly stated, is the most profound). If Paul had intended to provide this we would have expected him to have written *δι' αὐτόν* ("because of him," i.e. *διά* with the accusative rather than the genitive). Instead, "through him" (*δι' αὐτοῦ*) signifies that Christ is the mediator of the thanksgiving, a notion that is in view at Romans 1:8, 7:25 (and possibly 1 Cor 15:57; on the use of the *διά* phrases, such as "through our Lord Jesus Christ," in connection with rejoicing in God [Rom 5:11], exhorting the brethren [Rom 15:30], etc., see W. Kramer, *Christ, Lord, Son of God.* Tr. B. Hardy [SBT 50; London: SCM, 1966] 84–89; cf. O'Brien. *Introductory Thanksgivings,* 204–206). This is not to be understood to mean that as high priest Christ was presenting or transmitting each prayer to the Father (the view of O. Cullmann, *The Christology of the New Testament.* Tr. S. C. Guthrie and C. A. M. Hall. 2nd ed. [London: SCM, 1963] 107: 1st American edition [Philadelphia: Westminster, 1959]. Kramer, *Christ,* 88, rightly notes that exhortation passages such as this prove there is no idea of any "high priestly activity" on the part of the exalted Lord; cf. Deichgräber's comments, *Gotteshymnus,* 40), but that thanksgiving could now be addressed to God through him, the mediator, who had opened the way to the Father's presence. This the readers might do with confidence since Christ's death had torn down the separating curtain which had excluded a direct approach (Harder, *Paulus,* 163–99, has argued that "through Christ" is one of the significant distinguishing marks of Christian prayer, especially thanksgiving).

Explanation

The Colossian Christians are addressed by means of privileged titles: they are the elect of God, holy and beloved. That is, they are his chosen people whom he has set apart for himself and upon whom he has placed his love. These descriptions were employed not only of Israel in the OT but also of Christ himself in the NT. So the point of the readers' similarity to and identification with him is underscored in a context where they are said already to have put on the new man (v 10) and consequently must don the graces which are characteristic of him. In fact, the five so-called virtues listed here (note the two catalogs of vices in vv 5 and 8) are elsewhere predicated of God or Christ: "heartfelt compassion, kindness, lowliness, gentleness, longsuffering." Each of these graces with which the readers are to be clothed shows how they, as God's elect, should behave in their dealings with others, particularly with fellow-believers. As a result of their being clothed with "longsuffering" they are to show continual forbearance toward one another. Further, their relationships with each other should be characterized by mutual forgiveness. As the Lord freely forgave them, so when grievances arise they are to forgive each other. Love is the crowning grace which the new man is to put on as part of his distinctive dress, for love is the bond which produces perfection.

Christ's peace is to hold sway over every aspect of the readers' lives as they relate to one another; in other words, Christ himself, who is the Lord of peace, is to be present and ruling in their midst. And since the Colossians are said to have been called into the peace of Christ (that is, through the gospel), then the latter expression must also designate the realm or sphere in which the new man now lives. The readers are also admonished to let the word of Christ—the gospel message which centers on Christ—have its gracious and glorious way in their midst. If this occurs then the members of the congregation will mutually teach and admonish one another in a thoughtful and tactful way. Such mutual instruction and admonition will take place in Spirit-inspired psalms, hymns and songs as the Colossians sing thankfully to God with their whole being.

The paragraph with its injunctions is summed up in an exhortation that is universal in its scope, covering every aspect of life. Every activity is to be done in obedience to the Lord Jesus and accompanied by the giving of thanks to God through him. If the rich indwelling of the Word of Christ in the readers' lives is to be manifested in mutual teaching and admonition, as the Colossians thankfully sing to God, then it should also show its dynamic presence in this comprehensive way.

Behavior in the Christian Household (3:18–4:1)

Bibliography

Austgen, R. J. *Motivation,* 116–20. **Crouch, J. E.** *The Origin and Intention of the Colossian Haustafel.* FRLANT 109. Göttingen: Vandenhoeck und Ruprecht, 1972. **Goppelt, L.** "Jesus und die 'Haustafel'-Tradition." *Orienterung an Jesus. Zur Theologie der Synoptiker. Für Josef Schmid,* ed. P. Hoffmann, with N. Brox and W. Pesch. Freiburg: Herder, 1973, 93–106. **Hinson, E. G.**"The Christian Household in Colossians 3:18–4:1." *RevExp* 70 (1973) 495–506. **Kamlah, E.** " 'Ὑποτάσσεσθαι in den neutestamentlichen Haustafeln." *Verborum Veritas. Festschrift für Gustav Stählin zum 70. Geburtstag,* ed. O. Bocher and K. Haacker. Wuppertal: Brockhaus, 1970, 237–43. **Lillie, W.** "The Pauline House-tables." *ExpTim* 86 (1974–75) 179–83. **Martin, R. P.** "Virtue." *NIDNTT* 3, 928–32. **Merk, O.** *Handeln,* 214–23. **Rengstorf, K. H.** "Die neutestamentliche Mahnungen an die Frau, sich dem Manne unterzuordnen." *Verbum Dei manet in Aeternum. Festschrift für O. Schmitz,* ed. W. Foerster. Witten: Luther, 131–45. **Schrage, W.** *Einzelgebote.* ———. "Zur Ethik der neutestamentlichen Haustafeln." *NTS* 21 (1974–75) 1–22. **Schroeder, D.** "Lists, Ethical." *IDBSup,* 546, 547. **Schweizer, E.** *Text,* 195–209. ———. "Die Weltlichkeit des Neuen Testamentes: die Haustafeln." *Beiträge zur alttestamentlichen Theologie, Festschrift für Walther Zimmerli zum 70. Geburtstag,* ed. H. Donner, R. Hanhart and R. Smend. Göttingen: Vandenhoeck und Ruprecht, 1977, 397–413. **Zeilinger, F.** *Der Erstgeborene,* 68, 69.

Translation

18 *Wives, be subject to your husbands, as is fitting in the Lord.* 19 *Husbands, love your wives and do not be embittered with them.* 20 *Children, obey your parents in all things for this is pleasing in the Lord.* 21 *Fathers, do not provoke your children, lest they become discouraged.* 22 *Slaves, give entire obedience to your earthly masters, not with eye-service in order to please men, but with sincerity of heart as you reverence the Lord.* 23 *Whatever you do, work at it with all your heart, as working for the Lord not for men.* 24 *For you know that you will receive an inheritance from the Lord as a reward. Serve the Lord Christ.* 25 *For anyone who does wrong will be repaid for his wrong, and there is no favoritism.* 4:1 *Masters, treat your slaves justly and fairly, since you know that you too have a Master in heaven.*

Note: The Rules for the Household

Introduction

Colossians 3:18–4:1 contains a series of admonitions addressed successively to wives and husbands, children and fathers, slaves and masters. The paragraph is introduced without any connecting particle and constitutes an independent, self-contained paraenetic unit. Luther called this scheme of household duties a *Haustafel,* which means "a list of rules for the household," but it is usually translated into English as "house-table." The rules formulated to govern behavior patterns within the Christian household have been aptly described by Schroeder (*IDBSup*, 546, cf. his *Haustafeln* [Hamburg: unpublished doctoral dissertation, 1959]) as "station codes" for Christians are addressed according to their station in life. Each party is named (e.g. "wives"), a command is given (in the imperative mood, e.g. "Be subject to your husbands") and a motivating statement for the behavior is supplied (e.g. "as is fitting in the Lord"). Parallels are found in Ephesians 5:22–6:9; 1 Timothy 2:8–15; 6:1, 2; Titus 2:1–10; 1 Peter 2:18–3:7 and in the writings of the Apostolic Fathers (Did 4:9–11; Barn 19:5–7; 1 Clem 1:3; 21:6–9; Ignatius, *Poly* 4:1–6:2; Polycarp, *Phil* 4:2–6:1). However, in most of the latter passages (except Eph 5:22–6:9) there is an absence of the reciprocal obligations which are a distinctive mark of the "house-tables" and they do not spring out of a household situation (Schrage, *NTS* 21 [1974–75] 2, thus claims that *Haustafel* is not wholly adequate to describe the latter lists, while Schroeder, *IDBSup*, 546, classifies 1 Tim 2:8–15; 6:1, 2; Titus 2:1–10; 1 Clem 21:6–9 etc. as "church-order regulations"). The term "house-table" ought, therefore, to be limited to exhortations given in the characteristic form of Colossians 3:18–4:1 (cf. the Ephesian parallel) with its pairs and reciprocal duties (so Lillie, *ExpTim* 86 [1974–75] 180; for similar reasons Crouch, *Origin*, limits his inquiry to that of the Colossian *Haustafel*).

Backgrounds

New Testament scholars have developed no consensus concerning the possible origin and background to the house-tables. Diverse and competing theories have not been able to explain the formal and material similarities with earlier ethical teaching elsewhere on the one hand, as well as the undoubted differences with Colossians 3:18–4:1, the oldest extant house-table, on the other. So at the end of his historical survey Crouch concluded: "Historical study of the Christian *Haustafeln* is at an impasse" (*Origin*, 32). The following are some of the more significant alternatives:

(i) A Hellenistic Code

M. Dibelius (Dibelius-Greeven, 48–50), the first scholar to give serious attention to the question of background, claimed that the origin of the Christian house-tables was to be found in Hellenistic, and specifically Stoic, moral philosophy. Key expressions, such as "it is fitting" (*ἀνῆκεν*, Col 3:18), "it is pleasing," i.e. to God (*εὐάρεστον*, v 20), were appealed to in support since they are frequently found in Stoic literature, while the expression "in the Lord" (*ἐν κυρίῳ*, v 20) was said to be only loosely attached as a Christian addition.

K. Weidinger, a pupil of Dibelius, defended and expanded his teacher's thesis. He noted that the *Haustafel* schema was based on the Stoic concept of duty (*καθῆκον*) which in turn was an adaptation of "unwritten laws" (*νόμιμα ἄγραφα*): fear of the gods, honor toward parents, proper care of the dead, love of friends and fidelity toward country (cf. his *Die Haustafeln: Ein Stück urchristlicher Paränese* [UNT; Leipzig: J. C. Hinrichs, 1928] 27–34, 41, 42). There was no essential difference among Stoic, Hellenistic Jewish and Christian forms of these tables. Several writers mention similar obligations in tabulated form (e.g. Aristotle, *Pol* 1, 2; Seneca, *Ep* 94; Plutarch, *LibEd* 10; Epictetus, *Dissertationes*, 2, 10, 3, 7). A waning interest in an imminent Parousia and a growing recognition by Christians that they needed to come to terms with the world were the reasons (according to Dibelius) for the Christian adoption of such a schema. For Weidinger it was the need to regulate the inner life of the church on a nonenthusiastic, noneschatological basis (*Haustafeln*, 9; cf. Martin, *NIDNTT* 3, 931).

Although this theory has been popular, even axiomatic in some circles, it fails to account for the considerable differences in content between the Christian and non-Christian material, the different motivations and the unparalleled setting of the specific rubrics in Stoic writing. In the latter texts the stations are not addressed directly, nor is the imperative mood used; the naming of the station was sufficient to indicate the appropriate conduct (cf. Schroeder, *IDBSup*, 546).

(ii) A CHRISTIAN CODE

At the other end of the spectrum K. H. Rengstorf (*Mann und Frau im Urchristentum*) sought to explain the Christian house-tables as being uniquely Christian. For him the differences between the Christian *Haustafeln* and the Hellenistic and Jewish parallels prevent the conclusion that they are slightly Christianized versions of a non-Christian paraenetic piece. Because all the persons addressed in the house-tables are members of the household, the major impulse in their formation is the early Christian interest in the household (οἶκος). The emphasis is on the father as the head of the entire household rather than on sexual differences or distinctions in rank. According to Rengstorf the essentially Christian nature of the concerns of the house-tables may be compared with the similar elements in the infancy narratives of Luke 1, 2, where the home life of John the Baptist and Jesus are described. Joseph like Zechariah is head of the family, and the boy Jesus is submissive (ὑποτάσσομαι, "be subordinate," in Luke 2:51; it is a key term in the epistles and a designation of the duty of the wife is a specifically Christian creation, see below).

For Schroeder (*Haustafeln; IDBSup*, 546, 547) the NT station codes reflect the influence of diverse traditions: formally, with their direct address, imperative mood and motivating statements, they are indebted to OT apodictic law (cf. Deut 5:16). The content is drawn basically from the OT and Judaic tradition, though certain Greek ("what is fitting") and Christian (ἀγάπη, "love") concepts are added. The basic ethical conceptions of the NT station codes, according to Schroeder take us back to the teaching and example of Jesus himself. The occasion for the creation of the house-table was the gospel proclamation itself, and its setting in life was the teaching activity of the apostles. Specifically Paul created it because of a problem which in turn stemmed from his own declaration of the equality of all persons in Christ (Gal 3:28).

Both views have been subjected to a detailed critique by Crouch (*Origin*, 24–31, etc.) who prefers a background in the following:

(iii) A Hellenistic Jewish Code

With some variations several recent writers have traced the origin to Hellenistic Judaism, not in the sense that any exact parallel to the Colossian house-table is to be found in this source but that the material from which the *Haustafel* was formed came from Hellenistic Jewish sources (Crouch, *Origin,* Lohse, 154–57, Schweizer, for references see below; cf. Schrage, *NTS* 21 [1974–75] 7). Martin (*NIDNTT* 3, 931) speaks of a cluster of views that begin with the point of obedience to God's will, seen first in Jewish injunctions (so Lohmeyer, 152–55) and expanded to include material used in gentile missionary outreach by Hellenistic Judaism (Crouch, *Origin,* 84–101). The main sources are Philo, *Hypothetica* 7:1–9 (cf. *Decal* 165–67), Josephus, *Ap* 2, 190–219, and *Ps Phocylides* 175–227, an Alexandrian Jew. Following Crouch Martin points out that these writers "show some hint of the so-called Noachian laws by which the conduct of Gentiles was to be governed in matters of elementary morals (concerning immorality, idolatry, dietary rules)" (*NIDNTT* 3, 931). There were links between these Noachian laws and the "unwritten laws" (*νόμιμα ἄγραφα*), the basic moral and family duties of the Greeks. Here was a meeting place between Judaism and Hellenism where social duties were common to both cultures.

Lillie (*ExpTim* 86 [1974–75] 180, 181), while recognizing resemblances between the house-tables and Greek teachings, claims that the giving of good advice, particularly to such subordinates as wives, children or slaves, was something that both the Greek and later Roman Stoics loved to do. Further, Stoic teachings, diluted by popularizers, were part of the common culture of the later Hellenistic world, a culture in which Paul and other NT writers shared. Lillie, therefore, claims that the Jewish and OT influences appear far more important (cf. the quotation of the fifth commandment in the exhortation to children at Eph 6:2, 3 and the example of Sarah's attitude to her husband given to wives in 1 Pet 3:6). Lillie concludes that the first person to use this house-table pattern of teaching needed only to have known the conventional views of morality prevailing in the Hellenistic world and the OT and Jewish traditions that any educated Jew would possess.

Schweizer, who has written extensively on the subject (cf. 159–171 and *Festschrift für Zimmerli,* 397–413, *Text,* 195–209), follows the general line that the Hellenistic patterns have reached the NT mediated by Hellenistic Judaism. However, he recognized certain differences between those of Hellenism and Hellenistic Judaism (cf. *Text,* 201, 202): first, in the former it is the male, adult and free individual who is instructed how to act over against his wife, children and slaves. But the Hellenistic Jewish tables, e.g. Philo, influenced by the OT, side with the weak, the minor and the unfree (so Israel is reminded of her slavery in Egypt, the married life of the neighbor is protected, and the authority of parents over children is limited by the first commandment). Second, while the aim of the Greek ethical rules was the self-perfection of the individual who ought to have a right attitude to inferiors and their needs (since this was really for his good and harmonized with the all-embracing divine order of the cosmos), the central interest of the ethical tables shaped by the OT was the protection of the weak and the helpless. So the partner is always taken seriously and all human beings, not only men but also wives, children and slaves, are treated as ethically responsible subjects.

Schweizer (*Text*, 202–204) in his treatment of Colossians 3:18–4:1, the first Christian house-table, has summarized some of the significant differences between it and earlier models. So wives, children and slaves are addressed equally with their husbands, fathers and masters. Although this is not totally new, there are no extant examples which are as thoroughgoing as Colossians 3:18–4:1 in this emphasis on reciprocal obligations. Wives, children and slaves are ethically responsible to do "what is fitting" as well as husbands, fathers and masters. Further, the readers are admonished "in the Lord." This is no mere cipher, nor simply a loosely attached additional phrase (against Dibelius-Greeven, 49, and Weidinger, *Haustafeln;* so rightly Moule, 129, and Schweizer, in *Text*, 203; on the significance of the phrase see Schrage, *NTS* 21 [1974–75] 11, 19–22, and the exegesis below). Rather than living in conformity with the order of nature the reader is to regulate his life under the lordship of Christ and in conformity with his will. Finally, it is to be noted that the Colossian house-table follows on from chapter 3:17 and sets forth in concrete details some of those words and deeds to be done in the name of the Lord Jesus, giving thanks to God the Father through him. This naturally leads one to ask why Paul found it necessary to give this instruction here.

Occasion

The house-table may have been part of a larger complex of doctrinal and ethical material, that is, an early Christian catechism, which was easily learned by heart and given to new converts. But we have no direct evidence for this. Further, if the house-table scheme was integral to the early Christian catechism, why is there no evidence of it in the Thessalonian and Roman correspondence, or in 1 Corinthians where such a form would have been extremely appropriate? Why, too, do the *Haustafeln* not appear in James (the paraenetic character of which is undisputed), the Synoptic tradition or the Johannine literature? (For a critique of this view, presented with slight modifications by Seeberg, Carrington and Selwyn, see Crouch, *Origin*, 9–18.)

Dibelius considered that the Christian adoption of the house-table was to be found in a waning of an imminent Parousia while Weidinger understood it in terms of the need to regulate the inner life of the church on a nonenthusiastic, noneschatological basis (see above). But apart from the wider question as to whether the so-called delay of the Parousia played any part at all in the formation of the NT writings, any attempt to characterize the house-tables as protests against eschatological enthusiasm is unconvincing (cf. Schrage, *NTS* 21 [1974–75], 9, 10).

Others (including Crouch, *Origin*, 120–51, and Martin, *NIDNTT* 3, 931, 932) have argued that as Paul at 1 Corinthians 7:17–24 and 14:33–38 sought to correct a gnosticizing enthusiasm in Corinth based on a misunderstanding of the apostle's teaching in Galatians 3:27–29, to the effect that in Christ there was now the promise of social egalitarianism, so here the house-table of Colossians 3:18–4:1 confirms the restrictions as binding, thus safeguarding "the good order of the church against revolutionary attempts to undermine it by a false claim to unbridled freedom in the name of gnostic enlightenment and licence" (Martin, *NIDNTT* 3, 932). Although an overenthusiastic reception of the Pauline doctrine of freedom—such as is evident at Corinth—may have been a factor leading to the house-tables, it cannot be the only one since the emancipation of children was not an issue there (Schweizer, *Text,* 202; note also Schrage's criticisms, *NTS* 21 [1974–75] 4–6).

Particularly significant in the Colossians rule for the household are the references to the "Lord" (*κύριος*). The commands are furnished with the motivation "in the Lord" (*ἐν κυρίῳ*). So the readers are admonished "as is proper in the Lord" (*ὡς ἀνῆκεν ἐν κυρίῳ*, v 18), and "for this is pleasing in the Lord" (*τοῦτο γὰρ εὐάρεστόν ἐστιν ἐν κυρίῳ* v 20). Paul reminds them of the fear of the Lord (*φοβούμενοι τὸν κύριον*, v 22) and their conduct is regarded as done for the Lord (*ὡς τῷ κυρίῳ*, v 23). Reference is made to the Lord's judgment (vv 24, 25; 4:1), while they are admonished to "serve the Lord Christ" (*τῷ κυρίῳ Χριστῷ δουλεύετε*, 3:24). If the phrase "in the Lord" provides the motivation, then the other references show that the whole life, thought and conduct of believers (cf. v 17) is submitted to the lordship of Jesus Christ (Lohse, 156, 157; Schrage, *NTS* 21 [1974–75] 19–22, Schweizer, *Text,* 203). Yet the household rules indicate how this obedience is concretely expressed, and it may be because the devotees of the false teaching at Colossae were indifferent to mundane and domestic affairs. Perhaps with their concern for ascetic practices, heavenly worship and visions of divine mysteries the false teachers wished to keep themselves as pure as possible from all contact with the world, and Paul has to remind the congregation of the pernicious nature of this teaching, recalling them to the simple duties of family life. This might appear surprising since the apostle has already summoned his readers to "set their minds on things that are above," verse 2. Yet his idea of a life ruled from above where Christ is reigning is precisely that of a life in marriage, parenthood and everyday work (Schweizer, *Text,* 204). It is a life expressed in concrete statements, not in ideals, and as such follows on from and explains the injunction of verse 17, "and whatever you do, in word or deed, do all in the name of the Lord Jesus, giving thanks to God the Father through him."

Form/Structure/Setting

Colossians 3:18–4:1 is a self-contained paraenetic unit consisting of three pairs of reciprocal exhortations. In each case the exhortation deals with the proper kind of attitude or action which should be shown by one member to the other. The first member is exhorted to submission (v 18) or obedience (vv 20, 22) to the other. The relationships are set out in the most natural order, beginning with the closest—that of wife and husband—and concluding with the relationship between slave and master (cf. Crouch, *Origin,* 9). Each segment consists of an address (e.g. "wives," v 18; cf. vs 19, 20, 21, 22; 4:1), an exhortation in the imperative (e.g. "be subordinate to your husbands," v 18; cf. vv 19, 20, 21, 22; 4:1) and the reason or motivation for the behavior (e.g. "as is fitting in the Lord," v 18; cf. vv 20, 22; 4:1; no motivating statement accompanies the exhortations to husbands and fathers). The sentence structure of the house-table is not long and complicated (cf. Percy, *Probleme,* 36, and Bujard, *Untersuchungen,* 102, 103) as the opening two chapters of the letter are.

The exhortation to slaves (vv 22–25) is expanded and breaks the sequence somewhat. Verse 22 is a longer exhortation than the four previous admonitions and may be structured as follows:

22*a* οἱ δοῦλοι ὑπακούετε κατὰ πάντα τοῖς κατὰ σάρκα κυρίοις,
b μὴ ἐν ὀφθαλμοδουλίᾳ ὡς ἀνθρωπάρεσκοι,
c ἀλλ' ἐν ἁπλότητι καρδίας φοβούμενοι τὸν κύριον.
a "Slaves, give entire obedience to your earthly masters,
b not with eye-service in order to please men,
c but with sincerity of heart as you reverence the Lord."

The remainder of the admonition to slaves (vv 23–25) contains three dependent clauses (vv 23*a*, 24*a* and 25*a*), each of which is followed by a principal clause (vv 23*b*, 24*b* and 25*b*): cf. Zeilinger, *Der Erstgeborene,* 69.

Comment

In this household table Paul deals with concrete human relations within the ancient οἶκος ("house," "household"), not with abstract ordinances. The first pair of injunctions concerns wives and husbands, then children and fathers, finally slaves and masters. In each case the subordinate member is mentioned first and is exhorted to be subject (ὑποτάσσομαι) or to obey (ὑπακούω). Wives, children and slaves are addressed equally with their husbands, fathers and masters. They too are ethically responsible partners who are expected to do "what is fitting in the Lord" just as the male, the father and the free man. But the exhortations to subordination do not stand alone; immediately the second member of each pair is addressed and reminded of his responsibilities. The twin admonitions stand together and the first ought not to be interpreted apart from the second (so rightly Rengstorf, *Mann,* 46, Schroeder, *Haustafeln,* 123, 199, and Schrage, *NTS* 21 [1974–75] 12; against Crouch, *Origin,* 31). Each member of the family or household stands in his or her place within the created order (at 1 Cor 11:9 Paul expressly mentions the creation ordinances) and has certain responsibilities.

18. *αἱ γυναῖκες ὑποτάσσεσθε τοῖς ἀνδράσιν.* Wives are to be subordinate to their husbands. Here the use of the nominative case with the article (*αἱ γυναῖκες,* "wives") in address, instead of the vocative case, has been regarded by Schroeder (*Haustafeln,* 93, 94; cf. Lohmeyer, 156) as further evidence of the household table's indebtedness to the OT, since in the LXX the determinative Semitic vocative is rendered by the nominative with the article (cf. Hos 5:1). But nothing can be built on this since the use of the nominative with the article in address was not unknown in Greek (BDF, para. 147[3], Dibelius-Greeven, 45; cf. Merk, *Handeln,* 214).

The precise nature of the injunction has been a matter of some dispute among NT exegetes. So, for example, Lohse (157, 158) and Merk (*Handeln,* 215) claim that Christian wives are commanded to behave in accordance with the prevailing social order. It is argued that ὑποτάσσομαι ("be subordinate") is not to be interpreted as a specifically Christian word (as Rengstorf, *Mann,* 23, 24 and 30, claimed), nor are wives called upon to make a free decision in the matter (against E. Kähler, *Die Frau in den paulinischen Briefen* [Zurich/Frankfurt: Gotthelf, 1960] 156, who considered that being subject was a "free act of acknowledging the order which is established through the word of God in Jesus Christ," and that there was no trace of compulsion in the term). Instead, it was argued that this expression signifies no more and no less than that level of obedience which was customary and proper in such a relationship in the contemporary world (Merk, *Handeln,* 215, following Käsemann). And for Crouch (*Origin,* 109–111) the submission of the wife to her husband, which was a concern of Jewish propaganda (Philo, *Hyp* 7.3, and Josephus, *Ap* 2.201), shows that the woman is viewed as inferior.

But this rather popular line of interpretation is open to question at several points and in evaluating it one needs to examine the precise meaning of the verb. ὑποτάσσω, which appeared in Greek literature relatively late, in the active voice meant to "place under," "subordinate," and in the middle to "subject oneself" out of fear or to "submit voluntarily." In the LXX the word is not very common, but is employed in the active voice meaning to "place under," "subordinate," especially of God who makes creatures subject to man (LXX Ps 8:7), the people subject to David (143:2), to the nations (17:48), and the nations to the Israelites (46:4). The middle voice of the verb denotes to "subject oneself," "acquiesce in," and to "acknowledge someone's dominion or power," such as Yahweh's and his people's (1 Chr 22:18); it comes to be used meaning to "surrender to God" (Ps 36:7; 61:2, 6) and to "humble oneself before him" (2 Macc 9:12; for details see Delling, *TDNT* 8, 40).

Although the contrary impression is often given (Lohse, 157) the word "subordinate" was by no means widespread or commonplace in Greek literature dealing with marriage (Rengstorf, *Verbum Dei,* 131–45, found only two examples, Plutarch, *Conjugalia praecepta* 33, and Ps-Callisthenes 1, 22, 4, which are often cited by other commentators). The question, then, is what did Paul mean by using the term here? This verb occurs some twenty-three times in the Pauline corpus (τάγμα, "order," "division," and διαταγή, "ordinance," "direction," appear once each, τάξις, "order," twice and ὑποταγή, "subjection," "subordination," four times) and has to do with order. M. Barth (*Ephesians. Translation and Commentary on Chapters 4–6* [AB 34A; Garden City, NY: Doubleday, 1974], 4–6, 709–715; cf. Delling, *TDNT* 8, 41–45) discerns two groups of statements: *(a)* when the active ὑποτάσσω ("subordinate") is used (or the so-called divine passive) the power to subject belongs to God alone (1 Cor 15:24–28; Rom 8:20; Eph 1:21, 22; Phil 3:21; cf. Rom 13:1; Heb 2:8; 1 Pet 3:22; Luke 10:17, 20); *(b)* the apostle uses middle indicatives, participles or imperatives of the verb ὑποτάσσομαι (Robertson, *Grammar,* 807, suggests it may be a direct middle) to describe the subordination of Christ to God, members of the congregation to one another, believers with prophetic gifts, or wives, children and slaves (1 Cor 15:28; Eph 5:21; 1 Cor 14:32; Eph 5:22, etc.). In the forty or so NT occurrences the verb carries an overtone of authority and subjection or submission to it. Here at Colossians 3:18, as Schweizer

(164) claims, it denotes the subjection of oneself, as Christ subjected himself to the Father (1 Cor 15:28). The demand for mutual submission among Christians (Eph 5:21) shows that ὑποτάσσομαι ("be subordinate") bears a close relation to Christian ταπεινοφροσύνη ("humility"), as Delling (*TDNT* 8, 45) and Kamlah (*Verborum Veritas*, 237–43) have suggested. That the one verb can be used in an injunction to describe the attitude required of all Christians, whether in a "dominating" or a "subordinate" position, shows that the notion of inferior dignity need not be present in the term (a point confirmed at 1 Cor 15:28 with reference to Christ; cf. E. Kähler, "Zur 'Unterordnung' der Frau im Neuen Testament," *ZEE* [1959] 1–13, *Frau*, 7. Crouch, *Origin*, 110, in his concern to note the history of religions parallels has not given sufficient attention to the other Pauline uses of the term). Schrage (*NTS* 21 [1974–75] 12) and others claim that the basis, motivation and emphasis on the subordination of wives to husbands in the NT are different from similar injunctions elsewhere in the ancient world. The exhortation to be subordinate is balanced with the instruction to husbands to love their wives: the admonition is an appeal to free and responsible agents that can only be heeded voluntarily, never by the elimination or breaking of the human will, much less by means of a servile submissiveness (Barth, *Ephesians 4–6*, 609); and finally its motivation is "in the Lord" (see below).

ὡς ἀνῆκεν ἐν κυρίῳ. "As is fitting in the Lord." Paul is not suggesting here that the woman is naturally or spiritually inferior to the man, or the wife to the husband. But he does mention elsewhere that there is a divinely instituted hierarchy in the order of creation, and in this order the wife follows that of her husband (1 Cor 11:3, 7–9. The hierarchical argument for the subordination of wives is made more explicit at Eph 5:23, 24, "For the husband is head of the wife as Christ is the head of the church, his body, of which he is the Savior. Now as the church is subject to Christ, so also wives should be subject to their husbands in everything." Cf. Bruce, 289; note especially G. W. Knight III, *The New Testament Teaching on the Role Relationship of Men and Women* [Grand Rapids: Baker, 1977]; and J. B. Hurley, *Man and Woman in Biblical Perspective. A study in role relationships and authority* [Leicester: Inter-Varsity, 1981]; and for a different approach see P. K. Jewett, *Man as Male and Female: A Study in Sexual Relationships from a Theological Point of View* [Grand Rapids: Eerdmans, 1975]). The Christian wife should recognize and accept her subordinate place in this hierarchy, "as is fitting." This phrase, ὡς ἀνῆκεν (τὸ ἀνῆκον indicates what is proper, one's duty; cf. BAG, 66, and Schlier, *TDNT* 1, 360) has a Stoic ring about it and possibly came into Christian exhortation through the Hellenistic synagogue (note the similar expression τὸ καθῆκον, "the fitting," Schlier, *TDNT* 3, 437–40; here the imperfect ἀνῆκεν, "it is fitting," is used instead of the customary present tense, cf. BDF, para. 358[2], Turner, *Syntax*, 90). But the motivation is placed on a different footing from Stoic ideals with the words "in the Lord" (ἐν κυρίῳ goes with ὡς ἀνῆκεν, "as is fitting," rather than ὑποτάσσεσθε, "be subordinate," as the parallel in v 20 makes clear: so von Soden, 65, Abbott, 293, and Bruce, 289, 290). This expression may mean that the Lord Jesus is the criterion of what is fitting (cf. Schweizer, 165), or more likely it designates the proper attitude and behavior "within the new fellowship of those who own Christ as Lord" (Bruce,

289; cf. Best, *Body*, 4, and Moule, 129; on the significance of κύριος, "lord," in this household table, see 219).

19. The wife's subordination to her husband has its counterpart in the husband's duty to love his wife. This is not simply a matter of affectionate feeling (the more characteristic verb for this was φιλέω, to "feel or show affection") or sexual attraction (for which one would have expected ἐράω, to "love with sexual desire"); rather, it involves his unceasing care and loving service for her entire well-being. Crouch (*Origin*, 112; cf. Merk, *Handeln*, 216), rejecting the view that wherever ἀγαπάω (to "love") and ἀγάπη ("love") appear regardless of context they designate Christian love, claims that here in verse 19 "the normal, human love of a husband for his wife" is in view. There is nothing specifically Christian about this injunction since the verb ἀγαπάω (to "love") and its cognate noun were frequently used in other contexts of the love of a man for a woman (*Origin*, 111–13). However, although the terms were employed in a variety of senses in pre-Christian antiquity (cf. BAG, 4–6, Merk, *Handeln*, 216) they do not occur in any extrabiblical Hellenistic rules for the household (H. Greeven, "Zu den Aussagen des Neuen Testaments über die Ehe," *ZEE* 1 [1957] 122, Schrage, *NTS* 21 [1974–75] 12, 13 and Lohse, 158). Further, Paul has already made reference to "love" in this letter (2:2; 3:14) and the first recipients would have heard these household rules read publicly at the conclusion of that section in which they were exhorted to put on "love" as one of the graces of the new man. The injunction to husbands to love their wives is to be understood, in part at least, in the light of that preceding admonition. Finally, although no theological basis is added to the injunction—to this extent Lohse's comment is apt: "This command needs no justification, for the command of love is absolutely valid" (158)—the detailed presentation in the parallel passage, Ephesians 5:25–33 where Christ's love for the church is seen as the archetype of the husband's love for his wife, indicates what the author meant by "love." It is a love that is sacrificial, that disregards itself, which is defined by Christ's action (even if it is argued that the authorship of the two letters is different both spring from the Pauline school and must be said to reflect the same viewpoint; on the Ephesians passage see J. P. Sampley, *'And the Two Shall Become One Flesh.' A Study of Traditions in Ephesians 5:21–33* [SNTSMS 16; Cambridge: University Press, 1971] and Barth, *Ephesians 4–6*, 607–753).

If the husband heeds this apostolic injunction, he will not behave in an overbearing manner; all areas of married life will be characterized by this self-giving love and forgiveness (cf. 3:13). The original order of the Creator, which was troubled by the rule of sin and self-centeredness and which ended in the tyranny of eros and the slavery of sex (cf. 3:5), can be lived in love and forgiveness (cf. Schrage, *Einzelgebote*, 259).

καὶ μὴ πικραίνεσθε πρὸς αὐτάς. The positive injunction is now put negatively: husbands are not to be embittered against their wives. *πικραίνω* (to "make bitter," "embitter," BAG, 657, Michaelis, *TDNT* 6, 122–25), though appearing only here in an ethical context of the NT (cf. *πικρία*, "bitterness," in the short list of vices at Eph 4:31), was frequently used by classical writers from Plato onward (on the instances of the word-group in the LXX see Michaelis, *TDNT* 6, 122, 123). Christian husbands are not to become angry or incensed against their wives, either in thought or in word and deed. The preposition πρός ("against") is not attested with the verb in the LXX or Philo, and Michaelis (*TDNT* 6, 125; cf. Lohse, 158) has suggested that what may be especially in view is the bitterness vented on the wife though not caused by her. At all events, avoidance of bitterness is an expression of obedience to the commandment to love.

20. Next follow the mutual duties of children and parents. First, children are enjoined to obey their parents in all things. *τὰ τέκνα* ("children," note again the nominative case with the definite article is used for the vocative, see above 23) probably refers to children who are growing up and are still subject to their parents (cf. Eph 6:4, "bring them up") rather than those who have already grown up (though evidence for this latter interpretation is not lacking, note Lohse, 158). They are addressed as responsible persons within the congregation (Schweizer, 156; cf. Oepke, *TDNT* 5, 650) and this is noteworthy. The injunction to children, like that to slaves, is put rather more strongly than the one to wives. While the latter was expressed in the middle voice (*ὑποτάσσομαι*, "be subordinate"), suggesting voluntary submission, the admonitions to children and slaves are in the active imperative denoting absolute obedience (cf. Hinson, *RevExp* 70 [1973] 499, 500). The absoluteness of the command is strengthened by the phrase "in all things" (*κατὰ πάντα*, cf. v 22). Also the verb *ὑπακούω* (to "obey") is employed rather than *ὑποτάσσομαι* ("be subordinate") which may only sometimes imply obedience. The former term in Paul had special reference to one's submission to Christ, the gospel and the apostolic teaching (Rom 6:17, 10:16; Phil 2:12; 2 Thess 1:8, 3:14; cf. Matt 8:27; Mark 1:27; 4:41; Luke 8:25; Acts 6:7; Heb 5:9; 11:8; cf. *ὑπακοή*, "obedience," Rom 1:5; 5:19; 6:16; 15:18; 16:19, 26; 2 Cor 10:5, 6). The obedience of Christian children to their parents is all of a piece with their submission to Christ as the following words make plain. The unequivocal nature of this admonition to children is reminiscent of the OT. In the Decalog they are commanded to honor their parents and the promise of long life is attached (Exod 20:12; Deut 5:16; note how this is taken up at Eph 6:1–3). The expanded code of Exodus (21:15) ordered the death penalty for any child striking father or mother. In Judaism and in early Christianity the care of aged parents was regarded as a religious duty (1 Tim 5:4), their neglect, behavior worse than that of pagans (5:8; cf. Hinson, *RevExp* 70 [1973] 500). But in antiquity generally the emphasis on children's duties toward their parents was widespread, although in non-Christian parallels the demand was for honor rather than obedience (cf. Crouch, *Origin*, 114, for examples).

τοῦτο γὰρ εὐάρεστόν ἐστιν ἐν κυρίῳ. The motivation (*γάρ*, "for") given is that (lit.) "this is pleasing in the Lord." Although *εὐάρεστον* ("pleasing," "acceptable") was used widely outside the Bible (cf. Foerster, *TDNT* 1, 456, BAG, 318, and Merk, *Handeln*, 216) particularly on inscriptions (Priene, 114, 115, and Nisyros) originally to designate that which people considered proper (Dibelius-Greeven, 46, considered it points "clearly to an established social value"), in the NT it describes almost exclusively that conduct which is acceptable to God (at Tit 2:9 *εὐάρεστος* describes that which is acceptable to men). For Paul the term can designate the goal and motivation of the Christian's whole life (Rom 12:1, 2; 14:18; 2 Cor 5:9; Eph 5:10; Phil 4:18; cf. Col 1:10 where the similar term ἀρεσκεία is used of pleasing the Lord in all respects as the apostle's goal for the Colossians). Normally the expression "acceptable," or "pleasing" would be followed by the dative case "to the Lord" (τῷ κυρίῳ; cf. Turner, *Syntax*, 263; manuscript 81 al Clement of Alexandria [cf. Eph 5:10] have this reading; the RSV renders it as "this pleases the Lord") but here the additional phrase is "in the Lord" (ἐν κυρίῳ). This has been regarded as: *(a)* an unnecessary addition; *(b)* equivalent to a sort of conditional clause (so tentatively Moule, 130, referring to 1 Cor 7:39; Phil 2:19) meaning "provided that the children's obedience is ἐν Κυρίῳ, on a truly Christian level of motive"; *(c)* signifying "as judged by a Christian standard" (Lightfoot, 225); or, more likely, *(d)* obedience to parents is fit and proper in that sphere in which the Christian now lives, that is, in the new fellowship of those who own Christ as Lord (on this showing the parallel with v 18 is maintained; there may be, as some commentators suggest, a conscious qualifying of a traditional maxim by this addition: so Weidinger, *Haustafeln*, 51, Lohse, 159, Merk, *Handeln*, 217, and Martin, *NCB*, 120). Since Paul has a Christian family in view (ἐν κυρίῳ), he does not envisage the situation where parental orders might be contrary to the law of Christ. Clearly at that point the law of Christ must take precedence and children would have to obey God rather than men (cf. Acts 5:29).

21. *οἱ πατέρες, μὴ ἐρεθίζετε τὰ τέκνα ὑμῶν, ἵνα μὴ ἀθυμῶσιν.* If children are exhorted to render obedience to their parents, then the latter, especially fathers, are enjoined not to irritate or provoke their children lest they lose heart and become timid. (Bengel 2, 470, comments: "*Despondency* is the bane of youth.") While the children have to obey both parents (γονεῦσιν, v 20), fathers have a special responsibility toward them. Even if it is conceded that οἱ πατέρες here denotes "parents" (as in Heb 11:23, where it is stated that Moses was hidden "for three months by his parents," ὑπὸ τῶν πατέρων αὐτοῦ; cf. BAG, 635), certainly it is the fathers who are primarily in view. In contemporary society the Roman *patria potestas,* i.e. the authority and power of the head of the house, gave the father unlimited power over his children and this law exercised a considerable degree of influence in the Hellenistic culture generally (cf. Schrenk, *TDNT* 5, 950, 951). In Hellenistic Judaism severe punishment could be meted out for disobedient children (Philo's demand for severity on the part of parents has been attributed to this influence: Philo, *Hyp* 7.2; *Spec Leg* 2.232; cf. Josephus, *Ap* 2.206, 217; *Ant* 4.264, and note Crouch, *Origin*, 114–116). This is not to suggest, however, that the Roman period evidences no examples of tender love in the home (Moule, 129, claims it "would be unjust to paganism . . . to describe it only in lurid terms of infanticide and broken homes . . . And Judaism, even more obviously, was able to show splendid examples of such happiness"). But for all that the relationship ἐν κυρίῳ ("in the Lord") was new, and in this household table fathers are told nothing about their power of disposal over their children; instead their duties are spelled out (cf. Schrage, *NTS* 21 [1974–75] 15)—they are not to provoke or irritate them. ἐρεθίζω, used at 2 Corinthians 9:2 in a good sense of an encouraging example (the only other NT instance, see BAG, 308), here signifies to "irritate" either by nagging at them or by

deriding their efforts (Lohse, 159, Martin, *NCB*, 120, and BAG, 308, point out that in Epictetus, *Enchiridion* 20, the expression, "when someone irritates [ἐρεθίσῃ] you," refers back to "the man who reviles or strikes [ὁ λοιδορῶν ἢ ὁ τύπτων] you"; in the LXX it occurs at Num 14:8; Deut 21:20; Prov 19:7; 25:23, etc.).

Fathers are to obey the injunction so that their children (is the ὑμῶν, "your" inserted to remind fathers that the children belong to them? cf. von Soden, 65) do not become discouraged or think that it is useless trying to please them within the common life of the home (ἀθυμέω, to "be discouraged," "become timid," appears only here in the NT, though it turns up frequently in the LXX: e.g. Deut 28:65; 1 Kings 1:6, 7, 15:11; 2 Kings 6:8; 1 Chron 13:11, etc.; and was used from the fifth century B.C. on, cf. BAG, 21). The corresponding passage in Ephesians 6:4 sets the positive counterpart when it urges fathers to rear their children "in the discipline (παιδεία) and instruction (νουθεσία) of the Lord." There should be firm guidance, not servitude.

22. Christian slaves are next addressed and the opening exhortation parallels the injunction to children. In the list of household rules here and in Ephesians (6:5–9) the admonitions to slaves are more extensive than those to masters, and they have special encouragements attaching to them. This may, on the one hand, reflect the social structure of these churches (cf. Bruce, 293; in the household tables of 1 Pet 2:18–3:8 the admonitions to slaves have no correlative instructions to masters). Many commentators link this extended exhortation to slaves with the case of Onesimus whose name is mentioned at chapter 4:9. Certainly the companion letter to Philemon throws light on the mutual duties of slaves and masters within the Christian fellowship and "the transforming effect of this fellowship upon their relationship" but there is no basis for considering that Paul had Onesimus specially in mind in the present passage (Bruce, 293; see also Lohse, 159). Here the apostle is not making a social comment on a prevailing custom. He is addressing himself to Christian readers. The issue was not that of the acceptance of an institution sanctioned by law and part of the fabric of Graeco-Roman civilization; nor was it a question of how to react to a demand for its abolition (on the possible significance of the Letter to Philemon to these issues see below). Rather, it concerned the tension between the freedom given in Christ (cf. 3:11) and the "slavery" in which Christian slaves are to continue to serve their earthly masters (cf. 1 Cor 7:21–24).

Even those commentators who have asserted most forcefully that Paul took over and Christianized material from Hellenism or Hellenistic Judaism in the household tables concede that these injunctions have been newly formulated as specifically Christian instruction. So Dibelius-Greeven, 47, for example, states: "The whole section—in contrast to the preceding—has been formed out of original Christian ideas" (cf. Crouch, *Origin*, 116, 117).

οἱ δοῦλοι, ὑπακούετε κατὰ πάντα τοῖς κατὰ σάρκα κυρίοις. "Slaves, give entire obedience to your earthly masters" (NEB). Slaves who have become believers are to accept their station as slaves and to obey their earthly masters in everything. The expression *οἱ κατὰ σάρκα κύριοι* ("your masters according to the flesh") is not to be understood negatively or disparagingly, but rather shows that they are only lords within an earthly realm, within the sphere of human relations, in contrast to the Lord who is in heaven (cf. 4:1; Bruce, 293, makes the point that the expression *κατὰ σάρκα*, "according to the flesh," indicates the relationship between masters and slaves has particular reference to this present temporary world-order).

μὴ ἐν ὀφθαλμοδουλίᾳ ὡς ἀνθρωπάρεσκοι. "Not with eye-service as men pleasers." The obedience which the slaves must render their masters is described first negatively (*μὴ ἐν* . . . "not with . . ."), then positively (*ἀλλ' ἐν* . . . "but with . . ."). *ὀφθαλμοδουλία* ("eye-service," BAG, 599, Rengstorf, *TDNT* 2, 280; on the formation of the word see BDF, para. 115[1] and Moulton-Howard, *Grammar* 2, 271), a word not found before the Pauline writings (here and Eph 6:6), may have been coined by the apostle; it signified that service performed only to attract attention—and therefore superficial—not for its own sake nor to please God or one's own conscience (Moule, 130; note Theodoret's comment on Eph 6:6, 7, cited by Lohse, 160: "He calls eyeservice that type of service which does not issue from a sincere heart, but is content in mere external appearance"). Here at Colossians 3:22 if the plural is the correct reading then it describes those actions which originate in this dishonest attitude. Such persons are described as "men-pleasers" (*ἀνθρωπάρεσκος* which is found in the LXX at Ps 52:6; PsSol 4:7, 8, 19 and in the NT at Eph 6:6; note BAG, 67), i.e. those who try to please others in a position of superior authority rather than God (cf. Foerster, *TDNT* 1, 456).

ἀλλ' ἐν ἁπλότητι καρδίας, φοβούμενοι τὸν κύριον. By contrast (*ἀλλά*) Christian slaves are to serve conscientiously, out of pure motives: "But with sincerity of heart as you reverence the Lord." *ἐν ἁπλότητι καρδίας* means "with singleness of heart" (BAG, 85, 86, Bauernfeind, *TDNT* 1, 386, 387, and Lohse, 160; note the similar references in 1 Chr 29:17; Wisd 1:1; Test Reub 4:1; Test Sim 4:5; Test Levi 13:1) and denotes the innermost part of man as simple and sincere. As such his actions will not be guided by false, ulterior motives, but will be done in the fear of the Lord. These latter words "fearing the Lord" (*φοβούμενοι τὸν κύριον*) do not refer here to God as they do in the OT (and in Rev 15:4) but to Christ. Within the Old Testament the motives of fear and love stand side by side. The God who is great, mighty and terrible (Deut 10:17, 18; cf. 1 Chr 16:25) is gracious to man (Deut 6:5, 13). We can therefore understand the frequent address to men and women, which continues into the NT: "Fear not" (Gen 15:1; Judg 6:23; Isa 44:2, etc.). But God's grace and favor do not remove the note of solemnity in the address, and the motive of fear of God is significant in the laws of the Pentateuch (Lev 19:14, 32; Deut 13:11; 17:13, etc.) as well as being a decisive factor in OT piety generally (cf. Ps 103:11, 13, 17; Prov 1:7; 23:17, etc.). Within the NT *φόβος* and its cognates are used in the sense of fear, awe and reverence before God or Christ (e.g. Acts 9:31; 2 Cor 7:1; Eph 5:21; at 1 Pet 1:17 a life in fear is controlled by the seriousness of judgment and redemption from one's earlier life, while 3:6 makes it plain that fear of God rules out all human intimidation). Such reverence provides both the motive and manner of Christian conduct (Luke 18:2, 4; 1 Pet 2:17; Rev 11:18), not only in a general or basic sense but also in specific life situations within the structures of authority. Thus, the motive of fear turns up some seven times in the household tables (Col 3:22; Eph 6:5; 1 Pet 2:17, 18; 3:2, 6; cf. Eph 5:33). Christian slaves are above all else servants of Christ and they are to work first and foremost so as to please him. Not fear of an earthly master, but reverence for the Lord Christ should be their primary motive.

23. The comprehensive admonition of verse 17 ("whatever you do in word or deed do all in the name of the Lord Jesus"), addressed to all members of the congregation, is picked up here (ὃ ἐάν ποιῆτε, "whatever you do," is equivalent to κατὰ πάντα, "in everything," of v 22; elsewhere in the NT what is commanded or forbidden is put in a pronoun or relative clause with ποιέω, "do": 1 Cor 10:31; Phil 2:14; 1 Tim 4:16; 2 Pet 1:10; cf. Mark 7:13; Luke 3:19; John 4:29, 39; 7:51; Acts 16:18; 21:33; Rom 1:32; 2:3, so Braun, *TDNT* 6, 479) and applied more specifically to Christian slaves: whatever is assigned to them they should do with their whole heart. ἐκ ψυχῆς, which means literally "from the soul," here signifies "with a wholehearted endeavor" (the phrase is virtually equivalent to ἐκ καρδίας, "from the heart": so Mark 12:30, "You shall love the Lord your God with all your heart and with all your soul"; cf. LXX Prov 11:17; Ecclus 6:26; 7:29; 14:4; 19:16; 37:12; Test Gad 2:1; etc. Lohmeyer, 158) and clearly the apostle purposes to lift the slave's tasks above the level of compulsive necessity to that of joyful service (cf. Martin, *NCB*, 122, who rightly adds that either way the slave had no choice: he must either work or be punished for disobedience or idleness). It is just possible that ἐργάζεσθε ("do the work") is an advance upon ποιῆτε ("do"), because the things done are ἔργα ("works"; so Abbott, 294. Braun, *TDNT* 6, 478, regards the verbs as synonymous, and although ἐργάζομαι ["do the work"] may simply be a stylistic variant of ποιέω ["do"], this reference is different from v 17 where the latter verb is simply inferred in the principal clause; here a new verb is inserted with possibly a slightly different significance).

ὡς τῷ κυρίῳ καὶ οὐκ ἀνθρώποις. "As [working] for the Lord not for men." Clearly the faithful service to be performed by these Christian slaves and which the apostle here calls for, will benefit their masters. But the slaves are reminded of the ultimate reason or motivation for their conduct (ὡς, "as," often appears with a participle to indicate the reason or motivation for something happening; but the NT, like classical Greek, in abbreviated expressions will omit the participle when it is clear from the context as to what is meant: e.g. 2 Thess 2:2, see Robertson, *Grammar*, 1140; BDF, para. 425[4]): they are serving the Lord and not mere men (note the contrast between κύριος, "Lord," and ἄνθρωποι, "men"). As they engage in wholehearted work for their masters so in that very action they are serving their heavenly Lord.

24. Paul's ethical injunctions are next set within the context of future rewards and punishment (Steinmetz, *Heils-Zuversicht*, 31, notes that one of the few traces of future eschatology in the letter is found here). "Knowing" (εἰδότες, here and at 4:1) suggests that the apostle is recalling a pattern of teaching known to Christians: it is from the heavenly Lord that they will receive the inheritance as their reward. The term for "reward" (ἀνταπόδοσις, BAG, 73, Büchsel, *TDNT* 2, 169), which is attested from the time of Thucydides, occurs in the LXX, the papyri and inscriptions, usually in a bad sense denoting "the full recompense" (of divine judgment, e.g. Ps 68:22). Here, however, the only occurrence in the NT (the related ἀνταπόδομα, "repayment," appears

at Luke 14:12 and Rom 11:9), the term is used with a positive connotation, for the following words "of inheritance" (τῆς κληρονομίας) specify the content of that reward (most commentators and grammarians are agreed that the genitive is one of apposition or definition: see, for example, Robertson, *Grammar,* 498): it "consists in the inheritance" (cf. LXX Judg 9:16). Paul has already mentioned that an eternal inheritance has been prepared for the Colossians in heaven (1:5, 12, 27; 3:1–4; on the theme of inheritance see on 1:12 and the literature cited). He now asserts to the members of the congregation who were slaves, and under Roman law could never inherit anything, that their heavenly Lord (*ἀπὸ κυρίου,* lit. "from a Lord," stands first for emphasis; Lightfoot, 226, points out that the absence of the definite article from the phrase [cf. 4:1] is very remarkable because it has been studiously inserted elsewhere in the context of vv 22–24; in his paraphrase he thus attempts to catch the significance of this omission: "However you may be treated by your earthly masters, you still have *a* Master who will recompense you") can be trusted to give his reward at the end of the day. Retribution might be what the slave would normally expect from his earthly lord. This Lord is different giving as his reward an eternal inheritance of life in the age to come (see the rabbinic teaching about God's fairness in rewarding his faithful ones [*m. 'Abot* 2:16, "Faithful is thy taskmaster who shall pay thee the reward of thy labour. And know that the recompense of the reward of the righteous is for the time to come"] and note Martin's treatment, *NCB,* 123).

In using apparently mercenary terms such as "reward" and "punishment" the apostle is speaking of our relationship with God: reward is here described in terms of an inheritance that relates to life in the presence of God while punishment is deprivation of his fellowship and exclusion from his presence (Moule, 131).

Since none would wish to forfeit this precious gift through disobedience (Lohse, 161), Paul enjoins them to "serve the Lord Christ" (τῷ κυρίῳ Χριστῷ δουλεύετε; in the rather unusual expression "the Lord Christ," here and at Rom 16:18, the apostle is contrasting Christ *as Lord* with other lords; so Moule, 131). Although this short sentence might be either an indicative (Lightfoot, 227; cf. RSV, NIV) or an imperative (Moule, 131, Merk, *Handeln,* 218, Lohse, 161, Ernst, 237, Martin, *NCB,* 123; cf. NEB), since the verb δουλεύετε, "you serve," could be either, we prefer the latter (a. the best texts do not supply a preceding γάρ, "for," as represented in the AV; the indicative would be correct if the "for" were added [cf. the Byzantine text] and the sentence regarded as the motivation for the preceding; b. this injunction resumes the imperative ἐργάζεσθε, "do," of v 23; and c. the following connective particle γάρ, "for," of v 25, then gives the reason for this admonition). So the forceful injunctions to slaves (vv 22–25) conclude with this comprehensive admonition: "Serve the Lord Christ."

25. The ground (γάρ) for obeying the injunction to serve Christ as the Lord over all is now spelled out (Baumert, *Sterben,* 425, rightly observes that verse 25 is not simply a negative contrast to the previous statement about the reception of an inheritance, for this would require an adversative "but," δέ or ἀλλά; instead it is subordinated to the immediately preceding injunction, v 24*b*): ὁ γὰρ ἀδικῶν κομίσεται ὃ ἠδίκησεν κτλ. ("for the one who does wrong

shall receive again for the wrong that he has done," etc.). However, it is not patently clear to whom the words refer so that both ancient and modern commentators are divided as to whether it applies to slaves, masters or both. This general and inviolable principle is the same as the *lex talionis*, that is the punishment exactly fits the transgression (note the correspondence between ἀδικῶν, "he who does wrong," and ὃ ἠδίκησεν, "the wrong which he has done"; other examples of these "sentences of holy law" are 1 Cor 3:17; 14:38; 16:22*a;* Gal 1:9; cf. Käsemann, in *Questions*, 66–81, and note the view of K. Berger, "Die sogenannten 'Sätze heiligen Rechts' im Neuen Testament. Ihre Funktion und ihr Sitz im Leben," *TZ* 28 [1972] 305–330, who considers they are conditional relative clauses of wisdom origin having nothing to do with legal norms). κομίζω, meaning to "bring," is found here in the middle voice with the sense of "get (for oneself)," "receive" (BAG, 442, 443). Baumert (*Sterben*, 410–31) has made an exhaustive examination of the term and has argued that here the usage reminds one of the LXX background with its expression of bearing responsibility (Lev 20:17; Ezek 16:52, 54, 58): accordingly the term means the wrongdoer will have to bear the guilt and shame of his deed and be answerable before the judgment seat of Christ the *Lord* (*Sterben*, 424).

In favor of the view that there is a change of subject from slaves to masters it has been argued that Paul's connecting "for" (γάρ) is thus given its due weight, that the verb to "do wrong" (ἀδικέω, denoting any violation of human or divine law, cf. BAG, 17, Schrenk, *TDNT* 1, 157–61) is much more suitable to the master than the slave (the question has been raised as to how a slave with no legal rights could "act unjustly" against his master), and that the continuation of the apostle's instruction at chapter 4:1 for slaveowners to give their slaves what is just (τὸ δίκαιον) and fair, suggests that in verse 25 masters who were defrauding their slaves are in view. So the words are not only a sober reminder that all injustice will be accountable at the divine court (Martin, *NCB*, 124), but also an encouragement to the slave to regard himself as the servant of Christ and therefore not to be disheartened by unjust treatment, knowing that before the final tribunal there will be no respect of persons (Abbott, 295; also Meyer, 459, 460, and Martin, *NCB*, 123, 124, who has strongly advocated this). So this interpretation is parallel to Ephesians 6:9 where masters are admonished to treat their slaves decently "knowing that he, who is both their Master and yours is in heaven, and that there is no partiality with him" (Conzelmann, 153).

The second approach, claiming that the masters (κύριοι) are not addressed until chapter 4:1, considers it is more likely that verse 25 still refers to the slaves. Admittedly on this view there is some difficulty with the word ἀδικέω ("do wrong") which some advocates of the first interpretation claim is much more suitable to the master than the slave and, along with the term "favoritism" (προσωπολημψία), presupposes that the person punished is in a higher position. However, the verb ἀδικέω ("do wrong") is fairly general, designating any violation of law or illegal conduct, and it need not be restricted to masters. In fact, the same term is employed by the apostle in the companion letter to Philemon (v 18) with reference to Onesimus, Philemon's slave ("if he has wronged you" [εἰ δέ τι ἠδίκησέν σε], does not necessarily imply that Onesimus in running away had pilfered something from his master; he had already caused injury to Philemon's property simply by escaping, even if he had not stolen anything, see below). Others have taken the term at Colossians 3:25 as an indirect warning against rebelliousness (cf. Ernst, 237) or flattery as a cover for one's cunning (Baumert, *Sterben,* 425). Probably these suggestions are too specific, and the injunction if it does apply to slaves is a more general warning about all wrongdoing. They must not suppose that wicked actions have no significance before God because they are slaves or that indulgence would be granted because of extenuating circumstances (cf. Schlatter cited by Masson, 150, and Lohse, 161). Righteous behavior is required of slaves and masters alike (this could explain the word-correspondence of *τὸ δίκαιον,* "what is just," at 4:1; so while at Eph 6:9 it is the master who is reminded that God shows no partiality, here it is the slave: cf. Percy, *Probleme,* 401, Schrenk, *TDNT* 1, 160, Bruce, 295, Merk, *Handeln,* 218, Caird, 209, as well as earlier commentators such as Chrysostom and Bengel). At God's judgment bar there is no "partiality" or "bias" (*προσωπολημψία,* while occurring first in the NT [cf. Rom 2:11; Eph 6:9; James 2:1], may already have been in use in Hellenistic Judaism and was formed from the Hebraism *λαμβάνω πρόσωπον,* to "raise the face," found frequently in the OT to denote respect of persons: Lev 19:15; Deut 1:17; 16:19; cf. BAG, 720; Lohse, *TDNT* 6, 779, 780); he is neither biased nor does he allow himself to be influenced by appearances.

On balance we favor the second line of interpretation, that is, verse 25 is addressed to slaves. Some, recognizing the difficulty of making a choice between the alternatives, consider the words are addressed to both slaves and masters. Schweizer (168; cf. Lightfoot, 227) suggests that perhaps the sentence was deliberately left open so as to apply to all, while Ernst (237), concurring with the view that we have here a sentence of holy law (originally preached by charismatic prophets), claims that this is a generally valid apodictic sentence the judicial character of which is underscored by the housetable.

The ethical injunctions are set within the context of rewards and punishment in verses 24 and 25, and the judgment on disobedience is as sure as the reward for faithfulness. While the Bible generally, and Paul in particular, make it plain that salvation is according to grace, judgment is always according to works, good or bad, for believer and unbeliever alike. So to Christians the apostle writes: "For we must all appear before the judgment seat of Christ, that each one may receive what is due (*ἵνα κομίσηται,* the same verb as in Col 3:25) to him for the things done while in the body, whether good or bad" (2 Cor 5:10; cf. Rom 14:10–12; 1 Cor 3:12–15; 4:4, 5). Bruce, 295, comments:

> It may seem difficult to understand how one who by grace is blessed with God's salvation in Christ may yet before the divine tribunal "receive again the wrong that he has done." But it is in accordance with the teaching of Scripture throughout that judgment should "begin at the house of God"; and even if the tribunal be a domestic one, for members of the family of God, it is none the less a solemn reality.

4:1 At the conclusion of the household table the exhortation to slaves is balanced by a brief message to masters (*οἱ κύριοι*). Probably the Colossian congregation had fewer slaveowners among its converts than slaves. Yet the former had their responsibilities too. If slaves like Onesimus had their duties, then masters like Philemon had reciprocal responsibilities: they must treat their slaves justly and fairly (τὸ δίκαιον καὶ τὴν ἰσότητα τοῖς δούλοις παρέχεσθε). This admonition finds parallels in both Hellenistic and Jewish ethics. On the Greek side these appear as early as Plato (*Leges* 6.776d–788a) and Aristotle (*Politica* 1260b.6), while during the Roman period Seneca was the most ardent advocate of the humane treatment of slaves (note especially his forty-seventh letter to Lucilius, cf. J. N. Sevenster, *Paul and Seneca* [NovTSup 4; Leiden: Brill, 1961] 185–92; Crouch, *Origin*, 117–19). He does not attack the institution of slavery as such but accepts it as part of the existing social order. He feels great pity for slaves, expresses keen censure of the way they are treated and condemns the misuse of slaves for all kinds of contemptible tasks even though he recognizes some slaves are anything but faultless (cf. Sevenster, *Paul*, 186). Seldom do the Stoic codes, however, refer to the relations of masters to slaves. Palestinian Judaism accepted the institution of slavery, and slaves were viewed as the property of their masters (Str-B 4, 717). Hellenistic Jewish circles knew and used current Hellenistic appeals to masters to treat their slaves properly (so Ecclus 4:30, "Be not like a lion in your home, and tyrannous and terrible toward your slaves," also 7:20, 21; 33:31; Philo, *Spec Leg* 2:66–68, 89–91; 3:137–43; *Ps Phocylides* 224; see Crouch, *Origin*, 118, 119, for further examples).

The apostle does not command the masters to free their slaves, but he clearly "points to an amelioration of the slaves' lot" (Martin, *NCB*, 124): they are to treat them justly and fairly. "What is just or right" (τὸ δίκαιον, BAG, 196, comments: "The neuter denotes that which is obligatory in view of certain requirements of justice"; cf. Schrenk, *TDNT* 2, 187, 188; Hinson, *RevExp* 70 [1973] 505, following Hugedé, 197, suggests that it might refer to salary; the idea of honest remuneration might be implied in the notion of "fairness" especially as παρέχομαι rendered "treat" means literally to "grant," see BAG, 626) is paralleled by "what is fair" (τὴν ἰσότητα, BAG, 381, Stählin, *TDNT* 3, 354, 355). The relationship between the two was frequently discussed in the moral teaching and instruction of popular philosophy (the two terms were often treated as synonyms; Philo gives a detailed exposition of "fairness," ἰσότης, in *Rer div her* 141–206, calling it the "mother of justice" [μήτηρ δικαιοσύνης], *De spec leg* 4, 231; cf. Stählin, *TDNT* 3, 354, 355, Lohse, 162). Here the second term reinforces the first denoting "the spirit of equity as distinct from the letter of obligation" (Radford, 296, cited by Hinson, *RevExp* 70 [1973] 505; note Lightfoot, 228, who says, "the word naturally suggests an even-handed, impartial treatment," and Abbott, 296, who describes it as "what cannot be brought under positive rules, but is in accordance with the judgment of a fair mind," cf. Stählin, *TDNT* 3, 355; against Meyer, 461, 462, and others who suppose the meaning to be that slaves are to be treated as equals—but this is an obscure way of expressing such a thought). So any harsh measures of repression or victimization of those in a helpless position (Martin, *NCB*, 124) are clearly ruled out (cf. Eph 6:9).

εἰδότες ὅτι καὶ ὑμεῖς ἔχετε κύριον ἐν οὐρανῷ. "Because you know that you also have a Master in heaven" (NIV). The motivation for this just and fair treatment is basically the same as the slave's motive for obeying his master (v 24; note the repetition of εἰδότες, "knowing"). Masters also (καὶ ὑμεῖς, "you too"), like their slaves, are answerable to a greater Master in heaven (with the words κύριος ἐν οὐρανῷ, "a Master in heaven," one is reminded of 3:1–4—Christ is in heaven seated at the Father's right hand in the place of honor). This one Lord and Judge will decide whether these earthly masters have done what is truly just and fair. His will is the assessment that really counts. The relationship between masters and slaves has undergone a basic change. Both owe obedience to the one Lord, and therefore both have the true standard for their conduct toward one another (cf. Sevenster, *Paul*, 192; it is at this point of motivation that, for all their apparent similarities, Paul and Seneca part company).

Explanation

This paragraph with its injunctions regulating behavior patterns within the Christian household follows on from and explicates the injunction of verse 17, "and whatever you do, in word or deed, do all in the name of the Lord Jesus, giving thanks to God the Father through him." Particularly significant are the many references to "the Lord": several of the commands are furnished with the motivation "in the Lord" (vv 18, 20), while reference is made to fearing the Lord (v 22), conduct that is done for the Lord (v 23) and the Lord's rewarding judgment (vv 24, 25; 4:1). The whole of life, both thought and conduct, is to be submitted to the Lord Jesus Christ. No area of life stands outside his control; so there is no final distinction between the sacred and the secular. Yet the household rules indicate how this obedience is concretely expressed. Perhaps the devotees of the false teaching at Colossae were indifferent to mundane and domestic affairs. If so, then Paul has to indicate to the congregation that this teaching is pernicious, and that the Colossians are to be recalled to the simple duties of family life. The apostle has already summoned his readers to "set their minds on things that are above" (3:2), for a life ruled from above where Christ is reigning is precisely a life in marriage, parenthood and everyday work. Right behavior in these areas is the proper outworking of seeking the things above.

In this table or "station code" Paul deals with concrete human relations within the Christian household, not with abstract ordinances. The series of admonitions are addressed successively to wives and husbands, children and fathers, slaves and masters—from the closest relationship to the most distant. In each case the subordinate member is mentioned first: wives, children and slaves are addressed as ethically responsible partners who are expected to do "what is fitting in the Lord," just like husbands, fathers and masters. But the exhortations to subordination do not stand alone; immediately the second member of each pair is addressed and reminded of his responsibilities. The twin admonitions stand together and the first ought not to be interpreted apart from the second.

The admonition to wives is an appeal to free and responsible agents voluntarily to subordinate themselves to their husbands since this is entirely proper within the new fellowship of those who own Christ as Lord. The husband, for his part, is to show unceasing care and loving service for his wife's entire well-being. No theological basis is added to the injunction since "the command of love is absolutely valid" (Lohse). And the detailed presentation in the parallel passage (Eph 5:25–33), where Christ's love for the church is seen as the archetype of the husband's love for his wife, indicates what the author meant by "love."

Christian children are enjoined to obey their parents in all things. Such obedience is all of a piece with their submission to Christ as the following words show: "*for* this is pleasing in the Lord." At the same time parents, especially fathers, are not to irritate or provoke their children lest the latter become discouraged or think that it is useless trying to please the former within the life of the home. There should be firm guidance, not servitude (cf. Eph 6:4).

In the most extensive of the admonitions slaves who have become believers are to accept their station as slaves and to obey their earthly masters in everything. Their service is not to be superficial or performed only to attract attention; rather, Christian slaves are to serve conscientiously, out of pure motives: "with sincerity of heart as you reverence the Lord" (v 22). As they engage in wholehearted work for their masters so in that very action they are serving their heavenly Lord. They are to keep the transcendent end in view: a slave might normally expect retribution from an earthly master at the end of the day. This Master is different for he gives as his gracious reward an eternal inheritance of life in the age to come. A brief but solemn exhortation is now addressed to masters. They are not commanded to free their slaves, but to treat them justly and fairly. The motivation for this is basically the same as the slave's motive for obeying his master: both alike have a greater Master in heaven. Both owe obedience to that heavenly Lord. And thus their own relationships with each other are to be understood in the light of this.

Final Admonitions: Persistence in Prayer and Right Behavior toward Outsiders (4:2–6)

Bibliography

Brown, R. E. *Background,* 52–56. **Lövestam, E.** *Spiritual Wakefulness in the New Testament.* LUÅ 55/3 Lund: Gleerup, 1963, 75–77. **Merk, O.** *Handeln,* 224. **Pope, R. M.** "Studies in Pauline Vocabulary. Of Redeeming the Time." *ExpTim* 22 (1910–11) 552–54. **van Unnik, W. C.** "Die Rücksicht auf die Reaktion der Nicht-Christen als Motiv in der altchristlichen Paränese." *Judentum, Urchristentum,. Kirche. Festschrift für Joachim Jeremias,* ed. W. Eltester. BZNW 26; Berlin: Töpelmann, 1964, 221–34. **Zeilinger, F.** *Der Erstgeborene,* 70, 71, 94–116.

Translation

2 *Persevere in prayer as you watch for the Lord's return, and be thankful.* 3 *Intercede for us, too, that God may open a door for our message, so that we may proclaim the mystery of Christ, for which I am in chains,* 4 *that I may make it known, as I should.* 5 *Be wise in your behavior toward outsiders by snapping up every opportunity that comes.* 6 *Your speech should always be gracious, seasoned with salt, so that you may know how you should answer everyone.*

Form/Structure/Setting

This short paragraph of concluding exhortations, similar to those of 1 Thessalonians 5:12–22; Galatians 5:25–6:6 and Philippians 4:8, 9, ends the paraenetic section of the letter. These admonitions to intercession and missionary responsibility, following the household table with its injunctions to members in their various stations, are addressed to the whole congregation. In fact, the opening summons to prayer resumes the theme of chapter 3:17 where the Colossians were encouraged to give thanks to God the Father through Christ ("grace" and "the word" are additional links with 3:16, 17).

The paragraph contains three sentences: verses 2–4, which contain encouragements for prayer, thanksgiving and intercession, and verses 5 and 6 which give directions as to how the Colossians are to behave in their relationships with outsiders. Verses 2 and 5 each contain an introductory imperative (προσκαρτερεῖτε, "continue steadfastly," v 2, and περιπατεῖτε, "walk," v 5) and a following participle (γρηγοροῦντες, "being watchful," v 2, and ἐξαγοραζόμενοι, "making the most of," v 5) which provide a framework (Zeilinger, *Der Erstgeborene,* 70, regards these verses as an example of chiasmus) for the personal references to the work and destiny of the apostle in verses 3 and 4 (cf. Schweizer, 171). Within these latter verses a participial clause is followed by a series of dependent clauses and may be structured as follows:

3*a* (ἐν εὐχαριστίᾳ) προσευχόμενοι ἅμα καὶ περὶ ἡμῶν
b ἵνα ὁ θεὸς ἀνοίξῃ ἡμῖν θύραν τοῦ λόγου
c λαλῆσαι τὸ μυστήριον τοῦ Χριστοῦ
d δι᾽ ὃ καὶ δέδεμαι
4*a* ἵνα φανερώσω αὐτό
b ὡς δεῖ με λαλῆσαι
3*a* "(With thanksgiving). Intercede for us too
b that God may open a door for our message
c to proclaim the mystery of Christ
d for which I am in chains
4*a* that I may make it known,
b as I should."
(cf. Zeilinger, *Der Erstgeborene,* 70)

The final sentence, verse 6, is not attached grammatically to the preceding. No finite verb appears so a third person imperative or cohortative must be supplied, e.g. ὁ λόγος ὑμῶν πάντοτε [ἔστω] ἐν χάριτι ("your speech should always be gracious").

The next clause ἅλατι ἠρτυμένος ("seasoned with salt") is in apposition with λόγος ("speech"), while the final words, εἰδέναι πῶς κτλ. ("that you may know how . . ."), indicate the result. The style of this paragraph with its participles (vv 2, 3, 5 and 6), dependent relative sentence (v 3), ἵνα clauses (vv 3, 4), infinitives (vv 3, 4, 6) and circumstantial phrases (vv 2, 5, 6) is typical of the author (cf. Percy, *Probleme,* 34, and Bujard, *Untersuchungen,* 99, 120).

Comment

In a number of his letters the apostle exhorts his readers to pray and intercede regularly. Although these admonitions were usually short and concise they formed part of his regular teaching to his churches (Rom 12:12; Eph 6:18; Phil 4:6; Col 4:2; 1 Thess 5:17; 1 Tim 2:1). In addition he earnestly requests his readers to intercede for him in his costly work of spreading the gospel (Rom 15:30–32; 2 Cor 1:11; Eph 6:19; Phil 1:19; Col 4:3; 1 Thess 5:25; 2 Thess 3:1, 2; Phlm 22). In both Colossians and Ephesians (6:18–20) the general exhortation to pray constantly is immediately followed by the request for petition on the apostle's own behalf (cf. 1 Thess 5:17 and 25). Clearly Paul attached great importance to the mutual intercession of himself and his converts. Not only does he constantly pray for them all, but also he begs them to assume wider responsibilities in supporting him in petitionary prayer (cf. Wiles, *Prayers,* 283). When they interceded for him it was not the completing of some formality, but an actual cooperating with him, an assisting of him in prayer (2 Cor 1:11; cf. Phil 1:19). He earnestly desires this prayerful participation in his struggle for the gospel from churches which he founded, as well as from others in the gentile mission (Rom 15:30–32 and here at Col 4:3, 4). Such intercession is not confined to general matters. It names specific needs and concerns which arise from the missionary work of the moment (Delling, *Worship,* 127) and includes requests for a ministry that will be acceptable to the saints in Jerusalem, for deliverance from enemies of the gospel (Rom 15:30–32; 2 Thess 3:2) and for the proclamation with boldness of God's mystery, Christ (Eph 6:19; Col 4:2).

2. τῇ προσευχῇ προσκαρτερεῖτε. The congregation is exhorted to constant prayer. The verb προσκαρτερέω, which means to "adhere to," or "persist in," came to be used of a boat that always stands ready for someone (Mark 3:9), or an activity that one was devoted to or busily engaged in. It was in this latter sense that it came to be employed to denote continuance in prayer (Acts 1:14; Rom 12:12; Col 4:2; cf. Acts 2:42, 46) and the ministry of the Word (Acts 6:4; on the term and its cognate προσκαρτέρησις, "perseverance," "patience," see BAG, 715, Grundmann, *TDNT* 3, 618–20, and R. Kerkhoff, *Das unablässige Gebet. Beiträge zur Lehre vom immerwährenden Beten im Neuen Testament* [Munich: Zink, 1954] 39, 40). Here the injunction suggests determination in prayer, with the resolve not to give up (Luke 11:5–13) or grow weary (Luke 18:1–8). The content of this prayer (τῇ προσευχῇ) is not specifically mentioned, so it is sometimes assumed that all types of prayer are covered by the term. However, although προσευχή is, on occasion, used of prayer in general, in both Old and New Testaments it regularly signifies petition (1 Sam 7:27; cf. v 29; 2 Kings 19:4; 20:5; Pss 4:1; 6:9, etc.; Mark 9:29; Acts 10:31; 12:5; Rom 1:10; 15:30; James 5:17; in many other instances in the Greek Bible where it has been argued that προσευχή, "prayer," and its cognate verb προσεύχομαι, to "pray," bear a general sense of prayer, a case can be made for the rendering "petition"). Such a meaning fits the immediate context well. Since thanksgiving is to be an accompaniment of this prayerful activity then the thanksgiving itself (ἐν εὐχαριστίᾳ) is not included in the term προσευχή ("prayer"; against Conzelmann, *TDNT* 9, 414). Also the following participle προσευχόμενοι ("praying," v 3), which spells out the content of Paul's prayer request of the Colossians for himself and other messengers of the gospel, directs our attention to a particular form of petition, that is, intercession. The Colossian Christians are to persevere in petitionary prayer.

Especially significant are the remaining words of verse 2, γρηγοροῦντες ἐν αὐτῇ ἐν εὐχαριστίᾳ ("being watchful in it [i.e. prayer] with thanksgiving"). The participle γρηγοροῦντες ("be watchful") has been regarded as an independent command (Lohmeyer, 161, and Lohse, 164), with prayer as the right way to exercise watchfulness, or, as is more likely, an accompaniment of persevering prayer (cf. Meyer, 463, Abbott, 296, and Martin, *NCB,* 125). Jesus encouraged his disciples both in the Garden of Gethsemane (Mark 14:38) and in his eschatological admonitions (Luke 21:34–36; Mark 13:32–37) to "Watch and pray." Here Paul is not simply describing the believers' general stance to the effect that they should be watchful and pray at all times (Lohse, 165). Nor is he simply speaking of attention and engagement in prayer as opposed to a humdrum and lethargic praying (as Abbott, 296, Lightfoot, 229, Williams, 155, and Moule, 132, claim; cf. the NEB "with mind awake"). γρηγορέω ("be awake"), a term that seems to have been used regularly in catechetical contexts (cf. Selwyn, *1 Peter,* 439–66) has been interpreted in a more technical sense of the children of light being awake and renouncing the sleep of this world of darkness, with the mind directed toward Christ's coming and the consummation of the hope (Lövestam, *Wakefulness,* 75–77, following Lohmeyer, 161, and Benoit, 69. Cf. also Greeven, *Gebet,* 139, 140, and more recently Martin, *Lord,* 135, 136, who following Conzelmann, 155, inclines to this view). Certainly *γρηγορέω* with the figurative meaning to "be vigilant" turns up in contexts which refer to the Parousia, that day of the Lord which will come suddenly and unexpectedly (1 Thess 5:6; cf. Matt 24:42; 25:13; Mark 13:35, 37; Luke 12:37; Rev 3:3; 16:15; cf. Oepke, *TDNT* 2, 338). Both Lohse (164, 165) and Schweizer (172) consider that the vigilance is not motivated here by a reference to the day of the Lord. However, while the context of the passage does not contain any explicit eschatological suggestion (though cf. v 5 with its reference to redeeming the time, *καιρός*), it seems justifiable to assume that the concept of wakefulness had an eschatological character (note especially Lövestam's treatment, *Wakefulness*) and that the apostle is here encouraging his readers to be on the alert in expectation of the Lord's coming (Conzelmann, 155). Accordingly the prayer they are to persist in is for the coming of God's kingdom. The petition *Maranatha* ("Our Lord, come," 1 Cor 16:22; cf. Rev 22:20) is to be on their lips and in their hearts as they look forward in anticipation to Christ's glorious manifestation (Col 3:4). At the same time, thanksgiving is to be the accompaniment of this prayer (*ἐν αὐτῇ ἐν εὐχαριστίᾳ*)—that outward expression of gratitude to God the Father who has already freed them from a tyranny of darkness, transferred them into a kingdom in which his Son holds sway and given them a share in the inheritance of the saints in light (1:12–14).

3. The apostle's exhortation to persevering prayer is immediately followed by a request for the intercession of the Colossians for himself and his co-workers. He offers petition regularly for them (1:3, 9) and now asks that as they pray for the coming of the kingdom they will at the same time (*ἅμα* denotes the coincidence of two actions in time, BDF, para. 425[2], BAG, 42) consistently remember him before the throne of grace (*προσευχόμενοι*, "praying," a present tense, suggests an ongoing intercessory activity). Clearly he attached great importance to this regular, reciprocal intercession by his converts and other Christians in the gentile mission since he appeals for this prayerful support elsewhere (Rom 15:30–32; Eph 6:19; Phil 1:19; 1 Thess 5:25; 2 Thess 3:1, 2, and Phlm 22). He earnestly desired their understanding and help in his struggle for the gospel and there was no better way to express this than by intercessory prayer. The request is that they might pray "for us" (*περὶ ἡμῶν*, which corresponds to the *περὶ ὑμῶν προσευχόμενοι*, "praying for you," of 1:8; cf. v 9 and note the similar correspondence at 2 Thess 3:1 and 1:11; see Riesenfeld, *TDNT* 6, 54, and Wiles, *Prayers,* 259–84), a reference that no doubt includes his friends and colleagues mentioned later in the chapter who were messengers of the gospel (perhaps Timothy, [1:1] and Epaphras [4:12, 13] are especially in view; so Lightfoot, 229). But it is clear that Paul is thinking primarily of his own need for he slips into the first person singular later in the sentence ("for which I am in chains, that I may proclaim it clearly, as I should," vv 3b, 4).

ἵνα ὁ θεὸς ἀνοίξῃ ἡμῖν θύραν τοῦ λόγου. The content of the prayer (expressed by *ἵνα*, "that"; cf. Rom 15:31; Eph 6:19; 2 Thess 3:1) is not for the personal benefit of Paul and his companions but for the preaching of the gospel: it is that "God may open a door for our message." The image of an open door turns up in Hellenistic thought (Epictetus employs it in the sense of a person being free to go anywhere; "opened doors" is also a figure of literary activity, cf. Jeremias, *TDNT* 3, 174) as well as in later Judaism where man opens the door to God by repenting, while God opens the door to man by giving him opportunities for intercession or repentance, or by granting grace (Str-B 1, 458; 2, 728; 3, 484, 485, 631; Jeremias, *TDNT* 3, 174). Within the New Testament this picture of an open door, which is used in missionary contexts, denotes the provision of opportunity. God opens a door for the missionary by giving him a field in which to work (1 Cor 16:9; 2 Cor 2:12) and he opens a door of faith to Gentiles so that they might believe (Acts 14:27; elsewhere ἀνοίγω is used of the opening of the eyes, Luke 24:31; Acts 26:18; of the understanding, Luke 24:45; of the heart, Acts 16:14; and of Scripture, Luke 24:32; Acts 17:3). In Colossians 4:3 God is to be petitioned to open a door for the gospel message (several commentators, both ancient and modern, on the basis of Eph 6:19, have taken this to mean "the door of our speech," i.e. "our mouth," cf. Beza, Bengel; note also Lohmeyer, 161, who understands it of access by Paul to the right thing to say. But this interpretation is less likely)—this of course also means a door for the messenger, but here the emphasis falls upon the dynamic, almost personal, character of the Word (cf. 2 Thess 3:1, a prayer request, "Finally, brothers, pray for us that the message of the Lord may run and be honored"). Paul is concerned for an opportunity for effective evangelism; and it is just possible that he is asking them to pray for his release from prison (so many commentators; cf. Phlm 22, and on Paul's imprisonment see xlix–liv). On the other hand, even when he was at liberty such doors did not open up to him automatically (1 Cor 16:9; 2 Cor 2:12) and the apostle did not regard imprisonment as a serious interruption of his missionary work (Phil 1:12, 13; so Caird, 210). At the conclusion of the Book of Acts (28:30, 31) Luke indicates an open door was set before Paul in Rome. The opportunities were considerable though special wisdom was called for (cf. Bruce, 298).

The apostle earnestly desires that God would open a door for the word (and requests the Colossians to pray along these lines) λαλῆσαι τὸ μυστήριον τοῦ Χριστοῦ ("so that we may proclaim the mystery of Christ"; the infinitive λαλῆσαι, "to speak," "to proclaim," could be either one of result or intended result, which is tantamount to purpose, for the distinction between the two is a fine one, cf. Robertson, *Grammar,* 1089, 1090; see also Lightfoot, 229, Abbott, 297, Meyer, 465, Lohmeyer, 161). Once again in Colossians the word "mystery" is used to denote God's plan of salvation centered in Christ and which has special reference to Gentiles (cf. 1:26; 2:2 and see on these verses; here as at Rom 16:25 and Col 1:26 "mystery" is closely related to the message or Word of the gospel, for it is in the effective preaching and teaching of the gospel that the mystery is made known; cf. Brown, *Background,* 55; the genitive τοῦ Χριστοῦ, "of Christ," could be either epexegetic indicating that Christ himself is the mystery [so Feuillet, *Christ,* 292], or objective meaning "the mystery as it is revealed in the Messiah": Zeilinger, *Der Erstgeborene,* 113, claims both are possible).

δι' ὃ καὶ δέδεμαι, "For which I am in chains." It was on account of his apostolic activity in making known this mystery that Paul was imprisoned (on the use of δέω, to "bind," as signifying imprisonment see Matt 14:3; 27:2; Mark 6:17;

Acts 9:2, 14, 21; 12:6, etc. cf. Büchsel, *TDNT* 2, 60, and BAG, 177, 178). This is the only place in which Paul uses this verb in a literal sense, though he employs δεσμοί of his "bonds" or "fetters" at Philippians 1:7, 13, 14, 17; Colossians 4:18 and Philemon 10, 13 (cf. 2 Tim 2:9) as well as δέσμιος ("prisoner") at Philemon 1, 9 (cf. Eph 3:1; 4:1; 2 Tim 1:8). The transition to the singular was natural since he moved from what was common to himself and others to what was peculiar to himself (regarding his imprisonment, see the Introduction).

4. The verb φανερόω ("reveal," "make known," "show," cf. BAG, 852, 853, Bultmann/Lührmann, *TDNT* 9, 3–6, and see on 1:26) when used with reference to the manifestation of the mystery (1:26; Rom 16:26; 1 Tim 3:16) normally describes God's revelation. Here, although God is the person whom the Colossians are to petition to effect the opening of the door, it is the apostle who is said to reveal the previously hidden divine purpose (the ἵνα clause, "that . . . ," of v 4 is dependent on the preceding ἵνα ὁ θεὸς ἀνοίξῃ, "that God may open . . . ," of v 3; Lightfoot, 229, and Abbott, 297. Von Soden, 67, makes the clause dependent on δέδεμαι, "I am bound," and argues that Paul who was awaiting trial wished to make it clear to his judges as to what he preaches and why he must preach it). Further, this same verb "reveal" is not employed elsewhere to designate the apostolic proclamation (it is usually to "announce," καταγγέλλω, 1 Cor 2:1; "preach," εὐαγγελίζομαι, Eph 3:8; "speak," λαλέω, 1 Cor 2:7; Col 4:3, 4; "proclaim," κηρύσσω, 1 Cor 1:23, etc.). So when Paul's activity is described as making known the mystery its unique significance of being the proclamation of divine revelation is emphasized (Lohse, 165). What is elsewhere called the work of God is here said to be Paul's activity, no doubt because of his key role in the plan of God that includes Gentiles. His ministry has salvation historical significance. Yet it is no less the revelation of God for all that, since it is God who is asked to open a door for the Word, and it is he alone who can enable the apostle to publish the mystery openly and in a manner that Paul ought to: the final clause ὡς δεῖ με λαλῆσαι could refer to the necessity of the preaching (so keeping strictly to the meaning of δεῖ) and be rendered "since I am bound to speak it" (see 1 Cor 9:16; Acts 23:11; note Meyer, 466), or the manner of the proclamation (the rightness is then viewed with reference to "any given circumstances in which the apostle is called upon to speak," Moule, 133, cf. Dibelius-Greeven, 50, and Schweizer, 172) and so paraphrased as "in the way in which it is right that I should speak it." At first sight it might seem that only the first alternative gives the δεῖ, "it is necessary," its due weight. However, "a thing which is *necessary* if one is to do right in certain conditions is virtually what one *ought* to do" (Moule, 133). We therefore prefer the second alternative.

Accordingly the Colossians are to persevere in prayer with their eyes fixed on the second coming, at the same time interceding for the apostle whose ministry to Gentiles has a salvation historical significance in the purposes of God. Through him God reveals his divine purpose of blessing in Christ for Gentiles.

5. In the next injunction Paul turns from his personal situation to a general principle of Christian conduct, exhorting his readers to behave wisely toward

non-Christians: ἐν σοφίᾳ περιπατεῖτε πρὸς τοὺς ἔξω ("Be wise in the way you act toward outsiders"). "Wisdom" (σοφία), as we have noted, turns up in several important contexts of Colossians (1:9, 28; 2:3 and 3:16; see on these verses). The wisdom which the apostle sets forth is fundamentally different from that propounded by the false teachers. The latter is but an empty show of wisdom (λόγος . . . σοφίας, 2:23). Here "wisdom," which has to do with a knowledge of God's will (1:9) and walking worthily of the Lord (1:10; cf. Wilckens, *TDNT* 7, 523), is essentially practical and realistic. Like the Philippians (2:15, "so that you may become blameless and pure . . . shining like stars in the universe") these readers are to be godly, giving no occasion for valid criticism (cf. 1 Cor 10:32, "Give no offence to Jews or to Greeks or to the church of God"). They should be tactful on the one hand, yet bold in their Christian witness to outsiders on the other (several commentators, including von Soden, 68, Moule, 133, and Ernst, 239, in the light of the immediate context, consider the apostle has missionary responsibilities in view; Merk, *Handeln*, 224, following van Unnik, *Judentum*, 228, recognizes there is no explicit basis mentioned but thinks the motivation is drawn from the missionary possibilities in the situation). The expression "outsiders" (οἱ ἔξω corresponds to the rabbinic *ha-ḥîṣônîm*, "those who are outside," that is, either heretics or "the people of the land"; cf. 2 Macc 1:16; Thucyd. 5, 14, 3, and note Str-B 3, 362, Behm, *TDNT* 2, 575, 576, and BAG, 279) carries a semitechnical meaning and refers to non-Christians generally, especially pagans (1 Cor 5:12, 31; 1 Thess 4:12; cf. 1 Tim 3:7; *2 Clem* 13:1). Elsewhere in the exhortatory material of the NT the reaction of non-Christians to the behavior of believers plays a significant role: *(a)* the latter are to live in such a way that God's name is not dishonored, and *(b)* no occasion of stumbling should be given which would prevent men and women being saved (see 1 Cor 10:32, 33; Phil 2:14, 15; Col 4:5; 1 Thess 4:11, 12; 1 Tim 3:7; 6:1; Tit 2:8; 1 Pet 2:15; 3:1, 16; cf. van Unnik, *Judentum*, 221–34).

τὸν καιρὸν ἐξαγοραζόμενοι. Once again the participle has been regarded as having the force of an imperative (= "make the most of the time," so Lohse, 167, 168, who considers the command is not directly connected with the previous injunction about walking; however, Bruce, 299, who understands the words as an exhortation, correctly notes that they have special application to the readers' duties to their unbelieving neighbors while the parallel passage of Eph 5:15, 16 seems to have a more general reference to the duty of Christian prudence); on the other hand, it is quite natural to take the participle as specifying the means by which the command for the readers to conduct themselves wisely is to be carried out, that is, by "snapping up every opportunity that comes." The verb ἐξαγοράζω ("buy," "buy up," "redeem") is drawn from the commercial language of the market place (ἀγορά), and its prefix, the preposition ἐκ, denotes an intensive activity, a buying which exhausts the possibilities available (so Büchsel, *TDNT* 1, 128, who is followed by many commentators; on the middle voice as signifying the personal interest of the subject see von Soden, 68, and Robertson, *Grammar*, 810). The word καιρός ("time") here does not indicate a specific point of time (Gal 6:9; 1 Pet 1:5; 5:6), nor a particular period of time in salvation history, though it may suggest the paucity of time at one's disposal (cf. 1 Cor 7:29, "the time is short [ὁ καιρὸς συνεσταλμένος]," and Gal 6:10, "as we have opportunity [καιρόν], let us do good"). BAG, 271, concedes that one possible meaning of the phrase is "make the most of the time" since it is "severely limited because of the proximity of the Parousia as well as for other reasons." Robinson, *Ephesians,* 202, understood the same verb at Ephesians 5:16 and here in its more usual NT sense of to "rescue" time from the evil condition into which the present had fallen (the Ephesian parallel gives the reason: "because the days are evil"). But this is highly doubtful (cf. Moule's criticisms, 134). The Colossians context seems to demand a meaning such as "use to the full," "exploit" (cf. Martin, *NCB,* 127, and note Pope, *ExpTim* 22 [1910–11] 552–54).

6. Finally, the readers are exhorted to let their speech toward outsiders manifest both the grace and wisdom that Paul desires for his own utterance (Bruce, 299). ὁ λόγος ὑμῶν ("your speech") appears to be a deliberate echo of the apostle's preaching of the Word (λόγος) in verse 3 and includes both private conversation and public proclamation. That speech should always be (πάντοτε, "always," indicates a habitual character, while the imperative ἔστω, "be," is to be supplied, so Meyer, 467, von Soden, 68, Moulton, *Grammar* 1, 183, and Robertson, *Grammar,* 396; cf. Matt 27:19; 2 Cor 8:16) ἐν χάριτι, an expression that has been taken to mean: *(a)* "gracious," "charming" (lit. "with graciousness," BAG, 877, and many exegetes including Meyer, 467, Lightfoot, 230, and Dibelius-Greeven, 51, who claims that the formulation of the sentence must be based upon an idiomatic expression generally current at the time; note Moule, 135, Bruce, 299, Lohse, 168, Conzelmann, *TDNT* 9, 397, and Schweizer, 173; cf. "the gracious words" [οἱ λόγοι τῆς χάριτος, a genitive of quality] of Luke 4:22; Epict 3, 22, 90), *(b)* "with thanksgiving" (Ernst, 240, who adds that the speech of the Christian should be filled with thanksgiving since it should penetrate the whole of one's life; the same expression ἐν χάριτι has been taken as referring to thanksgiving at 3:16, see 210), and *(c)* "with (God's) grace," virtually referring to the gospel (Haupt considers God's grace is given directly to the hearers when Christians speak to outsiders about their faith; although Schweizer, 173, claims that the omission of the article makes it hard to understand it as God's grace, there are occasions in the Pauline corpus where χάρις without the article refers to God's grace, cf. Eph 2:5 with v 8). On contextual grounds our preference is *(a)* though it must be remembered that "grace" and "gracious" are intimately related and it is difficult to separate them (cf. Martin, *NCB,* 128). Here Paul is indicating that not only the content but also the manner of speaking are important when it comes to the influence the believer exerts on outsiders. Similarly at 1 Peter 3:15, 16 Christians are to defend their faith "with gentleness and respect."

ἅλατι ἠρτυμένος. "Seasoned with salt," which is the literal rendering of the Greek, is the second characteristic required of the Colossians' speech. Their words must not be dull or insipid but should be interesting and judiciously chosen. Salt was used in seasoning food and preserving it from corruption. The latter function may explain the parallel exhortation in Ephesians 4:29, "Do not let any unwholesome talk come out of your mouths, but only what is helpful for building others up according to their needs, that it may benefit those who listen" (NIV). Those who are the salt of the earth (Matt 5:13; Mark 9:49, 50; Luke 14:34) might be expected to have some savor about their language. This could be taken to mean "witty" since salt had this significance in pagan usage (apparently derived from the pungent power of salt) or "winsome," so that the Colossians' speaking was to exercise a wholesome influence in conversation which might otherwise become debased or crude. However, attention has been drawn to rabbinic parallels for a metaphorical use of salt as wisdom (cf. W. Nauck, "Salt as a Metaphor in Instructions for Discipleship," *ST* 6 [1952] 165–78; several church fathers, including Origen [*Hom in Gen* 5:12], took salt in this sense of wisdom; "the Torah is like salt" is a common comparison found among the rabbis, cf. Str-B 1, 232–36; 2, 21–23; 3, 631), while in Hellenistic contexts as well as rabbinic ones salt could describe the appropriate word used in speech (Plutarch, *De garrulitate* 23 [514, 515], which speaks of seasoning life with words; for further examples see Moule, 135, and Lohse, 168). Here Paul's statement has particular reference to Christians responding with the right word to those who ask questions of the community (*ἀποκρίνομαι*, "answer," is not found elsewhere in Paul), perhaps in connection with their beliefs and behavior. So not only must the addressees' conversation be opportune as regards the time; it must also be appropriate as regards the person (note the expression *ἑνὶ ἑκάστῳ*, "to each one"; cf. Caird's comment, 210: "*every one* is to be treated as an end in himself and not subjected to a stock harangue," cf. Lightfoot, 231, Abbott, 298, von Soden, 68). They are, in the words of Peter, "always [to] be prepared to give an answer to everyone who asks you to give the reason for the hope that you have" (1 Peter 3:15).

Explanation

This short paragraph with its admonitions that conclude the exhortatory section of the letter is, unlike the household table with its station codes, addressed to the whole congregation. The Colossians are to persist in petitionary prayer. Particularly is the cry *Maranatha* ("Our Lord, come") to be on their lips and in their hearts as they look forward in anticipation to Christ's glorious manifestation (3:4). Thanksgiving, the outward expression of gratitude to God the Father for having acted so graciously and decisively in his Son on their behalf, is to accompany this petition. The apostle who regularly remembered the Colossians in his prayers (1:3, 9–14), requests them to bring him and his coworkers before the throne of grace, praying that God would open a door for the gospel message, and thus for the messenger, which might well involve his release from prison. As apostle to the Gentiles, Paul has the great privilege of making known the previously hidden divine purpose, that purpose by which Gentiles are incorporated into the Messiah on an equal footing with Jews, and he now asks that the Colossians might pray to the living God to enable him to set forth that divine mystery in a plain and clear manner.

Turning from his personal situation to general principles of Christian conduct, Paul exhorts his readers to behave wisely toward non-Christians: the Colossians are to be tactful yet bold in their Christian witness as they make the most of every available opportunity, recognizing that their time is limited. Finally, as those who are to behave wisely toward "outsiders" they are admonished to let their speech manifest both the graciousness and wisdom that Paul desires for his own utterance. They are recipients of God's grace: let that grace be evident in the words they speak. Their conversation ought not to be dull or insipid; instead, they ought to choose the right word as they respond to each non-Christian who asks them questions about either their beliefs or behavior.

Personal Greetings and Instructions (4:7–18)

Bibliography

Anderson, C. P. "Who Wrote 'the Epistle from Laodicea'?" *JBL* 85 (1966) 436–40. **Ellis, E. E.** *Prophecy,* 3–22. **Ladd, G. E.** "Paul's Friends in Colossians 4:7–16." *RevExp* 70 (1973) 507–514. **Lähnemann, J.** *Kolosserbrief,* 57, 58, 177–81. **Lohse, E.** *Veritas,* 189–94. **Ollrog, W.-H.** *Paulus,* 238–40. **Zeilinger, F.** *Der Erstgeborene,* 71, 72. ———. "Die Träger der apostolischen Tradition im Kolosserbrief." *Jesus in der Verkündigung der Kirche,* ed. A. Fuchs. Freistadt: Plöchl, 1976, 175–90.

Translation

7 *Tychicus, my beloved brother, faithful minister and fellow-servant in the Lord,*
will tell you all the news about me. 8 *I am sending him to you for this purpose that*
you may know how we[a] *are, and that he may strengthen your hearts.* 9 *[He is coming]*
with Onesimus, the faithful and beloved brother, who is one of you. They will tell
you everything that is happening here.
10 *Aristarchus, my fellow-prisoner, sends you his greetings, as does Mark, the cousin*
of Barnabas. (You have already received instructions about him; if he comes to you,
welcome him.) 11 *Jesus who is called Justus also sends his greetings. These are the*
only Jewish Christians among my fellow-workers for the kingdom of God, and they
have been a comfort to me. 12 *Epaphras, who is one of you and a slave of Christ*
Jesus, sends his greetings. He is always striving [for the gospel] in prayer for you,
that you may stand forth perfect and be filled with everything that is God's will.
13 *For I can vouch for him that he works tirelessly for you and those at Laodicea*
and Hierapolis. 14 *Our dear friend Luke, the doctor, and Demas greet you.* 15 *Give*
my greetings to the brothers at Laodicea as well as to Nympha[b] *and the church in*
her house. 16 *After this letter has been read among you, see that it is also read in*
the congregation at Laodicea, and that you in turn read the one from Laodicea.
17 *Tell Archippus: "See to it that you complete the ministry you have received in the*
Lord."
18 *I, Paul, write this greeting in my own hand. Remember my bonds. Grace be*
with you.

Notes

[a] The reading *ἵνα γνῶτε τὰ περὶ ἡμῶν* ("that you may know how we are") has strong manuscript support (e.g. A B D* G P etc., that is, good representatives of the Alexandrian, Western and Eastern text types) and it best explains the origin of the other readings. Furthermore, this reading is consistent with the writer's declared purpose of Tychicus's visit (vv 7, 9). For further details see Metzger, *Textual Commentary,* 626.

[b] *τὴν κατ' οἶκον αὐτῆς ἐκκλησίαν.* "Nympha and the church that is in her house." The uncertainty of the gender of the name Νύμφα (feminine "Nympha") or Νυμφᾶς (masculine "Nymphas") led to variation in the following possessive pronoun between *αὐτῆς* ("her") and *αὐτοῦ* ("his"). Lightfoot, 241, suggested the original reading was *αὐτῶν* ("their," so ℵ A C P 33 81 Bohairic, Coptic, etc.) and that the original text read "Nymphas and his friends," which later copyists altered,

not realizing it was a common classical construction. This, however, has been rejected by recent commentators (Mussner, *ad loc.*, is an exception, supposing that the two names represent those of a married couple whose house was a meeting-place for Christian worship) on the grounds that the manuscript evidence is not sufficiently cogent (Moule, 28; cf. Metzger, *Textual Commentary*, 627: "The reading with αὐτῶν ['their'] arose when copyists included ἀδελφούς ['brothers'] in the reference"). Several modern translations (RSV, NEB, JB, NIV) prefer the feminine Nympha and render our expression "the church in her house" (this is the preference of the UBS Greek New Testament, based chiefly on the weight of B 6 424^c 1739 1877 1881 etc., so Metzger, *Textual Commentary*, 627). Lightfoot, 241, argued that the feminine is "in the highest degree improbable" because of its Doric form, but the denial was countered by Moulton (*Grammar 1*, 48) who saw here an Attic feminine form with a short *alpha*, and not the Doric form with a long *alpha*. It is possible that some scribes, considering the mention of a woman here rather unusual, altered the "her" to "his." Although the case for Nymphas as a man's name has been strongly presented by Moule, 28, and Masson, 156, on balance it seems preferable to understand the proper noun as feminine so that the phrase be rendered: "Nympha and the church that is in her house."

Form/Structure/Setting

As in his other letters (see 1 Cor 16:19–24; Rom 16:1–23; Philem 23–25; Phil 4:21–23; Eph 6:21–24) Paul concludes his epistle to the Colossians with personal greetings and instructions. This concluding paragraph comprises three sections: a reference to the messengers who will carry his letter to Colossae (vv 7–9), a series of greetings from a number of his associates who are acquainted with the Colossian church (vv 10–14), and his own greeting and brief instructions (vv 15–17). The final salutation is written in Paul's own hand and contains a request to remember his bonds as well as a prayer for grace (v 18).

Comment

Having finished dictating the substance of what he wanted to say to the Colossians, Paul sends messages and greetings to various people associated with the congregation. Tychicus and Onesimus will convey Paul's personal news to the Colossians who would naturally be keenly interested to learn how the apostle and Epaphras, the founder of the congregation, were getting on in prison. Much was done in the ancient world by word of mouth so that although a letter would contain the more urgent and doctrinal matters the ordinary remarks would be passed on orally.

7. Tychicus will be Paul's messenger to inform (γνωρίζω, "make known," which is used of God's making known the mystery, see on Col 1:27, is here [vv 7, 9] employed in a secular sense, cf. 1 Cor 12:3; 15:1, as it is on occasion in the LXX: 1 Kings 1:27; Neh 8:12; Prov 9:9; see Bultmann, *TDNT* 1, 718) the congregation about the apostle's personal situation (τὰ κατ' ἐμέ was a common expression to describe the situation of a person: e.g. Herodotus 7, 148; 1 Esd 9:17; Tobit 10:9; 2 Macc 3:40; Acts 24:22; 25:14; note especially Phil 1:12 and Eph 6:21; cf. Turner, *Syntax*, 15; the phrase is taken up again, with reference to Epaphras as well, in the following verses τὰ περὶ ἡμῶν, "how we are" [RSV], v 8, and τὰ ὧδε, "the things happening here," v 9). The wording here is almost identical with that of Ephesians 6:21, 22, and it is possible that Tychicus was the bearer of that letter as well as the one to Laodicea (see on v 16). He may have been Paul's special envoy at this time

to the churches of provincial Asia which had been established during the apostle's Ephesian ministry. In Acts 20:4 Tychicus (whose name is a common one in inscriptions found in Asia Minor, so BAG, 831), is mentioned as a native of the province of Asia who was with Paul in Greece and journeyed with him to Troas at the end of the third missionary journey. He accompanied Paul to Jerusalem when the latter took the collection from the gentile churches to their needy Jewish brethren in Jerusalem. According to 2 Timothy 4:12 Paul sent him on some undesignated mission to Ephesus, while later Paul planned to send either him or Artemas to Crete to take Titus' place (Tit 3:12). He along with several others appears to have been closely associated with Paul during the latter stages of his ministry (Ladd, *RevExp* 70 [1973] 507; Ellis, *Prophecy,* 4, 5, claims that Tychicus, along with eight other co-workers who continue in close association with the apostle to the end of his life, stands in an explicit subordination to Paul—as do Erastus, Mark, Timothy and Titus—serving him or being subject to his instructions).

He is commended as "the beloved brother and faithful minister and fellow-servant in the Lord" (*ὁ ἀγαπητὸς ἀδελφὸς καὶ πιστὸς διάκονος καὶ σύνδουλος ἐν κυρίῳ*). As noted in connection with Timothy at chapter 1:1 "brother" (*ἀδελφός*) may be used to describe a "helper" or "co-worker" of the apostle. The term "brethren" (*ἀδελφοί*) was Paul's favorite in referring to members of the communities to whom he was writing and was expressive of the very real relationships that exist between Christians as members of God's family (note especially 1 Cor 15:58; Rom 15:14; Phil 3:1; 4:1; Eph 6:10; cf. Banks, *Idea,* 61–71, for the treatment of Paul's family metaphors, and note R. P. Martin. *The Family and the Fellowship. New Testament Images of the Church.* Exeter: Paternoster; Grand Rapids, MI: Eerdmans, 1979, 123–25). Tychicus was obviously such a "brother" who was specially dear to the apostle. It is also possible that in this expression Paul is adding the thought that Tychicus was a particularly valued colleague. At any rate the latter point comes out in the following words "faithful minister" (*πιστὸς διάκονος*) which were previously used of Epaphras (see on 1:7; *διάκονος*, "servant," from which we get our title "deacon" [although there is nothing in the context to suggest it is employed in this technical sense, so Moule, 136, cf. Lohse, 171], also describes the ministry of Paul, 1:23, 25). Tychicus had rendered "reliable" (*πιστός*) service either to Paul, the Colossian church or to Christ. As a "fellow-servant in the Lord" (*σύνδουλος ἐν κυρίῳ*) it is just possible that Tychicus was (or at least had been, since he was now being sent as a messenger by Paul) a prisoner like Aristarchus (v 10) and Epaphras (Phlm 23). However, in the light of the application of this term *σύνδουλος* (lit. "fellow-slave") to Epaphras at 1:7 (see 15) this suggestion is doubtful. The phrase "in the Lord" (*ἐν κυρίῳ* is rendered by the TEV as "in the Lord's work" and the whole phrase "fellow-servant in the Lord" is taken to mean the "one who serves the Lord along with us" (so Bratcher and Nida, 103; cf. Bruce's rendering, 302, "[a faithful colleague and] helper in his service for the Lord"); alternatively it could mean he performs his task as one "in the Lord," that is, as a Christian (on the phrase *ἐν κυρίῳ*, "in the Lord," see the comments on the household table, 3:18–4:1; Lohse, 171, rightly notes that the phrase is to be connected materially with both *ἀδελφός*, "brother," and *διάκονος*, "minister").

8. Paul is sending Tychicus with his letter (*ἔπεμψα*, with most commenta-

tors, is to be understood as an epistolary aorist, that is, it views the action from the standpoint of the recipients as they read the letter, and so should be translated "I am sending"; the RSV rendering "I have sent" could be interpreted to mean Tychicus had been dispatched before Paul wrote to the Colossians; the Greek expression is like a covering note to a letter in which the bearer is mentioned) to the Colossians to give them all his news (εἰς αὐτὸ τοῦτο, "for the express purpose," is a "final" expression signifying the apostle's aim or intention and refers to "he [Tychicus] will tell" of v 7; Oepke, *TDNT* 2, 429; cf. John 18:37; Acts 9:21; 26:16; Rom 9:17; 14:9; 2 Cor 2:9; Eph 6:22; 1 Pet 4:6). The letter itself does not mention how Paul is getting on personally and the congregation wants to know how things are with him. But Tychicus will be able to give them all the details (ἵνα γνῶτε τὰ περὶ ἡμῶν: see the textual note above 245). At the same time as Paul's colleague and co-worker he will impress the apostle's teaching on the congregation and so strengthen their hearts (see on the same expression at 2:2; it is not simply through the passing on of information about Paul in prison that will be the instrument of strengthening but also by means of admonishing the congregation with Paul's teaching, cf. Zeilinger, *Jesus,* 179).

9. Along with Tychicus Paul is sending Onesimus who is called "the faithful and beloved brother" (ὁ πιστὸς καὶ ἀγαπητὸς ἀδελφός). Although some have argued there is no compelling reason to identify this Onesimus with the person of the same name in Philemon 10, and the name (meaning "useful") certainly was a common one among slaves during the period (cf. BAG, 570), the usual inference that it designates one and the same person is reasonable given the close verbal connections and the names common to the two letters (so Lohse, 171: "it must be supposed that one and the same Onesimus is meant," cf. Schweizer, 176). The details connected with his flight and how Paul persuaded him to return home are not mentioned (they would not be relevant in a letter to be read to the congregation). By describing him as "the faithful and beloved brother" Paul gives him the same predicates as Tychicus and Epaphras (though he is not called a διάκονος, "minister," or σύνδουλος, "fellow-slave") and this suggests that Onesimus the slave is to receive the same warm greeting from the Colossian church that would be extended to any visiting Christian. As one who is a native of Colossae (ὅς ἐστιν ἐξ ὑμῶν) he comes armed with a letter of commendation from the apostle to the Gentiles. (Because Philemon had been personally wronged it was proper that a personal letter should be sent to him, encouraging him to forgive his former slave, Bruce, 302.) He too along with Tychicus will inform (note the shift to the plural γνωρίσουσιν "they will make known") Paul's friends of "everything that has taken place here" (πάντα . . . τὰ ὧδε).

10. Greetings are now sent to the Colossian congregation by six of Paul's companions who are with him at the time of writing: three are of Jewish birth (Aristarchus, Mark and Jesus Justus) and three of Gentile birth (Epaphras, Luke and Demas). This list of greetings is surprisingly long and should be compared with Romans 16, although in the latter passage the greetings are, in the main, mostly from Paul to various individuals at Rome (on the question as to whether Rom 16 was an integral part of the epistle sent to Rome see Kümmel, *Introduction,* 314–20, and more recently H. Gamble Jr, *The Textual*

History of the Letter to the Romans [SD 42; Grand Rapids: Eerdmans, 1977] both of whom after careful examination defend the literary unity of the letter) while in the Colossian greetings these, in verses 10–14, are from Paul's friends to the whole congregation (Paul's own greetings occur at vv 15 and 18).

Aristarchus (the name was a common one, see BAG, 106) is the first-mentioned associate who passes on his greetings to the Colossians (*ἀσπάζομαι*, "greet," the basic meaning of which appears to be to "embrace," is the normal term used of greeting in the NT; forty-seven of its sixty occurrences are as an epistolary formula. It turns up in almost all the letters appearing in two forms: [1] an *imperative,* in which the writer asks his readers to present his greetings from a distance, so Col 4:15, "Give my greetings [*ἀσπάσασθε*] . . . . to Nympha and the church in her house," and Rom 16:3–16, or sends a greeting to all the members of the community, e.g. Col 4:15, "to the brothers at Laodicea," Phil 4:21; Heb 13:24; cf. Rom 16:16; 1 Cor 16:20; 2 Cor 13:12; 1 Thess 5:26; 1 Pet 5:14 where the holy kiss is part of the greeting. [2] *Indicative* greetings with *ἀσπάζεται*, etc., occur when fellow-Christians are absent at the time of writing: they are either mentioned by name [Col 4:10, 12, 14; Rom 16:21–23; 1 Cor 16:19; Philem 23, 24; 2 Tim 4:21] or referred to generally [1 Cor 16:20; Phil 4:21; Tit 3:15]. These greetings help to give the readers a clear picture of the circumstances in which the letter was written and to include friends and co-workers of the apostle in the fellowship he enjoys with the readers. Note also Phil 4:22; Heb 13:24; 2 John 13 and 3 John 15, where groups in the congregation send their greetings, presumably because of some particular relationship. On Paul's distinctive greeting see on v 18 Note Windisch, *TDNT* 1, 496–502, Gamble, *History,* 59, 60, 73–75, and also BAG, 116, 117, for papyri examples and references to the secondary literature).

Aristarchus appears in the narrative of Acts as a native of Thessalonica and a traveling companion of Paul (Acts 19:29; 20:40). His Christian origins may be traced back to Paul's ministry in Thessalonica (Acts 17:1–9). He was with the apostle at Ephesus and exposed to danger in the riot in the theater (19:29). Later he went to Jerusalem with Paul as one of the two delegates from the church at Thessalonica (20:4) and accompanied Paul and Luke when they sailed from Caesarea to Rome (27:2). Although Acts does not state explicitly that he journeyed with Paul all the way to Rome it is probable that he did (it has been suggested he went only as far as Myra, where Paul and Luke changed boats [27:5, 6], and then returned home to Thessalonica). Certainly if Colossians was written from Rome (see Introduction xlix–liv) then the reference to Aristarchus here could be taken to mean he remained with Paul on the journey and after reaching Rome. He is described as *ὁ συναιχμάλωτός μου*, which means literally "my fellow-prisoner of war," and perhaps we are to understand he was actually in prison with Paul (at Phlm 23 Epaphras receives this designation although Aristarchus is mentioned in the same sentence, while at Rom 16:7 Andronicus and Junia are called "fellow-prisoners" perhaps because of an imprisonment with Paul during his Ephesian ministry). It has been suggested that Aristarchus may have shared Paul's captivity voluntarily (Ramsay considered he could have passed as his servant, cf. Bruce, 305; while others conjectured Paul's helpers may have shared his imprisonment in turn, see Abbott, 300). The word could also be used in a figurative sense meaning "a prisoner of Christ," that is, one who has been taken captive by Christ to become a Christian and a fellow-worker of Paul (it has been argued that strictly speaking Paul was not a "prisoner of war," that in his imprisonment he does not describe himself as an αἰχμάλωτος, "captive," but always as a δέσμιος, "prisoner," and that his fondness for military images generally as well as his use of other terms in this word-group [so Rom 7:23; 2 Cor 10:5; cf. Eph 4:8; 2 Tim 3:6] suggest a metaphorical significance here, so Kittel, *TDNT* 1, 196, 197, Moule, 136, 137, and T. da Castel, Συναιχμάλωτος: "Compagno di Prigionia o Conquistato Assieme?" *Studiorum Paulinorum Congressus Internationalis Catholicus.* 2 vols. Rome: Pontifical Biblical Institute, 1963, 2. 417–28; cf. Dibelius-Greeven, 51, who however considers it to mean either "a fellow-Christian or fellow-worker," and Masson, 155). By way of response Lohse, 172, argues that since the term "fellow-prisoner" turns up without any further qualification ("of Christ" or its equivalent, as in Eph 3:1; 4:1) it is preferable to take the word literally. Further, it was not unnatural for Paul, who regarded himself as a soldier of Jesus Christ (note his application of the term "fellow-soldier," συστρατιώτης, to Archippus, Phlm 2, and Epaphroditus, Phil 2:25), to think of himself during his captivity as a prisoner of war (Bruce, 305; cf. also Ollrog, *Paulus,* 76).

Mark, the cousin of Barnabas (ὁ ἀνεψιός means "cousin," not "nephew" or "sister's son" as in KJV/AV; see BAG, 66) joins Aristarchus in sending greetings. The name no doubt refers to John Mark, who was from Jerusalem (Acts 12:12, 25) and who traveled with Paul and Barnabus to Cyprus on the first missionary journey. When they arrived in Perga on the mainland of Asia, Mark defected and returned to Jerusalem (Acts 13:13). Paul, judging this to be a weakness in Mark, refused to take him along with them again on the next journey. Barnabas and Paul had a sharp disagreement over the issue which resulted in the former taking his younger cousin back to Cyprus while Paul set off with Silas (Acts 15:36–41). Under the careful guidance of Barnabas, Mark redeemed his reputation so that here he and the apostle to the Gentiles are again on friendly terms, for Mark is with Paul in his imprisonment. He is mentioned again at Philemon 24 as Paul's "fellow-worker" (συνεργός) while at 2 Timothy 4:11, in a clear display of reconciliation, he is unhesitatingly commended as a faithful Christian worker. Elsewhere Mark appears as Peter's companion (1 Pet 5:13; note the tradition that Mark was Peter's attendant and the author of the second Gospel, the substance of which is Peter's preaching: Eusebius, *H.E.* 3. 39).

Paul refers to Barnabas as though he was well known at Colossae. Perhaps Mark at this stage was only slowly winning back his reputation in the Pauline churches and needs Paul's special plea (so Martin, *NCB,* 131). At any rate the community has already received instructions about him. If he comes they should welcome him (δέχομαι is the appropriate word for the hospitable reception of a guest or visitor: Matt 10:14, 40, 41; Mark 6:11; Luke 9:5, 53; 10:8, 10; John 4:45; Heb 11:31). It is not stated who gave these instructions (ἐντολαί). If they came from Paul himself then the words about the right reception of Mark probably give us the gist of them. But if, as seems more likely, the Colossians had received the communication about Mark from someone else (such as Peter or Barnabas) then Paul is here giving his personal confirmation of the "commandments." But we cannot be sure; nor do we know whether Mark made his way to Colossae or not.

11. The third person to send his greetings was Jesus, who is surnamed Justus. He is quite unknown to us apart from this reference to him as a Jewish Christian who was with Paul (it has been conjectured that at Phlm 23 the name "Jesus" ['Ἰησοῦς] should be read instead of "of Jesus" ['Ἰησοῦ]; on this reading there is a greeting to the Jesus Justus mentioned here in Colossians, see 307). "Jesus" ('Ἰησοῦς) was his Jewish name (the Greek form of "Joshua" or "Jeshua") and this was common among Jews (Acts 13:6) until the second century A.D. when it disappeared as a proper name, no doubt because of the conflict between the synagogue and the Church (Foerster, *TDNT* 3, 284–93, especially 285, 286; for detailed references to the widespread use of the name see BAG, 373, 374). Along with many other Jews who took a Hellenistic Roman name similar to their Hebrew or Aramaic name (a practice well illustrated in the case of Paul himself, Acts 13:9) this Jesus called himself "Justus" (a name that was commonly borne by Jews and proselytes: Acts 1:23; 18:7; see Lightfoot, 236; on the double name see BAG, 380, and Deissmann, *Bible Studies*, 315, 316).

These three men are said to be the only Jewish Christians who have remained faithful fellow-workers of Paul for the kingdom of God (the expression *οἱ ὄντες ἐκ περιτομῆς*, "those of the circumcision," is best connected with what follows, *οὗτοι μόνοι*, "these alone," so Abbott, 301, and Meyer, 473; note Moule's discussion, 137). The expression *οἱ ὄντες ἐκ περιτομῆς*, "those of the circumcision," is normally taken to refer to Jewish Christians generally (so most commentaries and note Meyer, *TDNT* 6, 81). However, E. E. Ellis ("The Circumcision Party and the Early Christian Mission," *Prophecy*, 116–28, published in an earlier form as " 'Those of the Circumcision' and the early Christian Mission," *SE* 4 [1968] 390–99) has put forward an interesting alternative: he claims that the generally accepted definition is neither self-evident from the passage nor does it accord with the meaning of the phrase elsewhere (the expression occurs six times in the NT: Acts 10:45; 11:2; Rom 4:12; Gal 2:12; Titus 1:10, as well as this passage; it does not turn up in the LXX or the intertestamental literature, while Justin's *Dialogue with Trypho* 1, 3 is the earliest parallel in the patristic writings, so Ellis, *Prophecy*, 116). "Those of the circumcision" is to be understood within the framework of a twofold diaspora mission (according to Ellis, *Prophecy*, 117–19, who follows Cullmann, Schmithals and others, the expressions "Hebrews and Hellenists" in Acts point primarily to distinctive Jewish attitudes toward the Jewish cultus and customs: "Hebrews designated those Jews with a strict, ritualist, viewpoint; and Hellenists those with a freer attitude toward the Jewish law and cultus" [118, 119]. Both Hebrews and Hellenists were present in pre-Christian Palestinian Judaism and from the beginning both were represented among the followers of Jesus. Ellis suggests that these differences in ritual and discipline between the two groups had important implications for the structure of the early Christian mission, a mission to the diaspora that had a twofold character). On this hypothesis our text is referring to Jewish Christian preachers who took a nonproselytizing attitude to the law and worked with Paul as they evangelized Jews. "Paul and certain Hebrews were pursuing their distinctive missions in a co-operative fashion" (Ellis, *Prophecy*, 124, who notes that this "venture in ecumenical Christianity" probably also occurred at Antioch [Acts 11:20], while Paul's Hebrew opponents of 2 Corinthians were the reverse; that Paul should say at Col 4:11 *οὗτοι μόνοι*, "these alone," suggests that the cooperative effort was failing). Martin, *NCB*, 143, claims this description of a concordat sounds a little too modern while Ladd, *RevExp* 70 (1973), 510, considers it is difficult to see any particular Jewish emphasis in the mention of the kingdom of God.

At any rate the apostle is grateful for their faithful presence: they are "fellow-workers for the kingdom of God" (*συνεργοὶ εἰς τὴν βασιλείαν τοῦ θεοῦ*) who have proved to be a comfort (*παρηγορία*) to him. *συνεργοί* are "helpers" or "fellow-workers" (BAG, 787, 788). It is not used of believers in general (at 1 Cor 3:9; 2 Cor 1:24 and 8:23 they are implicitly distinguished from the congregation) but describes those who are co-workers "with God" (1 Cor 3:9; 1 Thess 3:2), "in Christ" (Rom 16:3, 9) of Paul (Rom 16:21; Phil 2:25; Philem 1, 24), and for the Christian community (2 Cor 8:23; cf. 1 Cor 3:9; 2 Cor 1:24), qualifiers which indicate whose work it is, the sphere and company in which it is effected, and those who receive its benefits (so Ellis, in *Prophecy*, 6; cf. Bertram, *TDNT* 7, 871–76, and see further on Phlm 1). Instead of stating that these men work with him, the apostle says they are "fellow-workers for the kingdom of God." Usually in Paul the kingdom of God has a future reference, designating the believer's inheritance in the age to come (1 Cor 6:9, 10; 15:50; Gal 5:21; 1 Thess 2:12), and he retains the expression "the kingdom of Christ" for its present aspect (see on 1:13). However, Romans 14:17 shows that the kingdom of God has a present side to it and this appears to be its significance here. According to Acts 28:30, 31 Paul is said to have spent these two years in Rome "proclaiming the kingdom of God and telling the story of the Lord Jesus Christ"; during that time these three Jewish Christians assisted (or carried on their mission, if Ellis' interpretation is correct) and proved to be (*οἵτινες*, as a relative of quality, specifies their character) a great comfort to him (*παρηγορία*, "consolation," "comfort," occurs only here in the NT; cf. 4 Macc 5:12; 6:1. It often appears on funeral inscriptions, e.g. *Epigr Graec* 204, 12, "I have you as a comfort [*παρηγορίην*] even among the dead," also 261, 19, etc., used of consolation in the face of death's reality; see BAG, 626, MM, 494, and Lohse, 173, for further instances).

12. Epaphras also sends a special greeting to the congregation. The apostle has already mentioned him earlier in the letter as the one from whom the Colossians had learned the truth of the gospel (1:7). As a native of Colossae (*ὁ ἐξ ὑμῶν*) he had been the evangelist in his home town, as well as at Laodicea and Hierapolis, apparently having been sent there by Paul (see on 1:7). The latter calls Epaphras "a slave of Christ Jesus" (*δοῦλος Χριστοῦ* ['*Ἰησοῦ*]), a term which he elsewhere applies only to himself (Rom 1:1) and to Timothy (Phil 1:1). Epaphras is given this title of honor which speaks of him as an obedient slave of his Lord in the same service as Paul (at 1:7 he is called *σύνδουλος*, "a fellow-servant," a term also applied to Tychicus, 4:7). In fact, the apostle goes out of his way to stress the close correspondence between his own

ministry and that of Epaphras. Both are involved in the same struggle for the gospel (see below). Both are committed to urgent intercessory prayer as part of that struggle (1:9–11) while both are concerned for the full perfection and maturity of the Christians at Colossae and in the Lycus valley generally (1:28, 29; 2:1–5).

πάντοτε ἀγωνιζόμενος ὑπὲρ ὑμῶν ἐν ταῖς προσευχαῖς. "Regularly striving (for the gospel) through intercessory prayer for you." Epaphras was intimately acquainted with the affairs of the congregation. He, perhaps as no other, knew of the destructive nature of the false teaching and responded in regular, urgent intercession. The verb *ἀγωνιζόμενος* ("striving") has already been used (1:29; cf. the cognate noun *ἀγών*, "struggle," 2:1) of Paul's own costly apostolic mission, understood as a striving for the gospel (so Pfitzner, *Paul*, 109, 110). At Philippians 1:30 the believers at Philippi are said to be involved in the same struggle (*τὸν αὐτὸν ἀγῶνα ἔχοντες*) for the gospel as the apostle (cf. Rom 15:30–32). Here Epaphras is said to be engaged in the same struggle (*ἀγωνιζόμενος*, "striving," occurs in connection with Paul's colleague; *δοῦλος Χριστοῦ Ἰησοῦ*, "a slave of Christ Jesus," seems to tie his ministry in with Paul's; the purpose of his struggle on behalf of his fellow-believers at Colossae is phrased in similar terms to the goal of Paul's own activities, 1:28; 2:2; while *πόνος*, "toil," v 13, places him alongside Paul; Pfitzner, *Paul*, 125) and this finds particular expression in urgent and unceasing intercessions for his countrymen (*πάντοτε*, "always," together with *ἐν ταῖς προσευχαῖς*, lit. "in the prayers," refers to regular petitions being offered for the readers; it has already been suggested that the plurals "we give thanks," 1:3, and "we pray," 1:9, draw attention to the regular gathering together for prayer by Paul and his colleagues in connection with the Colossian Christians, see on 1:3, 9). Although Pfitzner (*Paul*, 128) is probably correct in recognizing that Paul's struggle (*agon*) is "untiring *toil and labour, an intense wrestling* and struggle for the spread, growth and strengthening of the faith as the goal of his mission," such striving comes to expression in Epaphras' petition.

At another level Paul was no doubt aware of the strenuousness of intercessory prayer (note his frequent references to the need for continued, unceasing intercessions) and such notions were probably not far from his thoughts in this passage (he was no doubt aware of a Jewish understanding of prayer, rooted in Jacob's well-known struggle with God, Gen 32:24–32; note too the central example in the NT, the struggle of Jesus in the Garden of Gethsemane: "And being in anguish [*ἀγωνία*] he prayed more earnestly," Luke 22:44).

ἵνα σταθῆτε τέλειοι καὶ πεπληροφορημένοι ἐν παντὶ θελήματι τοῦ θεοῦ. The substance of Epaphras' request (Robertson, *Grammar*, 991, Du Plessis, *Perfection*, 204, and note O'Brien, *Introductory Thanksgivings*, 30, regarding the different terms employed to describe the contents of prayers: e.g. object, subject, substance and purport) is that the Colossians "may stand forth perfect and be filled with everything that is God's will." *σταθῆτε* ("you may stand") is a passive voice and points to the divine activity. The reference to perfection (*τέλειος*) touches on one of the key issues at Colossae in which members of the congregation were encouraged by the false teachers to seek maturity or perfection through their philosophy (2:8) with its ascetic practices, visionary experiences and special revelations, rather than through Christ. Epaphras' concern, however, was like Paul's, namely, to "present every man perfect (τέλειος) in Christ" (1:28 see on that verse). To this end Paul toils, "striving" (ἀγωνιζόμενος) with all the energy which he mightily inspires within me" (1:29), and to this end Epaphras strives in prayer.

The maturity or perfection in Christ is further defined by the following expression "filled with everything that is God's will" (πεπληροφορημένοι ἐν παντὶ θελήματι τοῦ θεοῦ). The unusual verb πληροφορέω (see BAG, 670, and Delling, *TDNT* 6, 309, 310; the cognate noun πληροφορία, "fullness," appears at 2:2) can mean either "convince fully" (which is its significance at Rom 4:21 and 14:5) or "fill," "fulfill" (so 2 Tim 4:5, 17). Moule, 138, prefers the former and understands the phrase "in all the will of God" as attached to the verb. He thus renders the whole expression: "That you may stand firm in all the will of God . . . mature and complete (or convinced)" (see also Dibelius-Greeven). On this view Epaphras prays that the readers may be "fully convinced and certain" of the truth of Paul's gospel. But in our judgment is is better to regard the verb as taking the place of the more frequently used synonym πληρόω ("fill," "fulfill"; 1:9, 19; 2:9, 10; BAG, 670, notes that in this text as elsewhere some manuscripts replace the former verb with the more common πληρόω). The participle here reminds us of the teaching on "fullness" (πλήρωμα) which runs through the heresy as well as Paul's corrective (cf. Delling, *TDNT* 6, 310, Martin, *NCB*, 134, and Ladd, *RevExp* 70 [1973] 511). Accordingly, the prayer addressed to God recalls the polemic against the "philosophy." Christ is the one in whom the whole fullness of the Godhead dwells bodily (2:9). Only in him is fullness to be found. And the readers have been filled in Christ (2:10). Paul's co-worker now prays that they will stand firmly as "perfect," an eschatological perfection that occurs when they are "filled with everything that is God's will" (the preposition ἐν, follows the participle and signifies what one is "filled *with*," BDF, para. 172, Lohse, 173; also "the will of God" is understood as a totality which has its outworking in a variety of circumstances, cf. Delling, *TDNT* 8, 75, Schrage, *Einzelgebote*, 169). Once again it is noted that an emphasis in the letter on what has already been done in Christ in no way obviates the need to grow in him. The readers have already been filled in Christ. Epaphras now prays earnestly that they will attain to that eschatological perfection and fullness in him on the final day, as they make progress here and now.

13. Paul digresses to add an explicit testimony that Epaphras works tirelessly on behalf of the congregations in the Lycus valley. Why he had to work so hard (ἔχει πολὺν πόνον) is not indicated, though all kinds of suggestions have been made: that he had done his best to answer the claims of the heresy and then left Colossae to seek Paul's advice as to how to deal with the heretical propaganda (Lohmeyer, 169); or, that he had deserted his post having failed through incompetence to meet the arguments of the heretics and now needed to have his actions justified by Paul (Masson, 156). But there is nothing to suggest the latter reconstruction, and Paul's testimony is high praise indeed for one who had worked so hard. πόνος ("hard labor," "toil"; "pain," "distress," "affliction," BAG, 691) only turns up four times in the NT and three of these are in the Book of the Revelation (with the meaning "pain," or "distress," 16:10, 11; 21:4). The term was a common one for struggle in

battle and here, like the ἀγών ("struggle") word-group (see on v 12), is related to Paul and Epaphras' toil for the gospel.

ὑπὲρ ὑμῶν καὶ τῶν ἐν Λαοδικείᾳ καὶ τῶν ἐν Ἱεραπόλει. "For you as well as for those at Laodicea and Hierapolis." From the conjunction of the three names it is probable that Epaphras was the evangelist of all three congregations. He is commended by Paul to all three for his future ministry in the Lycus valley presumably because the dangers of the "philosophy" were affecting the whole area and his presence, under God, would be needed once again. We know little about the character of the churches in Hierapolis and Laodicea (the name Hierapolis means "sacred city" [on the spelling see BDF, para. 115(2)] and lay about twelve miles north-west of Colossae and six miles north of Laodicea; the latter, founded by Antiochus II about the middle of the third century B.C., lay further down the Lycus valley than Colossae). One of the seven letters in the Revelation is addressed to Laodicea (Rev 3:14–22). Apparently there were well-established churches in both cities and Epaphras had, under God, substantially contributed to their life and growth. See on verses 15, 16.

Within the list of greetings the name of Epaphras has been specially emphasized (cf. 1:7) and the question has been raised as to how this emphasis fits in with the origin and purpose of the letter. Marxsen (*Introduction*, 177–86) has argued that one of the chief reasons for this document, which is "a kind of pastoral letter" (180) was to give an apostolic authorization to Epaphras whose teaching represents the mind of Paul. The letter derives from the post-Pauline period—Paul himself would not have attacked the heresy in this manner. Epaphras stands in an apostolic succession now that the apostle is no longer alive. These characteristics, according to Marxsen, bear the marks of the "early catholicism" of the subapostolic age.

But the statements in the text give no basis for such far-reaching reconstructions. No passage can justify the assertion that Colossians is "a kind of pastoral letter" along the lines Marxsen suggested. The typical nature of Epaphras' office is nowhere mentioned, and it ought not to be overlooked that other persons in addition to Epaphras are especially mentioned (cf. Tychicus, 4:7). The title of honor, "a slave of Christ Jesus," has no official ring about it (cf. Phil 1:1 with reference to Timothy), while there is no suggestion of ongoing authority or apostolic succession bound up with any single person. Rather, there is a consciousness of brotherly service (in fact, Paul calls himself a "deacon," 1:24, and regards Epaphras as a fellow-servant of Christ, along with Tychicus, 4:7). Epaphras has founded the church (1:7), knew the destructive nature of the heresy as no other did (with the possible exception of Paul himself to whom Epaphras had reported the situation), obviously had a deep-seated concern for his fellow-Christians and continued to pray earnestly for their perfection and fullness. Epaphras was after all "one of them" as Paul especially mentions (ὁ ἐξ ὑμῶν, "one of you," immediately follows Epaphras' name in v 12). This actual background can satisfactorily explain the prominence given to him (for a critique of Marxsen's reconstructions see especially Ernst, 242–44, and Martin, *NCB*, 135; note also Lohse's variations [175–77, and in *Veritas*, 189–94] on Marxsen's treatment together with Ollrog's careful criticisms [*Paulus*, 238–40]; see Introduction xlvii–xlix).

14. Luke and Demas add their greetings. Both names recur in Philemon 24 as Paul's fellow-workers and at 2 Timothy 4:10, 11. Only here is Luke (on the name Λουκᾶς see BAG, 480) called "the beloved physician" (ὁ ἰατρὸς ὁ ἀγαπητός), and this has led to speculation that he was Paul's doctor during his imprisonment. But there is no evidence for this. Luke's profession was an unusual one so Paul mentions it, yet without further emphasis.

It is mainly on the basis of this verse, which separates him from Jewish Christians (οἱ ὄντες ἐκ περιτομῆς, v 11), that Luke was regarded as a Gentile Christian. Although this is possible, it is by no means certain, and if Ellis' arguments above about "those of the circumcision" referring not to Jewish Christians generally but to one group within a twofold diaspora mission are correct, then it is possible he was a Hellenistic Jew (see E. E. Ellis, *The Gospel of Luke* NCB; London: Nelson, 1966) 52, 53; and note the comments above; Deissmann, *Light from the Ancient East,* 437, 438, favored identifying him with the Lucius of Rom 16:21).

Little is known about Demas. In 2 Timothy 4:10 he is mentioned: "For Demas, in love with this present world, has deserted me." This statement seems to suggest that some temporal interest took Paul's fellow-worker (Phlm 24) off to Thessalonica at a time when the apostle would have valued his continued presence (Bruce, 308).

15. *ἀσπάσασθε τοὺς ἐν Λαοδικείᾳ ἀδελφούς.* Paul now asks the Colossians to convey his greetings to their fellow-Christians at Laodicea, which lay ten miles to the west. It is by no means clear why the apostle should send special greetings to the brethren in Laodicea when, according to the following verse, he is sending a separate letter to that church (Meyer, 477, supposed, without sufficient justification, that the brothers [οἱ ἀδελφοί] are a church distinct from the Laodicean church but in a filial relation with it meeting in the same house; Lightfoot, 241: the brothers are perhaps a Colossian family resident in Laodicea). Dibelius-Greeven, 52, suggested he wished to cement relations between the two churches in this way.

καὶ Νύμφαν καὶ τὴν κατ' οἶκον αὐτῆς ἐκκλησίαν. "And Nympha and the church that is in her house." It cannot be determined with certainty whether the greeting to Νύμφαν (Nympha) refers to a man (Νυμφᾶς, Nymphas, an abbreviated form of Νυμφόδωρος, Nymphrodorus; cf. Epaphras for Epaphroditus) or to a woman whose name was Νύμφα (Nympha). Since the earliest manuscripts had no accents by which the masculine and feminine forms might be distinguished, the only ancient evidence lies in the personal pronoun which follows: "in her/his/their house": (κατ' οἶκον αὐτῆς/αὐτοῦ/αὐτῶν)—the manuscripts vary considerably (see the textual note above), but on balance it appears preferable to understand the reference to a woman and render the whole phrase: "Nympha and the church that is in her house."

House-churches (on the meaning and use of ἐκκλησία see 57–61), are often mentioned in the NT letters. On occasion a whole congregation in one city might be small enough to meet in the home of one of its members, and it must be remembered that it was not until about the middle of the third century that early Christianity owned property for purposes of worship (see O. Cullmann, *Early Christian Worship.* Tr. A. S. Todd and J. B. Torrance [SBT 10; London: SCM, 1953] 9, 10). In other places house-churches appear to have been smaller circles of fellowship within the larger group. In addition to Nympha's house in Laodicea we know that in Colossae Philemon's house was used as a meeting-place (Phlm 2). At Philippi Lydia's home seems to have been used in this way (Acts 16: 15, 40) while at Corinth Gaius is described as "host . . . to the whole church" (Rom 16:23, the qualification "whole," ὅλη, would be unnecessary if the Christians at Corinth only ever met as a single group and implies that smaller groups also existed in the city; cf. 1 Cor 14:23). Aquila and Priscilla extended the hospitality of their home to house groups in the successive cities where they lived, e.g., in Ephesus (1 Cor 16:19) and Rome (Rom 16:5). Concerning the details of these house-churches we know little (note Banks, *Idea,* 45–50, and 226, 227, for further bibliographical details).

16. Paul's next instructions are significant. First, he expects the contents of this letter to be read out in the congregation. ἐπιστολή (a "letter," "epistle," BAG, 300, 301), a word which occurs some twenty-four times in the NT, here refers to the present letter (as Rom 16:22; 1 Thess 5:27; and 2 Thess 3:14: these latter verses are in the nature of a postscript, so Abbott, 304). ἀναγινώσκω, which in classical Greek had a range of meanings including to "know exactly," "know again," "acknowledge," in the NT is found only with the meaning "read," "read aloud." Usually reading the OT Scriptures was meant (cf. the fourteen Synoptic references, Acts 8:28, etc.), particularly in the synagogue service (Luke 4:16; Acts 13:15, 27; 15:21; 2 Cor 3:14, 15), but as here it was used of reading a letter (Acts 15:31; 2 Cor 1:13; 3:2) especially in the congregation (παρ' ὑμῖν, "among you," so Riesenfeld, *TDNT* 5, 732, is almost equivalent to ἐν . . . ἐκκλησίᾳ, "in . . . the assembly"). The Epistles of the NT were from the first intended to be read aloud in the Christian assembly (showing that they ranked equally with the OT), a point which is attested in one of Paul's earliest letters where he uses strong language in commanding that his letter be read aloud to all the brethren (1 Thess 5:27; Martin, *NCB,* 137, rightly observes that Marxsen's further argument, *Introduction,* 185, that the public reading of Paul's epistolary correspondence is a mark of subapostolic Christianity and therefore Colossians is a later post-Pauline writing, falls down).

Second, the Colossians are then to pass on this letter, or perhaps a copy of it, so that (ποιέω ἵνα means to "cause that," cf. John 11:37; Rev 13:15) it may be read in the congregation at Laodicea also.

Third, they are to obtain a certain letter from Laodicea and have it read publicly in church at Colossae. Much ink has been spilled, to little purpose, endeavoring to determine what this "letter from Laodicea" (τὴν ἐκ Λαοδικείας) actually was: *(a)* several of the early church fathers (Chrysostom, Theodore of Mopsuestia, and Theodoret) together with many other later writers including Beza, supposed this to have been a letter written from Laodicea to Paul. But by far the most likely meaning of the phrase is that the Colossians were to procure the letter from Laodicea (so Robertson, *Grammar,* 600, BDF, para. 437), an interpretation clearly supported by the context (so Dibelius-Greeven, 52, who considers the expression is from the standpoint of the Colossians and note Abbott's comments, 304, 305; ἵνα καὶ ὑμεῖς, "that you too," corresponds to the previous ἵνα καί, "that also," which refers to the Laodiceans reading the Colossians' letter; the parallelism implies that the Laodiceans, like the Colossians, will have received a letter, cf. Moule, 138, Bruce, 310, Loymeyer, 170, Anderson, *JBL* 85 [1966] 436, 437, Lohse, 174, 175, Martin, *NCB*, 138, and Schweizer, 179). *(b)* Marcion identified this letter with the Epistle to the Ephesians (a connection made in 1707 by John Mill and which received abundant support from Lightfoot, 272–98; note also J. Rutherford, "St. Paul's Epistle to the Laodiceans," *ExpTim* 19 [1907–08] 311–14). However, Ephesians was almost certainly written after Colossians, and not simply to one church in the province of Asia. If it was written after Colossians, then it is unlikely to have been mentioned in Colossians, unless 4:16 is a later addition but of this there is no evidence (Marcion's Apostolic Canon gave the title "To the Laodiceans" to the Epistle to the Ephesians, perhaps because it lacked the words "at Ephesus" in the first verse and he found what appeared to be a pointer to its destination in Col 4:16, so Bruce, 310, 311, following Souter). *(c)* The Epistle to Philemon has been identified with the "epistle from Laodicea," (J. Knox, *Philemon among the Letters of Paul.* 2nd ed. [London: Collins, 1960] 38–47), but this letter was private (see the full discussion of this point) and the delicacy of its appeal would be destroyed if Paul directed it to be read in public. Further, Philemon lived at Colossae (according to Col 4:9 Onesiumus is a slave of Philemon at Colossae) not Laodicea. *(d)* No extant Pauline letter seems adequately to fit the description and so we are left with the conclusion that the letter to the Laodiceans has not survived (the reference to a letter not obviously included in the canon led, at a later date, to the fabrication of the apocryphal "Epistle of Paul to the Laodiceans," which was made up of sentences gleaned from other Pauline letters; cf. the detailed treatment of Lightfoot, 272–98, Hennecke-Schneemelcher 2, 128–32).

Perhaps it perished accidentally (P. N. Harrison, "Onesimus and Philemon," *ATR* 32 [1950] 268–94, suggested it may have been destroyed during the earthquake in the Lycus valley of A.D. 60–61; Schmauch in the *Beiheft* to Lohmeyer's commentary, 85, considers the letter was meant for a splinter group of the Laodicean church which resided at Colossae and was destroyed once the church at Laodicea was united—but there is no evidence for this) and was not the only Pauline letter to have been lost (according to the most natural reading of 1 Cor 5:9 Paul had written an earlier letter to the Corinthians which has not survived).

Perhaps the Laodicean church required a letter along similar lines to the Epistle to the Colossians; yet the two were sufficiently different for Paul to direct that each letter should be read in the other church (Anderson, *JBL* 85 [1966] 436–40, submitted the view that Epaphras wrote the epistle to the Laodiceans because of his inability to accompany Tychicus on the return to the Lycus valley. Anderson claims we cannot discover a sufficient motive for Paul's writing the second letter. But this does not mean such a motive does not exist and, furthermore, why does not Paul say it is Epaphras' letter?). The philosophical ideas which were gaining currency in Colossae were probably very much alive in the Lycus neighborhood so that the exchange of both was important.

From this admonition one can understand how Paul's letters would be copied, disseminated and collected at an early date (Lohse, 175).

17. *καὶ εἴπατε Ἀρχίππῳ Βλέπε τὴν διακονίαν ἣν παρέλαβες ἐν κυρίῳ, ἵνα αὐτὴν πληροῖς*. A final word is directed to one member of the congregation—Archippus: "See to it that you complete the ministry you have received in the Lord." Archippus (Ἄρχιππος is widely attested as a proper name, so BAG, 113) is called "our fellow-soldier" by Paul at Philemon 2 (*ὁ συστρατιώτης ἡμῶν*; he is a member of Philemon's household, perhaps Philemon and Apphia's son: see 273), a designation employed figuratively of those who devote themselves to the service of the gospel (Phil 2:25). According to 2 Timothy 2: 2, 3 in the context of adherence to the apostolic teaching Timothy is encouraged to endure hardship "as a good soldier of Christ Jesus" (*ὡς καλὸς στρατιώτης Χριστοῦ Ἰησοῦ*). Most commenators recognize the difficulty of determining precisely what Archippus' task was. Knox *(Philemon)* imagined that Archippus was the owner of the slave, Onesimus, and that the letter to Philemon was really addressed to Archippus. In this case, the latter's "ministry" was that of receiving Onesimus as a brother. But this view is to be rejected (see the critique below 266–268) along with Goodspeed's suggestion that the task was that of appeasing or smoothing over Philemon because of the return of Onesimus. There is no indication that his ministry (*διακονία*) was that of a deacon (*διακονία* describes the discharge of service, not the exercise of the office of a deacon, Beyer, *TDNT* 2, 88), nor that he was to make a collection.

Merklein (*Amt,* 337–40; cf. Zeilinger, *Jesus,* 185–88), who understands *διάκονος* ("minister") and *διακονία* ("ministry") as traditional terms within Colossians, considers the ministry of preaching is the service Archippus is to fulfill. It is a ministry he has received in the Lord (*παρέλαβες ἐν κυρίῳ*; *παραλαμβάνω* is employed for the receiving of a tradition, see on 2:6) and involves the proclamation of the Pauline gospel (both Merklein and Zeilinger draw attention to the cluster of terms used in this connection: *παραλαμβάνω*, "receive," 2:6; *πληρόω*, "fulfill," 1:25; and *διάκονος*, "minister," 1:23, 25). As such Archippus is the guarantor to the Colossian congregation that they have received the apostolic gospel (for a qualification of this approach to traditional terms with special reference to Epaphras, see the Introduction xlvii–xlix).

18. The conclusion of the letter is brief. Having finished dictating, Paul takes up his pen to add a personal greeting in his own handwriting. The apostle always concluded his letters autobiographically even where there is no explicit acknowledgment of it (see Gamble's recent discussion and interaction with recent epistolary literature, *History,* 76–80, together with his treatment of 2 Thess 3:17). His personal signatures occur frequently (1 Cor 16:21; 2 Cor 10:1; Gal 6:11; Col 4:18; 2 Thess 3:17 and Philem 19) and were a common epistolary technique in the first century (Deissmann, *Light from the Ancient East,* 158, 159). Paul apparently employed the autograph with special nuances: because of a concern that forged letters in his name might be sent to churches or individuals (2 Thess 2:2), to give a quasi-legal commitment with his personal certification (Philem 19), or to add special emphasis to what has been said (so the reference to "large characters" in Gal 6:11).

μνημονεύετέ μου τῶν δεσμῶν. "Remember my bonds" is an appeal that is touching in its brevity and simplicity. The verb μνημονεύω, to "remember," also conveys the idea of "recognize" or "acknowledge" (Michel, *TDNT* 4, 682, 683) and so several have suggested the apostle is summoning the Colossians to respect his authority (Lohse, 177, Martin, *NCB*, 141; Philem 9 is usually drawn in, dubiously in our judgment, in support of this notion; see the exegesis below 290). But this is not really the point at issue. Paul has not had to assert his authority throughout the letter where it might have been expected, so why now? Rather, one biblical meaning of μνημονεύω is that of calling something to God's remembrance or of mentioning something to him in prayer (LXX 2 Sam 14:11; Ps 62:6; cf. Ps 6:5; in the NT note the use of μνείαν ποιοῦμαι, to "make mention," i.e. in prayer: Rom 1:9; Eph 1:16; 1 Thess 1:2; Philem 4; cf. 2 Tim 1:3; note Bartels, *NIDNTT* 3, 232, 242, and BAG, 525). Accordingly, these words are essentially a request for their continued prayers on his behalf (see vv 3, 4; Bruce, 313, cf. Wiles, *Prayers*, 260, who observes that such requests for prayer are frequently found in the closing passages of letters in the Pauline corpus: Rom 15:30–32; Eph 6:18–20; 1 Thess 5:25; 2 Thess 3:1–3; Philem 22; cf. Heb 13:18. Gamble, *History*, 81, notes that "prayer and remembrance are closely bound up in the Pauline letters"). That is not to suggest, however, that such remembrance could not take other forms as well (note Meyer, 483, Abbott, 307, 308), e.g., interest, concern, etc.

ἡ χάρις μεθ' ὑμῶν. "Grace be with you." As the opening epistolary greetings or benedictions of Paul's letters are quite stylized so too the χάρις ("grace") benediction was a frequent and formally consistent element in the conclusions of Paul's letters. Its uniformity of phraseology, structure and position is clear when a comparison is made (Rom 16:20, 24; 1 Cor 16:23; 2 Cor 13:13; Gal 6:18; Eph 6:24; Phil 4:23; Col 4:18; 1 Thess 5:28; 2 Thess 3:18; 1 Tim 6:12; 2 Tim 4:22; Titus 3:15; Philem 25; cf. Heb 13:25; Rev 22:21). Such a benediction brings the letter to a definitive conclusion and corresponds formally to the final wish of the secular letter (ἔρρωσο, "farewell," cf. Gamble, *History*, 65–67). The final benediction picks up the introductory greeting (1:2) where Paul desires that the Colossians may apprehend more fully the grace of God in which they stand (cf. Rom 5:2). At the same time the note of confidence is also struck (on the question as to whether the verb which has been omitted is an indicative, ἐστιν, "is," or optative, εἴη, "be," see Gamble, *History*, 66, 67, who claims that as a blessing the "grace-benediction" is neither a wish nor a statement but incorporates aspects of both: "Its wish character remains intact, even though qualified by confidence of its effectiveness"). God's grace will sustain the community, for it is by grace alone that they will stand.

Explanation

Paul concludes his letter to the Colossians in his usual way with personal greetings and instructions. First, he mentions Tychicus and Onesimus, bearers of the letter, who will convey his personal news to the congregation which would naturally be interested to know how he and Epaphras, the founder of the church, were getting on in prison. Next he sends greetings from six of his associates who are acquainted with the congregation: three are of Jewish birth (Aristarchus, Mark and Jesus Justus) and three from a Gentile background (Epaphras, Luke and Demas). The first three are the only Jewish Christians among his fellow-workers for the kingdom of God and Paul is grateful for their faithful presence. Among the latter group the apostle singles out Epaphras for special mention. As a native of Colossae he had been the evangelist in his home town (as well as at Laodicea and Hierapolis). He had engaged in the same struggle for the gospel as Paul and this found particular expression in his urgent intercessory prayers for the Colossians that they might come to fullness and maturity in Christ. Then Paul adds his own greetings and brief instructions: he expects the contents of this letter to be read out in the congregation. The Colossians are then to pass on the letter, or perhaps a copy of it, so that it may be read in the congregation at Laodicea as well, while the letter which has gone to Laodicea is to be read publicly in church at Colossae. Archippus, a member of the congregation, is told to complete the ministry he has received in the Lord. The final salutation is written in Paul's own hand and contains a request to remember his bonds, together with a benediction for God's grace.

Philemon

Introduction to Philemon

Bibliography

Bruce, F. F. *Paul*, 393–406. **Gayer, R.** *Die Stellung des Sklaven in den paulinischen Gemeinden und bei Paulus. Zugleich ein sozialgeschichtlich vergleichender Beitrag zur Wertung des Sklaven in der Antike.* Bern: Lang, 1976. **Greeven, H.** "Prüfung der Thesen von J. Knox zum Philemonbrief." *TLZ* 79 (1954) 373–78. **Guthrie, D.** *Introduction*, 247–54. **Hainz, J.** *Ekklesia. Strukturen paulinischer Gemeinde-Theologie und Gemeinde-Ordnung.* BU 9, Regensburg: F. Pustet, 1972, 199–209. **Harrison, P. N.** *ATR* 32 (1950) 268–94. **Jang, L. K.** *Der Philemonbrief im Zusammenhang mit dem theologischen Denken des Apostels Paulus.* Bonn: unpublished thesis, 1964. **Knox, J.** *Philemon.* **Kümmel, W. G.** *Introduction*, 348–50. **Suhl, A.** "Der Philemonbrief als Beispiel paulinischer Paränese." *Kairos* 15 (1973) 267–79. **Wickert, U.** "Der Philemonbrief—Privatbrief oder apostolisches Schreiben?" *ZNW* 52 (1961) 230–38.

The Nature of the Letter

The letter to Philemon is the shortest of all in the Pauline corpus (consisting of a mere 335 words in the original Greek), and is more closely related to the ordinary private and personal letters of the time—related in a way that others addressed by Paul either to communities or groups of communities are not (most scholars have recognized that Philemon stands near the ancient private letter: so for example, P. Wendland, *Die urchristlichen Literaturformen.* 3rd ed. [Tübingen: Mohr, 1912] 280, 281; note also Doty, *Letters*, 22, citing the work of J. L. White). This fact, however, does not indicate that the letter is simply a piece of private correspondence (cf. Roller, *Formular*, 147). Kümmel (*Introduction*, 249) states that Philemon is "like the longer letters of Paul . . . not private correspondence, but the instrument of early Christian missionary work" (cf. Suhl, *Kairos* 15 [1973] 267–79).

The precise nature of the letter to Philemon and the reasons for its inclusion in the canon have been the subject of discussion among scholars for some time—not least since 1935 when John Knox published his important little book, *Philemon among the Letters of Paul* (a revised edition appeared twenty-five years later). Knox considered that the letter was included in the Pauline corpus by one who played a prominent part in its publication—Onesimus, the runaway slave mentioned in this letter who, according to tradition, later became bishop of Ephesus.

The Recipient

The recipient of this letter is Philemon, who is described as Paul's "beloved fellow-worker" (v 1). Other names mentioned in the salutation are the sister Apphia, the fellow-soldier Archippus and the community assembled in Philemon's house (v 2). Since Colossians expressly mentions that Onesimus (4:9) and Archippus (4:17) belong to the church at Colossae, it can be assumed that Philemon, from whose house the slave Onesimus fled, also lived there. Philemon, who appears to have become a Christian through Paul (see on v 19)—possibly in Ephesus—had given concrete expression of his love for the saints (vv 5, 7). Apphia, whose name was peculiarly Phrygian and is mentioned alongside Philemon's, was probably his wife. Although Archippus has been thought by some to be a son of Philemon and Apphia, we have no certain means of knowing whether this is so or not.

According to Knox *(Philemon)* the letter was addressed to Archippus, Onesimus' owner. It is he rather than Philemon who is referred to in the second person singular from verses 4 to 24 of the letter, for it was in Archippus' house that the church met. Philemon was overseer of the churches of the Lycus valley. He lived at Laodicea and Paul arranged that the letter should reach Philemon first. Philemon would then use his influence with Archippus to ensure that Onesimus was released from slavery and was free to assist Paul in his ministry.

In spite of Knox's many penetrating insights (especially his comments concerning the reason for the epistle's inclusion within the canon, and whether or not Paul's request for/concerning Onesimus was accepted), his thesis has not found general acceptance among NT scholars (partial agreement with Knox has been expressed by Greeven, *TLZ* 79 [1954] 373–78) and according to Kümmel (*Introduction,* 349) is "controverted by the natural exegesis of Philem 1, 2 and Col 4:17." Philemon's name appears first in verse 1, and this, together with the phrase *κατ' οἰκόν σου* ("in your house", v 2) tells against Archippus as being the one primarily addressed (so Moule, 16, 17, among others; even in his second edition Knox has not effectively answered these criticisms of his reconstruction).

The Occasion of the Letter

The occasion of the letter may be inferred from its contents though some of the details are obscure. A slave named Onesimus had wronged his owner Philemon who was a Christian living at Colossae (vv 1, 2; cf. Col 4:9, 17) and had run off. Onesimus had in some way come into contact with the apostle, perhaps as a fellow-prisoner. However, if he had been apprehended by the authorities and thrown into prison it would have been their responsibility to take him back to his master. Perhaps he had sought refuge in Paul's company because he had heard his name mentioned in the house of his Christian master and had now hastened to him for help in his trouble.

The precise nature of Onesimus' offense is not certain and our understanding turns in part on the meaning of verse 18. It is usually assumed Onesimus had stolen his master's money and then absconded (so Caird, 222, 223, and Stuhlmacher, 49, among others who have made the suggestion with varying degrees of conviction). On the other hand, it is possible that the words, "if he has wronged you or owes you anything," simply indicate his running away meant he owed his master the value of the work that should have been done (cf. Lohmeyer, 190, Lohse, 204, Suhl, *Kairos* 15 [1973] 269, Martin, *NCB,*

167, and Gayer, *Stellung,* 230). Bruce (*Paul,* 400) wonders whether his master had sent him to fulfill some commission and Onesimus had overstayed his leave (on the whole discussion see on v 18).

But whatever the precise reasons for Onesimus' flight we do know that in the Roman world of Paul's day slaves did often run away. They joined groups of robbers and brigands, attempted to disappear in the subcultures of large cities, tried to flee abroad where they might be absorbed into the workforce, or sought asylum in a temple (cf. Stuhlmacher, 22, 23, and note the literature cited). Onesimus chose none of these methods of escape. Instead he sought refuge with the imprisoned apostle. Paul took an interest in him and Onesimus was subsequently converted to the Christian faith (v 10). The apostle clearly developed a great affection for him (at v 12 he describes him as "my very heart," τὰ ἐμὰ σπλάγχνα) and benefited from his ministry and service (vv 11, 13). He would dearly have wished to keep him so that he might take Philemon's place at his side in the service of the gospel. However, he had no right to retain Onesimus: not only would it have been illegal for Paul to act in this way (see particularly on v 12), but also it would have involved a breach of Christian fellowship between himself and Philemon (cf. Bruce, *Paul,* 406). So he sent him back with an accompanying letter.

At verse 10 the apostle mentions the *fact* of his request of Philemon for Onesimus. But the *content* of that request is not spelled out until seven verses later when he asks that Philemon might welcome his runaway slave as he would receive himself (v 17), that is, as a "beloved brother" (v 16). The apostle does not want the reconciliation between Philemon and Onesimus to collapse because of any demand for compensation, and so he asks that any outstanding damages resulting from Onesimus' flight (or absence) be charged to his own account. After all, did not Philemon owe his very self to Paul, since the latter was responsible for his conversion? Yet he refrains from issuing Philemon with any command (see the discussion on vv 8, 9), or from urging that Onesimus be given his freedom. The decision is to be Philemon's entirely, and Paul refuses to press him to act in any way that would suggest coercion or an intrusion into that decision (v 14). The apostle is confident that Philemon will be obedient to the will of God and he adds that the latter "will do even more than I say" (v 21). These words are tantalizing, and as we read between the lines it appears best to interpret the "more" as the desire of the apostle for Onesimus to be returned to him for the service of the gospel (see on v 21).

The bold request for Onesimus is carefully prepared by the writer as he uses gentle language (vv 8, 9) with its tones of entreaty, then leads on to an appeal for Philemon's willing cooperation and consent (v 14), and finally with his promissory note indicates his willingness to accept any liability Onesimus may have incurred (v 19). (Note the carefully structured paragraph of vv 8–20, 284–287.)

Knox argued that the letter to Philemon (which he took to be the "letter from Laodicea" of Col 4:16) should be read aloud in the church of Colossae to put pressure on Onesimus' owner (i.e. Archippus according to Knox; see above 266). But this is impossible. In his letter to the owner Paul has exercised discretion and tact, graciously making his request, rather than exercising any authority by way of demand. Also to suggest with Knox that the letter be read to the assembled church at Colossae would be entirely inconsistent with this exercise of tact (so Lightfoot, 279, who put the matter clearly: "Why should a letter, containing such intimate confidences, be read publicly in the Church, not only at Laodicea but at Colossae, by the express order of the Apostle? The tact and delicacy of the Apostle's pleading for Onesimus would be nullified at one stroke by the demand for publication." Cf. Harrison, *ATR* 32 [1950] 280; Bruce, *Paul*, 404, 405). Further, the inclusion of other Christians' names in the salutation (vv 1, 2) and benedictions (vv 3, 25) is due to Paul's courtesy. The body of the letter is addressed to an individual.

Wickert (*ZNW* 52 [1961] 230–38) correctly points out that Paul did not write simply as a private individual to Philemon, but as an apostle. However, he errs when he considers that Paul asserted his apostolic authority and made Philemon accede to his demands. This is the very thing Paul does not do (note the exegesis of vv 8, 9).

It is reasonable to infer from the preservation of the letter in the canon that Paul's request to Philemon about Onesimus was granted. Otherwise the letter would probably have been destroyed. Bruce (*Paul*, 406, following Knox, *Philemon*) claims it was preserved not only because "it accomplished its purpose so far as Philemon was concerned, but also because Onesimus treasured it as his charter of liberty." If the latter did subsequently become bishop of Ephesus and knew about the collection and publication of the Pauline corpus of letters, then he may have made sure that *his* Pauline letter found a place in the collection.

The Structure of the Letter

Paul's introductory greeting (vv 1–3) is followed by the thanksgiving paragraph (vv 4–7) which leads into (v 7) the body of the letter where the apostle develops his request for Onesimus (vv 8–20). A short list of greetings (vv 23, 24) and the benediction (v 25) form the conclusion.

In this epistle to Philemon the apostle employs the same basic structure he uses elsewhere in his letters. The thanksgiving paragraph (vv 4–7), which follows the usual introduction, is a relatively short and simple form of the first type of introductory thanksgiving (see on Col 1:3–8). This passage prepares the ground for the request that is to follow, a point that comes out in its general emphasis and in the repetition of specific words which the thanksgiving anticipates. The body of this epistle (vv 8–20), in which the intercession for Onesimus is made, is carefully structured so that the reader is gradually led to the actual request (see the section of vv 8–20 entitled "Form"). Paul gives a brief description of his situation (vv 8–12), indicating the basis of his appeal and stressing how dear Onesimus has become to him. He then looks back (vv 13, 14) to the time when the slave came to him seeking refuge, and tells why he did not keep Onesimus (cf. vv 15, 16). Only at the conclusion of this main section does he state the content of his request for the first time: "welcome him as me."

Place of Origin and Date

Paul writes as a prisoner (vv 1, 9, 10, 23), and a careful comparison of the names in the epistle with those of Colossians 4:7–17 shows that this letter was sent from the same place as Colossians (see above xlix–liv). Tychicus who was entrusted with this epistle had Onesimus as his companion on the journey to the Lycus valley, the same Onesimus mentioned in the letter to Philemon (v 12).

The precise location of Paul's imprisonment at the time of writing Colossians was discussed in the introduction to that letter (see xlix–liv), and of the three possibilities—Rome, Caesarea or Ephesus—it was considered that the balance of probability lay in favor of Rome. The most likely placing of the two letters is fairly early in Paul's (first) Roman imprisonment, i.e., A.D. 60–61.

Authenticity

Up to this point it has been assumed that Paul was the author of the letter. Only the most extreme negative critics have in the past disputed the Pauline authorship of the epistle. Because of its close connection with Colossians, which was thought to belong to the second century, the Tübingen school denied its authenticity, although Baur admitted its noble Christian spirit. The Dutch radical W. C. van Manen also took this line but such an approach may rightly be consigned to the eccentricities of NT scholarship. The letter was already included in Marcion's canon and there are good reasons for assuming we hear the authentic voice of Paul. "It breathes the great-hearted tenderness of the apostle and its dealing with an intensely difficult situation points to an author of much experience in handling social problems" (Guthrie, *Introduction,* 250, 251).

The Letter of Philemon and the Question of Slavery

The epistle brings into vivid focus the whole question of slavery in the early Christian church. From the "household table" of Colossians 3:18–4:1 (cf. Eph 6:5–9; 1 Cor 7:21–23; 1 Tim 6:1, 2; Titus 2:9, 10; 1 Pet 2:18–21) we have seen that Paul makes the following points: *(a)* slaves are involved in "serving Christ," *(b)* owners have "a master in heaven," *(c)* God deals impartially with master and slave, and *(d)* both are bond-servants of Christ. In the letter to Philemon Paul does not take up the question of slavery as such or even a particular instance of slavery. In his carefully chosen words of verses 16 and 17 ("no longer as a slave, but as one who is much more than a slave, as a beloved brother . . . receive him as you would receive me") he is dealing with the issue of brotherly love. He desires that Onesimus be welcomed back as a Christian brother and treated as he himself would be. He does not ask that Philemon should receive Onesimus back as a freed man or that he should free him immediately on his return (against Jang, *Philemonbrief,* 15; see on v 16).

Nevertheless as Bruce (*Paul,* 401) points out: "What this letter does is to bring us into an atmosphere in which the institution could only wilt and die." Onesimus as well as Philemon has been incorporated into the body of Christ and consequently the relationship of slave to slave owner within the context of the existing structures is to be conducted in the light of belonging to the same Lord. The relationship between the two men is deepened so that, in a sense, the terms "slave" and "master" are transcended. And although Onesimus' earthly freedom may be of positive value, finally it is of no ultimate significance to him as a Christian as to whether he is slave or free. In the end what matters is to have accepted God's call and to follow him (cf. 1 Cor 7:21–24, and see on Philem 16).

Analysis of Philemon

Vv 1–3	Introductory Greeting
4–7	Thanksgiving and Intercession for Philemon
8–20	Paul's Plea for Onesimus
21–25	Final Remarks and Greetings

Introductory Greeting (1–3)

Bibliography

(See on Colossians 1:1, 2)

Translation

[1] *Paul, a prisoner of Christ Jesus, and Timothy our brother. To Philemon our dear friend and fellow-worker,* [2] *to Apphia our sister, Archippus our fellow-soldier and to the church that meets in your house.* [3] *Grace and peace to you from God our Father and the Lord Jesus Christ.*

Form/Structure/Setting

The structure of Paul's introduction follows the pattern found elsewhere in his letters (see on Col 1:1, 2) with its mention of author (and his associate), addressee and a greeting.

Comment

1. Παῦλος δέσμιος Χριστοῦ Ἰησοῦ. "Paul, a prisoner of Christ Jesus." While Paul (on the name see Col 1:1) elsewhere commences his letters with the designations "a slave of Christ Jesus" (Rom 1:1; cf. Phil 1:1; Tit 1:1) and "called to be an apostle" (Rom 1:1; cf. 1 Cor 1:1; Gal 1:1, 2) or "an apostle of Christ Jesus" (2 Cor 1:1; Eph 1:1; Col 1:1; 1 Tim 1:1; 2 Tim 1:1), in Philemon 1 he calls himself δέσμιος Χριστοῦ Ἰησοῦ, "a prisoner of Christ Jesus." This unusual expression was corrected in the later manuscript tradition to bring it into line with the customary Pauline openings, but this text is certainly original (note vv 9 and 13 where the thought is repeated). δέσμιος ("prisoner," also Eph 3:1; 4:1; 2 Tim 1:8; Philem 9, as well as δεσμός, "bond," "fetter," at Phil 1:7, 13, 14, 17; Col 4:18; 2 Tim 2:9) is best understood of a literal imprisonment (so Kittel, *TDNT* 2, 43, asserts: "there can be no doubt that the actual imprisonment of Paul everywhere underlies the usage [of these references]"; see also Lohse, 189, Martin *NCB,* 158, Jang, *Philemonbrief,* 22, Hainz, *Ekklesia,* 200, Stuhlmacher, 29, and Gayer, *Stellung,* 228), from which Paul hopes soon to be released (v 22), rather than a metaphorical bondage (E. R. Goodenough, "Paul and Onesimus," *HTR* 22 [1929] 181–83) or a religious imprisonment (Reitzenstein sought to explain the meaning from parallels drawn from the mystery religions in which the devotee in the temple is "detained" by his god; for a critique see Lohse, 189). So at the outset reference is made to the apostle's situation: Paul is "in prison for the gospel" (ἐν τοῖς δεσμοῖς τοῦ εὐαγγελίου, v 13; the genitive Χριστοῦ Ἰησοῦ in the expression "prisoner *of Christ Jesus*" is best understood, with most commentators, to signify Paul has been imprisoned "for Christ's sake"; von Soden, 73, adds

that the genitive shows Christ is the owner of the prisoner and the cause of his imprisonment). The authoritative title of "apostle" is dropped, not because Paul has suddenly ceased to be an apostle, but because he has no intention of appealing to his apostolic authority. He desires to entreat Philemon (vv 8, 9) rather than command, and substitutes for the term "apostle" a "designation which would touch his friend's heart" (Lightfoot, 331, cf. Caird, 218; the reference to Paul's bonds is not to stress the apostle's authority as so many continental scholars argue).

Τιμόθεος ὁ ἀδελφός. "Timothy, our brother." Once again Paul associates Timothy with himself in the salutation (see on Col 1:1). When Paul names others along with himself in the address it is usually because of their relations with the church to which the letter is sent. Timothy was in Paul's company for much of his Ephesian ministry (cf. Acts 19:22; 2 Cor 1:1) and may have become acquainted with Philemon there. The mention of Timothy's name in no way suggests he is a joint author of the letter (so most exegetes), much less because Paul's request of Philemon is of general Christian interest (as Jang, *Philemonbrief,* 22, among others, argues; von Soden, 73, rightly claims that the addition of Timothy's name does not thereby give the writing an official character) or as a means of putting pressure on Philemon (see the discussion above).

Φιλήμονι τῷ ἀγαπητῷ καὶ συνεργῷ ἡμῶν. "To Philemon our dear friend and fellow-worker." Philemon (on the frequency of this name, see BAG, 859, and Lightfoot, 301, 302, for examples) whose name appears first is the real recipient of the letter (for a critique of Knox's view that Archippus is the person primarily addressed, see the Introduction 265). He is called "beloved" (*ἀγαπητός*), a term which Paul employs elsewhere to address the Christians at Rome (1:7) and the communities at Corinth (1 Cor 10:14; 15:58; 2 Cor 7:1; 12:19) and Philippi (Phil 2:12, 4:1; cf. 1 Thess 2:8). Here it has special significance: Philemon is precious to Paul and his colleague(s) (the Greek expression contains one definite article *τῷ*, "the," and one possessive pronoun *ἡμῶν*, "our," which apply to both nouns *ἀγαπητῷ*, "beloved," and *συνεργῷ*, "fellow-worker"): he belongs to a community of mutual love and has demonstrated his "love" (*ἀγάπη*) in the past (vv 5, 7). Paul now hopes that "for love's sake" (*διὰ τὴν ἀγάπην*, v 9) Philemon will grant his request so that Onesimus will be accepted as a "beloved brother" (*ἀδελφὸς ἀγαπητός*, v 16). The note of Christian love, struck in this opening address, echoes throughout the rest of the epistle (see below 276, etc.). Further, Philemon is called Paul's "fellow-worker" (*συνεργός*, see on Col 4:11). Ollrog, *Paulus,* 63–72, has recently suggested that *συνεργός* ("fellow-worker") was a general or comprehensive designation, perhaps including others such as *διάκονοι*, "ministers," for those who worked together with Paul as commissioned by God in the task of missionary preaching (Ollrog further suggests that the Pauline use of the term was distinctive, bound up with the particular nature of the proclamation of the gospel to Gentiles, *Paulus,* 67). The term in the first instance (cf. 1 Cor 3:4–9) describes the nature of the *ἔργον* (i.e. it is a joint work of proclaiming Christ) rather than the companionship, the persons with whom one worked. Whenever Paul wished to express his fellowship with his co-workers he noted this especially through additions such as "my" or "our" (as here at Phlm 1). Co-workers were not helpers of the apostle drawn in for his personal service. Rather, they were commissioned by God for the task of missionary preaching. Philemon, who seems to have owed his conversion to Paul, may have first met the apostle during the latter's ministry at Ephesus (see on v 19). Perhaps prior to his return to Colossae he had had a part in preaching the gospel of Christ here. At any rate, Paul regarded him as a valued colleague and dear friend.

2. Apphia, Archippus and the church that meets in Philemon's house (the *σου*, "your," is singular and refers back to Philemon) are also greeted by Paul. They are not named along with Philemon as recipients of the letter. The matter Paul is dealing with is a personal affair which concerns Philemon alone and the decision to be arrived at is not a concern of the entire community. The inclusion of other Christians' names in this salutation and the benedictions (vv 3, 25 where the plural "you," *ὑμῖν* and *ὑμῶν*, occurs) is due to the apostle's courtesy, but the body of the letter (vv 4–22) is addressed to an individual (for a critique of the prevailing view that Paul names others in the address since he wants them to know the contents of the letter and so put pressure on Onesimus' owner, see Introduction 267, 268). Apphia (*Ἀπφία*) was a peculiarly Phrygian name (see the examples cited by Lightfoot, 304–306, and MM, 73). Dibelius-Greeven, 111, cite an interesting grave inscription for an Apphia from Colossae: "Hermas in memory of Apphia his wife, daughter of Tryphon, a Colossian by birth." Apphia is called "sister" (*ἀδελφή*) and like Philemon was a Christian ("a *sister* in the faith," BAG, 15). Because her name immediately follows Philemon's it has been assumed from early times, probably correctly, that she was his wife (so Theodoret: "Paul . . . adds the name of the wife . . . to that of the husband," cited by Lohse, 190). As the person involved in the affairs of the household, she would wish to know about Onesimus, but the point of mentioning her in the greeting is one of courtesy; Paul's request is addressed to Philemon.

Archippus (*Ἄρχιππος*: see on Col 4:17) is mentioned next and called Paul's "fellow-soldier" (*συστρατιώτης*, see BAG, 795, and Bauernfeind, *TDNT* 7, 701–713). Paul does not speak of Christians generally as "soldiers," but instead reserves the term for himself and his co-workers (Pfitzner, *Paul,* 161; see also Ollrog, *Paulus,* 77) designating those who, like Epaphroditus (Phil 2:25), had played an important part in assisting him in his missionary labors, and had faithfully stood at his side through persecution and trial—perhaps even imprisonment. One cannot assert with Lohmeyer, 175, that the term denotes an appointed leader in the church holding a particular office. Archippus was a resident of Colossae, possibly a son of Philemon and Apphia (though we have no certain means of knowing), who was given a special admonition to fulfill the ministry (*διάκονια*) which he had received in the Lord (Col 4:17, see 259).

καὶ τῇ κατ' οἶκόν σου ἐκκλησίᾳ. "And the church that meets in your house." The list of persons greeted by the apostle concludes with the mention of the community that assembles in Philemon's house (the singular pronoun *σου*, "your," makes it clear Philemon is the real recipient of the letter; against Knox, *Philemon,* 54, see 266). Regarding house-churches see on Colossians 4:15 and note the literature cited there.

3. *Χάρις ὑμῖν καὶ εἰρήνη κτλ.* "Grace to you and peace, etc." On the opening epistolary greetings of Paul's letters see Colossians 1:2. Here the greeting (or benediction or blessing, as it is sometimes called) contains the additional words "and [from] the Lord Jesus Christ" (*καὶ [ἀπὸ] κυρίου Ἰησοῦ Χριστοῦ*) and this longer form is the more usual one. Paul's greeting indicates a deep prayerful concern for Philemon, Apphia, Archippus and the church that meets in Philemon's house, that they may understand and appreciate more fully the grace of God in which they stand and the relationship of peace that God has established with them in his Son, Jesus Christ.

Explanation

Paul commences his letter to Philemon in the usual way. After mentioning his own name as sender he includes that of Timothy who has been in his company for much of his Ephesian ministry and may have become acquainted with Philemon there. The latter, Paul's dear friend and fellow-worker, is the specific recipient of the epistle (vv 4 etc.). Although Apphia, Archippus and the church that meets in Philemon's house are included in Paul's greeting (cf. v 25), this is due to his courtesy but the body of the letter (vv 4–22 are in the singular) is addressed to one person, Philemon.

Paul's greeting indicates a deep prayerful concern for Philemon and his friends that they may understand and appreciate more fully the grace of God in which they stand and the relationship of peace that God has established with them.

Thanksgiving and Intercession for Philemon (4–7)

Bibliography

In addition to the bibliography to Colossians 1:3–8 note also: **Suhl, A.** *Kairos* 15 (1973) 267–79. **Wiles, G. P.** *Prayers,* 215–25. **Zmijewski, J.** "Beobachtungen zur Struktur des Philemonbriefes." *BibLeb* 15 (1974) 273–96.

Translation

[4] I always thank my God when I mention you in my prayers, [5] because I hear of your love for all the saints and your faith in the Lord Jesus. [6] I pray that your generosity, which arises from your faith, may lead you effectively into a deeper understanding and experience of every blessing which belongs to us[a] as fellow-members in the body of Christ. [7] For I have derived much joy and comfort from your love, because the hearts of the saints have been refreshed by you, my brother.

Note

[a] The phrase *ἐν ἡμῖν* ("among us") is not as well supported in the manuscript tradition (A C D K ψ etc.) as *ἐν ὑμῖν* ("among you") which is read by the Textus Receptus and other important manuscripts (P^{61} ℵ G P 33 etc.). However, the former is preferred since it is more expressive, binding Paul to the addressee, and it is more likely that copyists would have changed *ἡμῖν* ("us") to *ὑμῖν* ("you") to bring it into line with the other second person pronouns in the paragraph.

Form/Structure/Setting

The thanksgiving passage of the letter to Philemon, vv 4–6, as the second main section of the Pauline letter form (see Doty, *Letters,* 27–33, and on Col 1:3–8), is the shortest of all in the Pauline corpus. It comprises a mere forty-seven words and is approximately one seventh of the letter. This thanksgiving paragraph is short, not only because Philemon is the briefest of all the Pauline letters, but also since it is formally and functionally more closely related (as noted above, the thanksgiving passages in the papyrus letters are briefer than those of Paul) to the ordinary private and personal letters of the time—related in a way that the other letters in the Pauline corpus, addressed either to communities or groups of communities, are not.

Of the two basic types of structure noted in Paul's thanksgiving paragraphs (see 8, 9) the letter to Philemon, as in the companion letter to the Colossians, contains an introductory thanksgiving of the first type. It is, however, simpler in form than the other examples of this category having no pronominal phrase (item 4; such as *ὑπέρ σου,* "for you"), while there is only one causal participial clause (*ἀκούων σου τὴν ἀγάπην κτλ.,* "hearing of your love," etc.) and but one object of intercessory prayer (v 6). The basic structure of the passage is as follows: (1) the verb of thanksgiving (εὐχαριστῶ, "I give thanks," v 4), then (2) the personal object (τῷ θεῷ μου, "to my God," v 4) indicating the one who is thanked, (3) a temporal adverb (πάντοτε, "always," v 4) denoting the frequency with which thanksgiving is offered, (4) the pronominal phrase is omitted though its place is taken by means of the σου, "you," in (5) the temporal participial clause with its temporal adverbial phrase (μνείαν σου ποιούμενος ἐπὶ τῶν προσευχῶν, "when I remember you in my prayers," v 4)—an expression which explains the significance of the preceding adverb πάντοτε ("always"). A causal participial clause (6) ἀκούων σου τὴν ἀγάπην κτλ. ("for I hear of your love," etc., v 5) gives the reason which motivates Paul's prayer of thanksgiving, while the final feature of the section (7) is the ὅπως-clause of v 6 which spells out Paul's petition for Philemon and which is paraphrased as follows: "(I pray) that your generosity, which arises from your faith, may lead you effectively into a deeper understanding and experience of every blessing which belongs to us as fellow-members in the body of Christ" (for the detailed exegesis see below).

Most commentators treat the passage under review as extending from verses 4 to 7 (e.g. Dibelius-Greeven, 101, Vincent, 177, Friedrich, 192, Carson, 105, Moule, 140, and Lohse, 192). Although this division may be followed for the sake of convenience, it needs to be noted that the thanksgiving structure extends from verses 4 to 6, reaching its climax in the ὅπως-clause of verse 6. Verse 7, which refers once more to the love that Philemon has shown toward the saints, is a smooth and effective transition from the thanksgiving paragraph to the main purpose of the letter, a purpose which Paul promptly sets forth in verse 8 (so Schubert, *Form*, 5, Lohse, 192. Lohmeyer, 192, rightly observed that the thanksgiving period concluded at the end of v 6: "With these words the thanksgiving, in a strict sense, ends"; also correctly Suhl, *Kairos* 15 [1973] 271). Verse 7 is not a report of Paul's prayers for Philemon but is rather a statement telling the recipient why he had been refreshed and comforted (the attempt of Sanders, *JBL* 81 [1962] 358, to show that v 7, a "joygiving," was equivalent to a concluding thanksgiving which ended the period, fails as it appears to be straining the evidence unduly in an effort to fit the thanksgiving paragraphs into a liturgical mold).

This whole passage prepares the ground for the request that is to follow, a point that may be discerned not only in its general emphasis, but also in the repetition of specific words from the thanksgiving throughout the rest of the letter (Wiles, *Prayers*, 219). As Knox (*Philemon*, 19) has aptly remarked: "It is the overture in which each of the themes, to be later heard in a different, perhaps more specific, context, is given an anticipatory hearing." Terms (or their cognates) such as prayer (προσευχή, v 4, cf. v 22), love (ἀγάπη, v 5, cf. v 9), fellowship (κοινωνιά, v 6, cf. v 17), good (ἀγαθός, v 6, cf. v 14), heart (σπλάγχνα, v 7, cf. vv 12, 20), refresh (ἀναπαύω, v 7, cf. v 20) and brother (ἀδελφέ, v 7, cf. v 20) reappear in the body of the letter. The apostle had celebrated the generous character of the slave owner's relationships with his fellow-Christians. Paul too had been encouraged by this love and he now has a favor to ask. So he leads on to the request about Onesimus—the subject which prompted the writing of the letter.

Comment

4. εὐχαριστῶ τῷ θεῷ μου πάντοτε μνείαν σου ποιούμενος ἐπὶ τῶν προσευχῶν μου. "I always thank my God when I mention you in my prayers." Once again Paul begins a letter by mentioning that he gives thanks to God for the recipient (see on Col 1:3), in this case Philemon. Here, however, the singular εὐχαριστῶ ("I give thanks") is used. Although Timothy's name is joined with Paul's in the greeting, only the latter is the subject of this prinicpal verb. This is in contrast to the thanksgiving of the companion letter to the Colossians where Timothy is linked with the apostle in the giving of thanks (Col 1:3; though note the singular, referring to Paul alone, at Rom 1:8; 1 Cor 1:3; Phil 1:3; cf. Eph 1; 15, 16; 1 Tim 1:12; 2 Tim 1:3). Thanksgiving to God is uppermost in the apostle's mind as be begins to pen this letter. He does not congratulate Philemon but addresses his word of praise "to my God" (τῷ θεῷ μου). For Paul this is no vague or casual reference to whatever gods there might be. It is to the one true God that he offers his thanksgiving and stressing the consciousness of a personal relation to him he adds the pronoun "my" (μου). This phrase, with one exception, was used by the apostle in prayers or prayer reports (Rom 1:8; possibly 1 Cor 1:4; Phil 1:3, 4:19 and Phlm 4. 2 Cor 12:21 is not in a prayer context) and he has probably drawn from the wells of the Psalter for it (LXX Pss 3:8; 5:3; 7:2, 4, 7; 12:4; 17:3; 21:2, etc.; see Lohse, 192. Harder, *Paulus*, 67, 68, notes that in the pagan world of Paul's day it was the practice to increase the number of names and epithets in one's address to the gods. This sprang from uncertainty and scepticism. But Paul, like the Psalter, showed restraint using relatively few names—on occasion even Jews multiplied titles in their address to God: so 2 Macc 1:23–29). The person thanked for Philemon's progress is the God of the psalmists, known to Paul through Jesus Christ as "Father."

"Always" (πάντοτε) is attached to the main verb but does not designate unceasing thanksgiving (see on Col 1:3). Instead it is modified and explained by the phrase immediately following, "whenever I mention you in my prayers" (μνείαν σου ποιούμενος ἐπὶ τῶν προσευχῶν μου). When Paul states he gave thanks "continually" he means that he did not forget Philemon in his regular prayers—prayers which were centered in petitions though other types were no doubt included.

5. ἀκούων σου τὴν ἀγάπην κτλ. "Because I hear of your love . . . ." Paul's second participial clause is a causal one giving the ground or basis for his thanks to God. He has received a good report about Philemon's conduct and this news causes him to give thanks to God. (C. Spicq, *Agape in the New Testament* Vol. 2 Tr. M. A. McNamara and M. H. Richter. [St. Louis: Herder, 1965] 303, notes that the present participle ἀκούων, "hearing," expresses continuity and duration: "It suggests that St. Paul had received up-to-date information about Philemon from more than one source, or even that he was getting regular reports about him"; the use of this verb ἀκούω, "hear," does not mean that Philemon was unknown to Paul as Dibelius-Greeven, 103, implies and Knox, *Philemon*, 45, asserts.) Information probably came

from Epaphras (Col 1:7, 8; 4:12), and possibly from Onesimus, about Philemon's good standing in the Christian faith.

The apostle heard about Philemon's "love" (ἀγάπη) and "faith" (πίστις). But how are these words to be interpreted, and what are the respective objects of these two Christian graces? Commentators have been divided, giving answers along the following lines:

(1) πίστις is taken to mean "faithfulness" or "reliability" (cf. 3 John 5), so that both "love" and "faithfulness" are directed toward both the Lord Jesus and all God's people. Accordingly the NEB translates: "for I hear of your love and faith towards the Lord Jesus and towards all God's people" (see also Schlatter, 312, Vincent, 178, and Bruce, *Paul*, 393).

(2) Some take "love" and "faith" as being intimately linked (and render them as "piety" or "godliness") in an attitude which is shown to the Lord on the one hand and God's people on the other (Dibelius-Greeven, 103, Kramer, *Christ*, 47; cf. Spicq, *Agape* 2, 303, 304, and Carson, 105, 106, who are followed by K. Sullivan, "Epignosis in the Epistles of St. Paul," *Studiorum Paulinorum Congressus Internationalis Catholicus.* Vol. 2 [Rome: Pontifical Biblical Institute, 1963] 409). Advocates of this interpretation point out that love toward the Lord Jesus is closely linked with faith, because it is from faith that love grows and by faith love is nourished. Also the love which is shown to the brethren is love in the context of faith. The change of preposition from πρός ("to") to εἰς ("to") is then said to stress a difference in the relationships: to the Lord as object on the one hand, and to fellow-believers in a like relationship on the other (however, among advocates of this view there is no general agreement about the significance of the distinction, and in our judgment it is better to regard the change as simply a stylistic variation).

(3) A third interpretation sees in verse 5 an example of chiasmus, an *a b b a* pattern, in which Philemon's love is directed toward all God's people and his faith is in the Lord Jesus (among grammarians this is favored by BDF, para. 477[2], and Robertson, *Grammar*, 1200; commentators such as Lightfoot, 332, 333, Lohmeyer, 177, apparently Moule, 141, Friedrich, 192, Müller, 176, Lohse, 193, and Stuhlmacher, 32, 33, also follow this line; cf. Stauffer, *TDNT* i, 50, Greeven, *Gebet*, 177, Bultmann, *TDNT* 6, 212, and J. Jeremias, "Chiasmus in den Paulusbriefen," *ZNW* 49 [1958] 146). There are good reasons for taking the verse in this way: first, chiasmus is common enough in the NT (Jeremias, *ZNW* 49 [1958] 146, sees Semitic influences at work, cf. Ps 1:6). Second, here the usual order of graces for which the apostle gave thanks is reversed. Paul normally placed "faith" before "love." This reversal can be explained in terms of the situation which called forth the letter (although there is some textual support [D 69 1739 pesh.] for placing πίστις, "faith," before ἀγάπη, "love," this change of early scribes was made in the interests of uniformity, cf. Lohmeyer, 177). At the time of writing the apostle's attention was focused on Philemon's love. The word (i.e. ἀγάπη) appears again in verses 7 and 9, and Paul's request in connection with Onesimus is made on the basis of that Christian love. Paul was setting down his thoughts in the sequence in which they occurred to him. Having mentioned Philemon's love he refers to his faith. This leads on to the sphere of the faith (ἣν ἔχεις, "which you have," emphasizes that the faith is shown by one who is in the

Lord Jesus) which in turn directs one's thoughts to the range and comprehensiveness of the love, i.e. it has been shown in the past to all God's people. Finally, this interpretation is consistent with the introductory thanksgiving of the companion letter to the Colossian Christians: "because we have heard of your faith in Christ Jesus and of the love which you show to all God's people" (1:4). The variation in order can be adequately accounted for along the lines suggested, while the change in prepositions, from πρός to εἰς (each means "to") is to be seen as stylistic (cf. Moule, *Idiom Book,* 68, Turner, *Syntax,* 256, and Lohse, 193).

6. Paul's thanksgiving leads directly on to his petition—an intercession concerning Philemon's generosity. Although this verse contains no finite verb of petitionary prayer the ὅπως ("that") clause which states the content of the intercession (ὅπως, "that," is a stylistic equivalent of ἵνα, "that," which also begins the clause specifying the content of Paul's intercession at Eph 1:17; Phil 1:9; Col 1:9 [see 20]; 2 Thess 1:11; cf. εἰς τό, "that," at 1 Thess 3:10) is dependent on μνείαν σου ποιούμενος, the meaning of which is not something general such as "when I remember you," but is "when I make mention of you," i.e. "when I intercede for you" (this phrase and its syntactical equivalents προσευχόμενοι, "praying," Col 1:3, and δεήσιν ποιούμενος, "making request," Phil 1:4, occur in each of those thanksgiving paragraphs where intercessory prayer is mentioned, i.e. Schubert's type Ia and mixed types but not in the paragraphs that speak of thanksgiving alone, e.g. 1 Cor 1:4–9; 2 Thess 2:13, 14: for a structural and exegetical examination see his *Form,* 12, 54, 55, Wiles, *Prayers,* 218–25, and O'Brien, *Introductory Thanksgivings,* 7, 8, 54, 55. Lohse's failure to see this important structural point leads to his erroneous statement that v 6 does not depend on "when I remember" [μνείαν ποιούμενος], 193). However, this temporal participial clause is itself dependent on the principal verb "I give thanks" (εὐχαριστῶ). Grammatically and logically the intercessory prayer springs out of the prayer of thanksgiving (so Wiles, *Prayers,* 218, comments: "The intercessory prayer-report in this letter is interwoven more closely than usual within the thanksgiving period, both through syntax and through content"). It is as if Paul could not give thanks for the love and faith of his colleague Philemon without making intercession for him.

But the exact meaning of verse 6 is difficult to determine (for a recent discussion see G. Panikulam, *Koinōnia in the New Testament. A Dynamic Expression of Christian Life* [AnBib 85 Rome: Biblical Institute, 1979] 86–90). This is because there are several exegetical issues within the brief intercessory prayer: first, what is the meaning of ἡ κοινωνία τῆς πίστεώς σου? The following are some of the suggestions that have been made: *(a)* "the kindly deeds of charity which spring from your faith" (Lightfoot, 333, taking κοινωνία as especially referring to "contributions," "almsgiving"); *(b)* "the communication (to others) of your faith" (Vincent, 179); *(c)* "your fellowship with other Christians created by faith" (Lohmeyer, 178, who considers πίστεως, "of faith," is a genitive of origin; cf. E. W. Koch, "A Cameo of Koinonia. The Letter to Philemon," *Int* 17 [1963] 184); *(d)* "communion (with Christ) by faith"—i.e. faith-communion with Christ (Dibelius-Greeven, 103, H. Seesemann, *Der Begriff* KOINΩNIA *im Neuen Testament* [BZNW 14 Giessen: Töpelmann, 1933]

79–83, Hauck, *TDNT* 3, 805, Lohse, 193, 194, Stuhlmacher, 33, Jang, *Philemonbrief*, 27, 28, and Gayer, *Stellung*, 249); *(e)* "the faith in which you participate," i.e. your share in the faith; and *(f)* "the participation of other Christians in your faith" (J. Y. Campbell, *Three New Testament Studies* [Leiden: Brill, 1965] 18). Second, how is εἰς Χριστόν (lit. "to Christ") to be understood? Third, is it to be connected with ἐνεργής ("effective"), with παντὸς ἀγαθοῦ ("every good thing") or with ἐν ἐπιγνώσει ("with knowledge")? Finally, how is ἐν ἐπιγνώσει ("with knowledge") to be interpreted, and who is to attain to the *knowledge* in question—Philemon himself or those who notice and profit from his "fellowship of faith"?

Moule (142, 143), having outlined some of the difficulties of the verse and the attempts made at its solution, concluded with a touch of humor: "Unless and until further ἐπίγνωσις [knowledge] is given to Christian interpreters, the answers to these questions must remain obscure" (because of the difficulties A. R. George, *Communion with God in the New Testament* [London: Epworth, 1953] 183, does not commit himself to any alternative). Therefore the following suggestions are tentative: κοινωνία is understood in an active sense, not simply of almsgiving, although this is obviously covered, but in a wider sense referring to "generosity" or "liberality" (in our judgment κοινωνία at Phil 1:5 means the same thing: see the discussion in my *Introductory Thanksgivings*, 23–25; Wiles, *Prayers*, 223, adds the further point that κοινωνία, "generosity," prefigures the business language of v 17, see below 298, 299). τῆς πίστεως is treated as a genitive of origin indicating the source from which the kindness comes: "I pray that your generosity which springs from your faith (i.e. in the Lord Jesus) . . ." πίστις ("faith") has the same meaning as in verse 5, although the phrase in verse 6 throws the emphasis on the practical expression of the faith rather than on the faith itself or its object. According to this view ἐνεργής is to be understood as "effective" rather than "active," for the liberality of Philemon, according to Paul's statements in verses 5 and 7, had already been "active." The intercessory request of the apostle was that Philemon's liberality (and not that of others) might lead him effectively (that is, Paul wished Philemon's liberality to be especially effective in the case of Onesimus; on the nature of Paul's request see on v 17) into a deeper understanding (ἐν ἐπιγνώσει: ἐν marks the sphere in which something takes place, cf. 2 Cor 1:6; Col 1:29; note Vincent, 180) of all the blessings that belonged to him in Christ (ἐνεργὴς γένηται, lit. "may become effective," is to be taken with ἐν ἐπιγνώσει παντὸς ἀγαθοῦ, lit. "in a knowledge of every good thing"). πᾶν ἀγαθόν is understood to refer to "every blessing" which belongs to Philemon as a Christian (Lohmeyer, 179, maintained that this expression is a frequent designation for the will of God: so in Paul at Rom 2:10; 5:7; 7:13, 19; 9:11; 12:2, 9, 21; 13:3; 14:16; 15:2; Gal 6:10; 1 Thess 5:15. He drew a parallel between the function of the law for a Jew and the place of faith here for the Christian. Both are to be "active" in the believer, so that he may find out and do God's will [πᾶν ἀγαθόν]; however, it is doubtful whether many of Lohmeyer's references are to the will of God at all; also his case stands too heavily on a particular interpretation of εἰς Χριστόν ["into Christ"] which is questionable; see Moule, 143). In the present context ἐπίγνωσις conveys both the ideas of understanding and experience. The apostle's prayer was not simply that Philemon might understand or appreciate the treasures that belonged to him, but that he might also experience them. It is necessary to use two English words to translate this one Greek word, and therefore we render it by "understanding and experience" (cf. Bruce's rendering, "the experience and appreciation of every blessing," *Paul,* 393).

These Christian blessings of which the apostle has spoken do not belong to Philemon alone. They are for all who are incorporated "into Christ" (*εἰς Χριστόν*) and include Paul himself. There is considerable difference of opinion as to the meaning of this phrase. Lohmeyer (179), Wickert (*ZNW* 52 [1961] 230) and Suhl (*Kairos* 15 [1973] 271) treat it as an eschatological thrust in the passage, the latter two maintaining it has special reference to Christ as the final Judge. Others such as Moule (142, 143) consider the phrase means "bringing us into (closer) relation to Christ," while Lightfoot understands the expression as having reference to Christ as the goal (he considers the words ought to be connected with the main statement of the sentence, *ἐνεργὴς γένηται κτλ.* and paraphrases the whole: "as thou attainest to the perfect knowledge of every good thing bestowed upon us by God, looking unto and striving after Christ," 332, 334). Lohse renders the words as "for the glory of Christ"; their purpose is "to emphasize in conclusion that all active working of the faith—a faith which acts according to the knowledge of the good which God has bestowed on us—should be for the glory of Christ" (194, 195; cf. Vincent, 181, who regards the expression as meaning "unto Christ's glory," i.e. the advancement of his cause).

According to our suggestion the phrase *εἰς Χριστόν* refers to incorporation and is almost equivalent to *ἐν Χριστῷ* ("in Christ"; it is perhaps not without significance that where the person of Jesus is referred to in v 5 *Κύριον Ἰησοῦν*, "Lord Jesus," is used while the corporate reference in v 6 is to *εἰς Χριστόν*, "in Christ," which is how Kramer, *Christ,* 140, translates it; cf. also Percy, *Probleme,* 125). One can understand why Paul employed this expression, for in the *ὅπως* ("that") clause of verse 6 he had already used the preposition *ἐν* ("in") twice before penning the phrase in question. *ἐν* *Χριστῷ* ("*in* Christ") following hard upon *ἐν ἡμῖν* ("in us," "among us") would sound harsh. So the synonymous phrase *εἰς Χριστόν* ("in[to] Christ") has been chosen. Paul's intercessory prayer may thus be paraphrased: "I pray that your generosity, which arises from your faith, may lead you effectively into a deeper understanding and experience of every blessing which belongs to us as fellow-members in the body of Christ."

7. The apostle no longer reports his intercessory prayer which was offered to God but uses the language of direct address ("brother," *ἀδελφέ*) as he tells Philemon why he had been refreshed and comforted. This verse which refers once more to the love that Philemon has shown toward the saints is a smooth and effective transition from the thanksgiving paragraph to the main purpose of the letter, a purpose which Paul promptly sets forth in verse 8. In this simple transition important ideas from both the thanksgiving and the body of the letter are mentioned (or anticipated), e.g. "love" (vv 5, 9), "comfort" (cf. vv 9, 10), "heart" (vv 12, 20), "saints" (v 5), "refreshed" (v 20), and "brother" (v 20).

χαρὰν γὰρ πολλὴν ἔσχον καὶ παράκλησιν ἐπὶ τῇ ἀγάπῃ σου. "For I have derived much joy and comfort from your love." "For" (γάρ) gives the ground for Paul's thanksgiving (vv 4, 5) as he mentions again Philemon's love (cf. v 5) concretely demonstrated to the Colossian Christians. The apostle identifies himself with these fellow-believers, even with those he had not previously met (cf. Col 2:2), for he states that "joy and comfort" given to them is also given to him (Rom 12:9–13; 2 Cor 11:29; Caird, 220; Philemon's deeds of love have been a rich source of [ἐπί with the dative means "on account of," "from," see BAG, 287] joy and comfort to Paul, cf. Lohse, 195). He had written to the Corinthians in a similar vein at the joy (2 Cor 7:4) and comfort (7:7) he had experienced (cf. 7:13) in the context of his pastoral cares for this difficult congregation (on χαρά, "joy," bound up with his work as an apostle see Conzelmann, *TDNT* 9, 369, 370; on παράκλησις, "comfort," note Schmitz, *TDNT* 5, 793–99).

ὅτι τὰ σπλάγχνα τῶν ἁγίων ἀναπέπαυται διὰ σοῦ, ἀδελφέ. "Because the hearts of the saints have been refreshed by you, brother." These words elucidate or explain (ὅτι, "because") more particularly the expression "on account of your love" (Abbott, 181, and von Soden, 74). Some commentators (e.g. Ernst, 131) suggest that here Paul calls to mind the general distinguishing marks of Philemon's behavior as the presupposition for making his request. Others, however, consider he has in mind some particular instance of the kindness for which Philemon was distinguished. So Caird (220) says the perfect tense of "refreshed" (ἀναπέπαυται) seems to "point to some conspicuous act of generosity rather than to continual kindness" (see also Lohse, 195, and Scott, 105, who conjecture that the occasion for this may have been the earthquake of A.D. 60). But although this statement may indicate Paul has learned of one particular deed by which Philemon has helped the congregation we cannot be sure (the perfect tense may denote Philemon's regular acts by which the believers were refreshed, or the lasting effects of a signal instance). Either way the apostle does not detail Philemon's deed(s) of love. He simply spells out the effects: "the hearts of the saints have been refreshed." The expression τὰ σπλάγχνα, which frequently designates "pity," "sympathy" or "tender mercies," that is, an affection directed toward others (a meaning it carries at Col 3:12, see 198, 199), in its three occurrences within the letter to Philemon (cf. vv 12, 20) evidently means "inmost feelings," "very self" (so Moule, 144). It designates "the total personality at the deepest level. It . . . remains a very strong and forceful term which occurs only when Paul is speaking directly and personally . . . [it] is . . . used for the whole person which in the depths of its emotional life has experienced refreshment through consolation and love" (Köster, *TDNT* 7, 555). And the frequent occurrence of the term in this short letter shows the apostle's deep personal interest in the matter. Because Philemon had refreshed the hearts of other Christians, the apostle is confident he will not refuse his request in connection with Onesimus, described as "my heart" (τὰ ἐμὰ σπλάγχνα): so he encourages Philemon, "refresh my heart in Christ" (ἀνάπαυσόν μου τὰ σπλάγχνα ἐν Χριστῷ, v 20). ἀναπαύω (to "cause to rest," "give [someone] rest," "refresh"; in the passive of Titus' spirit being set at rest, 2 Cor 7:13; see BAG, 58, 59, Bauernfeind, *TDNT* 1, 350, and Hensel and Brown, *NIDNTT* 3, 254–58) was used *(a)* of taking one's rest, that is, in a normal bodily sense (Mark 14:41; Matt 26:45; in Attic

Greek prose it was almost a technical expression for the resting of soldiers); or *(b)* of calming someone who has become disturbed, or refreshing by giving pleasure, comfort or compensation (1 Cor 16:18; Phlm 7, 20). This might occur through Christian love, fellowship or action, or by means of news about these (see Hensel and Brown, *NIDNTT* 3, 256). Although the term frequently spoke of a temporary relief (so Lightfoot, 334, absolutely, but note Vincent's qualifications, 181) the refreshment promised by Christ to the weary (Matt 11: 28, 29) was not temporary, and the word was also used of the rest of the blessed dead (Rev 14:13).

Explanation

Although the epistle to Philemon is the briefest of all his letters Paul begins it in his customary way by reporting his thanksgiving to God for the love and faith of his reader. With slight variations the usual form of the thanksgiving paragraph has been followed here. Verses 4 to 7 are designed to prepare the way for the specific matter with which the letter is primarily concerned, namely, the request concerning Onesimus. The general emphasis of the passage, its tone and the specific terms which anticipate later references, serve this function of preparing for the central issue of the letter.

Giving thanks to God is uppermost in Paul's mind as he begins the passage. He has received good reports about Philemon's love actively demonstrated to all God's people, a love that arose out of his faith in the Lord Jesus. Paul's thanksgiving leads directly on to his petition—an intercession concerning Philemon's generosity. It is that his friend's liberality might lead him effectively into a deeper understanding of all the blessings that belong to him in Christ. These Christian blessings do not belong to Philemon alone. They are for all who are incorporated "into Christ" and include Paul himself.

At verse 7 he no longer reports his intercessory prayer which was offered to God but uses the language of direct address as he tells Philemon why he had been refreshed and comforted. The latter's love had been concretely shown to the Colossian Christians, and Paul can identify with these fellow-believers (some of whom he had not met; cf. Col 2:2) for he states that "joy and comfort" given to them is also received by him.

Paul's Plea for Onesimus (8–20)

Bibliography

Bjerkelund, C. J. *Parakalô,* 118–24. **Bruce, F. F.** *Paul,* 393–406. **Gayer, R.** *Stellung,* 223–66. **Goodenough, E. R.** *HTR* 22 (1929) 181–83. **Greeven, H.** *TLZ* 79 (1954) 373–78. **Knox, J.** *Philemon.* **Merk, O.** *Handeln,* 225–29. **Schütz, J. H.** *Paul,* 221–24. **Schweizer, E.** "Zum Sklavenproblem im Neuen Testament." *EvTh* 32 (1972) 502–506. **Suhl, A.** *Kairos* 15 (1973) 272–74. **Westermann, W. L.** *The Slave Systems of Greek and Roman Antiquity.* Philadelphia: American Philosophical Society, 1955, 102–109. **Wickert, U.** *ZNW* 52 (1961) 230–38. **Zmijewski, J.** *BibLeb* 15 (1974) 277–94.

Translation

8 *Therefore, although I am bold enough in Christ to command you to do what is fitting,* 9 *yet for love's sake I prefer to appeal to you. Although I am none other than Paul, an ambassador of Christ Jesus and now also his prisoner,* 10 *I appeal to you for my child Onesimus, whom I begot while in prison.* 11 *Previously he was useless to you, but now he has become useful both to you and to me.* 12 *I am sending him*[a]*—who is my very heart—back to you.* 13 *Indeed I would have liked to keep him with me so that he could take your place in helping me during my imprisonment for the gospel.* 14 *But I would not do anything without your consent, so that any favor you do will be spontaneous and not forced.* 15 *Perhaps for this reason he was separated from you for a little while so that you might have him back forever,* 16 *no longer as a slave, but as one who is much more than a slave, as a beloved brother, especially to me, but how much more to you, both in the flesh and in the Lord.*

17 *So then, if you consider me your partner, welcome him as you would me.* 18 *If he has wronged you or owes you anything, charge that to my account.* 19 *I Paul am writing this with my own hand. I will pay it—not to mention that you owe me your very self besides.* 20 *Yes, brother, I do wish that I may have some benefit from you in the Lord; refresh my heart in Christ.*

Note

[a] Although the general sense of the verse is clear the manuscript tradition has no uniform reading. That of א* A 33 best explains the origin of the other readings. προσλαβοῦ ("receive," from v 17) was introduced by copyists to smooth out the syntax, as also was the addition of συ ("you"). See Metzger, *Textual Commentary,* 655, 656, and Lohse, 201; see below on the apparently redundant αὐτόν ("him").

Form/Structure/Setting

With the opening words of verse 8, "Therefore . . ." (διό . . .), Paul commences the body of his letter to Philemon, the intercession for Onesimus, and this is a carefully structured paragraph extending from verses 8 to 20. Paul intercedes for Philemon's runaway slave, Onesimus, addressing Philemon in terms of Christian love and faith. He weighs his words carefully and structures the main part of the letter so that the addressee is gradually led to the actual request (Lohse, 197, 198).

First, Paul gives a brief description of his situation (vv 8–12). The opening sentence begins with the conjunction *διό* ("therefore") and a concessive participial clause *πολλὴν ἐν Χριστῷ παρρησίαν ἔχων ἐπιτάσσειν σοι* . . . ("although I am bold enough in Christ to command you . . ."). The principal clause which immediately follows, *διὰ τὴν ἀγάπην μᾶλλον παρακαλῶ* ("yet for love's sake I prefer to appeal to you"), stands in an adversative relation to the preceding (*μᾶλλον*, "yet," "rather"). A second participial clause *τοιοῦτος ὢν* . . . (which may be paraphrased as "although I am the sort of person . . ."), dependent on the main clause, names the subject *Παῦλος* ("Paul") and characterizes him as a *πρεσβύτης* ("ambassador") who is now also a *δέσμιος Χριστοῦ Ἰησοῦ* ("a prisoner of Christ Jesus"). Behind Paul's request stands one who is both an ambassador and a slave of Christ Jesus. In verse 10 the same finite verb *παρακαλῶ* ("I appeal") is repeated as Paul makes his request of the addressee (*σε*, "you"). Before he mentions the name of the runaway slave, he speaks of him as his child whom he has begotten in prison (v 10) and this stresses how dear and beloved he is to him. Just as Paul has previously (v 9) described himself by means of a contrasting statement, so here too in verse 11 he makes an antithetical assertion about Onesimus, playing on the words *ἄχρηστον—εὔχρηστον* ("useless"—"useful"); *τόν ποτέ σοι ἄχρηστον νυνὶ δὲ[καὶ] σοὶ καὶ ἐμοὶ εὔχρηστον* ("Previously he was useless to you, but now he has become useful both to you and to me"). By means of the pronouns in the dative case (*σοί, σοί, ἐμοί*, "you," "you," and "me") Paul underscores the personal relationships between Onesimus and Philemon on the one hand, and Onesimus and himself on the other. Verse 12 contains a relative clause *ὃν ἀνέπεμψά σοι* ("whom I am sending back to you"), while the noun clause attached to it *αὐτόν, τουτ' ἔστιν τὰ ἐμὰ σπλάγχνα* ("him, who is my very heart") spells out the close relationship—even identification—between Paul and the runaway slave.

In the second section (vv 13, 14) Paul looks back to the time when Onesimus came to him seeking refuge. Verse 13 commences with a relative pronoun *ὃν* ("whom," a further reference to Onesimus), and contains a finite verb of wishing, *ἐβουλόμην* ("I would have liked") to which an infinitive is attached (*κατέχειν*, "to retain"). A purpose *ἵνα* clause is dependent on the preceding. In verse 14 the construction is parallel though antithetical: *χωρὶς δὲ τῆς σῆς γνώμης* ("but without your consent"), which begins the clause, sets the contrast with what has gone before. Again a finite verb of wishing is used, *ἠθέλησα* ("I wanted," an aorist instead of an imperfect, cf. *ἐβουλόμην*, "I would have liked"), with an infinitive attached (*ποιῆσαι*, "to do"). Verse 14 also concludes with a purpose *ἵνα* clause that is dependent on the preceding, and within this telic construction a sharp antithesis is presented *μὴ ὡς κατὰ ἀνάγκην* . . . *ἀλλὰ κατὰ ἑκούσιον* ("not from compulsion . . . but from your own free will").

Verses 15 and 16 (which Zmijewski, *BibLeb* 15 [1974] 289, regards as a unity) are linked with the preceding by means of *γάρ* ("for") as Paul spells out an additional reason for his not detaining Onesimus. The sentence contains a sharp contrast between *πρὸς ὥραν* ("for a little while") of the principal clause and the *αἰώνιον* ("for ever") of the subordinate *ἵνα* clause, a contrast which finds its correspondence in the two verbs of these clauses, *χωρίζω* (to "separate") and *ἀπέχω* (to "have back"). God's activity is implied in the passive *ἐχωρίσθη* ("he was separated from") and therefore the purpose *ἵνα* clause which follows signifies the divine intention. Verse 16 contains a long addition which relates back to *αὐτόν* ("him," i.e. Onesimus), the object of the final verb *ἀπέχῃς* ("[that] you may have *him* back") and here Onesimus is described. For the first time it is stated that he is a slave; but this is immediately qualified by means of an antithesis: he is more than a slave (*οὐκέτι ὡς δοῦλον ἀλλὰ ὑπὲρ δοῦλον*). What this "more" signifies is expressed in the following appositional phrase which gives to him his Christian significance: he is *ἀδελφὸν ἀγαπητόν* ("a beloved brother"), and as such is referred to in the same way as Philemon himself (vv 7, 20). The latter part of the verse seeks to bring before Philemon the consequences of this, and a superlative formulation *μάλιστα* (here as an elative meaning "especially") is still further accented by *πόσῳ δὲ μᾶλλον* (lit. "how much more"). There is thus a double comparison. Onesimus has been a beloved brother to Paul in the highest sense. Even more will he be a beloved brother to Philemon, both as a slave and as one bound to him "in the Lord." (On the structure of vv 15 and 16 note especially Zmijewski, *BibLeb* 15 [1974] 289, 290.)

Verses 17–20 conclude the body of the letter. After his carefully worded preliminaries Paul for the first time states the content of his request of Philemon, *προσλαβοῦ αὐτὸν ὡς ἐμέ* ("receive him as me," v 17). The *οὖν* ("therefore") of verse 17 indicates a return to the main theme of the letter. The opening sentence (v 17) contains an introductory conditional clause, *εἰ οὖν με ἔχεις κοινωνόν* ("so then, if you consider me your partner") which is then followed by a principal clause with its verb in the imperative mood, *προσλάβοῦ αὐτὸν ὡς ἐμέ* ("receive him as me"). Verse 18 is exactly parallel: it also begins with an introductory conditional clause, *εἰ δέ τι ἠδίκησέν σε ἢ ὀφείλει* ("if he has wronged you or owes you anything") and it is followed by the principal clause with its verb an imperative, *τοῦτο ἐμοὶ ἐλλόγα* ("charge that to my account"). The opening words of verse 19, *ἐγὼ Παῦλος ἔγραψα τῇ ἐμῇ χειρί, ἐγὼ ἀποτίσω* ("I Paul am writing this with my own hand. I will pay it") are a parenthesis, a signed IOU, as the apostle undertakes to make good any loss incurred by Onesimus. Verse 19*b* picks up the thought of verse 18, and by means of an elliptical construction, *ἵνα μὴ λέγω σοι* ("not to mention to you"), Paul reminds Philemon that he, the addressee, is indebted to the apostle. The words are chosen carefully: *προσοφείλεις* ("you owe [besides]") corresponds to *ὀφείλει* ("[if] he owes," v 18), while there is an interesting interplay of first and second person pronouns (v 18, *σε . . . ἐμοί*, "you . . . to me"; v 19, *ἐγώ . . . σοι . . . σεαυτόν μοι*, "I . . . to you . . . yourself to me"). The final verse of the long paragraph which is made up of two sentences, verse 20*a* and 20*b*, echoes themes previously mentioned: *ἀδελφέ* ("brother"), *ἀνάπαυσον . . . τὰ σπλάγχνα* ("refresh the heart"). The personal relationships between sender and recipient, Paul and Philemon, which stood in the foreground at the commencement of the body of the letter, are again prominent. The two sentences, in which the apostle states his earnest wish that Philemon might fulfill his heart's desire, close with parallel ἐν phrases: ἐν κυρίῳ ("in the Lord") and ἐν Χριστῷ ("in Christ").

Comment

At the conclusion of the introductory thanksgiving Paul begins the main part of his letter to Philemon (vv 8–20), his intercession for Onesimus. In a carefully structured paragraph (see the preceding section) Paul leads on to his actual request of Philemon.

8. The body of the letter commences with the particle "therefore" (διό: see BAG, 198; several consider that the links with the preceding are not particularly strong: so Lohmeyer, 183, Sanders, *JBL* 81 [1962] 355, Lohse, 198, Suhl, *Kairos* 15 [1973] 272, Stuhlmacher, 36, and Gayer, *Stellung*, 250; however the linguistic and structural ties are considerable [see the preceding section] while the reference to "love" in v 9, the basis of Paul's request, is bound up with the ground of his thanksgiving mentioned in v 5) as Paul by means of a concessive clause (so Moule, 144, and his *Idiom Book*, 102, cf. Turner, *Syntax*, 157) makes an unusual assertion: "For this reason, although I am bold enough in Christ to command you to do what is fitting (v 8), yet for love's sake I prefer to appeal to you . . ." (v 9) (διό, πολλὴν ἐν Χριστῷ παρρησίαν ἔχων ἐπιτάσσειν σοι τὸ ἀνῆκον κτλ.). The term παρρησία which literally means "all speech" was used originally in the sphere of politics to signify the democratic right of a full citizen of a Greek city-state to speak out one's opinion freely. Later it was found as a characteristic of the relations between true friends in opposition to the feigned compliments of flatterers (see W. C. van Unnik, "The Christian's Freedom of Speech in the New Testament," *BJRL* 44 [1962] 466–88, cf. BAG, 630, 631, Schlier, *TDNT* 5, 871–86, and Hahn, in *NIDNTT* 2, 734–37). Neither noun nor cognate verb παρρησιάζομαι ("speak freely, openly, fearlessly") appears frequently in the LXX (van Unnik, *BJRL* 44 [1962] 472, comments that the word-group is "a marginal feature"; for details see Schlier, *TDNT* 5, 875–79, and Hahn, *NIDNTT* 2, 735, 736), but when we turn to the NT we note a considerable increase of instances (the noun appears thirty-one times, the verb nine: the former in the Pauline corpus at 2 Cor 3:12; 7:4; Eph 3:12; 6:19; Phil 1:20; Col 2:15, 1 Tim 3:13, Philem 8, and the latter at Eph 6:20; 1 Thess 2:2). No single English translation renders these occurrences with equal success (e.g. the NEB gives a variety of translations: "plainly," "bold," "boldness," "publicly," "openly," "confidence," while van Unnik opts for the phrase "freedom of speech"). The term in Paul can designate his openness and frankness toward men (2 Cor 3:12; 7:4; Eph 6:20; 1 Thess 2:2; 1 Tim 3:13; Phlm 8; cf. BAG, 630, Schlier, *TDNT* 5, 883, and Lohse, 198), a candor which is based on his openness toward God (2 Cor 3:12; Eph 3:12; Phil 1:20). Acts again and again reports how fearlessly Peter, Paul and others stood before the Jews or Gentiles and proclaimed the works of God (cf. Acts 2:29; 4:13, 29, 31; 28:31 for the noun, and 9:27, 28; 13:46; 14:3; 18:26; 19:8; 26:26). This boldness which provoked astonishment (4:13), division (14:3, 4) and persecution (9:27) is a fruit of the Spirit which is to be sought repeatedly (4:29–31). On occasion παρρησία in Paul can denote "frankness": at 2 Corinthians 7:4 the NEB rendering "I

am perfectly frank with you" (πολλή μοι παρρησία πρὸς ὑμᾶς) catches the nuance. In the strained relations which existed between Paul and the Christians in Corinth Paul finds the freedom to speak to them in all frankness and urges the Corinthians not to close their hearts (so van Unnik, *BJRL* 44 [1962] 473, 474). Connected with this, παρρησία can indicate that the relationship to other men is characterized by "openness" in the sense of affection. This is precisely what Paul means in Philemon 8: it is great boldness or openness (the πολλή, "much," indicates how much freedom Paul has) "in Christ" (ἐν Χριστῷ), i.e. because of their Christian relationships. No doubt Paul has in view their personal intimacy (a point brought out in the Greek through the balancing of first and second person singulars throughout the whole paragraph; see above) which probably began at the time of Philemon's conversion when Paul was the instrument God used (v 19). Philemon's fine Christian character, mentioned explicitly in the preceding verses, meant Paul could speak openly and with affection, while his responsibility as apostle to the Gentiles, of which the addressee was one, enabled him to speak boldly in Christ.

Many commentators suggest that παρρησία ("boldness," "openness") here is virtually equivalent to ἐξουσία ("authority," so Schlier, *TDNT* 5, 883, who is cited with approval by many, states: "we have an instance of παρρησία in much the same sense as ἐξουσία; cf. Lohse, 198, and note also Ernst, 133, and Merk, *Handeln*, 225, among others). Such an identification, however, is incorrect. The note of authority is struck in ἐπιτάσσειν not in παρρησία. Certainly the term ἐπιτάσσω ("order," "command"; BAG, 302; on the word-group see Delling, *TDNT* 8, 27–48) is a strong one. Although it does not appear elsewhere in the Pauline corpus the cognate noun does: ἐπιταγή ("command," "order," "injunction") turns up seven times (Rom 16:26; 1 Cor 7:6, 25; 2 Cor 8:8; 1 Tim 1:1; Tit 1:3; 2:15), and it is clear from the contexts that it means an authoritative command from one in a superior position (cf. Rom 16:26 which refers to an ἐπιταγή, "command," of the eternal God). ἐπιτάσσω (to "command") is found in the NT for the authoritative orders of Jesus to demons (Mark 1:27; 9:25 etc.), as well as the commands of Herod (Mark 6:27) and Ananïas (Acts 23:2). As in the LXX the term is restricted to situations involving obedience to an undisputed religious or political authority (Lohmeyer, 183; Schütz, *Paul*, 222; cf. Delling, *TDNT* 8, 36, 37).

τὸ ἀνῆκον denotes "what is fitting" (see above on Col 3:18) and has to do with the matter about which Paul writes to Philemon. It "does not mean the generally valid moral commandment" (so correctly Lohse, 198; against Schlier, *TDNT* 1, 360, who refers to "that which is almost legally obligatory," and Schütz, *Paul*, 222, who states that the term "presumes a binding authority, whether political or religious, to which one is obligated"), but what is proper for Philemon, as a Christian, to do in the circumstances concerning Onesimus. At this point Paul does not spell out the content of that duty, but only indicates he might have simply given a command about the matter.

9. Paul does not intend to enforce compliance with his word; rather he bases his appeal on other grounds: διὰ τὴν ἀγάπην μᾶλλον παρακαλῶ ("For love's sake I prefer to appeal to you"). The verb παρακαλῶ, which had a wealth of meanings in the Greek world of Paul's day (see above on 2:2,

and note the range of translations in BAG, 617) and could even connote "admonish," strikes the note of request or entreaty here (it is expressly distinguished from ἐπιτάσσω, "command," by means of the μᾶλλον, "rather," cf. Schmitz, *TDNT* 5, 795, and Bjerkelund, *Parakalô,* 188; Hainz's assertion, *Ekklesia,* 204, that "Paul commands even when he requests" is contradicted by the Greek antithetical construction with its concessive clause in v 8 and the μᾶλλον, "rather," of v 9, and tells us more about Hainz's own view of authority than Paul's). Bjerkelund (*Parakalô,* 119) notes that even a king can request and Paul chooses here to entreat rather than to command. He wants Philemon to consent freely (see v 14).

"For love's sake" (*διὰ τὴν ἀγάπην*) has been taken to mean love as such, that is, love as a principle, which governs Christians in their dealings and relations with each other, and which is regarded as the ground of Paul's appeal (so Wickert, *ZNW* 52 [1961] 236, "The common love urges that the request be made," cited by Lohse, 199; an alternative suggestion is to understand the love as Paul's, either for his child Onesimus or for Philemon). But the term "love" (*ἀγάπη*) has already been used twice in the previous paragraph (vv 5, 7) to denote Philemon's love concretely shown to the saints, and the most natural way of interpreting the expression here in verse 9 is along similar lines, so understanding the definite article "the" (*τήν,* in *διὰ τὴν ἀγάπην,* "for love's sake") as the article of renewed mention, pointing to the love previously referred to. (There would have to be strong contextual reasons for interpreting the term in a sense other than these two previous instances and, in our judgment, the context does not demand such a change in connotation; in fact, quite the reverse). It is precisely because Paul knows of Philemon's kindness and generosity in the past that he is able to entreat rather than command, and he looks forward to Philemon's love being shown once again, this time with reference to Onesimus (our exegesis of v 6 above synchronizes with this interpretation; it has already been shown that this letter has been carefully constructed, with the introductory thanksgiving paragraph anticipating themes in the body of the letter: *ἀγάπη,* "love," is the first of those themes to be taken up; O'Brien, *Introductory Thanksgivings,* 51, see also Dibelius-Greeven, 104, "trusting in the love of Philemon mentioned in 7," Friedrich, 191, Knox, *Philemon,* 19, Zmijewski, *BibLeb* 15 [1974] 278, and Gayer, *Stellung,* 251).

τοιοῦτος ὢν ὡς Παῦλος πρεσβύτης, νυνὶ δὲ καὶ δέσμιος Χριστοῦ Ἰησοῦ. "Although I am none other than Paul, an ambassador of Christ Jesus and now also his prisoner." In the second part of the sentence (a participial clause *τοιοῦτος ὢν* . . . , "since or though I am the sort of person . . " dependent on the principal clause) Paul describes himself as the one who makes the appeal (appositional expressions, usually for the sake of emphasis or special effect, occur at vv 9, 10, 11, 12, 16 and 19; note also the occurrences of *ὡς,* "as," at vv 9, 14, 16 and 17—here the particle "introduces the characteristic quality of a pers., thing or action, etc., referred to in the context," BAG, 898, cf. Lohse, 199, and when it follows *τοιοῦτος* it equals "in my character as," BAG, 821): first, he mentions his own name, "Paul" (Παῦλος occurs in the central sections of his letters at v 19, 2 Cor 10:1; Gal 5:2; Eph 3:1; Col 1:23; 1 Thess 2:18). The request of Philemon comes from one well-known to him—

Paul. Second, he calls himself πρεσβύτης, which some have taken as a reference to his age, and rendered "old man" (so BAG, 700, who discusses the stages of life through which one passes; Bornkamn, *TDNT* 6, 683, Lohse, 199, Stuhlmacher, 37, 38, and earlier commentators such as von Soden, 75, Vincent, 184, Dibelius-Greeven, 104, 105, and Friedrich, 193). Accordingly, Paul who thinks it enough to appeal to the love of Philemon, reinforces this with a reference to his age, his bonds, and the fact that he is a spiritual father to Onesimus. But the word πρεσβύτης was also used on occasion of an "envoy," or "ambassador" (2 Macc 11:34; 2 Chr 32: 31 [B]; 1 Macc 14:22; 15:17 [א], so Bornkamm, *TDNT* 6, 683, for references; strictly the Greek word for "ambassador" was πρεσβευτής, but Lightfoot, 336, 337, and Lohmeyer, 185, have shown that for some considerable period πρεσβύτης was used for both; either rendering is possible and so the context must determine the meaning here). If the translation "ambassador" is accepted, it would point to the authority granted to Paul, and so underline the fact that he speaks as an ambassador of Christ (cf. 2 Cor 5:20 and Eph 6:20, "for which [gospel] I am an ambassador [πρεσβεύω] in chains"). On this view the participle (ὤν) is concessive and parallel to the concessive clause of verse 8. It can thus be rendered: "although I am none other than Paul, an ambassador of Christ Jesus, and now also his prisoner" (cf. Moule, 144: others who understand πρεσβύτης here in the sense of πρεσβευτής, "ambassador," are Haupt, 201, 202, Robertson, *Grammar,* 201, T. Preiss, *Life in Christ.* Tr. H. Knight SBT 13 [London: SCM, 1954] 37, 38, Kümmel, *Introduction,* 349, Schmauch, *Beiheft,* 96, Wickert, *ZNW* 52 [1961] 235, Suhl, *Kairos* 15 [1973] 272, Martin, *NCB,* 163, Ernst, 133, 134, Caird, 221, Bruce, *Paul,* 393, Gayer, *Stellung,* 251, and Ollrog, *Paulus,* 102).

Finally, Paul is "a prisoner of Christ Jesus" (δέσμιος Χριστοῦ Ἰησοῦ, see on v 1), that is, he shares in Christ's sufferings right now (νυνί is a more emphatic adverb than νῦν, "now," and might suggest that Paul's imprisonment had only just begun at the time he wrote: see the Introduction above) as one faithful to his calling. Philemon will thus heed his words.

10. *παρακαλῶ σε περὶ τοῦ ἐμοῦ τέκνου, ὃν ἐγέννησα ἐν τοῖς δέσμοις Ὀνήσιμον.* "I appeal to you for my child whom I begot while in prison—Onesimus." The verb "I beseech, appeal" is repeated (παρακαλῶ) as Paul specifically mentions his request and therefore his purpose in writing the letter. Philemon is the person addressed (σε, "you," is the direct object of the verb), and Paul's request is not for himself but is an intercession for the one converted through his ministry while in prison and who is very dear to him—Onesimus. The Greek preposition περί here means "for," "on behalf of" (see 1 Cor 16:12; 2 Cor 12:8 and 2 Thess 2:1) rather than "about," "with reference to" (as Knox, *Philemon,* 20, has argued; for a critique see Greeven, *TLZ* 79 [1954] 373–78, esp. 374, Bjerkelund, *Parakalô,* 120, 121, Lohse, 199, and Suhl, *Kairos* 15 [1973] 272). Paul is interceding on Onesimus' behalf rather than making a request about him. The sentence is carefully constructed, for Onesimus' name stands last. This was probably the first news Philemon had received of his slave since he ran away and he might be expected to react negatively to the mention of his name. So with delicate tact Paul first establishes the central fact that Onesimus has become a Christian, converted during Paul's imprisonment.

In describing Onesimus as his child whom he had begotten (περὶ τοῦ ἐμοῦ τέκνου ὃν ἐγέννησα) Paul was using the imagery of spiritual parenthood which he employed elsewhere and which had its counterpart in Judaism, ultimately deriving from the OT. So he calls himself the father of an entire Christian community, the Corinthians whom he had begotten "in Christ Jesus through the gospel" (1 Cor 4:15; cf. Gal 4:19), while Timothy (1 Cor 4:17; 2 Tim 1:2) and Titus (Titus 1:4) he describes as his children (τέκνον occurs in each reference; cf. Rengstorf, *TDNT* 1, 668, and Schrenk, *TDNT* 5, 1005). In 1 Peter 1:3 God himself is spoken of as begetting Christians (cf. 1 Pet 2:2) and in James 1:18 of giving birth to them. The terms "father" and "son" with reference to a master and his disciple appear as early as 2 Kings 2:12 (of Elijah and Elisha respectively) while at the time of Jesus it was customary for a rabbi to call his pupil "my son." In this there was no thought of begetting but the notion is present in the statement of the Babylonian Talmud: "When a man teaches the son of another the Torah, the Scripture treats him as if he had begotten him" (*bSanh* 99b; cf. Str-B 3, 340, 341, for further rabbinic examples, note also Büchsel, *TDNT* 1, 665, 666). In addition, it was believed that the Jew who wins another to his faith (and this was an achievement of great magnitude, being compared with the creative work of God himself) satisfies in an ideal manner the injunction to be fruitful and multiply, which according to the rabbis was laid on all male Jews as a supreme command (see Rengstorf, *TDNT* 1, 666, 667). In the mystery religions although the terminology was somewhat similar (the mystagogue was regarded as the father of the initiate, cf. Dibelius-Greeven, 105) the ideas were different. Paul's act of begetting and his fatherhood were "through the gospel" (1 Cor 4:15).

That Onesimus (the Greek Ὀνήσιμον τόν ποτέ κτλ. is an accusative case, not a genitive in agreement with τοῦ ἐμοῦ τέκνου, "my child," and this may be due to an attraction to the relative sentence ὃν ἐγέννησα κτλ. ["whom I have begotten," etc.]: so Moule, 145, and Lohse, 200; Knox, *Philemon*, 21, takes it to mean that "Onesimus" was now first given to him as his "Christian" name) had been converted by Paul during the latter's imprisonment (which was no doubt a frustrating time) probably made him feel a special affection for Onesimus. The further point needs to be noted: if Onesimus was Paul's son, then that made him Philemon's brother. Paul will make this explicit a little later, but even now the implication is clear.

11. Several further statements about Onesimus are added (vv 11, 12). First, by means of a pun on the words ἄχρηστον/εὔχρηστον ("useless"/"useful") a sharp contrast is drawn between what Onesimus had once (ποτέ) been and what he had now (νυνὶ δέ) become in Christ: τόν ποτέ σοι ἄχρηστον νυνὶ δὲ [καὶ] σοὶ καὶ ἐμοὶ εὔχρηστον ("Previously he was useless to you, but now he has become useful [both] to you and to me"; within this clause there are two antitheses: ποτέ . . . νυνὶ δέ ["once . . . but now"] and ἄχρηστον . . . εὔχρηστον ["useless . . . useful"], as well as a parallel expression [καὶ] σοὶ καὶ ἐμοί ["[both] to you and to me"]). Commentators have drawn attention to the many extrabiblical instances of the play on the "useless/useful" contrast (Plato, *Republic* 411A, in the rabbinic tradition [*Midr Exod* 43, see Str-B 3, 668] as well as in the Shepherd of Hermas: *Vis* 3.6.7, "when you were rich, you were useless [ἄχρηστος], but now you are useful [εὔχρηστος] . . . Be useful to God"; and *Mand* 5. 6. 6: "long suffering . . . is useful to the Lord

. . . ill temper . . . is useless"; for further details see Lohse, 200). ἄχρηστος ("useless," "worthless," BAG, 128, which occurs only here in the New Testament) designates Onesimus with reference to his flight and the time before his conversion. Apparently he was useless even before he ran away. He was a Phrygian slave and as such "had confirmed the popular estimate of his class and nation by his own conduct" (Lightfoot, 310) since Phrygian slaves were proverbial for being unreliable and unfaithful. But a great change has occurred and Paul describes this by means of the "once—now" (ποτέ—νυνὶ δέ) contrast which he has employed previously (see on Col 1:21, 22; note also 2:13). This mighty transformation has been effected by Onesimus' conversion to Christ as Lord and he may now be described as εὔχρηστος ("useful," see BAG, 329; note also 2 Tim 2:21; 4:11; on the theological contrast drawn see Tachau, *Einst,* 87, 88, and Gayer, *Stellung,* 252) a description that truly fits his name for Onesimus means "profitable" or "useful" (BAG, 570). Paul can bear witness to this dramatic change (ἐμοί, "to me") and is confident he will give proof of his conversion as he is welcomed back to Colossae (σοί, "to you," rather unusually precedes καὶ ἐμοί, "and to me," so Lightfoot, 338; perhaps the word-order emphasizes that Philemon will have to satisfy himself that Onesimus has become a different person, cf. Lohse, 201).

12. With the mention of his sending Onesimus back to Philemon, Paul concludes the first section of the body of the letter: ὃν ἀνέπεμψά σοι, αὐτόν, τοῦτ' ἔστιν τὰ ἐμὰ σπλάγχνα ("I am sending him—who is my very heart—back to you" NIV). The verb ἀναπέμπω has the meaning to "send back," "return" (BAG, 59) and this is the way it has generally been understood. Knox (*Philemon,* 25), however, wishes to give a technical, legal sense to the verb, suggesting that Paul wishes to "refer Onesimus' case" to Philemon for Archippus' attention and decision. Onesimus' future, that is, whether he is to remain at Colossae or be free to be Paul's aide, is then a matter about which Paul seeks Philemon's consent (v 13). But here the verb seems to have the meaning "send back" (cf. Luke 23:15) and being an epistolary aorist (in which the writer puts himself at the point of time when the recipient is reading his letter; note Acts 23:30; Phil 2:28; Col 4:8, so most commentators and note Robertson, *Grammar,* 846, BDF, para. 334, and Turner, *Syntax,* 73) is to be translated by an English present tense "I am sending back." The pronoun αὐτόν ("him,") after the relative ὅν ("whom") appears to be redundant and is akin to a Hebrew construction (in which an indeclinable relative is qualified by a direct personal pronoun: Biblical Greek sometimes imitates this, e.g., Mark 7:25; see Moule, 145). It is probable though that the αὐτόν ("him") picks up again the relative pronoun before the sentence continues: so Moule paraphrases "whom I am sending . . . ; and when I say (I am sending) him, I mean my very self."

In the eastern part of the Roman Empire during this period, fugitive slaves who sought sanctuary in a household were likely to be given temporary protection by the householder until either a reconciliation with the master had been effected or else the slave had been put up for sale in the market and the resulting price paid to the owner (Goodenough, *HTR* 22 [1929] 181–83, drew attention to an Athenian law to this effect; it is suggested that this provision survived in Egypt under the Ptolemies and well into Roman imperial times as it influenced Ulpian's legislation early in the third century A.D.). The relevant Deuteronomic law ran as follows: "you shall not give up to his master a slave who has escaped from his master to you; he shall dwell with you, in your midst, in the place which he shall choose within one of your towns, where it pleases him best; you shall not oppress him" (Deut 23:15, 16). Although this law carried divine authority for Paul, as Bruce (*Paul,* 400) notes, "he would not invoke it without Philemon's consent, preferring Philemon to act like a Christian of his own free will" (note Bruce's whole discussion, *Paul,* 399, 400).

He therefore sends Onesimus back with this accompanying letter (for a further discussion of the Roman legal position in the various provinces see Stuhlmacher, 23, and especially notes 27 and 28 for further literature). But in so doing it was as if he was sending back himself: *τὰ ἐμὰ σπλάγχνα* means "my heart" but could be rendered "my very self." Köster (*TDNT* 7, 555) comments: "It is as if Paul, in the runaway slave, came to Philemon in person with his claim to experience love" (note also v 17 where the apostle writes: "welcome him as you would welcome me"; Onesimus has become very dear to him). The frequent use of this word *σπλάγχνα* ("heart," vs 7, 12, 20) shows how personally Paul was involved in the matter.

13. He now briefly describes what happened before he wrote his letter and sent Onesimus back: *ὃν ἐγὼ ἐβουλόμην πρὸς ἐμαυτὸν κατέχειν ἵνα ὑπὲρ σοῦ μοι διακονῇ κτλ.* ("Indeed I would have liked to keep him with me so that he could take your place in helping me . . ."). The verb "I would have liked" (*ἐβουλόμην*) expresses Paul's desire or personal preference. It speaks of an attainable wish but as the following verse, with its sharp contrast, makes plain Paul foregoes its realization: I "would have liked, but I do not, or did not do it" (BDF, para. 359[2]; cited by Lohse, 201, note Stuhlmacher, 40; the contrast between the two verbs of wishing *ἐβουλόμην* and *ἠθέλησα* lies not so much in their meaning as in the tenses: *ἐβουλόμην* as an imperfect describes a desire which Paul felt for a time while *ἠθέλησα*, an aorist, indicates his actual decision, cf. Burton, *Syntax,* 15, and for a similar use of *ἐβουλόμην* see Acts 25:22; note also Gal 4:20; Rom 9:3; against Robertson, *Grammar,* 886, 919, who thinks it is a courteous or polite use of the imperfect and rendered "I was just on the point of wishing"). Although *κατέχω* (a more emphatic form of *ἔχω*, "have") had a variety of meanings in extra-biblical Greek (cf. Hanse, *TDNT* 2, 829, and see BAG, 422, 423; it occurred as a technical term in the Hellenistic cult where the devotee was obliged to remain in the temple at the god's behest), the predominant use in both the LXX and the NT is to "hold fast" (see Luke 8:15; 1 Cor 11:2; 15:2; 1 Thess 5:21; Heb 3:6, 14; 10:23 etc.). Here it has the particular sense of to "retain" or "keep with" (*πρὸς ἐμαυτόν* means "with me"; see also Luke 4:42 for this sense: in v 15 the cognate *ἀπέχω*, to "receive in full," "keep" occurs). Onesimus had rendered faithful service to Paul and it had been the latter's wish that he would continue to give it in place of the absent Philemon. The expression *ὑπὲρ σοῦ* ("on your behalf," or more accurately "as your representative," so Deissmann, *Light from the Ancient East,* 335, Riesenfeld, *TDNT* 8, 513, Lohse, 202, Stuhlmacher, 40) is one of delicate tact for Paul assumes that Philemon would have wished to perform this service for him had it been possible (there

is some difference of opinion about the precise nature of the service: while the term διακονέω is as general as the English verb "serve," and might be understood in a variety of ways it probably does not designate menial or degrading work in prison [so rightly Bratcher and Nida, 126], but signifies "help," especially in the service of the gospel—note *εὐαγγέλιον*, "gospel," is used in this clause [cf. Acts 13:5; 24:23; Phil 2:25, 30]; see Lohmeyer, 173, 191, Gayer, *Stelling*, 241, and especially Ollrog, *Paulus*, 101–103. Stuhlmacher, 40, suggests Paul here means concrete help including the maintenance of regular contact with the outside world). At the same time the phrase may suggest that Onesimus is more than a mere substitute for Philemon, and if so then the relation of master and slave disappears for the moment (so Vincent, 186). It must also be remembered that Paul's circumstances are "in the bonds of the gospel" (ἐν τοῖς δεσμοῖς τοῦ εὐαγγελίου), that is, his imprisonment is for the gospel (BAG, 176, Moule, 146; cf. v 1, δέσμιος Χριστοῦ Ἰησοῦ, which may signify "a prisoner for the sake of Christ Jesus," so Friedrich, *TDNT* 2, 733, as well as one who belongs to Christ Jesus), or the gospel is the cause of his imprisonment since it had resulted from the preaching of the gospel (Vincent, 187; cf. Lightfoot, 339, who treats the genitive as one of origin). Probably both nuances are included and there is no need to choose between these alternatives.

14. But however much Paul was inclined to keep Onesimus he would do nothing without Philemon's consent: to have done so would at the least have involved a breach of Christian fellowship. He refuses to press Philemon to act in any way that would suggest coercion or an intrusion into the latter's decision: χωρὶς δὲ τῆς σῆς γνώμης οὐδὲν ἠθέλησα ποιῆσαι ("But I would not do anything without your consent"). γνώμη, a term which means "opinion" (1 Cor 7:25, 40; 2 Cor 8:10; cf. Ecclus 6:23; 2 Macc 14:20; 4 Macc 9:27), or "decision" (Acts 20:3; Rev 17:17; cf. examples in the papyri: *POxy* 54, 12; *PFay* 20, 4) has the connotation here of "previous knowledge" or "consent" (BAG, 163, Bultmann, *TDNT* 1, 717; the preposition χωρίς, "apart from" is found in place of ἄνευ, "without," which turns up only three times in the NT: Matt 10:29; 1 Pet 3:1; 4:9). On the aorist tense of the verb ἠθέλησα, see above at verse 13.

Paul's intention was ἵνα μὴ ὡς κατὰ ἀνάγκην τὸ ἀγαθόν σου ᾖ ἀλλὰ κατὰ ἑκούσιον ("so that any favor you do will be spontaneous and not forced"). His overriding concern is that Philemon should be free to decide for himself as to how he should act (so Schweizer, *EvTh* 32 [1972] 505); there should not be even the slightest hint of coercion or any intrusion into Philemon's decision (so ὡς, "as if," means it will not even have the appearance of being by constraint, Lightfoot, 340, von Soden, 76, Lohse, 202). The contrast μὴ ὡς κατὰ ἀνάγκην—ἀλλὰ κατὰ ἑκούσιον ("not by compulsion but of your own free will") was a common one, frequently found in the papyri (cf. Lohmeyer, 188, and Lohse, 202; note also 1 Pet 5:2 for the same antithesis). The first phrase (ἀνάγκη, "necessity," "compulsion," turns up in Paul at Rom 13:5; 1 Cor 7:26, 37; 9:16; 2 Cor 6:4; 9:7; 12:10; 1 Thess 3:7) refers to the outward pressure or force that is laid on someone by which he is forced to act in a certain way (Bratcher and Nida, 126); while the latter points to a decision that is freely arrived at (ἑκούσιος, "willing," "voluntary," occurs only here in the Pauline corpus; cf. Num 15:3, καθ' ἑκούσιον, of a "free-will offering," and Heb 10:26: note BAG, 243, and Hauck, *TDNT* 2, 470). The expression τὸ ἀγαθόν σου ("your good deed," here the neuter singular is used "in an individual sense of a particular definite thing or act," BDF, para. 263[1], see also Turner, *Syntax*, 13) is akin to the language of Paul's intercession for Philemon in verse 6 with its reference to "every blessing" (παντὸς ἀγαθοῦ). Up to this point nothing is stated explicitly about the nature of this good deed (Ernst, 135).

15. The apostle gives an additional reason for his decision (γάρ, "for," explains a further motive of ἠθέλησα, "I decided": Lightfoot, 340, Vincent, 188; cf. Zmijewski, *BibLeb* 15 [1974] 289; Knox, *Philemon*, 22–24, agrees that this sentence bears a close relation to the preceding but interprets the relationship differently; see below) not to detain Onesimus, namely, that he might well have acted contrary to God's hidden purpose: τάχα γὰρ διὰ τοῦτο ἐχωρίσθη πρὸς ὥραν ἵνα αἰώνιον αὐτὸν ἀπέχῃς ("perhaps the reason he was separated from you for a little while was that you might have him back for ever"). Within the sentence a sharp contrast is drawn between the πρὸς ὥραν ("for a little while") of the principal clause and the αἰώνιον ("for ever") of the ἵνα clause. This contrast finds its correspondence (cf. Zmijewski, *BibLeb* 15 [1974] 289) in the two verbs χωρίζω (to "separate") and ἀπέχω (to "have back"). The passive ἐχωρίσθη ("he was separated from") denotes that God's hidden purpose (in Hebrew the so-called "divine passive," especially in the apocalyptic literature, was employed to signify the hidden action of God as the person responsible for what was done; most commentators take this line, cf. for example Lohse, 202, Suhl, *Kairos* 15 [1973] 274, Martin, *NCB*, 166, Ernst, 135, Caird, 222) may have been behind this incident. But Paul puts forward this suggestion about God's purpose modestly with the adverb τάχα ("perhaps," "possibly," or "probably," so BAG, 806; it usually occurs with ἄν and the optative mood, but in the two NT passages where the word appears, Rom 5:7 and here, the indicative is used without ἄν: see BDF, para, 385[1]; note Wisd 13:6; *POxy* 40, 7; Philo, *Aet M* 54; Josephus, *Ant* 6, 33; 18, 277), since he is not assuming an acquaintance with God's designs. The language has been chosen carefully as Philemon's attention is turned from individual wrongs he may have incurred to God's providence which has made these wrongs work for good (note Chrysostom's comparison of Joseph who, when making himself known to his brothers said: "I am your brother Joseph, the one you sold into Egypt! And now, do not be distressed and do not be angry with yourselves for selling me here, because it was to save lives that God sent me ahead of you . . . So then, it was not you who sent me here, but God," Gen 45:4–8, NIV). πρὸς ὥραν means "for a while," "for a moment" (ὥρα, "hour," is used to denote "a short period of time": the same phrase occurs at John 5:35; 2 Cor 7:8; Gal 2:5; note also 1 Thess 2:17; Rev 17:12; 18:10, 17, 19, BAG, 896). The expression is indefinite and although the period of separation is not specified here "it was but 'an hour' as compared with its lasting consequences" (Vincent, 188).

If indeed God's hidden purpose lay behind this incident then the divine intention (διὰ τοῦτο, "for this reason," is explicated by the ἵνα clause which follows and which therefore spells out the purpose of Onesimus' separation;

Stauffer, *TDNT* 3, 329, and Zmijewski, *BibLeb* 15 [1974] 289, regard the *ἵνα* as a "theological" *ἵνα*; note the similar construction with *διὰ τοῦτο*, for this reason," followed by *ἵνα*, "that," at 2 Cor 13:10; 1 Tim 1:16, and see BAG, 597 under 2bβ) was that Philemon should receive him back in a new relationship that would endure for ever. There is some difference of opinion as to the significance of *ἀπέχῃς* in connection with *αἰώνιον*. The verb *ἀπέχω* was used in the active voice as a commercial technical term meaning to "receive [a sum] in full [and give a receipt for it]," a connotation it has at Philippians 4:8 ("I have received full payment [*ἀπέχω δὲ πάντα*], and more") in a context where other commercial terms and ideas are found (J. Gnilka, *Der Philipperbrief* [HTKNT 10/3; Frieburg: Herder, 1968] 179; for further examples from the papyri see Deissmann, *Light from the Ancient East*, 110–12, and BAG, 84, 85). The language of commerce is employed elsewhere in this letter to Philemon (note the exegesis of vv 17–19), and Knox (*Philemon*, 22–24) renders the whole phrase as "in order that you might freely relinquish your claim to him forever." It is not certain that this full commercial significance of the verb is to be pressed, and the usual rendering "that you may receive him back" seems preferable. But how is *αἰώνιον* to be interpreted? Moule (156) claims that in this context it appears to mean "for good" or "permanently," just as in Exodus 21:7 (cf. Deut 15:17) where the regulations for voluntary slavery speak of the Israelite being a "servant for life" (the LXX has *εἰς τὸν αἰῶνα* for the Hebrew *lᵉ ʿôlām*). Moule further states it should not be assumed (without additional evidence) that the term carries a deeper meaning here such as "forever," although on occasion *αἰώνιος* does have this connotation. The deeper relationship as Christians, it is argued, is described in the next verse (cf. Sasse, *TDNT* 1, 209, Merk, *Handeln*, 226, 227). But in our judgment Paul is already in verse 15 speaking of the new relationship of this master to his slave, a relationship in the Lord Jesus Christ which is "for ever." To get Onesimus back permanently means not to receive him back simply as a slave, but to acquire him permanently as a Christian brother (Gayer, *Stellung*, 243, argues that *αἰώνιον* cannot properly be understood in this context with reference to Onesimus' legal status as a slave for an unlimited period of time; his legal position as a slave is hardly in view at all: cf. Dibelius-Greeven, 107, Sevenster, *Paul*, 189, and H. Ridderbos, *Paul. An Outline of His Theology*. Tr. J. R. DeWitt [Grand Rapids, MI; Eerdmans, 1975] 318). Such an interpretation does not contradict the notion that subsequently he could be away from his master physically, sent back to minister to Paul (see on v 21 against Caird, 222).

16. The one whom Philemon will receive back for ever is "a beloved brother": *οὐκέτι ὡς δοῦλον ἀλλὰ ὑπὲρ δοῦλον, ἀδελφὸν ἀγαπητόν* ("no longer as a slave, but as one who is much more than a slave, as a beloved brother"). Grammatically this verse contains a long addition which stands in apposition to *αὐτόν* ("him") of the previous verse, and in these words Onesimus is described. For the first time the term "slave" (*δοῦλος*) is used with reference to him; but this is immediately qualified by means of an antithesis: he will be far more than a slave to his master. Again it is noted that Paul has chosen his words carefully: *οὐκέτι ὡς δοῦλον* ("no longer as a slave") is not stating that Philemon is to receive Onesimus back as a freed man and no longer a

slave, or that he is to free him immediately on his return (against Jang, *Philemonbrief,* 15, who suggests Paul is waiting for Philemon to give Onesimus his freedom). Rather, the ὡς ("as") "expresses the subjective evaluation of the relationship without calling its objective form into question" (von Soden, 76; who adds "therefore the line of thought found in 1 Cor 7:20–24 is not exceeded," cited by Lohse, 203, Gayer, *Stellung,* 236, and others; had Paul wished to describe the latter and therefore suggest that the runaway slave was to be freed, he would have simply written δοῦλον, "a slave," instead of ὡς δοῦλον, "as a slave," cf. Lightfoot, 340, 341, Vincent, 188, 189, Lohmeyer, 189, and Bratcher and Nida, 127, 128, with the latter's criticisms of the RSV rendering). In other words, whether Onesimus remained a slave or not, he could no longer be regarded *as* a slave. A change had been effected in him independent of his possible manumission (Lightfoot, 341, adds the further point that the negative οὐκέτι, "no longer," rather than μηκέτι, with the same meaning, describes the actual state of Onesimus, not the possible view of Philemon: "The 'no more as a slave' is an absolute fact, whether Philemon chooses to recognise it or not"). Instead (ἀλλά here is adversative) Onesimus is more than a slave (the preposition ὑπέρ with the accusative, having an original spatial meaning "beyond," is employed in a transferred sense denoting "exceeding," "above," "more than": 1 Cor 4:6; 10:13; 2 Cor 1:8; 8:3; 12:6, so Riesenfeld, *TDNT* 8, 515, BDF, para. 230, and BAG, 838, 839), and what this "more" signifies is expressed in the following words: he is "a beloved brother" (ἀδελφὸν ἀγαπητόν is in epexegetical apposition to ὑπὲρ δοῦλον, "more than a slave," so von Soden, 77, Vincent, 189, and Zmijewski, *BibLeb* 15 [1974] 289).

Contemporary popular philosophy, particularly Stoicism, had already recognized the idea of the equality of all men; so, for example, Seneca in his famous forty-seventh letter to Lucilius, in which he discourses at length on how to treat slaves, commented: "Kindly remember that he whom you call your slave sprang from the same stock, is smiled upon by the same skies, and on equal terms with yourself breathes, lives and dies" (*Epist* 47.10; cf. 44.1, "All men, if traced back to their original source, spring from the gods," and Pliny, *Epist* 9.21.24; note Sevenster, *Paul,* 185–92). Paul, however, appeals not as did pagan authors to their birth from the same stock or to the same path of life from birth to death, but to their common belonging to the same Lord (Paul is also different from the mystery religions which considered a slave who had been initiated was no longer reckoned as a slave, but lived with his former owner as a free man; cf. the treatment by Gayer, *Stellung,* 237–40, on the theme of the slave as a brother in popular philosophy, the mystery religions, the OT and Judaism. He concludes [240] that there was no religious fellowship in the ancient world which included a slave as a brother in a new relationship at such a deep personal level as we find here in Paul).

Onesimus, in being spoken of as "a [beloved] brother," is addressed in precisely the same way as Philemon (so vv 7, 20: ἀδελφέ, "brother"); he too has been incorporated into the body of Christ and consequently the relationship of slave owner to slave within the framework of the existing structures is to be conducted in the light of belonging to the same Lord (S. Schulz, *Gott ist kein Sklavenhalter. Die Geschichte einer verspäteten Revolution,* 1972, 183).

The relationship between the two men is deepened, the terms "master" and "slave" are transcended, as Paul in the final words of this verse attempts to bring before Philemon some of the consequences: *μάλιστα ἐμοί, πόσῳ δὲ μᾶλλον σοὶ καὶ ἐν σαρκὶ καὶ ἐν κυρίῳ.* ("Especially to me, but how much more to you, both in the flesh and in the Lord"). Paul's words contain a heightened comparison: *μάλιστα* which is superlative in form is used here as an elative with the meaning "especially" (also Acts 20:38; 1 Tim 4:10; 5:17; 2 Tim 4:13; Titus 1:10, see BAG, 488, 489, BDF, para. 60, Vincent, 189, Moule, 148, Lohse, 203, and Stuhlmacher, 42, against Lightfoot, 341). The comparison is then heightened by *πόσῳ μᾶλλον* ("how much more") which follows. If Onesimus is a beloved brother in the highest sense for Paul, then he is also for Philemon in a double sense: *καὶ ἐν σαρκὶ καὶ ἐν κυρίῳ,* that is, in a natural human relationship to Philemon (as his slave) and more than this, as one bound with him *ἐν κυρίῳ* ("in the Lord"). Cf. Zmijewski, *BibLeb* 15 (1974) 290. Philemon 16 is the only verse in which *σάρξ* ("flesh") and *κύριος* ("Lord") are linked together by *καί* ("and"; noted by Lohmeyer, 189, who is cited by later commentators). Here *σάρξ* "denotes the circle of purely human relations irrespective of the fact that the slave and his master are also believers in the Lord's kingdom . . . The reference is to social relations rather than kinship" (Schweizer, *TDNT* 7, 127; cf. Dibelius-Greeven, 106, "as a man and as a Christian," against Preiss, *Life,* 40). Schweizer rightly adds "it is especially plain that the two spheres are not mutually exclusive. But the sphere of *σάρξ* is not the decisive one." Onesimus' earthly relationship with Philemon is now determined by the union *ἐν κυρίῳ* ("in the Lord").

It is quite clear that in this letter Paul is not really dealing with the question of slavery as such or the resolution of a particular instance of slavery. In this verse, at least, he treats the question of brotherly love. Although Onesimus' earthly freedom may be of positive value, in the last analysis it is of no ultimate significance to him as a Christian as to whether he is slave or free. Finally what matters is to have accepted God's call and to follow him (1 Cor 7:21–24; on this see S. S. Bartchy, ΜΑΛΛΟΝ ΧΡΗΣΑΙ. *First-Century Slavery and the Interpretation of 1 Corinthians 7:21* [SBLDS 11; Missoula, MT: Scholar's Press, 1971] and Gayer, *Stellung,* 172–222).

17. Paul mentioned the fact of his request of Philemon for Onesimus in verse 10. Only here does he actually spell out its content (so Friedrich, 194, Suhl, *Kairos* 15 [1973] 274, Stuhlmacher, 49, and Gayer, *Stellung,* 234) and come to the real point of the letter (so rightly von Soden, 77, and Ernst, 136). In the previous verses (13–16) the apostle looked back to the time when Onesimus sought refuge with him. The runaway slave subsequently became a Christian and now Paul sends him back to Philemon as "a beloved brother" (v 16). Only after he has carefully made these remarks does Paul indicate the nature of his specific request (according to BDF, para. 451[1], "After parenthetical remarks *οὖν* ["therefore"] indicates a return to the main theme," i.e. the conjunction is resumptive; see also Lohse, 203): *εἰ οὖν με ἔχεις κοινωνόν, προσλαβοῦ αὐτὸν ὡς ἐμέ* ("So then, if you consider me your partner, welcome him as you would me"). He bases his appeal on the close tie that exists between himself and Philemon, a tie that is described by means of the word *κοινωνός*. This term ("companion," "partner," "sharer," according

to BAG, 439, 440) was used (in the plural) of those who shared common interests or engaged in the same endeavors (Lohse, 203; Lightfoot, 341, says κοινωνοί are those who have "common interests, common feelings, common work"). Although κοινωνός could designate a "business-partner" (cf. Luke 5:10) it is not employed here of business transactions (Campbell, *Studies*, 10, rightly observes that in "this whole passage Paul makes half-playful but very effective use of business terms in writing of the spiritual relationship between Philemon and himself"; but this does not mean κοινωνός is being used with a technical significance, "business-partner," as in Luke 5:10: note the criticisms of Ollrog, *Paulus*, 77). Nor is Paul referring especially to ties of friendship. Rather, Philemon's and his κοινωνία is that fellowship with God's Son, Jesus Christ our Lord, into which both of them have been called (1 Cor 1:9). This relationship has drawn them together in common activities, and thus κοινωνός in this context may have the added nuance of "co-worker" (note 2 Cor 8:23 where κοινωνός and συνεργός, "fellow-worker," are conjoined with reference to Titus).

Paul not only intercedes on behalf of Onesimus; he also identifies himself with him: "receive him *as me*" (ὡς ἐμέ). This last expression corresponds to his earlier statement in verse 12 that his returning Onesimus was equivalent to sending himself back (τὰ ἐμὰ σπλάγχνα, lit. "my heart"). Paul's request, which is short and concise (Lohmeyer, 189), means at least that Onesimus should be treated as a fellow-Christian just as Paul himself would be treated (M. McDermott, "The Biblical Doctrine of ΚΟΙΝΩΝΙΑ," *BZ* 19 [1975] 228, 229). In addition, if the suggestion above about κοινωνός having the nuance of "co-worker" is correct, then Paul's expression here may mean he wants Onesimus to be accepted back both as a Christian and as Paul's colleague (προσλαμβάνω was regularly used with κοινωνόν to mean to "take on as a partner": see LSJ, 1518, 1519; cf. MM, 549, and Knox, *Philemon*, 24).

18. In a sentence that is formally parallel to the preceding (see above) the apostle guards against any possible hindrances to Philemon's favorable reception of Onesimus. He thus speaks about the financial aspects of the slave's escape since he does not want the reconciliation between Philemon and Onesimus to collapse because of "any demand for compensation" (H. Gülzow, cited by Stuhlmacher, 49): εἰ δέ τι ἠδίκησέν ἢ ὀφείλει ("if he has wronged you or owes you anything") is an introductory conditional clause and has been taken: *(a)* as a sentence which is hypothetical only in form but which describes the actual offense of Onesimus. So Caird, 222, 223, comments: "Paul knows very well that Onesimus has *wronged* his master and owes him a considerable sum of money. He must have helped himself to at least enough to pay his way to Rome." But this conclusion is no more than an inference (the interpretation has been held with varying degrees of conviction: see Bratcher and Nida, 129, "it most certainly was not [doubtful]," though note their later qualification; Lightfoot, 341, said Onesimus "probably had robbed" Philemon; while Vincent, 190, speaks of Onesimus' "possibly" robbing his master; Stuhlmacher, 49, suggests that the double expression, ἠδίκησεν," "wronged" [see further on Col 3:25], and ὀφείλει, "owes," indicates Onesimus not only wronged his master by running away but also had pilfered some of his money; cf. Dibelius-Greeven, 106, Scott, 98, and Friedrich, 193).

(b) The sentence is a conditional one and may simply suggest that his overdue absence from Colossae (is it possible—as Bruce, *Paul,* 400, questions—that his master had sent him to Paul to fulfill some commission and that Onesimus overstayed his leave?) or his running away meant he owed his master the value of the work that should have been done (Martin, *NCB,* 167; Gayer, *Stellung,* 230, considers Paul might well have used ὅ, "whatever," rather than a conditional clause had he wished to make it plain that Onesimus had actually wronged his master; note also Lohmeyer, 190, Lohse, 204, and Suhl, *Kairos,* 15 [1973] 269).

Either way Philemon is asked to let the outstanding damages resulting from Onesimus' flight (or absence) be charged to the apostle's account: τοῦτο ἐμοὶ ἐλλόγα ("Put that on my bill"). ἐλλογέω (on the unusual formation ἐλλόγα see BDF, para. 90 and BAG, 252) was a commercial technical term meaning to "charge to someone's account" as the papyri show (*PStrassb* 1.32.10: "so that in this way he can settle accounts with him" [ἐνλογηθῇ]; for further examples see Preisker, *TDNT* 2, 516, 517, BAG, 252, and Lohse, 204; there is only one other instance in the NT, viz. Rom 5:13). As a father for his son (cf. v 10) Paul declares he is prepared to stand good for any damages.

19. ἐγὼ Παῦλος ἔγραψα τῇ ἐμῇ χειρί, ἐγὼ ἀποτίσω ("I Paul am writing this with my own hand. I will pay it"). These words of verse 19*a* are a parenthesis (Lohse, 204, Zmijewski, *BibLeb* 15 [1974] 290, 291, and Gayer, *Stellung,* 256) as Paul inserts his own legal promissory note or IOU (the introduction of his own name [see v 9] together with the twofold emphatic ἐγώ, "I," gives the statement the character of a formal and binding signature: see Lightfoot, 342, and Zmijewski, *BibLeb* 15 [1974] 291), undertaking to make compensation for the damages (ἀποτίνω, which occurs only here in the NT, is a legal technical term, found frequently in the papyri [cf. *POxy* 2.275.27], meaning to "make compensation," "pay the damages," see BAG, 101, cf. Deissmann, *Light from the Ancient East,* 332, who notes it is a much stronger term than ἀποδώσω, "I will give back"). The reference to Paul writing (ἔγραψα is an epistolary aorist: see on v 12) these words in his own hand was taken by Lightfoot, Roller and others to indicate that he composed and wrote the whole letter personally (Lightfoot, 342, Roller, *Formular,* 592, and Müller, 188; cf. Rom 16:22; 1 Cor 16:21; Gal 6:11; 2 Thess 3:17). Dibelius-Greeven drew the opposite conclusion, namely that the rest of the letter was dictated (106, 107; Scott, 112, note Friedrich, 195, Bratcher and Nida, 130: "Here Paul takes the stylus and writes these words himself." Cf. G. J. Bahr, "The Subscriptions in the Pauline Letters," *JBL* 87 [1968] 27–41, who suggests that the subscriptions had a legal function: they summarized the document in the contractor's own hand binding him to its details). But one cannot determine with certainty from these incidental remarks the manner in which Paul composed his letters; note Vincent, 190, Lohse, 204, and Doty, *Letters,* 41, who adds that in Hellenistic official letter records the writer might add a résumé of the document in his own writing showing he was aware of its contents and details. He thinks that such a situation is suggested by these remarks of Paul in verse 19.

After the parenthesis the rest of the sentence picks up the thought of verse 18: ἵνα μὴ λέγω σοι ὅτι καὶ σεαυτόν μοι προσοφείλεις ("not to mention that you owe me your very self besides"). In the opening words (ἵνα μὴ λέγω:

note the unusual *μή*, "not," with the indicative) a sort of elliptical construction is employed "in which the writer delicately protests against saying something which he nevertheless does say" (Vincent, 190; cf. BDF, para. 495[1], and note 2 Cor 9:4). If the discussion is to focus on debts then Paul reminds the addressee that it is he, Philemon, who is indebted to the apostle. (Mutual obligations have been established: cf. Rom 15:26, 27 and note Stuhlmacher's discussion, 50). The words have been chosen carefully—*προσοφείλεις* ("you owe [besides]," cf. *PHib* 63.14, "what you owe me [besides]," and note BAG, 717, who claims it is difficult to find any special force in the preposition *προσ-* and so to differentiate it from the simple verb, to "owe something") clearly corresponds to *ὀφείλει* ("[if] he owes") in the preceding verse while there is an interesting interplay of pronouns in the first and second persons (v 18 "if he has wronged *you* . . . charge that to *me*"; v 19, " . . . *I* will repay . . . *you* owe *yourself* to *me*")—as Paul indicates it was through him that Philemon had been converted (it has been suggested that Philemon's conversion was only indirectly due to Paul's ministry as he sent out his colleagues, especially Epaphras, to the Lycus valley region including Colossae: however, the expression appears to be stronger than this indicating Paul was personally and directly responsible for Philemon's conversion; the latter may have met Paul outside the Lycus Valley [cf. Col 2:2]; perhaps such an encounter took place on a visit to Ephesus). He therefore owed his spiritual life to Paul and that was a far greater debt than Onesimus had incurred and for which Paul would be responsible. The message is plain. Philemon will understand that Onesimus has experienced the same grace and mercy of God when he was converted. He should therefore receive him as a brother in Christ and not be angry with him even though there may be good grounds for it (Lohse, 205).

20. The principal section of the letter is concluded with Paul strengthening his request. He once again addresses Philemon as a Christian brother and expresses the wish that he may have great joy in him in the Lord: *ναί, ἀδελφέ, ἐγώ σου ὀναίμην ἐν κυρίῳ. ἀνάπαυσόν μου τὰ σπλάγχνα ἐν Χριστῷ* ("Yes, brother, I do wish that I may have some benefit from you in the Lord; refresh my heart in Christ"). The particle *ναί* ("yes," "indeed," "certainly"), which can denote affirmation, agreement or emphasis (BAG, 532, 533), here strengthens Paul's appeal (note Phil 4:3, "Yes indeed, I ask you too [*ναὶ ἐρωτῶ καὶ σέ*]," and cf. Matt 11:26; Luke 10:21; 11:51; 12:5). No fresh request is made beyond that of verse 17; Paul simply wishes that Philemon would fulfill his heart's desire. Once again *ἀδελφέ* ("brother," cf. v 7), the affectionate term of address, is used. Lightfoot (342) aptly remarks: "It is the entreaty of a brother to a brother on behalf of a brother" (see v 16 where the apostle had called Onesimus "a beloved brother," and note Friedrich, 195). This desire finds expression in a formula which was frequent in current usage although Paul uses it only here (the verb *ὀνίνημι* in the first person aorist optative meaning "may I have joy, profit or benefit," "may I enjoy" [with the genitive case of the thing or person that is the source of the joy] turns up frequently: Ignatius, *Eph* 2:2; *Mag* 2; 12:1; *Rom* 5:2; *Pol* 1:1; 6:2; for further examples see BAG, 570; the optative mood, which apart from this reference in the NT always occurs in the third person singular [cf. Burton, *Syntax*, 79, Moulton, *Prole-*

gomena, 195, Robertson, *Grammar,* 939], is used to denote an attainable wish: BDF, paras. 65[2], 384). Although the expression was often thought to continue the word-play on the name of Onesimus this is doubtful in the light of the frequent occurrence of the expression elsewhere (note the statement of BDF, para. 488[1b]; cf. Lohse, 205, Martin, *NCB,* 167, and Gayer, *Stellung,* 242). The apostle's earnest wish concerns the future of Onesimus. But Paul is closely and personally identified with him: the emphatic ἐγώ ("I") joins the cause of Onesimus with his own so that he, Paul, will also benefit from Philemon's action (cf. Lightfoot, 342, Lohmeyer, 191), and that "in the Lord" (ἐν κυρίῳ). This latter phrase has been understood as referring to Philemon's giving a benefit to Paul "in a Christian way" (so Martin, *NCB,* 167), i.e. by fulfilling his request; alternatively it is thought that by freeing Onesimus for the service of the gospel, the benefit will truly be "in the Lord" (Lohmeyer, 191; cf. Knox, *Philemon,* 25, and see below on v 21).

At the conclusion of his introductory thanksgiving paragraph Paul had referred to Philemon's acts of love by which "the hearts of the saints have been refreshed" (τὰ σπλάγχνα τῶν ἁγίων ἀναπέπαυται, v 7). Now in the final sentence of the body of the letter he clothes his request of Philemon with similar words in anticipation that this dear brother will once again act in love and "refresh the heart," this time the heart of the apostle (note the emphatic position of μου, "my," in <u>μου</u> τὰ σπλάγχνα, "my heart"), by fulfilling the express wish of verse 17 and so by receiving Onesimus in place of Paul himself (ἐν Χριστῷ, "in Christ," is here a stylistic variant of ἐν κυρίῳ, "in the Lord," cf. Moule, *Origin,* 59; Philemon's action of refreshing Paul will be a Christian one, effected on behalf of a brother who is "in Christ").

Explanation

In a carefully structured paragraph (vv 8–20) in which he weighs his words carefully, Paul makes his plea for Onesimus, Philemon's runaway slave. He begins with a brief description of his situation (vv 8–12), indicating that although he has the boldness or openness in Christ to command Philemon to do what is proper for him as a Christian in the circumstances concerning Onesimus, he refuses to enforce compliance with his word. Rather, he bases his appeal on other grounds, namely, Philemon's love. It is precisely because he knows of Philemon's kindness and generosity in the past that he is able to entreat, and he looks forward to Philemon's love being shown once again, this time with reference to Onesimus. Behind the request stands one who is both an ambassador and a slave of Christ Jesus and his plea is made on behalf of his child Onesimus, who was converted through his ministry while he was in prison. He indicates how very dear he has become to him by stating he is sending back one who is his very heart. As a Phrygian slave—and they were proverbial for being unreliable and unfaithful—he had previously been useless to Philemon. But a great change has occurred and Paul describes this by a "once-now" contrast. This mighty transformation had been effected by Onesimus' conversion to Christ as Lord, and he might now be called "useful," a description that truly fits his name for Onesimus means "profitable" or "useful." Paul would dearly have liked to retain Onesimus with him so that he might take Philemon's place in assisting him in the preaching of the gospel, especially as he was in prison on its account. But it would have been illegal for Paul to act in this way, apart from involving a breach of Christian fellowship between himself and Philemon. However, he would do nothing without the latter's consent or act in such a way that might suggest coercion or an intrusion into Philemon's decision. Further, had Paul detained Onesimus he might well have acted contrary to God's hidden purpose: "perhaps he (Onesimus) was separated from you for a little while so that you might have him back for ever." Paul puts forward this suggestion modestly, since he is not presuming to be acquainted with God's designs. At the same time his language, which has been chosen carefully, is intended to turn Philemon's attention from the individual wrongs he may have incurred to God's providence which has made these wrongs work for good (cf. Gen 45:4–8).

Finally, Paul spells out the specific content of his request: "welcome him as you would welcome me" (v 17). Although he has just referred to Onesimus as a "slave," Paul immediately qualifies this by means of an antithesis: he will be far more than a slave to his master—a beloved brother. And it is precisely in this capacity that he wants Philemon to receive Onesimus. He is not asking that Onesimus be received back as a freed man, or that Philemon is to free him immediately on his return. Onesimus, by being spoken of as a "brother," is addressed in exactly the same way as Philemon (cf. vv 7, 20): he too has been incorporated into the body of Christ. Thus the relationship between the two men is deepened so that, in a sense, the terms "master" and "slave" are transcended, and their behavior ought to be conducted in the light of their belonging to the same Lord. Although Onesimus' earthly freedom may be of positive value, finally it is of no ultimate significance to him as a Christian as to whether he is slave or free. In the end what matters is to have accepted God's call and to follow him (cf. 1 Cor 7:21–24).

To guard against any possible hindrances to Philemon's favorable reception of Onesimus, Paul urges that any outstanding damages resulting from the latter's flight (or absence) be charged to his own account. "Put that on my bill" are the words of the apostle's promissory note to which he then adds his own signature. He does not wish to mention it, but because Philemon himself has been converted through the ministry of Paul, he owes the apostle his own spiritual life and that is a far greater debt than Onesimus has incurred and for which Paul would be responsible. The message is plain. Philemon will understand that Onesimus has experienced the same grace and mercy of God when he was converted. He should therefore receive him as a brother in Christ and not be angry with him even though there may be good grounds for it. Paul concludes the body of his letter by strengthening his request and expressing the wish that Philemon may refresh his heart in Christ.

Final Remarks and Greetings (21–25)

Bibliography

Doty, W. G. *Letters,* 12, 36–42. **Funk, R. W.** "The Apostolic *Parousia:* Form and Significance." *Christian History and Interpretation. Studies Presented to John Knox,* ed. W. R. Farmer and others. Cambridge: University Press, 1967, 249–68. **Hainz, J.** *Ekklesia,* 206–209. **Mullins, T. Y.** "Visit Talk in New Testament Letters." *CBQ* 35 (1973) 350–58. **Wiles, G. P.** *Prayers,* 281–84.

Translation

[21] *Confident of your obedience, I write to you, knowing that you will do even more than I say.* [22] *At the same time, prepare a guest room for me, for I hope that I will be restored to you in answer to your prayers.*

[23] *Epaphras, my fellow-prisoner in Christ Jesus, sends you greetings.* [24] *As also do Mark, Aristarchus, Demas and Luke, my co-workers.* [25] *The grace of the*[a] *Lord Jesus Christ be with your spirit.*[b]

Notes

[a] The Textus Receptus adds ἡμῶν, "our," after κυρίου, "Lord": so A C D K 614 it vg etc. If the pronoun was present originally, then it is hard to explain its omission in ℵ P 33 81 and others. On the other hand, scribes were prone to introduce these sorts of expansions. The shorter reading is preferred (see Metzger, *Textual Commentary,* 658).

[b] Several manuscripts (ℵ C D[c]), versions and Fathers append a liturgical ἀμήν ("Amen"), but good representatives of the Alexandrian and Western text types (A D* 048 33 81 1881) have resisted this tendency.

Form/Structure/Setting

Paul brings his letter to Philemon to a conclusion with a few brief sentences. In verses 21 and 22 he assures Philemon of his confidence that the latter will certainly do what is right, and then announces he is planning to visit him. Paul's desire is that the intercessions of Philemon and his household for him will be heard so that he will be able to journey to Colossae in freedom. A short list of greetings (vv 23, 24) and the benediction (v 25) conclude the letter.

Comment

21. With his final remarks and greetings Paul brings the letter to Philemon to a close. He glances back at the matter previously mentioned and assures Philemon, as he writes to him, of his confidence in his obedience (πεποιθὼς τῇ ὑπακοῇ σου ἔγραψά σοι). The term ὑπακοή, which means "obedience" rather than "readiness" or "willingness" (cf. the "Bereitwilligkeit" of Dibelius-

Greeven, 106; Wickert, *ZNW* 52 [1961] 233, has argued against this translation and in favor of "obedience," the usual meaning of the term; cf. BAG, 837, and note Col 3:20 with reference to the cognate ὑπακούω, to "obey"), seems rather unusual here. Paul has expressly rejected the use of his apostolic right to command Philemon and instead bases his *appeal* on love (see the exegesis of vv 8, 9 above). Yet the term ὑπακοή ("obedience") is a strong one signifying men's obedience to God (Rom 6:16) or to his will as expressed in the gospel (Rom 15:18; 16:19), as well as to his chosen representatives, the apostle and his emissaries (2 Cor 7:15; 10:6). ὑπακοή is employed of Christ's obedience (Heb 5:8) to God (Rom 5:10) as well as of that obedience to Christ into which Paul intends to bring every thought captive (2 Cor 10:5). So does the presence of this authoritative term "obedience" suggest that when Paul referred to his request of or appeal to Philemon (v 9) he was simply speaking in a rhetorical fashion and that his apostolic authority was, in fact, being exercised in these words? Stuhlmacher (52) has rightly posed the question along these lines for he, as few other commentators, has seen the issue clearly (Dibelius-Greeven, 106, tried to solve the dilemma with the rendering of ὑπακοή as "willingness" or "readiness"). Others speak of "obedience" as being "the only appropriate response that the addressee can give to the word of the Apostle" (so Lohse, 206; cf. Wickert, *ZNW* 52 [1961] 233, and Hainz, *Ekklesia*, 206, 207); since Paul's request is the word of an apostle then Philemon is duty-bound to obey. But to interpret the statement along these lines is to fly in the face of the plain words of verses 8 and 9, and positive noises about Pauline dialectic (cf. Hainz, *Ekklesia*, 208) do not resolve the dilemma.

Paul has already made it clear in his introduction that he has interceded for Philemon regarding his understanding and generosity (see on v 6), a generosity that Paul obviously desires will be effective in the case of Onesimus. Such an intercession, like its parallels in his other introductory paragraphs (Phil 1: 9–11; Col 1:9, 10; 1 Thess 3:11–13; 2 Thess 1:11, 12), is a petition for a deeper understanding of God's will and the performance of it in love. Here the writer expresses his confidence that Philemon will be obedient to that will of God. He has prayed to that end, and there has been clear evidence of Philemon's obedience in the past, demonstrated so concretely in his continuous generosity as he has refreshed the hearts of the saints (v 7; cf. Stuhlmacher, 52, 53).

As Philemon is obedient to the will of God so Paul says he "knows that you will do even more than I say" (εἰδὼς ὅτι καὶ ὑπὲρ ἃ λέγω ποιήσεις). These words are tantalizing. The author has said expressly that he wants Philemon to receive Onesimus as he would himself (v 17). But what is the "more" that he so tactfully does not spell out? Preiss (*Life*, 36) thinks that Onesimus is to be received back home by Philemon for the service of the gospel, and not in order to be reinstated as a domestic slave. Lightfoot (343) discusses the possibility of manumission and comments: ". . . the idea would seem to be present to his thoughts, though the word never passes his lips." However, Dibelius-Greeven's remark (107) appears to be correct: "The legal side of the matter is not in view at all." In other words the issue is not simply the legal release of Onesimus. Paul has already indicated he would have liked to keep Onesimus so that he could have served with him in the gospel (note the exegesis of v 13). As we read between the lines it seems best to interpret the "more" as a desire of the apostle for Onesimus to be returned to him for the service of the gospel (so Lohmeyer, 191, Knox, *Philemon*, 24–26, Harrison, *ATR* 32 [1950] 276–80; Wiles, *Prayers*, 216, 221, Bruce, *Paul*, 406; for a contrary view see Wickert, *ZNW* 52 [1961] 230–38, and Lohse 206).

22. The writer then indicates that he hopes to come in person and visit Philemon. So he requests the latter to prepare quarters for him. No doubt by making this announcement he lends a certain emphasis to his intercession for Onesimus since he will obviously be able to see for himself how things have gone (cf. Lohse, 206, 207). References such as this to his future "presence" have been the subject of detailed epistolary study in recent times. It has been suggested that this feature at the close of the epistle, called a "travelogue," is no courtesy remark but a deliberately phrased convention, known from letter forms in the Greco-Roman world (Doty, *Letters*, 12, 36, 37, and Martin, *NCB*, 169). Funk (*History*, 249–68) has examined this travelogue form in some detail (notably at Rom 15:14–33; 1 Cor 4:14–21; Phil 2:19–24; 1 Thess 2:17–3:13 in addition to Phlm 21, 22) and understands it as one element of the "apostolic *Parousia*" in which Paul seeks to convey to the readers the presence of his apostolic authority and power. Mullins (*CBQ* 35 [1973] 350–58), however, has argued convincingly that these references to forthcoming visits by Paul denote a theme at the conclusions of his letters rather than a fixed formula.

ἅμα δὲ καὶ ἑτοίμαζέ μοι ξενίαν. "At the same time, prepare a guest room for me." On the adverb *ἅμα*, "at the same time," see on Colossians 4:3. Here it is attached to the immediately preceding words and signifies: "at the same time as your kindly action in connection with Onesimus." *ξενία* usually denotes "hospitality" or "entertainment" shown to a guest, but here it refers to the place where the guest is lodged, the "guest room" (Acts 28:23 and *Ps-Clem Hom* 12:2; see BAG, 547, and note Lightfoot's discussion, 343, of the Greek term and its Latin equivalent).

The ground for (*γάρ*) this request is that Paul hopes "to be restored to you in answer to your prayers" (*ἐλπίζω γὰρ ὅτι διὰ τῶν προσευχῶν ὑμῶν χαρισθήσομαι ὑμῖν*). As in the serious request of Philippians 1:19, so here too the author does not directly ask for their intercessions (*προσευχή* designates "petition for others," i.e. "intercession"), but tactfully takes it for granted that Philemon and those of his household (for the first time since v 3 the plural "you," *ὑμῶν*, is used; the change to the plural does not mean that the other members of the household are aware of the contents of the letter) are remembering him and his imprisonment constantly in prayer. This further suggests that Philemon's household are concerned not only about Paul's personal welfare, centering upon his release from prison, but also about the important ministry to which he is called and committed (note Wiles, *Prayers*, 281–83).

ἐλπίζω . . . χαρισθήσομαι ὑμῖν. Lit. "I hope . . . I will be granted to you." If the verb *ἐλπίζω* is being used in its normal NT sense of a firm hope or expectation then Paul is stating he is confident that he will soon be freed from prison (several commentators take it this way; Wiles, *Prayers*, 282, states, however, that "on this occasion, too [*sc.* as in Phil 1:19, 20], he is not sure of the outcome of his imprisonment: he is *hoping* to be granted to them through their prayers"). How or when this will occur is not known; such a decision rests entirely in God's hands who, it is hoped, will graciously restore Paul to the community (the Greek is expressive: the verb *χαρισθήσομαι* is in the passive indicating it is only God who can secure Paul's release—that is why he is to be petitioned in prayer—while the basic meaning of the word to "give freely or graciously as a favor" [see on Col 2:13, and note the parallel in Test Joseph 1:6, "I was in prison, and the Savior restored, *ἐχαρίτωσε*, me," cited by Lohse, 206] draws attention to the gracious nature of the divine action). Paul's hope for his release is not for his own sake but for the benefit of these Christians at Colossae (this is the significance of the plural *ὑμῖν*, "for you").

23. In the last two verses of the letter the apostle sends greetings (*ἀσπάζεται*: see on Col 4:10) from his co-workers to Philemon. The list of names, all of which occur in Col 4:10–14, begins with Epaphras who is described as "my fellow-prisoner in Christ Jesus" (*συναιχμάλωτός μου ἐν Χριστῷ Ἰησοῦ*). At Colossians 4:10 Aristarchus is called a fellow-prisoner (*συναιχμάλωτος*) of Paul. Although the term could be used in a figurative sense of one who had been taken captive by Christ and was a co-worker, in both places it is best understood as a description of a companion who is in prison with the apostle (so Lohse, 207, Martin, *NCB*, 169, Stuhlmacher, 55, and Ollrog, *Paulus*, 76). Here if Paul simply wanted to call Epaphras his "co-worker" the term *συνεργός* (v 24) would have been adequate. The presence of the two words in verses 23 and 24 suggests they are to be distinguished. Epaphras, the founder of the church at Colossae (see on Col 4:12, 13), shares Paul's confinement (note v 1). He is mentioned first since he was a Colossian (Col 4:12) and as the evangelist of Colossae was no doubt well known to Philemon.

It has been conjectured (E. Amling, "Eine Konjektur im Philemonbrief," *ZNW* 10 [1909] 261, 262) that the last two words in the preceding phrase "in Christ Jesus" (*ἐν Χριστῷ Ἰησοῦς*) should be separated by a comma so that the latter, "Jesus," then becomes the name of the man "Jesus called Justus" referred to in Colossians 4:11. On this view the list of names mentioned in Colossians 4:10–14 would then correspond with this list in Philemon 23, 24. It has been argued that if one reads "in Christ Jesus" instead of "in Christ, Jesus" it is the only place in the letter where the phrase occurs while elsewhere Paul employs "in Christ" (vv 8, 20) and "in the Lord" (vv 16, 20). But it is precarious to build too much on the evidence of such a short letter (of 335 words) especially as Paul does write "for Christ Jesus" in verses 1, 9 (Martin, *NCB*, 169; Stuhlmacher, 55, rightly contends that to conjecture the omission of the last letter *ς* of *Ἰησοῦς*, "Jesus," against the manuscript evidence is neither expedient nor likely; against Zahn whose suggestion is cited with approval by Lohse, 207, and Ollrog, *Paulus*, 49).

24. Mark, Aristarchus, Demas and Luke as Paul's fellow-workers also send their greetings (see on Col 4:10, 14). In contrast to the more complete list in Colossians 4 no details are given about those mentioned. However, they are styled "fellow-workers" (*συνεργοί*, see on Col 4:11 and Philem 1) a term already used of Philemon himself. Both senders and recipient of the greetings

were engaged in the task of proclaiming Christ, having been commissioned by God. They had labored together with Paul in the joint work of preaching the gospel, especially to Gentiles (cf. Ollrog, *Paulus*, 63–72; regarding the subject of Paul and his co-workers see 272, 273).

25. On the closing benediction, which was a regular and consistent element at the end of Paul's letters, see the comments on Colossians 4:18. As in its Colossian counterpart so here too the final benediction picks up the introductory greeting (v 3). Paul desires that Philemon and his "house community" (the plural ὑμῶν, "your," here corresponds to the ὑμῖν, "to you," of v 3) may apprehend more fully "the grace of the (or 'our,' see the note above 304) Lord Jesus Christ." At the same time the benediction strikes a note of confidence indicating that Christ's grace will remain with this house congregation. In place of the simple μεθ' ὑμῶν ("with you") the fuller expression μετὰ τοῦ πνεύματος ὑμῶν ("with your spirit") occurs, as in Galatians 6:18 and Philippians 4:23. πνεῦμα ("spirit") is found with an anthropological significance so that there is no difference in meaning between this phrase and the shorter "with you" (Schweizer, *TDNT* 6, 435).

Explanation

Paul closes his letter to Philemon with some final remarks and greetings. He has already interceded for his dear friend regarding his understanding and generosity (v 6), a generosity he trusts will be demonstrated toward Onesimus. Such an intercession is, in effect, a petition for a deeper understanding of God's will and the performance of it in love. Paul now expresses his confidence that Philemon will be obedient to that will of God and do even *more* than he has been requested, which was to receive Onesimus as a beloved brother, even as Paul himself. What this "more" is the author does not tell us, but it is just possible he is expressing the desire for Onesimus to be returned to him for the service of the gospel. Paul hopes to come in person and visit Philemon and if this occurs it will be because God has graciously answered the prayers of this house church. The announcement of this hope gives a certain emphasis to his intercession for Onesimus as it will enable him to see for himself as to how things have gone.

The apostle sends greetings to Philemon from five of his co-workers and then closes with a benediction that Christ's grace might remain with the members of this house church.

Bibliography

A. Texts, Commentaries and Reference Works
(Commentaries are cited by referring to the author's name and page number)

Abbott, T. K. *The Epistles to the Ephesians and to the Colossians.* ICC. Edinburgh: Clark, 1897.
Aland, K., Black, M., Martini, C. M., Metzger, B. M. and Wikgren, A. edd. *The Greek New Testament.* 3rd ed. New York: United Bible Societies, 1975.
Bauer, W. *A Greek-English Lexicon of the New Testament and Other Early Christian Literature.* Tr. and ed. from 5th German ed. Arndt, W. F. and Gingrich, F. W. 2nd ed. revised and augmented by F. W. Gingrich and Danker, F. W. Chicago: University Press, 1979.
Beare, F. W. *The Epistle to the Colossians.* IB 11. New York and Nashville: Abingdon, 1955.
Bengel, J. A. *New Testament Word Studies.* Vol. 2. Tr. Lewis, C. T. and Vincent, M. R. Grand Rapids, MI: Kregel, 1971.
Benoit, P. *Les Epîtres de Saint Paul aux Philippiens, aux Colossiens, à Philémon, aux Ephésiens.* La Sainte Bible. Paris: Editions du Cerf, 1949.
Blass, F. and Debrunner, A. *A Greek Grammar of the New Testament and Other Early Christian Literature.* Tr. and rev. from the 9th–10th German edition by Funk, R. W. Chicago: University Press, 1961.
Bratcher, R. G. and Nida, E. A. *A Translator's Handbook on Paul's Letters to the Colossians and to Philemon.* Stuttgart: United Bible Societies, 1977.
Brown, C. ed. *The New International Dictionary of New Testament Theology.* 3 vols. Exeter: Paternoster, 1975–78. American edition Grand Rapids, MI: Zondervan, 1975–78.
Bruce, F. F. in Simpson, E. K., and Bruce, F. F. *Commentary on the Epistles to the Ephesians and the Colossians.* NICNT. Grand Rapids, MI: Eerdmans, 1957.
Burton, E. de W. *Syntax of the Moods and Tenses in New Testament Greek.* 3rd ed. Edinburgh: Clark, 1898.
Caird, G. B. *Paul's Letters from Prison (Ephesians, Philippians, Colossians, Philemon) in the Revised Standard Version.* London and New York: Oxford University Press, 1976.
Carson, H. M. *Colossians and Philemon.* TNTC. London: Tyndale, 1960.
Conzelmann, H. *Die kleineren Briefe des Apostels Paulus. Der Brief an die Kolosser.* NTD 8. 10th ed. Göttingen: Vandenhoeck & Ruprecht, 1965.
Dibelius, M. *An die Kolosser, Epheser an Philemon.* HNT 12. 3rd ed. rev. by Greeven, H. Tübingen: Mohr, 1953.
Ernst, J. *Die Briefe an die Philipper, an Philemon, an die Kolosser, an die Epheser.* RNT. Regensburg: Pustet, 1974.
Field, F. *Notes on the Translation of the New Testament.* Cambridge: University Press, 1899.
Friedrich, G. *Die kleineren Briefe des Apostels Paulus. Der Brief an Philemon.* NTD 8. 10th ed. Göttingen: Vandenhoeck & Ruprecht, 1965.
Haupt, E. *Die Gefangenschaftsbriefe.* MeyerK 8–9. 8th ed. Vandenhoeck & Ruprecht, 1902.
Kittel, G. and Friedrich, G. eds. *Theological Dictionary of the New Testament.* 10 vols. Tr. Bromiley, G. W. Grand Rapids, MI: Eerdmans, 1964–76.
Lightfoot, J. B. *Saint Paul's Epistles to the Colossians and to Philemon.* 9th ed. London: Macmillan, 1890.
Lohmeyer, E. *Die Briefe an die Philipper, Kolosser und an Philemon.* MeyerK 9. 13th ed. Göttingen: Vandenhoeck & Ruprecht, 1964.
Lohse, E. *Colossians and Philemon.* Tr. Poehlmann, W. R., and Karris, R. J. from 14th German ed. Hermeneia. Philadelphia: Fortress, 1971.
Martin, R. P. *Colossians: The Church's Lord and the Christian's Liberty.* Exeter: Paternoster, 1972. (reprint) Palm Springs, CA: R. N. Haynes Publ. Co. 1982.
______. *Colossians and Philemon.* NCB. 3rd ed. London: Oliphants, 1981. Grand Rapids, MI: Eerdmans.
Masson, C. *L'Epître aux Colossiens.* CNT 10. Paris: Delachaux et Niestlé, 1950.
Metzger, B. M. *A Textual Commentary on the Greek New Testament.* London and New York: United Bible Societies, 1971.
Meyer, H. A. W. *Critical and Exegetical Handbook to the Epistles to the Philippians and Colossians.* Tr. Dickson, W. P. New York: Funk and Wagnalls, 1875.
Moule, C. F. D. *An Idiom Book of New Testament Greek.* Cambridge: University Press, 1953.
______. *The Epistles of Paul the Apostle to the Colossians and to Philemon.* Cambridge: University Press, 1962.
Moulton, J. H. *A Grammar of New Testament Greek.* Vol. 1. *Prolegomena.* 3rd ed. Edinburgh: Clark, 1908.
Moulton, J. H. and Howard, W. F. *A Grammar of New Testament Greek.* Vol. 2. *Accidence and Word-Formation.* Edinburgh: Clark, 1929.
Moulton, J. H. and Milligan, G. *The Vocabulary of the Greek Testament.* London: Hodder, 1930.
Müller, J. J. *The Epistles of Paul to the Philippians and to Philemon.* NICNT. Grand Rapids, MI: Eerdmans, 1955.
Nestle, E. and Aland, K. *Novum Testamentum Graece.* 26th ed. Aland, K., Black, M., Martini, C. M., Metzger, B. M., Wikgren, A. Stuttgart: Deutsche Bibelstiftung, 1979.
Radford, L. B. *The Epistle to the Colossians and the Epistle to Philemon.* WC. London: Methuen, 1931.

Robertson, A. T. *A Grammar of the Greek New Testament in the Light of Historical Research.* 4th ed. Nashville: Broadman, 1923.
Schlatter, A. *Der Brief an Philemon: Erläuterungen zum Neuen Testament* 2, Stuttgart: Calwer Verlag, 1909, 861–66.
Schmauch, W. *Beiheft* to Lohmeyer, E. *Die Briefe an die Philipper, Kolosser und an Philemon.* MeyerK 9. 13th ed. Göttingen: Vandenhoeck & Ruprecht, 1964.
Schweizer, E. *Der Brief an die Kolosser.* EKKNT. Zurich: Benziger, 1976.
Scott, E. F. *The Epistles of Paul to the Colossians, to Philemon and to the Ephesians.* MNTC. London: Hodder, 1930.
Stuhlmacher, P. *Der Brief an Philemon.* EKKNT. Zürich: Bensiger, 1975.
Thrall, M. E. *Greek Particles in the New Testament. Linguistic and Exegetical Studies.* NTTS 3. Leiden: Brill, 1962.
Turner, N. *Syntax* of J. H. Moulton, *A Grammar of New Testament Greek.* Vol. 3. Edinburgh: Clark, 1963.
Vincent, M. R. *The Epistles to the Philippians and to Philemon.* ICC. Edinburgh: Clark, 1897.
von Soden, H. *Die Briefe an die Kolosser, Epheser, Philemon; die Pastoralbriefe.* Hand-Commentar zum Neuen Testament 3,1. 2nd ed. Leipzig: 1893.
Williams, A. L. *The Epistles of Paul the Apostle to the Colossians and to Philemon.* The Cambridge Greek Testament for Schools and Colleges. Cambridge: University Press, 1907.
Zerwick, M. *Biblical Greek.* Tr. Smith, J. Rome: Pontifical Biblical Institute, 1963.

B. Studies, Articles, etc. relating to Colossians

Agnew, F. "On the Origin of the Term *Apostolos.*" *CBQ* 38 (1976) 49–53.
Aletti, J. N. *Colossiens, 1, 15–20. Genre et exégèse du texte Fonction de la thématique sapientelle.* AnBib 91. Rome: Biblical Institute. 1981.
Anderson, C. P. "Who Wrote 'the Epistle from Laodicea'?" *JBL* 85 (1966) 436–40.
Asting, R. *Die Verkündigung des Wortes im Urchristentum.* Stuttgart: Kohlhammer, 1939.
Austgen, R. J. *Natural Motivation in the Pauline Epistles.* 2nd ed. Notre Dame: University Press, 1969.
Bacchiocchi, S. *From Sabbath to Sunday. A Historical Investigation of the Rise of Sunday Observance in Early Christianity.* Rome: Pontifical Gregorian University, 1977.
Bammel, E. "Versuch zu Col 1:15–20." *ZNW* 52 (1961) 88–95.
Bandstra, A. J. "Did the Colossian Errorists Need a Mediator?" *New Dimensions in New Testament Study,* ed. Longenecker, R. N. and Tenney, M. C. Grand Rapids, MI: Zondervan, 1974, 329–43.
______. *The Law and the Elements of the World. An Exegetical Study in Aspects of Paul's Teaching.* Kampen: Kok, 1964. American edition, Grand Rapids, MI: Eerdmans.
Banks, R. J. *Paul's Idea of Community. The Early House Churches in Their Historical Setting.* Grand Rapids, MI: Eerdmans, 1980.
Barrett, C. K. *From First Adam to Last. A Study in Pauline Theology.* New York: Scribner's, 1962.
Barth, M. *Ephesians. Translation and Commentary on Chapters 1–6.* AB 34, 34A. Garden City, NY: Doubleday, 1974.
Bauckham, R. J. "Colossians 1:24 Again: The Apocalyptic Motif." *EvQ* 47 (1975) 168–70.
Baumert, N. *Täglich sterben und auferstehen. Der Literalsinn von 2 Kor 4,12–5,10.* SANT 84. Munich: Kösel, 1973.
Beasley-Murray, G. R. *Baptism in the New Testament.* London: Macmillan, 1962.
______. "The Second Chapter of Colossians." *RevExp* 70 (1973) 469–79.
Bedale, S. "The Meaning of κεφαλή in the Pauline Epistles." *JTS* 5 (1954) 211–15.
Benoit, P. "Corps, tête et plérôme dans les épîtres de la captivité." *RB* 63 (1956) 5–44.
______. "L'hymne christologique de Col 1, 15–20. Jugement critique sur l'état des recherches." *Christianity, Judaism and Other Greco-Roman Cults. Studies for Morton Smith at Sixty,* ed. Neusner, J. Part One. New Testament. SJLA 12. Leiden: Brill, 1975, 226–63.
______. "Qumran and the New Testament." *Paul and Qumran. Studies in New Testament Exegesis,* ed. Murphy-O'Connor, J. London: Chapman, 1968, 1–30.
Berger, K. "Apostelbrief und apostolische Rede/Zum Formular frühchristlicher Briefe." *ZNW* 65 (1974) 190–231.
______. "Die sogenannten 'Sätze heiligen Rechts' im Neuen Testament. Ihre Funktion und ihr Sitz im Leben." *TZ* 28 (1972) 305–330.
Best, E. *A Historical Study of the Exegesis of Col 2, 14.* Rome: unpublished thesis, 1956.
______. *One Body in Christ. A Study in the Relationship of the Church to Christ in the Epistles of the Apostle Paul.* London: SPCK, 1955.
Betz, O. "*Felsenmann und Felsengemeinde (Eine Parallele zu Mt. 16: 17–19 in den Qumranpsalmen).*" *ZNW* 48 (1957) 49–77.
Beyer, K. *Semitische Syntax im Neuen Testament.* SUNT 1. Göttingen: Vandenhoeck und Ruprecht, 1962.
Bieder, W. *Die Berufung im Neuen Testament.* ATANT 38. Zürich: Zwingli, 1961.
Biser, E. "Die Idee des Friedens nach den paulinischen Gefangenschaftsbriefen." *GuL* 27 (1954) 165–70.
Bjerkelund, C. J. *Parakalô. Form, Funktion und Sinn der parakalô-Sätze in den paulinischen Briefe.* Bibliotheca Theologica Norwegica 1. Oslo: Universitetsforlaget, 1967.
Black, M. *The Scrolls and Christian Origins.* New York: Scribner's, 1961.
Blanchette, O. A. "Does the Cheirographon of Col 2:14 Represent Christ himself?" *CBQ* 23 (1961) 306–312

Blinzler, J. "Lexikalisches zu dem Terminus τὰ στοιχεῖα τοῦ κόσμου bei Paulus." *Studiorum Paulinorum Congressus Internationalis Catholicus.* 2 vols. Rome: Pontifical Biblical Institute, 1963, 2. 429–43.
Bornkamm, G. "Baptism and New Life in Paul. Romans 6." *Early Christian Experience.* Tr. Hammer, P. L. London: SCM, 1969, 71–86. American edition, New York: Harper and Row, 1969.
———. "Die Hoffnung im Kolosserbrief. Zugleich ein Beitrag zur Frage der Echtheit des Briefes." *Studien zum Neuen Testament und zur Patristik. Erich Klostermann zum 90. Geburtstag dargebracht.* TU 77. Berlin: Akademie, 1961, 56–64. Reprinted in *Geschichte und Glaube 2. Gesammelte Aufsätze.* Vol. 4. BEvT 53. Munich: Kaiser, 1971, 206–213.
———. *Studien zu Antike und Urchristentum. Gesammelte Aufsätze.* Vol. 2. BEvT 28. Munich: Kaiser, 1959.
———. "The Heresy of Colossians." *Conflict at Colossae,* ed. Francis, F. O. and Meeks, W. A. 2nd ed. SBLSBS 4. Missoula, MT: Scholar's Press, 1975, 123–45. Originally published as "Die Häresie des Kolosserbriefs." *TLZ* 73 (1948) 11–20.
Bouttier, M. "*Complexio Oppositorum:* sur les Formules de 1 Cor. xii. 13; Gal. iii. 26–8; Col. iii. 10, 11." *NTS* 23 (1976–77) 1–19.
———. "Remarques sur la conscience apostolique de St. Paul." *OIKONOMIA. Heilsgeschichte als Thema der Theologie,* ed. Christ, F. Hamburg-Bergstedt: Reich, 1967, 100–108.
Bowen, C. R. "Are Paul's prison letters from Ephesus?" *AJT* 24 (1920) 112–35, 277–87.
———. "The Original Form of Paul's Letter to the Colossians." *JBL* 43 (1924) 177–206.
Bowers, W. P. "A Note on Colossians 1:27a." *Current Issues in Biblical and Patristic Interpretation. Studies in Honor of Merrill C. Tenney Presented by His Former Students,* ed. Hawthorne, G. F. Grand Rapids, MI: Eerdmans, 1975, 110–14.
Bradley, J. "The Religious Life-Setting of the Epistle to the Colossians." *StBibT* 2 (1972) 17–36.
Brown, R. E. *The Semitic Background of the Term "Mystery" in the New Testament.* FBBS 21. Philadelphia: Fortress, 1968.
Bruce, F. F. *Paul. Apostle of the Free Spirit.* Exeter: Paternoster, 1977. American edition, *Paul. Apostle of the Heart Set Free.* Grand Rapids, MI: Eerdmans, 1977.
———. *Tradition Old and New.* Exeter: Paternoster, 1970. American edition Grand Rapids, MI: Zondervan, 1970.
Bujard, W. *Stilanalytische Untersuchungen zum Kolosserbrief als Beitrag zur Methodik von Sprachvergleichen.* SUNT 11. Göttingen: Vandenhoeck & Ruprecht, 1973.
Bultmann, R. *Theology of the New Testament.* Vol. 1. Tr. K. Grobel, London: SCM, 1952. American edition NY: Scribner's, 1952.
Burger, C. *Schöpfung und Versöhnung. Studien zum liturgischen Gut im Kolosser- und Epheserbrief.* WMANT 46. Neukirchen: Neukirchener, 1975.
Burney, C. F. "Christ as the APXH of Creation." *JTS* 27 (1926) 160–77.
Caragounis, C. C. *The Ephesian Mysterion. Meaning and Content.* ConB, New Testament Series 8. Lund: Gleerup, 1977.
Carr, W. "Two Notes on Colossians." *JTS* 24 (1973) 492–500.
Cerfaux, L. *Christ in the Theology of St. Paul.* Tr. G. Webb and A. Walker. New York: Herder, 1959.
———. *The Church in the Theology of St. Paul.* Tr. G. Webb and A. Walker. New York: Herder, 1959.
Chadwick, H. "St. Paul and Philo of Alexandria." *BJRL* 48 (1965–66) 286–307.
Champion, L. G. *Benedictions and Doxologies in the Epistles of Paul.* Oxford: published privately, 1934.
Clark, K. W. "The Meaning of ἐνεργέω and καταργέω in the New Testament." *JBL* 54 (1935) 93–101.
Crouch, J. *The Origin and Intention of the Colossian Haustafel.* FRLANT 109. Göttingen: Vandenhoeck & Ruprecht, 1972.
Cullmann, O. *Early Christian Worship.* Tr. Todd, A. Stewart and Torrance, J. B. SBT 10. London: SCM, 1953.
———. *The Christology of the New Testament.* Tr. Guthrie, S. C. and Hall, C. A. M. 2nd ed. London: SCM, 1963. 1st American edition Philadelphia: Westminster, 1959.
———. "The Tradition." *The Early Church,* ed. Higgins, A. J. B. London: SCM, 1956, 59–99.
da Castel, T. "Συναιχμάλωτος: Compagno di Prigionia o Conquistato Assieme?" *Studiorum Paulinorum Congressus Internationalis Catholicus.* 2 vols. Rome: Pontifical Biblical Institute, 1963, 2. 417–28.
Dahl, N. A. "Anamnesis. Mémoire et Commémoration dans le Christianisme primitif." *ST* 1 (1948) 69–95.
———. "Form-Critical Observations on Early Christian Preaching." *Jesus in the Memory of the Early Church.* Minneapolis: Augsburg, 1976, 30–36.
Daniélou, J. "La Session à la droite du Père." *Studia Evangelica,* ed. Aland, K. and others. TU 73. Berlin: Akademie, 1959, 689–98.
Daube, D. "Participle and Imperative in 1 Peter." In Selwyn, E. G. *The First Epistle of St Peter.* London: Macmillan, 1947, 467–88.
Davies, W. D. *Paul and Rabbinic Judaism. Some Rabbinic Elements in Pauline Theology.* 2nd ed. London: SPCK, 1955. 4th American edition. Philadelphia: Fortress, 1980.
———. "Paul and the Dead Sea Scrolls: Flesh and Spirit." *The Scrolls and the New Testament,* ed. Stendahl, K. New York: Harper, 1957, 157–82.
———. *The Gospel and the Land.* Berkeley: University of California Press, 1974.
Deichgräber, R. *Gotteshymnus und Christushymnus in der frühen Christenheit. Untersuchungen zu Form, Sprache und Stil der frühchristlichen Hymnen.* SUNT 5. Göttingen: Vandenhoeck & Ruprecht, 1967.
Deissmann, A. *Bible Studies.* Tr. Grieve, A. Edinburgh: Clark, 1901.

———. *Light from the Ancient East.* Tr. Strachan, L. R. M. New York: Doran, 1927. Reprinted Grand Rapids, MI: Baker, 1927.
———. *Paul. A Study in Social and Religious History.* Tr. Wilson, W. E. 2nd ed. London: Hodder, 1926.
Delling, G. "Merkmale der Kirche nach den Neuen Testament." *NTS* 13 (1966–67) 297–316.
———. "Partizipiale Gottesprädikationen in den Briefen des Neuen Testaments." *ST* 17 (1963) 1–59.
———. *Worship in the New Testament.* Tr. Scott, P. London: Darton, Longman & Todd, 1962.
Dibelius, M. "The Isis Initiation in Apuleius and Related Initiatory Rites." *Conflict at Colossae,* ed. Francis, F. O. and Meeks, W. A. 2nd ed. SBLSBS 4. Missoula, MT: Scholar's Press, 1975, 61–121. Originally published as *Die Isisweihe bei Apuleius und verwandte Initiations-Riten.* SHAW. Ph. 8/4. Heidelberg: Winter, 1917.
Dodd, C. H. *New Testament Studies.* Manchester: University Press, 1953.
———. *The Bible and the Greeks.* London: Hodder, 1935.
———. *The Epistle of Paul to the Romans.* London: Hodder, 1932.
Doty, W. G. *Letters in Primitive Christianity.* Guides to Biblical Scholarship, NT Series. Philadelphia: Fortress, 1973.
Du Plessis, P. J. ΤΕΛΕΙΟΣ. *The Idea of Perfection in the New Testament.* Kampen: Kok, 1959.
Dumbrell, W. J. *The Meaning and Use of Ekklesia in the New Testament with Special Reference to its Old Testament Background.* University of London: Unpublished M.Th. thesis, 1966.
Duncan, G. S. *St. Paul's Ephesian Ministry. A Reconstruction with Special Reference to the Ephesian Origin of the Imprisonment Epistles.* London: Hodder, 1929.
Dunn, J. D. G. *Baptism in the Holy Spirit.* London: SCM, 1970. American edition SBT 15 2nd Ser. Naperville, IL: Allenson, 1970.
———. *Jesus and the Spirit. A Study of the Religious and Charismatic Experience of Jesus and the First Christians as Reflected in the New Testament.* Philadelphia: Westminster, 1975.
Dupont, J. *Gnosis. La connaissance religieuse dans les épîtres de saint Paul.* Paris: Gabalda, 1949.
———. ΣΥΝ ΧΡΙΣΤΩΙ. *L'union avec le Christ suivant saint Paul.* Paris: Desclée de Brouwer, 1952.
Durham, J. I. "*Šālôm* and the Presence of God." *Proclamation and Presence. Old Testament Essays in honour of Gwynne Henton Davies,* ed. Durham, J. I. and Porter, J. R. London: SCM, 1970, 272–93. American edition Richmond, VA: John Knox.
Easton, B. S. "New Testament Ethical Lists." *JBL* 51 (1932) 1–12.
Egan, R. B. "Lexical Evidence on Two Pauline Passages." *NovT* 19 (1977) 34–62.
Eitrem, S. "ΕΜΒΑΤΕΥΩ. Note sure Col 2, 18." *ST* 2 (1948) 90–94.
Ellis, E. E. "Paul and his Co-Workers." *NTS* 17 (1970–71) 437–52. Reprinted in *Prophecy and Hermeneutic in Early Christianity. New Testament Essays.* WUNT 18. Tübingen: Mohr, 1978, 3–22.
———. " 'Spiritual' Gifts in the Pauline Community." *NTS* 20 (1974) 128–44. Reprinted in *Prophecy,* 23–44.
———. "The Circumcision Party and the Early Christian Mission." *Prophecy,* 116–28. (Published in an earlier form as " 'Those of the Circumcision' and the early Christian Mission." *SE* 4 [1968]: 390–99).
———. *The Gospel of Luke.* NCB. London: Nelson, 1966.
Ernst, J. *Pleroma und Pleroma Christi. Geschichte und Deutung eines Begriffs der paulinischen Antilegomena.* BU 5. Regensburg: Pustet, 1970.
Feuillet, A. *Le Christ sagesse de Dieu d'après les épîtres pauliniennes.* Paris: Gabalda, 1966.
Foerster, W. "Die Irrlehrer des Kolosserbriefes." *Studia Biblica et Semitica. Prof. Th. C. Vriezen dedicata.* Wageningen: Veenman & Zonen, 1966, 71–80.
Francis, F. O. "Humility and Angelic Worship in Col 2:18." *Conflict at Colossae,* ed. Francis, F. O. and Meeks, W. A. 2nd ed. SBLSBS 4. Missoula, MT: Scholar's Press, 1975, 163–95. Originally published in *ST* 16 (1963) 109–134.
———. "The Background of ΕΜΒΑΤΕΥΕΙΝ (Col 2:18) in Legal Papyri and Oracle Inscriptions." ibid. 197–207.
Fridrichsen, A. "Charité et perfection. Observation sur Col. 3, 14." *SO* 19 (1939) 41–45.
———. "ΘΕΛΩΝ Col 2:18." *ZNW* 21 (1922) 135–37.
Friedrich, G. "Lohmeyers These über das paulinische Briefpräskript kritisch beleuchtet." *ZNW* 46 (1955) 272–74 and *TLZ* 81 (1956) 343–46.
Gabathuler, H. J. *Jesus Christus. Haupt der Kirche—Haupt der Welt. Der Christushymnus Colosser 1, 15–20 in der theologischen Forschung der letzten 130 Jahre.* ATANT 45. Zurich: Zwingli, 1965.
Gärtner, B. *The Temple and the Community in Qumran and the New Testament.* SNTSMS 1. Cambridge: University Press, 1965.
Gaffin, R. B. *The Centrality of the Resurrection. A Study in Paul's Soteriology.* Grand Rapids, MI: Baker, 1978.
Gamble, Jr., H. *The Textual History of the Letter to the Romans.* SD 42. Grand Rapids, MI: Eerdmans, 1977.
Gibbs, J. G. *Creation and Redemption. A Study in Pauline Theology.* NovTSup 26. Leiden: Brill, 1971.
Gnilka, J. *Der Philipperbrief.* HTKNT 10/3. Freiburg: Herder, 1968.
Goppelt, L. "Jesus und die 'Haustafel'—Tradition." *Orienterung an Jesus. Zur Theologie der Synoptiker. Für Josef Schmid,* ed. Hoffmann, P. with Brox, N. and Pesch, W. Freiburg: Herder, 1973, 93–106.
Gourges, M. *A la droite de Dieu.* Paris: Gabalda, 1978.
Grabner-Haider, A. *Paraklese und Eschatologie bei Paulus. Mensch und Welt im Anspruch der Zukunft Gottes.* NTAbh, NS 4. Münster: Aschendorff, 1968.
Grässer, E. "Kol 3, 1–4 als Beispiel einer Interpretation secundum homines recipientes." *ZTK* 64 (1967) 139–68.

Greeven, H. *Gebet und Eschatologie im Neuen Testament.* Gütersloh: Bertelsmann, 1931.

______. "Zu den Aussagen des Neuen Testaments über die Ehe." *ZEE* 1 (1957) 109–125.

Gundry, R. H. *SŌMA in Biblical Theology with Emphasis on Pauline Anthropology.* SNTSMS 29. Cambridge: University Press, 1976.

Gunther, J. J. *Paul: Messenger and Exile. A Study in the Chronology of His Life and Letters.* Valley Forge: Judson, 1972.

______. *St. Paul's Opponents and Their Background. A Study of Apocalyptic and Jewish Sectarian Teachings.* NovTSup 35. Leiden: Brill, 1973.

Guthrie, D. *New Testament Introduction. The Pauline Epistles.* London: Tyndale, 1961.

Hahn, F. "Der Apostolat im Urchristentum. Seine Eigenart und seine Voraussetzungen." *KD* 20 (1974) 54–77.

______. *Mission in the New Testament.* Tr. Clarke, F. London: SCM, 1965. American edition SBT 47; Naperville, Il: Allenson, 1965.

Hall, B. G. "Colossians II. 23." *ExpTim* 36 (1924–25) 285.

Halter, H. *Taufe und Ethos. Paulinische Kriterien für das Proprium christliche Moral.* Freiburg: Herder, 1977.

Hamerton-Kelly, R. G. *Pre-Existence, Wisdom and the Son of Man.* SNTSMS 21. Cambridge: University Press, 1973.

Hamman, A. *La Prière. I. Le Nouveau Testament.* Tournai: Desclée, 1959.

Hanson, A. T. *Studies in Paul's Technique and Theology.* London: SPCK, 1974.

Hanssler, B. "Zu Satzkonstruktion und Aussage in Kol 2, 23." *Wort Gottes in der Zeit. Festschrift für Karl Hermann Schelkle zum 65. Geburtstag,* ed. Feld, H. and Nolte, J. Düsseldorf: Patmos, 1973, 143–48.

Harder, G. *Paulus und das Gebet.* NTF 1S, 10. Gütersloh: Bertelsmann, 1936.

Harnack, A. von. "Κόπος (Κοπιᾶν, Οἱ Κοπιῶντες) im frühchristlichen Sprachgebrauch." *ZNW* 27 (1928) 1–10.

Harrison, P. N. "Onesimus and Philemon." *ATR* 32 (1950) 268–94.

Harrisville, R. A. "The Concept of Newness in the New Testament." *JBL* 74 (1955) 69–79.

Hay, D. M. *Glory at the Right Hand. Psalm 110 in Early Christianity.* SBLMS 18. Nashville: Abingdon, 1973.

Hegermann, H. *Die Vorstellung vom Schöpfungsmittler im hellenistischen Judentum und Urchristentum.* TU 82. Berlin: Akademie, 1961.

Hengel, M. *Judaism and Hellenism. Studies in their Encounter in Palestine during the Early Hellenistic Period.* 2 vols. Tr. Bowden, J. Philadelphia: Fortress, 1974.

Hester, J. D. *Paul's Concept of Inheritance. A Contribution to the Understanding of Heilsgeschichte.* Edinburgh: Oliver & Boyd, 1968.

Hill, D. *Greek Words and Hebrew Meanings. Studies in the Semantics of Soteriological Terms.* SNTSMS 5. Cambridge: University Press, 1967.

Hinson, E. G. "The Christian Household in Colossians 3:18–4:1." *RevExp* 70 (1973) 495–506.

Hollenbach, B. "Col. ii.23: Which Things lead to the Fulfilment of the Flesh." *NTS* 25 (1978–79) 254–61.

Hooker, M. D. "Philippians 2:6–11." *Jesus und Paulus. Festschrift für Werner Georg Kümmel zum 70. Geburtstag.* 2nd ed., ed. Ellis, E. E. and Grässer, E. Göttingen: Vandenhoeck & Ruprecht, 1978, 151–64.

______. "Were there False Teachers in Colossae?" *Christ and Spirit in the New Testament. Studies in honour of Charles Francis Digby Moule,* ed. Lindars, B. and Smalley, S. S. Cambridge: University Press, 1973, 315–31.

Hunter, A. M. *Paul and his Predecessors.* 2nd ed. London: SCM, 1961. American edition. Philadelphia: Westminster.

Hurley, J. B. *Man and Woman in Biblical Perspective. A study in role relationships and authority.* Leicester: Inter-Varsity, 1981.

Jensen, J. "Does *porneia* mean Fornication? A Critique of Bruce Malina." *NovT* 20 (1978) 161–84.

Jervell, J. *Imago Dei. Gen 1, 26f im Spätjudentum, in der Gnosis und in den paulinischen Briefen.* FRLANT 76. Göttingen: Vandenhoeck & Ruprecht, 1960.

Jewett, P. K. *Man as Male and Female: A Study in Sexual Relationships from a Theological Point of View.* Grand Rapids, MI: Eerdmans, 1975.

Jewett, R. "The Form and Function of the Homiletic Benediction." *ATR* 51 (1969) 18–34.

Johnson, S. E. "Unsolved Questions about Early Christianity in Anatolia." *Studies in New Testament and Early Christian Literature. Essays in Honor of Allen P. Wikgren,* ed. Aune, D. E. NovTSup 33. Leiden: Brill, 1972, 181–93.

Kähler, E. *Die Frau in den paulinischen Briefen.* Zurich/Frankfurt: Gotthelf, 1960.

______. "Zur 'Unterordnung' der Frau im Neuen Testament." *ZEE* (1959) 1–13.

Käsemann, E. "A Primitive Christian Baptismal Liturgy." *Essays on New Testament Themes.* Tr. Montague, W. J. London: SCM, 1964, 149–68. American edition. SBT 41. Naperville, Il: Allenson, 1964.

Käsemann, E. "Sentences of Holy Law in the New Testament." *New Testament Questions of Today.* Tr. Montague, W. J. London: SCM, 1969, 66–81.

______. "Worship in Everyday Life: a note on Romans 12." *New Testament Questions of Today.* Tr. Montague, W. J. London: SCM, 1969, 188–95.

Kamlah, E. *Die Form der katalogischen Paränese im Neuen Testament.* WUNT 7. Tübingen: Mohr, 1964.

______. "Ὑποτάσσεσθαι in den neutestamentlichen Haustafeln." *Verborum Veritas. Festschrift für Gustav Stählin zum 70. Geburtstag,* ed. Bocher, O. and Haacker, K. Wuppertal: Brockhaus, 1970, 237–43.

______. "Wie beurteilt Paulus sein Leiden? Ein Beitrag zur Untersuchung seiner Denkstruktur." *ZNW* 54 (1963) 217–32.

Karlson, G. "Formelhaftes in den Paulusbriefen." *Eranos* 54 (1956) 138–41.

Kasting, H. *Die Anfänge der urchristlichen Mission. Eine historische Untersuchung*. BEvT 55. Munich: Kaiser, 1969.
Kehl, N. *Der Christushymnus im Kolosserbrief. Eine motivgeschichtliche Untersuchung zu Kol 1, 12–20*. SBM 1. Stuttgart: Katholisches Bibelwerk, 1967.
______. "Erniedrigung und Erhöhung in Qumran und Kolossä." *ZKT* 91 (1969) 364–94.
Kerkhoff, R. *Das unablässige Gebet. Beiträge zur Lehre vom immerwährenden Beten im Neuen Testament*. Munich: Zink, 1954.
Kim, S. *An Exposition of Paul's Gospel in the Light of the Damascus Christophany. An Investigation into the Origin of Paul's Gospel*. University of Manchester: Unpublished Ph.D. thesis, 1977 [now published as *The Origin of Paul's Gospel*. WUNT, 2 Reihe 4. Tübingen: Mohr, 1981].
Kirk, J. A. "Apostleship since Rengstorf: Towards a Synthesis." *NTS* 21 (1974–75) 249–64.
Knight, III, G. W. *The New Testament Teaching on the Role Relationship of Men and Women*. Grand Rapids, MI: Baker, 1977.
Knox, W. L. *St Paul and the Church of the Gentiles*. Cambridge: University Press, 1939.
Kramer, W. *Christ, Lord, Son of God*. Tr. B. Hardy. SBT 50. London: SCM, 1966.
Kremer, J. *Was an den Leiden Christi noch mangelt. Eine interpretationsgeschichtliche und exegetische Untersuchung zu Kol. 1, 24b*. BBB 12. Bonn: Hanstein, 1956.
Kümmel, W. G. *Introduction to the New Testament*. Tr. Kee, H. C. 2nd ed. London: SCM, 1975. 17th American edition, Nashville, TN: Abingdon, 1975.
______. *The New Testament. The History of the Investigation of its Problems*. Tr. Gilmour, S. McLean, and Kee, H. C. London: SCM, 1972. American edition Nashville, TN: Abingdon, 1972.
Kuhn, H.-W. *Enderwartung und gegenwärtiges Heil. Untersuchungen zu den Gemeindeliedern von Qumran*. SUNT 4. Göttingen: Vandenhoeck & Ruprecht, 1966.
Ladd, G. E. "Paul's Friends in Colossians 4:7–16." *RevExp* 70 (1973) 507–514.
Lähnemann, J. *Der Kolosserbrief. Komposition, Situation und Argumentation*. SNT 3. Gütersloh: Mohn, 1971.
Larsson, E. *Christus als Vorbild. Eine Untersuchung zu den paulinischen Tauf- und Eikontexten*. ASNU 23. Uppsala: Gleerup, 1962.
Leaney, A. R. C. "Colossians ii. 21–23. (The use of πρός)." *ExpTim* 64 (1952–53) 92.
Lightfoot, J. B. *The Epistle of Paul to the Galatians*. 2nd American reprint edition. Grand Rapids, MI: Zondervan, 1957.
Lillie, W. "The Pauline House-tables." *ExpTim* 86 (1974–75) 179–83.
Lincoln, A. T. "A Re-Examination of 'The Heavenlies' in Ephesians." *NTS* 19 (1972–73) 468–83.
______. *The Heavenly Dimension. Studies in the Role of Heaven in Paul's Thought with Special Reference to His Eschatology*. University of Cambridge: Unpublished Ph.D. thesis, 1977 [now published as *Paradise Now and Not Yet: Studies in the Role of the Heavenly Dimension in Paul's Thought with Special Reference to Eschatology*. SNTSMS 41. Cambridge: University Press, 1981].
Loader, W. R. G. "Christ at the right hand—Ps. cx.1 in the New Testament." *NTS* 24 (1977–78) 199–217.
Lövestam, E. *Spiritual Wakefulness in the New Testament*. LUÅ 55/3. Lund: Gleerup, 1963.
Lohmeyer, E. "Probleme paulinischer Theologie. I. Briefliche Grussüberschriften." *ZNW* 26 (1927) 158–73.
Lohse, E. "Christologie und Ethik im Kolosserbrief." *Apophoreta. Festschrift für Ernst Haenchen*, ed. Eltester, W., and Kettler, F. H. BZNW 30. Berlin: Töpelmann, 1964, 157–68. Reprinted in *Die Einheit des Neuen Testaments. Exegetische Studien zur Theologie des Neuen Testaments*. 2nd ed. Göttingen: Vandenhoeck & Ruprecht, 1973, 249–61.
______. "Christusherrschaft und Kirche im Kolosserbrief." *NTS* 11 (1964–65) 203–216.
______. "Die Mitarbeiter des Apostels Paulus im Kolosserbrief." *Verborum Veritas. Festschrift für Gustav Stählin*, ed. Bocher, O. and Haacker, K. Wuppertal: Brockhaus, 1970, 189–94.
______. "Ein hymnisches Bekenntnis in Kolosser 2, 13c–15." *Mélanges Bibliques en hommage au R. P. Béda Rigaux*, ed. Descamps, A. and Halleux, A. de. Gembloux: Duculot, 1970, 427–35. Reprinted in *Einheit*, 276–84.
______. "Paränese und Kerygma im 1. Petrusbrief." *ZNW* 45 (1954) 68–89.
Lührmann, D. *Das Offenbarungsverständnis bei Paulus und in paulinischen Gemeinden*. WMANT 16. Neukirchener-Vluyn: Neukirchener, 1965.
Lyonnet, S. "L'hymne christologique de l'Epître aux Colossiens et la fête juive du Nouvel An." *RSR* 48 (1960) 92–100.
______. "Paul's Adversaries in Colossae." *Conflict at Colossae*, ed. Francis, F. O. and Meeks, W. A. 2nd ed. SBLSBS 4. Missoula, MT: Scholars Press, 1975, 147–61. Originally published as "L'étude du milieu littéraire et l'exégèse de Nouveau Testament: 4. Les adversaires de Paul à Colosses." *Bib* 37 (1956) 27–38; cf. also his article "L'Epître aux Colossiens (Col 2:18) et les mystères d'Apollon Clarien." *Bib* 43 (1962) 417–35.
McCown, W. "The Hymnic Structure of Colossians 1:15–20." *EvQ* 51 (1979) 156–62.
McDonald, J. I. H. *Kerygma and Didache. The articulation and structure of the earliest Christian message*. SNTSMS 37. Cambridge: University Press, 1980.
Macgregor, G. H. C. "The Concept of the Wrath of God in the New Testament." *NTS* 7 (1960–61) 101–109.
McKelvey, R. J. *The New Temple. The Church in the New Testament*. OTM 3. Oxford: University Press, 1969.
Magie, D. *Roman Rule in Asia Minor*. 2 vols. Princeton: University Press, 1950.
Malina, B. "Does *Porneia* mean Fornication?" *NovT* 14 (1972) 10–17.
Marchel, W. *Abba, Père! La prière du Christ et des chrétiens*. 2nd ed. AnBib 19A. Rome: Pontifical Biblical Institute, 1971.

Marshall, I. H. "New Wine in Old Wine Skins: V. The Biblical Use of the Word 'Ekklēsia'." *ExpTim* 84 (1972–73) 359–64.
______. "Palestinian and Hellenistic Christianity: Some Critical Comments." *NTS* 19 (1972–73) 271–87.
______. "The Christ-Hymn in Philippians 2:5–11." *TB* 19 (1968) 104–127.
Marshall, L. H. *The Challenge of New Testament Ethics.* London: Macmillan, 1947.
Martin, R. P. "An Early Christian Hymn (Col. 1:15–20)." *EvQ* 36 (1964) 195–205.
______. "Approaches to New Testament Exegesis." *New Testament Interpretation. Essays on Principles and Methods,* ed. Marshall, I. H. Exeter: Paternoster, 1977. 220–51. American edition Grand Rapids, MI: Eerdmans, 1977.
______. "Aspects of Worship in the New Testament Church." *Vox Evangelica* 2 (1963) 6–32.
______. *Carmen Christi. Philippians ii. 5–11 in Recent Interpretation in the Setting of Early Christian Worship.* SNTSMS 4. Cambridge: University Press, 1967.
______. "Reconciliation and Forgiveness in Colossians." *Reconciliation and Hope. New Testament Essays on Atonement and Eschatology presented to L. L. Morris on his 60th Birthday,* ed. R. Banks. Exeter: Paternoster, 1974, 104–124. American edition, Grand Rapids, MI: Eerdmans, 1974.
______. *The Family and the Fellowship. New Testament Images of the Church.* Exeter: Paternoster, 1979.
______. "Virtue." *NIDNTT* 3, 928–32.
______. *Reconciliation: A Study of Paul's Theology.* London: Marshall, Morgan and Scott. Atlanta, GA: John Knox, 1981.
Marxsen, W. *Introduction to the New Testament. An Approach to its Problems.* Tr. Buswell, G. Oxford: Blackwell's, 1968, 177–86. American edition, Philadelphia: Fortress, 1968.
Megas, G. "Das χειρόγραφον Adams. Ein Beitrag zu Kol 2:13–15." *ZNW* 27 (1928) 305–320.
Merk, O. *Handeln aus Glauben. Die Motivierungen der paulinischen Ethik.* Marburger Theologische Studien 5. Marburg: Elwert, 1968.
Merklein, H. *Das kirchliche Amt nach dem Epheserbrief.* SANT 33. Munich: Kösel, 1973.
Metzger, B. M. *The Text of the New Testament. Its Transmission, Corruption and Restoration.* 2nd ed. New York/London: Oxford University Press, 1968.
Meyer, H. A. W. *Critical and Exegetical Handbook to the Epistle to the Ephesians.* Tr. Evans, M. J. and Dickson, W. P. New York: Funk & Wagnalls, 1884.
Michaelis, W. *Versöhnung des Alls. Die frohe Botschaft von der Gnade Gottes.* Bern: Siloah, 1950.
Michl, J. "Die 'Versöhnung' (Kol 1, 20)." *TQ* 128 (1948) 442–62.
Mitton, C. L. *The Epistle to the Ephesians. Its Authorship, Origin and Purpose.* Oxford: University Press, 1951.
Montague, G. T. *Growth in Christ. A Study in Saint Paul's Theology of Progress.* Fribourg, Switz: Regina Mundi, 1961.
Morris, L. *The Apostolic Preaching of the Cross.* 3rd ed. London: Tyndale, 1965.
Moule, C. F. D. "Death 'to Sin,' 'to Law,' and 'to the World': a Note on certain Datives." *Mélanges Bibliques en hommage au R. P. Béda Rigaux,* ed. Descamps, A. and de Halleux, A. Gembloux: Duculot, 1970, 367–75.
______. "Further Reflexions on Philippians 2:5–11." *Apostolic History and the Gospel. Biblical and Historical Essays Presented to F. F. Bruce,* ed. Gasque, W. W. and Martin, R. P. Exeter: Paternoster, 1970, 264–76. American edition Grand Rapids, MI: Eerdmans, 1970.
______. " 'The New Life' in Colossians 3:1–17." *RevExp* 70 (1973) 481–93.
______. *The Origin of Christology.* Cambridge: University Press, 1977.
Münderlein, G. "Die Erwählung durch das Pleroma. Bemerkungen zu Kol. i.19." *NTS* 8 (1961–62) 264–76.
Mullins, T. Y. "Benediction as a NT Form." *AUSS* 15 (1977) 59–64.
______. "Disclosure. A Literary Form in the New Testament." *NovT* 7 (1964) 44–50.
Munck, J. *Paul and the Salvation of Mankind,* Tr. Clarke, F. London: SCM, 1959. American edition Richmond, VA: 1959.
Munn, G. L. "Introduction to Colossians." *SWJT* 16 (1973) 9–21.
Mussner, F. *Christus, das All und die Kirche. Studien zur Theologie des Epheserbriefes.* TTS 5. Trier: Paulinus, 1955.
Nauck, W. "Das οὖν-paräneticum." *ZNW* 49 (1958) 134, 135.
______. "Salt as a Metaphor in Instructions for Discipleship." *ST* 6 (1952) 165–78.
Nock, A. D. "The Vocabulary of the New Testament." *JBL* 52 (1933) 131–39.
Norden, E. *Agnostos Theos. Untersuchungen zur Formengeschichte religiöser Rede.* 4th ed. Darmstadt: Wissenschaftliche Buchgesellschaft, 1956.
O'Brien, P. T. "Col. 1:20 and the Reconciliation of All Things." *RTR* 33 (1974) 45–53.
______. *Introductory Thanksgivings in the Letters of Paul.* NovTSup 49. Leiden: Brill, 1977.
______. "Thanksgiving and the Gospel in Paul." *NTS* 21 (1974–75) 144–55.
______. "Thanksgiving within the Structure of Pauline Theology." *Pauline Studies in Honour of Professor F. F. Bruce,* ed. Hagner, D. A. and Harris, M. J. Grand Rapids, MI: Eerdmans, 1980, 50–66.
Ogg, G. *The Chronology of the Life of Paul.* London: Epworth, 1968. American edition, *The Odyssey of Paul.* Old Tappan, NJ: Revell.
Ollrog, W. H. *Paulus und seine Mitarbeiter. Untersuchungen zu Theorie und Praxis der paulinischen Mission.* WMANT 50. Neukirchen-Vluyn: Neukirchener, 1979.
O'Neill, J. C. "The Source of the Christology in Colossians." *NTS* 26 (1979–80) 87–100.

Overfield, P. D. "Pleroma: A Study in Content and Context." *NTS* 25 (1978–79) 384–96.

Percy, E. *Die Probleme der Kolosser- und Epheserbriefe.* SHVL 39. Lund: Gleerup, 1946.

Pfitzner, V. C. *Paul and the Agon Motif.* NovTSup 16. Leiden: Brill, 1967.

Pöhlmann, W. "Die hymnischen All-Prädikationen in Kol 1:15–20." *ZNW* 64 (1973) 53–74.

Polhill, J. B. "The Relationship Between Ephesians and Colossians." *RevExp* 70 (1973) 439–50.

Pope, R. M. "Studies in Pauline Vocabulary Of Redeeming the Time." *ExpTim* 22 (1910–11) 522–54.

Ramsay, W. M. *The Cities and Bishoprics of Phrygia.* Vol. 1. Oxford: University Press, 1895.

Reicke, B. "Caesarea, Rome and the Captivity Epistles." *Apostolic History and the Gospel. Biblical and Historical Essays presented to F. F. Bruce on his 60th Birthday,* ed. Gasque, W. W. and Martin, R. P. Exeter: Paternoster, 1970, 277–86. American edition, Grand Rapids, MI: Eerdmans, 1970.

———. "The Historical Setting of Colossians." *RevExp* 70 (1973) 429–38.

———. "Zum sprachlichen Verständnis vom Kol 2, 23." *ST* 6 (1952) 39–53.

Reitzenstein, R. *Hellenistic Mystery-Religions. Their Basic Ideas and Significance.* Tr. Steely, J. E. Pittsburg: Pickwick, 1978.

Rengstorf, K. H. "Die neutestamentliche Mahnungen an die Frau, sich dem Manne unterzuordnen." *Verbum Dei manet in Aeternum. Festschrift für O. Schmitz,* ed. Foerster, W. Witten: Luther, 1953, 131–45.

Reumann, J. "OIKONOMIA—Terms in Paul in Comparison with Lucan *Heilsgeschichte.*" *NTS* 13 (1966–67) 147–67.

Robinson, D. W. B. "Who Were the Saints?" *RTR* (1963) 45–53.

Robinson, J. A. *St Paul's Epistle to the Ephesians.* 2nd ed. London: Macmillan, 1909. American edition Grand Rapids, MI: Kregel, 1979.

Robinson, J. A. T. *The Body. A Study in Pauline Theology.* SBT 5. London: SCM, 1952.

Robinson, J. M. "A Formal Analysis of Colossians 1:15–20." *JBL* 76 (1957) 270–87.

Roels, E. D. *God's Mission. The Epistle to the Ephesians in Mission Perspective.* Franeker: Wever, 1962.

Roller, O. *Das Formular der paulinischen Briefe. Ein Beitrag zur Lehre vom antiken Briefe.* BWANT 4S, 6. Stuttgart: Kohlhammer, 1933.

Rutherford, J. "St. Paul's Epistle to the Laodiceans." *ExpTim* 19 (1907–08) 311–14.

Sampley, J. P. *"And the Two Shall Become One Flesh." A Study of Traditions in Ephesians 5:21–33.* SNTSMS 16. Cambridge: University Press, 1971.

Sanders, J. T. *The New Testament Christological Hymns. Their Historical Religious Background.* SNTSMS 15. Cambridge: University Press, 1971.

———. "The Transition from Opening Epistolary Thanksgiving to Body in the Letters of the Pauline Corpus." *JBL* 81 (1962) 348–62.

Satake, A. "Apostolat und Gnade bei Paulus." *NTS* 15 (1968–69) 96–107.

Schenk, W. *Der Segen im Neuen Testament. Eine begriffsanalytische Studie.* ThA 25. Berlin: Evangelische Verlagsanstalt. 1967.

Schenke, H. M. "Der Widerstreit gnostischer und kirchlicher Christologie im Spiegel des Kolosserbriefes." *ZTK* 61 (1964) 391–403.

Schille, G. *Frühchristliche Hymnen.* 2nd ed. Berlin: Evangelische Verlagsanstalt, 1965.

Schlier, H. *Principalities and Powers in the New Testament.* Questiones Disputatae 3. Freiburg: Herder, 1961.

Schnackenburg, R. *Baptism in the Thought of St. Paul. A Study in Pauline Theology.* Tr. Beasley-Murray, G. R. New York: Herder, 1964.

———. "Christus, Geist und Gemeinde (Eph. 4:1–16)." *Christ and Spirit in the New Testament. Studies in honour of Charles Francis Digby Moule,* ed. Lindars, B. and Smalley, S. S. Cambridge: University Press, 1973, 297–313.

———. "Der Neue Mensch—Mitte christlichen Weltverständnisses." *Schriften zum Neuen Testament. Exegese in Fortschritt und Wandel.* Munich: Kösel, 1971, 392–413.

———. "Die Aufnahme des Christushymnus durch den Verfasser des Kolosserbriefes." EKKNT Vorarbeiten 1. Neukirchen/Zürich: Neukirchener/Benziger, 1969, 33–50.

Schrage, W. *Die konkreten Einzelgebote in der paulinschen Paränese.* Gütersloh: Mohn, 1961.

———. " 'Ekklesia' und 'Synagoge.' Zum Ursprung des urchristlichen Kirchenbegriffs." *ZTK* 60 (1963) 178–202.

———. "Zur Ethik der neutestamentlichen Haustafeln." *NTS* 21 (1974–75) 1–22.

Schroeder, D. "Lists, Ethical." *IDBSup,* 546, 547.

Schubert, P. *Form and Function of the Pauline Thanksgivings.* BZNW 20. Berlin: Töpelmann, 1939.

Schütz, J. H. *Paul and the Anatomy of Apostolic Authority.* SNTSMS 26. Cambridge: University Press, 1975.

Schweizer, E. "Christianity of the Circumcised and Judaism of the Uncircumcised. The Background of Matthew and Colossians." *Jews, Greeks and Christians. Religious Cultures in Late Antiquity. Essays in Honor of William David Davies,* ed. Hamerton-Kelly, R. and Scroggs, R. Leiden: Brill, 1976, 245–60.

———. "Die 'Elemente der Welt' Gal 4, 3.9; Kol 2, 8.20." *Verborum Veritas. Festschrift für Gustav Stählin zum 70. Geburtstag,* ed. Bocher, O. and Haacker, K. Wuppertal: Brockhaus, 1970, 245–59. Reprinted in *Beiträge zur Theologie des Neuen Testaments. Neutestamentliche Aufsätze (1955–1970).* Zurich: Zwingli, 1970, 147–63.

———. "Die Kirche als Leib Christi in den paulinischen Antilegomena." *TLZ* 86 (1961) 241–56. Reprinted in *Neotestamentica: Deutsche und englische Aufsätze, 1951–1963.* Zurich: Zwingli, 1963, 293–316.

———. "Die Sünde in den Gliedern." *Abraham Unser Vater. Juden und Christen im Gespräch über die Bibel. Festschrift für Otto Michel zum 60. Geburtstag,* ed. Betz, O., Hengel, M. and Schmidt, P. AGSU 5. Leiden: Brill, 1963, 437–39.

______. "Die Weltlichkeit des Neuen Testamentes: die Haustafeln." *Beiträge zur alttestamentlichen Theologie, Festschrift für Walther Zimmerli zum 70. Geburtstag*, ed. Donner, H., Hanhart, R. and Smend, R. Göttingen: Vandenhoeck & Ruprecht, 1977, 397–413.

______. "Gottesgerechtigkeit und Lasterkataloge bei Paulus (inkl. Kol und Eph)." *Rechtfertigung. Festschrift für Ernst Käsemann zum 70. Geburtstag*, ed. Friedrich, J., Pöhlmann, W. and Stuhlmacher, P. Göttingen: Vandenhoeck & Ruprecht, 1976, 461–77.

______. "Kolosser 1, 15–20." EKKNT Vorarbeiten 1. Neukirchen/Zurich: Neukirchener/Benziger, 1969, 7–31. Reprinted in *Beiträge zur Theologie des Neuen Testaments. Neutestamentliche Aufsätze (1955–1970)*. Zurich: Zwingli, 1970, 113–45.

______. "Traditional ethical patterns in the Pauline and post-Pauline letters and their development (lists of vices and house-tables)." *Text and Interpretation. Studies in the New Testament presented to Matthew Black*, ed. Best, E. and Wilson, R. McL. Cambridge: University Press, 1979, 195–209.

______. "Zur neueren Forschung am Kolosserbrief (seit 1970)." *ThBer* 5 (1976) 163–91.

______. "Versöhnung des Alls. Kol 1, 20." *Jesus Christus in Historie und Theologie. Neutestamentliche Festschrift für Hans Conzelmann zum 60. Geburtstag*, ed. Strecker, G. Tübingen: Mohr, 1975, 487–501.

Scott, C. A. A. *Christianity according to St Paul.* Cambridge: University Press, 1927.

Scott, R. B. Y. "Wisdom in Creation: the *Āmôn* of Proverbs viii. 30." *VT* (1960) 213–23.

Seeberg, A. *Der Katechismus der Urchristenheit.* Leipzig: A. Deichertschen, 1903. Reprinted as TBü 26. Munich: Kaiser, 1966.

Sevenster, J. N. *Paul and Seneca.* NovTSup 4. Leiden: Brill, 1961.

Simon, M. "The Apostolic Decree and its Setting in the Ancient Church." *BJRL* 52 (1969–70) 437–60.

______. "The *religionsgeschichtliche Schule*, fifty years later." *RelS* 11 (1975) 135–44.

Smith, W. S. *Musical Aspects of the New Testament.* Amsterdam: Have, 1962.

Stanley, D. M. *Christ's Resurrection in Pauline Soteriology.* AnBib 13. Rome: Pontifical Biblical Institute, 1961.

Steinmetz, F. J. *Protologische Heils-Zuversicht. Die Strukturen des soteriologischen und christologischen Denkens im Kolosser- und Epheserbrief.* FTS 2. Frankfurt: Knecht, 1969.

Styler, G. M. "The Basis of Obligation in Paul's Christology and Ethics." *Christ and Spirit in the New Testament. In Honour of Charles Francis Digby Moule*, ed. Lindars, B. and Smalley, S. S. Cambridge: University Press, 1973, 175–87.

Synge, F. C. *St. Paul's Epistle to the Ephesians. A Theological Commentary.* London: SPCK, 1941.

Tachau, P. *"Einst" und "Jetzt" im Neuen Testament. Beobachtungen zu einem urchristlichen Predigtschema in der neutestamentlichen Briefliteratur und zu seiner Vorgeschichte.* FRLANT 105. Göttingen: Vandenhoeck & Ruprecht, 1972.

Tannehill, R. C. *Dying and Rising with Christ. A Study in Pauline Theology.* BZNW 32. Berlin: Töpelmann, 1967.

Thüsing, W. *Per Christum in Deum. Studien zum Verhältnis von Christozentrik und Theozentrik in den paulinischen Hauptbriefen.* 2nd ed. NTAbh NS, 1. Münster: Aschendorff, 1969.

Trench, R. C. *Synonyms of the New Testament.* Grand Rapids: Eerdmans, 1969 = 1880.

Trudinger, L. P. "A Further Brief Note on Colossians 1:24." *EvQ* 45 (1973) 36–38.

van der Horst, P. W. "Observations on a Pauline Expression." *NTS* 19 (1972–73) 181–87.

van Roon, A. *The Authenticity of Ephesians.* NovTSup 39. Tr. Prescod-Jokel, S. Leiden: Brill, 1974.

van Unnik, W. C. "Die Rücksicht auf die Reaktion der Nicht-Christen als Motiv in der altchristlichen Paränese." *Judentum, Urchristentum, Kirche. Festschrift für Joachim Jeremias*, ed. Eltester, W. BZNW 26. Berlin: Töpelmann, 1964, 221–34.

Vawter, B. "The Colossians Hymn and the Principle of Redaction." *CBQ* 33 (1971) 62–81.

Vögtle, A. *Das Neue Testament und die Zukunft des Kosmos.* Düsseldorf: Patmos, 1970.

______. *Die Tugend- und Lasterkataloge im Neuen Testament, exegetisch, religions- und formgeschichtlich untersucht.* NTAbh 16. Münster: Aschendorff, 1936.

Walter, N. "Die 'Handschrift in Satzungen' Kol 2:14." *ZNW* 70 (1979) 115–18.

Wambacq, B. N. " 'per eum reconciliare . . . quae in caelis sunt' Col 1, 20." *RB* 55 (1948) 35–42.

Wegenast, K. *Das Verständnis der Tradition bei Paulus und in den Deuteropaulinen.* WMANT 8. Neukirchen-Vluyn: Neukirchener, 1962.

Weidinger, K. *Die Haustafeln: Ein Stück urchristlicher Paränese.* UNT. Leipzig: J. C. Hinrichs, 1928.

Weiss, H. "The Law in the Epistle to the Colossians." *CBQ* 34 (1972) 294–314.

Wengst, K. *Christologische Formeln und Lieder des Urchristentums.* 2nd ed. SNT 7. Gütersloh: Mohn, 1972.

White, J. L. *The Form and Function of the Body of the Greek Letter: A Study of the Letter-Body in the Non-Literary Papyri and in Paul the Apostle.* SBLDS 2. Missoula, MT: Scholars Press, 1972.

Wibbing, S. *Die Tugend- und Lasterkataloge im Neuen Testament und ihre Traditionsgeschichte unter besonderer Berücksichtigung der Qumran texte.* BZNW 25. Berlin: Töpelmann, 1959.

Wiederkehr, D. *Die Theologie der Berufung in den Paulusbriefen.* Studia Friburgensia, NS 36. Freiburg, Schweiz: Universitätsverlag, 1963.

Wiles, G. P. *Paul's Intercessory Prayers: The Significance of the Intercessory Prayer Passages in the Letters of St. Paul.* SNTSMS 24. Cambridge: University Press, 1974.

Williams, A. L. "The Cult of Angels at Colossae." *JTS* 10 (1909) 413–38.

Williamson Jr., L. "Led in Triumph. Paul's Use of Thriambeuō." *Int* 22 (1968) 317–32.

Williamson, R. *Philo and the Epistle to the Hebrews.* ALGHJ 4. Leiden: Brill, 1970.

Wilson, R. McL. *Gnosis and the New Testament.* Philadelphia: Fortress, 1968.

Windisch, H. *Paulus und Christus. Ein biblisch-religionsgeschichtlicher Vergleich.* Leipzig: Heinrich, 1934.

Witt, R. E. *Isis in the Graeco-Roman World.* London: Thames & Hudson, 1971.

Wolter, M. *Rechtfertigung und zukünftiges Heil. Untersuchungen zu Röm 5, 1–11.* BZNW 43. Berlin: Walter de Gruyter, 1978.

Wulf, F. " 'Suchet, was droben ist, wo Christus ist, sitzend zur Rechten Gottes!' (Kol 3, 1)." *GuL* 41 (1968) 161–64.

Yamauchi, E. M. "Sectarian Parallels. Qumran and Colossae." *BSac* 121 (1964) 141–52.

Yates, R. "A Note on Colossians 1:24." *EvQ* 42 (1970) 88–92.

Zeilinger, F. *Der Erstgeborene der Schöpfung. Untersuchungen zur Formalstruktur und Theologie des Kolosserbriefes.* Vienna: Herder, 1974.

———. "Die Träger der apostolischen Tradition im Kolosserbrief." *Jesus in der Verkündigung der Kirche,* ed. Fuchs, A. Freistadt: Plöchl, 1976, 175–90.

C. Studies, Articles, etc. relating to Philemon

Amling, E. "Eine Konjektur im Philemonbrief." *ZNW* 10 (1909) 261, 262.

Bahr, G. J. "The Subscriptions in the Pauline Letters." *JBL* 87 (1968) 27–41.

Bartchy, S. S. ΜΑΛΛΟΝ ΧΡΗΣΑΙ. *First-Century Slavery and the Interpretation of 1 Corinthians 7:21.* SBLDS 11. Missoula, MT: Scholars Press, 1971.

Campbell, J. Y. *Three New Testament Studies.* Leiden: Brill, 1965.

Funk, R. W. "The Apostolic *Parousia:* Form and Significance." *Christian History and Interpretation. Studies Presented to John Knox,* ed. Farmer, W. R. and others. Cambridge: University Press, 1967, 249–68.

Gayer, R. *Die Stellung des Sklaven in den paulinischen Gemeinden und bei Paulus. Zugleich ein sozialgeschichtlich vergleichender Beitrag zur Wertung des Sklaven in der Antike.* Bern: Lang, 1976.

George, A. R. *Communion with God in the New Testament.* London: Epworth, 1953.

Goodenough, E. R. "Paul and Onesimus." *HTR* 22 (1929) 181–83.

Greeven, H. "Prüfung der Thesen von J. Knox zum Philemonbrief." *TLZ* 79 (1954) 373–78.

Hainz, J. *Ekklesia. Strukturen paulinischer Gemeinde-Theologie und Gemeinde-Ordnung.* BU 9. Regensburg: Pustet, 1972.

Jang, L. K. *Der Philemonbrief im Zusammenhang mit dem theologischen Denken des Apostels Paulus.* Bonn: unpublished thesis, 1964.

Jeremias, J. "Chiasmus in den Paulusbriefen." *ZNW* 49 (1958) 145–56.

Knox, J. *Philemon among the Letters of Paul.* 2nd ed. London: Collins, 1960.

Koch, E. W. "A Cameo of Koinonia. The Letter to Philemon." *Int* 17 (1963) 183–87.

McDermott, M. "The Biblical Doctrine of ΚΟΙΝΩΝΙΑ." *BZ* 19 (1975) 64–77, 219–33.

Mullins, T. Y. "Visit Talk in New Testament Letters." *CBQ* 35 (1973) 350–58.

Panikulam, G. *Koinōnia in the New Testament. A Dynamic Expression of Christian Life.* AnBib 85. Rome: Biblical Institute, 1979.

Preiss, T. *Life in Christ.* SBT 13. Tr. Knight, H. London: SCM, 1954.

Ridderbos, H. *Paul. An Outline of His Theology.* Tr. DeWitt, J. R. Grand Rapids, MI: Eerdmans, 1975.

Schulz, S. *Gott ist kein Sklavenhalter. Die Geschichte einer verspäteten Revolution.* 1972.

Schweizer, E. "Zum Sklavenproblem im Neuen Testament." *EvTh* 32 (1972) 502–506.

Seesemann, H. *Der Begriff* ΚΟΙΝΩΝΙΑ im Neuen Testament. BZNW 14. Giessen: Töpelmann, 1933.

Spicq, C. *Agape in the New Testament.* Vol. 2. Tr. McNamara, M. A. and Richter, M. H. St. Louis: Herder, 1965.

Suhl, A. "Der Philemonbrief als Beispiel paulinischer Paränese." *Kairos* 15 (1973) 267–79.

Sullivan, K. "Epignosis in the Epistles of St. Paul." *Studiorum Paulinorum Congressus Internationalis Catholicus.* Vol. 2. Rome: Pontifical Biblical Institute, 1963, 405–416.

van Unnik, W. C. "The Christian's Freedom of Speech in the New Testament." *BJRL* 44 (1962) 466–88.

Wendland, P. *Die urchristlichen Literaturformen.* 3rd ed. Tübingen: Mohr, 1912.

Westermann, W. L. *The Slave Systems of Greek and Roman Antiquity.* Philadelphia: American Philosophical Society, 1955.

Wickert, U. "Der Philemonbrief—Privatbrief oder apostolisches Schreiben?" *ZNW* 52 (1961) 230–38.

Zmijewksi, J. "Beobachtungen zur Struktur des Philemonbriefes." *BibLeb* 15 (1974) 273–96.

Author Index

Index of Principal Passages Cited

A. The Old Testament

B. Old Testament Apocrypha and Pseudepigrapha

C. The New Testament

Index of Principal Subjects

D. Pseudepigraphical and Early Patristic Books

E. The Dead Sea Scrolls

F. Rabbinic Literature

G. Hellenistic Authors

H. Nag Hammadi Tractates